$45

MAKING MUSIC MODERN

MAKING MUSIC MODERN
New York in the 1920s

CAROL J. OJA

OXFORD

UNIVERSITY PRESS

2000

OXFORD
UNIVERSITY PRESS

Oxford New York

Athens Auckland Bangkok Bogotá Buenos Aires Calcutta
Cape Town Chennai Dar es Salaam Delhi Florence Hong Kong Istanbul
Karachi Kuala Lumpur Madrid Melbourne Mexico City Mumbai
Nairobi Paris São Paulo Singapore Taipei Tokyo Toronto Warsaw

and associated companies in
Berlin Ibadan

Copyright © 2000 by Carol J. Oja

Published by Oxford University Press, Inc.
198 Madison Avenue, New York, New York 10016

Oxford is a registered trademark of Oxford University Press

Library of Congress Cataloging-in-Publication Data
Oja, Carol J., 1953–
Making music modern : New York in the 1920s / Carol J. Oja.
p. cm.
Includes bibliographical references, discography, and index.
ISBN 0-19-505849-6
1. Music—New York (State)—New York—20th century—History and criticism.
2. Composers—New York (State)—New York. I. Title.
ML200.8.N5 O43 2000
780'.9747'109042—dc21 99-052604

Epigraph sources:
Langston Hughes, "The Fascination of Cities," *Crisis* 31 (January 1926).
Gertrude Stein, "Composition as Explanation," in *What Are Masterpieces*
(London: Hogarth Press, 1926); reprinted in *Selected Writings of Gertrude Stein,*
ed. Carl Van Vechten (New York: Random House, 1946).

Manfred Bukofzer Publication Endowment
of the American Musicological Society
H. Earle Johnson Fund of the Society for American Music

1 2 3 4 5 6 7 8 9
Printed in the United States of America
on acid-free paper

to Mark, Wynn, and Zoe

Acknowledgments

If it takes a village to raise a child, it takes just as much support to produce a book. Since beginning this project nearly a dozen years ago, I have been extremely fortunate in receiving help from a wide network of friends, family, and professional colleagues.

I began research for the book under a Mellon Faculty Fellowship at Harvard University and continued it—in an especially intense blitz one summer at the Library of Congress—with a Grant-in-Aid from the American Council of Learned Societies. Since then, fellowships from the National Endowment for the Humanities and the National Humanities Center provided time for writing. At the National Humanities Center, I gained much from lunchtime chats with colleagues in other disciplines—many of whom are named below—who both challenged and expanded the directions I was pursuing. Additional research was funded by my two home institutions, with PSC-CUNY Faculty Research Awards from the City University of New York and Summer Research Grants from the College of William and Mary. These grants also helped pay for permissions.

The cost of publishing this book was assisted with generous subventions from the Manfred Bukofzer Publication Endowment of the American Musicological Society and the H. Earle Johnson Fund of the Society for American Music.

Numerous librarians helped clear through tangled thickets of primary sources. They include George Boziwick and John Shepherd at the Library for the Performing Arts of the New York Public Library, Elizabeth Auman and Wayne Shirley at the Music Division of the Library of Congress, Ken Crilly at the Irving S. Gilmore Music Library of Yale University, Mary Wallace Davidson at the Sibley Music Library of the Eastman School of Music, Sylvia Kennick Brown at the Paul Whiteman Archive of Williams College, Pamela Dunn at the Department of Special Collections of Stanford University Libraries, and Kristie French at the Oral History of the Arts Archive at California State University at Long Beach. I also received help from the staffs at Columbia University's Butler Library, Harvard University's Widener Library and Edna Kuhn Loeb Music Library, and the Museum of Modern Art Film Archive. The numerous interviews conducted by Vivian Perlis and her staff at the Yale School of Music's Oral History/American Music Archive brought me close to the spirit of the 1920s; they provide one of the richest sources available for writing about this period. Interviews conducted by the late Rita Mead, with transcripts housed at the Institute for Studies in American Music at Brooklyn College, were also invaluable. Special thanks go to the library staff at the National Humanities Center—including W. Alan Tuttle, Jean Houston, and Eliza Robertson—who performed wizardry in locating obscure research materials.

Encouragement from colleagues set me off on rewarding paths. When Samuel A. Floyd Jr., Director of the Center for Black Music Research at Columbia College in Chicago, invited me to write an article about William Grant Still for the *Black Music Research Journal,* he inspired me to look closely at Still's connection to the modernists. Similarly, when Adrienne Fried Block asked me to give a presentation for the Project for the Study of Women in Music at the Graduate Center of the City University of New York, I found myself intrigued with the role of women as patrons in the modernist movement. Judith Tick discussed almost every aspect of this book with me, providing a seemingly endless stream of provocative leads. Many other colleagues commented on all or part of the manuscript, generously offering time and suggestions. They include Mark Antliff, Philip Brett, Taylor Greer, H. Wiley Hitchcock, Joseph Horowitz, Ralph Locke, David Nicholls, Howard Pollack, Lawrence Rainey, Kitty Sklar, Joseph Straus, Mark Tucker, Patana Usuni, and Glenn Watkins.

Others who helped with ideas and materials include Charles Amirkhanian, Hilda Reis Bijur, Michael Broyles, Joan Cominos, Richard Crawford, Susan Feder, Peter Garland, John French, Erica E. Hirschler, Ellie Hisama, Lou Harrison, Elliott Hurwitt, Frederick A. Jacobi, Patricia Leighton, R. Allen Lott, Townsend Ludington, Olivia Mattis, Maurice Peress, Vivian Perlis, Richard Powell, Marion Walton Putnam, K. Robert Schwarz, Catherine Smith, Larry Starr, Larry Stempel, Judith Anne Still, Jay Sullivan, Anthony Tommasini, David Walker, Chou Wen-chung, Nan Werner, Linda Whitesitt, Ron Wiecki, and Sharon Wood. My students over the years—especially in seminars about modernism that I have given at Brooklyn College, the College of William and Mary, the Graduate School of CUNY, and Harvard University—continually enriched my perspective on the period.

For permissions, I am grateful to Charles Amirkhanian (estate of George Antheil), Jean Ashton (Rare Book and Manuscript Library, Columbia University), Thomas Broido (Theodore Presser Co.), Sylvia Kennick Brown (Paul Whiteman Archive at Williams College), Joan Cominos (daughter of Louis Gruenberg), Maria Elena Rico Covarrubias (daughter of Miguel Covarrubias), Ken Crilly (Yale University Music Library), Virginia Dajani (Executive Director of the American Academy of Arts and Letters), Kristie French (Oral History of the Arts Archive, California State University at Long Beach), Rosemarie Gawelko (Warner Bros.

Publications), Bernie Kalban (Edward B. Marks Music Company), Carolyn Kalett (Boosey & Hawkes, Inc.), Caroline Kane (European American Music), James M. Kendrick (Aaron Copland Fund for Music and the Virgil Thomson Foundation), Zoraya Mendez (G. Schirmer, Inc.), Harold L. Miller (Reference Archivist, State Historical Society of Wisconsin), Pamela Miller (Margun-Gunmar Music), Theresa Mora (Bobst Library Archives, New York University), Tim Noakes (Department of Special Collections, Stanford University Libraries), Vivian Perlis (Oral History/American Music at the Yale School of Music), John C. Putnam (son of Marion Walton Putnam), Therese Schneider (editorial director of *Musical America*), Mike Seeger (son of Ruth and Charles Seeger), Michael Stier (Condé Nast Publications), Richard Teitelbaum (for the Cowell estate), Roberto G. Trujillo (Head of Special Collections, Stanford University Libraries), Mary Vandenburg (Hal Leonard Publications), Electra Yourke (daughter of Nicolas Slonimsky), and Judith Anne Still (daughter of William Grant Still).

I owe much to Elliott Carter, Aaron Copland, Sidney Robertson Cowell, Minna Lederman, Marion Walton Putnam, and Virgil Thomson for sharing their memories of the 1920s.

For assistance with research queries and manuscript preparation (including musical examples), I am grateful for the help of Christine Aube, Jeremy Grimshaw, John Holzaepfel, Rob Nelson, Ruth Ochs, Ian Quinn, Kate Scott, David Smey, and Amy Speckart. Nancy Pardo (Institute for Studies in American Music at Brooklyn College) and Karen Carroll (National Humanities Center) helped type the appendix. When this book was a fledgling, Sheldon Meyer signed it up for Oxford University Press. Maribeth Payne, my editor after Sheldon's retirement, gently but firmly prodded me to let go of the manuscript when she felt it was ready. She, together with Scott Anderson, Maureen Buja, Jessica Ryan, and Jonathan Wiener, all expertly shepherded it through production and distribution.

I close as I opened, by returning to an image of children and family. My love and thanks go to Helen and Onni Oja, Louis L. Tucker and the late Beverley Tucker, Dorothy B. Jones, Carolyn Woollen Tucker, and Lance and Sheila Tucker—all of whom never stopped asking, "How's the book going?" To my children, Zoe and Wynn, who tumbled into the world as this project unfolded and delightfully kept my priorities in order. And to my husband, Mark Tucker, who not only improved the manuscript immensely through multiple critiques but shared with me the entire experience of shaping it—making it all a lot more pleasurable than it otherwise would have been.

CONTENTS

New York is truly the dream city—city
of the towers near God, city of hopes and
visions, of spires seeking in the windy
air loveliness and perfection.

—Langston Hughes, 1926

There is singularly nothing that makes a
difference a difference in beginning and
in the middle and in ending except that
each generation has something different
at which they are all looking.

—Gertrude Stein, 1926

MAKING MUSIC MODERN

Introduction

The Modern Music Shop

If you picked up a phone in Manhattan to call "DRY Dock 3732" at just about any point during the 1920s, a voice at the other end would have answered "Modern Music Shop," instantly connecting you with a source for the newest music, whether imported or domestic. Located at various times on East 48th Street, also on East Broadway, the shop was one of many signs that New York had become an international marketplace of modernism, rising up after World War I to join Paris, and to a lesser extent Berlin and Vienna, as one of the main sites where the newest compositions were written, performed, and discussed. Long past its early status as a colonial outpost, straining for credibility and currency, New York stood at the hub of the action, seen as "the capital of the musical world," as one contemporary observer put it.[1]

Already in the late nineteenth century New York was a major force on the international scene. But to young creative artists of the 1920s, it seemed to hold unprecedented charm and unlimited potential. As a talented new generation of American writers, musicians, and painters reached maturity—ranging from Langston Hughes and Ernest Hemingway to Josephine Baker, Duke Ellington, Arthur Dove, and Georgia O'Keeffe—it included composers who wrote music for the concert hall, most notably George Antheil, Aaron Copland, Henry Cowell, Ruth Crawford, George Gershwin, Roy Harris, Roger Sessions, William Grant Still, and Virgil Thomson. Riding a wave of postwar confidence, these young Americans staged a rebellion, challenging just about everything around them. Women gained the vote, African Americans asserted creative leadership, and Americans suddenly realized that the world was paying serious attention to what they did. It was a time when any idea seemed realizable, when taking risks was the order of the day.

Over the course of the decade, American concert-music composers explored an imaginative range of styles and ideologies, all under the banner of "modernism." Leaders emerged among them, first the French-American Edgard Varèse and by the second half of the decade, Copland and Cowell. Although strong rivalries developed, these composers shared an abundance of goodwill. They faced a common enemy, the "grey musty presence" that critic Paul Rosenfeld decried as suffocating the American concert experience, and they devised effective strategies to earn a position for themselves on the American cultural scene. Theirs was a collective effort—a movement forged of group grit. It made erratic progress, at times inching forward fitfully, at others taking giant leaps. By the time of the stock market crash in 1929 they had succeeded in putting in place essential institutional structures to help composers function in a democratic, capitalist society, and they had formulated an aesthetic agenda that dominated American musical life for decades to come.[2]

A string of events in January and February of 1924 made it clear that New York had become an energetic force in modern music. Within a few weeks, the New York premiere of Stravinsky's *Le Sacre du printemps* (a work from 1913) took place in a gala Carnegie Hall performance, the young Californian Henry Cowell made his debut in the same hall performing his tone-cluster compositions, and fifteen blocks downtown at Aeolian Hall George Gershwin premiered his genre-bending *Rhapsody in Blue*. During this same stint, Edgard Varèse's *Octandre* and Carl Ruggles's *Vox clamans in deserto* received their premieres, and the first issue appeared of the "League of Composers' Review," soon to be known as *Modern Music*, which immediately became the single most important forum for American modernist composers. Seemingly distant points of the new-music spectrum emerged almost simultaneously—American and European, mainline and offbeat, esoteric and accessible—only to reveal that they weren't so distant after all, that difference and diversity were at modernism's core.[3]

Given the plurality and mobility of American culture, New York was ideally suited to host the kaleidoscope of musical styles identified as modernist—or as "new music" or "ultra-modernist." The beauty of modernism was that it encompassed no dominating center or clear line of authority. Modernism was impossible to pin down. It embraced many styles. It did not even have a stable home. Yet it stood for one basic principle: iconoclastic, irreverent innovation, sometimes irreconcilable with the historic traditions that preceded it. It was an ideal to which composers and visual artists aspired, as much as fashion designers and machine manufacturers. As a term, modernism has since become problematic for its imprecision. Yet I use the word without apology here. Not only was it ubiquitous at the time, but it conveys the abundant "chaos," as contemporary commentators repeatedly put it, of the period's multiple modes of creative expression. As one cultural historian has observed, the word *modernism*, in spite of "all its vagueness, continues to convey a unique, almost spiritual authority."[4]

This book, then, looks at the extraordinary network of composers and ideologies that made up the modernist movement in New York City from World War I until the early years of the Depression. The city's overall cultural life has received rich treatment in *Terrible Honesty: Mongrel Manhattan in the 1920s* by Ann Douglas;

and studies such as *Modernist Culture in America*, edited by Daniel Joseph Singal, and *Skyscraper Primitives: Dada and the American Avant-Garde, 1910–1925*, by Dickran Tashjian, have shaped a broad-based perspective on modernism's manifestations in the New World. Yet concert music has been absent from their scope. Just as it is difficult to imagine the artistic ferment of early-twentieth-century Paris without including Claude Debussy, Erik Satie, or Igor Stravinsky or that of Vienna without Alban Berg, Arnold Schoenberg, or Anton Webern, so too did New York's composers figure crucially in the city's cultural identity.[5]

In exploring the various arenas in which musical modernism appeared in New York, I reexamine well-known figures and recover lost voices, discussing selected compositions within shifting historical frameworks. I have aimed for neither a chronological survey nor comprehensive coverage, and I adhere to no single method of musical analysis. Rather, I situate new concert music within what the composer Marc Blitzstein once called "the economic, spiritual, ethnic, and esthetic facts of our time." As the book unfolds, sources for many of the century's major musical movements appear, from the political activism of the 1930s to the postmodern pluralism and focus on spirituality so prevalent late in the century. Perhaps most tellingly, a vision emerges of a time when the status of academic formalism, which reigned so securely in the decades immediately after World War II, was by no means firmly established, and when interactions between popular musics and the concert sphere—or "lowbrow" and "highbrow" as they were once called—percolated provocatively.[6]

I have linked my discussion of composers and compositions to a series of issues that agitated artists and writers of the day, ranging from the rise of technology and hyperspace theory to the long reach of European neoclassicism and its implications for a postcolonial culture. The intersections of jazz and concert music emerge with greater clarity when considered together with changing American demographics and race relations. Music of the "Machine Age" takes on new meaning against a backdrop of American Dada. A discussion of patronage for composers branches out into the role of social feminism in the new-music movement, and one of theosophy's intersection with American modernism reveals a nearly forgotten chapter in the search for an indigenous species of dissonance. Subplots emerge as well, such as the growing Jewish presence among young American composers and the anti-Semitism it unleashed, the rising interest in composers of Latin America, and the omnipresent tensions of gender and sexuality, whether in the assertion of a masculine authority through modernist composition or the increasing visibility of composers who were homosexual. Along the way, I sketch portraits of an eclectic array of compositions, from Antheil's *Ballet Mécanique* to Copland's Piano Variations, Gershwin's *Concerto in F*, Marion Bauer's *Four Piano Pieces*, Cowell's *Irish Legends*, Crawford's *String Quartet 1931*, Ruggles's *Angels*, Sessions's Piano Sonata, Still's *Levee Land*, and Thomson's *Capital, Capitals*. Throughout, the reception of modernism in New York surfaces repeatedly, charting how opinion was shaped as controversial aesthetics clashed with established norms.

The book concludes with a composite listing of all the music performed on concerts sponsored by New York's modern-music societies during the 1920s.

"New York," within these frameworks, becomes more a lens for focusing on compositional trends than a geographic perimeter for discussion. The composers included here were continually on the move, sailing to Europe, driving to California, retreating to Vermont. Yet they returned regularly to the city, knowing it was the main place for their work to get noticed. "The air of New York was brilliant, revivifying," enthused Edna Ferber, author of the novel *Show Boat*. New York City placed young composers at an auspicious cultural crossroads. There they could stand, with all their belongings in one suitcase, free to roam in whatever direction their imaginations might lead.[7]

As work on this book progressed, I found myself increasingly at odds with some deeply enshrined myths about the 1920s—myths that have tended to caricature emerging composers of the time as either dashing young heroes or New World naifs. These are vestiges of earlier historical perspectives. The chest-thumping nationalism of the late Depression, World War II, and the Cold War yielded what one scholar has called the "myth and symbol" school of American history. In music's version of it, figures such as Copland and Cowell were portrayed as part of a posse of lone innovators storming the musical fortress that refused them entrance. Historians based their chronicles on an assumption of larger-than-life male autonomy, aiming to construct masters and masterworks, with less interest in the heterogeneity of communities. These composers have also been seen as America-first patriots, intensely driven to forge a native school of composition. The historiographic lineage of this perspective is too complex to recount in detail here. Suffice it to say that it has appeared in most histories of American music. Young composers of the 1920s rated some mention in John Tasker Howard's *Our American Music* (first edition, 1930), although, not surprisingly, they were presented as curiosities. Howard opened his twenty-two-page section on "The Modernists" with a story about a friend who was dining out with some young composers and told them of his musical son: "'Has he talent?' some one asked. 'I don't know,' said the father; 'if he hasn't, he can be a modernist composer.'" By the time of Gilbert Chase's *America's Music* in 1955, Copland, Cowell, and Harris had become proponents of nationalism, discussed, as they were, in a chapter titled "The Americanists." "Myth and symbol" turned into epic narrative in Wilfrid Mellers's bold and influential *Music in a New-Found Land* of 1964, in which American composers after World War I are subsumed under the heading, "The Pioneer and the Wilderness." In literary circles there was a parallel tendency, beginning with F. O. Matthiessen's *American Renaissance* of 1941 and Alfred Kazin's *On Native Grounds* of the following year.[8]

Politically, these books reflected the changing nature of American patriotism, first using it to confront economic crisis, then to thwart Hitler, and later to stop the spread of communism. Culturally, however, the motivation remained constant: to oppose the ingrained bias that assumed American creative art works to be inferior to those of Europe. In an understandable effort to gain credibility for their subject, historians and critics, as well as the composers themselves, often took part in a kind of compensatory boosterism. Much like the "Made in America" labels used late in the century to combat manufacturing imports, heart-on-sleeve nationalism made it clear that American composers were not simply clones of European models. "Listen to American music!" was the cry, and often it needed to be shouted from the rooftops.

The 1920s has receded far enough into the past so that boosterism and collective myth can yield to historical analysis. Rather than depicting young American composers of the period as earnestly striving for national identity through their music, I believe internationalism to have been an equally compelling force. Rather than imagining them as rugged daughters and sons of Paul Bunyan, single-handedly taming the American musical wilderness, I view them as part of an interdependent modernist community, one in which now-forgotten composers and new-music activists—many of them female—laid important groundwork. Rather than assuming them to have arrived for study in Europe ignorant of recent modernist advances, I probe their opportunities for encountering the newest ideas back home, whether in performance, published scores, or journalistic criticism. In the end, this batch of American composers appears to have been at once larger and smaller than its commonly accepted profile. These young people were products of a profoundly interconnected modernist network, which stretched across the ocean, across musical genres, across art forms.

Research for this book has been as varied as the coverage, largely drawing upon archival sources and contemporaneous periodical literature. My main goal has been to view the period as chronicled by its participants. In the process, I systematically read through such prominent music and general-interest periodicals as *Modern Music, Musical America, Musical Leader, American Mercury*, the *Bookman*, the *Dial*, the *Little Review, Vanity Fair*. Among these, particularly useful sources included the "little magazine" *Modern Music*, with its writings by contemporary composers, and the column "Music in New York," published weekly in the *Musical Leader* by critic and composer Marion Bauer, together with her sister Flora Bauer Bernstein. I combed the private correspondence of dozens of composers and new-music activists, most notably that of Antheil, Copland, Ruth Crawford, Minna Lederman, Claire Reis, Roger Sessions, Nicolas Slonimsky, Serge Koussevitzky, Charles Seeger, Irving Schwerké, the family of Alma Morgenthau (all at the Library of Congress); Charles Ives, Carl Ruggles, E. Robert Schmitz, Virgil Thomson (at Yale); Claire Reis and Blanche Walton (at the New York Public Library); and Dane Rudhyar (at Stanford). I profited from a substantial literature about the visual arts of the 1920s. And I conducted interviews with participants in the modernist movement, including Elliott Carter (then a youngster who attended concerts of new-music societies), Minna Lederman (editor of *Modern Music*), Copland, and Thomson. Although the last three died while this project was underway, I owe them much for recalling their youth with vividness and candor.

Enter the Moderns

Leo Ornstein

"Wild Man" of the 1910s

Perhaps the stronger the hold of the past the more violent
the need for freedom from it.

—Leo Ornstein

The decade between 1910 and 1920 was the mysterious Paleolithic period of
American modernist music. Occasional glints of activity were overshadowed by
a near single-minded focus on historic European repertories. Concert-goers were
far more likely to hear Schubert than Stravinsky, and they had little chance of
encountering music by a forward-looking composer born in America.

In the middle of this hazy, emergent scene, a charismatic keyboard virtuoso and
composer named Leo Ornstein dazzled New York with a series of four recitals at the
Bandbox Theatre in January and February 1915. This same theater served as home
to the Washington Square Players, a group also founded in 1915 to produce modernist drama. Ornstein's concerts "really startled musical New York and even
aroused orchestral conductors, in some measure, out of their lethargic method of
programme-making," recalled the critic Carl Van Vechten. They brought New
York "a breath of the intentions of modern thought as applied to music," declared
Alfred Stieglitz's daringly avant-garde art magazine, *291*. At them, Ornstein performed not only recent music by European composers, such as Arnold Schoenberg,
Alexander Scriabin, Maurice Ravel, Isaac Albeniz, Erich Korngold, and Cyril Scott,
but also adventurous new works of his own. Until the end of the 1910s, Ornstein
remained the touchstone of modernist musical expression in the city—"the high
apostle of the new art in America," as Van Vechten proclaimed. With a flair for flam-
boyance and self-promotion, Ornstein provided an early model of how a modernist
composer might make a career in the United States. He also embodied a classic

immigrant saga, arriving from the Ukraine and subsequently rising into a position of prominence in the creative arts.[1]

Ellis Island became one of the passageways through which early modernism entered America. Ornstein was the first major figure to emigrate, arriving in the United States in 1907. His family was fleeing the persecution of Jews that had followed the Russian Revolution of 1905. Born in 1893 in Kremenchug in the Ukraine, he was then fifteen and had already begun musical studies at the conservatory in Petrograd. The biggest wave of immigration occurred a few years later, in the midst of World War I. It preceded the later, better-known arrival of Europeans fleeing fascism during the 1930s and 1940s. The harpist and composer Carlos Salzedo came from Paris in 1909, not long after Ornstein. Then Edgard Varèse appeared in 1915, followed by Ernest Bloch, who arrived from Switzerland in 1916. Dane Rudhyar left Paris that same year, and the pianist and new-music organizer E. Robert Schmitz came in 1918. As performers, teachers, organizers, and music journalists, these men became activists for modernism, both in introducing new European works to America and in supporting the latest American compositions. They performed a function similar to that of foreign-born figures in the

Figure 1.1. Leo Ornstein at the piano (1915). Photo courtesy of Hilda Reis Bijur.

American visual arts, such as Marcel Duchamp, Joseph Stella, Max Weber, and Gaston Lachaise, who were major galvanizing forces among modernist painters in New York.[2]

Immediately after reaching the city, Ornstein set out to complete his education. He enrolled at the Institute of Musical Art (later to become The Juilliard School), where he worked with Bertha Fiering Tapper, a noted piano teacher of the day. Tapper (1859–1915) was an ardent mentor of the young virtuoso and an intriguing figure in her own right. Born in Norway, she had studied in Leipzig with Carl Reinecke and Louis Maas, and was friends with Edvard Grieg, for whom she edited two volumes of piano compositions. In 1910, she brought Ornstein to Europe for the first time and helped him make valuable contacts on an international circuit. After the two returned to New York, Ornstein staged his debut there at the New Amsterdam Theatre on 5 March 1911, where he offered a thoroughly conventional program of music by Bach, Beethoven, Chopin, and Anton Rubinstein. This was followed by similar concerts in Philadelphia and elsewhere.[3]

Sometime within the next two years, a flaming "futurist" emerged. (In the 1910s, just about any forward-looking artist was called a "futurist"; it was the hip label of the decade.) In 1913 Ornstein composed his *Dwarf Suite* and *Wild Men's Dance* before setting off with Tapper on a second tour of the continent. Europe

Figure 1.2. Bertha Fiering Tapper and her piano students (photo from the first half of 1910s). Tapper is seated in the center. To the right: Leo Ornstein and Claire Reis. To the left: Kay Swift and Pauline Mallet-Prevost (who later married Ornstein). Courtesy of Vivian Perlis.

intensified his attraction to modernism. In Berlin, Ornstein met Ferruccio Busoni, and in Paris, he fell in with M. D. Calvocoressi, a well-known music critic of the day. All the while, he continued to fashion himself into a latter-day Franz Liszt, integrating his own compositions into his concerts. He programmed contemporary European works as well. This pattern began when Ornstein participated in a series of lecture-recitals given by Calvocoressi in Paris in 1914, at which he performed music by Schoenberg and Cyril Scott, together with his own *Impressions de la Tamise* and *Danse Sauvage*. But his solo debut as a modernist virtuoso took place in London on 27 March 1914 at Steinway Hall, where he performed three chorales by Bach, as transcribed by Busoni, together with "a group of Schoenberg pieces," and his own Sonata (Op. 35), *Wild Men's Dance, Impressions of Notre Dame, Moods* (Op. 22), *Six Short Pieces* (Op. 19), and *Prelude* (Op. 20, No. 2). Other recitals in Paris and London established Ornstein's credentials abroad, an important step for gaining notice in New York. There were only occasional hints of chauvinist hoopla in the reception of Ornstein in America—little of the attitude of "here, finally, is a young American who can compete with the European masters" that greeted the generation of Aaron Copland and Henry Cowell. Rather, perspectives on him seemed to be shaped within an international perspective. He was seen more as Jewish than as American.[4]

Ornstein quickly built himself into something of a cult figure, especially for the tone clusters that became his trademark and for his capacity to mesmerize an audience. He transplanted the star magnetism of a nineteenth-century keyboard virtuoso into a modernist context. "You see a young man of a rather distraught, disheveled appearance and a sort of cowed, hang-dog manner slouch upon the stage," wrote the critic Charles L. Buchanan in 1916. "He sits before the piano in a crumpled-up, hesitating, half pathetic way. A lock of black hair falls over a frail, sensitive and not unprepossessing countenance." Once Ornstein dove into his own music, however, he transformed "pathetic" eccentricity into a sense of being "possesst [*sic*] by a bewildering and diabolic degree of energy." Commentators on both sides of the Atlantic noted the power of his presence. The *London Daily Telegraph* marveled over how Ornstein's listeners were "hypnotized as a rabbit by a snake," and Buchanan compared Ornstein's piano playing to the revivalist preaching of Billy Sunday.[5]

From 1916 through 1921, Ornstein presented a string of public performances that featured new music, especially his own compositions. Most took place on Saturday afternoons in Aeolian Hall. Ornstein's appeal was still on the rise, with one reviewer commenting that his recital in November of 1916 "was no less than a graduation into popularity for this young and revolutionary pianist" and that he had a "largely increased following." At that particular event, his *Impressions of the Thames* and *A la Chinoise* were "so enthusiastically" received that he added his *Wild Men's Dance* as an encore. A less well publicized series of four recitals, given by Ornstein during the spring of 1916 in the West Side home of Claire Raphael Reis, had significance in yet another dimension: it laid groundwork for the composers' organizations that were to have such an impact during the 1920s. Like Ornstein, Reis had also been a pupil of Tapper, and after their teacher died in 1915 she stepped in to take up the young virtuoso's cause. The "intimate" recitals she arranged were intended not only to promote Ornstein's career but, more significantly, to form a "nucleus" for "a modern music society." Her collaborator in this enterprise was the critic Paul Rosenfeld, one of the defining figures in American modernism.[6]

In 1922 Ornstein began to withdraw from the concert stage, just as a more broad-based modernist movement was emerging. He later claimed that he felt he could not "carry [his futurist style] any further without becoming completely and utterly unintelligible." He also was weary of coping with his "extreme nervousness" about performing in public. In the 1920s, Ornstein taught first at the Philadelphia Musical Academy and then at his own Ornstein School of Music, also in Philadelphia, where he remained until his retirement in 1953. (John Coltrane studied there.) Through the course of the decade, he reappeared occasionally—for the premiere of his Piano Concerto by Leopold Stokowski and the Philadelphia Orchestra in 1925 and that of his Piano Quintette at a League of Composers concert in 1928, among other sporadic events. But those appearances ended after 1930. By 1933, when Henry Cowell summarized the brief history of the modernist movement in *American Composers on American Music*, he addressed Ornstein's case in the first few pages of his introduction, saying Ornstein had "startled the world with his unheard-of discords and his renunciations of form." Then Cowell quickly dismissed him as "not [having] influenced the general trend since 1920 at the latest." Just as tellingly, he did not include a profile of Ornstein as one of his chapters.[7]

Such was Ornstein's curious story—rising rapidly on the New York scene and then virtually disappearing from sight. While Ornstein would have seemed a natural patriarch for radical young American composers of the 1920s, he never was acknowledged as such—perhaps because his teaching career in Philadelphia removed him from the center of new-music activity.

Despite this later eclipse, Ornstein was the single most important figure on the American modern-music scene in the 1910s. Even if his music is little performed today, a few of his titles have resonated across the decades—*Wild Men's Dance, Impressions of Notre Dame, Dwarf Suite, A la Chinoise*. These pieces all date between 1913 and 1918, and they share certain traits: programmatic titles, tone clusters, a percussive approach to the piano, a post-impressionist harmonic idiom, and fluid structures. Each has an improvisatory feeling—as though hatched before the listener's ears. Added to this, Ornstein was not only a captivating performer but also an effective image-maker. Playing off the nineteenth-century idealization of composition as being practiced by solitary geniuses who experienced lightning bolts of inspiration, Ornstein gave it an up-to-date slant. He claimed his music to be the product of "the irresistible urging of some mysterious spiritual force," suggesting a compulsion akin to automatic writing. In this construction, his mind and body were receptacles for creative messages conceived at a level beyond conscious control.[8]

This last notion smacked of the "vital impulse" articulated by the philosopher Henri Bergson, whose writings about creativity had a widespread impact on the development of modernism in both Europe and America. With a legion of followers among modernist painters, writers, and composers, Bergson strove for a view of art that would attain a spiritual resonance. Creative artists affected by his ideas included Wassily Kandinsky, William Butler Yeats, T. S. Eliot, James Joyce, Virginia Woolf, and Edgard Varèse. Bergson was the first to shape a "process philosophy, which rejected static values in favour of values of motion, change, and evolution." He urged his readers, "Always follow your inspiration." Bergson appeared to intellectuals of the early twentieth century "as a liberator sent to rescue mankind from the chains of scientific rationalism." He was viewed as "a champion of creativity and freedom in a world which seemed threatened by the ogres of materialism and determinism."9

Bergson's publications were easily accessible in New York. According to one scholar, Bergson turned "creativity and intuition" into the buzzwords of 1910. An English translation of *Creative Evolution* was published in the United States in 1911, four years after it appeared in France, and Bergson gave a series of much-publicized lectures at Columbia University in 1912–13. He was also an important force in the symbolist leanings manifested in Alfred Stieglitz's journal, *Camera Work*. An extract from *Creative Evolution* was published there in October 1911, and other Bergson essays followed in January and April 1912. Art historian Sherrye Cohn believes that *Camera Work*'s regular contributors, including especially the dadaist Marius de Zayas, "stressed the extra-intellectual, instinctual, and precognitive powers of the mind as indispensable to the creation and experience of art" and that they did so in part because of Bergson's impact.10

These were the very terms in which Ornstein discussed his creative method. A 1918 monograph about Ornstein by Frederick Martens, which is filled with quotations from the composer, lays out Ornstein's way of composing as having several key components. The pieces were "written at one sitting" and inspired by "a subtle musical intuition" rather than "a mathematical design." They were "never compose[d] at the piano," they were "developed in his mind" and in some cases not notated for years. Often he dictated them to his wife, the pianist Pauline Mallet-Prevost. According to historian Vivian Perlis, all his scores dating after their marriage in 1915 are in her hand. An extreme case of Ornstein's disregard for notation came with *Three Moods*, which he told Perlis had been in his memory for thirty years before he finally wrote it out in 1948. He had much to say about his unusual compositional process:

> To me, you see, music has absolutely no meaning if it doesn't have some
> emotional impact. I'm not interested in music as an intellectual [pursuit]—
> not at all, I'm bored to death with it. . . . And you see, what happened there
> apparently, there was some kind of emotional [energy] that drove the thing.
> And then, sort of instinctively and without knowing what it was all about,
> I grabbed at anything that was at hand to just get the thing down.

In an essay about Ornstein's music from 1916, Carl Van Vechten reported the same rationale: "The boy says only that he writes what he feels. He has no regard for the rules, although he has studied them enough to break them thoroughly. He thinks there is an underlying basis of theory for his method of composition, which may be formulated later. It is not his purpose to formulate it."[11]

Other commentators reported on Ornstein's "spiritual energy," his "simple, unspoiled, ardent, sensitive human" qualities, his "childlike" imagination, and his role as a "passive transmitter" of new sounds. These phrases resonate with Bergsonism, depicting creativity as a form of spiritual channeling, as an intuitive kind of primitivism, as sublimely antiformalist. They also fit with the notion of performance as catharsis. Bergson favored "intuition" over intellect, seeing it as constituting the "vital impulse" behind creativity. "But it is to the very inwardness of life that *intuition* leads us," he wrote in *Creative Evolution*; "by intuition I mean instinct that has become disinterested, self-conscious, capable of reflecting upon its object and of enlarging it indefinitely. . . . Intuition may enable us to grasp what it is that intelligence fails to give us, and indicate the means of supplementing it." This statement tied to the philosopher's focus on evolution, which underlay his

Figure 1.3. Leo Ornstein, photo by "Sarony," as published in *Musical Quarterly* (1918). Reproduced by permission of Oxford University Press.

belief that the more advanced states of human biology and social order were not necessarily better. Unleashing spontaneous impulses was fundamental to his theories. "For consciousness," Bergson continued, "corresponds exactly to the living being's power of choice; . . . consciousness is synonymous with invention and with freedom. Now, in the animal, invention is never anything but a variation on the theme of routine. . . . With man, consciousness breaks the chain. In man, and in man alone, it sets itself free."[12]

Ornstein deliberately cultivated these qualities of "freedom" and "invention," seeking to bring about the triumph of "instinct." He also promoted the notion of his music as thoroughly original—as being untouched by other new compositions. This last was a common stance for modernists of the early twentieth century. At the height of Ornstein's career, Martens claimed that "Ornstein has often been spoken of as an imitator of Schönberg; yet *The Wild Men's Dance*, and others of his more individual compositions, had been written before he had ever seen or heard anything by the Viennese composer." Ornstein also took part in promoting the purity of his originality: "When I wrote the 'Moods,' 'Wild Men's Dance,' 'Notre Dame Impressions' and 'Chinatown' [meaning probably *A la Chinoise*] I was unaware of any contemporary composers or compositions. I was not acquainted with any new music at all. I was brought up in the most rigid classical tradition. It has puzzled me greatly why I began to hear the things that I did since there was nothing in my musical background to explain the gap between my early training and what I suddenly was hearing." It is impossible to verify these claims, yet they raise intriguing issues. Certainly by 1914—and perhaps even earlier— Ornstein could not have maintained with any credibility to be living in a new-music vacuum, for around that date he met Calvocoressi and took on the role of proselytizer for fellow modernists, regularly performing compositions by Schoenberg, Stravinsky, and others.[13]

Ornstein's stance recalls that of Charles Ives, who also disavowed his connection to European modernism. In 1931 Ives told E. Robert Schmitz, "I have never heard nor seen a note of Schoenberg's music." Both Ives and Ornstein faced charges that their work was derivative; they were constantly being compared to Europeans, who were put up as the standard against which to measure American composers. In the case of Ives's outburst to Schmitz, he was defending himself against a review by Henri Prunières in which the French critic had said "there is no doubt that [Ives] knows his Schoenberg." Ornstein confronted the same comparisons, such as the following made by Winthrop Parkhurst in 1920: "Leo Ornstein is unquestionably a musical anarchist, . . . [but] he is neither the discoverer nor the actual creator of modern musical anarchy. On the contrary, his system of harmonic and contrapuntal polity is derived directly from and based directly on the heresies of half a dozen contemporaries and forerunners. Stravinsky, Schoenberg, Strauss, Scriabine: these are some of the men on whom he leans heavily for authority." The impulse to fend off such reductive comparisons with rising European titans—especially in a modernist climate—must have been great.[14]

There is a substantial body of music by Ornstein, much of it still in manuscript, with a few works published by small firms. It divides into three large groups: compositions from Ornstein's heyday in the 1910s, most written for solo piano; works from the 1920s, when he branched out into orchestral and chamber compositions; and a diminished but steady output through the subsequent decades that surged in the 1970s, when Ornstein returned energetically to composing after being rediscovered by the historian Vivian Perlis. The most "thrilling" pieces, as Paul Rosenfeld evaluated them, date from the 1910s and are distinguished by their "aesthetic of spontaneous, uncalculated, virginal response." These traits account for both their strengths and shortcomings.[15]

Of the fourteen solo piano works written by Ornstein during the 1910s, two will be looked at here: *Three Moods* of 1914 and *A la Chinoise* of 1918. Together they give a good sense of the dimensions of Ornstein's style, which added up to a quirky fusion of the old-fashioned and the avant-garde. As is typical of Ornstein's work from this period, these pieces follow a time-worn nineteenth-century custom of bearing titles that evoked some extra-musical image, whether the emotional states of "Anger," Grief," and "Joy" in *Three Moods* or impressions of a distant scene, as in *A la Chinoise*. Other examples of Ornstein's landscape pieces included *A Paris Street Scene at Night* (1912), *Impressions of Notre Dame* (1914), and *Impressions de la Tamise* (ca. 1914). Many of his works extended Debussyan practices. In "Grief," for example, there is a gently undulating bass and misty ambience. *A la Chinoise* includes filigreed sixteenth-note textures in its middle section, albeit with chromatic pitch constructions. There are also frequent pentatonic melodies.[16]

Yet these works break decisively with the past in a trait that became Ornstein's signature: chromatic tone clusters that are either delivered percussively (as in the heavy pounding bass clusters of "Anger") or, ironically enough, contained within the rippling, post-impressionistic textures described above. The latter occur in *A la Chinoise*, in which Ornstein presents a series of static thirty-second-note clusters (Example 1.1). Most clusters here are built of three to five notes, involving none of the fist or forearm groups soon to be devised by Henry Cowell. But they are striking for their chromaticism and their dogged repetitions. At the opening of *A la Chinoise*, for example, the undulating cluster pattern builds in volume until a pentatonic melody (the most common stereotype used to evoke Chinese musical practice) enters in the left hand, with clusters continuing above. Even a central section, which has far more hard-hitting clusters, still projects a five-pitch tune, although a more chromatic one than at the opening (Example 1.2). This technique of juxtaposing an experimental voice (here, the clusters) with a traditional one (the pentatonic melodies) bears comparison to a similar practice in Henry Cowell. In *The Tides of Manaunaun* (ca. 1917) Cowell assigned forearm black-key clusters to the left hand while the right hand carried a diatonic melody.

Besides clusters, Ornstein's other main trait during this period was the use of meandering structures, which seem hatched on the spot and improvisatory. They could easily be dismissed as shapeless. Yet they may well embody the spontaneity at the

Example 1.1. Ornstein, *A la Chinoise*, p. 1. © 1918 (Renewed 1945) Screen Gems-EMI Music Inc. All rights reserved. International copyright secured. Used by permission.

To Mr. Rudolf Ganz

A la Chinoise

LEO ORNSTEIN, Op. 39

core of Ornstein's Bergson-saturated compositional process. "Our personality," Bergson wrote, "which is being built up each instant with its accumulated experience, changes without ceasing. By changing, it prevents any state, although superficially identical with another, from ever repeating it in its very depth." *A la Chinoise* irregularly alternates sections of clusters and rapid runs—all delivered as a *perpetuum mobile* constructed of thirty-second notes. There is no conventional development of ideas; instead, snippets recur irregularly, with little seeming concern for tightly shaped organization. The structures of these pieces can perhaps best be understood if they are regarded as *performance* compositions—works inextricably connected to Ornstein's passionate keyboard persona. The impact of hearing Ornstein spin out his own compositions in front of an audience was clearly captivating, as the accounts already quoted attest. Yet like a jazz transcription, his music loses vitality on the printed page, needing the tone color, stage posture, and interpretative flair of its inventor to attain its original impact.[17]

Ornstein's compositions of the 1920s differed remarkably from those of the previous decade. More conservative, almost reactionary, they show a side that had been present in Ornstein early on. He had composed "impressionistic" pieces during the 1910s under the pseudonym "Vannin," and already in 1916, at the height of Ornstein's visibility as a "futurist," Van Vechten was puzzling over what he kindly called the "diversity" of Ornstein's style, in which the composer swung almost manically from being a wild man to a buttoned-down conservative. By the 1920s, it was the Ornstein of the tie and tails, rather than beret and cape, who dominated. The *Quintette for Piano and Strings*, composed in 1927 to a commission from Elizabeth Sprague Coolidge, gives a good sense of this new direction. Ornstein featured himself at the piano, as he had in the Piano Concerto of 1923. Yet because the piece involved other performers—rather than being for piano alone—it was, by necessity, fully notated right from the start, seeming less of a free-wheeling odyssey than Ornstein's earlier solo-piano works. The same idiosyncratic structures exist, but they now seem long and meandering rather than spontaneous. Folklike tunes evoking Russian scenes frequently appear within a lush, neoromantic harmonic idiom. Similar traits characterize the Piano Concerto. Whereas Ornstein had battered at tradition in the 1910s, devising a distinctive dissonance for a new age, in the 1920s he embraced it, settling down within a safe haven of rich harmonies and nostalgic memories of his homeland.[18]

Beyond his musical language, Ornstein's identity as a Jewish immigrant affected his reception and musical opportunities. As a Ukrainian who relocated to the United States, Ornstein was the first in a series of Eastern European Jews—or their children—who were to play a major role in American modernist composition. In the concert-music field, the most renowned case was Aaron Copland who, like Ornstein, represented a separate class of Jews from those of German descent who were already well established in New York. Carl Van Vechten identified Ornstein early on in terms of ethnicity and class, calling him "a poor Russian Jew music student." Others perceived the young virtuoso the same way. Ornstein's early affiliation with Bertha Fiering Tapper, for example, led to his friendship with Claire Raphael—later to become Claire Reis—who presented him in the "Four Intimate Recitals" that pointed toward later modern-music societies. A Scottish Jew, Reis married well, ascending into New York's German Jewish aristocracy, and she performed the same nurturing role with Ornstein that she later played with Copland.[19]

Other progressive Jewish intellectuals of the day took up Ornstein's cause, especially the novelist and cultural critic Waldo Frank and the critic Paul Rosenfeld. Frank attended at least some of Ornstein's musicales held in Tapper's apartment. He wrote of them at the time, calling the young Ukrainian-American an advocate of "musical anarchism," placing him alongside Stravinsky and Schoenberg as one of three great composers of the 1910s, and predicting that Ornstein "gives promise to be the greatest." Frank also recalled these informal recitals in his memoirs. Rosenfeld's connections to Ornstein began just as early and were longlasting. His reviews of Ornstein from the 1910s already show Rosenfeld to be a modernist insider, solidly supporting this young "ultra-modern" and wryly commenting on his reception by his more conservative colleagues. "Ornstein alone continues to represent to the critics, the composer delighting in ugliness for its own sake," wrote Rosenfeld in 1916. "And to the public [he is] the grand comic figure it demands the ultra-modern composer to be." As further evidence of Ornstein's connection to Frank and Rosenfeld, the young composer published an article about Stravinsky in *The Seven Arts*—a short-lived American modernist journal with which both critics were closely affiliated.[20]

Ornstein had the ability not only to shock but also to convert. He proved that an American—and an immigrant no less—could attract international attention as an innovative composer. He opened the door to experimentation and the use of unorthodox materials. And he showed that modernism could be successfully marketed through clever packaging.

In these incipient years of American modernism, a few composers bore witness to Ornstein's impact. Emerson Whithorne, who later helped found the American Music Guild, the International Composers' Guild, and the League of Composers, was among those who experienced an epiphany in Ornstein's presence. "Like a revelation the gorgeous cacophony overwhelmed me," he wrote of an Ornstein recital in St. Louis in 1917. "I then realized that my 'modern' songs, piano compositions and orchestral works were effete. . . . My music possessed no raw flavor of the primitive human. There was too much order and culture in it." Claire Reis confessed undergoing the same transformation under Ornstein's spell. And while the historical record is a bit dim, there remain isolated signs that burgeoning American modernists of the 1910s—most of whom would come into prominence a decade later—knew of Ornstein and reached out to him. In notes for lectures given at the Whitney Studio Club in 1922, Carl Ruggles called Ornstein "the first American composer who ever interested me." In 1928, Henry Cowell remembered that "when modern music was quite rare" Ornstein had "broke[n] with great suddenness into a highly dissonant and individual style." On another occasion Cowell recalled meeting Ruggles in 1917, at a time when "only two" other American composers "shared" his "intense delight in exploring free dissonance: Charles Seegar [*sic*] and Leo Ornstein." Further such testimony came from Dane Rudhyar, who met Ornstein during the summers of 1917 and 1918 at Seal Harbor, Maine, and who learned, through him, of "a young boy in California" named Henry Cowell who was writing clusters for his "whole arm." And George Antheil wrote in early 1922 of having given Ornstein one of his compositions "three years ago—a little piano piece which he liked and asked for."[21]

These connections with young modernists faded after Ornstein drew back from the concert scene in the early 1920s. Yet his daring spirit continued to have an impact, as did the power of his clusters. Antheil, Cowell, Rudhyar, and Ruggles may not have fully acknowledged their inheritance from Ornstein, but they tucked it away in their pockets as they set out on their own modernist adventures.

Creating a God

The Reception of Edgard Varèse

On my fifteenth birthday, my mother said she would spend
five dollars on me (a lot of money for us then), and asked me
what I wanted. I said, "Well, instead of buying me something, why don't you just let me make a long-distance
phone call?" (Nobody in our house had ever made a long-
distance phone call.)

I decided that I would call Edgard Varèse. . . . I don't remember exactly what I said when I finally spoke to him—
probably something articulate like "Gee I really dig your
music."

Varèse told me that he was working on a new piece called
"Déserts," which thrilled me since Lancaster, California, was
in the desert. When you're fifteen and living in the Mojave
Desert, and you find that the World's Greatest Composer
(who also looks like a mad scientist) is working in a secret
Greenwich Village laboratory on a "song about your hometown" (so to speak), you can get pretty excited.

—Frank Zappa, 1989

Musicians, critics, and historians love to love Edgard Varèse. Yet he and his supporters have not always seen it that way.

Within months of landing in New York Harbor in late December of 1915, the
thirty-one-year-old Frenchman entered the public eye, issuing periodic pronouncements through newspaper interviews and music magazines about the need for "new
instruments" and "new mechanical mediums which can lend themselves to every
expression of thought." He also criticized contemporary performers and audiences

for being "hypnotized by the past." Already he had formulated the principal themes of his entire career. Dark and handsome, with compelling self-confidence, Varèse quickly settled into a small community of French expatriate intellectuals and artists. He was closely identified with futurism and the machine movement. Like the "mad scientist" that Frank Zappa remembered, Varèse often was perceived as being out there in a creative orbit of his own, careening off into stratospheres of sonic discovery while mere mortals had not yet invented the practical means for realizing his visions. By the spring of 1927, when Varèse's *Arcana* received its premiere a few days after that of Antheil's *Ballet Mécanique*, the considerable power and status of the French-American were clearly apparent. Paul Rosenfeld hailed him in the *Dial* as a "new god." Olin Downes of the *New York Times* called him a "hero." Antheil, meanwhile, had produced a "flatulent" work of "blatant emptiness."[1]

Such praise clashes with the notion of an underappreciated genius or cultural tragedy portrayed by Varèse's supporters. He faced "only abuse and ridicule," wrote his student and amanuensis Chou Wen-Chung. "Few took him seriously," even though he was a "real composer," concurred the historian Wilfrid Mellers. He was "one of a now somewhat unjustly forgotten group of experimental composers of the '20s," lamented the composer Elliott Carter. "Varèse's time was long in coming, but he has made it into history at last," wrote the theorist Jonathan Bernard in the late 1980s.[2]

The myth of unjust neglect invites scrutiny. Not only was Varèse handled with consistent deference by the New York press during the 1920s, but in an even broader sense, he and his music have been chronicled and discussed at greater length than probably any other figure in this book. This has happened in part because Varèse emerged after World War II as a welcome ancestor for a new generation of American modernists, especially those involved in the electronic-music movement. His was the legacy they could comfortably claim from the 1920s. For Carter, Milton Babbitt, and a host of others, Varèse stood as an emblem of unadulterated high culture, quite literally lifted out of the Old World and into the New. No crossover figure when it came to genre, Varèse was a pure modernist, untainted by populist leanings.[3]

Historians of twentieth-century music have picked up this attitude, assessing Varèse's work with an exceptionally serious tone. Among Varèse's near-contemporaries in America, only Charles Ives can count on such treatment. But it is the collective weight of the Varèse bibliography that makes the biggest statement, including the valuable (if incomplete) memoirs of his wife Louise, as well as a growing series of studies produced by music theorists and historians.[4]

What has been forgotten is the degree to which this admiration for Varèse took shape from his earliest years in New York. Far from being ignored or harshly criticized during the 1910s and 1920s, as legend has it, Varèse was put on a pedestal. He became the matinee idol of modernism. If critics felt incomprehension in the face of his avant-garde scores, they assumed it to be *their* problem, not his. This is not to say that Varèse felt sufficiently appreciated in New York or that the artistic environment as a whole was as supportive—either spiritually or economically—as he might have required. But he loomed large, and he did so for reasons that turn out to be as intriguing as the attitude of reverence itself.

When Varèse arrived in New York in the midst of World War I, he joined the wave of European immigrants that also brought Ernest Bloch, E. Robert Schmitz, and Dane Rudhyar. His work ultimately may have come to define an important strain in the history of American music, but his European origins provided a strong international identity that he maintained throughout his career. This is crucial to remember. Not only did Varèse perceive himself as European, but others did as well.

Before arriving in America, Varèse (1883–1965) had studied at the Schola Cantorum in Paris and with Ferruccio Busoni in Berlin. He was already a well-established professional, having encountered some of Europe's leading artists and writers, including Guillaume Apollinaire, Fernand Léger, Pablo Picasso, Erik

Figure 2.1. Edgard Varèse, photo published in *Musical America* (5 December 1925). Courtesy of Musical America Archives.

Satie, and Richard Strauss. In New York, Varèse followed a typical pattern for newly arrived immigrants by immediately connecting with a community of expatriates from his home country. "I see only Europeans," he wrote his former mother-in-law during his first few months in the city. Varèse made his first significant connections with the French artists Marcel Duchamp and Francis Picabia; a later close colleague was Carlos Salzedo, with whom he founded the International Composers' Guild. Unlike immigrant laborers, however, who most often sought work within existing manufacturing and industrial systems, Varèse determined to create his own professional niche, asserting himself as an iconoclastic leader. He and his French confederates saw America as a land of opportunity, far from the war-bedraggled state of Europe. Duchamp enthusiastically declared America to hold the most promise for "the art of the future." The culture of Western Europe, by contrast, was "finished—dead." The headline of an interview with two of Varèse's other colleagues, the French cubists Albert Gleizes and Juliette Roche, declared, "New York Is More Alive and Stimulating than France Ever Was, Say Two French Painters." Roche breathlessly exclaimed, "Your city is beautiful! The lights, electric signs, most nourishing to artists." Varèse expressed some of the same wide-eyed idealism in notes for *Amériques* of 1918–21, his first score written after emigrating. There Varèse described America as embodying "all discoveries, all adventures, . . . the Unknown."[5]

At the same time as Varèse forged links with these fellow Frenchmen, his inspiration might also have come from an American artist: the photographer Alfred Stieglitz. Like Stieglitz, who established a series of galleries in New York to exhibit modern art, most notably the famous "291," Varèse aimed to make his mark in the United States not just as a creative artist in his own right but as a conductor and organizer of concerts—a figure who would actively introduce the latest compositions to his new home. "New York: Varèse, Conductor" is how Louise Varèse titled the chapter of her book that dealt with her husband's early years in the city. But Varèse aimed to define the role of conductor in a whole new way. Establishing a pattern for Pierre Boulez and Leonard Bernstein at mid-century, he determined to make contemporary music his focus. The fixation on historic European repertory that has so bedeviled progressive American musicians and critics throughout the century was already well ensconced, as was the star system of hiring Europeans—principally Germans—to conduct American orchestras. Among the reigning conductors then in New York were Walter Damrosch, Willem Mengelberg, Josef Stransky, and Arturo Toscanini—all highly visible, and all with little commitment to contemporary music. Varèse set out to challenge them. In a profile from 1916, three months after his arrival in New York, he was described as having "arranged for a tour with an orchestra, which he will conduct himself, and which will play in the main his own compositions." While this never seems to have materialized, it shows that he arrived with a mission in mind.[6]

When Varèse finally made his New York debut as a conductor on 1 April 1917, he compromised with conditions around him, already exhibiting the political acumen that was to serve him well over the years. Rather than proselytizing for modernism, he chose instead to program Berlioz's *Requiem*, and he did so as part of a "grandiose and solemn" concert staged as "a memorial in honor of all the soldiers who had been killed in the war." It was a cunning move. Varèse seized upon the obsession with war that was gripping Americans, as any contemporaneous newspaper or periodical showed. Furthermore, he took a cue from at least one star conductor of the day. Toscanini had been the feature of a profile in *Vanity Fair* just one year earlier, where he was shown rehearsing a "war concert" in Milan involving "over two thousand singers and musicians."[7]

Varèse's timing was brilliant. The day after the concert, President Wilson delivered a war message to Congress, and four days later (6 April), he declared war against Germany. Thus at the height of these traumatic events, a French conductor—significantly of the same nationality as America's ally—performed a French composition in the most populist of American forums—the Hippodrome on Sixth Avenue, which could hold an audience of up to six thousand. It was like choosing Yankee Stadium over Carnegie Hall. He also capitalized on another bit of recent publicity, commissioning a backdrop from Léon Bakst, set designer for Diaghilev, whose work had been in the news the previous winter when the Ballets Russes traveled to New York.[8]

The critics raved about Varèse's concert. He "seemed to possess the inspiration of genius," gushed the *Evening Mail*. He had presented Berlioz "in a veritable blaze of power," concurred Paul Rosenfeld. Even Varèse himself was satisfied, writing to his ex-mother-in-law: "It has been a marvelous debut. . . . The public adores me. Everyone predicts that I'll be one of their idols."[9]

This first venture established a tone for the reception of Varèse in New York over the next decade. By and large, "genius" and "power" were the very images that enshrined him. During the next few years, Varèse continued to pursue conducting opportunities. His nationality put him in the right place at the right time, contributing greatly to the speed with which he became established in New York. Once the United States declared war, Germans and German culture became targets of deep suspicion and even persecution. The same year as Varèse's Berlioz concert, the Metropolitan Opera banned productions of German works (a much more extreme measure than that taken in London, where Wagner, for instance, was performed in English translation), and the following year, Karl Muck, then conductor of the Boston Symphony Orchestra, was arrested as an enemy alien and imprisoned until the end of the war, when he returned to Germany. At the same time, the New York Philharmonic's programming of German works dropped from 60 percent in 1916–17 to 32 percent the next year. In an article in *Vanity Fair*, the critic Pitts Sanborn decried New York as having been "a suburb of Berlin, musically speaking." He went on: "Now is the time to shake our music free, to relieve us from the arrogant and narrow notion that all music made in Germany is divine." During these years, the German language was dropped from the curriculum in many American public schools, and everyday German terms were replaced. A "hamburger" became a "liberty sandwich," and "sauerkraut" was reborn as "liberty cabbage."[10]

Paul Rosenfeld called this period a "brief but terrible . . . orgy of musical witch-burning," and it had some potent by-products. As Americans rejected German culture, they discovered new repertories. "Banishment [of German music]," wrote the critic Henrietta Straus in the *Nation* in 1919, "forced us to explore the musical literature of other countries. . . . As a result, we have begun to recognize more than novelty in the works of Moussorgsky and Scriabine and Strawinsky, of Debussy and Ravel and Dukas."[11]

Varèse played a key role in this process of shifting cultural allegiance. After the Berlioz triumph, his next venture in March 1918 was to conduct the Cincinnati Symphony Orchestra. Varèse was hired to replace Ernst Kunwald, who had been jailed for being German, and he gave a program that was largely French. Reviving his mission of bringing modernism to America, he conducted Satie's *Gymnopédies*, Dukas's *L'Apprenti sorcier*, and Debussy's *Prélude à l'après-midi d'un faune*. These works, mostly new to his audience, were balanced by more familiar selections by Bizet and Borodin. Also included was the prelude to the first act of Wagner's *Lohengrin*, a surprising decision, given the political climate. With his contemporary offerings, Varèse recognized the necessity of educating his audience and invited the critic Carl Van Vechten to write program notes. Van Vechten was then one of the few Americans covering new music, and he had just published a profile of Satie in *Vanity Fair*. When trouble erupted in connection with this concert, it came not from the critics, who praised Varèse's performances, but from the orchestra's management, which was apparently scandalized that Varèse stayed in the same hotel as his future wife, Louise. As a result, the original plan for Varèse to go on tour with the orchestra was canceled.[12]

With his final, best-known attempt to establish himself as a conductor in America, Varèse was much more ambitious. He founded his own ensemble, the New Symphony Orchestra, which made its debut on 11–12 April 1919, and planned a season with two other pairs of concerts. Varèse envisioned this group as an alternative to New York's two reigning orchestras, the New York Philharmonic and New York Symphony Society. (In retrospect, it stands as a model for the American Composers Orchestra three-quarters of a century later.) His first program on 11 and 12 April included four works billed as a "first performance in New York": Debussy's "Gigues" from *Images*, Casella's *Notte di Maggio*, Bartók's *Deux Images*, and Gabriel Dupont's *Le Chant de la destinée*. Only one German composer was represented, and it was a safe choice—J. S. Bach. The remaining concerts were to include music by contemporary Americans (Charles Tomlinson Griffes, Charles Martin Loeffler, and Emerson Whithorne), as well as Europeans (Ferruccio Busoni, Maurice Ravel, Albert Roussel, and Jean Sibelius). One historic figure listed on an advance program—Jean-Philippe Rameau—was French; the other—César Franck—had a distinguished career as teacher and organist in France. Varèse continued to show keen awareness of the political climate. Peace was then being negotiated in Europe (the Treaty of Versailles was signed in late June), and Varèse's nationality remained an asset. A publicity flier for the concert opened by declaring that "Edgar Varèse . . . is a Frenchman. He was born in Paris and the major portion of his musical training was obtained in France." The third and fourth paragraphs (out of a total of five) focused on his French military service. Another timely political gesture came in organizing the group as a musicians' cooperative. These were the days when communism—fundamentally a cooperative concept—was first triumphing in Russia and Eastern Europe and still seemed an idealistic social experiment. That August, the Communist Labor Party of America was founded in Chicago.[13]

Varèse also showed strong publicity skills with the New Symphony Orchestra, lining up press in advance of the first concert. Interviews with him appeared at least twice in the *New York Times* and once in the *New York Telegraph*. In them, he seized a pulpit not only to promote his concerts but to further the broader cause of bringing modernist music to America. No distracted artist oblivious to practical strategies for success, Varèse showed real political savvy. He had likely watched his friend Marcel Duchamp "cultivate the scandal" that resulted after his ready-made sculpture *Fountain*—a urinal—was rejected from an exhibit by the Society of Independent Artists in 1917. According to one scholar, Duchamp immediately began "publicizing the incident and getting it written up in newspapers." Varèse's concerts were preceded by no similar act of audacity, but he showed himself just as aware of the power of the press. "I should like to propose a League of Nations in Art," Varèse wrote in a letter to the editor of the *Times*, published on 23 March. One month earlier, President Wilson had publicly unveiled a draft of the covenant for a League of Nations in conjunction with peace talks then underway in France. Unlike Wilson's vision, however, Varèse's league was somewhat anarchistic, needing "no covenants, no drafts, no high court of arbitration, no machinery to cause debate among politicians." Rather "it would exist solely in the mental attitude of the world." Varèse used this to advance an internationalist vision for modern music. "In art, as well as in politics, we have been jarred out of our traditional isolation. And the result will be good. . . . Art is nearer to the people than it was before the war. The great struggle has shown up the sham of conventionalism." Thus for Varèse the war had some positive repercussions, opening the possibility of a transatlantic community, of an art without geographic boundaries.[14]

Varèse also staged "an informal talk for readers of THE TIMES," which appeared on 30 March. It was essentially a press conference. Repeating a theme of one of his first interviews in America, he decried American musical organizations as "mausoleums, mortuaries of musical reminiscences." Then he made his pitch: "There is an urgent need for an organization that shall take what 'has been' for granted and lay stress upon 'what is'; an organization that will serve as the instrument through which living men may be heard." A similar interview appeared in the *Morning Telegraph* one week after the first pair of concerts.[15]

Yet despite this advance publicity, Varèse was unable to head off a mixed reception for his new orchestra. Louise Varèse perceived the reviews as containing "scarcely a good word." They sought, she continued, to "demolish the one conductor willing to jeopardize his career in order to bring such refreshment [i.e., new music] to New York." This may have signaled the beginning of the perception among Varèse loyalists that he was maligned and mishandled in the press. But it is important to separate out various components of the opinions expressed. The target of the criticism was Varèse's skill as a conductor, and attitudes about this point were fairly unanimous. An unidentified reviewer lamented in twisted syntax, "That [Varèse] has in him the making of a great conductor he did not demonstrate last night." Paul Rosenfeld, who was soon to become one of Varèse's biggest champions, agreed that he "limped pitifully through compositions by Bach and Debussy, Casella and Bartok." And the sixty-year-old James Gibbons Huneker, an eminent American critic, gently observed that Varèse was "evidently nervous," detailing a list of ways in which "his orchestra sounded like a wet hen." He ended supportively, expressing hope that Varèse would "do better" when he repeated the program. Most important to the story here, Huneker described Varèse as a figure whose "legend" was "already in circulation." This last was a key point, once again reinforced by the conductor's cultural credentials. "Mr. Varèse is French, and has had cosmopolitan experience," confirmed Huneker, who himself was described by Van Wyck Brooks as having a *"patrie psychique"* that "was always to be France, . . . a taste in which he resembled hundreds of New Yorkers."[16]

On the whole, then, these reviews did not summarily "demolish" Varèse. Rather, they criticized his competence on the podium while acknowledging the special aura that surrounded him.

So during the 1910s, a respectful tone emerged within discussions of Varèse. Yet dealing with a French-born conductor was one thing and confronting a modernist composer quite another. Varèse posed precisely this challenge in the ensuing decade, as he dramatically switched roles. The 1920s ultimately became the most productive creative stint of his life. As Ornstein retreated from the spotlight, Varèse stepped directly into it.

Amériques, the first of Varèse's compositions from this period, was probably begun in 1918 and completed in 1921. A series of major pieces followed: *Offrandes* in 1921, *Hyperprism* in 1922–23, *Octandre* in 1923, *Intégrales* in 1924–25, and *Arcana* in 1925–27. At the same time, Varèse clung to the core of his early mission in the city—that is, to present modern music. In 1921, together with Carlos Salzedo, he founded the International Composers' Guild (ICG); he continued to direct the organization until it folded in 1927. Varèse conducted only one performance for the ICG: the premiere of his own *Hyperprism* in March 1923. Otherwise, he consistently hired others.

Varèse's involvement in the ICG gave an enormous boost to his composing career by providing a forum for premieres of his *Offrandes, Hyperprism, Octandre,* and *Inté-*

grales. For *Amériques* and *Arcana*—both of which required full orchestra—premieres did not occur through the ICG but under the baton of Leopold Stokowski, who conducted them in subscription concerts of the Philadelphia Orchestra. This too grew out of Varèse's work with the ICG. Beginning in 1923, with the performance of Stravinsky's *Renard*, Varèse had engaged Stokowski occasionally for ICG concerts, building an alliance that ultimately opened up an exceptional opportunity for Varèse himself. Although Stokowski and the Philadelphia Orchestra programmed other contemporary music during this period, including some by Americans, the selections were limited—several works by Charles Tomlinson Griffes in 1919, *A Pilgrim Vision* by John Alden Carpenter in 1920, *El amor brujo* by Manuel de Falla in 1922, Piano Concerto No. 2 by Leo Ornstein in 1925, *Study in Sonority* by Wallingford Riegger in 1929.

The first of Varèse's compositions to receive its premiere in New York was *Offrandes*, which was performed at an ICG concert on 23 April 1922, conducted by Carlos Salzedo, with Nina Koshetz as soloist. The ICG was only in its initial season, and *Offrandes* attracted little critical attention, receiving a review in the *New York Times* that took up only a couple of inches of text buried at mid-page. But then *Offrandes* was not audaciously revolutionary. Written for soprano and small orchestra, with a prominent percussion section, it opens with a wash of strings, looking back more to Debussy than signaling a challenge to tradition. There are aspects of the innovations for which Varèse soon became famous: an erratic trumpet line that periodically pierces the gauzy texture, a prominent percussion section, and an episodic structure. Overall, though, *Offrandes* appears more like the opulent brocade of a turn-of-the-century salon than the clean linearity of a modernist interior.

This performance put at least one component of Varèse's critical reception in place. Winthrop Tryon, a strong journalistic supporter of Varèse during the 1920s, wrote an article about him the following summer for the *Christian Science Monitor.* Apparently Tryon did not review the premiere of *Offrandes*. But he attended rehearsals of it and was intrigued enough to interview Varèse in his New York apartment on 1 July, hoping to find out what other new pieces the composer was producing. Titled "New Instruments in Orchestra Are Needed, Says Mr. Varèse," this essay was one of a series of vehicles through which Varèse made his now-famous pronouncements about the need for new sound sources. Tryon described *Offrandes* briefly as having "a fine effect in performance," and he compared it favorably to other new works on the scene. *Offrandes*, observed Tryon, "seemed to me to say a thousand times more than things done after the manner of Brahms and Franck by conservative New York composers." As was to become the pattern in his interviews of Varèse, Tryon spent some time looking at the composer's latest manuscripts; he seemed comfortable with a score, and he reported what he saw. "He showed me, when I called on him," wrote the Boston-based critic, "the manuscript of an orchestral piece he is scoring on long sheets of paper specially ruled by a Parisian stationer, 52 lines to the page, and began pointing out parts not only for familiar musical instruments but also for a steamboat whistle, a rattle and a whip and I do not remember what other noise-making devices." This must have been *Amériques*.[17]

With this article, Tryon provided Varèse with a nationally distributed forum for airing his ideas, and Varèse used it well, giving a remarkable description of his music in which he not only articulated his innovations but also introduced a vocabulary that was to become commonplace in reviews of his music. "We should write today," he declared, "in a telegraphic style." Versions of the adjective "telegraphic" popped up constantly in writing about Varèse during the 1920s. His description of the overall shape of his works was equally self-aware and influential. "As for the technical aspects of modern music," Varèse continued, "we are working toward placing one harmonic plane against another and one volume of sound against another. The opposition of harmony to harmony, instead of note to note, will seem strange to anyone who thinks only in terms of the old instrumentation." This, then, was the concept of "sound masses," which later became a mainstay in describing the conceptual shape of Varèse's work. After endorsing "an enlarged percussion department," Varèse then concluded with one of the visionary statements for which he gained notoriety: "What we want is an instrument that will give us a continuous sound at any pitch. The composer and the electrician will perhaps have to labor together to get it. At any rate, we cannot keep on working in the old-school colors. Speed and synthesis are characteristics of our epoch. We need twentieth-century instruments to help us realize them in music."[18]

I quote this interview liberally to give a sense of how well Varèse communicated his mission and how seriously Winthrop Tryon treated it. Tryon uttered no criticisms in this essay, but rather let Varèse use the column as a platform to set out his progressive compositional agenda.

Varèse's next New York premiere—that of *Hyperprism* at an ICG concert on 4 March 1923, with Varèse himself conducting—also received modest critical attention. Varèse's reputation as a composer had not yet taken hold. W. J. Henderson, another old-guard American critic, reviewed it for the *Herald-Tribune*. Like Huneker writing about Varèse as conductor, Henderson handled Varèse respectfully, which was exceptional, given his usual "contempt" for contemporary music, as one scholar has put it. Henderson groused a bit but then paid his respects: "The name of Varèse will go down in musical history as that of a man who started something." Again, as with *Offrandes*, a scanty published reception of this premiere gives the sense of a small event performed for a community of insiders.[19]

The next performance of *Hyperprism* yielded an altogether different scenario. It put Varèse on the map as a composer in New York. Leopold Stokowski conducted the work with the Philadelphia Orchestra eight months after the ICG premiere, first in Philadelphia (7 November 1924), then in New York (16 December). Suddenly, there was abundant critical interest. This was a breakthrough score for Varèse, justifying the enthusiasm on musical grounds, yet it seems to have attracted attention largely because Stokowski chose to showcase it. A short chamber work for brass, woodwinds, and percussion—including siren—*Hyperprism* introduced the explosive, event-oriented style that became Varèse's signature. Built of a string of segments, each of which tends to reach a high point and then disappear, *Hyperprism* challenges longstanding conventions of form, texture, instrumentation, and dynamic pacing. At the opening, a trombone melody gains its character through erratic rhythms, extreme dynamic changes, and an initial fixation on the trombone's C-sharp, rather than through conventional pitch shaping (Example 2.1). Later in the flutes (m. 19ff.) and soon after that in the horns (m. 31ff.), there are melodies that follow more familiar procedures (neither is shown here). The first is angular in design and disjunct in pacing, yet tuneful; and the second invokes Wagnerian horns of doom—a nostalgic feature of which Varèse was fond. The percussion occasionally has sections in isolation. Throughout, however, its use is subtle and integrated into the ensemble. *Hyperprism* is perhaps most notable for shifting moments of sound and hard-edged timbres that collide, then disappear.[20]

Stokowski's performance of *Hyperprism* inspired a string of rave reviews, establishing a pattern that would obtain for the rest of the decade. Ursula Greville, who was visiting New York as a critic for the London journal *Sackbut*, proclaimed it "one of the most exciting things I have ever heard." More important, however, Lawrence Gilman, music critic for the recently merged *Herald-Tribune*, weighed in as a major supporter of Varèse—a role that he retained over the next several years. Gilman already had some history with Varèse, having written program notes for the debut of his New Symphony Orchestra in 1919. With *Hyperprism*, Gilman took part in some modernist myth making, calling the work "lonely, incomparable and unique," also "self-sprung and individual." And he confronted unbelievers—those who "say in their haste that such music affronts the sanctities of musical art and offends against reason"—by calmly declaring, "We are not one of these." This was a work that caught listeners' attention. Decades later, Minna Lederman, the editor of *Modern Music*, wrote to Louise Varèse asking which composition by her husband first used a siren. "I think I was present [at the concert]," Lederman recalled. "In retrospect it has seemed to me that nothing sounded or heard after that could equal its shock effect. Certainly things have been louder, more overwhelming—but these early works broke the barriers—for me at any rate." At the bottom of her carbon of the letter, Lederman scrawled "Hyperprism." Even today, *Hyperprism* stands out as barrier breaking, especially when compared to *Offrandes*. Its sections are splatted out, and its brevity is bracing.[21]

When *Octandre* received its premiere by the ICG on 13 January 1924, conducted by E. Robert Schmitz, another influential critic stepped forward to endorse Varèse. This was Paul Rosenfeld, perhaps the most important supporter of them all, given his role in shaping a vision of American modernism across art forms. Rosenfeld did not write for one of the daily newspapers but rather for the literary magazine the *Dial*. He came over to Varèse cautiously with *Hyperprism*, but with *Octandre*, he resoundingly joined Winthrop Tryon and Lawrence Gilman in a core triumvirate of

Example 2.1. Varèse, *Hyperprism*, p. 1. © Copyright 1986 by Casa Ricordi, a division of BMG Ricordi S.p.A. Reprinted by permission of Hendon Music, Inc., agent for Casa Ricordi.

N.Y. 2104

supporters. Varèse represented a rich blend of all that Rosenfeld valued most: a solid anchoring in European traditions, an uncompromising modernist stance, and an equally uncompromising commitment to "highbrow" values. The qualities in Varèse that captured the attention of modernists after World War II were the very ones that engaged Rosenfeld early on.

Rosenfeld ecstatically described *Octandre* as "hard of surface and machine-sharp of edge, . . . beautiful with intense economicality and concentratedness. The themes were stated in cablegram style." He held nothing back in this first endorsement of Varèse. A three-movement chamber work for woodwinds and brass with string bass, *Octandre* used no percussion whatsoever. Yet it took off from the style of *Hyperprism*. The opening oboe melody, for example, pastes together ever-changing snippets, each of which is a carefully shaped transposition of the opening four notes (Example 2.2). With no doubling among instruments, the textures are delectably transparent; each timbre resounds with a heightened sense of individuality. When the flute peals out a shrill C-sharp (rehearsal 1), it announces a section of pseudo-stasis. The flute pitch immediately moves down to a G-sharp and remains unchanged for over four measures, giving an illusion of repetition. But within this holding pattern lies a cauldron of activity. Rhythms change unpredictably, instruments appear and disappear. Suddenly, there is an explosive climax (final measure of example). These were characteristic gestures for Varèse: a meticulous attention to detail, an illusion of stasis, a sudden buildup.[22]

Rosenfeld recognized the distinctiveness of this composer's voice, endorsing him as a paragon of the "Machine Age," as well as a figure who could be placed alongside eminent European composers of the day. It was a bid for top-rank validation. "Varèse has already succeeded in achieving what Marinetti and his Italian group set out to do, and failed," Rosenfeld wrote at one point. But it was the conclusion that mattered most: "Last month, in this very space, we demanded to know who was the man destined to lead the art of music onward from Strawinsky's into fresh virgin realms of sound. One answer has come very quickly." Thus Varèse was not just moderately or locally recognized in Rosenfeld's eyes but seen as someone who could rival the biggest names across the ocean.[23]

With *Intégrales*, written for a similar ensemble, Varèse intensified his timbre-focused, event-oriented style. This time, however, Stokowski was the conductor, and the premiere took place at an ICG concert on 1 March 1925 in Aeolian Hall, giving another boost to Varèse's visibility. The work uses a type of ensemble that by then had become familiar—winds and brass, with, in this case, a prominent percussion battery. Like *Octandre* and *Hyperprism*, *Intégrales* presents sections with a static surface, punctuated by spasmodic interruptions. As sections come and go, they often run into gridlock, then suddenly and unpredictably resume forward motion.

Intégrales inspired Paul Rosenfeld to build on his previous rhetoric. Now, he not only praised Varèse's talents but also claimed him for the New World. "Varèse stems from the fat European soil," Rosenfeld acknowledged, but "he has come into

TO E. ROBERT SCHMITZ

OCTANDRE

BY

EDGARD VARÈSE

I

relationship with elements of American life, and found corresponding rhythms within himself set free." This continued a theme of his *Hyperprism* review, in which Rosenfeld had suggested that while still in France, "as a small boy," Varèse had read "some of the Leatherstocking stories, [and] the feeling of the prairies began to be associated in his mind with the sound of a very shrill, bitter-high whistle." Through such a validating construction, Varèse thus had a near-congenital connection to America and the machine, despite his European origins. Rosenfeld also built on the technological rhetoric introduced by the composer, adding to it images of "power" and "potency." His language resounds in retrospect with gendered meaning, at the same time as his machine imagery in part filled a metaphor gap, providing fresh vocabulary for unconventional repertory. Rosenfeld's prose on the whole tended toward the ornate, sometimes to the point of opacity, and he delighted in using extravagant extramusical references. With Varèse, he often spun descriptive orgies, conjuring up notions of Varèse as a state-of-the-art, testosterone-charged urban titan.[24]

One of the ways in which Rosenfeld did this in his review of *Intégrales* was to use the word *penetration*, which has since become ubiquitous in the literature about Varèse: "Varèse never has imitated the sounds of the city, as he is frequently supposed to do, or supposed to have been said to do by critical writers. His work is much more the penetration." This continued in the same review through a comparison of Varèse to the cubists, where a focus on "power" was coupled with a series of upward-thrusting images that gave off strong sexual overtones:

> Intégrales is informed with a genuine feeling of power. . . . The piece resembles nothing more than shining cubes of freshest brass and steel set into abrupt pulsating swing. . . . This music is built more vertically, moves more in solid masses of sound, and is held very rigorously in them. . . . The most powerful pronouncements merely force sound with sudden violence into the air, thrust it upward like the masses of two impenetrable bodies in collision. . . . The whole brought an amazing feeling of weighty power.

With this, Rosenfeld hailed Varèse for an eroticization of the machine, achieved by coupling mechanical images with ones of male potency. Such gendered language had surrounded Varèse from the very beginning of his career.[25]

With the New York premiere of *Amériques* on 13 April 1926, Varèse took another step forward. Stokowski again conducted, this time with the Philadelphia Orchestra in Carnegie Hall; the ICG was nowhere in sight. This was the second subscription concert at which Stokowski programmed a Varèse work. The critics' response remained as supportive as ever. Only Rosenfeld ventured any hesitation with the work, yet he did so with care and respect. With *Amériques*, Rosenfeld felt Varèse showed his "virtuosic genius with the orchestra," at the same time as he saw it occupying "a secondary place" when compared to "Hyperprism, Intégrales, and the other experiments in the simpler, directer, more positive forms made later by Varèse." This distinction, with which I agree, lends more weight to Rosenfeld's enthusiasm, especially in contrast to the unqualified huzzahs uttered by other critics.[26]

By the time of Stokowski's premiere of *Arcana* with the Philadelphia Orchestra in 1927 (Philadelphia, 8–9 April; New York, 12 April), Rosenfeld's praise dropped all qualifiers as he compared Varèse to Leonardo da Vinci. Olin Downes, as recounted earlier, declared Varèse a "hero." The audience reaction had been radically split—part hissing, part wild applause. But this, too, only added to the composer's luster: "Hissing is an honor rarely bestowed upon a composer in this town," wrote W. J. Henderson in the *New York Sun*. Praise of Varèse often came at the expense of George Antheil, whose *Ballet Mécanique* had been premiered a few days earlier. As the two main American composers connected with the machine, they were pitted against one another, score to score. While Antheil's ensemble of percussion, pianos, and machines banged, hammered, and roared, Varèse's string-based symphony was far more traditional. *Arcana*'s textures are dense, and its large percussion sections intricate and understated. While built on the same principles of explosive buildups and shifting planes of sound as his earlier chamber pieces, *Arcana* is ultimately huge and sprawling, lacking the taut concision that made the earlier works so compelling. But not a single critic uttered a negative word. A few months prior to the concert, Pitts Sanborn summarized the state of modernist composition in New York, vesting a royal sanctity in Varèse that was by then a common view. "The crown and sceptre of the left, however," wrote Sanborn, "the power that speaks to kindred power, and a big share of the glory, are vested in Edgar Varèse." He continued, "Mr. Varèse enjoys the incalculable advantage of being recognized in high places. . . . Mr. Varèse has arrived."[27]

By 1927, then, Varèse had attained considerable stature. All the time that Rosenfeld was building up Varèse's high-modernist potency, Gilman and Tryon continued to proclaim his genius. After the premiere of *Hyperprism*, Gilman called Varèse the "high priest of the International Composers' Guild," and after that of *Amériques*, he showed he had been reading Rosenfeld, hailing the work's "sense of power and release," its "violent, irrepressible exultation." And Tryon, for his part, continued to visit Varèse's studio, reporting on scores in progress. He too took part in the myth-making process, albeit with less histrionic delivery. Tryon followed Varèse to Paris in 1929, where he had temporarily relocated after the ICG folded in 1927, and he looked back on *Amériques*: "I felt it to be the first truly original composition in symphonic form ever written outside of Europe." He depicted Varèse as a modernist guru. "Musicians climb his stairs this winter, just as they did last; rue de Bourgogne, the same as Sullivan Street" (Sullivan Street was where Varèse had a house in Greenwich Village).[28]

Here, again, comparison to Varèse's counterparts in America is helpful. Stieglitz has been described by one art historian as having "an almost hypnotic presence in the art world of the 1920s in New York." Similarly, Marcel Duchamp was "celebrated" and "made famous" in New York, according to another scholar. "He was treated with curiosity, sometimes with bemusement or suspicion, but also with respect." Varèse inspired much the same aura.[29]

By the late 1920s, there were other signs that Varèse had clearly arrived. The British publishing firm of J. Curwen and Sons began issuing his scores in 1924—first *Hyperprism* and *Octandre* (1924), then *Amériques* (1925), and *Intégrales* (1926). *Offrandes* was published by C. C. Birchard in Boston in 1927, and *Arcana* by the Parisian firm of Max Eschig in 1931. This was an extraordinary achievement for a composer in America during the 1920s. Private modernist publishing firms, most notably New Music Quarterly Editions, begun in 1927 by Henry Cowell in California, and Cos Cob Press, founded by Alma Morgenthau Wertheim in New York in 1929, issued most scores composed by native-born Americans, and they did not start up until late in the decade. Added to this, C. C. Birchard published a twenty-four-page promotional booklet the same year it issued *Offrandes*. Authored by J. H. Klarén and titled *Edgar Varèse: Pioneer of New Music in America*, it was an unabashed marketing tool. There was a brief, highly flattering introductory essay, followed by snippets from Varèse's press over the course of the 1920s. Perhaps the most remarkable feature of this document was the quantity of positive press that was available to quote. Klarén did not just present brief "blurbs," to use the current jargon, but multiparagraph segments. A critical legacy was in place.

Capping it all off, Paul Rosenfeld's *An Hour with American Music* of 1929 concluded with a chapter on Varèse. The whole book built up to his imposing presence. "But the greatest fullness of power and of prophecy yet come to music in America, lodges in the orchestral composition of Edgar Varèse," Rosenfeld opened. He went on to sound an impassioned endorsement, placing his subject on a level with the great figures of Western Europe: "Edgar Varèse follows in the steps of Wagner, of Debussy, of the younger Strawinsky and of all the modern musicians not so much interested in the creation of beautiful objects as in the penetration and registration of the extant. He, too, is a kind of philosopher or sacred doctor." Later on, "he is the poet of the tall New Yorks."[30]

Given the substantial weight of this positive press and the strong recognition it carried of Varèse's compositional innovations, why did he and his supporters end up feeling as if New York had misunderstood him—as if neglect and even rejection had been his fate? Part of this, I believe, had to do with the construction of a double-headed myth, portraying Varèse not only as a unique modernist innovator unfettered by ghosts of the past but also as a misunderstood genius. The first part of this myth has been undergoing scrutiny for some time. With proclamations such as "I am the ancestor," Varèse attempted "a virtual parricide on musical tradition," as one scholar has put it. Varèse was not alone in assuming this posture. The futurists also fulminated in the face of tradition, and their attitude was symptomatic of a chronic condition. The young American writer Malcolm Cowley, for example, burned a volume of Chaucer during the early 1920s. To be modern, a creative artist needed to appear as new as possible, superseding all that had come before. In

Varèse's case, though, efforts to understand his links to Busoni, Debussy, Satie—even Wagner—have served to enrich his profile rather than diminish it.[31]

Critical rejection was another key part of structuring a modernist persona. While Winthrop Tryon observed that Varèse had an "unnecessary sensitiveness to criticism," there was more to the story than simply a thin skin. Bad reviews were often a painful reality for imaginative artists breaking with tradition. But they also became a badge of honor. Artists accepted by the establishment risked appearing less radical, but those vilified could be confident they were being sufficiently rebellious. A member of the avant-garde was a warrior, wary of compromise. At the same time, building a career required support in the press, and hungry egos yearned for the same thing. Thus earning approbation while claiming to be denounced gave a practical modernist the best of all circumstances. And so it may have gone with Varèse.[32]

There is yet another layer. When Varèse decided to leave New York in 1928, returning to his native France for five years, he set two concurrent streams in motion. First, his compositional output slowed remarkably. After a burst of productivity in the 1920s, he took three years to complete his next work, *Ionisation* (1930–31), and it, in turn, was not premiered until two years later, adding up to a total of six years since the premiere of *Arcana*. Second, he lost his two outlets for performance in New York. The ICG, as already noted, shut down in 1927. Less generally recognized, however, was Stokowski's decision to take a one-year sabbatical in 1928, complaining of shoulder problems. Thus, the same year that Varèse left for Paris, his principal promoter in the United States departed as well. During his years in exile, Varèse's main performance outlet became the Pan American Association of Composers, which he helped conceive in 1928. (He remained one of its nominal directors.) Nicolas Slonimsky conducted several of Varèse's compositions on concerts of the Pan American Association: *Intégrales* in 1931, *Arcana* in 1932, and *Octandre* in 1933. Since the first two of those performances took place in Paris and the third in Havana, they served an important purpose in disseminating Varèse's music. They did nothing, however, to enhance his standing in New York.

After so much compositional activity during the 1920s—with high-profile performances and critical approbation—Varèse faced a chasm in the United States. By the time of his next premiere—that of *Ionisation*, which was conducted by Slonimsky on 6 March 1933 in a Carnegie Hall concert for the Pan American Association—Varèse was back where he had started, having a new work unveiled by a small modernist organization that did not begin to garner the same critical attention as a major orchestra. Although *Ionisation* later entered music history as the first composition for an all-percussion ensemble—a position challenged here in the chapter about *Ballet Mécanique*—it was barely noticed after its premiere. Overall coverage of that concert was shockingly slight. An unsigned review in the *New York Times* was no more than 150 words long and simply recited a list of the compositions heard and performers involved. Another by "F.D.P" (Francis D. Perkins) in the *Herald-Tribune* was perhaps a hundred words longer, but it too said little. Varèse must have cringed to read only two sentences about *Ionisation*. The first of these simply described the piece as written for percussion, and the second took the form of an apology: "What with the vicissitudes of attending simultaneous musical performances at different points, the reviewer unfortunately missed Mr. Varese's first new work to be made public here in several years; accounts described the mass of sound to be most imposing, even overwhelming." Both the musical organization and the conductor were less celebrated than the days when Leopold Stokowski had presented Varèse's music with the Philadelphia Orchestra.[33]

The Varèse story from this point on is well known—the vastly diminished number of new compositions, the frustration at finding patronage, the search for technological breakthroughs to yield desired sound sources, and the wait until 1960 for his music from the 1920s to be released on recordings (Robert Craft conducted performances issued on Columbia Records). With *Déserts*, *Poème électronique*, and *Nocturnal*, written in the early 1950s, Varèse established himself as a pioneer of the electronic-music movement, and postwar American modernists, as noted at the opening of this chapter, seized him as a noble ancestor. Thus despite a gap in the middle, the critical advocacy of an earlier era was passed on to a new generation. Paul Rosenfeld handed a sacred scroll to Elliott Carter, Milton Babbitt, and their contemporaries, and it was inscribed with the image of a composer of impeccable high-culture credentials. The man who once stood as "a new god" rose again as a well-established deity.

The Arrival of European Modernism

The influence of new ideas and personalities is so rapidly felt throughout the world to-day that it is impossible for men in Madrid, Berlin or New York to work without thought of the evolution that is going on elsewhere.

—Exhibition of Modern Art,
Bourgeois Galleries, Fifth Avenue, 1916

On 17 February 1913, an "International Exhibition of Modern Art," better known as the "Armory Show," opened at New York's 69th Regiment Armory on Lexington Avenue and soon traveled to Boston and Chicago. It immediately created a sensation, especially with Marcel Duchamp's *Nude Descending a Staircase*, which was widely lampooned both for its cubist style and its unclothed subject. The show featured other European modernist painters, including Toulouse-Lautrec, Henri Matisse, and Pablo Picasso, as well as the work of young Americans such as John Marin and Marsden Hartley.

The Armory Show has since become a landmark in the history of modern art in New York, providing a fixed point in the transmission of the European avant-garde to America. "The moment belonged to the whole world," wrote art historian Meyer Schapiro. "Europe and America were now united in a common cultural destiny, and people here and abroad were experiencing the same modern art that surmounted local traditions."[1]

No such defining moment existed in music. There were the piano concerts of Ornstein and the New Symphony Orchestra of Varèse, to be sure. But they were isolated phenomena in a greater process of revelation and acquaintance—one that unfolded from the mid-1910s to the early 1920s as much through the dissemination of scores, commentary in the press, and informal exchange of information as it did through performance. It added up to a disorderly tale, and it is challenging to document. But it signaled a period of profound change, when the United States went from being years behind in hearing the newest European compositions, to attaining the status of a major international center. Increasingly, a composer or lover of new music did not have to sail across the ocean to hear the latest creations by European modernists. In 1915, the critic Carl Van Vechten railed against American conductors for introducing little of Stravinsky's music to the New World. But by 1925 conditions had altered so drastically that Henry Cowell could observe in *Musical America* that "Stravinsky is no longer an arch-fiend, a musical bogey to scare into submission the ears of refractory conservatory students. Eight years ago I was thought a raving lunatic because of giving a two-piano presentation of the 'Sacre'; now it is beginning to be regarded as almost passé by sophisticated concert-goers."[2]

The first period of the arrival of European modernism in New York—stretching from approximately 1914 to 1923—forms the subject of this chapter. This was the time when Copland, Cowell, Crawford, Thomson, and other American composers of the generation born around 1900 were adolescents. Their youth unfolded as modernism emerged. Even though so many of these figures eventually spent substantial residencies abroad, most of them first discovered the newest European music while still at home, and the ways they did so depended on a blend of socioeconomic background, education, geographic location, and serendipity. For some, the newest works were readily accessible in the United States, while for others they were totally unknown.

"During these formative years I had been gradually uncovering for myself the literature of music," recounted Aaron Copland in describing his discovery of the Great Tradition while growing up in Brooklyn. "Some instinct seemed to lead me logically from Chopin's waltzes to Haydn's sonatinas to Beethoven's sonatas to Wagner's operas. And from there it was but a step to Hugo Wolf's songs, to Debussy's preludes, and to Scriabin's piano poems." For this Brooklyn teenager, "modern music" meant Debussy and Scriabin, and his knowledge of the newest compositional styles broadened after arriving in Paris in 1921: "It was a fortunate time to be studying music in France. . . . Much of the music that had been written during the dark years of the war was now being heard for the first time. Schoenberg, Stravinsky, Bartók, Falla were all new names to me."[3]

Other budding modernists had different experiences. Like Copland, Virgil Thomson acknowledged Debussy and also Ravel as the reigning modernists in the Kansas City, Missouri, of his youth. Yet his experience with new European music while still in his native land ranged wider than Copland's. Thomson heard *Petrushka* in Kansas City during the 1916 nationwide tour by the Ballets Russes, and he had strong exposure to the music of both Stravinsky and Satie after beginning study at Harvard in 1919. Ruth Crawford represented yet another variation on this theme. European concert works—whether old or new—did not dominate the musical life of Jacksonville, Florida, during her adolescence there.

She later claimed her early artistic experience had "consisted of one concert each of [Percy] Grainger, Paderewski, and [Josef] Hofmann." Only after moving to Chicago in 1921 and beginning piano study with Djane Lavoie Herz did she encounter modernism: "I discovered Scriabin at this time; the music of Schönberg and Hindemith I did not hear until later; Stravinsky's *Sacre* and *L'Oiseau de Feu* came to me too about this time." In Philadelphia, George Antheil was having a similar experience. He wrote to his patron Mary Louise Curtis Bok in 1921, boasting, "There are few modern scores with which I am not a little acquainted—and of some (i.e., the Bloch Suite; Schönberg's Orchesterstücke) I know every note by heart." Antheil also encountered the music of Alfredo Casella, Les Six, Stravinsky, and Ornstein in Philadelphia and New York.[4]

These few testimonies confirm the slow but steady arrival of new European music during the 1910s. At first, it was being introduced with seemingly equal frequency in Boston and New York, also in Philadelphia and Chicago. But by the mid-1920s, New York emerged as the major site for such performances. This was an era before the widespread availability of recordings and radio. European modernism traveled through live performances, published scores, written accounts, and verbal testimony. A scattershot process of dissemination resulted, as is apparent in the performance history of selected European modernists who gained favor in the United States. All in all, composers and critics conveyed a sense of excitement, of uncovering treasures, and of struggling to maintain an edge of cultivation and currency.[5]

At first, Schoenberg seemed to be the European who most interested Americans. In December 1914, nearly two years after the Armory Show, Karl Muck conducted Schoenberg's *Five Orchestral Pieces* with the Boston Symphony Orchestra. This was a landmark event in Boston. "There were a few enthusiasts" in the audience, wrote Harvard English professor S. Foster Damon, "who mistook venerable Symphony Hall for a vaudeville theatre." But on the whole the reaction reflected indifference. "The majority read their programs," Damon continued, "making utterly no effort whatsoever to find out what the music was all about." Yet after five years had elapsed, Virgil Thomson heard about this performance when he began studying at Harvard. Schoenberg's piece "scandalized the hell" out of Archibald Davison, conductor of the Harvard Glee Club, Thomson recalled. Clearly the ongoing reverberation mattered as much as the performance itself. Once a major work such as *Five Orchestral Pieces* came into a city's musical orbit, it lingered.[6]

In January that same year, Schoenberg's earlier String Quartet in D Minor had received its New York premiere by the Flonzaley Quartet, one of the most accomplished ensembles of its day. On the whole, New Yorkers greeted the quartet more warmly than Bostonians had *Five Orchestral Pieces*. But then it was an earlier, more traditional composition. An unsigned review of the performance in the *New York Post* made it clear that this was the "first opportunity" for New Yorkers "to hear one of [Schoenberg's] larger works" and that "it is only within a few years that [he] has become so famous, or rather notorious." Intent on letting New Yorkers know where they stood in relation to major cities abroad, the critic informed readers that "only a few days ago some of [Schoenberg's] music was played in London, and the cable has told us how the audience and the critics were bewildered, annoyed, discouraged, dismayed."[7]

The Flonzaley Quartet worked hard to prepare the audience, staging two open rehearsals in advance of the concert. At the one on 28 December 1913, Kurt Schindler gave an introductory lecture explaining the piece. Schindler was an immigrant from Berlin who worked as music editor at G. Schirmer and conducted New York's Schola Cantorum. He presented an overview of Schoenberg's career and then introduced the audience to the music itself; the lecture was published immediately afterward. Schindler took care to reveal how the Flonzaley Quartet had come to perform the work, reassuring listeners with solid European endorsements that had local resonance. Adolfo Betti, first violinist with the ensemble and himself an immigrant from Italy, was introduced to the piece by Ferruccio Busoni, "who, during his last trip in America, spoke long and fervently to him of this neglected work." (Busoni had given concerts in the United States in 1910–11.) Schindler also informed his audience that Mahler thought highly of Schoenberg; Mahler, in turn, was a well-known figure in the city, having conducted the New York Philharmonic from 1909 to 1911.[8]

Between 1915 and the end of the decade, only a few subsequent Schoenberg performances seem to have occurred in New York. Most notably the Philharmonic-Symphony Society gave the American premiere of his orchestral tone poem *Pelleas and Melisande* in 1915, and Ornstein programmed the Opus 11 piano pieces on various recitals. The critic Carl Van Vechten reported in 1915 that "Charles Henry Cooper and Mrs. Arensberg played them [i.e., Schoenberg's piano pieces] in private." Not until the early 1920s, however—and then through the aegis of newly founded composer societies—did a substantial group of Schoenberg works reach the city. A comparison with the importation of Stravinsky's music provides clues about why this happened.[9]

"The name of Igor Stravinsky has crept across the Atlantic—thanks to America's newspapers, not to its orchestras," declared the *Boston Transcript* in May 1914, the same year as Schoenberg's *Five Orchestral Pieces* were heard there. But Stravinsky's orchestral compositions soon began appearing, and while they were by no means frequently performed, they surfaced with regularity on American programs up through the early 1920s. The Boston Symphony Orchestra performed *Fireworks* on 11 December 1914, and in January 1916 there were staged productions in New York of *Firebird* and *Petrushka*. These last occurred as part of a tour by Serge Diaghilev's Ballets Russes, which presented the works in New York before taking them across the country (these were the performances seen by Thomson in Kansas City). The tour, arranged by the Metropolitan Opera, was looked forward to with anticipation by New Yorkers. Edward L. Bernays, a nephew of Sigmund Freud, was

Figure 3.1. "Igor Strawinsky," photo from *Musical Quarterly* (1916). Reproduced by permission of Oxford University Press.

hired as publicist and "mounted a sophisticated campaign that publicized the ballet . . . [by] bombarding magazines, Sunday supplements, the music and women's page departments of daily newspapers." But the performances in New York ended up being a disappointment because the troupe's star dancer, Vaslav Nijinsky, arrived near the end of the engagement after he had been released as a prisoner of war; only then did the Ballets Russes realize expectations. That same March, Irene and Alice Lewisohn presented *Petrushka* at the Neighborhood Playhouse on Grand Street, with Charles Tomlinson Griffes and Lilly May Hyland at the piano. And three years later, in 1919, the work was again produced in New York, this time by the Metropolitan Opera with the choreography of Adolph Bolm, modeled on the original by Michel Fokine. These works were heard in concert renditions as well:

the Boston Symphony Orchestra performed the Suite from *Petrushka* in November 1920 and also the Suite from *Pulcinella* in December 1922.[10]

Stravinsky's chamber works had increasing exposure as well. Highlights included the Flonzaley String Quartet's presentation of his *Three Pieces for String Quartet* in 1915, one year after its composition. This was not a sympathetically received performance. There was some "un-Anglo-Saxon hissing," according to Paul Rosenfeld, but the audience was also "large and eagerly expectant," as *Musical America* reported. In the spring of 1918, the soprano Olga Haley and the London String Quartet performed *Pribautki* in New York. And by November 1920, when the Flonzaley Quartet gave the world premiere of Stravinsky's *Concertino for String Quartet*, which they had commissioned, a major change had occurred. No longer were New Yorkers hearing the second or third or seventh rendition of a piece, but they were watching it be unveiled.[11]

With increasing frequency, then, Americans living in major cities had opportunities to hear important new music by Schoenberg and Stravinsky not long after it was composed. Yet already in the 1910s Stravinsky was emerging as an American favorite, and by the mid-1920s he reigned triumphant. World War I had much to do with this. The anti-German sentiment that Varèse exploited in promoting his career as a conductor strongly affected Schoenberg's reception in the United States. From 1916 until the early 1920s, little of Schoenberg's music was heard in New York. When his *Five Orchestral Pieces* received its first New York performance in 1922 with the Philadelphia Orchestra conducted by Leopold Stokowski—eight years after the American premiere in Boston—Paul Rosenfeld sniffed a residue of wartime bias in the audience. "The assemblage sat like patients in dentist chairs, submitting resignedly to a disagreeable operation. What probably deterred from a more positive expression of distaste was a memory of certain hasty and mistaken prejudices, entertained in the same place." Not everyone reacted negatively, however. Years later, Henry Cowell recalled in a letter to Schoenberg (with a salutation "Dear Friend") that as a young man he had attended the performance and that the work was "marvellous."[12]

Other leading European modernists experienced varying visibility in the United States during this early period. Béla Bartók appears to have been among those who were little-performed, yet there were some intriguing exceptions. His piano music was performed by Heinrich Gebhard in Boston in 1912. The critic Lawrence Gilman later credited Gebhard as being "among the first, if not the first, to play Bartok's music in this country." The Boston Symphony Orchestra did not perform any of Bartók's music until 1926. Varèse conducted Bartók's *Deux Images pour Orchestre* (Op. 10) on concerts of his New Symphony Orchestra in April 1919, but the Hungarian's reputation did not take off in the city until the modern-music societies first performed his music, beginning in 1923.[13]

With Alexander Scriabin, the story was quite different. A slightly older figure than Bartók (Scriabin was born in 1872, Bartók in 1881) and citizen of a country with greater geopolitical significance, Scriabin enjoyed some fame in the United States during the early twentieth century.

All this began with Scriabin's visit to the United States in 1906, around the same time that Stieglitz began showing modern art in his New York gallery. Scriabin was remembered from that visit as "a shy little man with much wavy hair, a tiny Vandyke beard and clothes of fashion-plate elegance. He played [piano] extremely well and won resounding success." Then in 1908 Scriabin's *Poem of Ecstasy* was performed in New York by Modest Altschuler and the Russian Symphony Orchestra, and in 1915 Altschuler made an attempt, which failed, to present *Prometheus* with colored lights projected on a screen. This was not the first American performance of *Prometheus*, however; the Chicago Symphony Orchestra presented it without color organ on 5 March 1915, five days before Altschuler's event. Altschuler was a fellow Russian who had emigrated to the United States and in 1903 formed the Russian Symphony Society.[14]

By the early 1920s, a number of American composers and performers, especially Katherine Ruth Heyman and Dane Rudhyar, had come to regard Scriabin with worshipful respect. For both Heyman and Rudhyar, Scriabin represented a spiritual leader whose music embodied their deep connections to theosophy and the occult. But they were not alone, for by the mid-1920s Scriabin's reputation was soaring both in the United States and abroad. "Among European modernists his ghost disputes with the living Stravinsky the distinction of being the musical idol of the younger set," a commentator observed.[15]

Katherine Ruth Heyman was a prominent California-born pianist and composer who became Scriabin's disciple after first hearing his music in 1913. She shared aspects of his mystical aesthetic, maintaining as early as 1909 that she "felt certain colors" when playing the piano and that she had "psychic power" as a performer. According to her close friend and pupil Faubion Bowers, a biographer of Scriabin, there were eccentric aspects to her relationship with Scriabin. She claimed that she had "met Scriabin on the moon and had an affair with him" and that "she saw visions to his music . . . , violet ships on golden oceans of astral, ectoplasmic light." In 1916 Heyman brought to New York a lecture on "The Relationship of the Ultra-Modern to Archaic Music," which was mostly devoted to Scriabin. Heyman had earlier been giving this talk in California, and five years later it was published as a book. Heyman saw Scriabin as a redemptive force for Americans, declaring that "appreciation of Scriabin may mark the evolution of a nation's spiritual receptivity."[16]

In 1924 and 1927, when Heyman gave all-Scriabin recitals in New York, other American composers turned up with an interest in the Russian's music. Prior to the 1927 event, the young Elliott Carter wrote Charles Ives from Harvard, saying he hoped to see him there. Ives, in turn, was a patron of Heyman and discussed Scriabin not only with her but with his friend Clifton Furness. "I have been puttering around with the score of Scriabin's *Prometheus*," Furness wrote Ives in 1923,

Figure 3.2. "Katherine Ruth Heyman, the American Pianist, and a Snapshot Showing Her in Her New Automobile in London." Photo from *Musical America* (28 August 1909). Courtesy of Musical America Archives.

"and have started a piano transcription of it. . . . I am anxious for you to know it in one form or another. How much I have enjoyed thinking thru that Scriabin symphony that we played!" The French-American composer Dane Rudhyar became yet another devotee of Scriabin's music, as discussed in Chapter 6.[17]

Erik Satie also enjoyed a brief vogue in the United States. His *Gymnopédies* were first performed in Boston in January 1905 at a concert of the Orchestral Club given in Jordan Hall with Georges Longy conducting. Performances of his works were given in the United States during the 1910s by the pianists George Copeland and Leo Ornstein, the singer Eva Gauthier, and the conductor Edgard Varèse. But they were occasional events. Nonetheless, Satie had staunch early disciples in the United States. One of them, S. Foster Damon, introduced the young Virgil Thomson to the Frenchman's music soon after Thomson reached Harvard. Of all the composers in his generation, Thomson was to be most affected by Satie. Damon also appears to have written one of the earliest American articles about Satie. Titled simply "Eric [*sic*] Satie," the article appeared in the *Harvard Musical Review* in March 1914. Damon described Satie's piano music as "difficult to find"

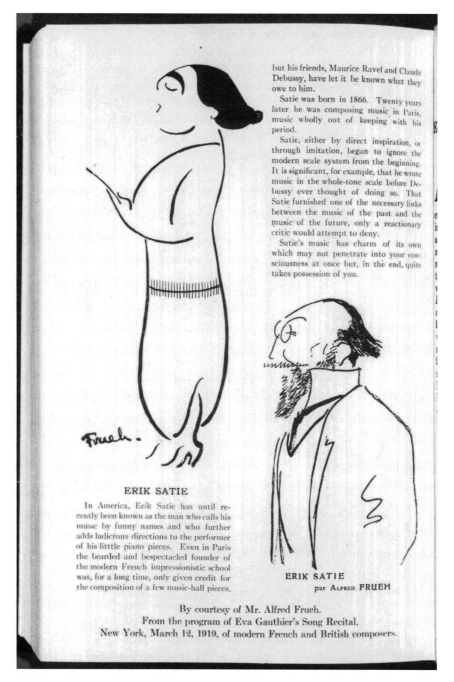

but his friends, Maurice Ravel and Claude Debussy, have let it be known what they owe to him.

Satie was born in 1866. Twenty years later he was composing music in Paris, music wholly out of keeping with his period.

Satie, either by direct inspiration, or through imitation, began to ignore the modern scale system from the beginning. It is significant, for example, that he wrote music in the whole-tone scale before Debussy ever thought of doing so. That Satie furnished one of the necessary links between the music of the past and the music of the future, only a reactionary critic would attempt to deny.

Satie's music has charm of its own which may not penetrate into your consciousness at once but, in the end, quite takes possession of you.

ERIK SATIE

In America, Erik Satie has until recently been known as the man who calls his music by funny names and who further adds ludicrous directions to the performer of his litttle piano pieces. Even in Paris the bearded and bespectacled founder of the modern French impressionistic school was, for a long time, only given credit for the composition of a few music-hall pieces.

ERIK SATIE
par ALFRED FRUEH

By courtesy of Mr. Alfred Frueh.
From the program of Eva Gauthier's Song Recital,
New York, March 12, 1919, of modern French and British composers.

Figure 3.3. Erik Satie and Eva Gauthier, caricatures by Alfred Frueh, as published in *Musical Quarterly* (1919). Reproduced by permission of Oxford University Press.

in Boston, so he discussed only a few works: the three *Gymnopédies*, *Sonneries de la Rose-Croix*, and *Embryons Desséchés*.[18]

Where Satie gained the most exposure in the United States was in an extraordinary series of articles published in the fashionable magazine *Vanity Fair* between 1921 and 1923. It included translations of four articles by Satie—"A Hymn in Praise of the Critics," "A Lecture on 'The Six,'" "A Learned Lecture on Music and Animals," and "Igor Stravinsky." No extensive introduction to Satie appeared; none seemed to be necessary. Over that same span of time, *Vanity Fair* also published articles about Satie and his circle. Paul Rosenfeld contributed two critical appraisals in 1921. In the second of them he discussed *Socrate* (the score had recently been published), claiming that it had turned "the clown of music" into "a grave and serene poet."[19]

Given Satie's irreverent, ironic style, these articles represented esoteric stuff for mass consumption—the kinds of pieces one might expect to find in "little magazines" such as *transatlantic*, the *Little Review*, or even the *Dial*. Their appearance in *Vanity Fair* suggests that Satie and issues of modernism in general were of as much interest to the smart set as they were to the impoverished intellectuals of Greenwich Village. This is a striking theme in the reception of European modernism in America: not only did it become more commonplace to hear such music by the mid-1920s, but in some circles it became downright fashionable.

Equally as striking was *Vanity Fair*'s focus on Satie and Les Six rather than on Ravel or more conservative French figures. Not only did the Satie group represent the latest artistic trends in Paris, but they articulated a disdain for the hallowed traditions of high art that probably appealed to a populist streak in Americans. Cultural hierarchy had long been a major issue for Americans, and in the 1920s it was tested strenuously.

As with all fads, the one for Satie seems to have passed quickly. By 1925, when he died, American obituaries pilloried him as a failed composer whose "sudden fame ruined him and decayed his art."[20]

The Satie saga is but one example of how ideas about European modernism often had as much impact as the music itself. As a result, performances yield only part of the picture. Journalism provided an equally powerful vehicle for transmission.

During the period 1915–20, European—not American—modernists drew the most attention in the United States. The American critics Carl Van Vechten and Paul Rosenfeld, both of whom are profiled in Chapter 18, established their voices as journalists by writing about the European scene. Van Vechten's *Music After the Great War* (1915) contained early assessments of the importance of Stravinsky and, to a lesser extent, Schoenberg and Satie. And Rosenfeld's *Musical Portraits: Interpretations of Twenty Modern Composers* (1920) included essays on Wagner, Strauss, Debussy, and Ravel alongside Scriabin, Stravinsky, and Schoenberg. The only "Americans" included in this volume were Ernest Bloch, Charles Martin Loeffler, and Leo Ornstein—all immigrants.

Another perspective on this process of dissemination came in 1914, with an exchange of letters between the Harvard composer E. B. Hill and Oscar Sonneck, editor of the soon-to-be-launched *Musical Quarterly*, which gives a rare firsthand view of how the process of dissemination was working. The two men discussed Hill's desire to write an article about Stravinsky for the new journal. Hill was obviously intrigued by the possibility, yet he struggled to locate information about the Russian composer. "Up to the present time, I have only been able to find one article on him by Vuillermoz, though doubtless there are many more," Hill wrote. "Nothing in English except a diffuse 'correspondence' in the transcript of the redoubtable H.T.P."[21]

Sonneck must have responded with a bibliography of writings about Stravinsky, and Hill, in turn, revealed that this literature was brand new to him and that he lacked access to some important Stravinsky scores. "I am greatly obliged to you for the list of articles on Stravinsky, two of them by Lalo & Vuillermoz I have seen," Hill replied. "Those by Calvocoressi and Montagu-Nathan I can look up here, the Russian article I may have to send for, if it can be issued to me." Hill named European critics who had published articles abroad within the last couple of years. But even this information left him wondering whether he knew enough to go into print. "I trust you will not think me vacillating if I tell you that I have come to the conclusion that an article on d'Indy may be the most satisfactory one to work out after all. Stravinsky, brilliant and interesting as he is, is still in a state of transition. Until I can get the piano score of 'The Nightingale' the 'mimed opera,' which is apparently published, since [Chalmers] Clifton refers to it in a letter to me, it would be difficult to realize whether the Sacre is a transitory stage in the direction of 'futurism' or whether it is permanent."[22]

Hill never did write about Stravinsky for the *Musical Quarterly*. Instead in 1915 he chose to publish an article about d'Indy. In 1914, though, he contributed an essay about Stravinsky to the *Harvard Musical Review*; this was the same spring as his correspondence with Sonneck. In it, Hill confessed to how Stravinsky's "violently revolutionary style" in *Le Sacre du printemps* was "difficult to reduce to a systematic analysis." He was respectful of what he saw. "There is nothing casual, accidental or amateurish in the musical style of Le Sacre," Hill continued. "It is the logical result of early 'futuristic' tendencies applied to an incredibly radical extent."[23]

Other American journalists focused in limited ways on Stravinsky, Schoenberg, and Scriabin, adding further support to a sense that these were the modernists with the most appeal in the 1910s. Still, information about them was just emerging. The second issue of the *Musical Quarterly* in 1916, for example, included articles about all three, each giving an overview of the composer's work. The most substantial was Egon Wellesz's essay on Schoenberg, which provided a nineteen-page summary of Schoenberg's career, proceeding work by work and culminating in *Pierrot lunaire*. "Never before has any artist gone so near to the limits of that which the human ear can comprehend," Wellesz commented. "The repeated renditions in Berlin and the numerous performances in the smaller cities of Germany, have contributed not a little toward making Schönberg's name popular."[24]

The single most striking characteristic of all the articles about European modernists published in the United States during this period was the degree to which they conveyed a sense of discovery. Compositions were often written about rather than heard; information was passed through magazines, newspapers, and personal correspondence. Yet no matter how sporadic this testimony might have been, interest among American composers and critics in the newest European works ran high. As the American modernist movement took off in the 1920s, this interest remained constant. What changed was the attitude of American composers toward themselves.

The Machine in
the Concert Hall

Engineers of Art

> There is a growing American music, and if this music can
> be kept free of European corruption it will answer every
> need of America. It is a music much more closely related to
> pile-drivers, electric dynamos, get-rich-quick, and rapid
> transit than to idle saunterings beside sentimental brooks—
> that is to say, it is modern and American, not European.
>
> —Gilbert Seldes, 1924

Ornstein and Varèse began imagining the dimensions of American modernism during the 1910s. But on the whole, the twentieth century dawned for American composers in the 1920s. No time of gentle change, this was a decade when iconoclastic ideas blasted through hallowed traditions. Machines often provided the horsepower to do so. What more audacious way to challenge conventional musical values than by introducing noise—raw, cacophonous sounds of industry and the city—into the hallowed realm of serious composition? And what better place to try this than in the United States, where the machine symbolized speed and invention, the triumph of humans over nature, and the New World's ascendancy over the Old?

The decade quickly became known as the "Machine Age"—a rubric that in a broader sense has been used to cover the entire interwar period. At the same time, machines became one of the signifiers of America as a whole, with especially strong resonance abroad. The glint of sun grazing the side of a skyscraper, the raucous blare of sirens, the shiny fenders of a Model T, the flash of figures on the silver screen—these were characteristic images of American urbanity in the 1920s. They signaled a new era of technological mastery and international status. Long conditioned not only to revering European culture but also to feeling overshadowed by it, Americans were suddenly "startled," as the young Edmund Wilson put it in 1922, to find Europeans "looking longingly" in their direction—not at their high art but at their skyscrapers, films, automobiles, and popular music. "From the other side of the ocean," Wilson observed, "the skyscrapers seem exotic, and the movies look like the record of a rich and heroic world full of new kinds of laughter and excitement." To Wilson, Europe seemed "exhausted" by World War I. By contrast, America had "energy" and "money." It was enviably "unencumbered by [Europe's] burden of conventions."[1]

For modernist composers in the United States, the machine had two powerful manifestations: it yielded new sound sources, and it provided new means of pre-

Figure 4.1. "Cubistic Phases of New York," photo of Manhattan by Ralph Steiner, from *Vanity Fair* (April 1928). Permission courtesy of Steiner estate.

serving and transmitting performances. Histories of the intersection of technology with music in America usually begin with John Cage's *Imaginary Landscape No. 1* of 1939, which combined two variable-speed record turntables with piano and percussion. But the saga needs to be expanded back to the 1920s, when a few composers were seizing common tools of industrialism as radical ingredients in a budding modernist aesthetic. They did so as part of a broad movement that also affected poets and painters, stretching from the New World to the Old and back again.

During the 1920s, the "machine" came to stand for a staggering array of technological developments. Widespread electrification of the home took place then, as did the rise of mass communication. The first American radio station (KDKA in Pittsburgh) appeared in 1920, and within five years there were 571 stations nationwide and over 2.75 million receivers—this in a country with an estimated population of 122 million. By 1929 the number of stations had reached nearly 700. The recording and film industries grew just as fast. Electrical recordings appeared in 1925, vastly improving the quality of sound, and in 1927 nearly a hundred million discs sold. The first sound film, *The Jazz Singer*, appeared that same year, and by decade's end there were some eight thousand movie theaters nationwide. Suddenly it was possible to communicate directly with a broad swath of Americans. With the flick of a dial, farmers in Nebraska could switch from hearing Lawrence Tibbett at the Metropolitan Opera to Duke Ellington at the Cotton Club, and they could do so at the same time as a steel worker in Indiana. By cranking up the Victrola, Americans could sample an even broader range of musical styles. "Highbrow" and "lowbrow" frequently inhabited the airwaves and record shelves side-by-side, often yielding unconventional mixes.[2]

Yet new music was not immediately part of the audio potpourri reaching the American masses. It found its niche in more elite spaces, with popular culture pressing insistently at the edges. In other words, the Machine Age brought composers a mixed blessing. At the same time as they experimented with new sound sources and benefited from scientific discoveries, they also encountered new problems with the rise of mass communication. "Composers were slow to realize that they were being faced with revolutionary changes," Aaron Copland later reflected. "One of the crucial questions of our times was injected: how are we to make contact with this enormously enlarged potential audience without sacrificing in any way the highest musical standards?" "Standards," for a composer such as Copland, might have been a euphemism for "modernist style," as opposed to a more consonant, generally appreciated tonal one, or it might have stood for "noncommercial music," as compared to the high-sales popular idioms that radio and recordings tended to favor.[3]

At the same time, mass communication intensified the competition between living composers and the growing canon of historic European repertories. In 1927 the conductor Walter Damrosch made some comments about a series of pilots for what soon became his highly successful weekly radio show on NBC, "Music Appreciation Hour," and in doing so he revealed something about the values with which mass media was being approached. Damrosch wrote with wide-eyed wonder of the "amazing results" of bringing *Tannhäuser* and Beethoven's Fifth Symphony to an audience of "three to four million, . . . reaching people from Minnesota and North Dakota to Louisiana and Texas." Copland's Piano Concerto or Henry Cowell's tone-cluster compositions were nowhere in his scheme. Rather Damrosch painted a warm and fuzzy picture of technology's promise and of how concert-hall chestnuts linked with an "Ozzie and Harriet" vision of America. Here is what young composers were up against: "I do not talk to an audience," Damrosch mused. "I talk to homes, to men in their shirt sleeves, and to mothers doing their family mending. Indeed, the radio should be a great home builder." Thus the radio melded "good music" and the family into a cozy image of edification and integrity, all for the purpose of buttressing conservative values. With its fundamental impulse to shatter tradition, modern music did not easily fit into such a framework, and it was not until the 1930s that new works by American composers began to be heard on the radio. In 1932, NBC sponsored a composition prize that resulted in a radio concert conducted by Eugene Goossens. Including the music of Philip James, Max Wald, Carl Eppert, Florence Galajikian, and Nicolai Berezowsky, the event did not feature composers on the cutting edge of modernism. One year later, the Pan American Association began a radio series on WEVD, and two years after that, the League of Composers started one on NBC.[4]

With recordings, the story was similar. In a special issue of *Modern Music* devoted to "Music and the Machine," published in 1931, Cowell wrote an article titled "Music of and for the Records" in which he assessed the situation for modernists on disc. "The recording of modern music has just begun," he announced at the outset. While "certain time-honored gumdrops were [being] duplicated innumerably by different artists for different companies," Cowell continued, "some of the world's greatest music went unrecorded." With recent work by European composers, it was possible to obtain several different releases of Stravinsky's *Le Sacre du printemps*, but "no composition of Schönberg can be obtained anywhere." Only the early *Verklärte Nacht* had been issued, according to Cowell's account, and by the early 1930s it was out of stock. American concert composers had fared even worse, with the one exception being George Gershwin, whose works such as *Rhapsody in Blue* and *American in Paris* were released soon after their composition. The young modernists waited until 1932 for the first commercial issue of one of their compositions—Roy Harris's *Concerto for Piano, Clarinet, and String Quartet*, which was released by Columbia. Two years later, Cowell began his "New Music Quarterly Recordings," which was devoted exclusively to the American avant-garde. But during the 1920s, American composers with a modernist bent were virtually shut out of the recording business.[5]

All this adds up to a scene in which the ideals of the Machine Age yielded new conceptual vistas but did so at a price. A potent wild card, machines and the ideology that surrounded them were among a few key elements that helped make American modernism into the high-stakes game that it quickly became.

Like most aspects of early twentieth-century American modernism, the machine movement had roots on both sides of the Atlantic. Its most commonly recognized origin reached to Italian futurists such as Filippo Marinetti and Luigi Russolo, who issued a string of fist-shaking proclamations during the first two decades of the century, setting in place some of the language and attitudes that were to characterize early modernism as a whole. The futurists scorned tradition. In painting, they threatened to destroy the museums of Italy, and in music, they challenged fundamental assumptions, claiming that noise had compositional validity. "Life in ancient times was silent," asserted Luigi Russolo in "The Art of Noises" from 1913. "In the nineteenth century, with the invention of machines, Noise was born. Today Noise is triumphant, and reigns supreme over the senses of men." Russolo went on to call for a "MUSIC OF NOISE," imploring composers to "break out of this narrow circle of pure musical sounds, and conquer the infinite variety of noise-sounds."[6]

This was an early shot in the modernist revolution, and its effect was felt in the United States. Alfred Stieglitz's magazine *Camera Work*, published in New York between 1903 and 1917, was one vehicle through which futurism was disseminated. In 1914, the experimental artist Mina Loy issued there a series of "Aphorisms on Futurism" in which she spun out pert, proto-Dada snippets such as "DIE in the Past/Live in the Future. . . . Consciousness has no climax." And a few American painters, most notably the Italian immigrant Joseph Stella, took up futurist ideals in their work. Stella's cubistic *Brooklyn Bridge* of 1919 was called by one contemporary commentator "a symbol of modern America," claiming that he had painted "the apotheosis of the bridge." Stella had a major show of his paintings at the Société Anonyme in 1923; that same year the *Little Review* published a "Stella Number" with sixteen reproductions of his paintings. "The average New Yorker who conceives his city as composed of noise, dirt and policemen," wrote the magazine's editor Jane Heap in a prologue to this issue, "will learn a great deal from this exhibition."[7]

Yet American-made machine art and music also could claim indigenous sources, distinct from the futurists, that dated back to the "rhetoric of the technological sublime" that the historian Leo Marx identified in his now-classic text, *The Machine in the Garden*. Marx examined the degree to which machines shaped Americans' view of themselves from the earliest days of the Republic, and he also considered how the machine came to symbolize America for Europeans. As the nineteenth century unfolded, the United States increasingly became associated with technological developments, obscuring European origins of the industrial revolution. Thus "a special affinity," as Marx puts it, took hold between Americans and the machine. Marx cites testimony from popular magazines of the nineteenth century in which new machines—especially railroads—were hailed as "objects of exalted power and grandeur." Seeming like seers of the Machine Age, the authors of these articles repeatedly hailed the artistic beauty of new contraptions.[8]

In the 1920s, Americans still felt as passionate about machines. Now, however, ardor for them was being articulated by progressive young modernists revolting against the inherited norms of European painting and concert music. These latter-day machine enthusiasts were less breathless and more hard-boiled, and they no longer needed classical references to validate their case. "If America has given or is to give anything to general aesthetics," asserted the modernist expatriate poet Ezra Pound, "it is presumably an aesthetic of machinery, of porcelain baths, of cubic rooms painted with Ripolin, hospital wards with patent dustproof corners and ventilating appliances." Pound's sidekick, the composer George Antheil, indulged in similar rhetoric. "This is by far my most radical work," Antheil wrote of his *Ballet Mécanique*. "It is the rhythm of machinery, presented as beautifully as an artist knows how. . . . The rhythms are steely and hard. It is the life, the manufacturing, the industry of today."[9]

But the machine also brought fear of dehumanization, of loss of connection with the land, of separation from primal essences. It became a symbol of how quickly the new was obliterating the old. Perhaps the most famous such outcry occurred in the first decade of the twentieth century in *The Education of Henry Adams* (published privately in 1907, publicly in 1918), where Adams set one chapter, "The Dynamo and the Virgin," in the Great Exposition in Paris of 1900. Adams recounted a spiritual epiphany in which he found himself in "the great gallery of machines" and "began to feel the forty-foot dynamos as a moral force, much as the early Christians felt the Cross." Soon he "began to pray to it," responding to a "natural expression of man before silent and infinite force." Heaven soon turned to hell for Adams, as he found himself "lying in the Gallery of Machines . . . , his historical neck broken by the sudden irruption of forces totally new." He was terrified in the face of change. Adams also provided a perfect example of how the machine movement was neither insular nor indigenous but rather the product of personalities and events on both sides of the Atlantic. This story, after all, is one of a young American traveling in Paris where he attends an international exposition and is overcome by a machine associated with his home country.[10]

Similarly, the mix of composers identified with the machine included both Europeans and Americans. Varèse and Antheil were the most prominent. Both had transatlantic careers of different natures. But there were others as well, and the music they produced fell into three loosely defined camps. First there was a somewhat esoteric group—even an obscure one—that wrote for new mechanical instruments, including the Estonian-American Nicolai Lopatnikoff in *Two Pieces for Mechanical Piano* (1927), the Russian-American Joseph Schillinger in *First Airphonic Suite for Theremin and Orchestra* (1929), and the California-born Cowell in *Concerto for Rhythmicon and Orchestra* (1931). All these pieces are known more by reputation than firsthand acquaintance. Few were performed in New York during the 1920s, and all remain in manuscript. Then there were works conceived together with experimental films. In addition to Antheil's *Ballet Mécanique*, which was intended to accompany a film by Fernand Léger, three Ralph Steiner films with modernist scores received premieres at the final concert of the Copland-Sessions series in March 1931: *Mechanical Principles* and *H_2O* by Colin McPhee and *Surf and Seaweed* by Marc

Blitzstein. They too are largely inaccessible for study. Both McPhee scores are lost, and Blitzstein's has been dismissed as including "tiny, awkward depictions of rock and seaweed formations." Finally, a number of works took the form of tone poems inspired by machines and the metropolis—or the "mechanical picturesque," as the British composer Constant Lambert later characterized them. These have had much more visibility. On the whole stylistically conservative, they were among the accessible offshoots of the machine movement. John Alden Carpenter's *Skyscrapers* (1923–24) was a Stravinsky-based paean to urban America. Frederick Converse's *Flivver Ten Million* (1926) was a self-styled "joyous epic" in lush, late-romantic style that depicted an assembly line in a Detroit automobile plant. And George Gershwin's *An American in Paris* (1928) simulated the sounds of taxis and street noises. In fact, machines popped up repeatedly with Gershwin. He claimed that the inspiration for *Rhapsody in Blue*, for example, came while on a "train, with its steely rhythms, its rattle-ty-bang that is often so stimulating to a composer." He concluded, "I frequently hear music in the very heart of noise."[11]

This last group of "mechanical picturesque" was not so different from parallel European machine compositions that were beginning to reach New York. Most famous was Arthur Honegger's *Pacific 231* (1923), which the composer conducted with the Philharmonic-Symphony Society on 19 January 1929 as part of a "Honegger Festival" presented by the Pro-Musica Society. A critic described it as one of Honegger's "best known works, so far as America is concerned." *Pacific 231* had previously been conducted at least twice in the city: initially by Walter Damrosch on 31 October 1924, just five months after its premiere in Paris, and subsequently by Serge Koussevitzky in 1927 and Arturo Toscanini in 1928. Damrosch broadcast the work over the radio the same spring as Toscanini's performance. *Skating Rink*, another machine-inspired work by Honegger, was programmed in New York during the 1923 tour of the Ballet Suédois. It depicted "a vast complex in which the human beings moved as regularly and monotonously as pistons or wheels." Other European machine conceptions that reached New York included Alexander Mossolov's *Factory: Music for Machines* (composed in 1927), performed by the Cleveland Orchestra in Carnegie Hall in 1930, and Prokofiev's ballet *Le Pas d'acier* (or *Age of Steel*, composed in 1924), presented early in 1931 by the League of Composers.[12]

This importation of machine compositions from abroad ran parallel to the arrival of paintings by figures such as Francis Picabia and Fernand Léger in New York's galleries. Picabia's impact is treated briefly in the next chapter. Léger's was multifaceted. He first traveled to the United States in 1923 with the avant-garde Ballet Suédois, which used his sets for *Skating Rink*. As an article in *Vanity Fair* showed, Milhaud's *La Création du monde* was also to have been performed during that tour; it, too, used Léger's sets (see Figure 4.2). It was dropped from the program, however. Soon after, Léger was being quoted in the *Little Review* for such homilies as "Beauty is everywhere." Outlining an "esthetics" of machine art, as Léger put it, he enjoined readers to appreciate "the order of the pots and pans on

An African Legend in Choreography

The Swedish Ballet, in New York Appearance, Unites Three French Artists in a Negro Ballet of the Creation

By GILBERT SELDES

THE natural advantage of a Frenchman setting out to write a negro ballet is that he escapes once for all the confusion between Africa and Alabam' which exists in the minds of most Americans. Like most alert Europeans, the creators of the negro ballet, which is the novelty of Rolf de Maré's season of the Swedish Ballet in New York, are perfectly well aware of the syncopation and the shuffle which the American negro has made characteristic in our music and dance. But they aren't compelled to remember it; and the use they have made of it is entirely legitimate —in the sense that they have returned to the African source, where their legend arose—centuries farther back, even, than the "spiritual"—and found there the appropriate rhythm and the proper movement for their ballet.

I was present once when the raw material of the choreography was being examined: a moving picture of certain African tribes in their native dances. But I have not seen the result, and it is only of the other factors that I have any real knowledge. The poem, the décor and the music are the work, in order, of Blaise Cendrars, Fernand Léger, and Darius Milhaud.

The last of these is now known in America, as he conducted the Philadelphia Orchestra for a time when Stokowski was absent, and his own works have been played more frequently, I believe, than those of any other of the group of *Les Six*.

From the piano version, played by the composer a few days after he had written it down, I can only judge that it is a characteristic work—so much depends on the orchestra for color and for mass. It seemed rather like his *L'Homme et Son Désir* which the Swedish Ballet will also produce; what there is of syncopation will hardly recall jazz; like syncopation in the work of Strawinsky, it hasnothing to do with impudence and is not necessarily concerned with gaiety. The poem, the legend itself, admits nothing cheap or trivial. In his work of collecting the Negro Anthology, Blaise Cendrars (whose adventures in America have little in common with those of Milhaud) arrived at an understanding of the almost terrifying simplicity with which the African negro expresses his relation to the universe. There is poetry in the Anthology of a high order; in the legend of this ballet, the beauty

THE NEGRO BALLET OF THE CREATION

The first of the curtains which Fernand Léger has designed for this ingenious ballet, which interprets in choreography the African Negro tradition of the Creation. Upon it are represented, in Léger's characteristic geometrical pattern, the gigantic figures of the three remote deities, Nzame, Nedere and N'kva. The curtain is in black and white, a few dashes of phosphorescence accentuating the white lines

Above, and to the left and right, are represented four of the structural costumes which Léger has invented for the Negro Ballet. While these are conceived in Léger's idiom, they reflect the actual characteristics of Negro ritualistic costumes

The setting at the opening of the ballet. The vague obscurity of clouds and forms represents the chaos before the world, and out of its pregnant stirrings, trees, bushes and, finally, animals and men, slowly take form and mingle their dance with that of the gods

is condensed. It is not, in the first place, a single poem, but the spirit of many. Reduced to the outline of a ballet, it still has its capacity to evoke images:

1. The curtain rises very slowly on a black stage. In the center is discovered a chaotic heap of confused bodies: it is the tumult before the creation. Three giant deities pass slowly. They are Nzame, Nedere and N'kva, the masters of creation. They consult each other, move around the chaotic mass, utter magic incantations.

2. The central mass stirs, leaps. A tree puts forth slowly, grows bigger, bigger still, rears itself upright, and when one of its buds falls on the ground, another tree springs up. When one of the leaves touches the ground, it grows bigger, swells, swells, trembles, begins to walk, and behold! an animal. An elephant which remains suspended in mid-air, a slow turtle, an awkward crab, monkeys sliding down from above. The stage grows lighter bit by bit during the creation, and as each new animal arrives there is a violent burst of light.

3. Each creature is a dancer spurting from the center, passing through its own evolutions, making a few steps, then entering softly into the circle, which little by little is created around the three deities. The circle opens; the three deities utter fresh incantations, and the chaos of the center is seen to boil; everything is in agitated movement; a monstrous leg appears, backs tremble, a hairy head shows itself, arms are thrust forth. Suddenly two torsos are upreared and clasp each other. It is the man and the woman, suddenly upright. They recognize each other; they stand face to face.

4. And while the couple execute the dance of desire and of fulfilment, all that remained of unformed beings on the ground appears quietly and mingles in the round, which dances in frenzy, to madness. They are the N'guils, the sorcerers, the magicians the masters of fetish.

5. The round grows calm, is checked, slows down, and dies slowly. The dancers disperse into small groups. The man and the woman are alone in an embrace which inundates them like a wave. It is Spring.

All of this is obviously on the side of *The Golden Bough* and not of *Batouala*; it is the reduction to choreography of one of those creation myths which fill the unconscious.

(Continued on page 92)

Figure 4.2. Fernand Léger, curtain and sets for Darius Milhaud's *La Création du monde*, as published in *Vanity Fair* (December 1923). © 2000 Artists Rights Society (ARS), New York/ADAGP, Paris.

the white wall of your kitchen," adding that this was "more" satisfying than what could be found "in your eighteenth century salon or in the official museums." Two years later, a major exhibit of Léger's paintings was mounted by the Société Anonyme at the Anderson Galleries—the site of many concerts given by the League of Composers.[13]

International exchange characterized yet another important facet of the machine movement in music: the invention of new mechanical instruments, which was being pursued energetically by a mix of American-born scientists and recent émigrés. Whether profiled in the popular press or in modernist magazines, these new devices generated considerable excitement. Among the instruments demonstrated in New York during the 1920s were the Theremin, the Clavilux, the Crea-tone, the Vitaphone, and the Martenot. All promised to liberate composers from the constraints of historic instruments, and all pointed enticingly to a yet-to-be envisioned future. At the same time, these new gadgets were often used to perform traditional European repertories, rather than to execute new music. Crossing a scientific frontier did not necessarily mean crossing an aesthetic one.

The appearance of each new instrument brought futuristic pronouncements. When in 1925 *Vanity Fair* ran a photo spread about the Clavilux (a light organ developed by Thomas Wilfred of Long Island), it predicted that "ten years from now, we shall all have light organs in our houses tucked away in a corner of the drawing room, just as we now have phonographs and radios." Was this a proto-television fantasy? Or the next year, after the first demonstration of the Vitaphone—a device for synchronizing sound with motion pictures—the composer and critic Marion Bauer and her sister Flora Bauer Bernstein, in their regular new-music column in the *Musical Leader*, mused about whether this new development might make it possible for composers to write scores for "either moving-picture stories or operas." The first sound film appeared the following year, in 1927. There was irony in the Bauers' perspective. Although sound films would soon become one of the great vehicles for mass entertainment, quickly begetting a whole new compositional genre of "film scores," the Bauers saw the Vitaphone as a weapon in the highbrow struggle, speculating that it would be "a most potent factor in the development of a national appreciation of good music." Just as Damrosch talked of radio in terms of artistic uplift, so too did film appear to have the same potential.[14]

The most famous of all these new instruments was the Theremin, devised by the Russian Leon Theremin in 1920 and first demonstrated in his home country. Theremin began an extended visit to the United States in 1927 (lasting until 1938), during which he gave many performances and continued refining his invention. Although his instrument was initially controlled by waving hands in front of an antenna, Theremin later added keyboards and fingerboards. But the earliest models, with eerie sounds produced by a performer coaxing music from the air, made listeners take notice. Theremin gave well-publicized demonstrations of the instrument in New York at a mixture of venues, ranging from the Plaza Hotel to

Figure 4.3. Leon Theremin demonstrating the instrument he invented; Carnegie Hall, 1928. Photo courtesty of Oliva Mattis.

Carnegie Hall, the Metropolitan Opera House, and Lewisohn Stadium. These events produced odd conjunctions. At a Plaza Hotel concert in January 1928, for example, Theremin performed Schubert's *Ave Maria* on his instrument.[15]

Another notable performer on the Theremin during this period was the Princess Jacques de Broglie, who first "cajoled" music from it in a setting that was a tribute to American eclecticism—the Seventh Annual Exposition of Women's Arts and Industries, held in the Astor Hotel in October 1928. There, amid the distribution of literature about "hairdressing, saving Riverside Drive for the Children, [and] modern furniture" and loudspeaker broadcasts of lectures by Mrs. Travis Whitney "on the progress of women in politics" and Mrs. Jacob Riis "on women in investment," the Princess de Broglie performed music by Granados and a Busoni arrangement of Liszt. Three months later, she gave a similar concert at Carnegie Hall featuring Franck and Bach. The new and the old were juxtaposed starkly. That same year, Theremin made a public statement about the relationship of contemporary compositions to his instrument. "To give a program of modern music," he told an interviewer in 1928, "would present the instrument as a freak." Yet he had tentative aspirations in that direction, with plans for "Hindemith, the Russian Vasilenko, and several French and American composers whose names, since they have not yet finished the numbers, I cannot disclose at present," to write new works for it.[16]

Theremin's most important contact with American new music came through Henry Cowell, with whom he devised the rhythmicon, the electronic instrument used in Cowell's Concerto for Rhythmicon and Orchestra. The rhythmicon could perform as many as sixteen rhythmic patterns simultaneously. Although Cowell wrote his concerto in 1931, it was not performed until 1971. However, the instrument alone was demonstrated in New York at the New School for Social Research in 1932.[17]

Another new electronic instrument—the Martenot—was also used for traditional repertory. Designed by the Frenchman Maurice Martenot, "a wireless instructor" who had "noticed that the apparatus for generating waves enabled the production of strangely beautiful sounds," Martenot first demonstrated his invention at the Salle Gaveau in Paris in 1928. Two years later, he played it in New York with the Philadelphia Orchestra, in a concert conducted by Stokowski. The program included works by Dietrich Buxtehude and Mozart.[18]

As these new inventions appeared, American composers began dreaming of future roles for the machine, setting in motion ideas and materials that were not fully realized until the second half of the century. The journal *Modern Music* was the primary forum for their writing on the subject. A 1929 article by Carol Bérard— identified in the magazine as a "composer and enthusiastic proponent of many advanced European tendencies in music," also as "director of the magazine, *La Revue internationale de musique et de danse*"—foreshadowed *musique concrète* and the music of John Cage. To a certain extent, Bérard did so by reiterating ideas of the futurists. Prophesying that "noise . . . holds the secret of the future," he posed a series of questions. "Why, and I have been asking this for fifteen years, are phonograph records not taken of noises such as those of a city at work, at play, even asleep? Of forests, . . . Of the tumult of the crowds, a factory in action, a moving train, a railway terminal, engines, showers, cries, rumblings? If noises were registered, they could be grouped, associated and carefully combined as are the timbres of various instruments in the routine orchestra, although with a different technique. . . . The future of music lies in the conquest, the subjugation and the organization of noise."[19]

Other such speculation appeared in *Modern Music*. Writing in 1927, the eminent German critic H. H. Stuckenschmidt praised Antheil's *Ballet Mécanique* for having "established all the basic principles of mechanical music," making one of the few positive comments about the work. He wondered whether permanent orchestras would even exist in fifty years and prophesied that by then "we shall make music mechanically." Anticipating the later work of figures such as Conlon Nancarrow and Varèse, whose music stretched beyond the capacities of human performers, Stuckenschmidt declared, "The artist is no longer content merely to express what is instrumentally feasible. Discarding the thought of the interpreter, he has begun to write, timidly and haltingly, music of a super-instrumental conception." This theme was picked up, with a more specific focus, by Henry Cowell in his article about the state of modern music on disc. He saw recordings not only as a tool for reproducing performances but also for actual composition. Cowell too seemed to envision Nancarrow on the horizon, at the same time as he shared his own ideas for the recently invented rhythmicon:

> The field of composition for phonograph records and player rolls is wide and offers many prospects, but the workers have been few. . . . One excellent line of possible development, which so far as I know has not yet been attempted, would be to work with subtle rhythms. To hear a harmony of several different rhythms played together is fascinating, and gives a curious esthetic pleasure. . . . Such rhythms are played by primitives at times, but our musicians find them almost if not entirely impossible to perform well. Why not hear music from player piano rolls on which have been punched holes giving the ratios of rhythms of the most exquisite subtlety?[20]

Thus the machine fueled the imagination, freeing composers to push beyond the limitations of acoustic instruments and human performers. By no means a circumscribed movement that yielded a few art works and then ended, the machine aesthetic projected outward like a beam of light, illuminating future potential and suggesting unexplored aesthetic territory. With the advent of subsequent waves of technology in the second half of the century—especially of the tape recorder and computer—its impact continued to be felt resoundingly.

Ballet Mécanique and International Modernist Networks

My reaction to New York is one of space, a city composed of parallel lines and dimensions which form beautiful white spaces.

—George Antheil, 1927

More than any other event, the Carnegie Hall premiere of George Antheil's *Ballet Mécanique* on 10 April 1927 brought music's role in the American machine movement into focus. "The first few minutes of the *Ballet* went off smoothly, and the audience listened to it carefully," recalled Donald Friede, its promoter and producer. "And then came the moment for the wind machine to be turned on—and all hell, in a minor way, broke loose." The propeller had mistakenly been aimed at the eleventh row, and when it gained full speed the effect was "disastrous. People clutched their programs, and women held onto their hats with both hands. Someone in the direct line of the wind tied a handkerchief to his cane and waved it wildly in the air in a sign of surrender." The final roar of the siren provoked even more disruption. "The mechanical-effects man," who had not had an opportunity to test the siren borrowed at the last minute from a fire department in New Jersey, "turned the crank wildly, while the audience, unable to contain itself any longer, burst once more into uncontrolled laughter. But there was no sound from the siren." After nearly a minute, the wail finally began. By then, the piece was almost over. As Eugene Goossens, conductor of the performance, took his bows, the siren finally "reached its full force." It succeeded in "drowning out the applause of the audience, covering the sound of the people picking up their coats and hats and leaving the auditorium."[1]

So ended the concert that Antheil had hoped would be a *succès de scandale*, like the riot that greeted Stravinsky's *Le Sacre du printemps* in Paris in 1913. *Ballet Mécanique* closed a program devoted entirely to Antheil's music, including his First String Quartet, Second Violin Sonata, and *Jazz Symphony*, the latter performed by W. C. Handy's Orchestra with the African American conductor Allie Ross. Up until this time, only one other American composer of concert music— Henry Cowell in 1924—had rented Carnegie Hall for a program of his own works. Antheil's concert was also unusual in challenging racial segregation and

Figure 5.1. George Antheil, in *Musical America* (16 April 1927). Courtesy of Musical America Archives.

in arranging a Dada spectacle that spurned longheld assumptions of concert decorum. A siren, airplane propellers, a player piano, ten conventional pianos, six xylophones, and a battery of other percussion instruments clustered on stage. Behind loomed a massive backdrop, which Friede recalled as depicting "a futuristic city of skyscrapers," together with "a series of enormous noise-making machines" and "a more-than-life-size figure of a man jumping off a diving board that seemed to be attached to a curved pipe of the sort generally used in connection with a toilet." This last was reminiscent of *Fountain*, the infamous Dada readymade by Duchamp. The event looked back to the fantastic nineteenth-century spectacles of P. T. Barnum and forward to John Cage's musical "circuses" of the 1960s.

Coincidentally, it occurred one evening after Serge Koussevitzky had performed Honegger's *Pacific 231* on the same stage and five weeks before the "Machine-Age Exposition," organized by Jane Heap (coeditor of the *Little Review*), opened in Steinway Hall. This much-discussed exhibit put real machines alongside paintings inspired by them, asserting both as art. As though to cap it all, Charles Lindbergh began his historic flight across the Atlantic on 20 May 1927.

A twenty-four-year-old New Jersey native who had been living in Paris since 1921, Antheil had envisioned the Carnegie concert as a triumph. As he wrote to his Philadelphia patron Mary Louise Curtis Bok: "For the first time . . . America will have a composer recognized in the one center of music in the world, . . . And the rest of my work will then be published by big concerns. The rest of my career will take care of itself." This was far from the result. Pilloried in the New York press, Antheil quickly retreated back to France, abandoning his machine style in favor of a more conservative idiom. The whole event became his *"nightmare,"* as he later called it.[2]

At once infamous and undervalued, *Ballet Mécanique* presents a vivid picture of modernism's international traffic. It drew upon the culture of Dada, with which Antheil came in contact as a teenager in the United States, and it was conceived together with a film by the Spanish cubist Fernand Léger. Furthermore, *Ballet Mécanique*'s position as an early percussion work gives it historic pride of place next to Edgard Varèse's *Ionisation* of 1929–31—especially for the degree to which it anticipated Cage's percussion works of the late 1930s and early 1940s. Virgil Thomson once called *Ballet Mécanique* Antheil's "most original piece." More than that, it represents one of the most provocative expressions of American musical modernism in the 1920s.[3]

The forces that shaped *Ballet Mécanique* reached back to Antheil's modernist awakening in the United States. In his autobiography, Antheil (1900–1959) depicted this time in stark terms, spinning a myth about himself as a congenital futurist, sprung not from the soil but from steel and concrete. "I had been born in Trenton, New Jersey, across the street from a very noisy machine shop," Antheil recalled. "A year later my parents moved several blocks away to across the street from an infinitely more silent but also infinitely more ominous structure, the Trenton

State Penitentiary. One of my first memories in life is of looking out of our front window to a brown wall and guard tower right across the street. My first memory of music is also connected with this view."[4]

But youth, for Antheil, brought more than simply "vistas of distant smoke-stacks." He also had access to high culture, encountering both historic European concert repertories and the latest modern compositions. In 1916, at the age of sixteen, Antheil began studying composition in Philadelphia with Constantin von Sternberg, a pupil of Franz Liszt. A staunch upholder of European traditions, Sternberg gave his student "a severe theoretical training" but had little interest in opening his ears to new sounds. Yet he recognized his young pupil's talent, recommending him to Mary Louise Curtis Bok, who became Antheil's patron for the next nineteen years (in 1924 Bok founded the Curtis Institute in Philadelphia).[5]

Study with Sternberg also brought Antheil another benefit: he now had regular access to a city exploding with new art, especially painters connected to the budding Dada movement. In 1919 Antheil extended his geographic range even further, taking the train regularly to New York where he began composition lessons with Ernest Bloch, who was more progressive than Sternberg though hardly radical. By 1921, if not before, Antheil's New York visits also included "gatherings of ultras," as he described them. There, in the earliest days of America's modern music movement, he met Leo Ornstein and Paul Rosenfeld, at the same time as his circle grew to include such figures as Alfred Stieglitz, the painter John Marin, and the *Little Review* editors Jane Heap and Margaret Anderson (with whom he shared a house in New Jersey during the summer of 1921). During this same period he was involved in plans to form a "modern artists society," which he termed "a rather international thing" that would involve Ezra Pound, Mary Garden, Picabia, and Picasso (spelled by Antheil "Piccazzo"). "It is a kind of society which will have as its object the propaganda of modern art," Antheil wrote to Bok in December of 1921, "and will among other things establish in New York City a kind of 'Salon' or meeting ground for the exchange of ideas, and a magazine devoted to the most modern art . . . *and* a small symphony orchestra especially designed to present modern and ultra-modern works." It is unclear whether or not these plans were tied to the founding of Varèse's International Composers' Guild, which issued a manifesto that July and gave its first concert in February 1922.[6]

All the while, Antheil devoured newly published compositions by Europeans, and in December 1921 he shared with Bok the intensity of his self-driven education:

> I am, beyond other things, also becoming acquainted—at odd moments with several new Strawinsky scores—the very latest, scarcely yet off print. They are "Renard" and "L'Histoire du Soldat" both of which are tragic and funny. I am also becoming acquainted with the very latest work of the now-famous Parisian "Six"—I mean their orchestral scores which are not known in America, as are the new Strawinsky scores.

Antheil's access to imported scores gives one of those rare views of how the dissemination of European modernism was taking place. *Renard* was published in Geneva in 1916, although it was not premiered until 1922, and the score to *Histoire du Soldat* was available in a suite arranged for violin, clarinet, and piano, published in London in 1920. As for "Les Six," Antheil had probably just finished reading the series of articles about this group of French composers that ran in *Vanity Fair* during the fall of 1921.[7]

While in Trenton, Antheil wrote his first machine-based work, *Second Sonata, "The Airplane"* for solo piano (1921). It launched a series of pieces inspired by technology that subsequently were composed abroad, including *Sonata Sauvage* (1922–23), *Third Sonata, "Death of Machines"* (1923), *Mechanisms* (ca. 1923, not extant), and ultimately *Ballet Mécanique* (begun in 1923). With the *Airplane Sonata*, Antheil revealed his exposure to various transatlantic modernist strains.

The *Airplane Sonata* grew out of a fashion for mythologizing aviation, whether in Filippo Marinetti's *Futurist Manifesto* of 1909, in which the airplane was viewed as an icon of industrial society, or the 1929 journal of the American poet Harry Crosby, who viewed the aviator as "the new Christ" and the airplane as "the new Cross." Antheil's sonata also showed a young composer drawing upon compositional techniques found in the scores he was studying. The result was in many ways tentative, even derivative. Stravinsky's impact was most noticeable, especially in Antheil's use of irregularly barred and accented rhythmic patterns. Throughout the *Airplane Sonata*, there are frequent changes of meter, at the same time as cross-rhythms challenge those shifting groups (Example 5.1). The opening left-hand ostinato, for example, sets up a pattern of three that begins to migrate off the beat, soon establishing itself against a metrical expectation of four. Stravinsky's shadow also falls over the form of the work, which uses a nondevelopmental, block structure.[8]

In other respects, the *Airplane Sonata* exhibits both traditional traits and cautious innovation. The opening cross-accented pattern forms the basis for a ritornello, a tried-and-true structural device that recurs regularly but briefly at five other points in the work (not illustrated here). At the same time, Antheil began to experiment with new techniques that soon became basic to his machine style. Most prominent among these is the use of near-literal repetition to generate a flat, mechanistic surface. One of the work's brief secondary patterns (first found in Example 5.1, mm. 15–17) recurs midway through the movement in a segment where it is hammered out irregularly (Example 5.2). Forward motion is suspended briefly, yielding a kind of mechanical stasis. This section is enhanced by the sonata's overall monochromatic surface, which uses few dynamic markings, thereby intensifying a sense of monotony. Yet another technique that became common in Antheil's machine works was the use of clusters. Here they appear only briefly (see the end of Example 5.1). Ultimately, the work did not sound much like an airplane but rather conjured up a more generic representation of a machine.

Example 5.1. Antheil, *Second Sonata, "The Airplane,"* p. 1. Published in *New Music* 4/3 (April 1931). Used by permission. Theodore Presser Co.

Example 5.2. Antheil, *Second Sonata*, mm. 44–55. Published in *New Music* 4/3 (April 1931). Used by permission. Theodore Presser Co.

Of the artistic currents that converged in the *Airplane Sonata*, the strongest came from Dada. Antheil's machine music has long been linked to this iconoclastic movement, yet it has been assumed that he encountered it in Europe after arriving there in 1922, not in the United States. But just as Antheil started venturing to Philadelphia in 1916 and New York three years later, Dada was gaining force in both cities. Francis Picabia and Marcel Duchamp, two of its key figures, were then recent arrivals in New York, as was Varèse. These Frenchmen launched artistic experiments amid a variegated swirl of ideologies and "isms," ranging from futurism to cubism, all of which fed into Dada.[9]

Antheil's contact with Dada can be loosely reconstructed, but then American Dada as a whole left a somewhat murky historical trail. In part this happened because of its pride in being a "matrix of nonsense," as one scholar has put it, also because of its disdain for labels. The last thing that these iconoclastic young Americans wanted, according to another scholar, was to be identified "yet again [with] something European." Beginning around 1916, a group of painters including Duchamp and Picabia, as well as Morton Schamberg, Charles Sheeler, Max Weber, and others, all pursued ideas related to Dada that soon cropped up in Antheil's music, whether glorifying the machine or lampooning the pretensions of high art—or both. Their work was being exhibited in both Philadelphia and New York. In iconography, technique, and attitude, these figures struck a pose strikingly similar to Antheil's own.[10]

Morton Schamberg was a Philadelphian whose work suggests much about the kind of art Antheil was viewing. Well known for championing the machine, Schamberg became prominent in Dada around 1916. He approached technology in two basic ways, either by rendering mechanical objects in technical detail or by transforming some aspect of a machine into an abstract, cubist-inspired design. The first of these was exemplified in *Machine Forms: The Well* (Figure 5.2), which precisely delineated the construction of a drill, and the second in *Composition* (Figure 5.3), which was inspired by images of a wheel and other basic geometric shapes. Around the same time, other Dadaists, most notably Duchamp, were going one step further by constructing so-called readymades in which found objects were simply presented as art, with no creative intervention. Duchamp's *Fountain* was perhaps the most notorious case. Designed for shock value, readymades issued a direct challenge about the nature of creative expression.[11]

Amid all this, in August 1917 Picabia published a drawing titled "Ballet Mécanique" on the cover of his own Dada magazine *391* (Figure 5.4). It depicted a car axle in graphic detail. This was one of three issues of the magazine published that summer in New York; Picabia had previously been sending it out from Barcelona, where he moved in August 1916. Antheil must have seen—or at least known of— the drawing. The title "Ballet Mécanique" resonated beyond Picabia and Antheil, turning up again in 1931 in a drawing by Charles Sheeler that depicts a Ford Motor Company plant outside of Detroit (Figure 5.5). The source for Sheeler's drawing, in turn, can be traced to a series of photographs by him of the same plant, commissioned by an advertising agency in 1927—the year of Antheil's Carnegie Hall performance.[12]

So when Antheil arrived in Europe in 1923 and began working on his own "Ballet Mécanique," he turned to an image already known in the United States and did so as part of a vital transatlantic aesthetic. Antheil shared with Schamberg, Picabia, and other Dada artists active in America a vision of experimentation and irreverence. His *Ballet Mécanique* was a percussive extravaganza that glorified technology by using actual machines, mechanical instruments, and principles of mechanical construction. It built on mechanistic techniques devised in his *Airplane Sonata* and subsequent machine compositions, and it combined the various approaches taken by

Figure 5.2. Morton Schamberg, *Machine Forms: The Well* (1916), oil on canvas, location unknown.

visual artists to the machine, fusing realistic technical rendering (in Antheil's case, simulating machine sounds) with fanciful reinterpretation (basing compositional experiments on recent scientific theories) and readymades (presenting machines as musical instruments).

Antheil connected *Ballet Mécanique* to machine ideology in a series of public and private statements, including a manifesto published both in the Dutch modernist magazine *De Stijl* in 1924–25 and its German counterpart *Der Querschnitt* in

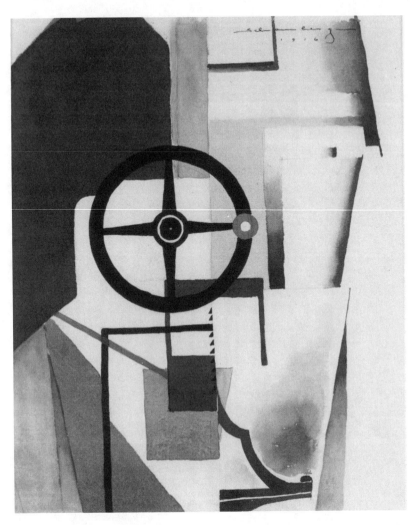

Figure 5.3. Morton Schamberg, *Composition* (1916), watercolor. Columbus Museum of Art, Ohio: Gift of Ferdinand Howald.

September 1925. He chose international forums to publicize his work, and his prose was consistently forceful, leaving no question of his aims. In the manifesto, portions of every line were shouted out in either capital letters or italics, just as Luigi Russolo had done over a decade earlier in "The Art of Noises." Also like the futurists, Antheil showed a complete disdain for modesty or subtlety: "My *Ballet Mécanique* is the first piece of music that has been composed OUT OF and FOR machines, ON EARTH." In private communications, his estimate of the work was equally audacious. "My first big work," he wrote to his friend Stanley Hart in 1925. "Scored for countless numbers of player pianos. All percussive. Like machines. All efficiency. NO LOVE. Written without sympathy. Written cold as an army operates. Revolutionary as

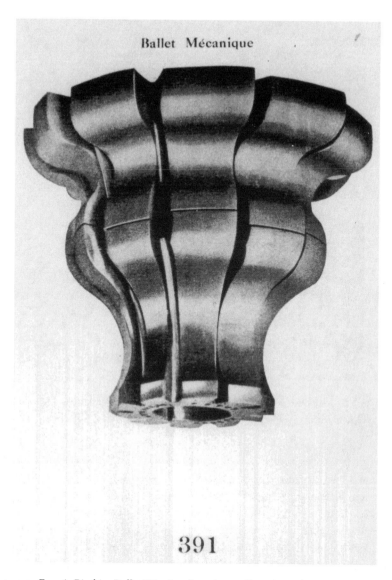

Figure 5.4. Francis Picabia, *Ballet Mécanique* (1917), pencil or charcoal on paper. Reproduced in the magazine *391* (August 1917). © 2000 Artists Rights Society (ARS), New York/ADAGP, Paris.

nothing has been revolutionary." This was the language of a generation that had just witnessed World War I, as well as the Russian Revolution, and it had an edge of megalomania. In these statements about *Ballet Mécanique*, Antheil also consistently drew comparisons with the visual arts, declaring at one point that painters affected his notion of a new music: "We of the future find our sense of organization from Picasso rather than Beethoven or Strawinsky for that matter."[13]

Figure 5.5. Charles Sheeler, *Ballet Mécanique*, 1931, conté-crayon drawing. University of Rochester, Memorial Art Gallery.

All this bluster accompanied some important musical innovations that are revealed in a long-neglected manuscript score from 1926. Most of the experimental sections are unknown today because Antheil removed them in 1953 when he reworked the score for publication (it was issued by Templeton six years later). The revised text has been the one used mostly by scholars and performers. In it, Antheil shortened the composition by ten minutes, aiming, in his words, to make it "more concise." In the process, he not only excised some of the more interesting passages but removed the pianola and added a glockenspiel, leaving the work with more tinkly effervescence than brute authority. Returning to the original manuscript uncovers a radically different composition.[14]

First among the intriguing traits of the original *Ballet Mécanique* is its use of silence. While Cage has been acclaimed as an innovator with silence—especially for *4′33″* of 1952—he had a significant predecessor in Antheil. Antheil, in turn, was making bold use of a technique being explored by some of his contemporaries. Toward the end of *Ballet Mécanique*, Antheil incorporated increasingly prolonged stretches of silence. The modules begin with moderate-sized units and eventually increase to a 64-beat gulf (Example 5.3). Occurring irregularly and disjunctly, these tears in the basic fabric of sound perilously suspend the musi-

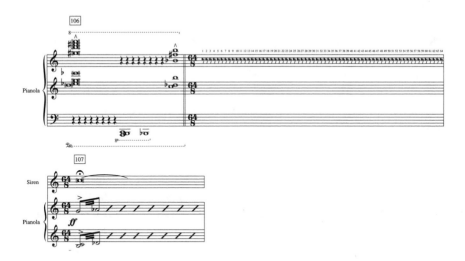

cal momentum, and they were announced by electric bells, which were a well-established Dada signifier. At what Tristan Tzara called "the début of Dadaism in Paris" in 1920, Tzara read a newspaper article while an electric bell rang so loudly that no one could hear what he said. Antheil had some comrades in his explorations of silence, most notably Erik Satie, whose "Vexations" from *Pages mystiques* of 1893–95 included instructions to open the piece with a period of silence. The brief composition was then to be played 840 times. Since "Vexations" was "for decades buried in obscurity," it is hard to guess whether Antheil knew it. But Cage seized upon it in 1963, giving an eighteen-hour performance in New York.[15]

When Antheil described his use of silence in *Ballet Mécanique*, he made no connection to ambient noise, as Cage later did, but rather based his theoretical justification on then-current theories about the fourth dimension, a facet of hyperspace theory ("hyperspace" refers to a space of more than three dimensions). He placed machine sounds in the foreground and a scientific theory in the background. Antheil spelled out the connection between *Ballet Mécanique* and the fourth dimension in his manifesto, where the opening sentence baldly declared that "My *Ballet Mécanique* is the new FOURTH DIMENSION of music." A few sentences later he continued, "My *Ballet Mécanique* comes out of the first and principal stuff of music—TIME-SPACE. . . . Can you dare to deny that TIME is the sole canvas of music? . . . Can you any longer dare to say that music is made of TONE and not of TIME?" With this, Antheil embraced a major artistic passion of the early twentieth century—one that also affected a variety of visual artists, especially the cubists, and drew its inspiration from theories about hyperspace that were popular then.[16]

Since Antheil's heyday, science has moved on to black holes and ten-dimensional time-space theory. But in the early twentieth century, it was the fourth dimension that loomed as an unseen component of space, beyond height, width, and depth. It hovered on a hazy border between true physics and pop cosmology. During Antheil's childhood, popular magazines in the United States generated considerable literature about the fourth dimension, especially in 1909 when *Scientific American* sponsored an essay contest for "the best popular explanation" of it. Even Willa Cather's *Song of the Lark* from 1915 used it to describe an abstracted quality in urban Americans: "New York people live a good deal in the fourth dimension, Doctor Archie. It's that you notice in their faces."[17]

Hyperspace theory offered visual artists on both sides of the Atlantic a tool for rationalizing experimental techniques. Most linked the fourth dimension with space rather than time. In 1910 the American painter Max Weber, who had just returned to his native country after an extended stay in France, published an article in Stieglitz's New York journal *Camera Work* titled "The Fourth Dimension from a Plastic Point of View." There he envisioned the fourth dimension as "the consciousness of a great and overwhelming sense of space-magnitude in all directions at one time." Others followed suit. Schamberg heralded the opening of the famous Armory Show in 1913 with an article for the *Philadelphia Inquirer* in which he examined the impact of the fourth dimension on avant-garde painting, equating it with the "harmonic use of what may arbitrarily be called volume." Three years later, Schamberg organized "Philadelphia's First Exhibition of Advanced Art," including paintings by dadaists and exponents of the fourth dimension, such as Weber, Duchamp, Picabia, and Man Ray. That same year Antheil began traveling to Philadelphia for composition lessons, giving him the opportunity to experience this very moment in American art.[18]

Yet for Antheil, unlike contemporary painters, it was the temporal facet of the fourth dimension that held the most appeal, inspiring the long stretches of silence at the end of *Ballet Mécanique*, as well as other experimental techniques. He turned in this direction just a few years after Albert Einstein announced his theory of relativity in 1919, which had shifted most discussions of the fourth dimension from space to time. In 1927, the year of *Ballet Mécanique*'s American debut, Antheil directly linked time and silence. "Time," wrote Antheil, is "the principal subject of my meditations. Time! Time must be filled—'it is the space of our musical canvas.'" He went on to call *Ballet Mécanique* "the dead line, the brink of the precipice. Here at the end of this composition where *in long stretches* no *single sound occurs and time itself acts as music* [Antheil's emphasis]." Through his passages of silence, then, Antheil aimed to project the fourth dimension by essentially suspending time, and silence became a compositional device to put alongside the various forms of "noise" advocated by the futurists.[19]

Antheil also drew upon theories about the fourth dimension to justify another experiment: the extreme use of repetition. While repetition is fundamental to *Ballet Mécanique*, it most often appears in small doses. But there is one point three-fifths of the way through the piece where a fluctuating pattern of clusters is repeated an extraordinary total of thirty-four times (Example 5.4 gives one occurrence of the pattern). At first it does so with subtle internal mutations. But once the pattern settles into a groove, the passage barrels forward with ear-numbing redundancy. This was the "final ten minutes [that] pounded away," as one reviewer complained. "Louder, and louder, colder and colder, as the pianists banged away at their instruments with the monotony of commercial business typists (half the pianists were women)." These were stereotypical machine-age images, yet they give a sense of the repetition's impact.[20]

This same passage also has an interesting parallel to the use of repetition in "Vexations" of Satie, as well as in the "Entr'acte symphonique" of his *Relâche* of 1924, which accompanied the interpolation of an abstract film by René Clair and Man Ray into a ballet with sets by Picabia. This film project was undertaken in Paris around the same time as *Ballet Mécanique*. The first section of *Relâche* consists of a single measure that recurs two dozen times. Yet it and *Ballet Mécanique* differ significantly in both harmonic language and overall character. Whereas Satie's redundancies are diatonic, Antheil's are mostly cluster-based and convey a stronger sense of assault.[21]

Antheil also proclaimed the form of *Ballet Mécanique* as among its key innovations, again drawing upon the fourth dimension for his rationale. He articulated an imaginative idea at the same time as he made fantastic claims for its realization. This was a pattern with Antheil. Repeatedly in his writings Antheil taunted his readers, daring them to question his credibility. "Everybody either thinks I'm a genius or a fake. Either is interesting," he declared at one point to a friend. And throughout his published statements—right through his autobiography of 1945—he darted back and forth between the visionary and the outrageous. Viewed sympathetically, Antheil's inflammatory rhetoric can be seen as fundamental to his Dada-based art. Viewed critically, it often crosses the line into the absurd.[22]

With his statements about form, Antheil became exceptionally audacious, claiming that the work "attain[ed] a single and gigantic form, . . . like a solid shaft of steel." Ten years later, he modified his stance somewhat but retained its core: "I personally consider that the *Ballet Mécanique* was important in one particular and that is that it was conceived in a new form, that form specifically being the filling out of a certain time canvas with musical abstractions and sound material composed and contrasted against one another with the thought of time values rather than tonal values." Antheil imagined the form of *Ballet Mécanique*, then, as both visual and physical, anticipating spatial compositions such as Varèse's *Poème électronique* of 1957–58 or even sculptural sound installations of the 1970s by Max Neuhaus. He saw it as a sonic counterpart of a sculpture or painting. At the core of this notion

Example 5.4. Antheil, *Ballet Mécanique*, p. 220 from autograph score. Copyright © 1959, 1961 (Renewed) by G. Schirmer, Inc. (ASCAP) and Templeton Music, a div. of Shawnee Press, Inc. International copyright secured. All rights reserved. Reprinted by permission.

was the "physicality" of *Ballet Mécanique*, and he shouted this out in the deliberately provocative conclusion to his manifesto: "Now I hope to present you with . . . THE FIRST PHYSICAL REALIZATION OF THE FOURTH DIMENSION. I am not presenting you with an abstraction. I am presenting you with a PHYSICALITY LIKE SEXUAL INTER-COURSE." Scatology was prevalent in Dada, whether in Duchamp's transformation of a urinal into a sculpture or in Act Two of *Relâche*, where Satie inscribed the words "ballet obcène [*sic*]."[23]

With *Ballet Mécanique*, Antheil managed to assert a strong physical authority, but he did so through hard-hitting timbres and repeated patterns, not through any exceptional structure. The work's force came mostly from its visceral sur-face—its relentless motion and timbral assault. When Antheil stepped down from the realm of visionary metaphors and attempted a straightforward descrip-tion of the work's structure, he claimed that the "formula" of *Ballet Mécanique* consisted of "AAAAAAAAAAAAAAAAAAAAAAAAA"—or a single section repeated twenty-five times. This, too, was far from the actual achievement. Although Antheil's repetition of patterns reached an unorthodox length in the section al-ready discussed, he by no means based an overall structure on such fundamen-tal redundancy. Rather, he used a series of patterns, often including internal repeats, that fill widely varying spans of time. Overall they added up to a form closer to the block structure of Stravinsky, also to that of Satie, than to any sculptural or physical entity.[24]

The opening of *Ballet Mécanique* illustrates how Antheil handled his patterns, attaining a musical parallel to the precise rendering of machines in paintings such as Morton Schamberg's *Machine Forms: The Well*. Even though Antheil later averred that he "had no idea . . . of *copying* a machine directly down into music," there are significant patches of *Ballet Mécanique* where he accomplished just that. Like rotating gears that periodically shift to new speeds, Antheil's patterns can be heard as simulating motoric action. Each repeats for a time and then is abruptly replaced by another. First, a multilayered ostinato in the pianolas irregularly os-cillates a small series of chords (Example 5.5). This initial pattern is then inter-rupted by erratic chromatic octaves (Example 5.5, page 2), and these octaves, in turn, assume different incarnations—repeated literally, placed in different ranges, lasting different lengths (not visible in Example 5.5). Next, a related pattern uses variants of the opening chords, and soon after that yet another pattern enters— this one syncopated and built of fifths. After the close of the opening section, a whole new unit of pendular clusters and glissandos abruptly introduces new tex-tures and wider registers.[25]

At the same time as this block structure is fundamentally Stravinskyan, it is based on contrast—a concept promoted by Fernand Léger, who directed the ex-perimental film that was intended to accompany Antheil's score. As already seen, Léger's work figured prominently in the machine art exhibited in New York, yet the nature of his collaboration with Antheil remains mysterious. In his autobiog-raphy, Antheil claimed that he initiated the project, but a monograph about Léger

Example 5.5. Antheil, *Ballet Mécanique*, pp. 1–2 from autograph score. Copyright © 1959, 1961 (Renewed) by G. Schirmer, Inc. (ASCAP) and Templeton Music, a div. of Shawnee Press, Inc. International copyright secured. All rights reserved. Reprinted by permission.

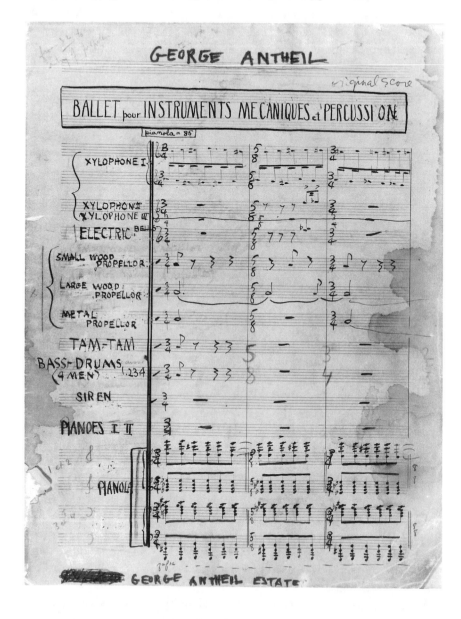

Example 5.5. (*continued*)

asserts that Antheil "saw and admired the film and composed the music shortly afterwards." The score and film were not performed together until 18 October 1935, when a version of Antheil's score for pianola alone was coordinated with the film at the Museum of Modern Art in New York.[26]

Léger provides another clue to the transatlantic reciprocity that defined Antheil's involvement in Dada and the machine aesthetic, and his film suggests an important corollary for some of the innovations in Antheil's score. The first installment of Léger's "Esthetics of the Machine" appeared in the same issue of Jane

Heap's *Little Review* as did an excerpt from Antheil's *Airplane Sonata*. Léger also attended Antheil's debut concert in Paris on 4 October 1923, at which the composer played his *Sonata Sauvage*, *Mechanisms*, and *Airplane Sonata*. That same year Léger declared "contrast" to be fundamental to his art, writing of "organization through contrast" and of contrast "as a method of creating an equivalence to life." With the film *Ballet Mécanique*, completed between 1923 and 1924, Léger put theory into practice, using chaotic simultaneity and abrupt juxtapositions of dissimilar objects. Built as a flickering montage—from an opening cubist rendition of Charlie Chaplin to shots from real life (traffic, feet in motion, a pulsating pile of quiche pans) and moving machinery—the film bears a close conceptual relation to the rapidly changing patterns in Antheil's score. Both film and music also use repeating motifs: in the film, the image of a woman's face recurs in increasingly distorted form, and in the music, the opening ostinato pattern returns in continually evolving incarnations. And both employ "contrast" to shift the scene abruptly and often unrelatedly, pasting together dissimilar sections into a kind of collage. Music and theater had a long, shared history. But this was an early instance in which aesthetic principles from a film turned up in a musical composition.[27]

Another striking aspect of *Ballet Mécanique* is its scoring for an ensemble of percussion and machines. Antheil's work stands near the head of a revolution extending from the Italian futurists through Varèse's *Ionisation* of 1929–31. Antheil's 1926 manuscript for *Ballet Mécanique* included three xylophones, electric bells, two wood propellers (one small, one large), a metal propeller, tamtam, four bass drums, siren, two pianos, and pianola. For the Carnegie Hall performance he expanded the scoring to six xylophones and ten pianos (the pianists included fellow modernist composers Aaron Copland and Colin McPhee, the ethnomusicologist George Herzog, and the new-music virtuoso Carol Robinson), reportedly also adding whistles, rattles, sewing machine motors, and two large pieces of tin. Here, too, Antheil built on foundations laid by earlier modernist compositions, especially Stravinsky's *Les Noces* of 1914–21, which used a percussion-based orchestra including four pianos, xylophone, timpani, a bell, and drums.[28]

At the core of Antheil's machines was the pianola (or player piano), suggesting yet another connection to Stravinsky, who had already written for the instrument when Antheil began *Ballet Mécanique*. A mechanical instrument popular in parlors early in the century, the pianola used pumping pedals to turn a prepunched paper roll and activate a keyboard. With its undifferentiated sound surface, the pianola contributed substantially to *Ballet Mécanique*'s motoric character.[29]

The remaining machines in *Ballet Mécanique* are essentially readymades: genuine mechanical objects that contribute unorthodox timbres and an aesthetic jolt. Yet Antheil did not just toss them in at random but worked them carefully into the score, often giving them structural significance. Whenever the siren enters, for example, the work seems to career forward, even to be on the verge of losing control. While the siren produces a sense of chaos so central to Dada, it also signals the appearance of new sections. At the opening, for example, the first such transition is heralded by a twelve-bar passage in which the siren gains momentum, wailing wildly as new material appears. Several other instances occur, most notably at the end of the final chasm of silence, where the siren propels the work to its conclusion with a sense of reckless abandon (see Example 5.3, Rehearsal No. 107). Airplane propellers also provide structural markers—most notably in the last part of the section of relentless repetition and at the beginning of the section featuring silence, where they combine with electric bell. By articulating internal subdivisions this way, machines emphasize the sense of cinematic contrast shared with Léger's film.

Pasting together the transatlantic migrations, Dada connections, hyperspace imaginings, and compositional advances of Antheil's *Ballet Mécanique* produces a collagelike historical profile, as richly chaotic as Dada itself. A few more pieces make up the mix, beginning with issues related to primitivism and, by extension, Antheil's stance on race. There is also the intense marketing strategy that built up to the work's New York premiere and the damning reception that resulted.

Gorham Munson, an American writer and contemporary of Antheil, observed the affinity between primitivism and the machine aesthetic early on, coining the phrase "skyscraper primitive," and Antheil himself clearly perceived primitivism as one of the pistons in his hard-pounding hymn of praise to the machine. All the banging, hammering, and siren-blowing of *Ballet Mécanique* create a visceral excitement; at the same time, the overall surface of the work is often flat and non-directional. Like the 1884 novel *Flatland: A Romance of Many Dimensions* by the British author Edwin Abbott, which helped popularize the idea of the fourth dimension, and the paintings of the cubists, which were so deeply affected by hyperspace theory, Antheil's *Ballet Mécanique* may have aimed to generate a sense of the fourth dimension by eliminating the third—that is, by creating the musical illusion of a two-dimensional surface. One contemporary artist exploring the same possibility was Max Weber, who in his article about the fourth dimension suggested that "splendid examples" of "the dimension of infinity" existed in "Archaic" art, as well as that of the Congo. On the other side of the Atlantic, Apollinaire made a similar connection, finding that the fourth dimension attracted "many young artists who contemplate Egyptian, negro, and oceanic sculptures, meditate on various scientific works, and live in anticipation of a sublime art." Links between primitivism and the machine were prevalent during this period, connecting an idealized past with an intimidating present.[30]

In 1923, Antheil mused about this unlikely pairing in relation to his machine-inspired sonatas: "I feel that in these few pages I have embraced all mankind, the fear, impossible hopes, and electricity of the unconscious from the primitive to the mind that dies in the airplane." While most of those works bore titles rife with mechanical imagery, one had a primitivist thrust: *Sonata Sauvage*, which had a first movement shockingly titled "Niggers." This sonata exposes another of the perplexing contradictions in Antheil's character: at the same time as he was capable of using such a crude slur, he could also summon up racial sensitivity. In a private letter from 1925, he claimed *Ballet Mécanique* to be "symbolic of New York crushing our negro," adding that it had "a primitive rhythm." And he made subsequent statements connecting *Ballet Mécanique* to African Americans. In publicity before the American premiere, he called *Ballet Mécanique* an attempt "to express America, Africa, and Steel," and in notes written during the first of a series of attempts to edit the score, he described its "first 'theme'" as characteristic "of mechanical scientific civilization" and its "second and third" themes as "barbaric ones, not unrelated to the American continent, Indian, Negro." Antheil's instrumentation fused the primitive and the mechanical, uniting brittle xylophones, resonant of their African forebears, with the various machines already cited.[31]

He also circulated in a Parisian community intrigued by African Americans. Dudley Murphey, one of Antheil's white American cohorts there, was cinematographer for Léger's *Ballet Mécanique* and went on to produce a number of important "race" films in the United States, including Bessie Smith's *St. Louis Blues* and Duke Ellington's *Black and Tan* (both 1929).

With *Ballet Mécanique*'s New York performance, Antheil aimed for a level of racial integration that was cropping up occasionally in new-music circles. It was by no means commonplace, however. Probably because W. C. Handy's Orchestra played the premiere of Antheil's *Jazz Symphony* that same evening, the concert attracted a more diverse audience than was customary. "Elite subscribers of the Beethoven Association and the Philadelphia Orchestra rubbed shoulders with habitués of night clubs and vaudeville artists," noted one chronicler. "All the gals and fellas of the Village were there," observed another. Yet a third critic recognized an exceptional racial mix: "The Horse-Shoe Circle of Boxes, almost as famous as the one at The Metropolitan, was filled with the most important people in the City; . . . to make it more amazing, [there was] one box, even, of negroes." And a fourth named some of the luminaries in attendance, including George Gershwin, Gilbert Seldes, Paul Robeson.[32]

The New York premiere of *Ballet Mécanique* also employed an exceptional focus on consumer marketing. Antheil approached the event more like a Broadway show than a sacrosanct recital. No elitist aiming for a rarefied atmosphere and select audience, Antheil wanted a big crowd—and a boisterous one at that. He hired Donald Friede as producer and publicist (Friede was then vice president of the publishing firm of Boni and Liveright), and Friede saturated the press with hype about a "sensational American modernist composer." From coverage of the event, it is clear that Friede did his job well. "The newspapers and periodicals of this most eager land have for the last two years been bursting with special stories, cabled accounts of sensational happenings overseas, photographs, [and] explications, all inspired by our young New Jersey maestro and his prodigious art!" wrote Lawrence Gilman in the *New York Herald-Tribune*. Just as Varèse had arranged a press conference in 1919, so too did Friede make his star attraction available to reporters.[33]

On top of his publicity blitz, Friede also sought to create a multifaceted spectacle rather than a conventionally sober concert. The machines on stage certainly added a theatrical element, as did two stage backdrops commissioned by Friede from Joseph Mullen, who was then in the midst of a brief career on Broadway. The sets were built by the Ward-Harvey Studios. Both stunned the audience. The one for *Ballet Mécanique*, described at the opening of this chapter, was somewhat benignly perceived, with its Dada vision of urban machinery. But the backdrop for the *Jazz Symphony* created a real stir. Modeled after nightclub sets of the day, it exploited sociopolitical taboos, showing "a gigantic Negro couple dancing the Charleston, the girl holding an American flag in her left hand, while the man clasped her ecstatically around the buttocks." These sets extended the practice at the time of having contemporary artists design backdrops for major musical productions, especially ballets. When Varèse conducted the Berlioz *Requiem* in 1917, it will be recalled, he commissioned a backdrop from Léon Bakst. But by turning to Joseph Mullen, Antheil transported this tradition into the realm of popular culture. He once used the term "cubistic Tin-Pan Alley" when describing one of his compositions. It applies to these sets as well.[34]

The cumulative hubris of *Ballet Mécanique*'s New York premiere provoked a hostile response, with critics calling the concert "a bitter disappointment" and dismissing the much-trumpeted *Ballet Mécanique* as "unconscionably boring, artless, and naive." Antheil and Friede pushed so hard for notoriety that their efforts backfired. As one headline put it, "Expected Riots Peter Out at George Antheil Concert—Sensation Fails to Materialize," typifying the critical response as a whole. Even a fellow composer was skeptical. A letter written by Charles Seeger, an "ultra-modern" of Antheil's day, to Carl Ruggles, another experimentalist, dismissed *Ballet Mécanique* as "good vaudeville," apparently seeing no redemption in its compositional experiments or its challenge to the privileged conventions of high art.[35]

With this very public failure in New York, Antheil's dream of becoming the dean of American composers quickly faded. Instead, he felt that the event had put him in "a wholly false light" and never completely pulled himself out of the resulting shadow. Prior to *Ballet Mécanique* fellow modernists had singled him out as exceptionally promising. As early as 1922, just after Antheil left for Europe, Paul Rosenfeld referred to him as a "youth from the Trenton suburbs who seems the most musically talented creature this country can have produced." And a string of Antheil's composer-contemporaries agreed. For them, he was no charlatan but a gifted musician. "A great deal of nonsense has been written about George Antheil," wrote Aaron Copland in a 1925 profile for *Modern Music*. "The real personality of this extremely talented young American composer has been cleverly concealed by a welter of words from the most varied sources." Virgil Thomson concurred, writing from Paris around 1926 to a friend at home that Antheil was "the first composer of our generation." In 1929 Marc Blitzstein concurred that "Antheil is easily the most naturally gifted composer of the four [i.e., a group including Antheil, Copland, Roger Sessions, and Carlos Chávez]." But this was two years after the Carnegie Hall concert, and he concluded with an indictment: "he is also the most defective."[36]

Antheil made an attempt to rehabilitate his status with an autobiography in 1945, published when he was forty-five, an early age for summing up a career. By titling the book "Bad Boy of Music," he still seemed to believe that scandal-mongering would yield results. But he continued to fade from view. In 1968, the composer and writer Ned Rorem gave a stark assessment of the degree to which Antheil's reputation had collapsed: "George Antheil. His name to our young is not even a name, and his performances number zero."[37]

Perceived for decades as a misfire—a *"flop mécanique"* according to its producer Donald Friede—*Ballet Mécanique* should no longer be dismissed as a dud. Rather it stands as a remarkable manifestation of the machine movement and Dada, showing energetic interchanges between musicians and visual artists during the 1910s and 1920s. Peeling away the excesses in Antheil's rhetoric and returning to the 1926 manuscript score reveals a composition of imagination and substance, especially for its use of avant-garde techniques such as silence and readymades, also for its foray into multimedia performance art. These traits, in turn, bear witness not only to raw native talent but also to a richly interconnected Western culture—one in which an eager young composer, hailing from a hometown better known for steel mills than high art, had opportunities to encounter new ideas of both European and American origin. With his noisy salute to the Machine Age, Antheil shouted in a transatlantic language, and he did so with distinctive American inflections.

Spirituality and American Dissonance

Dane Rudhyar's Vision of Dissonance

> To us, Dane Rudhyar's work, in its form and the pathos ex-
> haled by it, in its weaknesses and strengths, bad literature
> and realizations alike, presents itself quite simply as in-
> spired with the unconscious reality of America.
>
> —Paul Rosenfeld, 1925

Noise was but one tool for modernist composers in the early twentieth century.
For many, the principal challenge came in devising alternatives to the tonal system on which much Western music had been based. One particular group of
Americans—the "ultra-moderns" as they called themselves—took this mission
especially seriously. Including composers who spanned a range of styles, the
ultra-moderns seized experimentation as their rallying cry and dissonance as
their ideal.

One facet of the ultra-moderns' music—especially that of Carl Ruggles, Henry
Cowell, and Ruth Crawford—has been largely forgotten over time: the degree to
which they associated dissonance with spirituality. In this realm, the French-
American composer and philosopher Dane Rudhyar (1895–1985) became their
quiet leader. Rather than formulating specific methods for writing dissonant music,
Rudhyar assumed the role of high priest, exploring the connection of dissonance to
the spirit and advocating "a deeper, richer, more cosmic" form of creative expression. His perspective represented only one part of American ultra-modernism. But
it was influential for a time, and it affected the way some of the most difficult strains
of new music were being composed and perceived.[1]

Spinning metaphors that related dissonance to the soul, Rudhyar took a passion-
ately articulated antiformalist stance in which he raised issues that continued to

resonate throughout the entire century. A proto-multiculturalist, he helped expand the vision of American composers beyond the West. Spiritual rather than mathematical, intuitive rather than logical, he challenged the dominance of European cultural values, promoting instead a trans-Asian mix of religious philosophies and musical practices. All this was communicated in a series of articles, published mostly in music periodicals such as *Eolian Review* and *Musical America*, also in general-interest magazines. He produced a tremendous quantity of prose about music during the 1920s.

As modernism took hold, Rudhyar branded the music of his day as *"metaphysically aimless,"* calling upon composers to search for *"a new basis, a new soul, a new faith."* Staunchly opposed to neoclassicism and "neo-scholasticism" (his term for the music of Schoenberg), Rudhyar protested the dehumanization that he felt threatened early twentieth-century composition. These same concerns were being voiced at other points on the modernist spectrum. Even Jane Heap, one of the promoters of machine art, mused in 1925 that "a new mechanical world" had "bred

Figure 6.1. Photograph of Dane Rudhyar from *Musical America* (28 May 1927). Courtesy of Musical America Archives.

an incomplete man. His outer life is too full, his inner life empty." She concluded, "The desire for beauty has become a necessity." At the same time, there was a sense of almost over-rich creative potential, of a "chaotic superabundance of materials"— to quote Ruth Crawford. Artists and musicians repeatedly confessed to feeling overwhelmed by options; they faced a creative orbit dense enough to suffocate those who could not sort out its profusion.[2]

Rudhyar stepped in to clear the density by forging an alternate path, doing so in ways that suggest striking parallels with the acknowledged behind-the-scenes leader of the ultra-moderns, the composer and theorist Charles Seeger (1886–1979). Beginning in the 1910s, Seeger developed a systematic theory of "dissonant counterpoint"; Rudhyar, on the other hand, expressed little interest in systems of any kind, preferring poetic odysseys. Yet in many respects, the two men were not so far apart. Both sought to devise a dissonant form of musical expression emblematic of the New World, and their ideas affected the same group of composers. Rudhyar and Seeger were by no means personally sympathetic—in fact they had a rancorous debate in print in 1923. Yet no matter how opposed the two might have felt themselves to be, they stood on common ground, proposing separate yet interconnected rationales for exploring the uncharted waters of dissonant composition.[3]

In the intervening decades, Rudhyar's role has been largely eclipsed by Seeger's. But there have been isolated moments when his contribution has been acknowledged. In the 1970s, the composer Peter Garland devoted large sections of his "little magazine" *Soundings* to Rudhyar. In 1987, Gilbert Chase added him to the third edition of *America's Music*. And four years later Judith Tick studied his effect on the young Ruth Crawford. Beyond this, Rudhyar has been lost from view. In part this happened because he retreated from the new-music scene after 1930 or so. He essentially gave up composition as the Depression deepened and he found few opportunities "to continue the lecture-recitals on 'New Music'" that he "had been giving to small groups of people." Instead, he moved on to write about astrology, becoming a much-respected authority on the subject. This change in professional direction yielded yet another parallel with Seeger, who also retreated from modernism around the same time, becoming increasingly involved with vernacular musics during the Great Depression.[4]

Yet there was more to Rudhyar's disappearance from the history of modernist music than his early retirement from the subject. After World War II, the rise of academic musicology, music theory, and composition in American universities brought with it a high regard for para-scientific modes of discussing music. Serialism and set theory rose up then as the dominant means of producing and explaining compositions grounded in "post-tonal" idioms—music that in the 1920s had simply been termed "dissonant." To the extent that music of the American ultra-moderns was studied at all, it was considered for its particular post-tonal language. Seeger eventually emerged as a native progenitor of the ultra-moderns' post-tonality, while Rudhyar, if he had even been known then, would have been dismissed as lightweight in such a climate. As a result, memory faded of an era when a diversity of rationales for dissonance was being offered—when it was by no means certain that the more logically conceived notion would triumph.

Rudhyar's ideas, though, have floated down through the decades in the work of composers such as John Cage, Lou Harrison, and James Tenney, stretching right up to the ambient music of Harold Budd. As both composer and philosopher, Rudhyar opens striking perspectives on the early modernist movement in America. His conception of dissonance offers a path for exploring the spiritual inclinations of Ruggles, Cowell, and Crawford.

Born in France, Rudhyar joined others among his countrypersons—most notably Varèse and Duchamp—in immigrating to the United States in the midst of World War I. He arrived in 1916 and soon after took on the name of "Rudhyar," illustrating graphically his switch from the Old World to the New. Redefining himself in terms of ancient civilizations and astrology, Rudhyar confected a name with roots in the old Sanskrit root *rudra*, meaning dynamic action and the electrical power released during a storm. It also connected to the color red, which had appeal because his zodiac sign was Aries; it, in turn, was related to the red planet Mars. Over the next several years, Rudhyar meandered back and forth between Canada (Toronto and Montreal), New York, and Philadelphia, giving concerts and lectures.[5]

Although only twenty-one, he was already an active composer and author. His *Claude Debussy et son oeuvre* had been published in Paris in 1913 (when he was eighteen!), and he recalled later that it helped set his sights on America. "[Debussy's] music gave me the impression of an autumnal kind of state of the culture: the beautiful, golden, poignant feeling of the woods in France which are very beautiful but very nostalgic, not like the flamboyant New England woods at all. And so it occurred to me . . . that Debussy was a good symbol of the fact that our European culture had come to an Autumnal period, a Fall period." Upon reaching New York, Rudhyar made his North American debut as a composer in 1917, with Pierre Monteux conducting his *Symphonic Dance Poems* at the Metropolitan Opera. Then in early 1920 he moved to California, where he made his home. But Rudhyar remained fundamentally peripatetic, making a series of extended trips back to New York over the course of the 1920s. A prime example of the migrating geographic base of American modernism, Rudhyar anchored himself on the West Coast—a sympathetic environment for his deepening interest in the East—at the same time recognizing the professional need to gain visibility in New York. The impact of his ideas was felt in both locations.[6]

Like Duchamp and Varèse, Rudhyar saw American culture as a hopeful alternative to the wartime decay of Western Europe. Unlike them, he was attracted to esoteric philosophy, not Dada. During his early years in North America, Rudhyar immersed himself in the study of non-Western traditions, especially through long reading stints at the New York Public Library, where he explored Rosicrucianism, Buddhism, alchemy, and the Baha'i movement. He also read extensively about Asian musics. All this culminated in an interest in theosophy, which Rudhyar seems to have begun investigating seriously in Toronto during the winter of 1917–18, when he stayed with Djane and Siegfried Herz. Djane Herz was the same figure who in the next decade formed a salon in Chicago where the ultra-moderns gathered; there Ruth Crawford became absorbed in theosophy and first encountered both Rudhyar and Cowell. Rudhyar was active in new-music circles as well. He served on the "Composers' Committee" of Varèse's International Composers' Guild, and he took part in Cowell's New Music Society, as well as the Pan American Association of Composers. He became an American citizen in 1926.[7]

One early inspiration for Rudhyar's ideas lay in the writings of Henri Bergson, the French philosopher discussed in connection with Ornstein. A number of Bergsonian theories affected Rudhyar, including faith in the power of intuition, a tendency to use evolution as a model for a theory of creativity, and an openness to "deeper psychic states." All these played a role in Rudhyar's theories about dissonance in the New World. Rudhyar studied the writings of Bergson while still in Paris, and Bergson's name turns up occasionally in Rudhyar's publications. "This music is built in the manner of living organisms," he wrote when reflecting on Varèse's *Amériques*. "It is essentially Bergsonian in its principle of continuous unfolding. It has a tremendous 'vital impulse,' which refuses to become rigid, but keeps ever transforming, in a state of fluid becoming."[8]

Theosophy made the deepest impression on Rudhyar, infusing his publications during the 1920s. With this, he joined an international circuit of avant-garde writers and visual artists who were exploring its tenets as a way of giving meaning to radical creative expression. Claiming a continuity with ancient esoteric traditions, the modern theosophical movement took shape with the Theosophical Society, founded in New York in 1875 by Helena Blavatsky, Colonel William Olcott, William Quan Judge, and others. After Blavatsky's death in 1891, Annie Wood Besant assumed leadership, focusing on connections between theosophy and Hinduism. In membership and intensity, theosophy reached a peak in the late 1920s, encompassing some 7,000 adherents in the United States. It lives on, both in its many worldwide organizations and in the various New Age movements it has spawned.[9]

The word *theosophy* turns up only occasionally in Rudhyar's writings, yet its tenets inform almost every page, whether in direct doctrinal connections or in the wide-ranging spirit that characterized his thought. He espoused utopian notions of "universal brotherhoods," a core tenet of theosophy, and he absorbed its emphasis on cosmology. He also viewed the composer as a medium, modeling his notion on the role that Blavatsky assumed when she claimed to have received spiritual messages from the Mahatmas. (Mahatmas were "mysterious personages . . . who were perfected in former periods of evolution and thus serve as models of human development.") For Rudhyar, as he stated it, "the new composer" was "no longer a 'composer,' but an evoker, a magician. His material is his musical instrument, a living thing, a mysterious entity endowed with vital laws of its own, sneering at formulas, fearfully alive."[10]

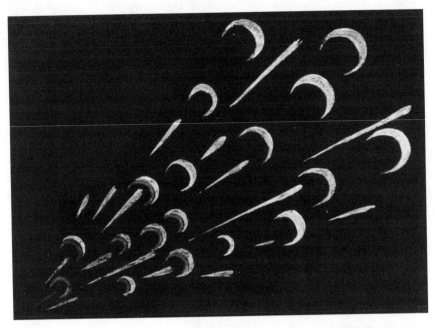

Figure 6.2. Annie Besant and Charles W. Leadbeater, *Thought-Forms (Sudden Fright)*, 1902. Location unknown.

Other artists of Rudhyar's day who investigated theosophy ranged from Wassily Kandinsky, Piet Mondrian, Franz Kupka, and T. S. Eliot, working in Europe, to Arthur Dove, Marsden Hartley, and Wallace Stevens in America. Rudhyar never cited any of these figures in his writings, and his ideas developed in distinct directions from theirs. But by evolving a spiritual philosophy of dissonance he was working in the same general orbit. The leading tract among painters was Kandinsky's *On the Spiritual in Art* of 1912, an excerpt from which appeared in Alfred Stieglitz's American journal *Camera Work* that July, almost immediately after its publication in Europe. Trying to ward off an art obsessed with form and devoid of humanity, Kandinsky defined the "responsibility" of the artist as recognizing that "his actions and thoughts and feelings . . . purify or infect the spiritual air" and that they "are the material for his creations." Kandinsky immersed himself in the writings of Blavatsky.[11]

Another predecessor to Rudhyar in fusing theosophy with new art was the Russian composer Alexander Scriabin, whom Rudhyar greatly admired. Rudhyar saw Scriabin as "the one great pioneer of the new music of a reborn Western civilization, the father of the future musician." For Rudhyar, the Russian mystic provided an antidote to "the Latin reactionaries and their apostle, Stravinsky" and the "rule-ordained" music of "Schoenberg's group."[12]

When Rudhyar began shaping his own ideas, he seized the printed word as a means of disseminating his progressive views, and he took up several themes, all of which centered around dissonance. The first of these articles appeared in 1920 in the *Musical Quarterly*. Titled "The Rise of the Musical Proletariat," it was written in French and translated into English by Frederick H. Martens, the same man who had published a biography of Leo Ornstein two years earlier. Rudhyar gave a grim diagnosis of composition at the dawn of the 1920s—"The music of to-day is built up on nothingness, on mortuary fragments"—and he focused on the inhibiting limitations of conventional notation, proposing the phonograph and electricity as offering new possibilities. "The phonograph . . . is led to play the same part which in the Orient is played by the oral transmission of music," Rudhyar wrote. Rudhyar also used this article to begin testing his theory of contemporary composition as reflecting a "social point of view" (although the title of this article uses a common Marxist term, the text does not display a Marxist perspective).[13]

With "The Relativity of Our Musical Conceptions," published in 1922, Rudhyar's ideas about "tone" moved to the fore. This was central to his philosophy of dissonance. Sounding a universalist theme basic to theosophy, Rudhyar opened by criticizing European culture for having ignored "the possibility of *another* Truth" drawn from the "discovery of Oriental civilization, art, [and] science." He declared in proto-Cageian terms that "every thing around us is sound." This, in turn, led to "tone," which for Rudhyar was different from the "note." Tone had multiple meanings. In one sense, it represented a multidimensional entity that included pitch, timbre, duration, and register. Webern, for one, was working at the same time with multiple pitch parameters; Rudhyar pursued a related goal through metaphysical arguments. "Tone" also had the character of a "living entit[y]," as in the Orient. Most fundamentally, though, it encompassed a pulsating sound, whether built up cumulatively or resonating in isolation, that filled the space around it.[14]

Throughout the course of the 1920s, "tone" remained at the core of Rudhyar's message to the world of music. He ardently preached what he termed "the gospel of tone," describing this concept in ways both complex and elusive. In 1926, he wrote how the truly new composer "deals now with *living matter* and no longer with patterns of notes. He takes with his powerful hand the throbbing instrumental matter, kneds [*sic*] it into the image of his own living human Soul." Thus "tone" not only encompassed a full composite of a sound's profile but aimed for something more intangible—the living, resounding spirit of sound. Listeners, moreover, played an active role in the creative process. The *experience* of "tone" was as important as the conception of it. Rudhyar challenged listeners, claiming that the new music "must be heard subjectively as Tone, not perceived objectively as a mass of melodic patterns, of recognizable themes and the like."[15]

In explaining his concept of sound, Rudhyar never resorted to technical descriptions. Doing so would have violated his campaign against formalism. Rather he tried to evoke the spirit of "tone." One exceptionally clear statement about it appeared in 1926 after Rudhyar heard cymbals—probably Chinese cymbals—in a piece by Henry Eichheim (most likely *Malay Mosaic*, which had been performed on a concert of the International Composers' Guild on 1 March 1925):

The shock of the cymbals produces a primary complex tone which at once grows by the cumulative resonance of all the sub-tones of the metallic mass. When this happens the tone produced can be truly said to be *alive*. Otherwise it is dead. Tones which do not grow are dead. This is why Scriabine piles up chords upon chords built upon the same modal group, Cowell tone-clusters upon tone-clusters; thus is produced the illusion—and at time[s] the reality—of the growth of tones; thus are cumulative resonances dealt with, and not singular, separative entities called notes.[16]

Once "tone" was defined in organic terms, it then became the basis for a new approach to dissonance. "Cumulative resonances" provided a means of introducing piles of seconds, as well as other intervals considered "dissonant" within traditional tonal practice.

Around this same time, Charles Seeger was developing his theory of "dissonant counterpoint," which he passed on to his students and colleagues—especially Ruggles, Cowell, and Crawford. His principal article about it—"On Dissonant Counterpoint"—appeared in *Modern Music* in 1930. There Seeger described "dissonant counterpoint" as "at first purely a school-room discipline." Seeger took the historic rules of counterpoint and inverted them, establishing "dissonance, rather than consonance, as the rule" and wrote about "the effect of this discipline" as "one of purification." This principle was then applied to other parameters of composition, so that rhythm or dynamics could also be "dissonated." Seeger's theory, in effect, took the form of a set of rules, as different as they could be from the metaphysical musings of Rudhyar. Yet as Taylor Greer points out, Seeger's ideas were based on a "fusion of reason and intuition." Seeger believed that the "mystic" and the "scientist" needed to be reconciled.[17]

Rudhyar's philosophy of dissonance had another component beyond "tone": he saw dissonance as part of a new postwar social order, with America becoming the site for a multicultural utopia. "I am working now in an (apparently) different line, dealing with international problems," he reported in a 1926 letter to Ruggles. Rudhyar was referring to a pamphlet he was writing titled "World-Americanism," which he explained as "merely another way of approaching the subject of the Great American Culture-to-be." Decades later he summarized this activity to Vivian Perlis: "That's why I came to America. The idea that European civilization was breaking down and that as a kind of seed of the past I could plant myself as it were, into a virgin soil. And all my life work has been to try to build up a foundation for a new civilization."[18]

Rudhyar believed that a new music would stride forth as part of this new civilization. Sounding at times like Charles Ives—with his notion of "the common universal mind" and belief that "all occupations of man's body and soul in their diversity come from but one mind and soul!"—Rudhyar aimed high, imagining composition as a noble calling that was linked to social constructions. "Notes stand as individuals, free, equal—like men in a perfect communistic civilization," he wrote. "The problem as a whole is much more complex than many composers believe it to be. For a sound to be free, that is atonal, is a great thing. The same, no doubt, for men. Yet men must live in society nowadays; sounds must live in symphonies, of whatever type they may be. Thus freedom is only relative. Some type of relationship must be evolved."[19]

Such a scheme provided a handy tool for giving meaning to dissonance. Like humans in an increasingly diverse social network, pitches considered dissonant could evolve new alignments to retain their essential difference yet achieve compatible coexistence. There was no better place to achieve such a multicultural sound, Rudhyar believed, than in the United States, with its rich mix of races and ethnicities.

Over the years, other American composers have waved related banners— whether Ives, whose cluster-rich song *Majority* has been described by Michael Broyles as "an incantation, a mystical statement of belief in the masses or the people"; or Duke Ellington, who played one of his recordings for a journalist and said, "That's the Negro's life. . . . Hear that chord! Dissonance is our way of life in America. We are something apart, yet an integral part." Similarly, Lou Harrison wrote about Ruggles's dissonant counterpoint in the 1940s, calling it "a community of singing lines, living a life of its own, . . . careful not to get ahead or behind in its rhythmic cooperation with the others."[20]

While most of Rudhyar's ideas on dissonance were set forth in articles during the 1920s, he also issued two important treatises, both of which are as forgotten as his more broadly disseminated writing. The first of these, *Dissonant Harmony*, appeared in 1928; by then Rudhyar felt his political ideas were important enough to state as part of the subtitle, "A New Principle of Musical and Social Organization." In *Dissonant Harmony*, Rudhyar continued his policy of offering no prescriptions for note choices or compositional procedure; rather he lectured on the need for both music and society to achieve spiritual "regeneration." Fixed rules would not govern the operations of a successful diverse society but rather "cosmic laws." All this had a musical corollary. "Dissonant music," wrote Rudhyar, "is thus the music of true and spiritual Democracy; the music of universal brotherhoods; music of Free Souls, not of personalities."[21]

The other visionary publication by Rudhyar is *The New Sense of Space*, a pamphlet published in 1930 together with five other essays and a reprint of *Dissonant Harmony*—all subsumed under the title *Art as Release of Power*. While *The New Sense of Space* restated many of Rudhyar's basic ideas, it also took some additional steps, proposing a view of the artistic process as reflecting "two opposite conceptions of Space." In one, embraced by formalists, space was viewed as "emptiness," as a "blank negation" onto which "esthetic forms are *projected*." In the other, artists who had undergone the spiritual and cultural transformation promoted by Rudhyar would conceive of space as "fulness of unconditioned Being" and perceive themselves as a kind of medium, permitting "forms" to be *"evolved out of it."* With such ideas, Rudhyar challenged the notion of composition as egoistical self-expression.

Rather, he advocated approaching it as a cooperative act, establishing parity between composers and their musical materials.[22]

With this attitude toward "space," Rudhyar also revealed the final basic component of his musical convictions—namely, his interest in Eastern philosophies. This too related—although often tangentially—to his philosophy of dissonance. Asian cultures, as fused and transmitted through theosophy, were central to Rudhyar's ideology, at the same time as he was not inclined to provide information either about specific Asian musical techniques that captured his attention or even about which cultures he was discussing. Rather, he had a kind of bear-hug approach, embracing "the East" generically and enthusiastically. His fascination with Scriabin, for example, was based in part on a belief that the Russian had "turned back to the East"—an opinion few others have shared. In California he came in contact with B. P. Wadia, who, according to Rudhyar, had been an important aide to Annie Besant, leader of the theosophists. Decades later, Rudhyar recalled that he had "tried to start a World Music Society, . . . but it was much too soon." He applied unsuccessfully for a Guggenheim fellowship to visit India, then wrote a book in 1926 titled *The Rebirth of Hindu Music*, which was published two years later by the Theosophical Publishing House in Madras (a firm once managed by Wadia). The book was written while Rudhyar was living briefly in Bryn Mawr, Pennsylvania; Rudhyar later complained that it was "never adequately distributed in America."[23]

At a time when a small group of American composers—including Cowell and Henry Eichheim—was beginning to explore the potential of various Asian repertories for modernist composition, Rudhyar stepped forward with a whole book on one culture. The musical interactions of East and West gained increasing importance as the twentieth century unfolded. Much of *The Rebirth of Hindu Music* contains theories published elsewhere by Rudhyar. But two crucial components are added: a strong statement about anti-imperialism and a desire to contribute to Indian culture. Rather than simply borrowing ideas and sounds from another realm, which was the most common Western approach to repertories from "the East," Rudhyar sought to honor its distinctiveness. He issued a call for Indians to "be true to their souls as Indians," to "reawaken in themselves the memory" of their impressive musical heritage, and he ended with a vaguely conceptualized plea for Indians to uncover their spiritual roots and share them with the world. Here again there was a parallel to Seeger. As the decades passed, Seeger's intellectual energy was increasingly directed to the study of musics outside of the European-American "classical" tradition. Eventually he came to be seen as one of the founders of the discipline of ethnomusicology in the United States. As in their other near-connections, Rudhyar and Seeger shared an interest in non-Western traditions, yet they exhibited it in entirely different ways.[24]

Rudhyar actively put his ideas about spirituality and dissonance into practice. Like Seeger, Rudhyar ended up having a far greater impact as philosopher and theorist than as composer; at the same time, he was more prolific in the realm of composition than Seeger ever became. A body of noteworthy music by him from the 1920s stood at the core of a developing ultra-modern idiom. It included several pieces for orchestra, some with titles evoking spiritual regeneration or Rudhyar's theory of "syntonic music" (or "the true dissonant music which moves spiritward"): *Soul Fire* (1920); *Syntony No. 1, From the Unreal Lead Us to the Real* (1919–21); *Syntony No. 2, Surge of Fire* (1921); and *Hero Chants* (1930). These are overshadowed, at least in public visibility during the 1920s, by a group of compositions for solo piano, some of which also carry titles redolent of spirituality: *15 Tone Poems* (1924–26), *Three Paeans* (1927), *Granites* (1929), *Nine Tetragrams* (*The Quest*, 1920; *Crucifixion*, 1926; *Rebirth*, 1927; *Adolescence*, 1925; *Solitude*, 1927; *Emergence*, 1929; *Tendrils*, 1924; *Primavera*, 1928; and *Summer Nights*, 1967); *Four Pentagrams* (*The Summons*, 1924; *The Enfoldment*, 1924; *Release*, 1926; *The Human Way*, 1926); and *Syntony* (*Dithyramb*, 1919; *Eclogue*, 1934; *Oracle*, 1934; *Apotheosis*, 1925; all revised in 1967). Of these, two groups of piano pieces were published in Cowell's *New Music*. *Paeans* appeared prominently in the second issue of the series (January 1928), following after Ruggles's *Men and Mountains*. It was dedicated "to my friend and co-worker Henry Cowell." *Granites* turned up seven years later (July 1935). Both works also had a performance life in New York: *Paeans* was heard at a Copland-Sessions concert on 6 May 1928, with Richard Buhlig at the piano, and *Granites* was performed by Rudhyar himself at a League of Composers' concert on 2 February 1930.[25]

Together, *Paeans* and *Granites* give a strong sense of Rudhyar's epic aims. He soared toward grand statement. The titles of his pieces not only are spiritual and metaphysical but many are also single, consonant-laden words. The titles and compositions share another trait as well: they are dissonant aphorisms pronounced by a sage. They give a sense of what Rudhyar was aiming for in his writings, at the same time as they show how thoroughly elusive "tone" could be. In introducing *Paeans*, Rudhyar defined the title conventionally as "odes of joy often sung [in Greece] to celebrate victories," adding his own interpretation: "But there are spiritual as well as physical victories." Each piece averages around thirty measures and contains tempo markings with spiritual coding: "With joyous exultation" in *Paean 1*, "Epic and Resonant" in *Paean 2*, and "With condensed strength and majesty," "With stark rigidity," "With a vibrant serenity," and "With triumphant exultation" in *Granites* 1, 2, 4, and 5 (unnumbered in the score). The music is vertically conceived, with thickly textured chords rolling upwards over the keyboard. Intervals of fourths, fifths, and seconds form the principal building blocks. *Paean 1*, for example, opens with the sense of the "living organism" articulated by Rudhyar (Example 6.1). In the first measure, two pairs of starkly exposed seconds with a downward jog are sequentially presented; the phrase then flits up through a series of fourths (both perfect and augmented), topped off by a final leap. In this brief temporal space a sonic spectrum of over four octaves is covered. Variants of these same melodic and intervallic ideas then fall (m. 2) and rise (m. 3) before reaching a static middle ground (m. 4)—this constructed almost fully of fourths. An even more powerful buildup

Example 6.1. Dane Rudhyar, *Paean 1*, p. 1. Published in *New Music* 1/2 (January 1928). Used by permission. Theodore Presser Co.

occurs next (mm. 5–7), cascading to a low point at the opening of m. 8. This massive ebbing and flowing realizes the "cumulative resonance" described in Rudhyar's writings. In introducing the work, he made this clear, stating that it "is not based . . . on melodic themes and the like. . . . Rather it is founded on the building of resonances or complex harmonies which are like vital seed-tones germinating, sprouting into vast trees of harmonies. It deals with Energies, not with so-called Form."[26]

Such sonic force fields were typical for Rudhyar, as were periods of relative stasis. Rudhyar marked the conclusion of *Paean 2* "Mighty. *Gong-like*" (Example 6.2). In it, he lined out three brief modules (mm. 15–17, 18–19, 21–23), where the composer most graphically realized his theory of "tone." Given the dynamic marking of *fff*, together with the striding pace of the work (a metronome marking of seventy quarter notes per minute), each of these modules gives an opportunity for spiraling swirls of sound—or "tone-masses"—which emanate from a basic chord and reach up to a high-pitched resonance.

Similarly, the pendular quartal and quintal harmonies of the final *Paean* have the cumulative impact of a gong, especially as they build to piles of resonating dissonances at the end. They generate a dense chromatic mass (no example included here).

Example 6.2. Rudhyar, *Paean 2*, mm. 15–end. Published in *New Music* 1/2 (January 1928). Used by permission. Theodore Presser Co.

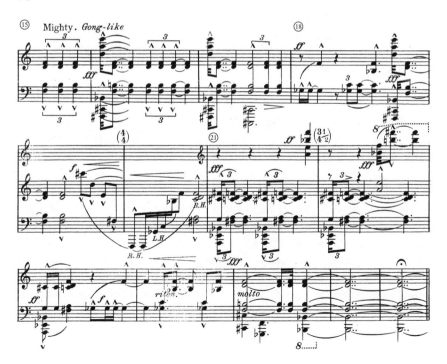

Thus "tone," as manifested in Rudhyar's own music, was achieved mainly through a buildup of sound. It aimed for an apotheosis where "tonality dies forever," as Rudhyar put it, and "a new type of harmony, of chords, is constituted; polyphony itself spreads vertiginously; . . . it vibrates as a whole, as a gigantic gong." In some ways, this harmonic conception seems related to Schoenberg's *Farben* from *Five Orchestral Pieces* of 1909. Yet Rudhyar would have sharply disavowed such a link, in large part because Schoenberg—like Stravinsky—represented the tyranny of Old World practices.[27]

Put next to the music of his close contemporaries, Rudhyar's style was "relentlessly harmonic in conception," as the theorist Joseph Straus has aptly described it, and stands apart from the contrapuntal inclination of Carl Ruggles and Ruth Crawford (especially by the late 1920s). Yet his insistence on massive sonorities and on glorying in the *resonance* of cumulative chords had strong ties to selected works by them, as well as to other American music of the period. One of the most surprising cases is Aaron Copland's Piano Variations of 1930, which shares melodic gestures with one of Rudhyar's *Granites* and conveys a similar spacious sense of authority—a subject to be discussed in Chapter 14. For some, Rudhyar's grandness simply did not work. When *Paeans* appeared in *New Music* in 1928, the young Elliott Carter wrote to Ives that "Rhudyar's [*sic*] Paeans are good but they seem a little too majestic, too much of his own greatness taken for granted." Others disagreed, though. Rudhyar's colleague John J. Becker called the *Paeans* "tremendously conceived and for me indescribably beautiful. Beautiful in their inherent contents and beautiful in their logical upbuilding." Carlos Chávez enthused about them as "powerfull [*sic*], intense" with "magnificence of mind and feeling." The critic Lawrence Gilman wrote of Rudhyar's *Moments*, another set of piano pieces from the 1920s, as "concentrated and interior," and Paul Rosenfeld responded to the work's "power, wild joy, and movement."[28]

All in all, Rudhyar fused an abundant array of ideas and influences into a distinctive vision of American dissonance. Like a comet blazing through the sky, his spiritual theory was intensely constructed and rapidly moving. It illuminated the horizon of a small group of composers for a short time. "Tone," with its accompanying notion of "cumulative resonance," advocated an approach to dissonance in which massive sounds piled up, filling the musical "space." And it connected to a utopian stance in which dissonant pitches represented peoples of disparate backgrounds. Given that Rudhyar avoided musical specificity and conveyed his ideas within the language of metaphysics and esoteric philosophy, he could continue to be ignored as representing a fringe perspective. But with the broad dissemination of non-Western religions during the late twentieth century and the appeal of so-called mystic composers such as Arvo Pärt or Sofia Gubaidulina, the ideas that Rudhyar promoted moved ever closer to the mainstream.

The Ecstasy of Carl Ruggles

No one else speaks with the deep exaltation that you do.

—Blanche Walton,
in a letter to Ruggles

With Dane Rudhyar, a figure whose reputation has faded over time, it takes effort to picture a fervent guru surrounded by a circle of disciples. But such a scene clearly existed. Rudhyar's closest bond during the early 1920s was with Carl Ruggles and Henry Cowell. Together, the three earnestly encouraged one another in their pursuit of a distinctive modernist idiom. Late in the decade, the young Ruth Crawford also entered their realm. Though never gaining full status in this nuclear brotherhood, she ended up being inspired most directly by Rudhyar.[1]

Among this select group of cohorts, Ruggles was the one most championed by Rudhyar himself. A New Englander by birth, Ruggles (1876–1971) gained a reputation as a salty eccentric, living in a converted Vermont schoolhouse and turning up regularly in New York for performances of his music. The 1920s was his most productive period as a composer. He wrote fewer than a dozen works during his lifetime, and most of them appeared in that decade, delivered straight into the hands of Edgard Varèse, whose International Composers' Guild provided a forum for their premieres.

Ruggles's music was consistently knotty and nontonal, posing stiff challenges for listeners. It was precisely to confront this challenge that Rudhyar stepped in. As critic and advocate, Rudhyar tried to enrich the listening experience by applying his spiritual philosophy of dissonance to Ruggles's music. Rudhyar published two portraits of Ruggles—the first in *Eolian Review* (1923), the second in *Musical America* (1927). He singled out no other American composer to this extent and had previously devoted an entire publication to only one figure: Claude Debussy. Both of Rudhyar's articles about Ruggles have an unacknowledged significance in the literature about the composer, for they appeared before writings about him by Charles Seeger, which have been cited as the first to be published. Ruggles's link to Seeger was certainly strong, especially while Seeger was evolving his theory of dissonant counterpoint; Ruggles himself once declared that "my style began with Seeger." In essence, Seeger became Ruggles's compositional coach, while Rudhyar was his interpreter.[2]

Rudhyar's connection to Ruggles remained tight throughout the early 1920s. He embraced Ruggles as a paragon of the nobility he hoped dissonance would achieve, and Ruggles responded to the strong support his colleague offered. Their relationship reveals much about the spiritual transcendence that has struck so many commentators on Ruggles's music. "The quality of sublimity which Ruggles professes as his desideratum," wrote the composer Lou Harrison in 1946, "is surely native to the spirit of great religious or philosophic composition in any age. . . . Sublimity in

Figure 7.1. "An Intimate Photograph of Carl Ruggles During a Vacation in Vermont," as published in *Musical America* (27 August 1927). Courtesy of Musical America Archives.

the sense of an elevated, individuated, new, explorative, serious adventure on the edge of faith." Rudhyar offers a key to understanding this sublime quality; in fact his theories illuminate a whole body of related adjectives used over the years to describe Ruggles's music. Neither he nor Ruggles were disciples of one another, yet they met for a time on the common ground of Whitmanesque mysticism and theosophical heterogeneity—two philosophical strains that fused in other artists early in the century—and Rudhyar articulated ideas sympathetic to the music Ruggles was composing.[3]

In many ways the two represented an odd match—an irascible, no-nonsense Yankee and a dreamy French mystic. The differences between them were legion. While Rudhyar was obsessed during the 1920s with explaining American dissonance, publishing hundreds of pages in the process, Ruggles focused all his energy on his own compositions, issuing no prose whatsoever. While Rudhyar linked his arguments to a utopian vision of an ethnically diverse society, Ruggles clung to a fading Anglo-Saxon past, tainting his reputation with anti-Semitic outbursts. At the same time, though, Ruggles's political leanings were decidedly liberal, even socialist; for example, he was a contributing editor to *New Masses.* While Rudhyar's compositional style was primarily homophonic, with resonating piles of dissonances, Ruggles's was largely contrapuntal, with scrupulous attention to the nonrepetition of pitches. Yet in some broad-sweeping, mutually supportive way they shared a passion for dissonance, and they found common ground in their aim to gain spiritual sustenance through ultra-modern creative expression.[4]

Beyond their metaphysical sympathies, the two also enjoyed a close friendship, as emerges in a small body of extant letters. Open affection consistently characterized their correspondence. At one point, Ruggles told Rudhyar that their friendship was "a great stimulus." After a performance of one of his pieces, Ruggles again articulated fondness: "My dear Rudhyar: Fine! It was wonderfully thoughtful of you to send me the account of the concert by airmail. . . . I'm so delighted you liked my Lilacs so much. It warms my heart, and gives me courage. Bless you." This probably followed a performance by the New Music Society in California on 25 October 1927. Several months later (March 1928) Rudhyar reported to Ruggles about his own *Five Stanzas* for twelve strings: "I think you would like them, and would love to dedicate them to you, if you will accept such a little offering presented in the spirit of deep companionship and true appreciation of what you represent in music." And that July Ruggles responded directly to Rudhyar's music, asking if his colleague had received a letter "in which I spoke of your 'Paeans,' and how fine they sounded." He must have heard Richard Buhlig's performance of the pieces at a Copland-Sessions concert in May 1928.[5]

Rudhyar and Ruggles also allied themselves against specific opponents in the avant-garde—most notably Varèse and Schoenberg. Even though Varèse was one of the most consistent promoters of Ruggles's music during the 1920s, as mentioned earlier, the two had some hefty rows. In 1926, when a disagreement erupted over the ICG's proposed premiere of *Sun-Treader,* Rudhyar was one of the people to whom Ruggles vented. Ruggles had demanded a small orchestra (as opposed to a chamber ensemble) and a concert date late in the season to give him more time to compose (the piece had been scheduled for November). But Varèse angrily refused and Ruggles responded by resigning from the Guild. "Varèse can't pull the Mussolini stuff with me," Ruggles wrote in a huff to Rudhyar. He then borrowed some of Rudhyar's own language: "You have expressed it exactly. His work is 'interesting—perhaps—but soulless.'" Someone, presumably Rudhyar, circled "perhaps" in the text. *Sun-Treader* never was performed by the ICG. Rather its premiere took place in Paris in February 1932, as part of a concert of the Pan American Association of Composers, conducted by Nicolas Slonimsky.[6]

With Schoenberg, Ruggles seemed to feel a sense of competition, if not acrimony; he and Rudhyar were bent on establishing Ruggles's superiority to the Viennese composer. At one point, Ruggles concurred with Rudhyar about his concept of "tone," but he did so as a way of criticizing Schoenberg: "Of course. It is the 'actual tone experience' which is the all important thing. *Music is no better than it sounds.* As you say, Schoenberg often looks well on paper—for example the Quintette for Woodwind[s] and Horn. There are fine places all through Schoenberg's work. But as a whole his brain runs away with his heart. And again, his melodic line, is as a general thing, dry, and uninspired, and unsustained." Ruggles must have been referring to passages about Schoenberg that were included in Rudhyar's 1927 essay about Ruggles, also to another article by Rudhyar published in *Musical America* that same summer, which analyzed the cultural politics behind the music of Stravinsky, Schoenberg, and Scriabin. In writing of Ruggles, Rudhyar criticized Schoenberg to establish the New Englander's merits: "Ruggles is finding his way mostly along the lines of pure polyphony; not, however, in the dry, dispersed and academic manner of a Schönberg juggling with intellectual problems, but in an intensely coherent, vital, and at times transparently pure manner." And when he wrote of the "Three S's," condemning Schoenberg's twelve-tone system as "neo-scholasticism," Rudhyar charged that he "HAD TO formulate new rules to stem the disintegration of his atonal material. These new rules are however purely intellectual, not born out of the very nature of Sound." But it was Rudhyar's final observation about Schoenberg that seems to have caught Ruggles's eye: "[His method] produces written music, *i.e.*, a music which looks most interesting when read; meaningless when heard."[7]

Interestingly, Henry Cowell also compared Ruggles and Schoenberg, although more temperately, in a 1925 article in *Musical America*. "The finest modern work produced in New York this year is the orchestral piece, 'Men and Mountains,' by the American, Carl Ruggles," wrote Cowell. He later made a Schoenberg comparison: "But there is a sophistication and a feeling of approaching decay in 'Pierrot' which is greatly in contrast to the exuberant upspringing of Ruggles' 'Mountains.'" Cowell made clear that he put the two side-by-side because "the spirit of their music is radically different, [yet] they have certain technical similarities." Like

Rudhyar and other American modernists of the 1920s, he was sensitive to how such comparisons diminished American composers.[8]

On the whole, Rudhyar's published statements about Ruggles were devoted to articulating a way of experiencing his colleague's music. In 1923, his first such article focused on *Angels*, which had been premiered at an International Composers' Guild concert on 17 December 1922. At this early date, Rudhyar did not ponder the mystical meaning of Ruggles's music. There was no mention of Whitman, none of spirituality. Rather he highlighted the composer's dissonant counterpoint, using it as a way to explore the political side of his own theory of dissonance. Rudhyar's ideas were still evolving, and he did not seem to have fully grasped the quality that attracted him to Ruggles's music. After declaring that "notes stand as individuals, free, equal," as quoted in the previous chapter, he then gave a mixed assessment of Ruggles, confessing to be "deeply moved and exalted by the purity of the lines and the serenity of the expression" in *Angels* at the same time as he found "an actual hearing" of the work "a disturbing and inharmonious thing." He called the "dissonant counterpoint" of *Angels* "beautifully serene" but claimed that because it was based on the "amorphous, amodal, duodecuple system"—probably referring to the traditional twelve notes of equal temperament—"it sounds to me out of tune, because unnatural." Rudhyar's technical language was utterly unorthodox; he seemed to make up words as he went along. This enraged Charles Seeger, to whom the work was dedicated. Not only was Seeger deeply invested in Ruggles, but he was also a man of punctilious precision. In "Reviewing a Review," published immediately after Rudhyar's essay in *Eolian Review*, Seeger angrily rebutted Rudhyar's "peculiar terminology, mis-statement and bad logic." This was not a cool response but a flaming dismissal. Many of the flaws identified by Seeger were present in Rudhyar's article, perhaps in part because Rudhyar was a nonnative speaker of English. Yet behind Rudhyar's garbled jargon lurked the spark of an attempt to describe the ineffable character of Ruggles's style. And it was within this realm that Rudhyar set himself apart from Seeger. "I may have been too cryptic in my dissertation upon the relations of tonality to modality and to scale," confessed Rudhyar in a response to Seeger, "but the obscurity comes mainly from the fact that I wrote from a philosophical standpoint trying to understand the *life* of music, whereas Mr. Seeger writes from a technical and dogmatic point of view analyzing what to me is but the *skeleton* of music."[9]

Four years later, when Rudhyar published his next profile of Ruggles, the New Englander had become for him a living example of the spiritual modernism that Rudhyar envisioned—a mystical sage who used dissonance to achieve an "ecstasy" that Rudhyar considered "intensely alive and transcendentally emotional." By this time, Rudhyar could precisely pinpoint the qualities that affected him, opening with a quotation from Ruggles: "Music which does not *surge* is not great music." Then Rudhyar moved on to Whitman, citing the poet's "beautiful words" that

Ruggles had used as an epigram for *Portals*, a work premiered by the ICG on 24 January 1926, a year before Rudhyar's article appeared:

What are those of the known
but to ascend and enter the Unknown?

Rudhyar credited "the mysticism and vibrant emotions of a Whitman" with having "awakened a deep response in the heart of Ruggles, one of the three or four real pioneers of the musical world." For Rudhyar, Ruggles transcended formalism, bringing a depth of meaning to his compositions that Rudhyar craved in contemporary music as a whole.[10]

Ruggles and Rudhyar were not alone in meeting at a juncture of spirituality and Whitman. Standing on a continuum of considerable historical reach, they could look back to Transcendentalist writers who discovered Asian religions in the early nineteenth century; ahead of them lay John Cage and poets of the Beat generation during the 1950s, with their immersion in Buddhism. Diverse artistic ancestors and spiritual writings also inspired other creative artists in the early twentieth century, including Max Weber, Albert Pinkham Ryder, and Arthur Dove, among a small group of contemporaneous American abstract painters. For them, as for others of the period, the ideas of Asian masters were paired with those of American Transcendentalists and their offspring, often under the umbrella of theosophy. "Emerson was one of the prophets of 'New America,' and Walt Whitman wrote its psalms," declared an unsigned author in an issue of *Current Literature* from 1909. "'New America' is nothing else than that mystical and spiritual America which centers predominantly about the recognition of new and hitherto unrecognized *powers of Mind*. . . . From the Orient, too, have come contributing influences—Madame Blavatsky with her Theosophy, and Swami Vivekananda with his Vedanta philosophy."[11]

Similarly in France, the country of Rudhyar's birth and youth, a "Whitmanian craze," as historian Betsy Erkkila has termed it, was playing out among avant-garde artists during the late nineteenth and early twentieth centuries. Those affected ranged from symbolists such as Maurice Maeterlinck and Stéphane Mallarmé to figures of the so-called *L'esprit nouveau* such as Blaise Cendrars and Guillaume Apollinaire. For the French, Whitman symbolized the "energy and apparent disorder" of the United States. Some went so far as to recommend him as "a guide for the social and cultural renewal of France." Although Whitman was not actively rediscovered in his home country until the 1920s, there were moments earlier in the century of strong identification with the spiritual force that he represented. In a 1909 essay titled "What I Feel About Walt Whitman," Ezra Pound acknowledged: "the vital part of my message, taken from the sap and fibre of America is the same as his." Ruggles's sympathy with Whitman seemed similarly physical, rooted in the American soil as much as in its literary imagination, and it became one of his links to Rudhyar.[12]

When Rudhyar publicly expressed admiration for Ruggles's music, he singled out one particular segment of it—the "Andantes"—which he believed to exemplify his spiritual theories of dissonance. Of these, *Angels* and *Lilacs* (the middle movement of *Men and Mountains*) held special meaning for Rudhyar, for he believed them to be infused with "an unearthly quality, a disembodied atmosphere which is essentially mystic." Listening to both works with Rudhyar's ideas in mind can deeply affect the way one experiences the music. Rather than focusing on their systematic use of dissonance, as is usually the case in writings about Ruggles, an auditor can take in their subliminal aura and ritualistic nobility. These are thoroughly subjective traits, impossible to quantify, challenging to evoke in prose. But they lie at the core of Rudhyar's ideology and the way in which he believed Ruggles to embody it. "If the composer had a profound and vital mind (and not merely an intellectual knowledge of technical mechanisms)," wrote Rudhyar at one point, "his emotions then would surge from a depth of being which would preclude sentimentalism. 'Intellectual grasp of materials' does not seem as important as a mental understanding of human life and of the problem confronting the human race. True creative power seems to me a combination of a profound, intense understanding of life and of a masterful control of emotions as well as technical means."[13]

In Ruggles, then, Rudhyar found a figure praised by many for his "intellectual grasp" while he himself valued his colleague's capacity to "surge from a depth."

Rudhyar's pulsating, organic sense of "tone" is fundamental to understanding the spiritual strain in Ruggles. Among the most striking traits of *Angels*, for example, are its close voicings, deliberate pacing, and intense vertical dissonance. The lens of Rudhyar brings them into focus as a beatific hymn. From the work's premiere in 1922, commentators were struck by its gorgeous resonance. Paul Rosenfeld singled out the "loveliness of the sound of the six close, dissonant, silver-snarling trumpets," and Rudhyar too declared the piece to be "beautifully serene," as already quoted. But Rudhyar probed the nature of this serenity, tying it to a "new sense of relationship between tones." He believed that Ruggles's careful way of sculpting vertical dissonance yielded "a cosmos, an organism of tones; it vibrates as a whole, as a gigantic gong. It is fulness of tone, a constant whirl of tone-energy."[14]

Angels does not generate the kind of motion that the term "whirl" suggests. Rather its tempo indication is "Serene," as is its overall character. A three-part work, *Angels* has opening and closing sections built of a five-note melodic pattern that rise in range and dynamic intensity. Both there and in the densely delineated dissonances of the central section, a series of buildups occurs—or "surges," in the language of Rudhyar. In the first section, the pattern appears twice in the upper voices (Example 7.1). The second time it is not only a third higher but grows slightly in length and dynamic intensity, extending to an auspicious pause. The texture is highly concentrated yet has none of the massive weight of Rudhyar's own music; rather there is a fundamental internal linearity and spaciousness of voicing.[15]

Example 7.1. Ruggles, *Angels*, p. 1. Used by permission. Theodore Presser Co.

Rudhyar found *Lilacs* to be just as affecting. Premiered by the ICG in December 1924, *Lilacs* shares many traits with *Angels*. Both are so short as to be epigrammatic. Both concentrate on intense, high-floating sounds. Both are virtually monochromatic—in *Angels* there are only trumpets and in *Lilacs* only strings. Ruggles wrote "With deep feeling" as the tempo indication for *Lilacs*, a designation like many of Rudhyar's. And he constructed it, like *Angels*, of brief melodic modules that "surge" toward a buildup of "tone"; in this case a falling second is the core pattern (Example 7.2). *Lilacs* falls into two sections, the first longer than the second. Through rising register and increasing dynamic thrust, each part swells deliberately. There is an intensely argued linear conception here, a trait more indebted to Seeger than Rudhyar, yet it is put to the service of constructing vertical masses rather than independently perceived lines.

Both *Angels* and *Lilacs* also project an ethereal sense of space—a quality that Rudhyar grappled with in his treatise on the topic. Here again, he sought to shape listeners' perceptions. For Rudhyar, as discussed previously, musical space was deeply metaphysical: "Space is in truth a most profound mystery." He saw it as a component that "makes a form esthetic and therefore meaningful in itself without need for further verbal intellectual explanation." In defining "space," he stumbled in a tangle of jargon, using terms like "*sonal energy*" and obliquely separating the "*inner*" from the "*outer*" space of a "tone" [Rudhyar's emphasis]. Yet at base he had a point. Rudhyar saw musical space as growing out of "a series of tones merging into each other." Like a yogi, "the *mind*" of listeners taking in this sound should be "still." The focus was not on an "analytical sense of successional relation (*i.e.* of exact intervals)" but rather on "a series of changing tones [that] are heard, and in a sense *nothing else*." "Space" also represented a fundamental paradox—embracing both "the fulness of Being" and utter "emptiness, absolute void."[16]

The "apt distant glow" of *Angels* and the "relative stillness" of *Lilacs*—both traits singled out by writers about Ruggles and typical of the language his works inspired—take on new meaning in light of this attitude toward space. Both *Angels* and *Lilacs*, despite their textural fullness, can be heard as projecting a "void." They convey a sense of other-worldly suspension, with "a series of tones merging into each other," as Rudhyar put it, each ending with a carefully voiced dissonant chord that wafts away into celestial oblivion.[17]

Throughout Ruggles's limited output, there are other works—or isolated moments within them—that benefit from having the spiritual theories of Rudhyar as a guide. By focusing on their cumulative resonance of "tone," together with the upward-sweeping motion that accompanied it and the projection of an ethereal sense of musical space, a listener can gain a kind of satisfaction that is akin to gazing from a wilderness mountaintop. This is the case in "A Clear Midnight," the third song of *Vox clamans in deserto*, which was premiered by the ICG in January 1924. The tempo indication reads "Slowly, with great tranquillity" and the text by Whitman sets a spiritual agenda: "This is thy house O soul, Thy free flight

Example 7.2. Ruggles, "Lilacs," from *Men and Mountains,* mm. 1–9. Used by permission. Theodore Presser Co.

into the wordless." Much of Ruggles's setting is couched in tight polyphony, which he worked out with advice from Seeger. But Rudhyar's "tone" clarifies individual moments throughout the work, as in a luminescent chord that first draws in the voice at the opening (Example 7.3). But the setting of the final line of text, "Night, sleep, death, and the stars," gains most from using Rudhyar as an interpretive guide. Heard as a sumptuous segment of surging "tone," a series of rising one-measure units in the piano initiate an ascent that culminates with the word "stars." There a tritone reiterates statically in the piano, surrounded by high-placed contrapuntal activity in the other voices. The work concludes within the next nine measures by floating upward to the same kind of high-flung chordal levitation that ended *Angels* and *Lilacs* (Example 7.4).[18]

Portals, with its epigram from Whitman (quoted previously), presents another such case. Its premiere by the ICG in January 1926 inspired Rosenfeld to compare Ruggles directly with Rudhyar: "Ruggles very definitely belongs in the band of Schoenberg, Rudhyar, Webern, and the rest who find the climate of music only at the pitch of ecstacy." That "pitch" occurs in two main sections, the slow-moving, homophonic "Lento" section, which surges upward, and the conclusion, "Slow and Serene," which floats even higher through a delicate counterpoint that rises to a limpid final chord. This last floating resonance spans nearly five octaves and sounds all but one of the pitches of the chromatic spectrum, positioning them carefully over an expansive range. Both this sort of chord quality and placement, as well as surge effect, became signatures of Ruggles's style. Looking back on the same kind

Example 7.3. Ruggles, "A Clear Midnight," from *Vox clamans in deserto,* mm. 5–7. Used by permission. Theodore Presser Co.

Example 7.4. Ruggles, "A Clear Midnight," last 4 measures [= p. 24]. Used by permission. Theodore Presser Co.

of conclusion to *Sun-Treader*, composed between 1926 and 1931, Ruggles himself exclaimed: "Jesus, that was a great chord!"[19]

Ruggles's spiritual journey continued after the 1920s, especially with *Evocations* of 1937–43, which Ruggles subtitled "Four Chants for Piano." There, the title hearkens back to Rudhyar, as does the "surging" style of the first brief work in the set.

A final connection between Ruggles and Rudhyar comes in a shared drive toward epic statement, toward "art as the release of power," to quote the title under which were subsumed Rudhyar's *Dissonant Harmony* and *The New Sense of Space* when they were published together in 1930. This is as evident in Ruggles's music as in the criticism generated by it, in which writers have focused not only on Ruggles's tendency toward the sublime but also on the "majesty" of his work. On first hearing, stately grandeur is perhaps the single most striking quality of Ruggles's music. *Men and Mountains* has it, in the bombastic counterpoint of "Men," the opening movement, and the archaic melodic line bellowed from a summit in "Marching Mountains." If anything, this trait increased with *Portals*. Its unison opening, upward-surging melodies, and deliberate pacing speak with a large utterance. Added to this, its melodic lines have a kind of "primal simplicity"—a quality that finds a visual counterpart in the abstract but spiritual evocations of nature by Arthur Dove. And the opening beat of the timpani in *Sun-Treader* announces the "monumental splendor" that John Kirkpatrick found gripping about this particular composition as a whole.[20]

Considering a title such as "Men and Mountains" with its epigram from Blake, "Great things are done when men and mountains meet," it is hard not to wonder about gendered meanings, especially when writings from Rudhyar are thrown in the mix. Both Ruggles and Rudhyar at times seemed as concerned with being ultra-male as ultra-modern. Spiritual power could be synonymous with masculine power, and utopian visions, be they ever so noble, were articulated within language void of feminine pronouns. Rudhyar's "The Rise of the Musical Proletariat" concluded, "There are some farsighted beings who anticipate and outstrip evolution itself, and such alone deserve to be called 'men!'" His 1928 treatise on dissonance took this even further: "Dissonant music is thus seen as being the music of civilization, the music of MAN." Although it can be argued convincingly that Rudhyar used "MAN" here as a synonym for "human," those capital letters convey a strong sense of maleness, especially since the word appears frequently in the treatise, and every time it is blared out the same way.[21]

Self-conscious masculinity surfaced in a 1926 letter from Rudhyar to Ruggles; it was part of their fraternal bond. Rudhyar wrote of Ruggles's close friend, the painter Rockwell Kent: "I saw Kent's exhibition which is wonderful. I got 2 photos of his works which I like immensely. He is a great artist and a real creator of the new Manhood." And a poem by Rudhyar from the 1930s resonates with the same fusion of massive landscape and maleness that is suggested by *Men and Mountains*:

White Thunder by Dane Rudhyar

Mirrors

The souls of strong men
are granite cliffs
dull and grey to passers by.

But the sun, pouring
upon their broken rocks
destiny sundered,
finds in them mirrors
that glitter.[22]

This is male affirmation. At times, though, such sentiments could turn ugly. To my knowledge, Rudhyar never took part in these negative transformations, but others in the circle surrounding him used gendered language as a weapon in the aesthetic battles they were waging. In the 1920s, many saw music as a feminized sphere and composition, by extension, as less than manly. Analyzing this attitude in 1927, the critic Henrietta Straus wrote in *Modern Music* that "during our struggles to become a nation" economic issues predominated. As a result, she concluded, "we had acquired a viewpoint of life as utilitarian and music did not fit into its scheme. Women might cultivate it as a parlor accomplishment, but certainly no manly men would pursue it seriously as a career—and few did. Like religion, it was left to the 'weaker sex' to uphold, with the result that to this day one sees more American women than men at a concert." Recurring backlashes erupted among men drawn to the arts. A particularly well-known case of this was Charles Ives, whose rhetoric contained gendered slurs that were mostly directed at the broad cultural changes surrounding him. Ives chafed at the commercialization that he believed to be engulfing the concert-music scene and often attacked the "ladies"—meaning essentially consumers—whom he felt influenced symphonic programming. Words like *emasculation* popped up when he decried the reign of the European canon. A 1922 letter from Ives to the violinist Jerome Goldstein shows that compositional experimentation inspired the same rhetorical gestures: "There is a remark in a symphony prospectus this year—'No music will be played that hasn't passed the experimental stage.' Whenever music passes that stage, it has started on it's [*sic*] way down. It has become but a sterile, withered old woman—It is dying; every great inspiration is but an experiment—though every experiment we know, is not a great inspiration." For Ives, "experimental" odysseys were synonymous with strapping youthful maleness.[23]

Gendered language was also used against the so-called neoclassicists of the day, a loosely structured group that ranged from Aaron Copland and Roger Sessions to Virgil Thomson, Walter Piston, and Roy Harris. Most of them studied or had extensive contact with Nadia Boulanger, a female teacher. And a few key figures, most notably Copland and Thomson, were gay. In aesthetic arguments of the period, as will be explored in Chapter 13, "neoclassicism" often was posed as the antithesis of "experimentation." Thus in a gendered scheme, neoclassicism became feminine—or "impotent," as Edgard Varèse was on record as saying—and experimentation was masculine, as Ives registered it. For Varèse, this gendered dichotomy led to some strong language in a letter to Ruggles, written in 1944 after receiving the newly published score for *Evocations*, and it had a direct relationship to spirituality. After praising *Evocations* as "beautiful" and saying that he had enjoyed reading through the pieces, Varèse then lashed out at the forces he felt were making it impossible for someone "healthy and white" to function as a composer in New York. In a stream of foul language, Varèse attacked Copland and his male friends, with explicit reference to their homosexuality, and then praised Ruggles for having composed "virile-spiritual" pieces. Ruggles's response to this letter is not known, but he clearly was perceived by Varèse as a sympathetic recipient. Intolerance on the part of certain modernists—whether directed at women, gays, Jews, or persons of color—surfaced repeatedly in the new-music movement.[24]

To return to Ruggles: his fusion of spirituality and dissonance aimed high on the whole, not low, and Rudhyar's ideas about "tone" and "space" open up new perceptual possibilities in approaching his music. Even Charles Seeger, in his articles from the early 1930s about the New Englander, recognized that dissonant counterpoint could not explain the total impact of his colleague's work. For Seeger, Ruggles's music yielded a "curious ratio between organization and fantasy." Seeger thoughtfully explored this mysterious side of his friend and colleague, reaching no real conclusion but recognizing, quite frankly, that "Ruggles' critique as a whole" yielded "unbalance, where a theoretical balance should be." He confronted an "enigma": "*the beauty is there* or *is near*" but "you cannot put your finger on it." Seeger continued, "You cannot point out any melody, passage or detail that even represents it or can be characterized as such. But you know, just as surely, that in hearing the work you have been in touch with or have had intimations of the sublime. . . . The critic who attempts in language to be logical can only go so far."[25]

This is what Rudhyar had been saying all along. His spiritual conception of dissonance clarified the elusive aspects of Ruggles's style, affirming the subjectiveness of the artistic experience. He turned the act of hearing the slow movements of Ruggles into a spiritual odyssey, an opportunity to journey into the "unknown" and explore the outer reaches of the soul.

Henry Cowell's "Throbbing Masses of Sounds"

I believe in music, in the force of its spirit, in its exaltation, its nobility, its humor, and in its power to penetrate to the basic fineness of every human being.

As a creator of music I express my creed in terms of the world of creative sound—the sound that flows through the mind of the composer with a concentrated intensity impossible to describe, the sound that is the very life of the composer . . so concrete, complete and full of dynamic force in the composer's mind and imagination.

—"Credo" by Henry Cowell (1954)

While Carl Ruggles soared toward the sublime, Henry Cowell kept his feet firmly planted on the ground. An inventor persistently pursuing new patents rather than a philosopher musing about the meaning of human existence, Cowell concentrated on the practical acts of composing and promoting the modernist cause. Above all he gained fame for his musical innovations during the 1910s and 1920s—especially for his use of clusters (which he defined as "chords built from major and minor seconds"), his conceptualization of the string piano (a technique of plucking and otherwise manipulating the piano strings rather than striking the keys), and his forays into complex rhythms. And as with Ruggles, Cowell's connection to the innovative theories of Charles Seeger deeply affected his own work. Cowell and Seeger explored "dissonant counterpoint" together, beginning in 1914 when Cowell studied with Seeger at the University of California, Berkeley, and they remained close friends over the years. Cowell chose the same route as Ornstein and Antheil, presenting himself to the public as both a radical composer and keyboard virtuoso. He made a debut at Carnegie Hall in 1924 and took several European concert tours during the 1920s. A committed activist for modernism in America, Cowell also founded the New Music Society in California in 1925, which initially presented concerts but soon added on the *New Music Quarterly*, a small publishing firm for new scores.[1]

Amid all this purposeful activity, Cowell (1897–1965) also felt the impact of spirituality on his evolving theories of new music. In the early stages of his exploration he had significant contact with Rudhyar. The two were both based in California during the 1920s, with frequent trips to New York, and they formed a bond for a time through shared connections in theosophical circles. In writings about spirituality and dissonance, Rudhyar repeatedly conjured up Cowell's clusters as exemplifying his ideals. By late in the decade, the language Rudhyar used for describing Cowell's music began to travel beyond spiritual circles, becoming enmeshed in the rhetoric surrounding these novel pitch constructions.

Rudhyar began his pronouncements about Cowell in 1922, when he singled out Cowell's clusters in "The Relativity of Our Musical Conceptions." Four years later, he extolled his colleague's "roaring pianism," citing clusters as "cumulative resonances" that exemplified "tone." But his biggest statement came at the conclusion of *The New Sense of Space*, where Cowell's clusters were posed as representing Rudhyar's ideal of a "new sense of tone-fulness, of synthetic resonance." With this "new type of piano playing," Rudhyar asserted, "the piano is a sort of big gong [and] the important factor in the instrument is not the keyboard, not even the separate strings, but the homogeneous sounding-board or table of resonance which, especially with the help of the pedal, gives birth to tone-masses, to complex, synthetic entities of sound." For Rudhyar, Cowell's clusters had an effect similar to that of an Asian gong; they resonated sympathetically in space rather than imposing themselves unnaturally upon it.[2]

Cowell became involved in theosophical circles before meeting Rudhyar, having been drawn into this world through his friendship with the Irish-American poet John Varian, whom he met around 1913. Varian introduced Cowell to the Temple of the People, a group of theosophists who lived in a community they called Halcyon, near Pismo Beach, California, about sixty miles north of Santa Barbara. It continues to flourish today. During the 1910s and 1920s, Cowell spent significant spans of time there, composing a series of works based on Irish mythology, some of them serving as incidental music for plays by Varian.[3]

Through his contact with Varian, Cowell became familiar with views he would soon encounter in Rudhyar. "There is a new race birthing here in the West," wrote Varian, outlining a vision of multicultural harmony. "In the ages coming, it will be a large factor in a new civilization now starting round the Pacific—of a quite different nature from that of the Atlantic. Oriental races will be in it. . . . We are germic embryonic seed of future majesties of growth." Cowell's connection with Rudhyar began when they met at Halcyon during the summer of 1920. Because of Varian, Cowell was primed for theories the French-American philosopher was then formulating. Rudhyar later recalled Halcyon's "vast beach" as having "marvellous, magical dunes" with "a very strong psychic atmosphere." Over the years, he mused with several different interviewers about meeting Cowell there. "I and these people I was staying with from Java were there," Rudhyar remembered, "and they had a convention [at Halcyon] and it was at that first evening of the convention that I was introduced to that young man, Henry Cowell, whom I knew was a composer. I had heard his name from Ornstein in 1917." He then went on to convey a sense of the peripatetic nature of both their lives at the time, suggesting how ideas germinating on the California coast might have meandered to the other side of the country. "Then we became very good friends," Rudhyar continued, "and then we started things together and occasionally, as he traveled a good deal and I was in California and he was in New York, so we saw each other when we were where we were."[4]

Cowell consistently sought mentors within the American modernist movement, with Ives ultimately becoming the most important one. But there were predecessors in that role. Ornstein was admired enormously by Cowell in the late 1910s and 1920s, even though Cowell largely seemed to have forgotten the older man in later years. Ruggles fit into this group as well, representing the apex of native modernism to many American composers during this period. And Seeger, mentioned earlier as a teacher and longtime cohort of Cowell, became an important adviser.

Rudhyar also served this mentoring function for Cowell, figuring prominently in Cowell's creative imagination for a brief time and then fading away. Even though Rudhyar, unlike these others, was of Cowell's generation, he seemed older, having had more professional experience by 1920. Rudhyar later suggested as much, recalling that when he was introduced to Cowell at Halcyon, he met "a younger man." He went on, "Of course I wasn't old. I was twenty-five. But he was even younger." (Cowell was twenty-three.)[5]

When Cowell launched his *New Music Quarterly* in 1927, he featured music by these mentors in the very first issues. Ruggles's *Men and Mountains,* Rudhyar's *Paeans,* and Ornstein's *Corpse* filled the first three volumes (published in 1927–28). The second movement of Ives's Fourth Symphony came out during the second season of the *New Music Quarterly.* Cowell had followed the same pattern when he launched the New Music Society two years earlier. Rudhyar appeared on his "Resident Cooperating Committee," together with Arthur Bliss and Henry Eichheim (all three lived in California), and the society's first program included Rudhyar's *Surge of Fire,* a score for orchestra and three pianos, together with Varèse's *Octandre,* Ornstein's *Musings of a Piano,* Ruggles's *Angels,* an improvisation by Feodor Kolin, Milhaud's Sonata for Two Violins and Piano, and Schoenberg's *Sechs kleine Klavierstücke.* Rita Mead called it a "quirk of history" that Rudhyar's work was "considered the high point of the concert," while *Octandre* "was dismissed as mere experimentalism." But Rudhyar's success might instead have reflected his strong position then among the ultra-moderns.[6]

As with Ruggles, there is a small group of letters between Rudhyar and Cowell to document their close relationship. The two were openly supportive of one another and shared modernist discoveries. "I am crazy to see you," Cowell wrote Rudhyar on a postcard from California around 1920. Cowell reported he was "coming to see the Pilgrimage Play next Sunday evening" and hoped to visit with Rudhyar because "Mrs. Stevenson told me you were still here." ("Mrs. Stevenson" was Christine Wetherhill Stevenson, who had hired Rudhyar to come to California in 1920 to write music for her theosophical Pilgrimage Play, *The Life of Christ*, which was produced on property now occupied by the Hollywood Bowl.) Another letter from Cowell, this one sent from New York City between 1920 and 1922, vividly conveys a time when modernist composers were just beginning to learn about one another. "Your most charming and beautiful letter, which I prize so highly—is with me," Cowell wrote Rudhyar. "I feel closely tied to you in some way, and everything you do is of vital interest and importance to me. There is only one other living in this country that I know of whom I consider writes really important music; this is Carl Ruggles. I am sending you a song by him." The song must have been *Toys*, composed in 1919 and published the next year. This suggests that Rudhyar may not have heard of Ruggles yet. But these new acquaintances took off quickly. By December 1922 Rudhyar was reviewing the New York premiere of Ruggles's *Men and Mountains* for *Eolian Review*.[7]

"I have just read your inspiring article in the Quarterly," opened another letter from Cowell to Rudhyar, this one from 1922. On the back, he wrote a six-measure cluster composition, "A Rudhyar" (Figure 8.1). In New York once again, Cowell was inspired to write by reading Rudhyar's "Relativity of our Musical Conceptions," published in the *Musical Quarterly* that January. In it, Rudhyar had singled out Cowell as an exemplary figure who together with Ornstein had "imperilled" traditional concepts of the "note" through his use of clusters. "It is the finest article I have ever read anywhere concerning music," Cowell continued. "The part

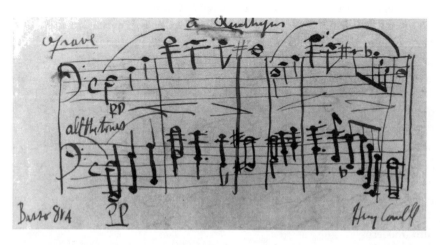

Figure 8.1. "A Rudhyar," by Henry Cowell. Courtesy of the Department of Special Collections, Stanford University Libraries.

about tones of different quality being altogether different, as though in pitch, is wonderful. And I have often wondered about the psychological relation of the octave. The single sound is indeed different from a note. The notation you propose is splendid. I feel honored that you mentioned me—thank you."[8]

Rudhyar's article clearly flattered the younger man. But it also contained a series of innovative ideas that might have caught Cowell's attention. Rudhyar's opening declaration, "The theory of Relativity is sweeping the intellectual world of to-day," found an echo in the introduction to Cowell's *New Musical Resources* of 1930, where he stated that his theory of overtone ratios "may be termed a theory of musical relativity." Rudhyar's challenge to Western musicians to consider "the possibility of *another* Truth" based in "Oriental civilization, art, science," prefigured Cowell's own exhortation to inhabit the "whole world of music," as he later put it. And his discussion of overtones and undertones connected with one of Cowell's obsessions, even though Rudhyar's technical description incorporated the sort of spiritual metaphors that Cowell never employed. "A dazzling profusion of new materials will flood the imagination of the future creators," Rudhyar wrote. "Not only upper partials will be used, but lower partials, as they have been detected recently in such abundance in the tone of bells. In fact, the prime sound— the only one we consider now—will appear then as a radiating center of dynamic tonal energy, as a Sun surrounded by the double series of planets, the over- and under-tones." From his earliest published article about clusters, titled "Harmonic Development in Music" and dating from 1921, Cowell connected clusters to the overtone series; throughout the years, over- and undertones were fundamental to many of his innovative theories.[9]

Nestled amid these personal ties and spiritual constructs were Cowell's clusters themselves—the thundering torrents of chromaticism that became his personal signature. As the scholar Michael Hicks has put it, there is likely "no 'true' origin to Cowell's clusters, no single mental or physical habit that spawned them." In other words, spirituality cannot be posed as their sole inspiration. But clusters became a staple in a substantial series of compositions by Cowell that had some connection to Irish mythology as retold by John Varian and to Cowell's alliance with the Temple of the People in Halcyon. They also became the compositional innovation that most intrigued Rudhyar. Cowell's involvement in Halcyon thus gave him the opportunity to write compositions exploiting an iconoclastic new chordal construction, and Rudhyar seized the resulting clusters as an example of his theory of "tone." Soon Cowell's cluster compositions began to be perceived by others within the language Rudhyar fashioned. They were "evidence again and again of a fine spirituality," as one writer—*not* Rudhyar—put it in an article for the California *Carmelite* written late in the 1920s. Undergirded with a noble purpose, clusters transcended any association with raucous noise and became instead manifestations of an abiding "sense of power"; their physicality also gave them the same masculine connotations that surrounded Ruggles's work. With this encoding, clusters could no longer be dismissed as an ultra-modern antic or a mere technical innovation but rather became a deeply moving spiritual experience.[10]

Cowell developed two concurrent strains of cluster compositions, writing accessible works with a clearly spelled-out program connected to Irish mythology—which I am labeling "programmatic mystic"—as well as more densely difficult compositions, often with no apparent program, which have been viewed as separate from any spiritual agenda. David Nicholls has dubbed this second group "violent"; Hicks calls them "futuristic"; Steven Johnson dubs them "the virtuoso pieces." To me, they simply seem an extension of the mystic works—what I am labeling "abstract mystic"—in part because the two types share compositional devices but also because they were perceived by Rudhyar and others within the same spiritually conditioned mode of listening. Both types of clusters emerged concurrently. Early "programmatic mystic" compositions first appeared around 1916 (*March Men of the Earth*) and 1917 (various compositions for *The Building of Bamba*), just as Cowell became connected with Halcyon. But a large group of them dates from between 1923 and 1926, all with titles conveying primeval images: *The Vision of Oma, The Fire of the Cauldron, March of the Feet of Eldana, The Ballet of Midyar, Domnu*, and *The Mother of Waters*, to single out a few. Many of these works originated in connection with Varian's writings. At the same time, the "abstract mystic" cluster works were also being written, including *Dynamic Motion* (1916), *Antinomy* (1917), and *Tiger* (ca. 1926), also *Advertisement* (1917) and *Piece for Piano (Paris, 1924)* (the first three titles vaguely resonant of spiritual implications, the last two not so).[11]

Three Irish Legends—initially known as *Three Irish Myths*—exemplify the "programmatic mystic." These pieces were performed frequently by Cowell during the 1920s and enjoyed a respectful reception by critics. Furthermore, they had the exceptional honor of being published then (they were issued "separately but in a series" by the German firm of Breitkopf and Härtel in 1922, one of the earliest publication dates for any work by an American modernist of Cowell's generation). Included in this set are *The Tides of Manaunaun*, written to accompany a pageant by Varian, *The Building of Bamba*, of 1917; *The Hero Sun*, dated 1922; and *The Voice of Lir*, dated 20 November 1922. Cowell performed the three together at a concert in St. Mark's Hall in New York City on 11 May 1922. He immediately took them west for concerts at a private home in Denver, the Palo Alto Women's Clubhouse, and the Recreation Center auditorium in Santa Barbara—all modest venues. *Three Irish Legends* followed him to prominence as well. He performed them on his first European tour in 1923 and at his Carnegie Hall debut on 4 February 1924. By July 1935, when Cowell gave a lecture-recital at the San Francisco studio of Rudolph Schaeffer, the critic Marjory M. Fisher—a frequent contributor to *Musical America* as well as to local San Francisco papers—made it clear just how well known these pieces had become: "Mr. Cowell played nothing we had not heard before. The numbers inspired by Irish myths which we have been hearing at more or less regular intervals for the past decade seem to stand the test of time and repetition." And so they did during the course of the 1920s, often being singled out on pro-

Figure 8.2. "Henry Cowell, Composer and Pianist, Back from an European Tour, Prepares to Startle America," published in *Musical America* (16 February 1924). Courtesy of Musical America Archives.

grams as the works that proved Cowell's experiments with clusters to be "really worth while" or "effective." As *Musical America* put it, "Mr. Cowell is a composer who has made distinct contributions, particularly with his 'Irish Myths.'" Thus Cowell's musical response to the epic tales of Varian not only gained him notice but brought a respectful reception.[12]

The last of the *Three Irish Legends*, titled *The Voice of Lir*, illustrates how Cowell's cluster writing emanated from Varian's retelling of ancient Irish tales. It is a highly accessible composition—almost shockingly so for a work by a so-called ultra-modernist—and thoroughly programmatic. Like the other *Irish Legends* and the bulk of Cowell's music inspired by Varian, *The Voice of Lir* opens with a "story according to John Varian," detailing the Celtic myth it evokes. The "story" is virtually the same in program notes for Cowell's Carnegie Hall debut as in the published score:

> Lir of the half tongue was the father of the gods, and of the universe. When he gave the orders for creation, the gods who executed his commands understood but half of what he said, owing to his having only half a tongue; with the result that for everything that has been created there is an unexpressed and concealed counterpart, which is the other half of Lir's plan of creation.

With this tale as its epigram, *The Voice of Lir* seems more closely related to the tone poems of Hector Berlioz or Richard Strauss than to the noise making of the futurists. A critic heard *The Tides of Manaunaun*, another of the *Irish Legends*, just that way in 1920, calling it "a tone-picture of primeval chaos."[13]

With their low register and lumbering pace, the clusters of *The Voice of Lir* set a murky, mysterious scene. They present a densely dissonant chromatic spectrum, saturating the space they inhabit either with all the chromatic pitches or, less often, with white- or black-key subunits. Yet no matter how dissonant the clusters, they are tamed by strong doses of accessibility in the harmonic, melodic, and rhythmic shaping of the work. Cowell himself told an interviewer in 1925 that the clusters in *The Voice of Lir* "move in such fashion as to flood the bass and, at the same time, form a bass counterpoint. . . . [The piece] sounds much more concordant than one might imagine." These are palatable clusters, with an experimental technique swathed in familiar gestures.[14]

In *The Voice of Lir*, Cowell achieves this accessibility through a series of cluster patterns, all of which repeat predictably. Above them is a melody that thickens in texture as it approaches the work's highpoint (Example 8.1, m. 26). The first of the patterns opens and closes the work, girding it with stable pillars and consisting of a descending three-cluster module that repeats fourteen times at the opening, nine at the conclusion. There are only two slight variants in it and both are critically placed: first where the melody enters (m. 3), and second when the top note moves a half step lower to yield a cadence on descending parallel sevenths (final measure). In between, there are two other bass cluster patterns, the second of which appears at the section of widest range and greatest emotional intensity (m. 21ff.). There the piece becomes acrobatic, with the pianist sounding thickly doubled triads with both hands, then swooping down low in between melody chords to interject a double-forearmed combination of black-key and white-key clusters. The span of the cluster covers two octaves. Another striking trait of *The Voice of Lir*, as with the other two *Irish Legends*, is its slow, majestic tempo. All three works open with "Largo," presenting another case of the mythic grandeur so prized by Rudhyar and Ruggles.

The Voice of Lir, together with the other two *Irish Legends*, is thus accessible through its overriding consonance and rhythmic regularity. Johnson speculates that "despite their exotic attitudes," the audiences at Halcyon "probably favored conservative music," and *The Voice of Lir* bears witness to how Cowell may have met the practical demands of specific assignments. It also shows how he functioned on multiple stylistic tracks, consistently producing audience-friendly works—often with some base in traditional repertories—alongside more challenging ones. At once a constructor of clusters and practitioner of common triadic constructions, Cowell was irrepressibly eclectic. In the mid-1920s he retorted to an interviewer, when asked if he felt any kinship with Bartók and Schoenberg, that "they seem to be striving for dissonance while I am seeking a richer and fuller harmony, by using hitherto untouched resources of the piano. . . . Above all, I avoid novelty for its own sake."[15]

While it is easy to label Cowell as a daring experimentalist, he had strong ties to tradition. But then so did theosophy. Johnson muses that Cowell's involvement

Example 8.1. Cowell, *The Voice of Lir,* pp. 1–2. Copyright © 1922 (Renewed) by Associated Music Publishers, Inc. (BMI). International copyright secured. All rights reserved. Reprinted by permission.

To Edna L. Smith

3. THE VOICE OF LIR

Story according to John Varian

Lir of the half tongue was the father of the gods, and of the universe. When he gave the orders for creation, the gods who executed his commands understood but half of what he said, owing to his having only half a tongue; with the result that for everything that has been created there is an unexpressed and concealed counterpart, which is the other half of Lir's plan of creation.

Henry Cowell

AMP-7795

Meno mosso

in Halcyon reinforced his interest in science—both because Varian's children were scientific experimenters and because theosophy in general preached a respect for science. But it may also have kept Cowell rooted in music's version of the "Ancient Traditions," a term for the eclectic mix of time-honored writings that came together in theosophy. Both Rudhyar and Cowell often devoted a portion of their articles to invoking the European musical tradition that had preceded them. For Rudhyar, this was a way of exposing the Old World's decadence. For Cowell, it justified musical experiments as growing out of an age-old lineage. Taking a stance typical for him, Cowell wrote in 1927: "Modernist music is distinctly not attempting to disregard the classics but rather to do exactly what those same classics accomplished in their day—to add new principles to what had been established before." This statement defies the stereotype of a tradition-bashing modernist. It also connects Cowell to the neoclassicists—a notion he would have been appalled to realize.[16]

While producing cluster compositions directly linked to Varian, Cowell also wrote cluster pieces that do not evoke the inchoate murmurs of pagan gods but rather have a pointillistic, percussive thrust. Yet they shared techniques with the "programmatic mystic" compositions and came to be perceived, by a widening network of critics, in spiritual terms. These "abstract mystic" works were more tied to the ultra-modern aims of Rudhyar than to the mythological bent of Varian.

Dynamic Motion, dated by Cowell as 1916, is a cluster tour de force, using the brief patterns of *The Voice of Lir* but aiming for a distinctly different effect. Program notes for one of Cowell's concerts extol it as "probably the most ultra modern piece ever composed." Johnson associates the clusters in *Dynamic Motion* with those of Ornstein, whom Cowell met in New York the year that it was composed. In contrast to *The Voice of Lir*, there is no story at the opening of *Dynamic Motion*, and the tempo marking is "Allegro" rather than "Largo." Its patterns do not lend stability but aim for asymmetry and unpredictability, yielding erratic splashes of chromatic color rather than graspable melodic units. *The Voice of Lir* has regularity at its core— especially in its repetitiveness—but *Dynamic Motion* swiftly changes textures, ranges, phrase lengths, and rhythmic patterns. The opening, for example, splices together a series of irregular modules, beginning with a four-bar segment (Example 8.2, mm. 1–4), followed by five different groups of two bars (mm. 5–6, 7–8, 9–10, 11–12, 13–14), one of one bar (m. 15), and a final one of two bars (mm. 16–17). Yet despite all the ways in which this passage differs from *The Voice of Lir*, it shares with it a tendency toward upward-sweeping gestures, repeated drives to massive fortissimos, and an exploration of the full range of the keyboard—in other words, the signal traits of Rudhyar's "tone." This is especially striking in the rolled clusters three-quarters of the way through, which rapidly leap up over five octaves (Example 8.3). With the whole note at the end of this segment (Example 8.3, m. 47), also with the earlier use of a repeated single cluster (Example 8.4), the work can be described as generating cumulative reverberations that yield "tones" that "grow,"

DYNAMIC MOTION

Henry Cowell

Example 8.3. Cowell, *Dynamic Motion,* mm. 44–47. Copyright © 1922 (Renewed) by Associated Music Publishers, Inc. (BMI). International copyright secured. All rights reserved. Reprinted by permission.

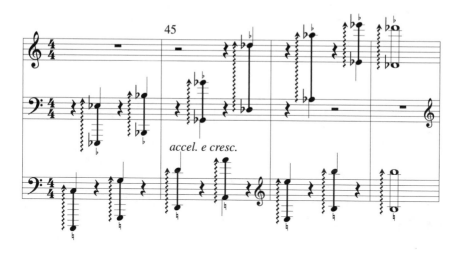

Example 8.4. Cowell, *Dynamic Motion,* mm. 23–28. Copyright © 1922 (Renewed) by Associated Music Publishers, Inc. (BMI). International copyright secured. All rights reserved. Reprinted by permission.

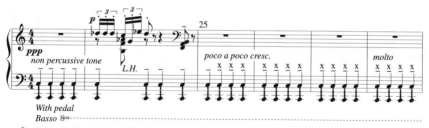

ˣLay left hand on keys, then press left hand down with right fist.

to evoke Rudhyar's images. The piano becomes a "table of resonance" and the sound "extends in space," filling it with a rich sonic spectrum.[17]

Piece for Piano (Paris, 1924), which despite its title probably dates from 1923, presents an even subtler integration of these same techniques. While *Dynamic Motion* gained some following—Paul Rosenfeld singled it out in Cowell's 1924 New York debut program, together with *Antinomy* and *The Voice of Lir,* for its "new lovely rolling sounds"—*Piece for Piano* seems to have had a rockier launching. A critic who heard Cowell perform it in Palo Alto in 1925 called it "one of his most intricate and least popular studies." Like *Dynamic Motion* it is built of brief patterns, highly varied in texture and range. Yet the result is even more pointillistic, more collagelike, more given to unpredictably exploring musical space (Example 8.5). In addition to

Example 8.5. Cowell, *Piece for Piano,* p. 1. Copyright © 1982 by Associated Music Publishers, Inc. (BMI). International copyright secured. All rights reserved. Reprinted by permission.

PIECE FOR PIANO WITH STRINGS

Henry Cowell

AMP-7795

combining various types of clusters with sparely textured dissonant pitch constructions, Cowell incorporates string-piano techniques, directing the player at isolated points to pluck a melody while a wide-spanning cluster pattern sounds concurrently (not shown here). Like *Dynamic Motion*, *Piece for Piano* is a consistently dissonant work, with none of the comforting consonances of *The Voice of Lir*. Consider the opening melodic idea, for example. After a passage of relatively static gonglike clusters, the texture and range change as a five-pitch module begins to descend in an inner voice (m. 9). It reappears in several gapped-pitch incarnations: in the same voice with a different shape (m. 11); simultaneously in the bass below; and inverted in the lower voice of the right hand (m. 19). Dissonance and tonal disruption are the goals, not affable accommodation.[18]

Piece for Piano (Paris, 1924) and *Dynamic Motion* thus represent a strain of Cowell's cluster compositions that has little overt connection to spirituality. Yet, as with much abstract painting and dissonant music of the early twentieth century, spirituality—especially as conveyed through theosophy—provided a way of bringing meaning to them. Rudhyar heard Cowell's clusters as resonating gongs, articulating for listeners a way of experiencing extraordinary new sounds. Other writers of the time had related responses, if not directly influenced by Rudhyar (for it is impossible to gauge the impact of his writing) at least sharing a set of aesthetic values. As a result, a new, antiformalist vocabulary emerged to convey the effect of this music. This language may even have played a role in gaining its acceptance, transforming an image of Cowell as vaudevillian acrobat at the keyboard—even as a clown—into one of him as high priest, who like Sarastro in Mozart's *Magic Flute* intones noble incantations. "Henry Cowell has invented new ways of experiencing sound," wrote an anonymous critic in a California paper, the *Carmelite*, in 1929. "Instead of observing it objectively and analytically, as with the old music, you must enter the whole wave of it, become drowned in it, become overwhelmed in its mass and volume. To attempt to separate it into its component parts, pitches, intervals, triads, sevenths, fifteenths, is irrelevant. . . . This is direct and im-mediate [*sic*] music, which does not require the functioning of that intermediary and often impeding tool the intellect, for its most complete experience." This writer singled out *Tiger, Dynamic Motion*, and *Antinomy*—all works from the "abstract mystic" strain of cluster compositions—as especially strong examples of these traits, calling them "simple utterances of the sense of power."[19]

Given the origin of this criticism in a paper published in Carmel, a beach community a hundred miles north of Halcyon, it might well be dismissed as a neighborly perspective on Cowell. But such ideas were traveling outside of West Coast spiritual circles, as a profile of Cowell by Nicolas Slonimsky, published in New England in March 1929 (six months before the excerpt above), suggests. Slonimsky was trying to prepare Boston audiences for an upcoming visit by Cowell, and he quoted at length from "an impression of [Cowell's music by] a professor of a western university." This appeared in no surfside daily but the *Boston Evening Transcript*:

His creations bring one at the strike of a tone-cluster into the very texture of our contemporary world whence one directly experiences the swift and immense dynamism of primal world-destroying and world-creating forces. From the softest murmurings of the piano we ascend with Henry Cowell, by virtue of his original means of tone-production, to planes of being where we recognize a strongly rhythmic cosmos sublimely shaping itself out of weltering chaos by a clash of energies that augments in tonal volume, pyramids its effects into overarching claps of thunder, till in this titanic struggle we behold a world-structure in motion, and quake within to live through the cosmic ordeal. A world structure in motion! Dynamic architectonics! The architecture of the universe breathed upon, stirred by creative impulse into life![20]

By providing a platform to mainstream this spiritually based way of hearing clusters, Slonimsky helped validate a compositional device dismissed by some reviewers as "ugly and meaningless noises." But Slonimsky was not alone. The same impulse turned up in a promotional brochure for Cowell, probably issued around 1930. Its first paragraph describes Cowell with tempered spiritual language: "Certain of his works contain 'tone clusters' for which he has developed a new technique that produces great sweeps of orchestral sound as a basis for the beautiful melodies which exquisitely express the cosmic spirit of the Irish myths in many of his compositions. . . . Hearing Henry Cowell is to experience important new music of exceptional beauty and unique piano virtuosity, which is of greatest interest and capable of deep and strong musical feelings." Another far less overt but striking case of mainstreaming a spiritual aesthetic came in a 1931 essay about Cowell by the critic Isaac Goldberg, best known for his writings about popular music, who granted credibility to Cowell's clusters because of their "imposing effect." He wrote this after hearing Cowell perform at a "mixed gathering" at George Gershwin's "modernist penthouse apartment on top of 33 Riverside Drive." "I am of those who are convinced that [Cowell's clusters] are not mere *loudnesses*," observed Goldberg. "The piano seems to acquire new stature, new expressiveness. It thunders. . . . Cowell, beyond a doubt, has added to the tonal and the expressive range of the pianoforte,—to its majesty of utterance, to its delicacy of suggestion." "New expressiveness" through a "majesty of utterance": this is precisely what spiritually based dissonance sought to attain.[21]

As for Cowell himself, he kept his connections to theosophy hazy, whether to obscure deliberately a troubled part of his past, which involved allegations of a homosexual encounter at Halcyon, or because his own interests as a writer and thinker reached in more concrete, scientific directions. Yet despite the glaring fact that Cowell did not mention spirituality in any of his publications from the 1920s, he had irrefutable connections to it through his association with Halcyon and his ties to both Varian and Rudhyar. All this occurred during a formative phase when Cowell was defining himself as an experimentalist and exploring all sorts of contexts in which to imagine new sounds.[22]

There are a few revealing moments, however, when Rudhyar and the rhetoric of spirituality emanate from Cowell's prose. Although little inclined during the 1920s to write about specific composers, Cowell singled out Rudhyar in 1927 as part of a small group at the "forefront" of writing "compositions that are not mere echoes and imitations of Europe, but alive with the vitality of new growth from new soil." With images of "new growth" and "new soil," Cowell's language echoed that of Rudhyar and Varian. Two years later Cowell gave a lucid although not particularly literary explanation of "tone," showing himself conversant with Rudhyar's theories. "Dane Rudhyar . . . writes consistently and individually, and has many interesting theories concerning tone, one of which is that all tone complexes should be regarded as a unit," Cowell offered. "In so far as a single tone is made up of a fundamental and its overtones, he does not think it is any more a unit than a complex formed by the union of several tones. This would do away with the idea of discord and concord, a complex of sound being judged according to the form taken by its component parts, much as molecules can be classified by different juxtapositions of atoms."[23]

But the most striking use of spiritually infused language occurred at the conclusion of *New Musical Resources*, Cowell's ultra-modern magnum opus, which was designed as a technical primer for experimentalists. Rudhyar was not mentioned specifically (nor were many other composers). But spiritual ideals can be teased from a passage at the end of the book. After more than 130 densely packed pages about overtones, dissonant counterpoint, scales of rhythm, and clusters, Cowell suddenly shifted gears, winding up with a homily about the meaning of all the technical information he had delivered. This was no sermon from a pulpit but rather a quiet, passing acknowledgment, crucially positioned, that new music did not consist only of iconoclastic materials and innovative architecture. "For the sake of the exquisiteness of emotion which music may express, as well as for the sake of perfection of the music itself, therefore," Cowell wrote, "there is a place for the formalization and coordination of different contemporary musical resources by means of their common relationship with the overtone series, which, although it forms a mathematical, acoustical, and historical gauge, is not merely a matter of arithmetic, theory, and pedantry, but is itself a *living essence* from which musicality springs [my emphasis]."[24]

Although not clearly or forcefully articulated, Cowell acknowledged that modernist music needed to add up to more than the sum of its parts. To have real meaning, it needed to transcend mechanical innovation and deliver emotional sustenance.

A quarter of a century later, after Rudhyar had become an astrologer and Beat poets roamed the California coastline, Cowell wrote a "Credo" professing his beliefs as a composer, a segment of which opened this chapter. It is a more open avowal of spiritual concerns than anything penned in Cowell's youth. With words like *exaltation, power,* and *dynamic force,* his language resonated with values of a bygone era, suggesting that spirituality was not some passing fad for him but a profound component of his character as a composer. Rudhyar's teachings, alongside Varian's mythological writings, had made a difference, not only in how Cowell viewed himself but also in how others came to perceive his music.

Ruth Crawford and the Apotheosis of Spiritual Dissonance

Lightly sprinting, . . .
To feel our bodies yield, answer, become one
      with air
No longer flesh but spirit
      Fluid,
      Uncontained . . .

—Ruth Crawford, 1928

Alone among the ultra-moderns, Ruth Crawford became a rapt disciple of Dane Rudhyar, recalling that "a definite turning point" occurred for her in 1925, when as a student in Chicago taking piano lessons with Djane Lavoie Herz she met the French-American composer and philosopher. Soon she fell under his spell, "worshipping" him "intellectually," finding herself "dazzled by his erudition." She revered him as an "idol." Thus one of America's most uncompromising modernists—a composer who within a few years was to be hailed for her proto-serial writing and heterophonic ideal—encountered spiritual theories during a formative period in her compositional development. Crawford was never promoted or explicated by Rudhyar, as was the case with Ruggles and Cowell. He never cited her music in his articles, and no letters survive to document their relationship. Rather, she stood apart in actually applying his theories to her compositions and gaining little attention from him for the results. In an interview with the pianist and composer Sorrel Doris Hays conducted some sixty years later, Rudhyar sounded paternalistic about Crawford, crediting some of his own piano works with inspiring the "first really interesting music Crawford wrote."[1]

When Crawford (1901–53) came to know Rudhyar in 1925, it was some five years after Cowell and Ruggles had done so. She was then an emerging composer, and she was also a young woman, with gender circumscribing her relationship to Rudhyar as much as professional status. At the time they met, Rudhyar was staying in Djane Herz's Chicago apartment for a few months, and Crawford was teaching at the American Conservatory. Herz was a theosophist and Scriabin enthusiast whom, it will be recalled, Rudhyar had met soon after arriving in North America. Three years later Crawford's exposure to Rudhyar's ideas deepened when he returned to Chicago to give a lecture on "The Meaning of the New Dissonant Music" for the local chapter of Pro Musica. The event also included a concert of his compositions: *Moments: Tone Poems for Piano* (Nos. 1, 7, 11, 17, 19), *Ravishments* (Nos. 6 and 11), *Songs from Exile* (Nos. 4 and 13), and *Triptych* (No. 2). There Rudhyar espoused the spiritual and political theory of dissonance found in his periodical writings and in *Dissonant Harmony*, which was published that same year.

Figure 9.1. Djane Lavoie Herz and Ruth Crawford, near Lake Michigan. Chicago, ca. 1925. Courtesy of the Estate of Ruth Crawford Seeger.

Crawford quoted whole excerpts from his talk in her diary, marveling at his "vision of the brotherhood of man, which blends all as human beings, despite slight exteriors which are discordant." Beyond sympathizing with Rudhyar's racial politics, Crawford, like Ruggles, met him on the common ground of American Transcendentalism and Whitman. "She regarded Emerson and Thoreau as intellectual and spiritual ancestors," states her biographer Judith Tick. Whitman provided her "a model for the spiritualizing of the vernacular."[2]

During this period, Crawford wrote a series of works directly reflecting Rudhyar's ideas about "tone" yet did so within her own distinctive leaning toward linear construction. Two of them—her Sonata for Violin and Piano of 1926 and her Piano Prelude No. 6 of the following year—abundantly manifest Rudhyar's ideas. In both, Crawford used techniques that had become standard within the spiritual vocabulary.

The third movement of the Violin Sonata proclaims its connection to spirituality from the outset with the tempo indication "Mistico, intenso." It opens with low-lying dissonant chords in the piano, which are to be played "sonoro" (Example 9.1). They evoke resonating masses of "tone" through their sustained, near-parallel motion. The movement surges twice in range, texture, and dynamics—the first time at a point halfway through and the last building up tumultuously to a segue into the final movement.

With Piano Prelude No. 6, dedicated to Djane Herz, Crawford applied Rudhyarisms even more overtly (Example 9.2). The tempo indication "Andante Mystico" again declares her agenda, and the work delivers pulsating waves of sound. The

Example 9.1. Crawford, Violin Sonata, 3rd movement, 1st two systems. Used by permission. Theodore Presser Co.

Example 9.2. Crawford, Prelude No. 6, p. 1. Used by permission. Theodore Presser Co.

right hand presents a brief upward-arching pattern over and over, repeating and transforming it. This pattern, in turn, has been described as "thick resonating chords . . . deconstructed into intervallic components." In other words, the densely clotted sonorities of Rudhyar's style were transformed by Crawford into openly voiced intervals that satisfied her own desire for textural clarity. The pedal enhances the overall surge effect, bleeding the resonance of each pattern into the next. Although the upward motion here suggests the power sweeps of Rudhyar, Cowell, and Ruggles, it has none of the same dramatic posturing. Rather it wafts into the sublime.[3]

Crawford's Prelude No. 9 presents a different case, having what Tick has revealed as a "hidden [spiritual] meaning." Crawford again evokes repeated gonglike dissonances, here even more delicately positioned in musical space, with a wide-spanning range and overall surging buildup. Yet she gave no mystical indications on this score. Her method was publicly covert but privately explicit, for she recorded in her diary that the prelude had a "program from Laotze's *Tao*"—a revelation redolent of Cowell's mystical cluster compositions based on ancient Irish legends. Through the work, Crawford sought to evoke "calm," recalling Djane Herz's "distinction between the artist and the mystic: the latter is simply farther along the road which the former is travelling: he has gone beyond the need for expression."[4]

After composing these works infused with spirituality, Crawford moved in 1929 to New York City, where her music had already been performed on programs of the League of Composers and Copland-Sessions Concerts. There she launched a more illustrious phase of her career, studying composition with Charles Seeger and beginning to write the challenging works that have since gained considerable acclaim, especially her *String Quartet 1931*.

Yet when Crawford began to work with Seeger, she did not renounce one guru and submit to another. No wayward convert, she imaginatively fused and transformed the ideas of both Rudhyar and Seeger. As she continued to draw upon each, her life became a pageant vérité of the tensions between spirituality and formalism that charged ultra-modern composition in the 1920s. In one of the most celebrated love stories in American music, Crawford married Seeger in 1931, forging a personal as well as professional alliance. Their shared devotion during the 1930s and 1940s to the study of American folksong has since become famous, but during the years of their courtship they also collaborated in the pursuit of "dissonant counterpoint." When Seeger drafted a treatise on the subject, he dedicated one version of the typescript "To Ruth Crawford of whose studies these pages are a record and without whose collaboration and inspiration they would not have been written."[5]

Alongside Crawford's brilliance as a practitioner of "dissonant counterpoint," her sympathy for spirituality remained strong. A documentable flash of it came in 1930 when she received a commission from the Women's University Glee Club in New York, conducted by Gerald Reynolds, and responded with a set of *Chants for Women's Chorus*. This group of works showed the universal embrace of theosophy in its text, for which Crawford invented "a language of my own," as she put it, using "consonants and vowels in a kind of chant which sounds quite Eastern," as well as in its

Asian-influenced style of intonation. These are beautiful compositions—arcane and ethereal with the voices tightly woven in persistent dissonance.[6]

Chants for Women's Chorus stands as Crawford's public farewell to spirituality, seeming to represent a final burst of "tone" and Asian associations before she immersed herself in the precision of dissonant counterpoint. Yet I wonder if she continued to fuse the two strains in at least one of her later compositions. Could the "tragic power," as Tick has eloquently put it, of the now-famous third movement of Crawford's *String Quartet 1931* be as much an outgrowth of the spirituality of Rudhyar as the formalist doctrine of Seeger? Could this yin and yang of American ultra-modernism have come together profoundly in a work best known for its inclination toward total organization? I believe this movement may well represent the apotheosis of Rudhyar's philosophy of dissonance.[7]

The third movement of Crawford's *String Quartet 1931* is best known for its canon of dynamics—an idiosyncratic adaptation of Seeger's "dissonant counterpoint" to one particular parameter of composition (Example 9.3). As has been frequently discussed in the years since, Seeger's influence is prominent in the piece—in its intellectual rigor, its drive toward independence of voices, and its thoroughgoing application of dissonant counterpoint. Each line sustains unbroken throughout, with dynamics that fluctuate more rapidly than the pitches, producing a seamless elasticity that is shattered by the climax near the end of the work—a section of the piece added seven years after its initial composition. There are pitch changes throughout, but they occur slowly and almost imperceptibly, each line buffeting off the others with carefully calculated dissonance. The result is a melody that migrates from one instrument to another, producing "a kind of *Klangfarbenmelodie*," as Joseph Straus has characterized it. Crawford "dissonates" dynamics—to use a term common to her and Seeger—with no two dynamic levels occurring simultaneously. Patterns emerge from the oscillating sequence of dynamic intensity.[8]

While most commentators have focused on the systematic planning of this movement, some composers and critics over the years have mused over its ineffable aura. The ultra-modern composer Adolph Weiss once called the quartet "spiritual in spite of method," and Straus has marveled at how the third movement "evok[es] masses of sound moving through space, colliding, expanding, breaking apart" through the use of "continuous sustained notes." Tick views it as testimony to her theory that Crawford sought to honor both "heart and head" in her "new style" of the 1930s. And Crawford herself avowed the year the quartet was composed, "Music must flow. It must be a thread unwinding, a thread from no one knows just where. It must not be a problem in mathematics, writing music." She also noted in a letter to the composer Vivian Fine that Seeger's treatise on dissonant counterpoint was a "medium" for her own compositional exploration, showing that spiritual allusions continued to suffuse her thoughts.[9]

Hearing this movement against a backdrop of Rudhyar's ideas—especially his idea of "tone"—its "tragic power" and serpentine sublimity assume a new meaning.

Example 9.3. Crawford, *String Quartet 1931*, 3rd movement, p. 1. Used by permission. Theodore Presser Co.

The most striking evidence of this comes with its overall upward-surging sweep and sustained textures. It creeps aloft, beginning low on a C-sharp one octave beneath middle C (viola) and soaring up over three octaves to a high E (violin) at the climax. At the same time, the seamless interplay of dynamics results in a relentlessly sustained texture. Whereas in Prelude No. 6, heavy piano pedaling connected one sonority to another, here stringed instruments achieve the same effect by playing "sempre legatissimo." By dissonating dynamics and pitch and using an overall slithering linearity, Crawford subtly reimagined traits that had almost become clichés in the spiritual language emanating from Rudhyar.

Recalling some of Rudhyar's statements about "tone" with Crawford's quartet in mind reinforces this interpretation. In one of his earliest articles, Rudhyar called "tone" a product of *"modulations of sounds*, or melody," describing an active musical texture in which "living organisms [react] directly upon other living organisms, visible or invisible." "Modulations of sounds" captures evocatively the slowly mutating character of the third movement. On another occasion, Rudhyar described traits meaningful to him in Varèse's *Amériques*, using images that could just as easily have been written about Crawford's quartet. He valued how *Amériques* represented a process of "continuous unfolding," how it kept "ever transforming, in a state of fluid becoming." With its sinuous lines, the quartet's third movement brilliantly embodies the concepts of "continuous unfolding" and "fluid becoming."[10]

At another point, Rudhyar talked of "tone" as "a new type of harmony, of chords" in which "polyphony itself spreads vertiginously." The word *vertiginous* is especially striking in connection with the quartet, for it implies a sense of motion and precarious balance that is basic to this movement. Crawford's malleable sound masses, with their irregular vacillations in and out of sonic prominence, defy traditional expectations for forward momentum. She achieved a whole new kind of "relationship between tones" with her fluctuating canon of dynamics.[11]

Crawford's music has long been seen as an avatar of the new American modernism—a sonic vision so distinct from its European counterparts that, as Straus puts it, "the musical gestures of European classical music are consistently absent." Rudhyar's spiritual notions about dissonance give another perspective on how such a style came to be. After hearing Rudhyar lecture in Chicago in 1928, Crawford confided to her diary "that dissonance is all a matter of point of view." Her notion of American dissonance drew upon multiple "points of view," each reshaped imaginatively according to her own instincts and talent.[12]

Reviving Rudhyar's spiritual theories not only makes it possible to grasp a shared strain in the music of Ruggles, Cowell, and Crawford but also suggests that the vivid cultural metaphors about "pluralism" and "diversity" applied by historians to the whole body of ultra-modern composition turn out to have a basis in ideas being developed as this music was composed. In the conclusion to *American Experimental Music*, David Nicholls declared that "the concept of plurality" is as fundamental "to the methods of organising materials" used by American ultra-moderns as it is "to the materials themselves." In other words, the fractured hymn-tune quotations of Ives and their disjunct layering with seemingly unrelated materials, the dissonant counterpoint of composers in the orbit of Seeger, the conjunction of clusters and diatonic melodies in the music of Cowell, the heterophonic textures of Crawford—all shared a culturally based inclination to champion difference, multiplicity, whichever term best fits. Rudhyar's theories resonated with this very premise: that the new American music of the 1920s needed to mirror a pluralistic society, that dissonance was a key to achieving this, and that musical structures should be devised to celebrate diversity rather than coerce it into conformity.[13]

Rudhyar's philosophy of dissonance by no means displayed the full spectrum of ideas that converged in the music of Ruggles, Cowell, and Crawford. But it yielded one significant component. Once the story of American composition readmits Rudhyar, it becomes clear that this particular group of ultra-moderns tended to both the intellect and the spirit and that it was fortunate to have leaders advocating both perspectives. We need to begin balancing our fascination with the craft of this music by attaining a grasp of its meaning.

Myths and Institutions

A Forgotten Vanguard

The Legacy of Marion Bauer, Frederick Jacobi,
Emerson Whithorne, and Louis Gruenberg

> In our humble opinion, there is a dearth in all musical composition at the present time EXCEPT in America. In the last few years, our composers seem to have evolved an idiom to which we might attach the label "Made in America," and which might be developed into a valuable and interesting contribution to the world stream of contemporary music.
>
> —Marion Bauer and Flora Bauer, 1927

American composers not only explored new compositional byways during the 1920s but they also sought ways to bring their work before the public. They were good at it, often finding others willing to invest time and money in devising opportunities for performance and publication. As a result, a string of new-music organizations appeared in New York: the Franco-American Musical Society, later called Pro Musica (founded in 1920); the International Composers' Guild (ICG) (1921); the League of Composers (1923); the Pan American Association of Composers; and the Copland-Sessions Concerts (both 1928). These followed parallel ventures in the visual arts. During the first two decades of the century, Alfred Stieglitz's Gallery 291 exhibited new European and American art, while selected dealers such as Stephan Bourgeois began featuring modernist painting. The Whitney Studio Club opened in 1918 to promote living American artists, and the Société Anonyme was founded in 1920 by Marcel Duchamp and Katherine Dreier as an artist-initiated organization for exhibiting the newest art.[1]

All these enterprises faced a tug between importing European modernism and supporting the homegrown variety. For a time, especially during the early 1920s, European music and paintings had an edge, for reasons to be explored in later chapters. Yet this inclination to gaze across the Atlantic made the existence of one of the more modest composer organizations, the American Music Guild (AMG), all the more remarkable. Established in 1921, the AMG had one goal: to provide a forum for music by Americans. It generated a much-needed counterforce to the other guild (the ICG), also to Pro Musica, and it became a model for the League of Composers. In addition, a small cluster of related enterprises surrounded the AMG, and these too were noteworthy. They included the Composers' Music Corporation, founded in 1918 to publish new American works, and the Modern Music Shop, which sold new scores—both European and American—in the early 1920s, when dissemination of this music remained limited.

No angry bunch of upstarts, the AMG generated faint ripples on the New York modernist scene. It was not the biggest or most visible show in town, but in the early years of the decade, it was one center of composer activity. Most notable among the AMG's members were Marion Bauer, Frederick Jacobi, Emerson Whithorne, and Louis Gruenberg—all participants in a vanguard that was ultimately forgotten. Born in the 1880s and early 1890s, these composers were in their thirties during the 1920s—roughly ten years older than Copland, Cowell, and their contemporaries and just as much younger than established composers of the day, such as E. B. Hill and Daniel Gregory Mason. In short, they were wedged between generations. During the early 1920s, they appeared as promising figures in contemporary American composition, being among the first Americans—beyond Ornstein and Varèse—to be labeled as "modernist." Yet their fate ended up being similar to that of Van Wyck Brooks, Waldo Frank, and other American writers born in the 1880s: having the vision to imagine a new life for America's creative artists, setting precedents for realizing it, and ultimately being overshadowed by a dazzling crop of young people. Stylistically, they represented a solid conservative strain that held firm throughout the entire century.

The historic importance of the American Music Guild was recognized as soon as it appeared. "Suddenly . . . the unexpected and long-awaited thing has happened," wrote a reviewer after the AMG's first public concert on 22 April 1922. "Something definite and constructive and absolutely real has been done for the American composer." Others concurred. "It was, indeed, a . . . truthful picture of American musical production at the moment when its grand general uselessness is commencing to shrink before sudden unexpected flashes and rumblings of latent power," wrote Paul Rosenfeld in typically tortured language. For Rosenfeld, the concert stood at a crossroads between "the great dreary empty past" and "the young uncertain fitful future." It revealed "the promise of coming years." In addition to composers already mentioned, founders of the AMG also included Sandor Harmati, Charles Haubiel, A. Walter Kramer, Harold Morris, Albert Stoessel, and Deems Taylor—a solid batch of composers, some of whom also occupied well-respected positions as music critics, performers, and teachers.[2]

Following a convention of the day, the AMG issued a manifesto, which was published in the program for its first concert at the MacDowell Gallery in Manhattan. Rather than being a histrionic call to battle, as had been the case for the manifesto of the International Composers' Guild issued only two months earlier, the AMG politely listed its members and stated that it was intent on "furthering interest in American music."[3]

But then the goal of the group was simply to generate a sense of community and to give local composers performance opportunities. "I can attest to the stimulating effect of the short-lived organization in fulfilling its mission," reported Marion Bauer retrospectively. "It gave the members a definite opportunity to measure their talents and to seek the right channels for further development." By all accounts the AMG's events had the companionable feel of family gatherings rather than counterculture happenings. In fact, they began informally, both in composers' homes and at the New York Public Library. Highlights of the public concerts during 1922 and 1923 included performances of Gruenberg's Concerto for Piano in One Movement (composed in 1915), Bauer's Sonata for Violin and Piano in G Minor (1922), Whithorne's Three Fragments from *New York Days and Nights* (1922), and Jacobi's Three Preludes for Violin (1921). Charles Martin Loeffler's Two Rhapsodies for Oboe, Viola, and Piano (1901) and Edward MacDowell's *Sonata eroica* (1894–95) turned up as well, revealing the group's sympathy for music of the American past, and Ornstein's Sonata for Two Pianos (date unknown) suggested the AMG was willing to take some chances. Most of these pieces had been recently composed and represented a transitional state between early-twentieth-century idioms—especially the lush textures and altered harmonies of French impressionism—and the varied approaches to dissonance that characterized modernism in the late 1920s.[4]

The AMG gave special support to the music of Charles Tomlinson Griffes, a contemporary of theirs (born in 1884) who died prematurely in 1920. His Piano Sonata (1917–18), *White Peacock* (1915), and *Five Poems of Ancient China and Japan* (1917) were performed by the AMG in 1923. The group donated proceeds from its first season to help support the processing of Griffes's music manuscripts at the New York Public Library, and both Bauer and Jacobi published articles in *Modern Music* promoting his work. Jacobi credited Griffes with helping release American music from its "bondage to Germany," also with introducing "a certain element of daring and independence, *an experimental frame of mind* [Jacobi's italics]." But Griffes also provided a link to the past. "His experimentation was not the half-cocked star-shooting we so frequently meet with now-a-days," Jacobi continued. "It was the searching of a mature and serious-minded human being, fully aware of what has been done in the past, eager to enlarge his means of expression and ours, by the conscious and legitimate development of his own individuality and genius."[5]

The AMG's exclusive attention to composers working in the United States was unmatched by any other new-music organization of the day. Yet the group suffered for its national focus. "We wish to state most emphatically," read a defensive disclaimer in a promotional pamphlet for the 1922–23 season, "that we are not actuated in the least by any chauvinistic state of mind that seeks to blind people by furiously waving the American Flag. We are merely endeavoring, by combining our strength and sincerely cooperating, to gain the necessary recognition and opportunities for the serious American composer that will enable him to take his place with the rest of the world's present-day composers." That season the group reached its peak, giving six concerts. The next year (1923–24) it presented only three, and with that its public events ended. Lack of money seems to have contributed to the group's demise. It operated "without private patronage or public support," while outside funding was essential to both the ICG and the League of Composers.[6]

No challenger of tradition, the AMG simply paid tribute to the idea of supporting native composers, and it did so during an important early period, when American composition was in flux and attitudes toward it were being shaped. Once the League of Composers was formed, Gruenberg and Whithorne joined its founding executive board and Jacobi its advisory board (he soon moved up to the executive board). Bauer became an official part of the new enterprise in its third season. Ultimately, the League subsumed and eclipsed the AMG. As a result, the story of the AMG has virtually been written out of the history of American composition.

Even less well known than the AMG but of related historic interest was the Composers' Music Corporation, an early composer-operated publishing firm. Founded in 1918, three years before the AMG, it involved some of the same composers and initially established the same priority—"to stimulate native American composition," as its catalog proclaimed. By 1920 it had broadened its scope to "include works by many distinguished foreign writers, both living in America and abroad," making it a force in the internationalizing of American modernism. But it also retained a loyalty to native figures. The last catalog that I have been able to locate—issued in October 1922—includes over 250 titles; the firm was listed in Manhattan telephone directories from 1920 to 1927.[7]

Finding a publisher was one of the main problems confronted by American composers in the late 1910s and 1920s, especially as their music ventured past nineteenth-century conventions and took on various modernist traits. Pieces written in a less familiar style posed a greater commercial risk. The Composers' Music Corporation faced this issue squarely, aiming "to bring forth the music of new and talented writers as well as the latest compositions of those of established reputation; to publish music only of artistic merit in an artistic manner, in editions free from the commercialism unfortunately so prevalent." It sought to overcome the "lack of confidence on the part of [commercial] publishers [which had] prevented the widespread acceptance and encouragement of the work of young composers." Whithorne served as the corporation's vice president from 1920 to around 1923; both he and Gruenberg were represented in its catalog.[8]

There was some precedent for the work of the Composers' Music Corporation, especially in Arthur Farwell's Wa-Wan Press, which had issued the music of Americans from its base in Boston between 1901 and 1912, and Serge Koussevitzky's Paris firm of Editions russes de musique, which beginning in 1909 published the work of Stravinsky, Scriabin, and others. Yet the Composers' Music Corporation, to the best of my knowledge, was the first such undertaking in postwar New York. It was followed by the Society for the Publication of American Music, a juried enterprise begun in 1922, which lasted considerably longer (until 1969) but issued only one or two scores per year during the 1920s. At the end of the decade, two other composer publishing enterprises emerged, first Cowell's *New Music Quarterly*, launched on the West Coast in 1927, and then Cos Cob Press in New York, founded in 1929 by Alma Morgenthau Wertheim, who recruited as two of her close advisers Emerson Whithorne and Louis Gruenberg, both veterans of the Composers' Music Corporation. The corporation also served as American "agent" for *The Chesterian*, *The Sackbut*, and *La revue musicale*, helping to disseminate information about European modernism.[9]

As much as anything, the catalogue of the Composers' Music Corporation highlighted the transitional posture of composers surrounding the forgotten vanguard. In 1922 it listed the music of Richard Hammond, Albert Spalding, and Fannie Charles Dillon—all figures anchored in a bygone era—at the same time as it issued early scores by Gruenberg and Whithorne. It also took on a number of composers of the forgotten vanguard's generation: Elliot Griffis, Charles Haubiel, Katherine Heyman, James H. Rogers, Lazare Saminsky, and Alexander Steinert. Ultimately these were not the most adventuresome figures of the 1920s, but they enjoyed visibility for a few short years.

An intriguing offshoot of the Composers' Music Corporation was the "Modern Music Shop," which was located for a time at the corporation's headquarters at 14 East 48th Street, also at 219 East Broadway. It appeared in Manhattan phone directories from 1921 to 1929. An ad for the shop was published on the inside front cover of a 1922 issue of the *Little Review*, the prominent avant-garde literary magazine associated with Machine Age ideology and edited by Margaret Anderson and Jane Heap (Figure 10.1). There musicians could purchase "publications of leading contemporary composers," together with "a large selection of imported modern music" and "standard editions in the classics." The Modern Music Shop was yet another link in the chain of composers and organizations that gave coherence to the early modernist movement in America.[10]

Bauer, Gruenberg, Jacobi, and Whithorne were recognized during the early 1920s as young, talented, New York-based composers. "A Group of the Younger American Composers: Creators of Music Who, Though of Various Schools, Can All Be Classed as Modernists," read the caption of a photo spread in *Vanity Fair* (September 1923) that pictured Gruenberg, Jacobi, and Whithorne (Figure 10.2). These were the Americans getting performed and winning prizes. As early as

Figure 10.1. Ad for the Modern Music Shop, as published on the inside front cover of the *Little Review* (Spring 1922).

1919, Jacobi was identified as "one of the most promising of the young school of American musicians." This was echoed a decade later when *Modern Music* deemed him "one of America's most representative composers." In 1920 Gruenberg won the prestigious Flagler Prize for his composition *The Hill of Dreams*. The next season both Gruenberg and Whithorne had works premiered by the Philharmonic-Symphony Society of New York, a distinction conferred on few Americans of the day. And in 1923, a critic dubbed Whithorne "composer laureate of New York."[11]

A Group of the Younger American Composers
Creators of Music Who, Though of Various Schools, Can All Be Classed as Modernists

Figure 10.2. "A Group of the Younger American Composers: Creators of Music Who, Though of Various Schools, Can All Be Classed as Modernists." Emerson Whithorne (upper right), Frederick Jacobi (center), Louis Gruenberg (lower right), as pictured in *Vanity Fair* (September 1923). Reproduced by permission of Condé Nast Publications.

Bauer did not inspire such expansive proclamations. Yet her music consistently appeared on programs alongside that of Gruenberg, Jacobi, and Whithorne, and her work as a music critic—most notably for the *Musical Leader* in Chicago—gave her a strong voice in shaping opinion about musical modernism. She struggled harder than her colleagues for recognition as a composer.

In Western Europe, this same group was viewed as typifying American composition. Even Bauer's works seemed to gain more attention abroad. In October 1922, the Russian-American composer Lazare Saminsky—himself an important figure in the International Composers' Guild and later the League of Composers—gave a lecture titled "Les jeunes compositeurs américains" at l'Ecole normale de musique in Paris. The composers highlighted by him included Bauer, Jacobi, Whithorne, and Gruenberg. Throughout the decade, these same figures continued to receive notice in France. Saminsky included their music on several concerts that he conducted with the Colonne Orchestra in 1923 and 1924, and the Franco-American Musical Society (or Pro Musica Society) programmed their works in Paris. Even more significant was the presence of music by these composers on international new-music festivals. Theirs were the names representing the United States. At the Salzburg Festival of Contemporary Music in 1923, Whithorne's *New York Days and Nights* appeared as the sole American representative. At the festival of the International Society for Contemporary Music (ISCM) in 1925, Gruenberg's *Daniel Jazz* joined works by Henry Eichheim and Carl Ruggles as the American entries. And at ISCM in 1926, Frederick Jacobi's *String Quartet on Indian Themes* was the only American composition heard.[12]

Composers of the forgotten vanguard were agents of change. Yet by the mid-to-late 1920s the momentum they helped initiate spun beyond their control. This turns up in their music as much as in their organizational activities.

Marion Bauer (1887–1955) was a gifted composer. Her works from the late 1910s and early 1920s showed a fusion of traits associated with late romanticism and impressionism, while those from the mid-1920s moved toward greater dissonance and emotional dispassion. *From the New Hampshire Woods* of 1921, a suite of three piano works ("White Birches," "Indian Pipes," and "Pine-Trees"), represents the early Bauer. Using titles evocative of nature and opening with sentimental epigrams by William Rose Benét and M. Hardwicke Nevin, she lent the work a whiff of Mac-Dowell. *From the New Hampshire Woods* was located not far from the older composer's *Woodland Sketches* and *New England Idyl*. The same was true of the work's visual presentation, which evoked the world of the parlor in its sheet-music format and, more pointedly, in its cover art, which presented a pretty engraving of forest birches. Yet these nostalgic associations were not fully realized in the music itself. "White Birches" tumbles limpidly down from a suspended melody, recalling somewhat the texture and motion of Brahms's *Intermezzi* but growing more directly out of the Preludes of Scriabin and the Piano Sonata of Griffes. The tonality is wayward, with persistent chromatic alterations and constant forward motion.[13]

Figure 10.3. Marion Bauer (undated photo), New York University Archives.

Three years later, Bauer took bolder steps with *Turbulence* (Op. 17, No. 2) of 1924. The title remains pictorially evocative and the textures are as consistent as "White Birches"; also the work rushes from a harmonically ambiguous opening to a comfortably resolved conclusion (Example 10.1). Yet where "White Birches" flowed smoothly, *Turbulence* moves in fits and starts, building up short, self-contained modules, some of which remain static while others press urgently ahead. Harmonically, the work also shows a change, incorporating a more pervasive use of dissonance. The first three measures, for example, are built from a chromatic set of seven pitches.[14]

By the time of *Four Piano Pieces*, Op. 21, published by Cos Cob Press in 1930, Bauer continued to rely on the post-impressionistic textures of her earlier works while becoming increasingly adventuresome harmonically. In "Chromaticon," the first piece from this group, she used a chromatically saturated palette, introducing eleven different pitches in the first measure (Example 10.2). The piece falls into two sections, both of which build to a series of powerful chords—or "arbitrary" ones as she termed similar constructions in her *Twentieth Century Music* (first

Example 10.2. Bauer, "Chromaticon," from *Four Piano Pieces,* Op. 21, p. 1. © Copyright 1930 by Boosey & Hawkes, Inc. Renewed. Reprinted by permission of Boosey & Hawkes, Inc.

TO ALMA M. WERTHEIM

FOUR PIANO PIECES

I

CHROMATICON^{*)}

Marion Bauer, Op. 21, № 1

*) *Accidentals apply to individual notes only; they are not effective through the measure*

Example 10.3. Bauer, "Chromaticon." mm. 45–56. © Copyright 1930 by Boosey & Hawkes, Inc. Renewed. Reprinted by permission of Boosey & Hawkes, Inc.

edition, 1933). At the conclusion these chords are more extended and bombastic than in the middle, progressing in contrary motion and with bitonal independence. The climactic chord three measures from the end uses the same three pitches that opened the work (Example 10.3).[15]

Bauer recognized the confluence of old and new in her music. In 1925, she described her "tendencies" as "modern," saying she was "not afraid of dissonance." But she hastened to add that she did not fear "a melodic line," realizing "that it is a new kind of melodic line, and not the square tune of the Romantic period." She went on: "We must reflect the period in which we live, but we must include the past in our knowledge."[16]

Frederick Jacobi (1891–1952) was stylistically the most conservative composer in this group. On the one hand, he proclaimed himself as "intensely interested in contemporary music," while on the other he believed that to be "durable" art must have "its roots firmly imbedded in the past." Ultimately gaining recognition for his synagogue compositions, which he began writing in the early 1930s, Jacobi was active in the new-music movement of the previous decade. Yet his compositions had little modernist edge. Bauer discussed Jacobi's work briefly in her *Twentieth Century Music*, saying that it had "leanings toward Impressionism" and that his "*Cello Concerto*"—meaning probably the *Three Psalms* for cello and orchestra of 1932—showed aspects of the "new romanticism."[17]

One distinguishing aspect of Jacobi's music during the 1920s was his devotion to Native American sources. With *Indian Dances* for orchestra of 1927, he aimed for "a series of impressions of the great ritualistic dances which take place still today among the Pueblos and Navajos of New Mexico and Arizona." These pieces, as he put it, were by no means "a reconstruction" of the original sources. "The treatment is completely free," he continued, "for the composer has felt that the least photographic method would bring him closest to the essence, the spirit, he was seeking." This sort of freely interpretative approach placed Jacobi in the same orbit as Bauer in *From the New Hampshire Woods*. Yet it contained its own blend of old and new. Jacobi's interest in Native Americans can be viewed as an extension of the "Indianist" composers earlier in the century—including Charles Wakefield Cadman, Thurlow Lieurance, Arthur Farwell, even MacDowell. At the same time, it had a contemporary inflection, connecting with the exploration of so-called primitive cultures by European artists and composers during the 1910s and 1920s, as well as a resurgent interest in the culture of Native Americans—especially those of the Southwest. He stood close to Griffes, whose *Two Sketches for String Quartet Based on Indian Themes* appeared in 1918; a few years after Jacobi's quartet, Mrs. H. H. A. Beach wrote a String Quartet (1929), which was based on Inuit melodies.[18]

Jacobi's *String Quartet on Indian Themes* of 1924 was relatively well known in its day, premiered on a 1926 concert of the League of Composers and published by the Society for the Publication of American Music that same year. As in the later *Indian Dances*, Jacobi aimed for ethnographic authority, identifying the sources for his themes. "Those in the second movement are taken from Natalie Curtis' 'The Indians' Book,'" wrote Jacobi. Those "in the third movement were noted by the composer during a recent stay in New Mexico. They are parts of the ritualistic dances of the villages of Santa Clara and Tesuque: Rain Dances, Corn Dances and War Dances." Jacobi jettisoned the rich textures of Griffes in favor of brittle clarity, often doubling voices so that two or at most three parts sound simultaneously. The opening of the quartet's third movement shows both Jacobi's mode of representing Native American tradition and his identity as a modernist (Example 10.4). In the viola, an open fifth on D-sharp is reiterated like a tom-tom throughout the first section. Yet it gets a chromatic jolt, both with the accompanying E in the cello and with the violin melody, which is initially built of four pitches also based on E.[19]

A skilled craftsman of gentle inspiration, Jacobi exemplified one stage in the post-romantic idiom that meandered through American composition during the entire twentieth century. As a teacher of composition, he helped shape that strain. He began teaching at The Juilliard School in 1936, and his students eventually included Jack Beeson, Norman Dello Joio, Robert Starer, and Robert Ward. They are among the leading composers who have traveled the same tonal road as Jacobi, and they have consistently seemed unperturbed as a parade of modernist fashions has passed them by.

Example 10.4. Frederick Jacobi, *String Quartet on Indian Themes,* third movement, p. 1. © Copyright 1954. Reprinted by permission of Carl Fischer, Inc.

III

Emerson Whithorne (1884–1958) was as active among fellow composers as Jacobi but enjoyed greater visibility during the 1920s. His music was frequently performed by both new-music groups and established orchestras, and it fell into complete obscurity afterwards. Even a partial list of Whithorne's performances gives a sense of his standing during his heyday. *The Rain* and *In the Court of Pomegranates* were performed by the New York Philharmonic Society in 1918 and 1922, respectively; *Poem for Piano and Orchestra* by the Chicago Symphony Orchestra in 1926; *The Aeroplane* by the Cleveland Orchestra in 1927; and *Fata Morgana* by the New York Philharmonic in 1928. Added to that, John Tasker Howard published a monograph about Whithorne in 1929.

Whithorne's *New York Days and Nights* of 1920–23, the only American entry in the Salzburg Festival of 1923, was Whithorne's best-known piece of the period. The work was so successful, in fact, that Whithorne characterized the sheet music for it, published by the Composers' Music Corporation, as a "big seller," and in 1924, when the bandleader Vincent Lopez presented a concert at the Metropolitan Opera House, he included a movement from it ("Pell Street"). Whithorne "may be mentioned in the same sentence with Varese, Antheil and Cowell," wrote John Tasker Howard in his 1929 monograph about Whithorne, "and we may also judge his work in comparison with our less revolutionary Griffes, and even the more popular [Deems] Taylor." While the first part of Howard's comparison now seems a long stretch, it was typical for the day, capturing a sense of the generational limbo in which Whithorne found himself.[20]

Like Bauer's *From the New Hampshire Woods*, *New York Days and Nights* has roots in the piano studio and the parlor. The second movement, "Chimes of Saint Patrick's," is prefaced with a prose epigram by the composer. "The tumultuous chiming of bells high in the twin steeples," he wrote; "a great organ intoning the solemn *Dies Irae*; vivid patches of color stretching in rich patterns across the pavement of the nave, dropped down from high warm-hued windows." The musical style is grounded in French Impressionism, especially with openly voiced chords descending in parallel motion to simulate the peal of bells (Example 10.5). Harmonically Whithorne differs radically from Bauer around the same date. Showing none of her boldness, the opening of the "Chimes of Saint Patrick's" presents a textbook case of bitonality. Similar but isolated moments occur throughout the other movements. On the whole, though, this is a thoroughly diatonic work.[21]

The same composer who could unabashedly evoke scenes of New York City was also a founding board member of both the International Composers' Guild and the Pan American Association. It is hard to imagine the impression that Whithorne's *New York Days and Nights* must have made at the 1923 Salzburg Festival, appearing on a program with Berg's Second String Quartet, Schoenberg's *Das Buch der hängenden Gärten*, and Stravinsky's Three Pieces for String Quartet. Yet there it stood as representative of a rising cultural force, "a block in the foundation of the skyscraper of American composition," as Marion Bauer once characterized the work.[22]

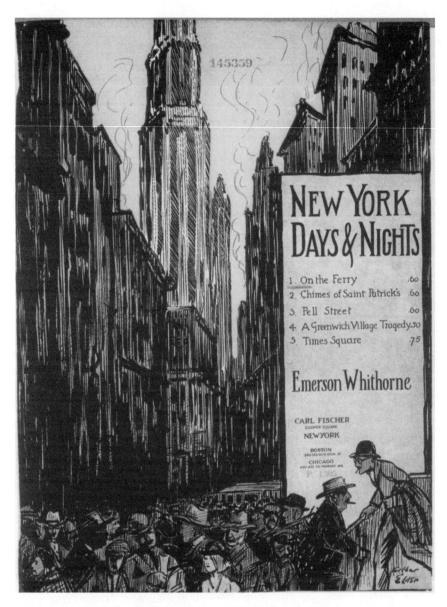

Figure 10.4. Cover by Arthur Elden to Emerson Whithorne's *New York Days and Nights* (1922), published by Carl Fischer in New York.

Example 10.5. Emerson Whithorne, "Chimes of Saint Patrick's," *New York Days and Nights,* p. 1. © Copyright 1923. Reprinted by permission of Carl Fischer, Inc.

Chimes of Saint Patrick's

Louis Gruenberg (1884–1964) left a large body of music, and he too enjoyed critical recognition during the 1920s. "The supreme function of the creative artist is to seek new forms of expression," he wrote in the second issue of *Modern Music.* "There is, however, great danger in a search for new impressions without an adequate foundation of technique and knowledge of what has been done up to the present."[23]

Gruenberg's *Polychromatics* joined Whithorne's *Greek Impressions* as the only other American contribution to the first program of the International Composers' Guild in February 1922. Gruenberg had forged alliances in the transatlantic composers' community, having spent long periods living abroad. He studied first in Berlin in 1905 and then with Ferruccio Busoni in Vienna in 1908. He returned to the United States in 1914 and visited Europe frequently in the years ahead. Gruenberg conducted the much-publicized American premiere of *Pierrot lunaire* in 1923, had a substantial series of his works published by Universal Edition in Vienna from 1924 to 1929, and was active in the International Society for Contemporary Music, serving as president of the United States section from 1928 to 1932. His music from the 1920s reflects these many Germanic connections, exhibiting a density that was alien to Bauer, Jacobi, or Whithorne.[24]

Gruenberg's solo cantata *Daniel Jazz* of 1924, which enjoyed some fame during the 1920s, was premiered at a 1925 concert by the League of Composers. It was heard again that same year at the ISCM Festival in Venice, where Alfredo Casella declared it to have enjoyed "great success." *Daniel Jazz* is set to a narrative poem by Vachel Lindsay that retells the story of Daniel in the lion's den. In his setting of it, Gruenberg exploits the vibrant energy of the language, conveying a frolicking, circuslike quality similar to that of *General William Booth Enters Into Heaven* (1914), Ives's setting of another Lindsay poem. Where Ives presented multilayered chaos, Gruenberg conveyed a more orderly concept of fun. Lindsay himself was famous for chanting his poems before audiences—especially *The Congo: A Study of the Negro Race* of 1914—making him "an early variant of today's performance artist," as one scholar has put it. Gruenberg shared with Lindsay a fascination with African American culture. In Gruenberg's case it culminated with his opera, *The Emperor Jones*, premiered in 1933 at the Metropolitan Opera.[25]

With its playful rhythms and brittle sound, *Daniel Jazz* stands with a group of works from the late 1910s and early 1920s that use chamber ensembles, popular rhythms, and crisp linear clarity. Paul Hindemith's one-act opera *Das Nusch-Nuschi*, first performed in Stuttgart in 1921, exhibited a similar sense of arch humor, and his dance pantomime *Der Dämon* of 1922 showed similarities in linear independence and scoring. Hindemith's flute, clarinet, horn, trumpet, piano, and string quartet of *Der Dämon* compare loosely with Gruenberg's clarinet, trumpet, percussion, string quartet, and piano. Both had roots in the scoring for *Pierrot lunaire*, which although configured differently also used eight instruments, including winds, strings, and piano.

Despite connections to these European colleagues, Gruenberg had a style of his own. *Daniel Jazz* used a thicker textural density than is common in Hindemith, and ostinato passages, so basic to the music of Stravinsky, Hindemith, and others, were not part of Gruenberg's scheme (Example 10.6). Even his use of tonality, while it gestured toward early Hindemith, has its own special character. *Daniel Jazz*'s clear tonal focus (E-flat major) is most strongly apparent in the vocal line, which maintains a traditional tonal anchor with frequent uses of a flat third—the work's one bow to the "jazz" in its title. The instrumental part also often implies

Example 10.6. Louis Gruenberg, *Daniel Jazz*, mm. 1–12. © Copyright 1925 by Universal Edition. Copyright renewed. All rights reserved. Used by permission of European American Music Distributors Corporation, sole U.S. and Canadian agent for Universal Edition.

THE DANIEL JAZZ
(Vachel Lindsay)
For a voice and eight instruments

DANIEL JAZZ
Deutsch von R. St. Hoffmann

Louis Gruenberg, Op. 21
(1924 - II.)

Universal-Edition Nr. 7765

U. E. 7765

E-flat. Often chromatic runs splash across the texture, as with the clarinet at the opening and again in measure 4.

Overall, composers of the forgotten vanguard get a mixed assessment. Historically, both their music and their organizational activities held significance, revealing a palpable confrontation with shifting cultural currents. Musically, the results were varied. They envisioned an American modernist frontier but never fully crossed its borders. Ultimately even their best works and most earnest efforts could not overcome their problematic historical position. Decades later, Virgil Thomson, a member of the generation that superseded Whithorne and his contemporaries, mused about Whithorne. In the process, he put his finger on the unfortunate timing that plagued the whole bunch:

> Emerson Whithorne was not a bad composer. He was simply not a chum of ours—he wasn't a modernist composer. He wasn't of any group involving Harvard or Boulanger or Copland or any of that. But he was a perfectly well-schooled composer. He was closer to Gruenberg. . . . But they were no part of what we considered a modern movement, nor were they part of the American academic standard movement, like Hill, Carpenter, Mason, and all those.[26]

Like commuters who emerge baffled from the subway, peering in all directions to ground their location, Whithorne, Gruenberg, Bauer, and Jacobi were disoriented by the fast-paced changes around them. Theirs was not an enviable position, but it is worth remembering.

Organizing the Moderns

Americans of all ages, all conditions, and all dispositions constantly form associations. . . . Wherever at the head of some new undertaking you see the government in France, or a man of rank in England, in the United States you will be sure to find an association.

—Alexis de Tocqueville,
Democracy in America, 1835

I'm glad you made all those connections in Europe. It will give you <u>power</u>.

—Carl Ruggles, in a letter
to Henry Cowell, 1926

We are provincials no longer, declared President Woodrow Wilson in his second inaugural address of 1917, signaling the end of postcolonial isolation and the beginning of international leadership. Once World War I was over, transatlantic relations in music reflected such sentiments as much as they did in politics, and France, America's wartime ally, became its peacetime friend. Forces of internationalization resounded throughout the new-music scene. In 1920, the Prix de Rome was first awarded, launching a fellowship program for creative artists at the American Academy in Rome that continues to the present. The Conservatoire Américain at Fontainebleau opened the following year in France, initiating an ambitious, long-reaching Franco-American interchange. There and then the young Nadia Boulanger welcomed Aaron Copland as a pupil, the first of many gifted American musicians who entered her studio during the next half of the century.

These programs extended patterns of the past—especially in sending American creative artists abroad to study—but they did so with a new twist. The country that had led the way to victory in an international conflict was no longer content simply to worship European cultural heroes. It also expected parity in return.[1]

The composer societies that arose in New York during the 1920s strongly reflected these changes, even though one of the myths surrounding them has exaggerated their commitment to American composers. They did reach out to Americans somewhat by the late 1920s and emphatically in the 1930s. But in the early 1920s, the American Music Guild was the only organization devoted to national activism; for the others, Americans took a back seat. Instead, there was a drive to make New York a major port on a bustling transatlantic modernist circuit.

Two waves of activity resulted. At first, the goal was to educate the New York concert-going public about the most recent music from abroad, and the importation of European modernism dominated. Two of the earliest composer societies—the Franco-American Musical Society (later called Pro Musica) and the International Composers' Guild (ICG)—unabashedly proclaimed a transatlantic mission. Like Methodists bringing the Gospel to China, the founders of these groups aimed to convert the canon worshipers in Carnegie Hall. The League of Composers—New York's other new-music organization from this first wave—initially did much the same, declaring in a manifesto issued in conjunction with its founding in 1923 that the group's goal was to program "music representative of the present time" and to choose it "regardless of nationality or school of composer." Rather than an organization with a "strong national bias," as is commonly assumed, the league exerted as much of an internationalizing force in its early years as either the ICG or Pro Musica.[2]

In 1928, a second wave of composer societies appeared in New York, resulting in the Copland-Sessions Concerts and the Pan American Association. These organizations were largely founded by young Americans, and they signaled a new direction, focusing far more aggressively on composers in the United States. Yet internationalization continued to play a role for them as well; this time, though, it took the form of displaying American talent in Europe. They combated provincialism aggressively, caring little about the importation of European modernism but rather working to establish American modernism both at home and abroad.

There is a second myth pervading the history of these composer organizations. It tells of two opposing factions emerging from the ICG and League, producing strains in American composition that remained at odds throughout the course of the entire century. "There is a fundamental schism in American music, one that has existed since the 1920s," asserted the composer Peter Garland in the early 1990s. "This split has created a condition where there are now (and always have been) two kinds of American music: the 'official' and the 'real.'"[3]

On one side, according to this plot line, stood the "ultra-moderns"—the "real" according to Garland or the "experimentalists," as they are more generally known—including John J. Becker, Henry Cowell, Ruth Crawford, Charles Ives,

Dane Rudhyar, Carl Ruggles, Charles Seeger, Nicolas Slonimsky, Edgard Varèse, and Adolph Weiss. They are posed as inheritors of the radical spirit that began with Ornstein and Varèse and that first found a haven in New York within the International Composers' Guild, later within the Pan American Association. Opposite them stood a group—"official" according to Garland—to which no tidy label applied. Called at various times "neoclassicists" or the "Boulangerie," this stratum included Marc Blitzstein, Israel Citkowitz, Theodore Chanler, Aaron Copland, Roy Harris, Walter Piston, Roger Sessions, and Virgil Thomson. Many of them studied and lived abroad, mostly working with Boulanger, and they have been linked to the League of Composers and, by extension, the Copland-Sessions Concerts. These two contingents have been depicted as yielding a tense historical drama—a kind of "us" and "them" showdown, pitting "the first generation of American composers to step out from the shadow of European models," in the words of Joseph Straus, against "acceptable Europeanised modernists," as David Nicholls has put it. This perspective has usually come from those sympathetic to the ultra-moderns. Steven Gilbert wrote in the early 1970s of "two rival camps," asserting that composers affiliated with the League enjoyed the upper hand and "found little trouble in securing commercial publication" (the historical record shows this to have been far from the case). A similar view was expressed by Olivia Mattis in the 1990s, "While Copland, Blitzstein, Gershwin and the others went to Paris in order to complete their educations, and returned with an internalization of the neoclassicism of Stravinsky and Les Six, the Pan-American Association came in order to present an American music, fully formed, to European audiences." Neoclassicism—an aesthetic with internationalism at its base—was often the offending issue, and "internationalization" a dirty word.[4]

If these truisms of American music historiography deserve at least partly to be reshaped, as I argue here, what vision might replace them? How much did New York's new-music societies support American composers during the 1920s, and in what ways? What value did they place on importing modernism from abroad? Was the schism between these groups really so deep at such an early date?

With the Franco-American Musical Society, established in New York in 1920 "by a group of American and French musicians and American music lovers" and renamed the Pro Musica Society in 1925, there has never been much question about its international thrust. Its founder and director, the pianist E. Robert Schmitz, was a French immigrant who proclaimed "internationalization in music" as the organization's "ideal" and remained committed to that goal. A 1922 article about Schmitz in the Paris edition of the *Chicago Tribune* gave a sense of how he perceived the United States as a modernist backwater:

> His [Schmitz's] fight for modern international music has been heroic in the
> country where Beethoven, Wagner and especially Brahms are worshipped perhaps
> even more passionately than in Germany. Mr. Schmitz does not neglect these

great masters but he believes in evolution and modernism, and has been struck by the fact that America, as a nation, is very fond of music, yet thoroughly ignorant, except for an elite, of musical expression since the end of the last century.

By 1923, Schmitz's society had grown remarkably. Its impact reached far beyond New York City, with the founding of nearly forty chapters in cities and towns across the country, including Chicago, Denver, Detroit, Kansas City, Los Angeles, Madison, Philadelphia, and Poughkeepsie. These regional affiliates disseminated modern music to the continent at large. National membership for the organization totaled approximately 600 in 1924; by 1928 it had reached over 3,500. That same year the Pro Musica Society began a series of "International Referendum" concerts in New York, Paris, and the regional chapters. The referenda were designed to "give equal opportunity to the various countries for the expression of their musical tendencies."[5]

The term "equal opportunity" gained currency much later in the century as a founding principle of affirmative action programs, the flurry of initiatives intended to aid women and persons of color in obtaining education and employment. It serves as a handy metaphor for grasping the position of American composers within

Figure 11.1. Rehearsal for an "International Referendum" concert given by the Franco-American Society. Seated: Greta Torpadie (soprano) and Carlos Salzedo (pianist). Standing, left to right: José Delaquerriere (tenor), Claudio Arrau (pianist), Richard P. Hammond (composer), Richard Hale (baritone), and Arthur Bliss (composer). Inset: E. Robert Schmitz (pianist). Photo published in *Musical America* (23 February 1924). Courtesy of Musical America Archives.

New York's new-music societies in the 1920s. With Pro Musica, its programs largely featured European modernists, at the same time as they gave occasional but significant space to Americans. A gradual process of integration was underway, and it was implemented through programming's version of tokenism. In the first two seasons, only one American composition appeared on any of Pro Musica's New York concerts: Leo Sowerby's *Serenade in G*. Throughout the decade, Pro Musica continued the practice of presenting one or occasionally two compositions by an American on each of its programs. As a result, the group kept new American works subsidiary to their European counterparts, at the same time as it made the positive gesture of including them. Working toward the same goal, the society in 1922 founded a music library in Paris of scores by Americans.[6]

Most of the American music presented on Pro Musica's concerts came from composers whose style was rooted in French idioms, including Charles Tomlinson Griffes, Charles Martin Loeffler, and Richard Hammond—the same figures embraced by the American Music Guild. In the midst of all this there was one daring stroke: a series of premieres of the music of Charles Ives. This was an important period for Ives, when his music was first being discovered by young American modernists. In February 1925, Hans Barth and Sigmund Klein performed the "Largo" and "Allegro" from his *Three Quarter-Tone Pieces* at a Pro Musica concert; in January 1927, the first and second movements of his Fourth Symphony were conducted by Eugene Goossens with members of the New York Philharmonic; and in November 1928, *The Celestial Railroad* was performed by pianist Anton Rovinsky.

As for Pro Musica's European repertory, it was largely French—initially Debussy, Fauré, and Ravel, later Milhaud and Honegger. There was also a reasonable representation of Russian (Prokofiev), Italian (Alfredo Casella), and British composers (Frank Bridge), as well as a few works by Germans and Austrians, both of which had become problematic national groups for New Yorkers in the early 1920s. A letter from Schmitz to Alban Berg, written in 1925, gives a sense of the outreach techniques used by Pro Musica. Schmitz had visited Berg in Vienna the previous summer and wrote afterward to inquire about new works by the composer. He reassured Berg that Pro Musica was making a special effort to include composers from "Central Europe," and his programs show this to have been at least modestly the case. Greta Torpadie sang Berg's *Dem Schmerz sein Recht* and Webern's *So ich traurig bin* in January 1925; Egon Wellesz's String Quartet, Op. 28, No. 4, appeared on a concert in March 1926. Although Berg ended up contributing a "Letter from Vienna" to the *Pro Musica Quarterly* in 1925—a fairly significant coup for Schmitz—no more music by him appeared on the New York programs of Pro Musica for the remainder of the decade. Thus even though Schmitz gestured toward national balances, he mostly ended up supporting the French composers with whom he was comfortable.[7]

"Internationalization" and the leadership of French immigrants also dominated the International Composers' Guild. Here, though, the tale of how the group interacted with American composers becomes more tangled. All of the ICG's concerts took place in New York City, with none of the ambitious cross-country network created by Pro Musica. Yet it joined Pro Musica in maintaining strong contacts across the Atlantic. Among the ICG's models were a number of new-music organizations that recently had been formed abroad, including Schoenberg's Verein für musikalische Privataufführungen, which existed in Vienna from 1918 to 1923, and Casella's Società Nazionale di Musica (later the Società Italiana di Musica Moderna), which lasted in Rome from 1917 to 1919. In 1923, the ICG formed affiliations with at least two European groups: the Internationale Komponisten-Gilde, founded that year by Varèse and Ferruccio Busoni in Berlin, and the Corporazione delle Nuove Musiche, established by Casella and others.[8]

More than anything else, the ICG demonstrated how New York was becoming an international bazaar for modernist music. This was not a case of imposing

Figure 11.2. Miguel Covarrubias, "Two Types of Symphony Orchestras—Ancient and the Modern. A Comparison of Classical, and Contemporary Musical Methods." As published in *Vanity Fair* (March 1927). Permission courtesy Maria Elena Rico Covarrubias.

European culture wholesale on a colonial outpost but rather of forming a coalition of Americans and Europeans who envisioned a glorious future for New York as a cosmopolitan center of the avant-garde. The ICG's two composer-directors—Varèse and Carlos Salzedo—were both recent immigrants from France. But its patrons, most notably Gertrude Vanderbilt Whitney, and its energetic "executive secretary" Claire Reis were all American. Such a mix also characterized its "board of technical advisors." The initial group included Casella (Italian), Acario Cotapos (Chilean), Karol Szymanowski (Polish); and Carl Engel, A. Walter Kramer, Julius Mattfeld, and Emerson Whithorne (all American).

Taking a significant step beyond Schmitz's concentration on a Paris–New York axis, Varèse and Salzedo aimed to bring broad international coverage to their organization. "The aim of the International Composers' Guild is to centralize the works of the day," proclaimed the closing salvo of the ICG's manifesto. "The International Composers' Guild disapproves of all 'isms'; denies the existence of schools; recognizes only the individual." The image of "centralizing" is a potent one, conjuring

up a force that would gather together modernist compositions from distant points of the globe and supply a forum for them, perhaps gaining power for the movement in the process. A flyer for the ICG's 1923–24 season addressed its transatlantic mandate more explicitly: "Since 1921 the International Composers' Guild has been helping New York to get acquainted with *new music from all parts of the world*." The results bore this out. By the time the ICG disbanded in 1927, it had introduced New Yorkers to a substantial series of new European compositions. In fact, such works dominated its programs: 69 percent of the works performed by the ICG were European, 17 percent were by foreign-born American nationals (Carl Engel, Louis Gruenberg, Colin McPhee, Leo Ornstein, Dane Rudhyar, Salzedo, and Varèse), and the remaining 14 percent came from composers born in the United States.[9]

The European programming of the ICG resulted in some notable American premieres, with works by Stravinsky and Schoenberg at the fore. *Pierrot lunaire* was first heard in New York on an ICG concert in 1923 (see Chapter 17). Stravinsky's *Renard* had its New York unveiling through ICG in December 1923, *Les Noces* in February 1926, and the Octet in April 1927. Excerpts from Schoenberg's *Das Buch der hängenden Gärten* were performed in February 1924 and his *Serenade* turned up in March the following year. But the ICG was not solely a Schoenberg-Stravinsky show. A wide array of European modernist works appeared on its programs, including those of Casella, Gian Francesco Malipiero, Ildebrando Pizzetti, Ottorino Respighi, Vittorio Rieti (Italian); Maurice Délage, Arthur Honegger, Charles Koechlin, Arthur Lourié, Milhaud, Francis Poulenc, Ravel, Satie, Florent Schmitt (French); Hindemith (German); Nikolai Miaskovsky, Prokofiev, Nina Koshetz (Russian); Lord Berners, Arthur Bliss, Ralph Vaughan Williams (British); Bartók (Hungarian); Karol Szymanowski (Polish); Berg and Webern (Austrian). Fulfilling the notion of a "League of Nations in Art," as Varèse had proposed in his letter to the editor of the *New York Times* in 1919, the ICG sought to hear the voices of all.

Useful parallels for grasping the ICG's mission can be found within New York's modern-art community of the same period. Just as European new-music organizations served as a model for the group, so too did similar initiatives among visual artists nearby. The Société Anonyme was one such endeavor. Founded in 1920, a year before the ICG, this American organization with a French name was begun by Marcel Duchamp, the French artist and soulmate of Varèse who was then living in New York, and by Katherine Dreier, a progressive American crusader for modern art. They added up to a pair much like Varèse and Claire Reis. During its first season, extending from April 1920 to June 1921, the Société Anonyme presented a string of six-week exhibits of work by contemporary Europeans, with an occasional American thrown in. These included Francis Picabia, Kurt Schwitters, Georges Braque, Juan Gris, Picasso, Kandinsky, and Marsden Hartley.

The work of Alfred Stieglitz also helps clarify the ICG, especially in providing a perspective for the organization's selective support of American-born composers and American nationals (both of which are subsumed below under "Americans"). Parallels between Stieglitz and Varèse have already been established: Stieglitz exhibited the new art of Europeans just as Varèse conducted and programmed their music. Both worked to transform the artistic climate of New York. Yet Stieglitz also nurtured a group of native-born painters, including Arthur Dove, John Marin, and Georgia O'Keeffe, and it is on this point that comparisons to Varèse grow shaky. While Varèse integrated American composers into his concerts, he favored a small and curious group. Unlike Stieglitz, Varèse encouraged no stable of like-minded souls. Viewed critically, Varèse can be seen as programming the music of a few Americans who genuinely interested him but largely turning to those who were in a position to help his cause. He also featured his own music prominently. Viewed more charitably, he appears as having had the foresight to champion one key American modernist—Carl Ruggles. On the whole, though, he reacted to the American composition scene rather than actively shaping it.[10]

The ICG's programming of music by Americans, then, yielded a mixed profile. The American composer it most frequently featured—beyond Varèse and Ruggles himself—was Carlos Salzedo, a well-known French-American harpist and cofounder of the ICG with Varèse. Other Americans appearing on the ICG's programs tended to represent the generation born in the 1880s. They made up a surprisingly conservative group, given the ICG's reputation for fostering avant-garde American composition. Early on, these composers included Carl Engel, Louis Gruenberg, Frederick Jacobi, A. Walter Kramer, Alexander Steinert, and Emerson Whithorne; there were also single performances of music by Ornstein and Rudhyar. This was in large part the same group that made up the American Music Guild, providing yet one more example of the prominence that composers in the forgotten vanguard held in the early 1920s.

After the League split from the ICG in 1923, the number of Americans on the ICG's programs decreased significantly, yet new names began to creep in, including Samuel Barlow and Henry Eichheim (both little known today), together with composers from a new generation—William Grant Still, Henry Cowell, Carlos Chávez, Colin McPhee. Most of this last group received single performances. Also significant is the list of names absent from the ICG's roster. There were no performances of music by John J. Becker, Ruth Crawford, Charles Ives, or Wallingford Riegger—all connected historiographically with the ultra-moderns. And there were none of Antheil, Copland, Harris, Sessions, or Thomson. None either of Marion Bauer. The ICG showed little inclination to include works by young Americans. Antheil's *Ballet Mécanique*, for example, was to have been performed on an ICG program in November 1925, but the December concert that year (none occurred in November) included instead works by Hindemith, Schmitt, Lourié, Casella, and Rudhyar.[11]

Given the modest presence on ICG concerts of music by composers now labeled as "ultra-modern," it is hard to see the organization as a significant breeding ground for that strain in American composition. The ICG's contribution to ultra-modernism was largely confined to its support of music by Ruggles and Varèse.

The ICG disbanded in 1927 when Varèse declared victory in the battle to establish modern music in New York. He publicly proclaimed "satisfaction" that the group's "purpose" was "accomplished," leaving "to other organizations the purely managerial task of continuing to entertain a public which now takes pleasure in hearing (thanks to its new ears) the works of its young contemporaries." It was a disingenuous communiqué, as Varèse's wife pointed out. Privately, Varèse confided to Ruggles that the ICG's concerts had become "routine like—a snobs affair—too fashionable and established: no more fighting." The modernist rebel yearned for skirmishes rather than security. Within a year, Varèse nominally surfaced again as an organizer—this time through the Pan American Association.[12]

In turning to the early history of the League of Composers, the second myth being highlighted here comes even more prominently into view—that two opposing factions emerged in American composition and fought it out through the remainder of the century. The myth certainly has substance, but it oversimplifies a tale laced with inconsistencies and contradictions, and it thoroughly obscures the stages through which relationships progressed within the modern-music community.

To be sure, the League was founded in 1923 because of a rift between Varèse and members of his governing board. The splinter group included Claire Reis, the ICG's executive director; Minna Lederman, its publicist; Alma Morgenthau Wertheim, one of its patrons; and Louis Gruenberg, Frederick Jacobi, and Emerson Whithorne, three of its most visible American composers. They collectively disagreed with Varèse over whether the ICG's successful performance of *Pierrot lunaire* should be repeated. (Varèse had a policy of never repeating a work on his programs, and he refused to budge.) There were administrative tensions as well, and charges of anti-Semitism were leveled against several ICG members by some of the League's founders. There was also resistance on the part of some male composers in the ICG to the increasing power exerted by a triumvirate of women who were not composers—Reis, Lederman, and Wertheim. Tensions clearly existed, and even the principal protagonists wavered in assessing just how deep a divide resulted. Aaron Copland, who was not on the scene for the schism but later became identified with the League, gave conflicting opinions at different points in his life. Looking back from the relatively close perspective of the 1940s, he saw the separation between the ICG and League as benignly replacing "one forward-looking group" with "two." Decades later, though, he viewed it quite differently: "The competition between the International Composers' Guild (ICG) and the League of Composers was such that a composer could not be allied with both. Since the League had presented my music first in New York, I could have no connection with the ICG." It is intriguing to examine just how much these hardened distinctions were reflected in the League's early programming.[13]

In many respects, there was not much difference at all between programs of the ICG and the early League. This was especially apparent in their commitment to internationalism. From its inception, the League proclaimed it would "effect co-operation between composers of all nations," and its transatlantic mission was af-firmed time and again. A review in the *Musical Leader* of the League's first concert on 11 November 1923 stated that the League planned to "present new and sig-nificant music by living composers of all nations." And years later, Claire Reis, who immediately had assumed leadership of the new organization, rearticulated the same ecumenical credo. "The League of Composers . . . had a very broad plat-form: music of all nations, music of all trends and of all nationalities, as long as they were contemporaries."[14]

There were other parallels to the ICG. Both organizations fought to gain more than counterculture success, graduating from small offbeat performance spaces to large mainstream concert halls. The ICG began in the Greenwich Village The-atre, then moved up to the Klaw Theatre in midtown, then in 1924 to Aeolian Hall—the same place where Gershwin's *Rhapsody in Blue* had received its premiere that February. The League followed a similar path, initiating its concerts in the Klaw Theatre, to which Claire Reis had free access, and moving in 1925 to Town Hall. Both groups also aimed for mainstream status by engaging star conductors of the day. Those for the ICG included Leopold Stokowski, who conducted *Renard* in 1923 and Schoenberg's *Serenade* and Varèse's *Intégrales* in 1925. At various points, the ICG also engaged Fritz Reiner, Otto Klemperer, and Artur Rodzinski. With the League, the most consistently visible conductor-luminary was Serge Koussevitzky, who in 1925 began offering an annual concert under the organi-zation's sponsorship. But there were other major names as well: Tullio Serafin, Willem Mengelberg, Pierre Monteux.[15]

At the same time as both groups ascended to upscale venues and big-name con-ductors, they also featured some of the same European composers. Given that these two organizations ostensibly were opposed ideologically, they might well have reached out to different strains within the European avant-garde. But such was far from the case. Scanning the ICG's programs for its entire life (1921–27) and the League's for its first seven years (1923–30) gives a sense of whose music was heard where. Stravinsky was equally welcomed in both realms. He had more works performed than any other European, and the ICG took the lead in doing so, programming a total of thirteen of his compositions. The League performed eleven. The next most popular European was Hindemith, but his record with the two groups was more unbalanced: the ICG performed only three of his works, while the League presented nine. Other performances were distributed as follows: Casella (five by the ICG, one by the League), Honegger (two by the ICG, five by the League), Malipiero (three and four), Ravel (four and two), Milhaud (two and three), Schoenberg (four and five), and Webern (three and two). These numbers show the League to have held its own in programming European composers. They also suggest that aesthetic allegiances were not so firmly in place. At the same time as the League has been branded with advancing neoclassicism, an aesthetic that traced its roots in part to Stravinsky, it was the ICG, not the League, that performed more of his compositions. Similarly, the League showed no more favor toward Ravel or Milhaud than did the ICG, and its commitment to the music of Schoenberg—a modernist with whom many of the ultra-moderns felt kinship—was no less than its competitor.

In spite of these similarities, the League increasingly outpaced the ICG in both the size and number of its performances. It was a bigger success. More than anything else, this probably fed the bad feelings among the ultra-moderns. From the outset, the League offered five concerts per season, as opposed to three by the Guild, and in 1925 it took a step beyond simply hiring prominent conductors and initiated a series of star-studded stage productions featuring major European and American performers, designers, directors, and choreographers. Some of these figures already had well-established reputations, such as the choreographer Adolph Bolm, who began with the Ballets Russes and directed his own Ballet Intime. Others, such as Martha Graham and Rouben Mamoulian, were at the beginning of illustrious careers.

The staged performances included De Falla's puppet opera *El Retablo de Maese Pedro*, presented initially in 1925 and again in 1928. In the 1925 version, Willem Mengelberg conducted members of the New York Philharmonic Society and donated his services; Wanda Landowska was the harpsichordist; and the production was designed by Remo Bufano. In 1927, the League presented an evening of ballets, with Tullio Serafin conducting, Adolph Bolm as choreographer, and Ruth Page as principal dancer. The works included *The Tragedy of the Cello* by Alexander Tansman (an arrangement of the composer's *Sextuor* from 1924), *Visual Mysticism* by Alexander Scriabin (a reworking of three of his piano preludes), *Voyage to the East* by Richard Hammond, and *The Rivals: A Chinese Legend* by Henry Eichheim. The next year the League staged *Histoire du soldat*, directed by Michio Ito with assistance from Irene Lewisohn. In 1929 it produced *Les Noces* with a battery of composer-pianists: Marc Blitzstein, Aaron Copland, Louis Gruenberg, and Frederick Jacobi. Then in 1930, there was a double bill: Schoenberg's *Die glückliche Hand*, with Doris Humphrey and Charles Weidman among the mimes, and Stravinsky's *Le Sacre du printemps*, with Martha Graham as principal dancer. Staging for the Schoenberg was directed by Rouben Mamoulian, with costumes and scenery by Robert Edmond Jones.[16]

These productions by the League focused heavily on European compositions, and they represented yet another important step in placing New York on an international performance circuit. The League's 1928 production of *Histoire du soldat*, for example, was only the fifth staging of the work, the previous ones having occurred in Lausanne, Hamburg, London, and Münster. With *Les Noces*, its 1929 performance in New York was preceded only by the work's 1923 Paris premiere and productions in London and Buenos Aires. With *Le Sacre du printemps*, the League's 1930 staging followed a small cluster of prior productions: the work's 1913 Paris premiere, with choreography by Nijinsky, which had been repeated that same year in London, and a new conception of it, with choreography by Leonide Massine, which had appeared first in Paris in 1920 and the following year in London. The League, as already noted, also used Massine's choreography, with adaptations by Martha Graham, and commissioned new costumes and scenery from Nicholas Roerich, who had also been involved with the Paris premiere.[17]

The League exhibited a steady commitment to European composers in other realms as well. Two of its four commissions during the 1920s went to Europeans— Béla Bartók for *Village Scenes*, premiered by the League in November 1926, and Anton Webern for *Symphony for Chamber Ensemble* (Op. 21), first performed by the League in December 1929. The others were issued to Aaron Copland for *Music for the Theatre* (premiered in 1925) and Emerson Whithorne for *Saturday's Child* (premiered in 1926). Similarly, the League's journal *League of Composers' Review*—or *Modern Music*, as it later came to be called—began with an almost exclusive focus on the European scene. "Stravinsky, Picasso, Cocteau, Satie, and the Group of Six," wrote the magazine's editor Minna Lederman, "these were the preoccupations of the Europeans whose comment dominated the *Review*'s first numbers." The very first issue included feature pieces on Schoenberg and Stravinsky, the Italian avant-garde, Les Six, and contemporary English composers, and the *Musical Courier* criticized the new publication for this continental focus, hoping that "the next number will get round to something a little nearer home." Which is exactly what *Modern Music* did, eventually developing a whole new breed of American composer-critics who assessed one another's work.[18]

With the early years of the League, though, where did American compositions fit in? Initially, hardly at all. During its first year, the League's only bow to the music of its own country came in a special lecture-recital about jazz, at which Vincent Lopez performed with his orchestra and E. B. Hill and Gilbert Seldes spoke. The only American composition that season was a Piano Quintet by Ernest Bloch (Bloch had emigrated to the United States a few years earlier). When a composition by an American-born composer finally appeared during the second season, it was placed within an international context. The piece was *Assyrian Prayers* by Frederick Jacobi, and it was identified as the American contribution to "An International Program of Chamber Music." As the decade progressed, American music gained more and more visibility, yet it did so through a slow process that began with small, segregated concerts rather than a prominent presence on the League's main agenda.[19]

The first American composers presented by the League were drawn mostly from the generation of the 1880s, including many of the same figures featured by the American Music Guild and the ICG—especially Bauer, Gruenberg, Jacobi, and Whithorne. At the same time, a new direction was signaled at the opening of the 1924–25 season when the critic Olin Downes gave a lecture titled "The Younger Generation in Music." The accompanying program included a sturdy European contingent, with works by Georges Migot, Eric Fogg, Alois Hába, Daniel Lazarus, and Ernst Krenek. Yet alongside them were Copland's *Passacaglia* and *The Cat and the Mouse*, Antheil's *Jazz Sonata*, songs by Bernard Rogers (*In the Gold*

Room and *Notturno*), and songs by Richard Hammond (*Dans les montagnes* and *Les trois princesses*). According to Copland, these concerts were organized by Marion Bauer, and they represented a revolutionary new step. After a year's hiatus, the League resumed its "Recital of New Music by Young Americans" in February 1927, and one such event occurred each season through the end of the decade.[20]

The League thus reached out to American youth more systematically than the ICG, and while it often did so along expected party lines, the exceptions were significant enough to note. The inaugural young composers' event in 1924 included the mixed bag of participants listed above, none of whom fits into a tidy aesthetic package. With the concert in February 1927, there was yet another kind of mix, with Ruth Crawford standing alongside Copland, Blitzstein, Chanler, Evelyn Berckman, and Randall Thompson—Crawford probably having been included because she was friends with Marion Bauer. From then until the end of the decade, expected borders were crossed regularly. In March 1929, Cowell's *Trio* (probably his *Four Combinations for Three Instruments* of 1924) appeared on one of the young composers' concerts. And the League's 1929–30 season brought three events that trounced aesthetic expectations by including a series of pieces by composers considered as "ultra-modern": Riegger's *Suite for Flute Alone* and Rudhyar's *Granites* (performed in February 1930); Slonimsky's *Studies in Black and White* (March); and Crawford's "Home Thoughts," "White Moon," "Joy," and "Sunsets"; Weiss's *Sonata da camera*; and Ornstein's Quartette Op. 99 (April). A modernist movement divided? Perhaps, but by no means consistently.

These concerts of music by young Americans were decidedly modest events—scheduled in the afternoon and often given at the Anderson Galleries, a building filled with exhibit spaces. It was a small venue compared to Town Hall. Yet it was a significant location in the history of American art. In December 1925, Stieglitz opened the Intimate Gallery in the same building. Its purpose was for "the Intimate study of Seven Americans"—namely Arthur Dove, Marsden Hartley, John Marin, Charles Demuth, Paul Strand, Georgia O'Keeffe, and Stieglitz himself. The League, then, chose an auspicious alternative location to profile contemporary American composers.[21]

All the while that the modernist movement was gaining coherence in New York City, a related momentum was underway on the West Coast. While not at the core of our story, it nonetheless held important implications for the type of composer societies that characterized the second wave of activity in New York and for the specific aesthetic divisions beginning to take shape.

In 1925, the young Henry Cowell issued a flyer announcing the formation of "The New Music Society of California." The group was "affiliated with the International Composers' Guild of New York, Inc." and devoted to presenting "the works of the most discussed composers of so-called ultra-modern tendencies, such as Strawinsky, Schoenberg, Ruggles, Rudhyar, etc." The first concert, on 22 October 1925 at the ballroom of the Biltmore Hotel in Los Angeles, was an ambitious event for orchestra, and it marked a significant step beyond the token inclusion of Americans by the ICG and League. Of the seven works performed, five were by composers living in the United States (only one of them—Ruggles—was native-born). The program included Milhaud's Sonata for Two Violins and Piano, Ornstein's *Musings of a Piano*, Rudhyar's *Surge of Fire*, Varèse's *Octandre*, Ruggles's *Angels*, Schoenberg's *Sechs kleine Klavierstücke*, and a piano improvisation by Feodor Kolin, a Russian-Polish-American from Los Angeles who "had developed theories based on the combined use of light, dramatic movements, and perfumes." Kolin believed "in the freedom of the improvisation spirit" and claimed himself to be "a reincarnation of either Schumann or Schubert." The Little Symphony performed, with Adolph Tandler conducting.[22]

The New Music Society presented only one concert that first year, as well as in the 1926–27 season. This last again included music by Milhaud, Ruggles, Schoenberg, and Rudhyar, adding works by Casella and Cowell. Again, the national profile was evenly balanced. But New Music's most broadly felt initiative was the publication of *New Music: A Quarterly of Modern Compositions*, first issued in October 1927. In these volumes of scores, the tendency toward equal representation of Americans, as exhibited in the group's early concerts, gave way to outright advocacy, and ramifications of that policy were felt almost immediately on the East Coast. Published scores were not just local phenomena but objects with mobility. To be sure, works by Europeans appeared in *New Music*, but they did so belatedly and incidentally with the publication in 1930 of Webern's *Geistlicher Volkstext* (Op. 17, No. 2) and two years later of Schoenberg's *Klavierstück* (Op. 33b). The main goal, as an announcement at the founding of the publication put it, was to promote "the modern American composer," to issue "ultra-modern works," and to defy commercial publishers "unwilling to risk losing money" by printing new scores. During its first three years, *New Music* released the following works, nearly all by Americans (or by composers in the midst of extended residencies in the United States):

1927–28

Ruggles, *Men and Mountains*
Rudhyar, *Paeans*
Ornstein, *The Corpse*
Imre Weisshaus, *Six Pieces for Solo Voice*
Chávez, *Sonatina for Violin and Piano*

1928–29

Ruth Crawford, *Four Preludes*
Ives, *Fourth Symphony* (second movement)
Adolph Weiss, *Six Preludes for Piano*
Copland, *As It Fell Upon a Day*

1929–30

Nicolas Slonimsky, *Studies in Black and White*
John J. Becker, *Symphonia Brevis*
Ruggles, *Portals*
Wallingford Riegger, *Suite for Flute Alone*
Colin McPhee, *Kinesis* and *Invention*[23]

The composers on this list uniformly fit *New Music*'s founding criteria—"moderns" who were largely American and composed music that entailed a financial "risk." All were points of pride. In addition, these figures fell mostly into the ultra-modern camp. The only unambiguous exception was Copland—although he was certainly a significant one. Both Chávez and McPhee were perceived, at different times, as standing on either side of the aesthetic dividing line.

Thus Cowell, from his base in San Francisco, set up an organization that initially gave a limited number of concerts but did so with an eye toward showcasing American composers, and then branched into a publication series through which he sought to shape a particular strain of American modernism, including composers he saw as having "developed indigenous materials" or being "specially interested in expressing some phase of the American spirit in their works." Cowell had Europeans on his mind, to be sure, but he saw them more as recipients of new American scores than as transmitters of exemplary models. His goal with *New Music* was to disseminate American music as broadly as possible. "It would be very greatly appreciated on my part," he wrote to the critic Irving Schwerké in Paris, just as *New Music* got underway, "if you could put me in touch with a list of addresses of people in Europe who might be interested in receiving announcements of 'New Music' since I am particularly eager to introduce the finest examples of modern American composition into European circles." In this way, an important new perspective entered in America's relation to European modernism, shifting the emphasis to exporting American works abroad. During *New Music*'s first year, Cowell immediately built a subscription base of around six hundred. Although a high concentration of those subscribers was on the East Coast of the United States, others were scattered throughout the country and overseas, among them Darius Milhaud, Nadia Boulanger, Alban Berg, Artur Schnabel, Ernst Krenek, Albert Roussel.[24]

Thus in a fundamentally peripatetic era, when modernists criss-crossed the Atlantic and the continental United States, the New Music Society added a new geographic dimension to the American composers' movement. Its support of native talent realigned the field on which modernism gained ground in the New World, and its dissemination of contemporary scores signaled a revolution on the most practical of levels. Once Cowell's enterprise is factored into the picture, the American modern-music scene seems less place-based than fluid and fundamentally in transit. New York, in this scenario, resembles a busy crossroads where composers who faced east to Europe greeted those looking west toward the Pacific—or elsewhere in the country. In an era when the automobile made transcontinental travel easier and telephone lines increasingly linked the continent—from approximately 7.5 million phones in 1920 to over 20 million a decade later—a geographically dispersed modernist movement was possible in a way that could not have been the case even a decade earlier. Cowell himself exemplified this mobility, frequently motoring cross-country, giving concerts along the way and maintaining a presence on the modernist scene in New York.

With the founding of its *Quarterly*, the New Music Society also crystallized the notion of an ultra-modern contingent among young American composers. Yet I believe that ultra-modernism was, in large part, a construction of Cowell, who aimed to promote not just American composers but also those whom he considered kindred spirits. It never became a distinct stylistic sphere so much as a geographic protest, embracing figures writing new scores on the West Coast, the Middle West, and Vermont—anywhere outside of New York City. Ultra-modernism stood for an assertion of regional validity, a reaction against the perceived hegemony of East Coast institutions. Yet while ultra-modern composers embraced their difference from those in New York, they still actively sought acceptance there. They aimed to have it both ways: to distinguish themselves from New York-based composers—especially those surrounding Copland—and to gain the recognition that performances in the city could bring.

Which leads to the second wave of performance organizations in New York City. In the spring of 1928 both the Pan American Association of Composers and the Copland-Sessions Concerts were founded. Sibling societies from birth, they embodied the drama of shared needs and intense rivalries within the American modernist movement. Both groups proclaimed American composers as their focus. Both signaled the emergence of leaders from a new generation—Cowell on the one hand, Copland and Sessions on the other. Both strove to empower youthful voices and disseminate their music in New York and abroad, building on the young-composer concerts of the League and the initiatives of the New Music Society.

At the same time, profound contrasts marked the two organizations. Each employed strikingly different rhetoric and selected its governing board from different constituencies. In many ways, the Pan American Association became an East Coast extension of the New Music Society, concentrating its efforts on building an ultra-modern group—or at least on generating the appearance of one. Overall, the Pan American Association exhibited far greater partisanship in its programming than did the Copland-Sessions Concerts. This resulted in a situation where composers within the ultra-modern camp appeared on the Copland-Sessions Concerts, but the ultra-moderns seldom reciprocated.

When the Pan American Association took off in New York in February 1928, its initial executive board consisted of Edgard Varèse (president), Henry Cowell, Carlos Chávez, Carl Ruggles, and Emerson Whithorne (vice presidents), forming a coalition that cut across generational lines. It is this lineage from Varèse and Ruggles to Cowell and Chávez that has contributed to a sense of an ultra-modern family (with Whithorne's role totally ignored), stretching from the ICG to the Pan American Association. But it was Cowell and the mission of the New Music Society that propelled the Pan American Association—not Varèse and the ICG. A decisive reorientation had occurred. Rather than trumpeting itself as "international" as the ICG had done, this new group declared itself to be "Pan American," addressing itself "exclusively [to] composers who are citizens of the countries of North, Central and South America." Thus the Pan American Association completely rejected the programming policy of the ICG, at the same time as its emphasis was not narrowly nationalistic. "Encouragement may be derived from the fact," its manifesto continued, "that whereas a few years ago it would have been impossible to find a sufficient number of American composers with new musical ideals to form such an association, today there is a sizable group of progressive men and women who, although representing many different tendencies, are banded together through serious and sincere interest in furthering all the finest music being written in the Americas." At the same time as this group embodied the spirit of the New Music Society, it issued a new geographic challenge: "It is the hope of the association," to quote again from the manifesto, "that [its performances] . . . will stimulate composers to make still greater effort toward creating a distinctive music of the Western Hemisphere." The Pan American Association seemed to thrive on representing forces from outside New York, building on the New Music Society's defiant projection of anti-establishment separateness and geographic difference. As though in reaction to this new direction, Varèse withdrew almost immediately from active leadership in the Pan American Association, heading to Paris in October of 1928 and staying there for the next five years. He became "Honorary President" of the new association, and Cowell assumed active leadership.[25]

The Pan American Association lasted until 1934, and its impact was felt most solidly in the thirties. As had been the case with the New Music Society, this East Coast group got off to a slow start, giving only one concert in New York City during the twenties, an event that took place in March 1929 and was solely devoted to Latin American composers, including Chávez, Villa-Lobos, Alejandro Caturla, Amadeo Roldán, and Raúl Paniagua. (This appears in retrospect to have been a forerunner of the series "Sonidos de las Americas" of the American Composers Orchestra, begun in 1993.) The Pan American Association's next concert in April 1930 focused on the North American ultra-moderns as we conceive of them today, including music by Antheil, Henry Brant, Cowell, Ruth Crawford, Vivian Fine, Ives, Rudhyar, Gerald Strang, Imre Weisshaus, together with that of Chávez and Caturla. It was the first occasion on which this group appeared as a united front in New York City. Prior to these two concerts, the Pan American Association seemed to have trouble getting in gear. In November 1928, Cowell wrote to Charles Ives: "I regret to say, that I believe the lack of success of this organization is because certain composers blocked any action, thru jealousy that other composers' works would be presented to conductors! I think some working plan may be found for the association later, and all the troubles ironed out." The internal cross-sniping that had characterized the ICG was also present among the Pan Americans. Seeger wrote to Ruggles that he did "not take" the music of Adolph Weiss "very seriously" and even more surprisingly, he declared that Cowell "on anything but the piano, is simply awful. I think he will find a better metier in experimental and speculative musicology." The critic Isaac Goldberg characterized the group aptly as "a motley crew."[26]

By the early 1930s, the "troubles" plaguing the organization had been "ironed out." Beginning in 1931, it sponsored an important series of concerts abroad, all conducted by Nicolas Slonimsky. The first took place on 6 June in Paris. The program included Weiss's *American Life*, Ruggles's *Men and Mountains*, Cowell's *Synchrony*, Ives's *Three Places in New England*, and Roldán's *La Rebambaramba*. These programs further solidified the notion of an ultra-modern group. A second concert, with an entirely different program, occurred there five days later. Then in late winter of 1932, Slonimsky and the association became even more ambitious, offering two concerts in Paris (21 and 25 February) and one in Berlin (5 March). From then until the group ceased operation in 1934, there were two concerts in Havana, interwoven with an increasingly substantial series in New York.[27]

With the Pan American Association, as with the Pro Musica Society, Charles Ives enters the story as a significant figure. His music appeared on nearly half the association's concerts, both at home and abroad, providing a major forum for the emergence of his work. Just as significantly, Ives became a patron for the group, as he was also doing for Pro Musica and *New Music*. "You gave me a sum of money to apportion between New Music and the Pan American Association for Composers," Cowell wrote to Ives on 24 November 1928. "I apportioned $125.00 to the latter, and have been holding it for them, pending the time they show some action, and need it." Ives went on to subsidize the concerts that Slonimsky conducted abroad.[28]

Thus Ives—the quintessential powerless figure in American composition, the composer whose music had received few public performances before the 1920s and who has come to symbolize the cruel rejection that American creative artists can face—provided the necessary financial base not only for his own music to be unveiled but also for a certain strain of composition to be promoted. Again, Cowell was a crucial figure. He seized upon Ives to help construct "a usable past," to provide an ancestor for the ultra-modern group he sought to build. "Charles E. Ives is the father of indigenous American art-music," wrote Cowell in the opening salvo of an essay about Ives for his *American Composers on American Music* of 1933. "At the same time," he continued, Ives "is in the vanguard of the most forward-looking and experimental composers of today."[29]

If an ultra-modern contingent in American composition did not gain ground in New York until the 1930s, as the tale of the Pan American Association suggests, how did the composers who have come to be identified with that group fit into New York's new-music scene in the late 1920s? The answer, surprisingly enough, lies within the history of a parallel composer organization—the Copland-Sessions Concerts.

Long seen as a promoter of the "Boulangerie," the Copland-Sessions Concerts initially had much more diverse programming than has been acknowledged. Begun by its two namesakes in the fall of 1928 and concluded in the spring of 1931, the series encompassed ten concerts. Like the Pan American Association, the Copland-Sessions Concerts scheduled performances abroad—one in Paris in June 1929 and another in London in December 1931. The series sprinted ahead of the Pan American Association, both in presenting new music in New York and disseminating it to the continent.[30]

During its first season, the Copland-Sessions Concerts delivered programs that cut across the perceived factions in New York. In April 1928, works by Theodore Chanler, Walter Piston, and Virgil Thomson appeared, fitting the usual image of this enterprise. All three were pupils of Boulanger, and all had substantial Parisian experience. But alongside them stood a Sonata and Three Sonatinas by Carlos Chávez, who simultaneously was working as one of the vice presidents of the newly formed Pan American Association. The next concert, given one month later, defied assumptions even more blatantly. Yes, there were sonatas by Robert Delaney and Robert Sessions, a quintet by W. Quincy Porter, and *Two Pieces for String Quartet* by Copland. But more striking was a performance by Richard Buhlig, a pianist from the West Coast who had been a teacher of Henry Cowell and later taught John Cage. Buhlig selected a group of works by ultra-moderns: *Two Preludes* by Ruth Crawford, *Three Preludes* by Adolph Weiss, and *Three Paeans* by Dane Rudhyar.

This might be an unimportant detail if it were not for a jolting fact: this particular Copland-Sessions concert marked the first time that composers of the ultra-modern contingent had their music performed as a group—albeit a small one—on a concert in New York. It predated their appearance as an even larger group on the Pan American Association's concert in 1930. Before this Copland-Sessions concert in 1928, Crawford's only previous performance in New York had been the year before in a League of Composers' concert; Rudhyar's music had appeared twice before on programs by the International Composers' Guild; and this was Weiss's debut on a New York new-music event. Another notable fact: all these works had a recent or imminent connection to publication in *New Music*. Rudhyar's *Three Paeans* had just appeared there in January 1928; Crawford's *Preludes* came out several months later (October 1928); and Weiss's *Preludes* appeared the following spring (April 1929). This was tangible evidence that the *Quarterly* was yielding practical results. An ultra-modern presence was also strongly felt at the opening of the second Copland-Sessions season, with the performance of Cowell's *Paragraphs for Two Violins and Cello*—in his case it was the second appearance of a score by him on a new-music concert in the city. The first had been with his *Ensemble for String Quintet with Thunder Sticks* at the ICG in 1925.

There was yet another connection between the Copland-Sessions Concerts and the ultra-moderns. On 13 April 1930, the music of three young Hungarians—Istvan Szelenyi, Pál Kadosa, and Imre Weisshaus—was heard on the series. These were figures championed by Cowell. In June 1927, he had brought them to the attention of American musicians through an article in *Musical America*, and he had published Weisshaus's *Six Pieces for Solo Voice* in the April 1928 issue of *New Music*. Cowell also reported in 1928 about "a week of modern Hungarian music" in New York the previous fall. It included a performance by the New York Philharmonic of an orchestral suite from Zoltán Kodály's *Háry Janos*, as well as a recital by Weisshaus, who performed his own music together with that of Kadosa, and it concluded with Béla Bartók making his debut as a piano soloist with the Philharmonic. Thus Copland and Sessions programmed music by Hungarian composers known slightly to New Yorkers, who had been first discovered by Cowell.[31]

By 1930, though, intersections were diminishing between ultra-modern composers and the Copland-Sessions Concerts. Copland's and Sessions's series increasingly included music largely from within the extended realm of the Boulangerie—in short, it began to assume the image with which it has since been perceived. This is the point—around 1930–31—when the notion of two separate factions emerged in New York among the young generation of Americans. It paralleled precisely the rise in activity of the Pan American Association and was reinforced by the founding of Cos Cob Press, which as a parallel venture to *New Music* provided publication opportunities to composers who were coming to public notice within the Copland-Sessions Concerts.[32]

If an ideological flash point ignited rivalries between the two groups, it was neoclassicism. For some, the Copland-Sessions Concerts appeared as an advocate of the aesthetic. Seeming to be a political ideology so pernicious that it demanded aggressive opposition, neoclassicism had risen within the final years of the 1920s to challenge basic tenets of radical modernism. Many cried out against it. Varèse called upon fellow composers to "combat" neoclassicism. "We had rejected the neo-classicism of a war-weary Paris," recalled Wallingford Riegger, treasurer of the Pan American Association, "and had struck out for ourselves, each in his own way."[33]

Yet no matter how much composers associated with ultra-modernism may have disagreed with the compositional ideologies they believed Copland and his concert series to be promoting, they did not turn down opportunities to get their work performed. Any division in the modernist ranks at this stage of the movement seems to have been pressed from one side but largely ignored by the other—which adds even more support to my contention that the outsider status railed against by composers identified with ultra-modernism was largely of their own doing. Cowell and his comrades do not appear to have been rejected by Copland, Sessions, or any of the figures surrounding them but chose on their own to form a separate modernist community. By doing so they took a gamble: in order to claim a distinctive identity, they bet they could establish a strong enough power base in New York to become self-sufficient. They cherished their outsider status, but they also competed for turf on the inside.

Composer societies did not provide the only havens for performance of new music in New York during the 1920s. There were isolated artists and ensembles who took up the cause in solo concerts—the singer Eva Gauthier, the New World String Quartet founded by Varèse and Stokowski in 1927, and the Little Symphony, conducted by the French-American flutist Georges Barrère. And there were scattered venues that provided a forum for the new, most often sponsored by underground networks of the avant-garde or progressive political organizations. Early on, one significant such space was the Whitney Studio Club, a forerunner of the Whitney Museum of American Art. In March and April 1922, Ruggles presented there a series of "three talks on Modern Music." Titled "The Present Situation in American Music," "The Historical Background of Music," and "Technique and Phantasy in the Study of Composition," they were advertised as being "preliminary to the formation of a class in Composition which will be conducted by Mr. Ruggles next winter at the Club." Cowell heard at least one of those lectures, later recalling that Ruggles had the text of his lecture "written out carefully on an armful of the familiar butcher's paper which he deposited in a heap on the grand piano" (among Ruggles's many eccentric habits, he composed on brown butcher paper). The wife of Henry Hadley, a conservative American composer of Ruggles's generation, also sat in the audience. As Cowell recalled, her presence "did not deter [Ruggles] from opening his lecture with this remark: 'I thought that music had reached the lowest possible point when I heard the works of John Alden Carpenter. Now, however, I have been examining the scores of Mr. Henry Hadley!'" Another venue for discussing new music was the Society for Ethical Culture, where on 14 December 1924, a program took place titled "Open Forum: Modernism in Music." Charles Seeger appeared as "speaker" and Cowell as "composer-pianist," with performance of compositions by Cowell, Ruggles, Stravinsky, and Scriabin.[34]

Most significant, the New School for Social Research hosted all types of alternative artistic expression. Copland gave an annual lecture series there on modern music, beginning in 1927, and he also "arranged," as the programs put it, concerts of modern music. One on 28 December 1927 included his own *Nocturne* and *Serenade* for violin and "Four Piano Compositions" by Cowell, together with music of Hindemith, Krenek, Ravel, Stravinsky, and Webern. He was involved in yet another series of concerts at the New School—this one given in the spring of 1928 and "arranged" together with Edgard Varèse, again defying the notion of fixed divisions within the new-music ranks. These included a mixture of European modernists, plus Copland, Cowell, and Chávez. Cowell began teaching his now-famous "Music of the World's Peoples" course at the New School in 1928. It, too, included a series of concerts.[35]

Collectively, these alternative spaces generated a counterforce to New York's longstanding musical institutions, which were too busy marketing European warhorses to pay much attention to the creative activity surrounding them. The New York Philharmonic Society, most notably, managed to ignore almost entirely the young generation of American composers active in the 1920s. The only exceptions were George Gershwin, whose *Concerto in F* was performed in 1925 and 1928 (the latter time with *American in Paris*); Howard Hanson, whose *Pan and the Priest* turned up in 1926; and Leo Sowerby, whose *Irish Washerwoman* appeared two years later. There were other orchestras, especially the Boston Symphony Orchestra and the Philadelphia Orchestra, that brought new American music on tour to New York. The Boston Symphony Orchestra gave regular concerts there under Serge Koussevitzky, and it championed Copland vigorously, with limited performances also of works by other young composers, including Vladimir Dukelsky (Vernon Duke) and Sessions. The orchestra also began appearing on concerts of the League of Composers in 1925, performing largely European modernist music. Koussevitzky paid no attention to the ultra-moderns, even though Slonimsky worked as his assistant for a couple of years. The role of performing music by the ultra-moderns fell to Leopold Stokowski, who as part of his New York concerts with the Philadelphia Orchestra presented Varèse's *Amériques* and *Arcana* (in 1926 and 1927, respectively), Ornstein's *Piano Concerto* (in 1925), and Riegger's *Study in Sonority* (1929).[36]

Amid all this, an unusual ensemble deserves notice: the "Conductorless Symphony Orchestra," which played a small but intriguing role in furthering the cause of the ultra-moderns. Founded in 1928—the same year as the Copland-Sessions Concerts and the Pan American Association—it was initially called the "American Symphonic Ensemble (A Symphony Orchestra without Conductor)." The group apparently presented three concerts its first season (1928–29) and six the next, when it was renamed the "Conductorless Symphony Orchestra." All took place in Carnegie Hall. Designed according to a communist model, the group was "a thoroughly co-operative organization" in which the workers—that is, the performers—put up expenses for the first concert "out of their own pockets." It challenged the traditions basic to American orchestras, whether those of private patronage, the predominance of historic European repertory, or the reign of star conductors. It shifted both financial power and artistic decision-making to the players. A flyer for its 1929–30 season stated, "The interpretation (decided upon in advance by a small committee) is modified in rehearsal by suggestions from the players. The final arbiter on interpretation is the Composer himself who by his expression marks in the score has indicated his ideas." The ideology behind this group lay in the Soviet Union, as did an actual model—the Persimfons Orchestra, which Henry Cowell reported on in a 1929 article about his recent trip to "radical Russia."[37]

There was a battery of composers allied with the Conductorless Orchestra, including Louis Gruenberg, Carlos Salzedo, and Adolph Weiss, who were members of its "Committee on Interpretation," and reviews quoted in one of its flyers focused on the "vitality" of the orchestra's performances, as well as its "uncanny precision," giving a sense that empowered players made music with pleasure. Its programs on the whole were loaded with historic European repertory, yet the group intended "to play one novelty (wherever possible, an American novelty) at each concert." It managed to do so at least twice: on 26 October 1929, when Ruggles's

Portals was performed, and on 26 April 1930, when the first two movements of Cowell's Concerto for Piano and Orchestra received their premiere, with the composer as soloist. By then, the financial ideal of the group had been compromised, if not abandoned. In reporting to Ruggles about rehearsals for *Portals*, Weiss acknowledged that "Mr. Hazard very kindly gave us $1000. In fact all your friends were a wonderful asset for the cause of the Conductorless Orchestra. Thousand thanks to you!" By linking left-wing politics with performance, the Conductorless Symphony Orchestra appears as a predecessor to the Composers' Collective of the 1930s.[38]

All in all, the organizations formed during the 1920s provided a foundation for new music to flourish. They took practical steps at a critical time and created a sense of community. Although we have come to view the generation of composers born around 1900 through a nationalist lens, in large part because so much of their work turned in that direction during the Depression and World War II, they launched their careers on a playing field after World War I where transatlantic relations loomed above all else.

At the same time, competing ideological groups were not battling in New York during the 1920s quite as agressively as legend would have us believe. The newest generation of composers was more intent on gaining recognition than squabbling.

Women Patrons and Activists

It was not that ladies were inferior to men; it was that they were different. Their mission was to inspire others to achievement rather than to achieve themselves. Indirectly, by means of tact and a spotless name, a lady could accomplish much. But if she rushed into the fray herself she would be first censured, then despised, and finally ignored.

—E. M. Forster,
A Room with a View, 1908

The modern-music organizations that sprang up in New York during the 1920s made composers their focus. Yet the establishment of these institutions by no means involved only composers but rather an intricate network of publishers, promoters, performers, editors, and patrons. No movement of isolated trailblazers, American modernism grew out of an interconnected community. With energy and imagination, a series of women worked intensely and often anonymously to give composers viability on the American cultural scene. "I do not think there has ever been a country whose musical development has been fostered so almost exclusively by women as America," attested Walter Damrosch, conductor of the New York Symphony Society, in 1923. While Damrosch was reflecting on the past—looking back on a culture in which women had played key roles in establishing prominent musical institutions such as the New York Philharmonic and the Metropolitan Opera—he suggested much about the scene in which the avant-garde was taking hold.[1]

Yet Damrosch also pinpointed the limitation of women's involvement in music: they "fostered" its growth. Among American modernist composers, few were female. There were only Marion Bauer, already discussed as a member of the

American Music Guild, and Ruth Crawford Seeger, a much more widely acclaimed figure. Some women specialized in performing new repertory—most notably the singers Eva Gauthier, Greta Torpadie, and Radiana Pazmor. Others edited New York's composer magazines. Minna Lederman was best known among them for her work at the helm of *Modern Music*, the "little magazine" of the League of Composers. Louise Varèse, wife of the composer and herself a noted French translator, worked with Carlos Salzedo to edit *Eolian Review*, a harp journal that became a forum for the International Composers' Guild; she also wrote exceptionally informative program notes for the ICG. And Ely Jade, a pseudonym for Germaine Schmitz, edited *Pro Musica Quarterly*, the publication of Pro Musica, which in turn was directed by her husband E. Robert Schmitz.[2]

The focus in this chapter will be on yet another sector of female activity within New York's modern-music community—the patronage of Gertrude Vanderbilt Whitney, Alma Morgenthau Wertheim, and Blanche Walton, and the organizational achievement of Claire Reis. These women have largely been absent from chronicles of the period, partly because they chose to keep a low profile and documentation of their work is uneven, but also because of lingering attitudes about gender and the writing of history. Exploring their contribution broadens our perspective on the modernist movement as a whole, revealing close connections between patterns of patronage and institutional organization in literature, art, and music, and suggesting what might on the surface seem an unlikely alliance, between social feminism and the American avant-garde. It also raises questions about the degree to which women became scapegoats amid a growing tension between "high" and "low" culture.

In 1925, George Antheil, the brash young American who two years later was to achieve notoriety for the premiere of his *Ballet Mécanique* in Carnegie Hall, wrote to Mary Louise Curtis Bok, the woman who was generously financing his work. He was in Paris, she in Philadelphia. Antheil's outcry was typical of the histrionic rhetoric in which he specialized at the same time as it articulated the central economic issue for his generation:

> If you want composers like Beethoven or Chopin, you shall have to be prepared
> to do what the princes of other days did for these people. The joke of it is that
> the rich and wealthy people of our States want these thing[s] WITHOUT PAYING
> FOR THEM. For NOTHING! The princes of other days had to pay for them. So will
> the princes of today.[3]

Antheil made his appeal, of course, not to the American equivalent of a prince but rather a princess, as did so many of his contemporaries. Women, more than men, stepped forward as patrons of the American musical avant-garde. Alongside Mary Louise Curtis Bok in Philadelphia, a growing cluster of women patrons invested their energy and capital into young, often experimental, composers. This was not only a musical phenomenon or an American one: wealthy European women subsidized the avant-garde in music, and women on both sides of the Atlantic supported writers and visual artists. Private patronage experienced a major revival during the 1920s. In Paris, the Princesse de Polignac (an American from the Singer sewing machine family) assisted Igor Stravinsky; he dedicated his Piano Sonata of 1924 to her, and many of his new compositions received private hearings in her salon. She also subsidized Ravel and Satie, among others. Well-to-do women also supported writers and painters of the period—for example Lady Gregory, who financed Yeats; Harriet Shaw Weaver, who subsidized Joyce; and Mabel Dodge Luhan, who supported D. H. Lawrence and others. "A striking characteristic of the twentieth-century avant-garde, after all, was its determinedly anti-commercial cast," observe the literary critics Sandra Gilbert and Susan Gubar. "Perhaps there has been no circle of writers since the sixteenth century which was more dependent on private patronage, and, like such sixteenth-century figures as Sidney and Spenser, many prominent modernists were subsidized by a series of wealthy women or publicized by a set of powerful women." Similarly, historian Dorothy Brown writes of how patronage was a "feminized" area during the 1920s, similar to teaching, social work, nursing, and librarianship. And Minna Lederman, longtime editor of *Modern Music*, once commented that the rich felt a deep responsibility to support the arts during the 1920s. Being a patron, she said, was "like tithing."[4]

Such was certainly the case with Gertrude Vanderbilt Whitney, Alma Morgenthau Wertheim, and Blanche Walton, who provided essential financial help and moral support to New York's concert-music composers. They were establishing new models for the support of composers in America, building on a brief but rapidly changing history. In the late nineteenth century, as a wealthy class rose to prominence through expanding railroads, mines, and industry, it became involved in supporting cultural improvement. In music, most of that support had gone toward performance, not composition, and its focus had been on European repertory. Just as the notion of being a patron followed European models, so too did the choice of music to support. The same occurred with American museums: undertaking the purchase and exhibition of European masterworks insured an aura of sophistication and cultivation—essentially guaranteed an importance—that the acquisition and display of American works simply could not match. America's wealthy citizens munificently funded the Metropolitan Museum of Art, the Metropolitan Opera, the New York Philharmonic, and Carnegie Hall, but with the exception of Isabella Stewart Gardner, who in Boston at the turn of the century subsidized the composer Charles Martin Loeffler, they paid little attention to native composers.[5]

Things began changing in the late 1910s, however, especially with the work of Elizabeth Sprague Coolidge in Massachusetts and Washington, D.C., and by the early 1920s patronage of composers was becoming more frequent. Though many patrons continued to support the performance of European masterworks, others reached out to native composers, and they made quite a difference. Suddenly an ambitious generation of young musicians could devote themselves fully to practicing their art.[6]

Gertrude Whitney, Alma Wertheim, and Blanche Walton, then, were continuing an old tradition but approaching it in a new way. Each allied herself with a different faction of the avant-garde, and each shaped her giving according to her own resources and interests. On a personal level, each sought satisfaction by contributing to a cause that seemed both adventuresome and important. In an institutional sense, the three helped establish a network for the early performance and reception of the avant-garde in New York.

Although remembered primarily as a patron of visual artists, Gertrude Vanderbilt Whitney (1875–1942) advanced modernism in America in a variety of art forms, focusing her musical benefaction on Edgard Varèse. An accomplished sculptor, she was a major underwriter of the famous 1913 Armory Show, and her Whitney Studio Club, located on West Eighth Street in Greenwich Village, led to the founding of the Whitney Museum of American Art in 1931. Her involvement in new music, while less celebrated, had a similar purpose: to promote modernism in a society reluctant to accept it. In 1917 she helped underwrite Varèse's performance of the Berlioz *Requiem* at the Hippodrome, and two years later, she was among a group of four women who formed an "executive committee" for his New Symphony Orchestra. More important was her position as "one of the principal sponsors" of the International Composers' Guild, founded in 1921. Whitney not only gave direct financial support to the group but also housed its office at the Whitney Studio Club from mid-1923 to late 1925. This was the same space where Ruggles gave his lectures on modernist music in 1922. In retrospect, Whitney's connection to Varèse seems logical. The ICG's emphasis on European modernism served the same purpose in music as the Armory Show had in art, and its occasional focus on American composers found a parallel in the efforts of the Whitney Studio Club.[7]

In supporting the ICG, Gertrude Whitney followed a philanthropic model set by older members of her family, most of them male, but she did so in her own special way. Among the inheritors of the Vanderbilt family fortune, built on ships and railroads, she expanded her financial base by marrying Harry Payne Whitney, whose money lay largely in oil and tobacco. The Whitneys and Vanderbilts had strong awareness of an obligation to distribute their wealth. They tended to subsidize major educational and cultural institutions such as Columbia University and the Metropolitan Museum of Art. Gertrude, by contrast, shaped her own vision of philanthropy by supporting living artists. It was a riskier choice. But it helped give her life meaning, relieving what one historian has described as "the inchoate sense of uselessness" that consumed wealthy young women of the day. The novels of Henry James and Edith Wharton are filled with characters whose lives were awash in time for leisure and constricted by social conventions. According to a British census from 1911, 52,432 men and 195,712 women possessed "Private Means" but were "Without Specified Occupations." Wealthy American women existed in comparably disproportionate numbers. "I pity, I pity above all that class of people who have no necessity to work," lamented Whitney to her journal in 1901. She went on to condemn the wealthy as "the great and grand unemployed—the dregs of humanity." To counter this fate and to attain a sense of self-worth, Whitney became a patron.[8]

Details about Whitney's support of Varèse and the International Composers' Guild remain sketchy, in part because Varèse's papers are inaccessible to scholars, also because little information about this facet of Whitney's work survives in the literature about her. In 1921 she gave Varèse what has been described by his wife, Louise, as "an adequate allowance" so that he could focus on composition. It is unclear how long this subsidy lasted. She also hosted lectures and postconcert social events. After the ICG's first concert in February 1922, for example, she threw a party at the Whitney Club that was attended "by practically the entire audience," as Louise Varèse later recalled, and in subsequent years there were social events for composers at the Whitney Studio Club and at the home of Juliana Force, Whitney's secretary and active liaison to artists. But few other particulars about her work have been uncovered. "No one will ever know the extent of the private benefactions Mrs. Whitney performed through Mrs. {Juliana} Force," observed the painter John Sloan as he looked back over Whitney's patronage of visual artists. "The records have been destroyed, probably at Mrs. Whitney's request. But . . . I was one of innumerable artists whose studio rent was paid, or pictures purchased just at the right time to keep the wolf from the door, or hospital expenses covered, or a trip to Europe made possible." In music, her legacy has a similar conjunction of vagueness and timeliness.[9]

As a result, the importance of Whitney's music patronage could easily be obscured. Yet her assistance in launching the International Composers' Guild made her one of the earliest patrons to subsidize modern music in New York City. By extending the kind of support already being given visual artists to those who wrote music, Whitney's efforts in the late 1910s and early 1920s helped turn the attention of American patrons away from performance of European classics. A kind of venture capitalist for new music, she subsidized a key modernist and his institutional forum, betting that her investment would yield a more vital and imaginative creative environment.

Alma Morgenthau Wertheim (1887–1953) was only a decade younger than Gertrude Whitney, but those few years made her more a character of the twentieth century than the nineteenth. Assertive in her patronage of new music and personally active in shaping its institutions, she did not coolly write checks and retreat to the sidelines but rather threw herself energetically into the causes she supported. While Whitney's deepest connection had been to the visual arts and her direct participation in new music had been slight, Wertheim took a composer-focused approach. But then Wertheim's own creative life lay in music. She was an amateur singer who occasionally presented recitals and studied at some point with Lotte Lehmann. Both Wertheim and Whitney followed the same unwritten code, however, muting their identities in connection with the enterprises they sponsored.[10]

A child of Jewish financiers, Wertheim began her support for new music within Whitney's orbit, becoming one of several subsidiary patrons of the ICG. Her first husband, Maurice Wertheim, owned a Wall Street investment firm and was involved in a parallel philanthropic endeavor with the Theatre Guild, an early organization for the production of modern drama. He knew Claire Reis as early as the 1910s, and it was Reis with whom Alma Wertheim collaborated at the ICG. "Alma Morgenthau Wertheim was giving money generously to pay the back debts and to help establish this organization," Reis later recalled. In 1922, Wertheim also published an article in the *New York Times*, promoting the ICG's work. All this unraveled the next year, when Wertheim joined with Reis, Minna Lederman, and a small group of composers to form the League of Composers. By doing so, she left behind the subsidiary role she had played to Whitney at the ICG and stepped forward as principal underwriter of the new society. "For those first three or four years [of the League]," recalled Reis, "she met the gap between a wider public and the money we needed."[11]

Wertheim earnestly took up the League's mission, becoming a member of its board and playing a major role in launching it. Her contributions took many forms. When Lazare Saminsky's opera *The Gagliarda of a Merry Plague* was presented during the League's second season, "Alma Wertheim offered to lend her own personal furniture to set the stage, and she did," recalled Reis. In addition, "she would bring sandwiches to feed the rehearsal artists so that they would stay longer, and there wasn't a union rule at that point." Wertheim also subsidized the League's journal *Modern Music* for its first few years, contributing $1,500 annually to its publication costs; this was a substantial sum in the mid-1920s. There, too, she became personally involved, contributing what Reis described as "little 'Guatemala' drawings, . . . that she had on stones." During the first two years of the magazine's existence, her "drawings" appeared on the magazine's title page, decorating the borders and providing a central logo (Figure 12.1). During the next two years, only her logo was used, and with the sixth volume of the magazine (1928–29), her art work disappeared entirely. Wertheim received no credit in the magazine for either her financial support or artistic contribution.[12]

Wertheim's intense absorption in the League and its magazine came to a fiery conclusion. When her logo disappeared from *Modern Music*, so too did her name from the list of the League's Executive Board. She never turned up again in the magazine's pages. Decades later, Minna Lederman recalled Wertheim as "a very special figure in her own circle . . . with beautiful taste for decor, personal and otherwise, and a very hot, passionate temperament." Reis concurred, "She was very active, very dedicated and very generous. She was a temperamental person, and the final upshot with Alma was unfortunate, . . . because she had been really the one patron to give a large sum." That "upshot" occurred either late in the 1927–28

VOL. II   APRIL 1925   NO. 2

THE
LEAGUE *of* COMPOSERS'
REVIEW

IN THIS ISSUE

PUBLISHED BY THE LEAGUE OF COMPOSERS, INC.

FIFTY CENTS A COPY

Figure 12.1. Cover of *The League of Composers' Review* (April 1925), with a border design by Alma Wertheim. Soon after, the magazine was retitled *Modern Music*. Permission courtesy of the estate of Minna Lederman.

concert season or early in 1928–29, when Wertheim "demanded" for her patronage, as Reis recounted the story, "the right" to have her drawings published in the magazine. Lederman and Reis refused, and, according to Lederman, Wertheim "left the League and the magazine high and dry." There were other strains among them. "She did not like to have Minna and myself—the other two women," recalled Reis, "too active in suggestions which some of the rest of the board of composers would follow." As Wertheim strained not only to provide financial support but also to gain an occupation for herself, she felt that she was not being taken seriously. "Both Minna and I would bring in new ideas which the composers would think about carefully and very often accept," Reis recalled. "It was at that point that Alma differed—who was more of an amateur I think in her point of view musically than Minna and I were; . . . We both had a very professional point of view." There was no close-knit sisterhood within this female leadership but rather a strain that grew out of different generational and social expectations, clashing temperaments, and—perhaps—different intellectual thrusts. "The Alma Morgenthau chapter was very bloody," Reis's daughter Hilda told me. "My mother and Alma didn't get along at all."[13]

During these same years, Wertheim also subsidized a select group of American composers. Aaron Copland was a central recipient of her help and became a kind of hub around which her patronage spun. Ironically, considering that the modern-music movement focused on breaking decisively with the past, Copland's link to Wertheim began within the social conventions of old New York. In 1925 he made at least two pilgrimages to her Upper East Side apartment for tea. Both times he played some of his music, and as a result she handed him a check for $1,000. "I don't know how, without that, I would have managed in the year that followed while I was composing *Music for the Theatre*," Copland later recalled. Wertheim's patronage of him gives an exceptional view of how networks of support were formed. Not only was Copland being subsidized by Wertheim while he wrote this composition for chamber orchestra, but he had been paid a commission for the work from the League of Composers, the organization for which she labored so ardently. Wertheim also helped others. She presented Roy Harris with at least $1,800 so he could study with Nadia Boulanger (she may have done so for several consecutive years), and she provided smaller cash stipends to Israel Citkowitz, a young composer championed by Copland during the 1920s.[14]

Ultimately the most monumental component of Wertheim's patronage came with the founding of Cos Cob Press in 1929, which over the next nine years published thirty-five volumes of music by young Americans. A parallel venture to the *New Music Quarterly*, which had started up two years earlier, Wertheim's press took its name from the town of Cos Cob, Connecticut, where she owned a home, and it began after she had abandoned her tie to the League. A 1927 article in the *New York Times* shows that the League then had a plan "under consideration . . . for the publication of new music." This was never realized through the organization itself but instead became the singular mission of Alma Wertheim. When the press was launched, an unsigned article about it appeared in *Musical America*, which included a photograph of Wertheim together with her principal advisers, Copland, Gruenberg, and Whithorne (Figure 12.2). It boldly quoted her, "There is a growing conviction that American composition is becoming independent, authentic, and truly of this continent, and that American composers, particularly those who are writing music in the larger forms, find it difficult to have their works published and almost equally difficult to have them performed." A similar announcement also appeared in the *New York Times*. Cos Cob Press gained distinction as Copland's first major American publisher; by 1937, it had issued eight works by

Figure 12.2. Alma Wertheim, Louis Gruenberg, Aaron Copland, and Emerson Whithorne. Photograph from an article in *Musical America* announcing the founding of Cos Cob Press (25 February 1929). Courtesy of Musical America Archives.

him. Music by Marion Bauer, Carlos Chávez, Israel Citkowitz, Louis Gruenberg, Roy Harris, Charles Ives, Walter Piston, Roger Sessions, Virgil Thomson, and Emerson Whithorne formed the remaining bulk of the press's catalogue; for many composers, these scores represented their debut in print.[15]

When Wertheim incorporated Cos Cob Press on 23 January 1929, she was its sole stockholder, and she remained its only patron even though her assets declined after the stock market crash in October 1929. She divorced Maurice Wertheim that same year. With Cos Cob Press, Wertheim took on a function that had become familiar for women during the 1920s—especially in Paris, where they were publishing the work of young writers. For example, Nancy Cunard ran the Hours Press late in the decade and counted Samuel Beckett among her major literary discoveries, and Caresse Crosby started Black Sun Press with her husband Harry, managing it single-handedly after his death. In Wertheim's case, she became just as actively involved in her press as she had in the League of Composers. This time, however, she held more power, designing the cover used for the scores—vindicating her artistic ability after being rejected by *Modern Music*—and serving on the press's selection committee. In 1938, Cos Cob Press was subsumed by Arrow Music Press, a composer-initiated venture, and in 1956 both were bought out by Boosey and Hawkes.[16]

No matter how substantial Wertheim's contribution to the new-music movement, it has faded with the passage of time. In part this had to do with record-keeping and the social constriction against acknowledging financial contributions in print. The Morgenthau Archive at the Library of Congress contains materials mostly about male family members, especially Alma's father, the financier and ambassador Henry Morgenthau, and her brother, Henry Morgenthau Jr., who was secretary of the treasury under Franklin Roosevelt. Even though one of her daughters was the late historian Barbara Tuchman, few of her personal papers appear to have been saved. Most of the remaining documentation appears in archival collections for the League of Composers and Cos Cob Press. With the latter enterprise, she made herself far more visible publicly than had earlier been the case. At the same time, though, her name does not appear on any of the press's published scores—not even to acknowledge her cover design.[17]

Wertheim, then, assumed the roles of both patron and activist, combining the two in different proportions according to the setting in which she found herself. She made a major contribution to building a base for the avant-garde in New York, at the same time as her own role within the modernist movement was riddled with conflicts.

Blanche Wetherill Walton (1871–1963) was an altogether different kind of patron. While Whitney allied herself with Varèse and the International Composers' Guild and Wertheim focused on Copland and the League of Composers, Walton took on another corner of the new-music community, becoming a close friend of Henry Cowell and some of his ultra-modern comrades, including Ruth Crawford, Carl

Ruggles, and Charles Seeger. By no means as wealthy as Whitney or Wertheim, she gave modest cash stipends. Her biggest contribution came through offering room and board to composers and presiding over a kind of salon for modernists. In other words, she exploited the traditional female domain of the home as a way of fostering the American avant-garde, becoming a domestic impresario. "Keep on," enjoined Carl Ruggles in a 1928 letter to her, "and you will become such a power in musical circles that all we poor, damned composers will have to do is to take our scores and our troubles to you and everything will be 'velvet.'"[18]

Like Whitney and Wertheim, Walton took up her work as part of a search for personal satisfaction. Unlike them, she had professional potential as a musician. A gifted pianist who had studied with MacDowell, she was later described by Cowell as "a pianist of professional calibre in the days when a public career was unthinkable for a girl of good family." Instead, after losing her husband in a train accident in 1901 and raising two children on her own, she sought a new life in contemporary music, and her various residences in and around New York City— in Bronxville, at West 68th Street and Central Park West, and near Washington Square—became havens for experimentalists. She must have been inspired, at least in part, by the philanthropy of Edward De Coppet, for whom her husband had worked. De Coppet was a major music patron in New York early in the century,

Figure 12.3. Marion Walton Putnam and Blanche Walton in the early 1930s. Photograph in the collection of Marion Walton Putnam.

most noted for founding and supporting the Flonzaley Quartet, an ensemble holding the status of the Juilliard Quartet decades later. Like Whitney and Wertheim, Walton chose instead to reach out to counterculture artists. "The one contribution I could make to the gifted and struggling pioneer composer was to turn my apartment on Central Park West into a meeting place," Walton later recalled. "It was then a shabby elderly house which had a large corner room which proved to be excellent for a music room with Steinway piano. My rooms were comfortably apart which left other rooms for visiting composers, of whom Cowell was a frequent one."[19]

Walton was involved in the American modernist movement from the very beginning of the decade. A few remaining letters, housed within a small collection of her papers at the New York Public Library, suggest the dimensions of her efforts. She gave some money to the International Composers' Guild, but not major sums. "We appreciate so much the spirit in which [your gift] is given," acknowledged Varèse in 1924, "needing as we do moral support as much as financial, and we thank you heartily for both." More important, she helped support Cowell's New Music Society, when it was founded in California in 1925, as well as his *New Music Quarterly*, and Cowell, in turn, shaped her choice of composers to support. Walton met him through the singer Radiana Pazmor during a visit to California in the early 1920s. She gave Ruggles and Cowell a place to stay for long periods, and during the winter of 1929–30 the young Ruth Crawford lived with Walton while she began studying with Seeger. "How I wish I might have been with you if only to thank you for your great kindness to Miss Crawford," wrote Mrs. Edward MacDowell to Walton in December 1929, after declining Walton's invitation to a musicale she hosted at which Crawford's Suite No. 2 for Four Strings and Piano received its premiere. "I am sure of her talent," MacDowell declared supportively, "and you are doing a fine thing in helping her to live under such lovely conditions." Walton helped others, including Béla Bartók, who used her West 68th Street apartment as a base during his 1927 tour of the United States. She also hosted the first meeting of the American Musicological Society at her apartment in 1930. Cowell, Joseph Schillinger, Seeger, Joseph Yasser, and Otto Kinkeldey all attended.[20]

Walton produced at least two major events built around Aaron Copland, providing more evidence that dividing lines between composer-factions were not so rigidly in place during the 1920s. Sometime in 1929, she gave a musicale of his work, featuring the newly composed trio, *Vitebsk*. And she threw a large party after a Copland-Sessions concert—probably the one on 13 April 1930. This last was a remarkable event not only because of the considerable support it showed for Copland but also because of its exceptional documentation; a guest list survives that was sent by Copland to Walton, and it provides an unusual view of how the social events hosted by women helped composers build a power base. The Copland-Sessions program that evening had included new Hungarian works by Istvan Szelenyi, Pál Kadosa, and Imre Weisshaus, and the invited guests featured a number of Hungarians—the Hungarian Consul General, the violinist Leopold Auer, the violinist and composer Sandor Harmati. Walton was likely inspired to focus on this particular Copland-Sessions event by Cowell's connection to these young Hungarians. She also may have taken an interest in them through her association with Bartók. There was a small Polish contingent as well, in deference to a work by the Polish composer Jerzy Fitelberg that had been performed. The other invitees brought together New York's power structure in modern music. There was Claire Reis of the League of Composers (together with her husband Arthur), as well as cofounders Emerson Whithorne and Frederick Jacobi. (Interestingly, Copland, in his annotations on the list of names, felt the need to identify Jacobi to Walton as an "American composer," suggesting that she did not know him.) Also included were Arthur Judson and F. C. Coppicus, two of the most important concert managers of the day, and the British critic and composer Leigh Henry, as well as Robert Simon of the *New Yorker*. No frivolous bash, this party was intended to cement old alliances and forge new ones. Yet another perspective on Walton's social events appears in a letter she wrote to Ruth Crawford before a party given after a concert by the Pan American Association on 31 January 1931 (which included the premiere of Ives's *Three Places in New England*). "Don't I wish you could come!" Walton exclaimed to Crawford. "This will draw I hope all the best of the composers and musicians in N.Y. You know what my affairs are like so you can picture it—the crowd, the meeting of friends and rivals, the ice cream and the prohibition wine!"[21]

Walton's musical activities continued at least through the 1930s, but they dropped off sharply after 1929. "During the crash," recalled Marion Walton Putnam, "mother lost a great deal of money, and she had to give up the apartment on 68th Street."[22]

Because Walton did not take on huge financial responsibilities with new music, as Whitney and Wertheim were doing, or step forward as an outspoken activist, as was the case with Wertheim and Reis, her legacy is more difficult to assess. Measured against today's standards of feminine achievement, her work could easily be devalued because of its domestic nature. Yet by providing lodging to struggling young composers and by hosting musicales, as well as after-concert parties, she formed a kind of private club in New York for radical thinkers who shuttled in from elsewhere. In the process, she became "one of the most important and best beloved sponsors that modern music has had here," wrote Cowell in 1959 in conjunction with a concert given in her honor. "Much of the activity of composers of modern music was centered in her home," he continued, "and we owe to her hospitality an early focusing of modern musical thought in New York. She created a stimulating atmosphere where nothing but generosity toward divergent ideas was possible." That "generosity" provided a small group of composers an opportunity to gain a hearing in the American capital of new music.[23]

As patrons, then, Whitney, Wertheim, and Walton helped build a foundation upon which modern music could get established in New York. Yet no matter how critical their role, it fit into a well-established hierarchy based on gender and occupation, making these women patrons subsidiary to the mostly male composers they assisted. An important part of a patron's role was to stay modestly in the background, nurturing and assisting but being cautious about the amount of attention she drew to her own contribution. Louise Varèse called Gertrude Whitney "self-effacing," and the same adjective could be applied in varying degrees to all three. A woman's place as patron was to be selfless as well as generous. Her creative energy went into discovering and encouraging others, not into highlighting her own contribution.[24]

A far different profile, however, characterized Claire Raphael Reis (1888–1978), perhaps the single most indispensable woman to modernist musicians in New York. Outspoken and highly visible, she served first as executive director of the International Composers' Guild and later assumed the same capacity with the League of Composers. Her "luminous, nourishing energy," as the writer Waldo Frank once characterized it, became legendary, and her administrative talent made it possible for modernist composers to form an institutional base in the city.[25]

Diverse ideologies converged to inspire Reis. Ironically, given modern music's elite audience, she approached her task with the tools and ideals of a settlement-house volunteer. If Gertrude Whitney embodied the high-society ambivalence of a Henry James character, Claire Reis reflected the social mission of Jane Addams or Lillian Wald. A consummate organizer, she had deep roots in two important feminized spheres—social service and the woman's club—and she embraced the goals of social feminism: to promote reform through vigorous action. While her female contemporaries labored for the rights of children, new immigrants, and the poor, Reis took on another of society's underdogs: the composer. She shared progressive roots and an intense commitment to activism with Katherine Dreier, the driving force behind New York's Société Anonyme.[26]

Reis's career also reveals much about early musical modernism in New York—especially the years between 1910 and 1920. Like Blanche Walton, Reis was a gifted pianist inhibited from becoming a professional by the conventions of her time and class. While Reis later claimed that her teachers had encouraged a concert career, "playing for charity was my mother's idea of bringing up a musical daughter." And musical charity became her principal pursuit. Born in Brownsville, Texas, to a Jewish family, Reis moved to New York with her mother, sister, and brother shortly after her father's death in 1898. And there she happened upon modernism while both she and it were young, especially through piano studies with Bertha Fiering Tapper at the New York Institute of Musical Art (now The Juilliard School); this was the same Tapper who taught Ornstein. Reis later recalled bringing the writer Waldo Frank and the critic Paul Rosenfeld, both good friends of hers, to hear Ornstein play at one of Tapper's Saturday-afternoon musicales. Ornstein not only performed his own new works but also presented the latest compositions of Schoenberg, Satie, Stravinsky, and others. Frank vividly recounted one of Tapper's afternoons, which probably took place in 1914:

Figure 12.4. Claire Reis and her husband Arthur Reis in the 1910s. Photograph courtesy of Hilda Reis Bijur.

The long room [in Tapper's home on Riverside Drive] with a façade of windows giving on the Hudson was astir like a convention of birds with the elegant gentlemen and ladies perched on their camp stools. . . . [After Ornstein played some Debussy, Ravel, and Albéniz], Mrs. Tapper stood up and announced to her guests that Leo would now play some of his own music. Leo responded with a voluminous, cacophonous broadside of chords that seemed about to blow the instrument in the air and break the windows. Chaos spoke. Ladies laughed hysterically. The music growled like a beast, clanged like metal on metal, smouldered before it burst again, and suddenly subsided. Leo drooped over the keys, like a spent male after coitus, his head down as if he were praying. . . . Claire and I shouldered through the throng to the piano which might have been a guillotine. I noted that there was blood on the keys. . . . I loved the music.

The scene described so extravagantly by Frank abounds with jolting juxtapositions. Here was an "elegant" audience, seeming like the epitome of old New York, taking in modernist experimentations. And here was an event adventuresomely produced by a woman, yet "ladies" were the portion of the audience depicted as incapable of handling the music's newness. By contrast, Ornstein was empowered with the ultimate image of male prowess.[27]

Reis capitalized vigorously on this and other such events. Coming in contact with Ornstein "was really the beginning, the ear opening, if not the eye opener for me," she later acknowledged. In the spring of 1916, eight months after Tapper's death, Reis took up her teacher's mission, presenting Ornstein in a series of "Four Informal Recitals" at her home on Madison Avenue. Those concerts were an important harbinger of the 1920s, as much for giving new direction to Reis's work in music as for laying crucial groundwork for the composer societies that would make modern music flourish in New York. Rosenfeld had proposed the concerts in letters to Reis, viewing them not only as a way of promoting Ornstein but also as a means of "giving a comprehensive course in modern piano music." As he continued, a vision of Reis's future unfolded:

> The point is, that in the back of my mind there is a desire to help organize a modern music club, . . . and I wonder whether an audience gotten together for Leo's recital couldn't help form a nucleus for such a society? There's really a crying need for such an organization to make headway against the sluggish conservatism in musical circles. . . . You remember speaking of a similar matter, don't you, during our talks last spring?

Although no such organization materialized immediately, Rosenfeld's letter shows that the idea for the International Composers' Guild and the League of Composers was germinating in the mid-1910s, several years before either organization came into existence.[28]

Reis made other early alliances that helped in her later work with the ICG and the League. One of these was with Irene Schwarcz, a fine pianist and fellow student (with Reis) of Tapper who married Frederick Jacobi. Schwarcz's name appears on recital programs with Reis as early as 1908 (Ornstein and Katherine (Kay) Swift, the composer for musical theater, also took part in those same events). During the 1920s, Schwarcz became a frequent performer on modern-music concerts, and her husband joined with Reis in founding the League of Composers. Another of Reis's early friendships was with the composer Louis Gruenberg, who of course joined her among the League's founders. The two met in Germany around 1904, when Reis was studying there.

During these years of piano study and growing contact with modernist musicians, Reis was working to help the poor. In 1911, she fulfilled her mother's commitment to musical charity by establishing the People's Music League, an organization that presented some two hundred free concerts each year for newly arrived immigrants. The concerts were given in New York schools. It was an extension of the settlement house—of places such as Henry Street Settlement House in

New York or Hull House in Chicago where struggling newcomers to America could obtain educational and social services. Reis's involvement in the enterprise came about through the aegis of Maurice Wertheim, husband of Alma Morgenthau, who gave her a letter of introduction to Frederic Howe of the People's Institute. Wertheim's wife Alma in turn became a member of the advisory council of the People's Music League. For Reis, this was her "first satisfying experience combining music and social service in a civic project . . . [It] stirred great sympathy [for] people poor and hungry for music." The concerts included standard European concert repertory, together with European folksongs and a few American compositions. One event featured works by Dudley Buck and Will Marion Cook, and performers for other concerts included Greta Torpadie and Eva Gauthier. Bands and orchestras made up of workers also appeared, including an ensemble from the Cloak Makers' Union.[29]

For the tenth anniversary of the People's Music League, Reis tried something new: a concert of contemporary music, which included works by Rebecca Clarke, Gruenberg, Jacobi, A. Walter Kramer, Lazare Saminsky, and Deems Taylor, some of whom would become prominent in the League of Composers. It took place at Cooper Union, just a few blocks south of Union Square, on 12 February 1922. For Reis, it was a pivotal event. "My reputation with the Cooper Union Composers' concert," she later recalled, "led me into the next phase of music—this time with a feeling of service to *composers.* . . . My sympathy for the masses and for music seemed to begin a new chapter; *sympathy for the composers.* I had not lost sight of the masses entirely, but they were now transformed into the concert-going public, and for them the goal I quickly realised involved EDUCATION."[30]

This, in turn, led to the next stage of Reis's career. That fall, after the People's Music League had ended, Reis became executive director of the International Composers' Guild. Her success with the composers' concert at Cooper Union made her a desirable candidate, and according to Louise Varèse, Reis was proposed for the ICG post—an unpaid one—by her old friend Louis Gruenberg. It was a productive but unhappy appointment. She was the one who moved concerts uptown to the Klaw Theater, which she obtained from a family friend at low rent; she added to the board Alma Wertheim and the art dealer Stephan Bourgeois, well known for his exhibits of modernist painting; she brought the ICG out of debt; and she organized the mundane details involved in producing events—all "the folding, stuffing, licking, stamping, and the meetings," as Louise Varèse put it. Just as significantly, in a city where space was at a premium—especially in the borough of Manhattan—she made her apartment available for ICG business. Nineteen rehearsals of *Pierrot lunaire,* for example, took place in her living room before the famous 1923 American premiere.[31]

Yet, according to Louise Varèse, Reis "took over" the Guild, and her husband disdained the after-concert receptions that Reis hosted as "those delicatessen parties." In part, he might have been resisting an assertive female, at the same time as his language had an edge of anti-Semitism. Most of those who defected from the ICG to form the League were Jewish: Jacobi, Gruenberg, Lederman, Reis, and Wertheim. The bigotry of at least one ICG member, Carl Ruggles, was well known at the time, and it continued over the course of his life. "I agree with *Adolph* [Weiss] and [Carlos] *Salzedo*," Ruggles wrote to Henry Cowell, "that it is a great mistake to have that filthy bunch of Juilliard Jews in the Pan American [Association]." Cowell too was known to single out ethnicity, albeit with much less inflamed language. "How you will shine among the Jews!" he wrote to Ruggles in 1931, just days after Ansermet had conducted an ISCM concert in Berlin that included Copland's *First Symphony*, Gruenberg's *Jazz Suite*, and Ruggles's *Portals*. Over the years, the League continued to be the target of anti-Semitism. Virgil Thomson, to cite a particularly well-known example, called the group the "League of Jewish Composers," venting his irritation that the League did not sponsor a performance of his work until February 1933; he felt ignored by its leaders in the 1920s, and he never let go of a feeling of exclusion.[32]

Yet none of this was so clear-cut. Reis vehemently denied that anti-Semitism had played any role in the split between the Guild and the League. When asked directly about this by Vivian Perlis during the 1970s, Reis firmly replied, "No, I definitely don't think there was any anti-Semitism at all. Salzedo was a Jew, Varèse's best friend." Yet when I later told Minna Lederman about Reis's statement, she was shocked to discover that Salzedo was Jewish and recalled him as an anti-Semite.[33]

Reis's account of the schism focused on two points: the "great disorder" of the Guild's board meetings and the degree to which some members of the organization took pride in obscurity: "People like Ruggles would loudly voice their opinions. His was: If more than a dozen people [were] in [the] hall they were catering to the public." While Ruggles and other modernists believed that broad audience appeal threatened artistic corruption, Reis had a more populist perspective. In 1923, she published an article in the Guild's unofficial journal, *Eolian Review*, in which she argued that the audience for new music might develop not from the "so-called musically educated class," as she put it, but from those less committed to the European classics. It was a radical idea. "'The man on the street,' as signified by the average person without esthetic standards which belong to the past," Reis continued, "this man can hear, can see, can sense an art belonging to his age because it is part of his life, because he has not been educated to accept *definite laws based upon tradition*." In other words, modernist composers might circumvent audiences of the Philharmonic or the Metropolitan Opera, instead reaching out to the unprejudiced masses whose horizons were not limited to "the canon," as we have come to call it. Reis never spelled out who would make up this new constituency, but it seems likely she had in mind the same working-class audience that had participated in the People's Music League. She was applying social feminism to contemporary composition.[34]

Reis's article was greeted with charges hurled at other social feminists of the day. Jerome Hart, a conservative music critic, wrote that her theory gave evidence of the depths to which supporters of modernist music had plunged. "Of course, this is but a phase of present-day unrest and revolutionism, which finds its extreme expression in Bolshevism," Hart wrote, "under which anarchists are elevated into prime ministers, incendiaries and criminals into judges, and all the rules of decent and orderly living are thrown into the discard. It is but a passing phase, in which ugliness, both moral and physical, boldly asserts itself." Hart published this not long after the Red Scare of 1919–20, when the epithet "Bolshevist" had been hurled at many espousing new ideas. This backlash hit social feminists especially hard. The pioneering Sheppard-Towner Maternity and Infancy Protection Act of 1921, for which women had campaigned vigorously, was dubbed "Bolshevist" by its opponents, and four years later such name-calling defeated an anti-child-labor initiative in Congress. By viewing both the music that Reis supported and the audience she anticipated as subversive, Hart echoed the posture of the composer and critic Daniel Gregory Mason, a professor of music at Columbia University and notorious reactionary who spoke out against both modernism and jazz. At the same time, Hart foreshadowed charges that composers, especially those involved in any way with folksong, faced decades later during the McCarthy hearings.[35]

Thus Reis's work in social service prepared her for activism in new music. As leader of the group that seceded from the ICG to form the League of Composers, she became executive director of the new organization, a successor in name as well as spirit to the People's Music League. Reis conceived the organization in a democratic spirit, in direct opposition to the governing structure of the ICG, where she was among those who felt Varèse had been a "dictator," and she followed the model of other leagues that were being founded in the late 1910s and early 1920s. Some, such as the National League of Women Voters and the Women's International League for Peace and Freedom, were inspired by women activists (the second of these had Jane Addams as its president). Another, the League of Nations, obviously had a broader base.[36]

From the outset Reis mobilized the composers' league. She organized its concerts, staged publicity campaigns, negotiated with conductors and performers, hosted social functions, raised money, provided office space in her home, and made her car and chauffeur available for conducting business. Directing the League became the equivalent of a full-time job, though her position was never salaried. Copland later characterized her as "a pro" whose "day was as highly organized as that of any modern career woman," and his words provide an important clue to the context in which she should be viewed. By no means a radical feminist, Reis fit into a particular breed of "modern" woman. Proud to have marched with the suffragists—or so her daughter, Hilda Bijur, recalled—she embraced a feminist ideal that combined activism with a Victorian sense of womanly duty. As one historian has observed, social feminists did not campaign for suffrage to advance themselves but rather "to win the power to clean up America. Social feminism was serviceable and safe." Reis later acknowledged her model to be one of social feminism's great architects, Jane Addams, who advocated combining home and family with public service. Addams also supported volunteerism for women, and

Reis later articulated the same philosophy: "In those days if a girl did not need to earn money, neither Jane Addams nor Lillian Wald—both very modern, liberal women—[did. They] were adamant that girls should not work for money." To Reis and others of her generation, social service was modern, and volunteering provided an acceptable way of accomplishing it.[37]

Also striking was Reis's connection to the Auxiliary of the New York Philharmonic and to the Women's City Club of New York, begun in 1916 by a group of suffragists. Both presented her with well-tested models for running organizations and raising money. In the early twentieth century, the women's club movement was widespread, providing the principal means for women to become active outside the home. More immediately germane to the story here, however, was the Philharmonic's Auxiliary, which was founded during the 1921–22 concert season, though its roots reached back at least to 1909. Reis had joined during its second season. "I never felt that I was needed [by the Philharmonic]," she later averred. "But I did feel I was needed in the League, and therefore I had a greater sense of wanting to do what I could." Nonetheless, when she formed her own auxiliary within the League in 1927, she modeled it directly on what she had observed at the Philharmonic. She approached this new board cunningly, aware that its members expected the same cultural cachet from the League as they were gaining through the Philharmonic, and she used their money solely to finance the League's elaborate stage productions, as well as to support appearances on its programs by world-renowned conductors. Each of the thirty-five or so members of the League's auxiliary—the majority of whom were female—gave small gifts of approximately one or two hundred dollars, and some were recruited from the Philharmonic, notably the Countess Mercati, who had also served on the executive committee for Varèse's New Symphony Orchestra, and Mrs. Charles (Minnie) Guggenheimer, who not only helped Varèse's orchestra but also founded the famous Lewisohn Stadium Concerts in 1918, an inexpensive and popular summer series by the Philharmonic that she directed for some fifty years.[38]

On one occasion Reis tried to stretch the auxiliary's musical taste by asking its members to contribute to a composers' fund, which would commission new American works, and she met flat refusal: "We were keenly disappointed when not a single response came from any of the hundred-odd 'pillars of art,' although they had gladly spent $250 for a box from which to see and be seen for one evening. . . . They seemed little aware of the composer as a fellow human being."[39]

Others recognized that the role of the League's auxiliary was carefully circumscribed, and its members often faced scorn as a result. Minna Lederman recalled that the women of the auxiliary were referred to disdainfully as "the ladies." "I don't think," she went on, "they gave money except when there was an opera coming on. . . . They did so then because of the glamour of the conductor." Analogous groups confronted the same attitude. Louise Varèse, for example, recalled somewhat disparagingly that Varèse's New Symphony Orchestra had a "large Ladies' Committee" that did "whatever ladies' committees do."[40]

Among Reis's many other achievements during this period, a final item deserves attention: her publication in 1930 of *American Composers of Today*, the first catalog of music by living American composers. While the compilation of bibliographies and work lists has become commonplace, in 1930, for the generation of American composers that was just gaining visibility, such a source was unique. It served as an invaluable means of giving conductors, performers, publishers, and critics a sense of existing contemporary literature, and it made access to these works possible. Two years later Reis produced a revision of the catalogue with two-and-a-half times as many entries (expanding from 55 names to 135). Subsequent editions appeared in 1938 and 1947. She went on to become one of the founders of the New York City Center and the Hunter College Opera Workshop, among other endeavors.[41]

Change often produces a backlash, and such was certainly the case with the involvement of women in new music during the 1920s. While female leaders of composer organizations may have disparaged the social pretensions of "the ladies" on their auxiliary boards, they too became targets of gendered stereotypes. Collectively, these women represented rapid social and cultural change, and they highlighted the dependency of composers on a fragile but complex modernist community. At the same time as a new American art was being born, the struggle of the "New Woman" continued to unfold. She threatened cherished traditions, especially in the first decade after the Nineteenth Amendment (ratified in 1920), when women had gained the right to vote. As Minna Lederman put it, "We thought we could do anything." Some composers expressed gratitude for all the good work and hard cash they received. Copland and Cowell, most notably, acknowledged their debt to Reis and Walton. Others all but demonized their benefactors. Music critics tended to launch the most generalized attacks, targeting women as a group rather than singling out individuals.[42]

The decade opened with a categorical indictment of women patrons, penned by no less than the critic Paul Rosenfeld—the same man who was a close friend of Claire Reis and who, at least aesthetically, was one of the most progressive voices in American modernism. In a 1920 article for the *Dial*, written to mark the end of Varèse's tenure with the New Symphony Orchestra, Rosenfeld analyzed the orchestra's failure to succeed in performing contemporary music as "one of the innumerable consequences of the fact that in America musical organizations have patronesses more often than they have patrons. Great musical bodies cannot exist in America today, it is a commonplace, without subsidies," he continued. (This, recall, was the group subsidized primarily by Gertrude Whitney.) "But in our civilization," Rosenfeld went on, "the man is not interested in art. . . . The control of the purer forms of music are almost entirely left to the distaff side. . . . But, unfortunately, the control by women of art is not the health of art. . . . In consequence, artistic activity remains, for the majority of those who engage in it, a lightly social expression." According to Rosenfeld's reasoning, women contaminated the very art that they nurtured. They made it "lightly social" rather than heavily intellectual, and by extension they kept American music-making a dilettante's delectation rather than a world-class professional enterprise. His rationale left the male conductor of that orchestra completely unaccountable for its failure.[43]

Rosenfeld's critique recalled—albeit inadvertently—the "Introduction" to Willa Cather's *My Ántonia*, published two years earlier, where Cather described a chance encounter with a man from her hometown, while both were on a train crossing Iowa. She claimed that his story about Ántonia inspired her book. Then she mused a bit about her male friend—Jim Burden—and his wife, whom Cather said she did "not like." "She is handsome, energetic, executive," Cather went on, "but to me she seems unimpressionable and temperamentally incapable of enthusiasm." Cather disparaged the woman as finding it "worth while to play the patroness to a group of young poets and painters of advanced ideas and mediocre ability."[44]

Other damning pronouncements about women appeared throughout the 1920s. One of the most widely read must have been that of Deems Taylor, who contributed an essay on music to *Civilization in the United States* (1922), edited by Harold Stearns, which was an important contemporaneous assessment of American culture. In it, Taylor featured women as first-string players in American music and blamed them for much of its limitations. "Women," wrote Taylor, "constitute ninety per cent of those who support music in this country. . . . It is no disparagement of their activities to say that such a state of affairs is unhealthy." Rather than criticizing women for being lightweight, as Rosenfeld had done, Taylor disdained them for encouraging chauvinism among American composers, claiming that "the feminine influence helps to increase the insularity of our musicians." He also stated that women "must assume responsibility for our excessive cult of the performer."[45]

In 1928, a year after Varèse's International Composers' Guild had come to an end, Rosenfeld weighed in again about the position of women in modern music. His biases remained intact. By setting up straw women, he illustrated the kind of rhetoric that was being used to divide the ICG and the League. This was not the men against the boys, but the men against the women. In an article titled "Thanks to the International Guild," Rosenfeld hailed the group for its achievements and drew a gendered comparison to the League, which he claimed had "a social function where the performance of music served the ambitions of mediocrities; handsomely dressed people conversed up and down the aisles; and music preluded to an apotheosis of personal projections and chicken salad in close quarters." Women are indicted here by implication. But the impression of the League as socially upscale—or "lightly social," to recall Rosenfeld's earlier formulation—was not new. Gendered rhetoric—whether direct or implied—had become a means of characterizing the League as less adventuresome than the ICG. In an unsigned review from 1926 in the *Christian Science Monitor*, to provide another example, the League was characterized as entertaining "a rather good-humored, even indulgent, notion of its responsibilities to the public" and with offering programs that favored "music which is fanciful and entertaining, rather than that which is intellectual and uncompromising." Although women took no direct hit here, their leadership of the League unleashed a particular kind of disdain, which turned up whether or not gender was invoked directly. As late as 1981, the composer Jerome Moross dismissed the League as not being "a dues paying organization, but . . . a pet project of two rich ladies who were constantly struggling over the leadership."[46]

While the League suffered scorn as a result of its female directors, critics connected women to the new-music movement in an even broader sense, questioning whether those on the "distaff side" were capable of intellectual engagement with the bold new sounds they fostered. Satire became a frequent weapon. In 1926, the critic W. J. Henderson published an article in the *New Yorker*, titled "The Modern Music Jag," in which he sarcastically pointed out that women were giving up the Charleston for another fad: new music. Three years later, *Vanity Fair* published a caricature by the famed artist Miguel Covarrubias captioned "A Salon Recital of Modern Music: One of Those Awesomely Elegant Evenings Which Society Has to Suffer," which ridiculed the wealthy women who presented musicales of new compositions (Figure 12.5). Granted, the assembled audience featured women *and* men of affluence, but the caption initially singled out "Mrs. Bartow Blodgett, the monumental matron at left-center," who had presented "the entertainment" pictured. "Her mother, Mrs. Holzderber," is immediately to the right; she "is resting easily on her pearl dog-collar." A wealthy social class is under scrutiny here, but women are used to highlight its absurdities. Even in the socially conscious 1930s when Marc Blitzstein composed *The Cradle Will Rock*, a leftist-inspired musical-theater work for which he wrote both text and music, he depicted a painter and composer who mocked their patron as "a stupid woman . . . what she doesn't know about music would put Heifetz back on his feet again." Blitzstein at least exposed the hypocrisy of creative artists by having his two characters turn about and eagerly accept an invitation to visit their patron's country home for the weekend. But he drew on a well-established cultural stereotype to make his point.[47]

There were many sources for this gendered rhetoric. By the early twentieth century, the extended realm of concert music in America had come to be seen as a feminized sphere, as the issues extending from Ruggles and spirituality have already shown. As hostesses of the parlor, as supporters of the opera and symphony, as teachers, and as vigorous local activists through music clubs, women had gained sovereignty over certain aspects of music making in the United States. They had come to be closely identified with "classical" music, provoking a strong reaction. For one thing, this gave music a disturbing whiff of effeminacy, leading some male musicians to a "manliness complex," as a 1924 editorial in *Musical America* put it. This had as much to do with the sexual identity of men, of course, as it did with their attitude toward females. "It was true as a general thing that a certain type of man, who did not look physically very strong, almost always went in for the arts," mused the character Bruce Dudley in Sherwood Anderson's novel *Dark Laughter* of 1925. "When a fellow like himself went out with his wife among the so-called artists, went

Figure 12.5. Miguel Covarrubias, "A Salon Recital of Modern Music: One of Those Awesomely Elegant Evenings Which Society Has to Suffer—Seen by Covarrubias," as published in *Vanity Fair* (February 1929). The caption reads as follows: "In the forefront of mondaine [*sic*] musical circles is M. Pierre Paravent, the most recently imported Parisian pianist. Not to have heard Paravent is to be completely out of the present season. He has therefore been rented for the evening by Mrs. Bartow Blodgett, the monumental matron at left-center, for the entertainment of a number of tremendously important people. This he is endeavouring to do by rendering a program of his own compositions, in which he specializes. This is no stuff for weaklings and the auditors are taking it according to their several capabilities. The hostess is flanked by her daughter who is entranced by both the piece and the performer, and by her mother, Mrs. Holzderber, who is resting easily on her pearl dog-collar. In the center row, from left to right, are Horace Bankhead, critic, Lady Cragsmoor and lorgnette, Mrs. Dapper, wearing her famous *Mona Lisa* smile, and the young Camberwells who are plotting an escape. In the background two low-browed husbands are talking about the stock market while the host, at right, ponders grimly on the cost of all this noise Paravent produces." Permission courtesy of Maria Elena Rico Covarrubias.

into a room where a lot of them had congregated, he so often got an impression, not of masculine strength and virility, but of something on the whole feminine." This reinforces my earlier point that women did not present the only threat to "manliness"; modernism's many homosexual composers also were targeted. Individual professional frustrations were easily vented at the expense of whole classes of musicians. "I know I am in a perpetual stew and rage over my inability to transfer my feelings and impressions to paper," lamented Louis Gruenberg decades later to Claire Reis. His concern? American music, as he saw it, was in a "sad state . . . since the politicians and homosexuals are dominating it."[48]

On the female side of this equation, women not only became identified with classical music, but they were associated with the practices of a bygone era—with the Genteel Tradition of the late nineteenth century—at the same time as they were perceived as agents of "conspicuous consumption," to use the famous phrase of Thorstein Veblen. Thus women became easy targets in the complex tangle of antitradition and anticommercialism that were fundamental to the modernist movement. Increasingly, consonant music—especially the pretty sort representing long-standing European traditions—was linked with women or effeminacy, while dissonance was quickly labeled "manly" or "virile." These last could be terms of approbation, as Ruggles's case made clear. Other instances abounded. "But there is a pretty high average in ideas and workmanship, and an especially high one in virility," responded a critic to one of the Copland-Sessions concerts. But gendered labels could also become a critical weapon, especially in branding older composers whose music was not perched on the cutting edge. "Perhaps its chief lack," wrote a critic about John Alden Carpenter's *Skyscrapers*, "was that of virile masculinity in the Coney Island scene." "Loeffler is one of those exquisites whose refinement is unfortunately accompanied by sterility, perhaps even results from it," observed Paul Rosenfeld about Charles Martin Loeffler. "His art is indeed, in . . . the dangerous vicinity of those amiable gentlemen, the Chadwicks and the Converses and all the other highly respectable and sterile 'American composers.'" This recalls, once again, the gendered outbursts of Charles Ives.[49]

"It is indeed striking," writes the cultural critic Andreas Huyssen, "to observe how the political, psychological, and aesthetic discourse around the turn of the century consistently and obsessively genders mass culture and the masses as feminine, while high culture, whether traditional or modern, clearly remains the privileged realm of male activities." Male apprehension about "the 'wrong' kind of success," meaning commodification, went hand-in-hand with "the persistent gendering as feminine of that which is devalued." Male modernists exemplified this paradigm. They constructed an image of aesthetic autonomy, and they needed to separate themselves out not only from the commercial world of popular music but also from the mainstream success of those who were marketing European classics to the masses. At the same time, though, the ICG and the League—the havens for modernists within the dominant musical culture—both bought into these mainstream values when they hired illustrious conductors, such as Stokowski,

Koussevitzky, or Fritz Reiner, and when they moved their events out of low-rent venues and into the most prized concert spaces of the day. Since women were in the position not only of financing these upscale ventures but also of producing and promoting them—probably even of conceiving the idea of aspiring to them—they were disdained for the very success they facilitated. Male modernists often seemed to want it both ways—to maintain their aesthetic elitism and achieve widespread acclaim. Women patrons and administrators became convenient scapegoats for their ambivalence.[50]

Other issues existed as well. Just as gender dichotomies frequently overlapped with distinctions between new and old, between appealing to the elite and the masses, so they did in the growing tension between "high" and "low." Popular music, when criticized in the insider's lingo of modernist composers, was often gendered as female. "Yes, we want our musical tastes to be governed by the young sophisticates rather than by Mrs. Carrie Jacobs Bond," wrote the composer and conductor Nicolas Slonimsky in 1929, providing a prime illustration of how this process worked (Bond was a turn-of-the-century composer of popular songs, most notably *I Love You Truly*). Slonimsky could just as easily have conjured up Paul Dresser or Charles K. Harris, but Bond exemplified far more vividly the saccharine, commercially tainted art form that the modernists disdained. Several years earlier, George Antheil made the same connection when he attacked popular songs of earlier generations. "I pride myself with the fact that most of the themes are not original," he wrote a friend in 1925 about the tunes he had quoted in his Second Sonata for Violin, Piano, and Bass-Drums. He then continued with an obscene and gendered slur as a way of distancing himself from the material he borrowed: "'In the shade of the Old Apple Tree,' 'Hochee chooche' [*sic*], 'Darling, you are growing older,' and all the most vomiting, repulsive material possible. This sonata is like Joyce, and like spew . . . nevertheless it is electrical. For the first time in the history of the concert stage, the world is allowed to gaze raptuously [*sic*] into an open cunt." In other words, Antheil did not quote these tunes out of sentimental attachment but as a way of making a political statement about the degradation that he imagined himself to be exposing. Although he specialized in this sort of modernist machismo, he felt free to indulge in obscenities because he was writing privately to a male buddy.[51]

By now it should be clear that Antheil and some of his contemporaries were lashing out at the very hands that supported them. Consistently, it was only the male perspective on this gender struggle that gained a forum. How did the women who were playing such a crucial role in American modernism react to these tirades? On at least one occasion, Antheil's patron Mary Louise Curtis Bok took him to task for his chest-puffing rhetoric. "To be virile in Art," she wrote in a letter of 1930, "one does not necessarily have to exceed the bounds of good taste." She launched no defense of herself or of women in general, nor did she attack the composers and critics who were making her and her ilk the target of all that they believed had gone wrong with American musical culture. Beyond that, I have found little record of women's response. Reis saved W. J. Henderson's satiric essay from the *New Yorker* as part of her papers, but she did so without comment.[52]

Perhaps the attitude of Minna Lederman, whom I knew well for the final fifteen years of her life, provides a revealing example. Although a tough professional, cunning political strategist, and brilliant editor, she never questioned the degree to which she helped build a modernist world that was largely male, and she saw criticisms of wealthy female patrons, the League's Auxiliary Board, or even Claire Reis as being directed at another species. She called Alma Wertheim "silly," for example. In many ways, Lederman viewed herself as one of the guys, and her sense of being exceptional may have been more common than we now imagine. Some, perhaps most, of the women attacked by composers and critics may have believed that the bigotry they witnessed was directed at someone else. Seeing themselves as strong intellectuals and gifted administrators, not as representatives of ugly stereotypes, they may have positioned themselves high above the gendered invective that surrounded them. Whatever their reaction, they had no forum for public rebuttal.[53]

Women patrons and activists, in short, came to symbolize far more than the sum of their monetary contributions or number of hours volunteered, and they were easy targets for the frustrations of modernists and their critics. Social discourse at the time permitted gendered bigotry. At the very least, though, this rhetoric exemplifies just how deeply women had become embedded in the institutional foundations upon which American modernism was being built. Women provided abundant opportunities for a whole generation of talented young composers to rise tall and strong, and they put in place blueprints for practical success that continued to serve composers throughout the course of the twentieth century.

New World Neoclassicism

13

Neoclassicism

"Orthodox Europeanism" or Empowering Internationalism?

Back to Principles!—not to classical forms.
Back to the Nature of Sound!—not to tonalities.
We must STUDY, not European theories about music, but
MUSIC in a permanent, changeless, universal sense.

—Dane Rudhyar, 1927

Labels in art are popular, easy to make, equally confusing,
and usually wrong somewhere.

—Charles Ives

Artists and intellectuals chronically avoid being aligned with "isms," and the stylistic designation "neoclassicism" met with especially strong resistance from young American composers during the 1920s. Although slippery to define, neoclassicism popped up all across the Western modernist spectrum, often encompassing stylistic principles of "clarity" and "simplicity" and a broad range of attempts in art, music, and literature to re-imagine materials from the past. Neoclassicism could be arch or sober, overt or subtle. Whatever its profile, as a loosely defined aesthetic it affected a significant body of American works written late in the decade. These included compositions by Aaron Copland, Virgil Thomson, Roy Harris, Roger Sessions, Carlos Chávez, Walter Piston, and other newcomers to the scene. The impact of neoclassicism on American composition did not end with the crash of 1929, however. In the politically charged climate of the 1930s, styles shaped within the aesthetic became the basis for some of these same composers to devise works with a nationalist message; at the same time, neoclassicism was viewed as a decadent symbol of modernism's elitist impulses, becoming a target for polemics decrying "art for art's sake." Well beyond World War II, it continued to define a rich strain in American composition.[1]

Composers associated with neoclassicism, though, have gained little strength from their numbers. Copland is the one among them who has enjoyed consistent success in the concert hall, but it is a success often regarded with suspicion because of the widespread popularity accompanying it. Recordings made at the close of the twentieth century by conductors such as Gerard Schwarz and Leonard Slatkin raised the visibility of other Americans connected to neoclassicism, whether Harris, Piston, or figures of a later generation such as David Diamond and William Schuman. Yet on the whole these composers have occupied a second rank in the elusive realm of historiographic respect. Often they are perceived by historians and critics as more traditional—even "academic" or "Europeanized," to recall that formulation—and they have been overshadowed by Ives, Ruggles, Cage, and others lionized as indigenous mavericks.

Consider the conjunctions that defined neoclassicism in the New World. Looked at positively, its international underpinning made neoclassicism a handy tool for Americans aiming to find parity with their transatlantic peers. Here was an aesthetic that consciously defied geographic borders, zealously embracing such goals as objectivity, coolness, and dispassion. Like the "International Style" that coalesced in architecture beginning in the early 1920s, led by Le Corbusier, Gropius, Mies van der Rohe, and Philip Johnson, neoclassicism sought a postwar neutrality, positing a style that followed certain abstract principles and was practiced with individual manifestations around the Western world.[2]

Aaron Copland, the energetic leader among Americans drawn to neoclassicism, emphasized this international inclination in an article about his teacher, Nadia Boulanger, who in turn has been seen by many as the great purveyor of neoclassicism's ideals to America. Composers studying with her learned the latest scores of European composers tied to the aesthetic, especially those of Stravinsky, and in testimony after testimony they applauded her emphasis on one of the central tenets of neoclassicism: "purity" of style. They also responded to the sense that she "never singled out an American composer as different, as such, from a French composer or a Spanish composer," as Copland put it. Rather she sought to cultivate "the profound personality that can create great music and consider[ed] such a personality as beyond a question of territorial boundaries." The ecumenical spirit of the League of Nations infused artistic trends. American neoclassicism responded as much to postwar transatlantic politics as it did to anything else.[3]

Looked at negatively, as was the tendency of American composers outside the Paris-New York axis, neoclassicism appeared not as an agent of opportunity but as a pernicious force, destroying a nascent national autonomy just as it gained momentum. It could inspire virulent prose. Dane Rudhyar, Henry Cowell, Charles Seeger, and Edgard Varèse were among those who argued strenuously that it was the latest installment in a long series of independence-stifling colonial impositions. "It is a strictly European attitude," wrote Rudhyar in a passionate denunciation of neoclassicism's evils. "The crux of the whole matter is whether or not one . . . wishes to identify oneself with the spirit of orthodox Europeanism." Cowell defined a neoclassicist as a "curiosity," characterizing such a figure as "a composer who has been a modern in the vanguard, and who later renounces modernism in an attempt to reduplicate a bygone style." Writing at the onset of the Depression, Seeger grouped neoclassicism with "neo-Romanticism" as "mere conscience-quieters for workers in a pampered art who are at their wits' ends for a compass, a course, and a hand at the helm." Varèse decried the "neo-classical ideal" as "zealously academic" and inhibiting the "creative effort": "It is lassitude constructing a theory by which to excuse itself and this theory has become the fashion."[4]

Like many aspects of modernism, then, neoclassicism gained mixed responses from composers in the New World. In some ways it polarized them. Yet Europeans were also uncomfortable with its inherent tug between tradition and innovation. In fact, neoclassicism had been a problematic notion since the term was first applied to a retrospective strain of composition on the continent around the turn of the century. Arising concurrently with the growth of musicology and its archaeological efforts to dig up music from the past, neoclassicism was beset early on by pejorative connotations. After World War I it underwent a transformation, coming to embody a sense of order in a society unraveled by an unprecedented international conflict. In other words, it responded to the same social and political conditions that turned some composers toward the systematic pursuit of dissonance and others toward the machine. Yet unlike these parallel modernist preoccupations, the basic impulse of neoclassicism was reactionary, countering the freewheeling, tradition-blasting inclinations of early twentieth-century experimental modernism.

For a time, the term covered such a broad span of different figures and musical manifestations as to be nearly meaningless. This last is a key point in grasping how neoclassicism played out in America. In an illuminating study of how the word *neoclassicism* was used in Europe, Scott Messing has observed that "for every cautionary statement warning against the term because of its ambiguity," it appeared just as many times with the "apparent assumption that the reader would know the precise connotation the author intended." It paralleled "modernism" in being both vague and pervasive. Whether neoclassicism meant something quite specific or vexingly general depended on one's perspective.[5]

Despite the open-ended meanings of the term neoclassicism, it came to identify certain prominent composers and specific traits in their works. In Europe, neoclassicism was most notably associated with the music of Stravinsky, beginning with *Pulcinella* of 1919–20 and continuing through *The Rake's Progress* of 1948–51. According to Messing, the term was first applied to Stravinsky in a 1923 article by Boris de Schloezer. A host of other composers fell within its orbit, ranging from Ravel and Milhaud in France to Krenek and Hindemith in Germany. Regardless of the national origin of the composers involved, neoclassicism was consistently associated with notions of "simplicity," "clarity," and "purity" and with a "new impersonal approach to music." These descriptive labels were omnipresent enough that it is impossible to avoid their redundancy. As early as 1912 Ferruccio Busoni wrote of the need for "a new classic art," one that is "beautiful, great, simple, impressive." And this idea continued to hold appeal, whether it was Apollinaire writing in 1917 of "l'esprit nouveau . . . inheriting from the classics a good solid sense" or the Italian artist Gino Severini calling in 1921 for a new trend in the arts based upon "geometric principles of proportion" as opposed to "the personal whim of impressionism and the experimental nature of cubism." With the declaration of war against Germany in 1914, "nothing less than modern culture itself was besieged," writes art historian Kenneth E. Silver. "The war gave the conservative forces in France the ammunition they needed to go on the offensive. Cubism in particular, one of the most obvious expressions of the modern spirit, was seen as the advance guard of the enemy." Out of this emerged such works as Picasso's *Villa Medici* and *Portrait of Olga* from 1917—spare, linearly precise, determinedly anti-abstract.[6]

Young Americans who developed an interest in neoclassicism during the 1920s tended to avoid the term even as they subscribed to the core principles it embodied. Those principles, in turn, became code words for the aesthetic. Quincy Porter, for example, who was an American pupil of Vincent d'Indy and lived for part of the 1920s in Paris, never mentioned neoclassicism when asked by the American music critic Irving Schwerké around 1930 to share his compositional creed. But he singled out its key qualities as his own: "Tendencies—?: toward simplicity and lyricism, economy. Particular admiration for Orlando di Lassus, etc., Bach, later Beethoven and much of Brahms." Taking a more aggressive posture, Roy Harris attacked the aesthetic outright while implementing some of its ideals. Harris warned his friend Aaron Copland that he should "avoid neo-classicism like the pest that it is." This advice was given in 1928, while Harris studied with Boulanger and worked on his Sonata for Piano, a work that can be viewed as embodying many conventions of neoclassicism. Years later, when he looked back on this period, Harris acknowledged having valued certain attitudes associated with the aesthetic: "I subscribed to a series of all the Beethoven string quartets [in the 1920s], bought the scores and studied them in minute detail. . . . Beethoven became a wise, confiding, copiously illustrative teacher. . . . I also turned to Bach's rich contrapuntal textures and long, direct musical structures. I learned about the passion and discipline of uninterrupted eloquence. . . . In short, I became a profound believer in discipline, form, both organic and autogenetic."[7]

The young Americans who shunned an identification with neoclassicism did so for one central reason: its origins were European, both in the earliest figures to embrace its precepts and the history to which it responded. Thus ideologically they distanced themselves from the aesthetic, while in practice they shaped their own versions of it, producing a diverse set of compositions inflected in basic ways by its values. They formed a separate sect within neoclassicism, one that held much in common with practice on the continent yet had its own distinct history. The result was a syncretic process of international exchange in which aspects of neoclassicism were manipulated and fused to form different breeds in different contexts. The Satie-like clarity of Thomson stands apart from the characteristic open chord voicings of Copland or the austere utterances of Sessions.

During this same period, surrealism was migrating to America, and its transmission from the Old World to the New offers a useful parallel to what happened with neoclassicism. Surrealism underwent a complex process of mutation that "was never neat or orderly," as the cultural historian Dickran Tashjian has observed. "Surrealism was hardly transferred in pristine form to an American avant-garde, which in any case did not exist whole to receive it." So too with neoclassicism, where neither the lines of communication between America and Europe nor the resulting metamorphoses were systematic or coherent.[8]

Much of the ambivalence of American composers toward neoclassicism, then, hung on the question of whether the aesthetic yielded "orthodox Europeanism," as Rudhyar charged, or whether it represented an empowering form of internationalism. Was it a means of squashing national autonomy or of leveling the playing field with colleagues in Europe? Looking back at the experience of their American forebears such as Horatio Parker and John Knowles Paine, Copland later lamented that they "accepted an artistic authority that came from abroad, and seemed intent on conforming to that authority." Young Americans of the 1920s, by contrast, were painfully aware that their hard-won gains in prestige and independence could easily be diminished if their artistic sovereignty came into question. Ruggles's desire to see himself as superior to Schoenberg was part of this attitude, and the generation born around 1900 felt this impulse with collective urgency, believing that a strong national identity would make an international standing possible. Three decades later Copland still puzzled over his generation's relationship to developments abroad: "We have inherited everything they [i.e., the Europeans] are and know; and we shall have to absorb it and make it completely our own before we can hope for the unadulterated American creation."[9]

A sense of the diversity within American neoclassicism as practiced in these early years comes from selected works performed in the Copland-Sessions Concerts, the series of programs that took place between 1928 and 1931. These concerts have already been posed as representing no single aesthetic stance; the music of so-called ultra-moderns appeared prominently on them. Yet a significant group of composers on the series was made up of those who had studied with Boulanger or who had spent time in France.

The manifesto of the Copland-Sessions Concerts proclaimed that they were to be devoted to "the younger generation of American composers" (mostly under thirty-five, as it turned out) and that they hoped "to stimulate composers to more prolific activity and to develop a stronger sense of solidarity among the creators of a growing American music." During an interview in his Upper West Side apartment at the beginning of the 1929–30 concert season, Copland stated that composers on his series wanted to be taken seriously for "honestly conceived" works, without the national imprint of jazz, which "Europeans," he claimed, were "wont to hail as American, and therefore truly vital." He also made it clear that "modern music is no longer in the experimental stage," a point especially relevant to the discussion here. In his politic way, Copland was promoting abstract composition in long-established forms that did not feel burdened to include overt Americanisms. He was also distancing himself and his coterie from the term "experimental," which conjured up a sense not only of scientific discovery but also of being in a trial stage. Copland aimed to present a mature and fully formulated contingent.[10]

To gain a sense of the range of American compositions from the late 1920s that can be loosely claimed as neoclassical, a group of works performed on the Copland-Sessions Concerts will be profiled in the chapters that follow. Included are Copland's *Piano Variations* of 1930, Thomson's *Capital, Capitals* of 1927, Harris's Sonata for Piano of 1928, Walter Piston's *Three Pieces for Flute, Clarinet, and Bassoon* of 1925, and piano sonatas by Sessions and Chávez (composed in 1928–30 and 1928).

The traditional titles of "sonata," "variations," and "pieces" that stand at the head of these works reveal just how much neoclassicism was affecting American composition, especially when put alongside the number of related titles performed in the Copland-Sessions Concerts as a whole (there were also a fair number of "quartets"). These genres stood at the core of the European tradition. But after Stravinsky's Octet and Piano Sonata (1923 and 1924), to single out two landmarks in European neoclassicism, standard structures suddenly signified the cutting edge of composition rather than the dustbin of historic practice.

These selected works from the Copland-Sessions Concerts give no sense of being churned out of a neoclassical mill or of straining under a stultifying doctrine. Rather they exhibit sprightly responses to varying aspects of the aesthetic, showing how American composers achieved individuality while responding to a transnational set of aesthetic values.

14

The Transatlantic Gaze of Aaron Copland

> Charles can no longer pay attention to one source of infor-
> mation at a time. He is Modern Man, programmed to take
> in several story lines, several plots at once. He cannot quite
> unravel them, but he cannot do without the conflicting im-
> pulses, the disparate stimuli.
>
> —Margaret Drabble, *A Natural Curiosity*

More than any other composer in the generation born around 1900, Aaron Copland has come to be seen as championing an idiom that was identifiably American. Some of his compositions—*Fanfare for the Common Man, Lincoln Portrait, Appalachian Spring*—have become virtual signifiers of American culture. They beam out from television commercials and herald affairs of state. They waft over FM radio. Yet they are but one part of Copland's multifaceted output, and they date from the years immediately surrounding World War II.

In the 1920s, Copland had his feet planted just as firmly in Europe as he did in the United States. The *Piano Variations*, composed in 1930 and performed on the Copland-Sessions Concerts in 1931, gives a strong sense of how this came to be. There is no denying that Copland began pursuing a nationalist voice during the 1920s. At the same time, he kept pace with the latest developments abroad. In the realm of image, which remains fragile in discussing the relationship of American composers to Western Europe, acknowledging such a link could easily cause Copland to be dubbed a Europhile. But the reality was more subtle than that. During this period Copland grasped the importance of having both an international purview and a national one. His transatlantic gaze was deeply intertwined with his personal response to neoclassicism.[1]

In many ways, Copland became a prototype of the fusion between national strength and international standing that was being imagined during the 1920s by visionaries of a postwar American cultural renaissance. Notable in advocating this concept was a young American writer named Robert Coady, perhaps best known for starting a "little magazine" called *The Soil* in 1922. Coady conceived of his publication as "aggressively American," boasting that it "roared New York." It was also a central part of his notion that nationalism and internationalism were fundamentally interrelated. "An Internationalist is a nationalist whose product, in any field, has reached the quality of world beneficence," wrote Coady. "Internationalism is not destructive of nationalism, but depended [*sic*] on nationalism." Coady formed an organization called the American Tradition League, and in doing so, he issued a manifesto that seems today like a blueprint for Copland's activities during the 1920s. Calling for "the interplay of national cultures," Coady identified a national identity as the key to international success. "Internationalism cannot be agitated into sudden completion but must grow and can grow only as national cultures grow." Thus the goal of nationalism was not purely chauvinistic but also cosmopolitan.[2]

During the 1920s Copland determinedly subscribed to these same ideals. He worked to build his reputation both at home and abroad, at the same time as he sought to forge a style reflecting a transnational synthesis. Neoclassicism yielded a framework for doing so.

Copland provided a perfect example of how Europe, which had always loomed large for American musicians, now did so in a new way. Copland's first composition teacher, Rubin Goldmark, with whom he studied in Brooklyn from 1917 to 1921, had himself studied with Robert Fuchs at the Vienna Conservatory late in the nineteenth century. As Copland later put it, his teacher "felt 'at home' with our European musical heritage." Yet while composers of Copland's generation subscribed to some of the same practices as their forebears, they pushed those patterns in new directions. So when Copland sailed for Paris to study in 1921, he broke a long-standing American tradition of going to Germany or Austria, and he used the experience as a means of achieving self-discovery rather than cultural upgrading. As has been abundantly documented in succeeding decades, he and scores of other American exiles discovered the glories of their native land while abroad, recognizing the vogue for American culture that was sweeping the continent. "Suppose that one could discover America not by returning to it, but by sailing away from it," mused an unsigned "comment" in a 1923 issue of the *Dial*, one of the periodicals Copland asked his parents to send him while living abroad.[3]

Copland did just that. Rather than seeking out a famous teacher such as Vincent d'Indy, Copland chose to study with Nadia Boulanger, then young and little known. As Copland later acknowledged, it was Boulanger who inspired him to pursue the fusion of nationalism and internationalism that would define his career—a fusion directly in synch with her own deeply held ideals about neoclassicism.

Figure 14.1. Nadia Boulanger with her students in 1923. Left to right: Eyvind Hesselberg, unidentified, Robert Delaney, unidentified, Boulanger, Aaron Copland, Mario Braggioti, Melville Smith, unidentified, and Armand Marquint. Copland Collection, Library of Congress. Reprinted by permission of The Aaron Copland Fund for Music, Inc., copyright owner.

Copland saw Boulanger as having a "faith in the future of America" that was "striking," yet she threw "each pupil back on the strength or weakness of his own individuality."[4]

Once Copland returned to New York in 1924, others stepped in to reinforce this attitude, mostly notably Paul Rosenfeld, whose cultural values were firmly grounded in Europe. He envisioned a native form of creative expression that could be "grouped without impertinence with classic European works." Copland was among the first Americans of his generation to be championed by this maverick, and he quickly came to be seen by Rosenfeld as the great hope for American composition. Reviewing the premiere of Copland's Symphony for Organ and Orchestra, conducted on 11 January 1925 by Walter Damrosch with the New York Symphony Orchestra and Nadia Boulanger as soloist, Rosenfeld began by hailing Copland's music with typically oblique, quasi-mystical language, praising it for "at all times" having "a thingness." But he quickly picked up steam, ending with an effusive encomium: "No American not yet twenty-five years of age, not Glenway Wescott even, has won artistic spurs more honourably and certainly than young Aaron Copland of Brooklyn. He already stands with the earth-sprung talents to which the civilized community can look for sustenance." "Civilized" was the key word here. Rosenfeld's credo, as will be explored more fully in Chapter 18, was built in no small part on a belief that new music needed to meet long-established criteria for high art. The same beliefs informed his support of Copland.[5]

Copland's European connections, then, were reinforced by Rosenfeld, as well as by the modernist climate in New York, with the high value it placed on new music from abroad. Over the course of the 1920s, Copland (1900–1990) kept his transatlantic ties strong by visiting the continent frequently, and he played a public role in encouraging Euro-American communication by publishing essays and reviews commenting on his experiences. Through those trips and articles, Copland's relationship to neoclassicism emerged with clarity.

After three years of study in France, Copland went abroad nearly once a year, using the time to compose as well as to attend international new-music festivals. At the latter, he kept abreast of modernist trends. In 1923, before returning to the United States from France, Copland attended ISCM's second festival in Salzburg with his friend Harold Clurman and later recalled, "I reported on the festival to Boulanger, relating that Stravinsky and Ravel were still the most popular composers." He was at the Zurich festival in 1926 and the one in Frankfurt the next year, as well as Oxford and London in 1931 and the festival of German chamber music at Baden-Baden in 1927—many of which he covered for *Modern Music*. In 1929 he produced a concert in Paris for the Copland-Sessions series, and in 1931 he did so in London.[6]

During this same period, Copland also gained force as a critic, most notably in articles for *Modern Music* but also in *Musical Quarterly*, the *New Republic*, *Musical America*, and the *New York Times*. While today he is remembered for his advocacy of American composers, then he wrote just as frequently about European developments.

Copland's articles began appearing as soon as he returned from France in 1924. He took a reverential view of Gabriel Fauré, for example, as expressed in a 1924 article for *Musical Quarterly*. This was an attitude he must have inherited from Boulanger. Copland mused over Fauré's "curious and unique" position and wondered why he was "ignored outside his country." According to John Kirkpatrick, who befriended Copland while both studied with Boulanger, Copland had played with the letters "GABRIELFAURE" in composing his Rondino of 1923. In 1925, Copland took up Mahler's cause in a letter to the *New York Times*, where he addressed the antagonism toward Mahler that he felt existed among New York critics. Copland called "quite justified" their reservations about the "bombastic, longwinded, banal" qualities of Mahler's music. Then he cited several works, including the Second and Eighth Symphonies and *Das Lied von der Erde*, that showed Mahler as "a composer of today," hailing the "big simple lines" and "extraordinary economy" in his orchestration and the degree to which his music possessed "that individual quality that we demand from every great composer." Within the context of Copland's relationship to neoclassicism, these were striking traits to isolate.[7]

In "What Europe Means to the Aspiring Composer," another article from the same year (1925), Copland listed the virtues of European training and described in detail the inadequacies that most Americans faced when encountering a European teacher: "As time goes on it becomes more and more clear that what he has studied at home under the names of harmony, counterpoint and fugue is but vaguely related to what his European teacher understands under these headings." The "embarrassing" limitations recited by Copland may well have come from his own experience, including the inability to "read in half a dozen different clefs" and to take down "musical dictation at a vertiginous speed." Five years later he wrote a tribute to his own European education in "A Note on Nadia Boulanger."[8]

At the same time, Copland was gaining stature as a spokesperson for his own generation in the United States. This was especially evident in a small but subsequently well-known series of articles published in *Modern Music*, beginning with "America's Young Men of Promise" of 1926. There, he brought to the fore names such as George Antheil, Henry Cowell, and Virgil Thomson, who were just coming to public recognition. Yet he still used European contextualizing, opening with a paragraph that cited Liszt, Satie, Busoni, Schoenberg, and Casella as composers concerned with the "fascinating diversion" of identifying "rising young talent"—which Copland then proceeded to do himself. Exemplars from abroad justified his advocacy at home. This article, with its final, now-famous declaration that "the day of the neglected American composer is over," not only became the equivalent of a press release announcing the arrival of Copland's generation, but also heralded Copland's debut as the spokesperson for that cause. Modeled perhaps on a well-known article of 1921 by Malcolm Cowley, discussing "This Youngest Generation" of American writers, Copland's "Young Men of Promise" was followed by a series of similar assessments, most notably in 1933 and 1936.[9]

By the second half of the 1920s, with high visibility in print, natural gifts as an organizer, and growing stature in the League of Composers, Copland had become the unchallenged leader both of the New York sect of neoclassically oriented composers and, in some respects, of the American compositional scene as a whole. Henry Cowell exerted a parallel authority during this same period. With Copland, it is hard to pinpoint exactly when his leadership coalesced—perhaps with "America's Young Men of Promise" in 1926 but certainly with the inception of the Copland-Sessions Concerts two years later. By 1929, when Cos Cob Press was launched through the largesse of Copland's patron, Alma Morgenthau Wertheim, he moved into publishing, becoming an adviser to Wertheim and gaining considerable power by doing so. That same year, a brief biography of Copland on the back flap of *Modern Music* cited him as being "regarded by most of America's youngest generation of composers as its spokesman."[10]

Letters and published documents of the period show Copland to have had a talent both for handling the practical side of his own career and for promoting the work of his contemporaries. He seemed naturally generous. "Aaron's view of contemporary composition was not the old trick of we're all in competition with one another," declared Virgil Thomson toward the end of his life. "He saw it more like the Fifth Avenue Merchants' Association—we get together and make it work! He was very good at that." Others concurred. "God bless your Good Samaritan conscience," wrote Roy Harris to Copland in 1928. "I was thinking the other day that one reason the French 6 were so colorless was because they had no contrasts, no Aaron to explain them—and no etcher like Chavez—and no scholastic gormand [sic] like Roger—and no black sheep like Anteil [sic] and no romantic hay seed antiquity like myself. (I suppose I might mention a few others but then that's your territory.) For instance the half baked Gershwin and the super jazz hound—blue devil Copland. Anyhow old boy I wish [I] could put my arms around you now and tell you how grateful I am to you for your generous spirit which is holding us all together." There were many munificences as the years passed, but the most concentrated record of Copland's embracing outreach during this period appears in letters connected with his work for Cos Cob Press, where he consistently advocated music by his American contemporaries. At the same time, his own compositions appeared steadily under the Cos Cob imprint. Thus a balance between personal ambition and collegial service remained consistently in place.[11]

Perhaps the responsibility of leadership increasingly directed Copland's efforts and ideology toward national issues. This certainly was the case as he reached the end of the 1920s and moved into the next turbulent decade—producing the figure who has lived on in historical memory. There were plenty of intimations of such a change. In a 1930 tribute to Boulanger, Copland grumbled about the "current European fashion to be conscious of Americans as Americans rather than as men"; Boulanger stood out for him as being free of such "a condescending attitude." But the next year, right after returning from a trip to Berlin, he shared his evolving stance with Carlos Chávez, "All you wrote about music in America awoke a responsive echo in my heart. I am through with Europe Carlos, and I believe as you do, that our salvation must come from ourselves and that we must fight the foreign element in America which ignores American music." Toughened by experience, Copland was no longer the twenty-year-old idealist who believed that talent alone could bring respect for American composers in an international arena. At the same time, he increasingly viewed art as a public occupation that brought moral responsibility. The notion of art as private creative expression had become passé.[12]

That change in attitude takes us well into the Great Depression. But such a journey is necessary to understand how historical perspectives on Copland have been formed. By the mid-1940s, the image of Copland reflected American flags and folk tunes more than it did oceanliners. Looking back at the 1920s, I am intrigued by the way that Copland forged his own form of transnationalism, shaping a style of American traits, European traditions, and transatlantic modernist associations. The drive within neoclassicism to synthesize materials at hand—rather than search for new ones—gave coherence to his mission.

The apotheosis of this period for Copland came with his *Piano Variations* of 1930, which immediately achieved iconic status among early-twentieth-century compositions. It was premiered at a concert of the League of Composers in January 1931 with Copland at the piano, and it also appeared on the final London program of the Copland-Sessions Concerts in December that same year. Constructed of a theme and twenty variations, the *Variations* are muscular and hard-hitting. Every note emanates from an initial four-note motive, with consistent angularity and dissonance. Octave displacement and exploitation of register are critical to the work, and the syncopations of jazz—incorporated so literally in Copland's *Piano Concerto* of 1926—have been subtly integrated and personalized, as in the seventeenth variation, where a two-voice counterpoint is set up in octaves, grouped in shifting, cross-accented compounds of two and three.

When interpreted against the backdrop of the published statements by Copland just discussed and against his active presence on the continent, the *Piano Variations* reveals Copland's effort to carve out a personal stance within modernism's many strains. Among them, neoclassicism emerged as the most powerful potential rationale for his aesthetic identity. It is at once a problematic and appropriate term to apply to the work. Most productively, the *Piano Variations* can be connected to the "cultural sense" of neoclassicism, as Scott Messing has termed it—meaning both its aesthetic values and the language used to describe them—which has consistently inflected discussions of the work. This has most notably been the case in the writings of Arthur Berger, who more than anyone else established the norms according to which Copland continues to be judged. Beginning with a 1934 article in the short-lived *Musical Mercury* and continuing in his 1953 book about Copland's music, Berger laid out the language that has become basic to criticism of Copland. Core concepts in neoclassicism—or "code words" as I called them earlier—suffuse his argument. Within the first sentence of Berger's historic early article about the *Piano Variations* he described its "economy of means" and "careful workmanship." In the next paragraph he addressed European connections, acknowledging that Copland had an "affinity" with Stravinsky that was "profound," also that he was "indebted to Schönberg." Parity was defensively assumed, and Copland was affirmed as no "mere imitator."[13]

With this, Berger established a perspective on Copland that emphasized traits with high status among neoclassicists. In an even broader sense, he confidently asserted an international context for Copland, deliberately refusing to view him in provincial terms. Yet Berger had significant predecessors, some of whom, like himself, were affected by neoclassicism in their own compositions. A striking case came in a "thumbnail history" of "new music" written by Marc Blitzstein in the early 1930s, in which he wrote about the *Piano Variations* with a neoclassically based language; he too assumed a European context. Blitzstein described the work as "preoccupied with form, no longer with matière, color, or a good 'spot.' The large-scale conception, the continuous line achieved, the success of the architecture, make it very likely that this work is in the vanguard of the day's trend."[14]

The *Piano Variations* culminated a whole series of works by Copland that had at least some intersection with neoclassicism. The first were composed in Paris early in the decade while he was a pupil of Boulanger. They include *Four Motets* (1921) and *Passacaglia* (1922), works described by John Kirkpatrick in 1928 as "excellent specimens of the degree of stylistic purity" demanded by Boulanger in forms in which "all" her pupils write. Already Copland exhibited a style "thrifty to the point of miserliness," as Blitzstein observed in yet another essay, pinpointing traits that became Copland's signature. Other works showed these same characteristics in varying degrees, including *Two Pieces for String Quartet* (1923–28), *Music for the Theatre* (1925), *Concerto for Piano* (1926), and especially *Symphonic Ode* (1928–29) and *Vitebsk* (1929)—the last with a virulent austerity that foretold the aura of *Piano Variations* as much as its musical style. Jazz was also a significant component in a number of these works, especially the Concerto, which is discussed in Chapter 20.[15]

Thus the *Piano Variations* extended an exploration of linearity and resonant dissonance that had preoccupied Copland throughout the 1920s, at the same time as it grew out of his own adaptation of neoclassicism. By the late 1920s, the reactionary tendencies of the aesthetic underpinned Copland's own philosophy, fueling a growing conviction that experimentalism had had its day and the principal challenge was to consolidate the many advances of the previous quarter century. This posture is crucial to understanding the *Piano Variations*, and it emerges in a series of Copland's reports from European new-music festivals. "But it is not so easy to be an *enfant terrible* as it used to be and nothing is more painful than the spectacle of a composer trying too hard to be revolutionary," Copland observed in 1927 after attending the festival of German chamber music in Baden-Baden. The next year, Copland pursued the same theme: "Modern music is no longer in the experimental stage. . . . These younger composers [Hindemith, Milhaud, Prokofiev, Krenek] . . . no longer seek new harmonies or rhythms, but are content to make use of the materials added to the technical equipment of composers during the years 1895–1920. . . . It promises an end of useless turmoil, a period of repose in which the full energy of the composer may be directed toward the creation of perfected masterworks."[16]

Other American artists of the late 1920s outside of music were expressing the same urge. "Self-expression is not enough; experiment is not enough; the recording of special moments or cases is not enough," wrote Jane Heap—introduced earlier as curator of the "Machine Age" exposition in 1927—in the final issue of the *Little Review*. "All of the arts have broken faith or lost connection with their origin and function," she continued. "They have ceased to be concerned with the legitimate and permanent material of art." In other words, the rage against historical traditions that had inflamed early-twentieth-century modernists had been spent, as the past and present began to fuse productively once again. Literary historians have termed this impulse "high modernism," a time of summation and consolidation. "The high modernists no longer need to rebel against history," writes literary historian Art Berman. "They are not newly forging modernism but have taken possession of modernism."[17]

Viewed in this light, the *Piano Variations* seems like a summation, both of Copland's work to date and of the music around him. He approached the *Variations* with a self-conscious mission: to draw upon the materials at hand, much like the pragmatic impulses of hardworking immigrant families such as his own, and to make a grand statement, or, as he put it, a "masterwork." "I am anxious above all things to perfect myself. I am bourgeois to the core!" confided Copland to his journal at an unguarded moment in March 1928. "This seemingly gratuitous 'perfectionnement' (since I wish it for no reasons of worldly glory or heavenly bliss) comes from an inborn sense of economy, getting the best possible out of my own being. H. [Harold Clurman?] is amused when I pass a store and say 'Too bad, they couldn't make it pay.' I am anxious to become a more profound person because it supremely satisfies my sense of economy (order) that one being should render the utmost possible profit (good)."[18]

Once Copland's pragmatic "sense of economy" and drive to consolidate existing materials are held up for scrutiny, other ties to neoclassicism suggest themselves. First is its historical thrust, described by Messing as the impulse to "borrow from, [be] modeled on, or allude to a work or composer from an earlier era, often from the eighteenth century, but equally from any composition *regardless of period* that has somehow entered into the canon of 'great art'" [my emphasis]. For Copland, in the *Piano Variations*, the main bow toward the Great European Tradition came in his decision to use the long-valued variations form, with its links to bravura keyboard works by Bach, Beethoven, Schumann, Brahms, and others. But in a broader sense, he was brimming with the entire canon of piano literature as he began to imagine this composition, having brought "tons" of music with him to study in Bedford, New York, where he began sketching the piece during January of 1930. Gerald Sykes, his housemate that winter, later recalled that Copland "began by playing works from as far back as the fifteenth century, then [went] on to piano pieces by Mozart, Haydn, and others. . . . [Then to] Brahms and Schumann. He developed an affection for Liszt." In conceiving the *Piano Variations*, then, Copland was ambitious, aiming to write a work that would take its place in a long line of keyboard masterpieces. He deliberately avoided the kind of historical vacuum so prized by radical modernists but instead bathed unabashedly in tradition.[19]

Yet another component of the "modeling" that infused the *Piano Variations* came through its very personal transformation of a host of compositions from the early twentieth century. None is explicitly evoked. In fact, most attempts to identify a direct lineage between the *Piano Variations* and modernist compositions that immediately preceded it quickly reinforce Copland's individuality. In a profile of Copland, published in *Modern Music* in 1932, Virgil Thomson branded his colleague as exhibiting "eclecticism"—and it was not a compliment. Yet Thomson managed to pinpoint a key aspect of the *Piano Variations*, which with some historical distance can be explored without incriminating implications. Viewed against Copland's writings of the late 1920s, in the *Variations* Copland simply seemed to be following his own exhortation by making powerful, imaginative use of "materials added to the technical equipment of composers during the years 1895–1920."[20]

The array of possible early-twentieth-century models that informed the *Piano Variations* adds up to a richly textured family portrait. Some connections are immediately apparent, others are subtly submerged. Copland himself acknowledged one main contemporary source—Arnold Schoenberg, whose twelve-tone method Copland claimed to have adapted, although "in my own way." Copland's knowledge of Schoenberg's system is clear from the outset, with the sharply chiseled pitch module that generates much of the *Variations* in proto-serial fashion, even with the indication in the first left-hand note to "press down silently" (perhaps modeled on Schoenberg's Opus 11) (Example 14.1). As Arthur Berger demonstrated decades ago, Copland followed some of Schoenberg's basic principles—especially his "metamorphosis of tones" and his use of octave displacement. But he by no means stuck to Schoenberg's rigorous scheme of not repeating pitches. The composer Marc Blitzstein had identified Copland's affinity to Schoenberg much earlier—perhaps even before the *Variations* was composed—but he did so more generally, asserting that the same impulse "toward discipline, away from experiment" provoked the development of both serialism and neoclassicism. It was the technique of Schoenberg that Copland emulated, rather than the texture or overall surface of his music. Copland's *Piano Variations* was far leaner and more austere in outlook than works from around the same time by Schoenberg.[21]

Other possible sources of varying origins converged in the *Piano Variations*, each of them illuminating specific characteristics of the work. Like a rock musician with a sampler, Copland pulled in gestures from this composer and that—all reprocessed in a personal way. For example, Copland heard Béla Bartók's Piano Sonata at the Baden-Baden chamber-music festival in 1927 and reviewed it for *Modern Music*, singling out its "incisive rhythms, its hard unsentimental quality"—traits prized in his *Variations* as well. Similarly, Copland reported on Webern's *Five Orchestral Pieces* from the Zurich ISCM festival in 1926, expressing unqualified admiration for Webern, whom Copland perceived as "a super-sensitive musician." He admired Webern's ultra-economy, again highlighting a trait that can be traced to the *Variations*: "Where one [i.e., Hindemith] writes four pages, the other [Webern] writes four measures. . . . One listens breathlessly: each piece lasts but a few seconds and each separate note seems filled with meaning." This, in turn, connects to the tendency of the *Variations* to spareness and economy.[22]

Stravinsky also looms. Blitzstein linked Copland to the Stravinsky of *Les Noces*, which others have done as well, suggesting that the *Variations* "stem[med] directly" from Stravinsky's score and finding in it a "prototype" of a "peculiarly intense and pure Primitivism." For Berger, on the other hand, the connection between Copland and Stravinsky was, as he first viewed it, more subtle and generalized; it was an "affinity," as noted already. Later, he zeroed in on the *Octet*, from which he claimed Copland to have derived the *Variations'* theme (specifically from the theme and first variation of the *Octet*'s second movement).[23]

Example 14.1. Copland, *Piano Variations*, p. 1. © Copyright 1932, 1959 by The Aaron Copland Fund for Music, Inc. Renewed. Boosey & Hawkes, Inc., sole licensee. Reprinted by permission of The Aaron Copland Fund for Music, Inc., and Boosey & Hawkes, Inc.

PIANO VARIATIONS

But I wonder if the Stravinsky of *Oedipus Rex*, which was premiered in Paris on 30 May 1927, may have lurked in the shadows as well, perhaps affecting two striking characteristics of the *Variations*—its stentorian declamation and its authoritative, broad-sweeping sense of grandeur. Copland openly admired this particular Stravinsky work. He reviewed its Paris premiere for the *New Republic* and featured the piece in his lectures at the New School for Social Research. In a 1929 interview about the Copland-Sessions Concerts, he "confessed a fondness, even a downright admiration" for it. *Oedipus Rex* generated considerable private discussion among Copland and his composer-colleagues as well. For example, his friend Israel Citkowitz wrote Copland soon after the premiere of *Oedipus*, pointing out specific parts of the work that he found potent. "[*Oedipus*] made a wonderful impression on me," wrote Citkowitz, "in spite of some things which I disliked very much. But the opening chorus and some of the recitatives, and the whole of the last half of the 2nd act . . . all wonderful."[24]

By connecting the work to *Oedipus Rex*, I refer to no quotations or transferred segments, rather to a common sensibility. The *Variations* open with a "Grave" tempo, and the materials unfold deliberately, setting a lofty tone from the outset. This quality is maintained throughout, emerging most notably at the conclusion, where weighty chords and a sprawling range yield a massive close (Example 14.2). Copland strove for this trait, writing to Israel Citkowitz in the midst of composing the piece, "It is a big work both in dimensions and meaning." He went on to perform the piece himself frequently, adopting a keyboard style that further enhanced its grandness. "To have the *Variations* played for one by the composer is a rare experience," wrote Arthur Berger. "The brilliance, the hardness are characteristic and as important in the communication of the work as the precise notes and rhythms." Right after the work's premiere, Paul Rosenfeld recognized this same effect, giving a typically extravagant assessment of its conclusion, which he saw as "a tragic peroration that seems to tear the whole edifice of things apart."[25]

The impulse for grand statement, in turn, stretches well beyond the *Piano Variations* to encompass a prominent series of American works from the late 1920s. It has already been discussed in the music of Carl Ruggles, and it is found in other composers as well, as in *Symphony on a Hymn Tune* by Virgil Thomson, which has opening and closing sections that unfold in a solemn brass fanfare based on medieval organum. Similarly, the first movement of Roy Harris's Piano Sonata conveys a sense of archaic majesty through open intervals—first octaves, then fifths.

Copland had his own history of lofty proclamations, especially in the opening of *Music for the Theatre* of 1925, where a brass fanfare sets a stately scene. He and his contemporaries were not timidly stepping forward but loudly proclaiming their arrival. In a profile of Copland for *Modern Music*, Thomson noticed this inclination toward grandness among his contemporaries—not only Copland—and he decried it, claiming that American composers faced a "problem of rhetoric" and that they were guilty of "forcing . . . every idea into the key of the *grandiose* and the *sublime*." He considered the result to be "false" and "frightfully monotonous." In typical

Example 14.2. Copland, *Piano Variations*, last page. © Copyright 1932, 1959 by The Aaron Copland Fund for Music, Inc. Renewed. Boosey & Hawkes, Inc., sole licensee. Reprinted by permission of The Aaron Copland Fund for Music, Inc., and Boosey & Hawkes, Inc.

fashion, Thomson put his finger on a salient trait, giving a sarcastic poke where affirmation or cool observation might have been possible.[26]

Also intriguing are potential connections between the *Piano Variations* of Copland and *Granites* by Dane Rudhyar. While Rudhyar fancied a thickness of texture alien to Copland's ear, he produced a body of piano music notable for epic statement and angular gestures. Over the course of the 1920s, Rudhyar's thick masses of sound were pared down a bit, and by the time of *Granites*, composed in August of 1929 in Carmel, California, and performed (perhaps premiered) by Rudhyar at a League of Composers concert in New York on 2 February 1930, they had become more linear. The League concert came just as Copland began immersing himself in the *Variations* (recall he had moved to Bedford in January for a secluded work stint). I do not know whether or not he attended Rudhyar's premiere. But the opening of *Granites* has a similar-enough conception to the *Piano Variations* to warrant attention (Example 14.3). Both employ a strong attack, singling out individual notes, and both have a similar melodic and rhythmic profile to their opening gestures. According to sketches for Copland's theme, he had already conceived of it before Rudhyar's *Granites* was performed at the League; the basic idea was his own. But the shaping of it—gesturally, rhythmically, spatially—merits comparison to Rudhyar.[27]

The works intersect again at their conclusions. After an ecstatic buildup that was typical for Rudhyar, *Granites* culminates in a descending three-note motive, drawn from the opening, which is punched out before a definitive concluding chord (Example 14.4). Copland, too, returns to the opening gesture—this time with only three notes, yielding a literal reduction of what had occurred at the opening. Then he finishes with what seems his own tensile version of a Rudhyaresque conclusion: lots of big sounds spanning the breadth of the keyboard, "surging" to a fierce resonance (Example 14.2). Copland certainly knew Rudhyar's earlier works, especially *Three Paeans*, which was performed on a Copland-Sessions concert in May 1928. In other words, there had been time for the grandiloquence of Rudhyar to settle in.

Example 14.3. Dane Rudhyar, *Granites,* mm. 1–4. Used by permission. Theodore Presser Co.

Example 14.4. Rudhyar, *Granites*, last two systems. Used by permission. Theodore Presser Co.

For Copland, then, the *Piano Variations* was not simply another composition. With its considerable length (approximately twelve minutes), its spacious use of register, and its hard-hitting attack, the work demanded to be noticed. The composer who had come to be seen as a leader in organizing the American modernist cause aimed to exert compositional authority as well—to write a "great" work that would take its place alongside revered masterpieces of the European past and present. No counterculture retreat into a realm reserved for outsiders, the *Piano Variations* represented a bid for membership in the most exclusive club around—the international new-music community—and the application came from a young man whose nationality by no means assured him entrance. For Copland, neoclassicism not only shaped the overall character of his music—especially in its carefully crafted lines and open textures—but encouraged him to consolidate and personalize traits that he admired in the modernist orbit that surrounded him. Ultimately, the language that he shaped under its influence became one of the most well known in twentieth-century composition.

15

Virgil Thomson's "Cocktail of Culture"

> The twenties had been a peaceful and busy time, with lots
> of parties and dancing and casual sex-lives, and with minor
> new movements in music, art, and poetry every year.
>
> —Virgil Thomson

For Virgil Thomson, the very mention of "neoclassicism" could inspire a sneer, usually exposing a response somewhere between ambivalence and downright disgust. Yet he had been weaned on the aesthetic. Thomson not only studied with Boulanger, like so many others, but he had admired the music of Stravinsky and contemporary French composers since his undergraduate studies at Harvard with E. B. Hill, before ever touching European soil. Later Thomson emerged as one of the most outspoken critics of neoclassicism, at one point disparaging it as a "*lingua franca*" that was essentially "an indigestible mixture, . . . a cocktail of culture." He specialized in such contradictions. One day, in his role as music critic, which he performed with devastating panache beginning in the early 1920s, he would pen a sharp attack on a fellow composer, acting like a sniper outside a fort. The next, when promoting his own music, he maneuvered comfortably on the inside, arranging performances within composer societies and establishing friendships—albeit tenuous ones—with some of the same colleagues he had just criticized so strenuously.[1]

Contradictory behavior characterized Thomson and his music throughout his career, and it is intriguingly present in *Capital, Capitals*, a work from 1927 that was among the more radical offshoots of neoclassicism in America. It was performed twice on the Copland-Sessions Concerts, first in New York in February 1929 and two years later in London. But since then it has been largely forgotten— overshadowed by Thomson's opera *Four Saints in Three Acts* and *Symphony on a*

Hymn Tune, written immediately afterward. *Capital, Capitals* is a key transitional work, reflecting a time when Thomson switched from a branch of neoclassicism that exhibited the acerbic harmonic edge of Stravinsky to one that embraced the ultra-diatonicism of Satie. It is daring for its simplicity rather than its complexity. But the internal tensions in *Capital, Capitals* reached beyond neoclassicism to involve an impish fusion of sacred and secular, both in its particular blend of historic styles and in the way it encoded a homosexual message within an aura of high church.

Completed in April 1927, *Capital, Capitals* dates from the middle of a three-year period of consolidation for Thomson, during which he moved from one strong female force to another, concluding composition lessons with Boulanger and beginning a close collaboration with the writer Gertrude Stein. After composing his *Sonata da Chiesa* (February 1926), a self-described neoclassical "graduation piece" that fused baroque forms with bitonality, Thomson quickly turned out a cluster of compositions that blended Dadaesque satire, super-simple harmonies, and references to both historic European repertories and American hymnody. A few of these enjoyed a prominent position within the Copland-Sessions Concerts. In addition to *Capital, Capitals*, Thomson's *Five Phrases from the Song of Solomon* was sung by Radiana Pazmor at the inaugural concert of the series in April 1928, and *Susie Asado* and *Preciosilla*, together with three other Thomson songs, were heard on the Paris program of June 1929.[2]

With *Capital, Capitals*, Thomson (1896–1989) stepped into a new stylistic period, moving closer than ever before to "the greatest audacity—simplicity," for which Jean Cocteau had praised Satie in *Le Coq et l'arlequin*, an influential pamphlet of 1918 that became a call to arms for neoclassicists. Selections from Cocteau's text were published in *Vanity Fair* in October 1922 just as Thomson returned from his first full year in Paris to begin a final stint at Harvard. For Cocteau, Satie was the master simplifier, and Thomson felt the same way. He had discovered Satie's music through S. Foster Damon, a teacher and friend at Harvard, and when he returned to Cambridge during the fall of Cocteau's article, he brought with him Satie's *Socrate*, which he performed the following spring on campus.[3]

This time of transition resulted in two songs—*Susie Asado* (1926) and *Preciosilla* (1927)—together with *Capital, Capitals*. All three featured texts by Stein. The two solo songs give a sense of how Thomson's new style was evolving. In *Susie Asado*, Thomson delivered the text with a clear, simple melody, but he laced the accompaniment with "wrong-note" dissonances. The piano part is a paragon of concision, using four discrete patterns made up of independent rhythmic units. First there is a broken triad in eighth notes, then a C-minor scale harmonized at the seventh below, followed by organum-inspired open fifths and a single B-flat with upper grace note (Example 15.1; the last two patterns do not appear in this example). Meanwhile, the melody is diction-obsessed, delivering the text with matter-of-fact clarity. Yet despite all this simplicity, the melody and accompaniment are both more ornate than in *Capital, Capitals*.

Figure 15.1. Virgil Thomson and Gertrude Stein looking at the score for *Four Saints in Three Acts*, Paris, 1934. Thomson Collection, Yale University. Reprinted by permission of Virgil Thomson Foundation, copyright owner.

Preciosilla, completed in early February 1927, exhibited the same crystalline texture. But it took another step as well, eliminating the dissonant flavoring of *Susie Asado* and opting instead for unambiguous diatonicism. Thomson, in the estimation of John Cage, "chose to appear outlandishly behind the times because the words he was setting were outlandishly ahead of them." Using a sober baroque frame, Thomson shaped his score as an early eighteenth-century recitative and aria, imitating the form and stylistic gestures of the idiom precisely. It is a straightforward revival of a long-defunct style.[4]

Susie Asado

GERTRUDE STEIN   VIRGIL THOMSON

Capital, Capitals, by contrast, involves a cluster of delightfully eccentric twists. Its scoring for a quartet of men recalls the a cappella glee club of Thomson's alma mater as much as it evokes a medieval monastery. Its harmonic language is unremittingly diatonic. And its references to historic styles run the gamut from ancient European religious idioms to beloved American hymns. When Thomson later critized his contemporary Aaron Copland for "eclecticism" and derided neoclassicism as "a cocktail of culture," he singled out traits characteristic of his own music.

Even the premiere of *Capital, Capitals* was unconventional, occurring at a midnight costume ball in June 1927, given by the Duchesse de Clermont-Tonnerre. The event was a Dada spectacle, as Thomson's account revealed. "My *Capital, Capitals* has created considerable curiosity," wrote Thomson to his college friend Briggs Buchanan, using aphoristic prose reminiscent of Jean Cocteau:

> Given privately at the house of the Duchesse de Clermont-Tonnerre. Great costume ball. At midnight divertissement artistique, namely the capitals. Four men & a piano. Text by Gertrude Stein. Time twenty minutes flat. All singing antiphonal. Never sing together. Not a sacred work but sounds sort of so. Seems to remind everyone of what he heard in childhood.
>
> Fania Marinoff [?]—Jewish synagogue
> Miguel Covarrubias—Mexican church
> Mary Butts—Greek chants
> Jean Cocteau—Catholic liturgy
> Edward Ashcroft—Gilbert & Sullivan patter
>
> Since its performance there has been a stream of visitors to my door, including the above for purposes of hearing said work and others. All French people at the Duchesse's. More dukes than you could see for the ambassadors. Not the Princesse crowd. Cocteau came to see me more or less as their representative, I presume. His comment after my music was "At last a table that stands on four legs, a door that really opens and shuts." The French who know no English [at] all exclaim [*sic*] "What an extraordinary sense of English prosody!" I suppose they mean that it is English that sounds like English.[5]

Thomson later identified the Duchesse de Clermont-Tonnerre (also known as Elizabeth de Gramont) as "a member of [Natalie] Barney's feminist literary group that called itself l'Académie des Femmes." An American of French ancestry, the Duchesse enjoyed considerable affluence before her divorce in 1920, entertaining lavishly at her home on rue Raynouard, which had magnificent gardens sloping down to the Seine. But she was a writer and representative of the radical chic, not just a professional hostess. Around the same time, she was collaborating with Arthur Honegger, probably authoring the scenario for his obscure, unpublished ballet *Roses de métal* of 1928. Like her friend Natalie Barney, another American living abroad, the Duchesse was openly lesbian, hosting "Fridays" through "l'Académie des Femmes" for a series of notable women. Gertrude Stein's "Friday" took place on 4 February 1927 and included a performance by Thomson of *Susie Asado* and *Preciosilla*.[6]

The music to *Capital, Capitals* was as unusual as the circumstances of its debut. Adding up to slightly over fifteen minutes in C major, it employed a melody delivered with churchly intonation and an accompaniment that drew upon the conventions of Italian recitative, sparely supporting the text's delivery (Example 15.2). Throughout, there is a tongue-in-cheek humor, in both the text and music. The four voices never overlap, so they form no mass sound. Rather they pass the lines of chant back and forth from one singer to another, achieving an odd sort of timbral polyphony. Thus the vocal texture is effectively monophonic yet gives an illusion of multiple levels of activity. Thomson had a longtime passion for chant, beginning with excursions during the 1910s to St. Mary's Episcopal Church in Kansas City, where, as he reported to a hometown friend, "they have incense, and a male choir; they sing the creed and use only Gregorian music."[7]

John Cage later commented on the "static nature" of *Capital, Capitals*. "The fact that the piece takes a long time to accomplish nothing," he wrote, "is the secret of its strength and its effectiveness." It is static partly because the accompaniment is constructed of alternating modules. They do not build in any way, certainly not to a climax. Rather one simply hooks onto another. Furthermore, the chant has a non-directional quality.[8]

Yet another striking characteristic of the work is its diatonic chasteness. Like a grandfather to Terry Riley's famous *In C*, which essentially launched the minimalist movement forty years later, *Capital, Capitals* keeps "C" omnipresent in the melody, with reiterations of the pitch interrupted occasionally by full or partial C-major scales. Throughout much of the accompaniment there are no triads—only repeated pitches and stepwise motion. At a few isolated points, triads do suddenly pop up, and they have a stunning effect. The first such moment occurs at the words "Decide . . . My side. At my side," where piano and voice use broken triads (Example 15.3). Simultaneously, the piano switches from approximating the accompaniment for recitative to delivering a two-voice invention. Another quite different episode is found at "Cannot express can express tenderness," where chant gives way to arialike lyricism in the melody (Example 15.4). This, in turn, responds to the image of "tenderness" in the text. At the same moment, the chord voicing in the piano changes as well, directly imitating an American hymn. A work suffused with the darkened murmur of a continental cathedral suddenly lets in the sunlight of a clapboard sanctuary on the Great Plains.[9]

These same excerpts also provide a clue to how *Capital, Capitals* encodes a string of homosexual allusions within its churchliness. Deciding "to reside at my side" and talking of "tenderness" could be loaded. While Stein's texts have often inspired scholars to puzzle out their "dissociative rhetoric," as Harold Bloom has termed their playful redundancies and non sequiturs, they have been explored by others for their coherence. According to the literary critic Lisa Ruddick, Stein does not just deliver "formal word play but also, often in the same words, a variety of

Example 15.2. Thomson, *Capital, Capitals,* p. 1. Used by permission. Theodore Presser Co.

witty, subversive, and veiled messages," and she believes that Stein expressed her own lesbian sexuality with increasing openness beginning with *Tender Buttons* of 1914. Although Ruddick does not analyze *Capital, Capitals*, she suggests a way of interpreting Stein that can be applied to this lesser-known poem, igniting a string of suggestive sexual images. Following is a concordance of such moments, keyed to page numbers in Thomson's published score:

"tenderly" (12)

"In the third place the third capital is aroused." (13)

"hearty kisses" (14)

"tenderness" (15)

"Capitals are plenty there are plenty of capitals.
Why do they enjoy capitals and why are capitals rapidly united.
We unite ourselves together.
The capital seems to be the capital.
A capital is not easily undertaken nor is it easily aroused nor indeed is it impervious.
Thoroughly.
And very pleasantly.
Nearer to it than that.
Eagerly.

They are.

They do.

They will.

They are to-night." (20–21)

"Permit me to do this and
also permit me to assure
you that coming again is not as pleasant as coming
again and again and
coming again and again is
very nearly the best
way of establishing where
there is the most pleasure." (22)[10]

Occasionally, Thomson highlights these words, as with the hymn chords that call attention to "tenderness." But just as often, he treats the suggestive language like everything else, intoning it in chant-derived melodic lines and integrating it into the bulk of Stein's patter.

Capital, Capitals did not represent the first time that Thomson mixed sex, religion, and music. Among his unpublished writings is a little-known essay titled "My Jesus, I Love Thee," which may have been the article that H. L. Mencken rejected for the *American Mercury* in October 1924. Thomson submitted a piece then about hymns, and Mencken responded by writing, "Your investigations of the hymns are a bit shaky to begin with and you discover nothing new about their contents." It is also possible that "My Jesus, I Love Thee" was written as a response to that rejection. Dated "Paris, 1925," it was probably written by Thomson right after returning there that fall following three years in the United States.[11]

Whatever its initial purpose, "My Jesus, I Love Thee" brings a gay perspective to Baptist hymn texts, using a sassy tone and delivering a thoroughly blasphemous message. Thomson initially catches the reader off guard, lining out a matter-of-fact comparison of the contents of a hymnal from 1917 (*Treasury of Song*, published in Dallas) with another unnamed hymnal of 1843. Both were presumably relics of his childhood. At the bottom of a numerical tabulation of tune types, Thomson suddenly exposed his agenda:

86 of these hymns are evangelical exhortations,

28 explain the benefits of conversion, . . .

1 is about Mother,

1 recalls with pleasure a little brown church in the wildwood, and

91 confess erotic feeling for the person of Jesus.[12]

Thomson then proceeded to read beloved gospel texts as covert bearers of a homosexual message, citing their "tenderest references to Jesus's breast" and their ecstatic emphasis on "the joy with which He will be united to each of us privately and personally." Applying the Freudian lingo so popular during the 1920s, Thomson believed these text writers to have been victims of "an eroticism turned inward by taboos." According to his reasoning, "God the Father scarcely interests them. Jesus, the perfect, though very human, 'lover of my soul,' is the deity."

With this argument in place, Thomson went on to quote some widely known hymntext snippets, loading them with homoerotic implications:

"Love is the theme," "love for you, love for me." It is the "old, old story." "Tenderly pleading," He waited "all the night long," "knocking, knocking at the gate." Those who had "tasted his delights" called to me "in His name." . . . "Resist Him no More!" "Let Him have His way with Thee!"

He ended with a twist illuminating Thomson himself, who kept his own sexual preference carefully hidden. "All this," he wrote of hymn texts, "is simply a fixation of the libido upon an unattainable object." Then he proceeded to construct an argument that replaced oft-repeated Christian mantras with an earthly counterpart. "Heaven" became "that ultimate Paris," and "love for Jesus" transformed into "yearning" restricted by an "imaginary social code." This added up to, "The unattainable object has two advantages. It does not tempt to infractions of that imaginary social code which is such a terror to Americans. . . . All the material necessary for a love-affair being thus comprised within the ego, consummation is no longer endangered. SUCCESS is assured. The present becomes endurable; and the faith, the hope, the great yearning are projected toward that ultimate Paris to which wicked Americans make pilgrimages in this life, the poor or the timid in the next." Renowned for his clear, unadorned prose, Thomson's language here was uncharacteristically convoluted, and he again lapsed into Freudian lingo.

With "My Jesus, I Love Thee," Thomson boldly revealed himself, deliberately linking poetry, religion, and sexuality. He mocked the dearly beloved "tunes of long ago" as bearers of earthly passion. Yet he took this step within the safe haven of an article that remained unpublished. For Thomson and most other Americans of his day, homosexuality was hidden from public view, cloaked in gestures of conventional respectability. He fantasized an outing for these texts much as he might have desired one for himself. Over the years, Thomson seemed to delight in sending out erotic teasers, such as the way he publicized his habit of composing in bed—albeit in the bed of repose not lust. Unlike Benjamin Britten, who managed both to live openly with his lover Peter Pears and to remain officially in the closet, Thomson struck a consistently enigmatic pose for public view. His sexuality has been explored sensitively by his biographer Anthony Tommasini, who conveys a vivid sense of the social codes within which Thomson maneuvered.[13]

A slight leap is needed to get from "My Jesus, I Love Thee" to *Capital, Capitals*, but the landing feels solid. In both, Thomson turns to traditions he reveres, splicing together disparate fragments to generate a state-of-the-art collage. He is fond of those traditions at the same time as he violates them. In lectures at the New

School for Social Research during the late 1920s, Copland described Thomson as writing "two kinds of music: religious and profane." Those two strains fused overtly, if heretically, in the prose of "My Jesus, I Love Thee," and they joined again in *Capital, Capitals*, with their blasphemous message covertly concealed.[14]

In later years, Thomson never particularly singled out *Capital, Capitals* for any reason. Rather he focused on *Four Saints in Three Acts* and *Symphony on a Hymn Tune*, larger compositions of the same period that were written in the more conventionally favored forms of opera and symphony. Both these works also fused sacred and secular, integrating hymn tunes and doing so with blatant impertinence. With *Capital, Capitals*, though, Thomson found the voice that so distinguished him from other neoclassically inclined American composers. His particular "cocktail of culture" yielded an arch blend of New World and Old, of hallowed and hedonistic. And it blithely snubbed dissonance—a realm so privileged at the time—to deliver secret messages with seeming innocence. Artifice reigned. Neoclassicism could lurk behind many different compositional styles, and this one was particularly distinctive.

A Quartet of
New World Neoclassicists

What has not yet been proven, is that our young musicians
are sufficiently strong to go to the past, to go to the European experimenters, as they must in order to develop their
purely intellectual comprehension of their art, and still continue to express themselves freshly.

—Paul Rosenfeld (1922)

Above all else, the Copland-Sessions Concerts celebrated youth, giving performance opportunities to composers who would eventually emerge as leaders in the
United States. The stylistic range of music performed on the series was far broader
than is generally recognized, as already discussed. Yet there is no denying that one
of its main constituencies was made up of composers with varying inclinations
toward neoclassicism. Four will form the focus of this chapter: Roger Sessions,
Walter Piston, Roy Harris, and Carlos Chávez. But others on the Copland-Sessions
series also fell in some way under the rubric of neoclassicism, including Marc
Blitzstein, Theodore Chanler, Israel Citkowitz, George Antheil, Robert Russell
Bennett, Paul Bowles, Robert Delaney, Vladimir Dukelsky, Colin McPhee, and
W. Quincy Porter.

When placed alongside Copland and Thomson, the quartet of Sessions, Piston,
Harris, and Chávez broadens our perspective on the diversity of American attitudes toward neoclassicism. Sessions and Piston both adopted fairly traditional
stances toward the aesthetic yet achieved quite different results. Harris and
Chávez, on the other hand, took much more idiosyncratic approaches. All four
negotiated individual contracts with this transatlantic aesthetic in some of their
earliest mature works.[1]

Among American composers born around the turn-of-the century, Roger Sessions (1896–1985) was the one most comfortable with his connection to the music and traditions of Western Europe. He lived abroad from 1926 to 1933, with a few significant breaks in between. Yet unlike fellow expatriates of the period—most notably George Antheil and Virgil Thomson—Sessions did not rediscover the culture of his homeland on foreign soil. Rather he became a fervent internationalist. Sessions alone, among compatriots of his generation, made statements such as the following, "I am aware of the strong influence in my work of two, above all, among modern composers—Bloch and Stravinsky. These influences I have tried to absorb rather than to escape, since I have no sympathy with consciously sought originality." There were no encoded messages here—rather, a frank admission of kinship. Being so open about historic connections was unusual for a modernist, and trumpeting European roots was especially taboo for one who also happened to be American.[2]

Sessions ultimately became famous for his advocacy of an international outlook, but its early manifestation is of interest here. After attending concerts by the

Figure 16.1. Roger Huntington Sessions, photo by Standiford Studio, published in *Musical America* (9 February 1924). Courtesy of Musical America Archives.

International Society for Contemporary Music in Geneva in 1929, where his own First Symphony appeared on the program, Sessions reported to Copland, "I was struck by the way in which musicians from all over the Western world are more and more achieving a kind of common idiom. I don't mean of course that we have gotten as far as in the 18th century, of course, where French and Italian and German composers wrote in a kind of grand European style; but nevertheless it seemed to me that something approaching that comes nearer every year." Among Americans, Sessions was the principal figure to advocate a style that would transcend geographic borders, and neoclassicism provided the framework for doing so. Like the other Americans profiled here, he by no means embraced the principles of neoclassicism wholesale during the 1920s, and he certainly did not spend an entire career as one of its disciples. Yet he became a beneficiary of the kind of open passport that it offered. "Sessions had always rightly insisted that the American past is the European past," his student and advocate Edward T. Cone observed, "and that the foundation provided by the great line [in music] is basic to the development of music in the United States as well as in Europe."[3]

Not long after the opening of the 1920s, Sessions was singled out as a gifted member of his generation. When his incidental music to Leonid Andreyeff's *Black Maskers* was premiered in Northampton, Massachusetts, in 1923, Paul Rosenfeld journeyed up to hear it, enthusing at length about Sessions as a long-awaited native talent: "Only a brief while since, we had been wondering whether the arrival of a musician with enough chaos in him to make a world were truly possible in America; wishing indeed for the tone such an apparition would give to life, . . . that golden gift is among us to-day." Rosenfeld held Sessions up to well-established notions about European high art. He declared *Black Maskers* to be "no happy hit such as many slight talents make once in their lives; . . . the author is an artist." In other words, Sessions waved a banner for the Great Tradition, unsullied by the lower forms (as Rosenfeld saw them) of Tin Pan Alley. Rosenfeld also argued for the work's ethnic integrity, proclaiming that Sessions's "gift . . . comes as it must inevitably have come, as the voice of the living young people in a compromised and shoddy world. No Indian or negro, or bastard Scottish tunes. Absolutely, no red white and blue. Rather, the grey on grey of Russia. That, is more American." This was Rosenfeld's rebuttal of the influential view of Antonín Dvořák, who during an extended visit to the United States (1892–95) offered that American composers should find their identity in indigenous vernacular traditions. Rosenfeld made it clear that Sessions was no "mongrel," to use a catchword adopted by cultural historian Ann Douglas. By contrast, he lifted Sessions high above the teeming masses.[4]

Sessions's Sonata for Piano, one of his main compositions from the 1920s, exemplifies the strong continental aura of his style. The work quickly gained respect. An incomplete version was performed by John Duke at a Copland-Sessions concert on 6 May 1928. It then consisted of two movements, and Duke apparently improvised a conclusion. Sessions took two more years to finish the piece, and the full composition received its premiere by Frank Mannheimer on 3 March

1930. It was subsequently performed at the Oxford ISCM concert in 1931, after which Copland hailed its "'universal' style" and proclaimed it "a cornerstone upon which to base an American music."[5]

The Sonata has deep, immediately audible connections to neoclassicism—or as Sessions put it in a program note, it was "built on the general lines of classic form." Sessions seemed drawn to the dispassionate, even clinical nature of the aesthetic. To a listener acquainted with Sessions's later serial works, through which he "acquired a reputation for ponderousness" as Cowell once put it, the Piano Sonata is surprisingly accessible. It is also solidly in the "Stravinsky camp," as the composer himself acknowledged and a glance at the opening segment shows (Example 16.1). Sessions notates the work on three staves, a practice that comes directly out of Stravinsky's scores during the period, most notably the Piano Sonata of 1924. The work's stark linearity and bitonal emphasis have ties to Stravinsky as well. Sessions's Sonata has no clear division into separate movements. Rather it falls into six contiguous segments, characterized by contrasting tempos, textures, rhythms, and pitch materials. The lyrical opening Andante recurs twice to become a ritornello framing the first portion of the piece—another Stravinskian trait. Because of it, the work subdivides into two large sections, the first encompassing the initial five parts (Andante, Allegro, Andante, Poco meno mosso, Tempo I [a return of the Andante]) and the second consisting of the final Molto vivace.[6]

The Sonata has two main historical models, Bach and Beethoven, both filtered through the lens of Stravinsky. Sessions's link to Bach is especially striking in the concluding "Molto vivace," a black-key perpetuum mobile with long stretches of two-voice writing. With its crisp articulation and tied notes, the right-hand line recalls Bach's keyboard preludes, while the left hand has the frenetic motion of a baroque countermelody. All these materials are delivered with modernist shaping. Accents shift continually to create internal cross-stresses, as well as asymmetric rhythmic counterpoint between the hands. And the faux-pentatonicism of the right hand at the opening of this section, together with the conscious use of sevenths on strong beats, stands distinct from practices of the early eighteenth century. Meanwhile, the opening of the "Andante" (the second section of the work) recalls Beethoven, with its octave pyrotechnics and third-based textures.[7]

One of the more intriguing aspects of Sessions's Sonata is its rhythm, which is handled in a manner different from Copland, Harris, or others among his American contemporaries. Sessions did not make a distinctive American approach to rhythm the heart of his modernist mission. Yet he joined his American contemporaries in exploring syncopation and asymmetric patterns. Years later, Elliott Carter singled out Sessions for his "technique of irregular grouping," as exhibited both in the Sonata and the First Symphony. The Allegro (second section of the Sonata) is particularly interesting in this regard. There the basic rhythmic unit constantly mutates, beginning with an eighth note and changing first to triplets, then to sixteenths.[8]

Example 16.1. Roger Sessions, Piano Sonata No.1, first movement, p. 1. © B. Schott's Soehne, Mainz, 1931. © Renewed. All rights reserved. Used by permission of European American Music Distributors Corporation, sole U.S. and Canadian agent for Universal Edition.

SONATA

Overall, the Sonata by Sessions shows a buttoned-down side of modernism—or in the words of Marc Blitzstein, Sessions had "a gift rich in austerity." Thoroughly allied with historic European forms, he appears in it as a youthful neoclassicist, sufficiently skilled to say something fresh within a language developed abroad. The Sonata was published by the prestigious German firm of B. Schott's Söhne of Mainz and Leipzig in 1931, a rare achievement for a young American then, which gives added testimony to the international currency of Sessions's craft.[9]

Walter Piston's *Three Pieces for Flute, Clarinet, and Bassoon* clung even more tightly to conventional expectations of neoclassicism. Written in 1925, while Piston (1894–1976) studied with Boulanger, it showed a young composer eagerly absorbing the new music around him. It also revealed exquisite craftsmanship. The work was premiered in May 1925 at a "Concert de musique américaine" given at the Salle Gaveau by the Société Musicale Indépendante, and in April 1928 it was heard on the inaugural concert of the Copland-Sessions Concerts. Published by the *New Music Quarterly* in 1933, it had the distinction of being released on Cowell's New Music Quarterly Recordings two years later—yet another example of how stylistic divisions among American composers were not so fiercely enforced during this early period.

Neoclassicism suffuses *Three Pieces*, from its crystalline textures to its carefully contained formal structures. There is an intentional anonymity here, beginning with a neutral title—not only "Three Pieces" but also the individual movement names, "I," "II," and "III." This is a work consciously void of extra-musical references, whether national, poetic, or personal. Even its tempo indications appear in Italian, the international language of music. Throughout, there are irregularly overlapping melodic patterns (often ostinatos) and strict stratification of the three instruments. Clarity reigns. Piston would later cite Bach as a primary model for *Three Pieces*—a hero he shared with other neoclassicists—and added that "certainly Hindemith had something to do with it." Composers whom he also acknowledged as important to his early development included Stravinsky, Hindemith, Schoenberg, and Webern.[10]

The first piece, marked "Allegro Scherzando," is constructed with the linear independence so valued by neoclassicists and falls into three parts. An ostinato in the bassoon continually shifts accents by challenging ⅜ time with a steady pattern of four eighth notes (Example 16.2). Above this, the clarinet sounds a separate pattern, this one conforming to ¾ and built of two alternating melodic figures. Over it all, the flute floats with a descending melody. This stratification is maintained throughout the movement, as the instruments frequently shift roles but the layering of materials remains constant.

Linear autonomy also characterizes the second piece ("Lento"). It is short and also fits into a three-part form. Yet now the flute and clarinet cling much closer together, growing in serpentine fashion out of a common G-sharp, to which they both creep back at the end. The third piece ("Allegro") is a perpetuum mobile, energetically contrasting with the first two movements at the same time as it

Example 16.2. Walter Piston, Three Pieces for Flute, Clarinet, and Bassoon, Movement 1, p. 1. Copyright © 1933 (Renewed) by Associated Music Publishers, Inc. (BMI). International copyright secured. All rights reserved. Reprinted by permission.

adheres to the same fundamental principles: a three-part form, irregularly shifting ostinatos, complete sovereignty of each instrument.

Piston later described the *Three Pieces* as "concise pencil drawings." In doing so he not only called upon an image natural to the husband of an artist (Piston's wife, Kathryn Nason, was a painter) but the medium that he selected tells much about this work. Avoiding the emotional intensity of broad-brushed oil paints or the liminal atmosphere of a watercolor, Piston chose "pencil," with its capacity for precise containment. In a profile of Piston for Cowell's historic *American Composers on American Music*, Nicolas Slonimsky isolated these same qualities, ending with the code words of neoclassicism: Piston is "a builder of a future academic style, taking this definition without any derogatory implications. . . . He is an American composer speaking the international idiom of absolute music."[11]

When Roy Harris's Sonata for Piano appeared on a Copland-Sessions concert in February 1929, it left one critic looking a bit perplexed. Kenneth Burke, a poet and cultural commentator who had replaced Rosenfeld as music critic for the *Dial*, claimed that it "confirmed" his "admiration" for the composer and went on opaquely: "[Harris] lacks the independence and individuality of a Hindemith, he cannot carry music so far into the uncharted—but he is scrupulous in taking no theoretic step which he does not duplicate by the imagination." In other words, Harris (1898–1979) was not as adventuresome as at least one of Burke's favorite European composers, but he had a creative voice all his own. The Sonata fared less well in subsequent evaluations. Virgil Thomson called it "a coarse work and laborious," while Henry Cowell grouped it with other early compositions in which Harris "aims for continuous form, but cannot achieve it always, so that the works often 'blow up' and the form seems to explode and disappear."[12]

Such mixed commentary, leaning toward the negative, continued to haunt Harris through the years. At one moment, he could be branded as inept, poorly schooled, lacking refinement. At another he was perceived as an intriguing figure who was "naturally conservative musically," as Cowell put it, but had managed to shape a distinctive personal idiom within fundamentally conventional means. "He is in no sense a 'neo' classicist," Cowell declared. As Isaac Goldberg wrote in response to the landmark recording of Harris's Concerto for Piano, Clarinet, and String Quartet in 1933—already mentioned as the first commercial release of a work by one of the young American modernists—"I am a practised [*sic*] listener to the most *ultra* music; and Mr. Harris's recorded concerto is by no means ultra. . . . I cannot hear anything like genuine greatness in the composition, yet there is the token of an unmistakable individuality."[13]

Whatever qualifiers might be used, something about Harris's music was clearly new, not simply rehashed. Harris worked unapologetically with long-existing materials, respecting the tradition in which they were conceived at the same time giving them a personal stamp. Like his trademark method of evolving an entire composition from an opening cell, Harris methodically progressed as a craftsman

Figure 16.2. Roy Harris against the Manhattan skyline (1931). Nicolas Slonimsky Collection, Library of Congress. Reproduced by permission of Electra Yourke.

from a youthful beginning in the Sonata, a work brimming with promise despite its clumsy architecture, to the mature language of works such as his Third Symphony of 1939.

Anyone confronting Harris's music must also face the hard-sell pitch he made on his own behalf. He had the instincts of a publicist, constructing a myth about himself as a rough-hewn cowboy straight off the Midwestern plains. Harris was much like Antheil in the importance he assigned to image making, but he devised an entirely different persona. Rather than painting himself in the steely gray hues of the Machine Age, the Oklahoma-born Harris took a regional approach by placing himself against the golden landscape of the American past. He was quite successful at it. Critics and commentators did not challenge or deride his image, as they did with Antheil; rather they bought it wholesale. Isaac Goldberg romantically sketched him as a "young tonal Lochinvar from the West . . . [who] carries in his veins the blood of pioneers," and Cowell wrote of his "plain, driving force, undampable conviction, ruggedness." Friends perceived him similarly. "He . . . looked very wild and worn; but gave off a wonderful western farmer air in the middle of the Place de la Concorde," wrote Mary Churchill, patron to Copland as well as his concert series, after she ran into Harris at a Paris bank.[14]

Behind this facade of a pioneer, Harris in the late 1920s was working through his particular version of the American transnational struggle—sorting through European music both past and present, self-consciously aiming to articulate national traits, and searching for a way to express his own vision. The Sonata for Piano exposes his turbulence and influences. Historically one of the more important works by Americans within the orbit of neoclassicism, the Sonata gives a revealing view of how disparate cultural spheres could be nimbly negotiated.

The Sonata is shaped conventionally in three movements: Prelude, Andante Ostinato, and Scherzo. Harris's models in the Sonata are readily apparent: Beethoven, in its cellular construction and recurring thick textures; Bach, in the playful inventionlike counterpoint of the closing Scherzo; and Stravinsky, in the decision to write a sonata and obeisance to earlier masters. The first two were acknowledged by Harris two decades later (as already quoted) and clearly audible. But the last is more subtle; Harris's music had a fundamentally different conception from Stravinsky's—lusher, less acerbic, more openly emotive.

Perhaps the most striking trait of Harris's Sonata is the degree to which it has its own eccentric personality. The opening has an archaic grandeur, built of organum-like octaves, fourths, and fifths—a device also used by Virgil Thomson in his Prelude for Piano of 1921, as well as the opening of his *Symphony on a Hymn Tune* of 1928, the same year Harris began his Sonata (Example 16.3). As a whole, the Sonata is distinguished by thick textures, often chordally conceived, as well as a thoroughgoing employment of counterpoint—what Harris himself dubbed "chordal counterpoint."[15]

Among the Sonata's other notable characteristics is its jarring sectionalism. As soon as Harris starts to cruise within any given segment, he switches gears. Continuity is not the goal here. The thematic idea at the opening, for example, is built of variants of two different one-measure modules. When a new section enters, it is set off with strikingly different rhythms from the first—a repeated sequence of sixteenths, triplets, and eighths. The first movement breaks down into five sharply delineated sections, each of which grows out of a core cell from the opening—using a technique later dubbed as "autogenetic" by Harris himself. Disruptive events characterize this structure more than ongoing flow, and this continues to be the case in the final two movements.[16]

Yet another key trait of Harris's Sonata is its inventive approach to rhythm. Elliott Carter, who commented on Sessions's rhythmic personality, also wrote of Harris's, noting his tendency to write "long, continuously developing melodies in which groups of two, three, four or five units . . . are joined together to produce irregular stresses," principles that are clearly evident in this early work. Looking

again at the opening, the accent constantly shifts, often knocking cellular phrase groups akimbo. The first measure builds a unit of five out of two plus three, yet the accents are placed as three plus two, creating an internal cross-accent. The second measure unambiguously presents two plus three; the third expands the opening module over six beats (to equal three plus three); and the fourth disrupts the internal symmetry of the six-beat units by placing an accent on the second beat. A few weeks prior to the debut of this work, Harris wrote a letter to Copland, including a "program" for the Sonata, in which he described it as conceived of "germ ideas" and identified his "rhythmic germ of 5 (stated in 2nd measure)." Harris presented the work in traditional analytic language, using terms such as "exposition" and "organic"; he saw the "climax" of the first movement coming with the introduction of a "3rd rhythmic & melodic motive $^{11}/_8$—group of 4 + group of 3 + group of 4. This motive becomes the foundation of the 2nd movement."[17]

Besides being premiered at one of the Copland-Sessions Concerts, Harris's Sonata received another boost from Copland when it was published by Alma Wertheim's Cos Cob Press in 1931. The pianist Harry Cumpson, who had premiered the work, edited it for publication.

Harris's biographer, Dan Stehman, called the Sonata a "grandly scaled 'serious' effort by a fledgling composer," while Cowell disparaged it as being "influenced by the modern French," making it "not . . . his best, which is his ruggedly-American self." Yet it has considerable strength and charm. Ultimately Harris became best known as a symphonist, especially for his Third Symphony, which drew on the same stylistic principles as the Sonata. The Symphony remains one of the few pieces by this generation of American neoclassicists to enter the American orchestral repertory.[18]

Carlos Chávez's Sonata for Piano of 1928 was premiered with Piston's *Three Pieces for Flute, Clarinet, and Bassoon* on the opening night of the Copland-Sessions Concerts, and it took listeners down an even more unusual byway within the neoclassical aesthetic than that of Harris. In many ways, the work does not fit comfortably within the rubric. As with much of Chávez's music, the Sonata's overall character resonates with the ancient grandeur of his native Mexico. Yet there is nothing obvious about this connection—no flashes of regional color or direct quotation from folk sources. Rather, it is suggestively evocative. At the same time, the Sonata is less touched by European models than any other composition discussed in this chapter, perhaps because Chávez (1899–1978) had none of the same training abroad as his contemporaries. It inhabits a more austere sonic realm than Harris or Thomson—one that is closer to Dane Rudhyar, Carl Ruggles, or the Copland of the *Piano Variations* than to Stravinsky or any continental modernist of the day.

Conceived in four movements, the Sonata's key features include melodic angularity, a percussive approach to the piano, construction in taut one- or two-measure units, pointillistic manipulation of register, consistent rhythmic irregularity, and a harmonic profile that blends frequent vertical seconds, sevenths, and ninths with sudden unisons—or "hollow octaves," as Paul Rosenfeld described them (Example 16.4). Like Sessions and Harris, Chávez had an individual approach to rhythm, building it of discrete patterns. The first pattern at the opening fills two measures; the next pattern takes up three, expanding considerably in range; and the third grows to four measures, bringing in an oscillating left-hand module. The remainder of the movement transforms and reiterates these patterns, either whole or in part, adding up to a tight construction based on cellular units with no conventional organic development. During this same period, Chávez also produced three sonatinas—for cello and piano, piano solo, and violin and piano. All were performed on the same Copland-Sessions concert as the Sonata.[19]

Responses to Chávez by his American contemporaries are as intriguing as the Sonata itself. In the early 1940s Copland looked back on this work as a pugnacious declaration of a modernist's inner vision, describing it as "hermetic and inaccessible," with "a certain downrightness . . . that seems to imply, 'This is how it is, and you can either like it or leave it.'" He also keenly isolated the very traits that make the piece stand out:

> Its four movements are no doubt too continuously taut, too highly condensed
> for common consumption. It contains a profusion of short melodic germs, none
> of which is developed in the conventional manner. The piano writing is thin and
> hard, without lushness of timbre. The general style is contrapuntal, with sudden
> unexpected mixtures of acid dissonances and bright, clear unisons.[20]

In earlier critiques of the Sonata, Paul Rosenfeld mused about some of the same issues, embroidering a characteristic profusion of images. But he put a finger on the delicate balance that characterized the Sonata, with its juxtaposition of startlingly original elements alongside those grounded in European traditions. Writing in 1928, immediately after the Sonata's premiere, Rosenfeld located Chávez securely within the neoclassical spectrum, exclaiming, "An original classical music!" He saw Chávez as distinct from "the Stravinskies" because his works did not "embody a return, like the precise, architectural, and 'pure' composition of the Stravinskies." Furthermore, the Sonata and other compositions by Chávez did not "merely chill and disaffect," like "the great mass of their European companions and competitors," but "move by an eminent involuntariness and virginity."[21]

Four years later, in a profile of Chávez for *Modern Music*, Rosenfeld turned to gendered images, in part assessing the Mexican's work for the degree to which it conveyed a sense of being "masculine." "Chavez's music is a dance of the male on the American soil," Rosenfeld declared at the opening. Later, he took up this theme again. "There is no voluptuousness in the score," he wrote. "Yet there is a perfect logic here. . . . And the American man dances in it: goodhumored, robust, mocking, ultimately detached: in the plenitude of liberated energies, in joyous reserve, in derisive impenetrability. But it is not singular; all Chavez is such a rhythmic expression of masculine completeness and independence on the American soil." In

Example 16.4. Carlos Chávez, Sonata, 1st movement, p. 1. Published in *New Music* 6/2 (January 1933). © 1933/1965. CPP/Belwin Music. All rights reserved.

a final huzzah, Rosenfeld used this male construction to characterize Chávez's particular fusion of neoclassicism and personal identity, posing his style as a transatlantic male alliance. "The robustness, astringency, flintiness of these forms in tone, bare of romantic expansivity and ornamentation, are universally masculine; and the extreme contraction of form, the laconism, the dryness, the abruptness, are masculine of the new world."[22]

With a Kirk Douglas image of "laconism" and "abruptness," Rosenfeld validated neoclassicism as an aesthetic conveying virility. His language stands out in a compositional realm where many of its American practitioners were gay—most notably, Copland and Thomson, also Blitzstein, Bowles, Citkowitz, and McPhee. On at least one occasion, this same kind of image was used within the group itself, when Harris wrote Copland—perhaps in 1926—commenting on a work-in-progress. "Glad you have written new work," declared Harris, with back-slapping affirmation. "Harp, viola, and flute sounds Ravel-ian—I hope not. It would be a pity for an American to become so emasculated." This in turn makes Virgil Thomson's covert homoerotic agenda in *Capital, Capitals* all the more intriguing. If maleness was one goal in American neoclassical expression, Thomson may have cleverly concealed his message within an aesthetic perceived by some as ultra-male.[23]

Returning to Chávez: at the same time as his Sonata was unusual for the day, so too was his position in New York. Disappointed by his first trip in 1922 to Europe (twenty-seven years passed before he went again), Chávez first came to the United States in December 1923, staying until March 1924, and he returned again in 1926 for a two-year residency. In other words, New York became Paris for this young man from Mexico City. While in the United States, he not only gained considerable status but also linked up compatibly with various modernist factions. His music appeared on concerts by the International Composers' Guild, beginning with his *Tres exágonos* in February 1925 and continuing more notably with the premiere of *H.P.* in November 1926, at the same time as it appeared on three different Copland-Sessions concerts. The League of Composers did not program a Chávez composition until 1930. In September 1928, Chávez was the subject of a cover story in *Musical America*. He also received an entire chapter of his own in Rosenfeld's *An Hour with American Music* of 1929 (only Varèse rated the same treatment), and another in Cowell's *American Composers on American Music* of 1933. Furthermore, an unusually high number of Chávez's compositions from this period gained publication through American modernist outlets. Cos Cob Press issued his Sonatina for Piano in 1930, and by 1933 Henry Cowell's *New Music Quarterly* had included three of his works, including the Sonata.[24]

Even though he had broad-based ties in New York, Chávez's strongest ally there was Copland. His Sonata for Piano was dedicated to Copland, and the two became close personal friends and professional co-advocates, resulting in a kind of composer exchange program. Although in 1928 Copland declined Chávez's first invitation to Mexico City, where Chávez wanted to conduct Copland's Piano Concerto in his new post with the Orquesta Sinfónica de México, he did travel there for a performance of the *Ode* in 1932, beginning a series of important residencies south of the border. The two men's relationship, in turn, was the most visible part of a vital bond that existed at the time between composers of the United States and Latin America. One early manifestation of it was the Pan American Association of Composers, discussed previously, for which Chávez joined Cowell and Varèse as a cofounder in 1928; Copland had works performed by the organization but was not part of its governing body. Later, the modernist movement found some support in the Pan American Union, an official multigovernment agency that for a time underwrote north-south composer exchanges. Charles Seeger directed its Music Division from 1941 to 1953. This is an auspicious but little explored area of American musical history that is deeply enmeshed in national politics—initially of World War II and ultimately the Cold War. In the 1920s Chávez and Copland were both at the forefront of early efforts to shape a fraternity of composers in all parts of the Americas.[25]

Taken as a group, then, the American composers singled out here for their engagement with neoclassicism produced scores exhibiting as many differences as they did common traits. There was a leaning toward spare textures, asymmetric cross-accents, independence among voices, and pattern-based writing. The notions of "simplicity," "balance," and "purity" linked to the aesthetic can meaningfully be projected on these scores, even as composers and commentators discussed them in those terms. But these shared inclinations manifested themselves in diverse ways, and through it all, the term neoclassicism barely turned up.

No matter how varied the resulting compositions, there is no denying that they grew out of the same transatlantic aesthetic and that it had a substantial impact. American composers may not have wanted to be identified directly with neoclassicism, and historians may have avoided the term as well. But the record shows that neoclassicism migrated fluidly between the New World and the Old, affected by patterns of dissemination that were as diverse as the music produced. As discussed in the first of these chapters about neoclassicism, the aesthetic seemed destined for such a fate, both in Europe and America. Even though "the presence of neoclassicism . . . was so rife that almost every major figure composing during the first three decades of this century was tied, loosely or umbilically, to this term," Scott Messing writes, "a collation of usages produced such a variety of meaning that the expression seemed to possess no syntactical weight whatsoever." Through it all, there was an overriding assumption that the meaning of the term was understood by all. As neoclassicism hovered over both Europe and America in the early twentieth century, providing a common atmosphere of musical values, its practitioners— especially those who were American—often posed behind a mask.[26]

The postcolonial fear of yielding cultural turf has already been discussed in connection with the shaky reputation of neoclassicism in America, but another aspect needs to be addressed as well—that is, the perception, as the decades passed, that a core group of American composers associated with neoclassicism held an inordinate amount of political power and that they tended to dispense favors to composers just like themselves. This was tightly bound to perceived rivalries between composer societies, as explored earlier, and to a growing sense of opposing schools of American composition. During the 1920s, there was more cooperation than rivalry, but from the 1930s on, a competitive spirit gained force, as selected composers testified, and the main target was Copland. Cowell wrote to Ruggles in 1931 about a review of a concert in Berlin that had been conducted by Ernest Ansermet, revealing raw musical antagonism. Works by Copland, Sessions, Gruenberg, and Ruggles were on the program. "You will note," Cowell remarked, "he [i.e., the reviewer, H. H. Stuckenschmidt] says Copland is a Ravel imitator" and that "Sessions COULD be much better, if he were not under the domination of Copland!" Looking back on his unsuccessful application for a Guggenheim Fellowship in 1926, another composer—this time, Dane Rudhyar—lashed out at Copland but focused explicitly on politics. "I had a very fine letter [of reference] from Salzedo [and] Stokowski," Rudhyar recalled. "But apparently [that] did not make any impression because the group of Copland and that neo-classical thing, you see, was in complete control of the so-called 'new movement.' And they kind of blocked—consciously or half-consciously—everything that I was trying to do." Yet another later composer—Peter Garland, a self-proclaimed disciple of Cowell, Rudhyar, and Ruggles—has raised questions not only about American composers associated with neoclassicism but also those who adopted serialism after World War II (a movement that included some of the same figures and their students). His main targets were Milton Babbitt, Charles Wuorinen, and Elliott Carter. "What has been so heinous about these people," Garland wrote, "is not so much their dry and lifeless music, but the increasingly negative political role they began to play in American music. . . . Like Copland, Thomson and others before them, these composers—because of their 'respected' academic positions—were called upon to judge contests, award prizes and commissions."[27]

Garland brings the story well past mid-century. My point here is not to support or refute his claims but to show how the attitude he and Rudhyar projected has gotten linked with perceptions about neoclassicism in America. Politics and style became intermeshed.

Returning to the decades between the wars, the neoclassicists themselves declared a unified front for a time. Virgil Thomson suggested that he, Harris, Piston, and Sessions rallied around Copland during the 1930s. "All were to serve under his leadership as a sort of commando unit for penetrating one after another the reactionary strongholds." Thomson asserted this military analogy with swagger and pride, although the word *neoclassicism* remained unspoken. But others who were either outside the battalion or felt mowed down by its advances did not share such a charitable view.[28]

Of this group, Piston and Sessions went on to become two of the most influential American teachers of composition during the twentieth century—this in a century when, as Thomson put it, "a university rather than a conservatoire background" became most common for American composers. Piston's base was at

Harvard, Sessions's at Princeton and The Juilliard School. Between them, they exerted considerable power, shaping several generations of American composers. Piston's pupils included Leonard Bernstein (one leader on the American scene who never became ensconced in the academy), as well as Elliott Carter (who held sporadic teaching posts at Columbia, Yale, The Juilliard School, and elsewhere), Arthur Berger, Irving Fine, and Harold Shapero (the last three had distinguished careers at Brandeis University). Sessions's students included Milton Babbitt and Edward T. Cone (both with major careers at Princeton), Leon Kirchner and Donald Martino (both ended up at Harvard), and Hugo Weisgall and David Del Tredici (both at the City University of New York). It was an overwhelmingly male contingent.[29]

The nature of the power held by Copland and Thomson had different manifestations because both seized public forums rather than academic ones. By positioning Copland at the head of his "commando unit," Thomson acknowledged the strong leadership role that his colleague asserted. Copland also gained considerable visibility early on, especially through performances of his music by the Boston Symphony Orchestra, conducted by Serge Koussevitzky—himself an important link between American composers and the neoclassicism of his Russian colleague Stravinsky. As a teacher, Copland never held a long-term university position, but he had considerable impact both through private lessons and, after 1940, through the summer school at the Berkshire Music Center (Tanglewood), where he was chair of the faculty until 1965. But Copland's main base came through his successful organizing efforts, beginning with Cos Cob Press and the Copland-Sessions Concerts and continuing through the years to touch most of the major composer institutions in New York. He brought practical skill, energy, and coherence to the American compositional scene. In the process, as is the case with any leader, he exercised personal taste and selectivity—which meant that some composers were excluded. No matter how many figures he assisted, how much music he put in circulation, or how catholic his outreach, Copland had special inclinations toward certain composers, and those who felt themselves to be outside his circle never forgave him. As his influence grew, so did resentment.

Thomson's impact came most profoundly in his work as a critic. Beginning in the early 1920s with reviews for the *Boston Evening Transcript* and feature pieces for *Vanity Fair*, Thomson moved on to *Modern Music*, eventually becoming music critic for the *New York Herald-Tribune* in 1940. Through these writings he became one of the most prominent opinion shapers of the second and third quarters of the twentieth century. He held nothing sacred—not even music by other "commandos"—but he put his weight behind the development of an American school of symphonic and operatic composition. As a teacher and mentor, Thomson was attracted more to free-floating figures than to those in the orbit of Copland, Sessions, or Piston. Most prominent in his circle were Ned Rorem, Lou Harrison, and John Cage. Thomson held no ongoing university appointment.

Politically, Roy Harris was the least visible member of the "unit." Beginning in the late 1930s, he moved through a series of university positions, none of which lasted long-term, and he had a few notable pupils, especially William Schuman and Peter Schickele (P. D. Q. Bach). Thomson included him within the group for musical reasons, as one of the progenitors of an American symphonic tradition.

Readers will note that Carlos Chávez has dropped out of this story, simply because in the late 1920s his base of activity shifted back to his native Mexico, where he assumed a level of musical power comparable to his "commando" colleagues in America. In 1928, Chávez took over the Orquesta Sinfónica de México, which had begun haltingly the previous year, and he also stepped in as director of the National Conservatory of Music in Mexico City. His ongoing interactions with Copland have already been discussed.

This is a succinct summary of subtle cultural and political currents that wafted over decades—a subject complex enough to deserve a book of its own. But it is pertinent here because the power accumulated by American composers associated with neoclassicism played a role in making the aesthetic so intensely maligned, causing composers linked to it to renounce or cover up their connection. While the aesthetic's European roots gave it dubious standing during the 1920s, its reputation grew even shakier as time passed. Nationalist pressures of the Depression and World War II entered the scene, and they were only compounded by growing issues of power and jealousy.

But the "commando unit" has long since passed away, and the power centers of American music have undergone vigorous challenge. Universities remain a haven for composers at the same time as a few figures in recent generations have successfully soared past them with stunning and influential freelance careers. Perhaps the time has come when we can begin acknowledging, without prejudice, that the impact of neoclassicism in the United States had merit. In an age when cultural diversity is cherished so dearly, this particular transnational exchange—even though it involved Europe rather than Asia or Africa—needs to be viewed not as a postcolonial concession but as part of the great American mix.

European Modernists
and American Critics

Europeans in Performance and on Tour

The port of New York lies on a single plane with all the world to-day. . . . The sun is rising overhead, the sun which once shone brightly on Europe alone and threw slanting rays merely upon New York. The sun has moved across the Atlantic.

—Paul Rosenfeld, 1924

While American neoclassicists obscured their stylistic connection to Western Europe, these same composers and their American contemporaries worked to foster transatlantic performance opportunities. The founding of New York's modern-music societies in the early 1920s generated a booming trade in European modernism, and other strategic points of Euro-American contact occurred, including especially the New York premieres of *Pierrot lunaire* and *Le Sacre du printemps*, the establishment of the International Society for Contemporary Music, and the American tours of European composers. All reinforce my fundamental assertion: that the tie binding American culture to Europe may have reconfigured during the 1920s but it remained securely in place. The change had to do with attitude more than anything else. At mid-decade the novelist Sherwood Anderson gave voice to how he and his compatriots viewed this new but old relationship. "Had I myself come to New York, half wanting to go on to Europe and not quite daring?" Anderson mused. "At least there was not in me the naïve faith in Europe my father must have had. I found myself able to go into the presence of men who had spent years in Europe without trembling, visibly at least, but something pulled."[1]

Something certainly "pulled" when it came to *Le Sacre du printemps* and *Pierrot lunaire*, modernist milestones premiered abroad in 1912 and 1913, respectively, which in the early 1920s had not yet reached a New York concert stage. "'Le Sacre' . . . is Strawinsky's masterwork," wrote Paul Rosenfeld in 1920. "To us, at this moment, 'Le Sacre du printemps' appears one of those compositions that mark off the musical miles." Years later, George Antheil looked back on America's failure to mount an early performance of this landmark as one of his reasons for not returning to the United States from Paris. "In 1922 America did not even yet know whether it could accept as music 'Le Sacre du Printemps.' In 1922 America the prevailing fashion in composition was Debussy-Ravel, plus some Ernest Bloch."[2]

All that began to change when *Le Sacre du printemps* finally reached the New World. Its premieres there in several major cities marked a significant rite of its own: the passage from postwar isolationism to international engagement. The official American premiere took place in Philadelphia on 3 March 1922, with Leopold Stokowski conducting the Philadelphia Orchestra. Yet reception of the work was tepid, and the significance of the event was largely symbolic. With its first New York performance on 31 January 1924 by Pierre Monteux and the Boston Symphony Orchestra, the effect was strong and immediate. The orchestra played "superbly" and the audience responded enthusiastically, with "cheers ringing out for the conductor and his men." "I want to tell you that I played the *Sacre* in Boston last week and here in New York last night with enormous success in both cities," Monteux reported enthusiastically to Stravinsky. "But you must understand that the success was as great as it was ten years ago on the rue de Clichy, except that here it was *unanimous*. . . . I myself do not recall having given a performance of the *Sacre* even approaching these [Monteux's emphasis]."[3]

No matter how frustrated Americans felt at waiting for their own premiere of *Le Sacre du printemps*, they could take comfort in the fact that they did not wait alone. This was not simply a case of the cultural lag so quickly pinned on Americans in relation to European culture but rather of a process of dissemination that had been slowed worldwide during the war. Before *Le Sacre du printemps* reached Philadelphia in 1922, it received concert premieres only in London, Saint Petersburg, and Moscow. By the time of the New York performance two years later, there was a burst of activity across the Western world, including national premieres in Berlin, Rome, Geneva, and Leipzig.[4]

Before its premieres in the United States, *Le Sacre du printemps* was known to American musicians either through hearing performances abroad or, more usually, through playing the two-piano arrangement. Virgil Thomson, for example, recalled performing the two-piano version while a student at Harvard; E. B. Hill included the piece in his course there on Russian music. The critic Deems Taylor referred to it in 1920 as his only means of hearing the work. And Carl Ruggles used this same version, as performed by Mrs. Alexander Block and Madame Artur Nikoloric, to illustrate one of his lectures about modern music at the Whitney Studio Club in April

1922. These were but a few examples of a fairly common phenomenon. There was no recording of the work at this early date.[5]

But even though *Le Sacre du printemps* had been known in the United States for years, and even though other countries also waited for a premiere, its performances by American orchestras brought a profound psychological change, one that was acknowledged repeatedly by writers of the time. Reporting on the 1923–24 concert season in *Modern Music*, Pitts Sanborn declared, "The fact of prime importance in last season's record is that through it Stravinsky has 'arrived' in New York. He is now quite definitely one of the composers that everybody may not worship but still accepts." The young Virgil Thomson observed the same thing: "For there is no concealing the fact, disconcerting though it be, that Stravinsky is the fashion. A single short piece by him on any concert program will sell out the house." And when Rosenfeld commented on this new attitude, he attributed it not only to the American premiere of *Le Sacre du printemps* but also to that of *Renard* by the International Composers' Guild nearly two months earlier. "Strawinsky a success in New York!" exclaimed Rosenfeld. "But it was yesterday only that the Concertino was hissed, whole families uniting in the sport; and day before yesterday only that a Philharmonic audience sat mute motionless aghast during a parade of little Fireworks."[6]

By 1928, *Le Sacre du printemps* had become so fashionable that F. Scott and Zelda Fitzgerald used it to entertain guests at a party they gave in a house they had recently rented near Wilmington, Delaware. "Scott met his guests at the door," recalled Edmund Wilson. Then, "we were next taken into a room," Wilson continued, "where we were given, for our entertainment, a choice of listening to records—which were still a novelty then—of *Le Sacre du Printemps* or of looking at an album of photographs of horribly mutilated soldiers."[7]

Equally significant was the American premiere of Arnold Schoenberg's *Pierrot lunaire* on 4 February 1923 at a concert of the International Composers' Guild. The program opened with works by Charles Koechlin, Satie, and Milhaud; *Pierrot lunaire* took up the second half. Like *Le Sacre du printemps*, *Pierrot lunaire* arrived in New York as a notorious, middle-aged icon of modernism, having received its European premiere eleven years earlier. Also like it, the New York debut of *Pierrot* occurred at a time when the work was being revived elsewhere, following a hiatus during the war. Beginning in April 1921, the Society for Private Performances in Vienna presented *Pierrot lunaire* in performances conducted by both Erwin Stein and Schoenberg. They initially took place in Vienna and were repeated several times over the next eighteen months in both Vienna and Prague. Then in 1922, Milhaud conducted the work in Paris. Soon after being performed in New York by the ICG, the work was introduced to Italy, conducted by Alfredo Casella and presented by his Corporazione delle Nuove Musiche, which recently had made a formal affiliation with the ICG.[8]

Pierrot lunaire was the perfect choice for an ICG program, because of both its status and its scoring for chamber ensemble. Besides, Varèse had rare personal experience with the piece, having been among the composers who heard it at a private performance at Busoni's home in Berlin prior to the premiere in 1912. Then during a visit to Europe in 1921 or 1922, Louis Gruenberg attended a performance of the work. He subsequently conducted it in New York, with the Swedish-American soprano Greta Torpadie as vocalist. As with the premiere in Berlin, the performers in New York found the work difficult, so much so that the planned performance date of 21 January had to be postponed to 4 February. Twenty-two rehearsals were required—eighteen fewer, however, than in 1912. These were the rehearsals that took place in Claire Reis's apartment. By all accounts, the resulting performance was highly successful. As with *Le Sacre du printemps*, the audience responded enthusiastically. Thanks to intense promotion by the ICG's executive director Claire Reis and by Minna Lederman, the house sold out. Reis later recalled that between two and three hundred people had to be turned away. The audience was distinguished, including the composers Alfredo Casella, Georges Enesco, and Milhaud, and the conductors Willem Mengelberg and Leopold Stokowski. One month later, Carlos Salzedo described these dignitaries as "amazed at the reception" given to *Pierrot* in New York and "no less amazed at the possibility of producing it with such an incomparable artist as Greta Torpadie . . . , a precise and intelligent conductor as the composer Louis Gruenberg, a superb pianist as Leroy Shield, and others." The *New York Times* reported that "the younger and youngest generations of the local musical intelligentsia were enthusiastically present. There were also musicians of the elder line, curious, but less enthusiastic." Charles Ives was even invited, though whether or not he went is not known. Ives's friend Clifton Furness wrote him, asking if he would like to attend either the concert or a semipublic rehearsal scheduled for the preceding Sunday. "Perhaps you would rather go with me to the rehearsal than to the whole concert, if the other numbers on the programme do not interest you particularly," Furness suggested. "I enclose announcement of the other numbers. The Schönberg, at least will be worth hearing. I'm sure Carl Engle [*sic*], of the Music Library of the Library of Congress, gave a very interesting diatribe on it yesterday afternoon. I would have asked you to venture it, but anticipated a bore—on the contrary he dropped some really stimulating ideas, about which I'll tell you when I see you." In a letter of 1931, subsequently published in the *Memos*, Ives claimed to "have never heard nor seen a note of Schoenberg's music."[9]

Pierrot lunaire received a varied critical response in New York. The older, more conservative forces on New York's newspapers, such as H. E. Krehbiel and Henry T. Finck, were predictably disgusted by the piece. But Pitts Sanborn, writing in the *New York Globe*, acknowledged that the performance had been "painstaking" and that the work was "one of the most typical and significant compositions of one of the most important of living composers." And Richard Aldrich of the *New York Times* acknowledged the significance of the concert: "A momentous event in the musical world, long expected, loudly heralded, at least once postponed, occurred last evening in New York: the first performance in America of Arnold Schoenberg's 'melodrama,' called 'Pierrot Lunaire.'" He went on, "You either liked it and accepted it or you did not." Modernism's champion, Paul Rosenfeld, not only com-

Figure 17.1. "Greta Torpadie, Soprano, and Her Associates—Louis Gruenberg, Conductor; Jacob Mestechkin, Violinist; Leroy Shield, Pianist; William Durieux, 'Cellist; George Possell, Flautist; and Robert Lindemann, Clarinetist—Rehearsing Schönberg's 'Pierrot Lunaire,' for Its First American Performance." Photo published in *Musical America* (20 January 1923). Courtesy of Musical America Archives.

mended the endeavor but also observed that the musicians acted more maturely than had been the case for previous performances of modern music in New York: "When Eva Gauthier gave the three Japanese melodies of Stravinsky; when Vera Janacopoulous presented the Pribaoutki of the same composer, the musicians came on the stage grinning, to let the audience know they at least were not balmy. . . . But, during the Schoenberg, the playing was rich and smooth and telling." In April 1924, *Vanity Fair* added to the kudos by inducting Schoenberg into its "Hall of Fame," a regular photo section featuring current personalities.[10]

Varèse had negotiated directly with Schoenberg about performing *Pierrot*, a process that was anything but amiable. He wrote the composer in August 1922, telling him that a performance was planned on 18 January 1923 and asking him to join the Composers' Committee of the ICG. Schoenberg responded angrily. He berated Varèse for including "no single German among 27 composers performed!" and he was distressed that a performance had been scheduled "without asking me whether you *can and may* do so [Schoenberg's emphasis]." He went on to question

Varèse's ability to find competent performers. It appears that Varèse did not respond directly, but that Max von Recklinghausen, secretary of the ICG's Executive Board, did so on behalf of the organization. He defended the absence of German composers on the ICG's previous programs, claiming that "we approached a number of composers in Germany at the founding of the Guild, but received no answer from them" and went on to tell Schoenberg that in order "to direct all the details of the performance" of *Pierrot lunaire* he "would have to come to New York to conduct the work." He also endorsed the performers who would be appearing in New York: "Greta Torpadie, Swedish singer, trained in Europe, very well known here, a splendid musician, familiar with your style and possessing an excellent German pronunciation," and "Louis Grunberg [*sic*], composer and pianist pupil of Busoni; One of the first to defend your music in Germany. You will remember a letter of thanks to him on one occasion."[11]

Another decisive event in the relationship of American and European modernists came in 1923 with the founding of the International Society for Contemporary Music (ISCM). This was far less glamorous. There was no photo spread in *Vanity Fair* to announce it. But its importance—both practically and symbolically—was tremendous.

In the summer of 1922, the Salzburg Festival of Chamber Music had proven that a postwar international forum could be launched to promote modernism, and that August a group of composers gathered to devise an ongoing international organization. This resulted in the ISCM, and the need for it was felt as acutely in the United States as it was in Western Europe. "In fact," mused the composer Richard Hammond, "a more universal exchange of music and musical ideas would result in obvious advantages, for in an era of almost instantaneous verbal communication over vast distances, it is inexcusable that eleven years should pass before a work so important as *Le Sacre du printemps* reaches America."[12]

Yet one early decision made by founders of the ISCM shows how Americans had to fight to gain a position on the international scene. The draft constitution of the ISCM defined "contemporary" as "music of all European countries written within the last fifteen years," thereby excluding Americans. But American composers responded aggressively. Members of the International Composers' Guild met in New York in January 1923—a month before the New York premiere of *Pierrot lunaire*—to debate whether the United States should demand representation in the venture. Those present included Claire Reis, then executive director of the ICG, Edgard Varèse, Lazare Saminsky, Alfred Human of *Musical America*, Carlos Salzedo, Frank Patterson of the *Musical Courier*, Henry F. Gilbert, William C. Tuthill, Alma Wertheim, Chalmers Clifton, Louis Gruenberg, and Minna Lederman. Exclaiming that the language in the draft must have represented "an oversight," the American group decided to request that it be amended, and they appointed Oscar Sonneck as chair of a committee to write a constitution for their national affiliate. Their effort succeeded, and the United States became an equal partner in the ISCM. The English critic and historian Edward J. Dent served as the ISCM's chairman, and the new international organization set up an office in London. Conflicts over national representation apparently continued. Writing in the very first issue of *Modern Music*, the Danish oboist and conductor Svend B. Felumb talked of the "dissatisfaction following last summer's Salzburg performance" of the ISCM, wondering "whether the society should strive to be judiciously international or simply to represent new music." Yet for Americans it brought significant international exposure. Over the remainder of the 1920s, music by Copland, Eichheim, Gruenberg, Jacobi, Ruggles, Sessions, and Whithorne appeared on the ISCM's annual festivals; Gershwin's *An American in Paris* was performed in 1931. And American composers, as has been discussed with Copland, attended those events and learned from them.[13]

At the same time as American composers established this foothold abroad, their European colleagues were clamoring to visit the United States. The climate, both politically and economically, was right for it. As an audience grew in New York for the newest European compositions, interest rose not only in hearing the music but also in meeting the composers who had written it. And so a string of major European composers visited America, including Milhaud in 1922–23; Stravinsky, Alfredo Casella, and Germaine Tailleferre in 1925; Prokofiev and Milhaud in 1926; Bartók in 1927–28; Ravel in 1928; and Honegger and Milhaud in 1929. "The Invasion of America by the Great Musicians: We Suddenly Find Ourselves the Custodians of the Musical Culture of the World," declared a headline in a 1925 issue of *Vanity Fair*. These tours were highly publicized, and the composers often criss-crossed the United States; for some this was a prelude to immigrating during the 1930s. Like Ole Bull, Jenny Lind, Anton Rubinstein, or Sigismond Thalberg during the nineteenth century, these latter-day Europeans brought continental culture to major cities and remote outposts, and like Antonín Dvořák late in the previous century, they occasionally lectured Americans about the direction their music should be taking.[14]

Treated as a celebrity event, the arrival of each European modernist made the news. There was usually a photograph in *Musical America* showing the composer stepping off the ship, and interviews followed in the New York papers. Most composers immediately had a major orchestral performance. There were private auditions as well—often at the home of a wealthy woman patron—and there were appearances with the composer societies. This was followed by some travel, perhaps just to Boston and Philadelphia or, more likely, across the continent, often under the auspices of the Pro Musica Society. At some point, each was inducted into the *Vanity Fair* "Hall of Fame."

The American tours of Stravinsky and Bartók give a sense of how these visits unfolded. Stravinsky made his American debut on 8–10 January 1925 as guest conductor of the Philharmonic Society of New York. He was treated like a star. The kickoff was devoted solely to Stravinsky's music, including *Song of the Volga Boatmen, Fireworks, Scherzo fantastique, Le Chant du rossignol, Suite from Pulcinella, Suite*

Figure 17.2. Igor Stravinsky, with the conductor Wilhelm Furtwängler, during Stravinsky's 1925 tour of the United States. Photo published in *Musical America* (24 January 1925). Courtesy of Musical America Archives.

from L'Oiseau de feu (replaced on one program by *Suite from Petrushka*). *Le Sacre du printemps* had been scheduled for the final concert but was dropped; apparently there was not enough rehearsal time to get it into shape. The audience was "huge and lustrous and clamorous," giving an unabashedly rousing reception. It may even have been a little jaded by then. "In the year 1925," reported Oscar Thompson in *Musical America*, the "lack of outrage for the ear doubtless left some thrill-hunters a little disappointed."[15]

American reviewers had no compunction about leveling criticisms at Stravinsky's performance. This could be viewed as yet another manifestation of the curmudgeonly attitude of New York critics toward new music, or, more likely, it was a sign that they were not intimidated by the luster of a European luminary. Lawrence Gilman described Stravinsky as "a slight, nervous, baldescent, goggled, pleasantly homely figure, looking somewhat like one of Mr. Wells's great-orbed Martians," and no critic seemed overly impressed by his conducting. Oscar Thompson was not afraid to state with deadpan frankness that "there was no disposition to regard Stravinsky as an electrifying conductor." Gilman concurred: "It would be excessive to say that he threw much new light upon the question of the interpretation of his works."[16]

On 15 January, the composer appeared "in recital of his own compositions" at the Fifth Avenue home of Mrs. Vincent Astor. The event was given "for the benefit of the Mental Hygiene Committee of the New York State Charities Aid Association." Greta Torpadie, the soprano who two years earlier had introduced *Pierrot lunaire* to America, performed with him, as did the violinist Scipione Guidi and clarinetist Simeon Bellison. The program included two groups of songs and a trio arrangement of *Histoire du soldat*. Before the end of January, Stravinsky traveled to Boston, where he played his Piano Concerto with Koussevitzky and the Boston Symphony Orchestra. Then he went back to New York to perform in a concert of his chamber music at Aeolian Hall with Greta Torpadie and to attend a performance of *Le Sacre du printemps* conducted by Wilhelm Furtwängler. This last "drew such a large audience to Carnegie Hall . . . that it was necessary to limit standees." Stravinsky then headed off to Philadelphia for another conducting engagement. But that was not all. In early February, he returned to New York to play his Piano Concerto with the Philharmonic under Mengelberg. From then through the first week of March, he traveled to give performances in Cleveland, Philadelphia, Chicago, and Cincinnati.[17]

When Bartók set shore in New York in December 1927, he may have been a less celebrated modernist than Stravinsky, but his arrival still inspired considerable hoopla. "Previous visits of other revolutionaries, such as Stravinsky and Strauss, were fairly sensational, yes, but they came before the brand new tidal wave of American public opinion on modern music had gotten under way," declared *Musical America*. After comparing the importance of his visit to that of the famous Armory Show, the author continued: "Perhaps it is Bartók's destiny to be one of the first great radical composers to ride the crest of it. As yet he is a musical dark horse." That same month, Bartók's picture appeared in *Vanity Fair*, together with that of Sir Thomas Beecham, Vladimir Horowitz, Beatrice Harrison (a British cellist), and Maurice Ravel, bearing the caption "On Our Musical Visiting List."[18]

Prior to this visit, Bartók's music had been infrequently performed in the United States. There was an initial introduction of *Deux Images* by Varèse's New Symphony Orchestra in 1919, followed by the American premiere of the Second String Quartet by the International Composers' Guild in March 1923. Immediately before the ICG's performance, Bartók's photograph had been published in *Vanity Fair*'s Hall of Fame, still well in advance of his visit nearly five years later. Clearly the ICG, not just the League of Composers, knew how to exploit fashionable components of the press. Later that summer, Paul Rosenfeld published a feature piece about Bartók in the same magazine, hailing the ICG's performance of

Figure 17.3. "Bela Bartok, Hungarian Composer, Upon His Arrival Here for a Concert Tour of Ten Weeks." Photo published in *Musical America* (31 December 1927). Courtesy of Musical America Archives.

the quartet as "stand[ing] apart" from its previous endeavors: "While the others brought to the public compositions by men whose work was already known to it, this brought to it a work by a significant composer who had hitherto been nothing but a name." As early as 1924, E. Robert Schmitz had invited Bartók to visit the United States under the auspices of Pro Musica, and Bartók responded by saying that the Baldwin Piano Company had already engaged him as pianist for a ten-week American tour in 1926. This was canceled because of poor health.[19]

Bartók's American debut finally took place on 22 December 1927 with the New York Philharmonic. "He is as great a master of composition as any living, and finer than many of the dead to whom we devote nine-tenths of our concert programs," wrote Henry Cowell afterward. The original plan had been for the composer to perform his new Piano Concerto No. 1, but it had to be scuttled. The orchestra announced that it had insufficient rehearsal time to conquer the piece, and instead, it presented his Rhapsody for Piano and Orchestra, with the composer as soloist. Irving Weil, writing in *Musical America*, speculated that Mengelberg, who conducted the concert, was simply afraid to tackle the concerto, and Olin Downes in the *New York Times* expressed disappointment not only at the substitution of the "immature and rather old-fashioned Rhapsody" but that even in this work the orchestra was "far from finished or precise in its accord with the soloist or vivid in the presentation of the orchestral part."[20]

The concerto was finally performed in New York on 13 February 1928 by Fritz Reiner and the Cincinnati Orchestra. Bartók was at the piano, and Cowell in the audience. "New loveliness was revealed in each succeeding measure; and counterpoint of lines formed by percussion instruments, which were used canonically, was a unique musical element introduced," Cowell observed. Between his New York debut and the concerto's performance, Bartók traveled across the country under the sponsorship of the Pro Musica Society. On 15 January he was in Seattle, the 17th in Portland, the 21st in Denver, the 23rd in Kansas City, and the 25th in St. Paul. His final stop was in Chicago before the tour wound up in New York with a Pro Musica concert of his music on 5 February.[21]

Money made these tours mighty appealing to European composers. Robert Craft and Vera Stravinsky reported that "Stravinsky's 1925 American tour was the most lucrative of his life"—enough so that afterward he employed a chauffeur. And while the financial details of Bartók's visit remain obscure, he wrote E. Robert Schmitz in July 1928 after returning to Hungary from America, saying that he hoped to come to the United States again in 1929–30 or 1930–31. He wanted fifteen engagements for $7,000 over the course of two months; he was guaranteed an additional $100 per concert by the Baldwin Piano Company.[22]

In spite of different musical styles and nationalities, most of these Europeans arrived in the United States eager to hear jazz, which for them represented the core of American music. Soon after Stravinsky docked, the *New York Times* described him as "going at evening to dine and to hear on its native heath the dance music that the Old World has called American jazz." Variations of the same story were repeated time and again. Bartók asked about "the latest things in American jazz . . . pretty nearly as soon as he was down the gangplank." Besides going to hear the music, some European composers lectured Americans on its value. In an interview with Marion Bauer, Bartók, speaking as ethnomusicologist more than composer, urged white Americans to leap the racial divide and discover African American jazz. "He [Bartók] finds that the Jazz band has also been harmed by its popularity," reported Bauer. "He feels that we must get back to the source and get the Negro music in its unspoiled, natural state, in order for it to have a worth-while influence on art."[23]

Milhaud and Ravel took a different approach, affirming the importance of jazz to concert-music composers. They knew this was a sensitive topic in the United States, yet they spoke out firmly about it. "One thing I want to emphasize very particularly and that is the beneficial influence upon all music of jazz," exhorted Milhaud during his visit in 1923. "It has been enormous and in my opinion, an influence for good. It is a new idea and has brought in new rhythms and almost, one might say, new forms. . . . All great composers, you know, have written in the dance form popular at the time. . . . There is no reason, therefore, why the best modern composers should hesitate to write jazz. They have excellent precedents. I intend to compose a jazz Sonata, and I have already done a number of jazz pieces. Listen!"[24]

During his visit in 1928, Ravel did more than simply admonish American composers; he leveled some criticisms in the process. "But in the field of composition I have found my earlier impressions of American music confirmed," Ravel began. "I think you have too little realization of yourselves and that you still look too far away over the water. An artist should be international in his judgments and esthetic appreciations and incorrigibly national when it comes to the province of creative art. I think you know that I greatly admire and value—more, I think, than many American composers—American jazz. . . . I am waiting to see more Americans appear with the honesty and vision to realize the significance of their popular product, and the technic and imagination to base an original and creative art upon it."[25]

By 1929, when Arthur Honegger visited, Olin Downes of the *New York Times* felt compelled to suggest: "We do not commend to him American jazz, which too many European musicians have striven to imitate." He also expressed the hope that "Mr. Honegger will leave us a somewhat different man than he came, and enriched in other ways than the merely pecuniary."[26]

Through these tours and premieres, New York not only caught up with Western Europe in presenting continental modernism but also became a desirable locale in its own right. Even though visiting European luminaries seemed to pay little attention to American composers of concert music—at least there is scant record of it—they helped alter the overall climate for modernism. As every year passed, New York seemed less provincial, and its young composers benefited from the difference.

Visionary Critics

When one is in Paris one is in Paris; when one is in Amsterdam one is in Amsterdam; . . . but one may be in New York and a great many other places simultaneously.

—Carl Van Vechten, *In the Garrett*, 1920

Paul Rosenfeld has heard my music and likes it. (He has advised me to burn MacDowell and Franck in effigy.)

—Letter from Roy Harris
to Aaron Copland, [1926]

As contemporary European music arrived in the United States and Americans devised their own brands of modernism, a new generation of critics took on a parallel challenge, attempting to interpret these fast-breaking developments for a public that was often bewildered. Faced with an art that could seem unfathomable, they sought to divine its essence. While their ranks were not large—in fact more American critics of the day berated the modernists than backed them—a few key figures rallied to the cause of the avant-garde, with two, in particular, leading the charge. The first, Carl Van Vechten, wrote perceptive, even prescient evaluations of new music during the mid-1910s, just as the modernist movement began taking hold in New York. This phase of his career was brief, and by the early 1920s, he embarked on his better-known work as a champion of African American culture. At about the time that Van Vechten's interests were shifting, another critic stepped in: Paul Rosenfeld, who became an advocate of modernism in all the arts. Both flourished within the medium of the essay, not daily journalism. Both agitated for cultural change, and both grappled with contemporary European figures and American popular idioms. But they ended up in very different positions. Van Vechten's role in early-twentieth-century modernism is now largely forgotten, while Rosenfeld is lionized as one of modernism's great interpreters.[1]

To Americans of the mid-1910s, Van Vechten appeared as an emissary from abroad, sending home news of the new as he heard it unfolding in Paris. Even when reporting from New York, his focus was on European developments as transmitted there. One of the most significant aspects of Van Vechten's criticism of modern music was how early it appeared, mainly between 1915 and 1920, when the works of Schoenberg, Stravinsky, and their European colleagues were first reaching America. He took the lead in recognizing the importance of this music, publishing essays about a select group of European composers in a series of books, most notably *Music After the Great War* (1915), *Music and Bad Manners* (1916), *Interpreters and Interpretations* (1917), and *Red* (1925).[2]

New music represented the second stage of Van Vechten's career as a critic. Born in 1880, he belonged to the generation of John Alden Carpenter and Charles Ives, not of Copland and Sessions, and at first he had worked as a journeyman music critic, serving as assistant to Richard Aldrich at the *New York Times*. In 1915 he decided to change course. "I have determined to be a writer," he later explained to his brother, "not a journalist or a scribbler but a writer." Van Vechten believed that in newspaper work "the hurry produced by the demand for copy makes one fall into routine expressions which eventually spoil a style." By forsaking daily papers, Van Vechten gave himself freedom to choose his own topics, even esoteric ones such as contemporary composers.[3]

Van Vechten possessed a capacity to form opinions quickly and state them with absolute confidence. He also loved to venture into unexplored terrain. Witnessing the Paris premiere of Stravinsky's *Le Sacre du printemps*, he immediately knew he was encountering something "most extraordinary," as he wrote his wife Fania Marinoff. "Both the music and the dancing were of an originality appalling. . . . And how wildly beautiful it was." He wrote a vivid account of the event in *Music After the Great War*. Over the next several years, Van Vechten went on to become an active proselytizer for Stravinsky, contributing some of the earliest literature about the Russian. He predicted fame for this rising figure, calling him "perhaps the greatest of the musicians of the immediate future," and he published major essays about Stravinsky in 1915 and 1916.[4]

Two of these essays vividly convey Stravinsky's standing at this early date. In writing of the Ballets Russes, one year before its visit to New York in 1916, Van Vechten perceived the essential role of the troupe in "bringing some of the most radical and anarchistic of modern composers to a hearing before the public." "Igor Strawinsky: A New Composer," an essay devoted solely to the young Russian, also arrived like a telegram over the water. In it, Van Vechten gave a compact and informative profile of the composer, doing so at a time when few such digests of his work had yet been published. Van Vechten began by tracing his personal discovery of the composer and showed direct acquaintance with Stravinsky's music; he made it clear that few of his readers had had the same opportunities to obtain scores or hear pieces.[5]

Van Vechten also stood out for his capacity to discuss musical texts, rather than impressionistically dance around them. Discussing *Le Sacre du printemps* in *Music After the Great War*, for example, he managed to capture its unconventional sense of narrative, as well as its new approach to rhythm and harmony. At a time when no technical language existed to grapple with these phenomena, he could easily have avoided the challenge. Instead, he found his own way to convey the innovations he heard. "The lack of a fable, the early and uncertain setting of the action, offered Strawinsky an opportunity which he seized with avidity," Van Vechten observed. "The music is not descriptive, it is rhythmical. All rhythms are beaten into the ears, one after another, and sometimes with complexities which seem decidedly un-rhythmic on paper, but when carried out in performance assume a regularity of beat which a simple four-four time could not equal." He then confronted Stravinsky's harmonic style: "In many cases his chord-formations could not be described in academic terms; the instruments employed add to the strangeness of the sounds. I remember one passage in which the entire corps of dancers is engaged in shivering, trembling from head to toe, to music which trembles also. It makes my flesh creep even to think of it again. At the beginning of the ballet the adolescents pound the earth with their feet, while a little old woman runs in and out between their legs, to the reiterated beat of a chord of F flat, A flat, C flat, F flat; G, B flat, D flat, and E flat, all in the bass (begin from below and read in order), while an occasional flute or a piccolo screams its way in high treble. Try this on your piano."[6]

At the end, Van Vechten attempted to contextualize Stravinsky's particular brand of the new, giving a sense of the impressionist climate in which his music emerged:

> This young Russian has appeared in an epoch in which the ambition of most composers seems to be to dream, to write their symbolic visions in terms of the mist, to harmonize the imperceptible. Strawinsky sweeps away this vague atmosphere with one gesture; his idea of movement is Dionysian; he overwhelms us with his speed. . . . His gifts to future composers are his conciseness, his development of the complexities of rhythm, and his invention of chord-formation. His use of dissonance is an art in itself.[7]

In "A New Principle in Music" in *Music and Bad Manners*, Van Vechten analyzed Stravinsky's innovations as an orchestrator. He recognized that the Russian made "new use of the modern orchestra, completely upsetting the old academic ideas about 'balance of tone,' and proving to his own satisfaction the value of 'pure tone,' in the same sense that the painter speaks of pure colour." He grasped Stravinsky's technique of applying chamber principles to the full orchestra, avoiding doublings as much as possible.[8]

Yet Van Vechten did not indiscriminately boost all Stravinsky performances. He lambasted the Ballets Russes for bringing "the dregs" of the company to New York for a series of "highly advertised" appearances. "To those enthusiasts, and they included practically every one who had seen the Ballet in its greater glory, who had prepared their friends for an overwhelmingly brilliant spectacle," he lamented, "the early performances in January, 1916, at the Century Theatre were a great disappointment." Only when Nijinsky arrived on 12 April, well into the troupe's appearance, did the level of performance pick up, and Van Vechten described at length his extraordinary impact on stage.[9]

Through all this advocacy of Stravinsky, Van Vechten simultaneously decried the degree to which he felt concert programming in New York had become stultifying. In "The Bridge Burners," published in *Music and Bad Manners*, he again invoked Stravinsky, but this time his real goal was to counter the conservative opinions of his former boss, Richard Aldrich of the *New York Times*. Van Vechten was merciless. From the opening sentence—"It is from the enemy that one learns"—he came out swinging. In covering the Flonzaley Quartet's performance of *Three Pieces for String Quartet* by Stravinsky in November 1915, Aldrich had written that the music "seems to be conditioned on an accompaniment of something else to explain it from beginning to end," which Van Vechten interpreted as implying that it was incomprehensible without a program. Van Vechten spewed twelve pages in response, first defending the history of program music, then refuting the notion that Stravinsky's work fit that classification. He included brash lines such as "it seems a bit thick to jump on Strawinsky for writing music which has to be explained." Although obviously frustrated by Aldrich, Van Vechten also aimed his remarks at a bigger audience, seeking to shake concert-goers out of their torpor. His conclusion to "The Bridge Burners" made this clear:

> We may be on the verge of a still greater revolution in art than any through which we have yet passed; new banners may be unfurled, and new strongholds captured. . . . Try to admit as much to yourself. Go hear the new music; listen to it and see if you can't enjoy it. Perhaps you can't. At any rate you will find in time that you won't listen to second-rate imitations of the giant works of the past any longer. Your ears will make progress in spite of you and I shouldn't wonder at all if five years more would make Schoenberg and Strawinsky and Ornstein a trifle old fashioned.[10]

With salvos such as this, Van Vechten contributed to the campaign to reform concert programming that Virgil Thomson, most notably, took part in thirty years later. "Symphony concerts, then, as they exist in America—and to a lesser degree elsewhere—are museums," Van Vechten declared in *Music After the Great War*. He reflected on how the music of Bach, Haydn, and Mozart was being rendered inappropriately by oversized orchestras designed for nineteenth-century repertory. But his main gripe had to do with "the organization [i.e., American orchestras] and its supporters," which he felt to be "corrupted by cobwebs." He continued, "They are things of the past that persist in going on. A live orchestra, built on living principles, which played new music if it played at all, would serve not only to develop new composers, but also new ideas." Here, too, he berated music critics, this time as "cataloguers of the museum" who were unable "to accept any innovations after a diminished seventh." Van Vechten wrote this before Varèse's venture with the New Symphony Orchestra and before the birth of any of the composer societies; he called for change before composer-activists began implementing it.[11]

Where Van Vechten fell short was in evaluating contemporary American concert composers. "I shall not hesitate on the music of America," he declared in *Music After the Great War*. But he did not address the music of American composers of the mid-1910s—whether George Chadwick or Henry Gilbert or Charles Martin Loeffler—and, not surprisingly, he did not seem to know about Charles Ives. Disliking the little American concert music that he heard, Van Vechten dismissed the whole shebang: "One cannot speak with too great enthusiasm of Ethelbert Nevin and Edward MacDowell—there is no immediate promise of important development." This attitude may explain why Van Vechten completely passed over the generation of concert composers born around 1900. He also ignored Copland, Cowell, Thomson, even Varèse, creating no line of continuity with his early criticism of European modernism. He became friends with some young composers, most notably Copland and Colin McPhee; in McPhee's case Van Vechten even went to hear performances of his music. But he never wrote about it.[12]

Instead, during the early 1920s, Van Vechten made a break with the concert tradition altogether and turned instead to popular music, African American jazz, and blues, launching the third phase of his work as a critic. In writing about these idioms, Van Vechten was intrigued by the newest, most innovative work, just as he had been with European modernism, and he seemed to revel in expressing opinions that must have struck many readers as outrageous. Rumblings of this change appeared already in the late 1910s, when he wrote about American popular songs, although his focus then still remained on white Americans. "When some curious critic, a hundred years hence, searches through the available archives in an attempt to discover what was the state of American music at the beginning of the Twentieth Century do you fancy he will take the trouble to exhume and dig into the ponderous scores of Henry Hadley, Arthur Foote, Ernest Schelling, George W. Chadwick, Horatio W. Parker and the rest of the recognizedly 'important' composers of the present day?" he wrote in "The Great American Composer," published in *Vanity Fair* in 1917. "But if he is lucky enough to run across copies of *Waiting for the Robert E. Lee, Alexander's Ragtime Band*, or *Hello Frisco*, which are scarcely mentioned in the literature of our time, his face will light up. . . . Lewis F. Muir, Irving Berlin, and Louis A. Hirsch [are] the true grandfathers of the Great American Composer of the year 2001."[13]

While Van Vechten may have been impatient with American composers of concert music, his recognition of popular idioms was visionary—a view that was seized upon by Gilbert Seldes in *The Seven Lively Arts* within a few years. Van Vechten was slightly off target with the specific figures highlighted—Muir and Hirsch have hardly survived as major songwriters—but there was freshness to his thinking. The careers of a group of gifted American songwriters soon took off, including those of Jerome Kern, George Gershwin, and Cole Porter. Not surprisingly, then, when Van Vechten finally did write an essay surveying the career of a white American composer who had made a significant contribution to the concert repertory, the subject was George Gershwin and the date was 1925, not long after the premiere of *Rhapsody in Blue*.[14]

When Van Vechten published *Red* in 1925, his last volume of essays about music, he had come to the conclusion that jazz "may not be the last hope of American music, nor yet the best hope, but at present, I am convinced, it is its only hope." That statement reflected a new conviction. By then, he had lost interest in Stravinsky and Schoenberg. *Red* opened with "A Valedictory," in which Van Vechten bade farewell to music criticism and passed on his mission to "the younger generation, who are hereby given permission to transfer what I said ten years ago about Stravinsky and Satie to Darius Milhaud and the young Italians." Van Vechten devoted a good portion of the essay to an expansive assessment of his own achievement as a music critic. He pointed out that he had been "about ten years ahead of most of the other critics and the orchestral conductors who make out programs" and concluded: "The job of music critic in New York, therefore, is certainly not an ideal occupation for a man with imagination and foresight." The same year that *Red* was published Van Vechten made his switch to African American topics definitive, especially with a series of articles in *Vanity Fair* on spirituals, the blues, and black theater. During this same period, he also wrote some successful novels, most notoriously *Nigger Heaven* of 1926.[15]

Paul Rosenfeld cut a figure quite different from Carl Van Vechten: a prolific and widely recognized critic of American modernist music, a confirmed elitist who disdained jazz as well as other American popular and vernacular idioms, and an advocate not just of the European avant-garde but also of its burgeoning counterpart in the United States. While Van Vechten ended up championing the American music that was most distinct from European traditions, Rosenfeld demanded that the new American modernism take its place in a continental lineage. Yet the two shared a fundamental desire to encourage the acceptance of European modernism in America and a view of criticism as a creative endeavor. Both, too, had the independent means to support their choice of vocation—Van Vechten more modestly so than Rosenfeld.

In retrospect, Rosenfeld took off where the older critic ended. Born in 1890, making him ten years junior to Van Vechten, Rosenfeld published his first music criticism in 1916, just as Van Vechten's interest in modernism peaked, and he made his mark by covering the very American figures that Van Vechten ignored. By the late 1910s, as the older man ended up completely disillusioned with

American concert composers and convinced that popular song writers, blues singers, and jazz musicians were emerging as the New World's musical luminaries, the younger one stepped in to champion those Americans who were devising a distinctive response to European models. Like Van Vechten, Rosenfeld was also a visionary, although a more conservative one. He was unreformedly "highbrow," as his colleague Van Wyck Brooks defined the term.[16]

Like Van Vechten, Rosenfeld's great awakening to modernist music came while traveling abroad—in his case, during a visit in 1914 to London where he first heard the music of Scriabin. Prior to that, as Rosenfeld later recalled, "Music I thought had ended with César Franck." Not long after returning to New York, Rosenfeld encountered the startling performances of Leo Ornstein and joined his friend Claire Reis in exploring avenues for bringing modernist music to America. With Waldo Frank and Van Wyck Brooks he founded *The Seven Arts*, a "little magazine" that lasted from November 1916 to October 1917. There and at the *New Republic* Rosenfeld began writing music criticism. In 1920 he initiated "Music Chronicle" for the *Dial*, a magazine that was stepping forth as a center for opinion about American literature and art, and he continued there until 1927, completing his longest and most important stint as a critic. In the early 1920s he also published a series of essays in *Vanity Fair*. At the same time Rosenfeld, like Van Vechten, regularly issued anthologies of his writing. The first of these, *Musical Portraits*, appeared in 1920, and during the next decade six more books followed. Rosenfeld's productivity dropped off in the 1930s when only one title appeared: *Discoveries of a Music Critic.*[17]

Rosenfeld's heyday, then, was in the 1920s. He was the period's most illustrious critic of new music, and he had much to do with shaping the course of modernism in America. Rosenfeld flourished amid the decade's extravagant idealism, achieving distinction for writing about painting and literature, as well as music. Once the radical politics and financial strains of the Depression descended, his power diminished. Although Rosenfeld's achievements as critic during the 1920s have been widely acclaimed, many aspects of his work remain unexamined. His preconceptions, which circumscribed his views of American modernism, have been accepted without question.[18]

Much about Rosenfeld's early perspective came out of his work with Waldo Frank and Van Wyck Brooks on *The Seven Arts*. The writer Gorham Munson called the publication "a bonfire burning in a depressing gray fog." Founded on the eve of America's involvement in World War I, the magazine radiated an optimistic outlook for the arts in America. "We are in the first days of a renascent period, a time which means for America the beginning of that national self-consciousness which is the beginning of greatness," declared its editors in an opening manifesto. "The arts are not only the expression of the national life but a means to its enhancement." That affirming message became the foundation for Rosenfeld's entire body of writing. He entered the 1920s determined to uncover "greatness" in American composition, and by the end of the decade he had accomplished his mission. Yet he was never a jingoistic advocate of just any homegrown product. Rosenfeld set high standards for his compatriots and shaped those standards according to his knowledge of European modernism.[19]

Beginning with his very first book, *Musical Portraits* of 1920, Rosenfeld searched for the Great American Composer—someone who could enter the international arena with parity and pride. But he conceded that the field of contenders at the time was limited. In his next major publication, *Musical Chronicle* of 1923, Rosenfeld still strained for an American to promote. The American Music Guild (see Chapter 10) and John Alden Carpenter turned up on his list of contenders but he wrote tepidly of them and continued to wait "for the talent that can grow in intellectual mastery and still utter itself in freshness." With *Port of New York*, published one year later, Rosenfeld's wait was over. He sensed "a new spirit dawning in American life, . . . awaken[ing] a sense of wealth, of confidence, and of power which was not there before." The book included a profile of one young native-born composer, Roger Sessions, amid fourteen essays on progressive American painters and writers. Rosenfeld saw Sessions as a kind of messiah, and he openly confessed relief that the savior had appeared in the respectable garb of a concert-music composer.[20]

Throughout the decade, Rosenfeld discovered other new figures, including Copland, Varèse, and Ruggles, each one reconfirming his faith in America's potential. His writing appeared mostly in the *Dial*, and much of it was reprinted in his various anthologies. By the time of *An Hour with American Music* in 1929, he had synthesized these individual essays into a grand theory of American music. This extraordinary little book may be the most underacclaimed of Rosenfeld's publications. It has much historical significance, not only representing the culmination of Rosenfeld's efforts to advance modernist music in America but also giving unique firsthand accounts of young composers as their work was being discovered. In it Rosenfeld unveiled his perspective on the history of American music. In so doing, he revealed much about attitudes during the 1920s—especially the narcissistic self-confidence of Americans.[21]

With this book, Rosenfeld solidified the Darwinian framework that informed much of his writing. The book opened in Rosenfeld's version of an abyss, facing head-on the music perceived by him as the greatest threat to concert idioms, "American music is not jazz. Jazz is not music. Jazz remains a striking indigenous product, a small, sounding folk-chaos, counterpart of other national developments." To defend his dismissal of jazz, Rosenfeld sought to define "music," and did so by calling up the names "Bach and Beethoven, Mozart, Wagner and Brahms" as being "what jazz from the beginning is not: the product of a sympathetic treatment of the sonorous medium." He then went on for several pages lauding the glories of these historic Europeans and finally completed the punch: "And to-day a force related to theirs is at work in America. This is one of the most significant aspects of the national situation. We have an American music: there existing a body of sonorous work, not jazz, made by persons associated with the American community, to be grouped without impertinence with classic European works." That premise generated the rest of the volume. Early American composers were dismissed for being imitative colonialists, for their "assimilation of European motives, figures and ideas" and lack of "original expression." The nineteenth century was a time when "determined musicians, men like [John Knowles] Paine and Lowell Mason, were forceless; weak personalities." Real composition dawned with MacDowell, "the first American to deserve the name of composer." Yet Rosenfeld saw MacDowell as a flawed provincial. Foreshadowing the language of Ives in the *Memos*, he described MacDowell as having "succumbed to 'nice' and 'respectable' emotions."[22]

Not until the 1920s, with the arrival of Sessions, Copland, Harris, Ruggles, and Varèse, did an American music appear that could be placed alongside European. With them, Rosenfeld found the "most advanced sort of product." This was the essential point for him—that American modernism must conform to long-established European standards at the same time as it found its own distinctive manifestations. Not surprisingly, then, Rosenfeld was selective in championing Americans of the decade, showing little sympathy for more offbeat figures like Henry Cowell and calling a crossover musician like George Gershwin "assuredly a gifted composer of the lower, unpretentious order." He credited Virgil Thomson with a style that was "individual" though "neither strong nor unclouded."[23]

And so a paradox surfaced. At the same time as Rosenfeld criticized some contemporary American composers for being too derivative of European modernists, he was unable to break free of constant comparisons with Europeans. He championed a national form of creativity, yet he could only understand the composers and genres who spoke a certain language. George Antheil's *Ballet Mécanique* was dismissed as too derivative of Stravinsky: "a skyscraper built of girders synthesized from Les Noces, Le Sacre and Petrushka, and dependent for support on associated ideas." At the same time, Adolph Weiss was compared to a European in ways that worked both for and against him. On the one hand, "The dependence of [Weiss's] works on Schoenberg is even more pronounced than the dependence of the Sessions symphony on Strawinsky." On the other, "Weiss's music has a stronger relation to diatonism [*sic*] than to the atonality so characteristic of Schoenberg's; and his expression is more simply lyrical, more innocently human, than Schoenberg's fiercer, tortured one." In fact, Rosenfeld invoked the names of Stravinsky, Schoenberg, Satie, or Milhaud in the discussion of almost every contemporary American. Rosenfeld aimed to place these Americans in an international context. Yet he used this "cosmopolitan intelligence," as Edmund Wilson once put it, to varying purposes, alternately damning and supporting, always comparing. The end result was that he seemed, again according to Wilson, "more like a European among us than like an indigenous American."[24]

Rosenfeld's view of American musical history as progressing from rudimentary beginnings to civilized sophistication had precedents among his colleages at *Seven Arts*, especially in two books: *America's Coming-of-Age* (1915) by Van Wyck Brooks and *Our America* (1919) by Waldo Frank. "When I began first to read him," Sherwood Anderson wrote to Rosenfeld about Brooks, "his voice was a great shout saying, 'You are on the right road. You may never get to the sacred city but you have put your feet on the right road.'" With *America's Coming-of-Age*, Brooks defined themes that resounded with the up-and-coming generation of American modernists. Like Rosenfeld, he made severe judgments about early America, observing of its writers, for example, "Something, in American literature, has always been wanting—every one, I think, feels that." He sought intensely for a "usable past." Yet Brooks articulated exuberant optimism for the future, "It is true that under the glassy, brassy surface of American jocosity and business there is a pulp and a quick, and this pulpy quick, this nervous and acutely self-critical vitality, is in our day in a strange ferment. A fresh and more sensitive emotion seems to be running up and down even the old Yankee backbone—that unblossoming stalk."[25]

Frank's *Our America* expanded on these same themes and became, in turn, a model for both the structure and substance of *An Hour with American Music*. One of Rosenfeld's contemporaries called *Our America* "the bible of the oncoming generation." Frank also looked to the future, calling his country "a hidden treasure" and adding that "for us of the younger generation, America is a promise and a dream." Like Brooks and Rosenfeld he saw much of America before the twentieth century as a cultural prehistory, valuing most those figures who represented extensions of European practices. Frank came down hard on *Huckleberry Finn* by Mark Twain: "It must go down in history, not as the expression of a rich national culture like the books of Chaucer, Rabelais, Cervantes, but as the voice of American chaos, the voice of a precultural epoch." On the other hand, he devoted an entire chapter to "The Multitudes in Whitman," extolling the writer's achievements. Frank viewed Whitman as an international figure, avoiding any whiff of chauvinism: "The critics, therefore, who interpret Whitman as . . . 'father of the American tongue,' 'propagandist of American cultural liberation' dangerously reduce him. He was these things. But he was far more. To call him American in the sense of explanation is to reduce him also. . . . The whole world can claim Walt Whitman best."[26]

Many of these same notions were fundamental to Rosenfeld's thinking. He was intent on viewing American composers as part of a greater international scene; he had enormous difficulty with American music before the twentieth century; and he placed considerable faith in the future. Perhaps most striking was the degree to which Frank and Rosenfeld were prophets of a new American art at the same time as they clung to European ideals.

Rosenfeld's criticism also contained bluntly expressed prejudices. Although an open-minded promoter of new works at a time when few critics bothered to give them a chance, his tolerance had limits. Rosenfeld disdained almost any vernacular idiom, regardless of what cultural group it represented. Placing together white-American folk styles and black-American spirituals, he conceded that both had "charm" but were largely derivative of "extra-American" sources. To him, "The old-world folk tunes have a sad habit of deteriorating in the new world."[27]

Rosenfeld's writing also displayed a strain of misogyny. In ridiculing MacDowell, for example, he claimed that the composer "minces and simpers, maidenly, and ruffled. He is nothing if not a daughter of the American Revolution." He called his childhood piano teacher in Poughkeepsie "pathetic [and] bosomy," and his criticism of the French composer Germaine Tailleferre showed open gender bias:

> Tailleferre has nothing of great novelty to say. There is certain charm and cleverness in what she writes that is feminine. . . . But her talent is very frail; and her inclusion in the group [i.e., Les Six] must be attributed chiefly to a fine enthusiasm for the sex on the part of the five male members. Honegger is a more respectable musician than is the lady.

By contrast, Rosenfeld dealt respectfully with Ruth Crawford in *An Hour with American Music*, calling her "the most distinguished woman-composer in the younger ranks"; yet it was circumscribed praise, and it was all that he had to say about her.[28]

With yet another issue of minority status—Rosenfeld's own Jewishness—he stepped forward boldly. One of his biographers, Hugh M. Potter, has claimed that although Rosenfeld's upbringing was secular, being Jewish deeply affected his identity. Certainly it entered his music criticism, where he openly evaluated Ernest Bloch, Leo Ornstein, and Arnold Schoenberg according to traits he believed to be Jewish. With Ornstein and Bloch, Rosenfeld extolled their connection to an ancient heritage. He wrote that Ornstein "is the resurrection of the most entombed of spirits, that of the outlaw European Jew. . . . He is Lazarus emerging in his grave clothes into the new world." With Bloch, Rosenfeld encountered music "that is a large, a poignant, an authentic expression of what is racial in the Jew." He continued: "There are moments when this music makes one feel as though an element that had remained unchanged throughout three thousand years, an element that is in every Jew and by which every Jew must know himself and his descent, were caught up in it and fixed there."[29]

With Schoenberg, however, the issue of Jewishness had a double edge. In 1920 Rosenfeld evoked Jewish imagery as a means of criticizing Schoenberg: "But it is in the piano-music that the sonorities are most rudely neglected. . . . They smell of the synagogue as much as they do of the laboratory. Beside the Doctor of Music there stands the Talmudic Jew, the man all intellect and no feeling, who subtilizes over musical art as though it were the Law." Yet by 1925 he grouped Schoenberg favorably with Bloch, declaring that "the modern orientation has been particularly inviting to the Jewish temperament."[30]

Waldo Frank enters this facet of Rosenfeld's sensibility as well. *Our America* included a chapter titled "The Chosen People," which outlined the contribution of Jews in the United States. Such a section was unusual for a history of American culture. Like Rosenfeld, Frank placed a number of contemporary Jewish figures within an ongoing continuum of Jewish history, and later on in the book, he assessed Alfred Stieglitz as "a true Jew. He takes up the ancient destiny where the degenerate Jews whom we have observed had let it fall." He also declared, "Others in New York are marking this new rising of the Jew. Plenty of others." Such bold proclamations of ethnicity were more easily—even naively—articulated in the 1920s, before the Nazis came to power. Yet they still provoked difficulties. The music historian John Tasker Howard wrote with nervousness about the rise of the "New York Jew," and Daniel Gregory Mason made repeated pronouncements about a Jewish threat, stating on one occasion, "And our whole contemporary aesthetic attitude toward instrumental music, especially in New York, is dominated by Jewish tastes and standards, with their Oriental extravagance, their sensuous brilliancy and intellectual facility and superficiality, their general tendency to exaggeration and disproportion." By proudly highlighting Jewishness, Rosenfeld unintentionally stepped into one of the uglier areas of music criticism.[31]

At the same time, Rosenfeld did not champion Jewish composers at the expense of Gentiles. On the contrary, he showed no such bias in making his evaluations. Throughout the years Rosenfeld supported many non-Jews, especially Varèse, Ruggles, Harris, and Sessions; conversely, he was extremely critical of Gershwin, one of the more famous Jewish composers of the day. In fact, the great apotheosis of *An Hour with American Music* came not in the work of Copland or Bloch but of Varèse, whose compositions contained "the greatest fullness of power and of prophecy yet come to music in America."[32]

Those who evaluated Rosenfeld during the 1920s objected less to his biases than to his flowery prose. "Impressionistic" was a word that popped up frequently in evaluations of his writing. "The style which, in the whole of 'Musical Portraits' and in the best of this book, seems to flash with something of the quick clear colours of the music itself, has a tendency to become florid or viscous," complained Edmund Wilson in a 1924 review of *Musical Chronicle*. "Mr. Rosenfeld expands impressions and ideas which would be far more effective if stated more tersely and with a more careful economy of images, into veritable oceans of prose." Certainly *Musical Chronicle* contained some of the more "viscous" language of Rosenfeld's career, as the opening paragraph of his essay about Bartók shows. Although the full effect relies on wading through a mass of verbiage, a small sample of Rosenfeld's prose conveys its flavor:

> In forests, sometimes, a stranger sprouts among familiar plants. Migrating birds have brought a seed from distant parts, and left a foreigner to spring far from his folk in the presence of species unrelated to him. We chance upon the little pieces of Belá Bartók with a surprise identical to that roused in us by sight of one of these wandering growths. They also, "Esquisses" and "Bagatelles," are curious and apart among the organisms 'mid which they push.[33]

Here Rosenfeld is at his most extreme, painting a wash of images rather than specifically describing music. But the near-opaque prose of *Musical Chronicle* was balanced by other books in which Rosenfeld's love of word rhythm and sensory impression yielded cogent results. His section about Aaron Copland in *An Hour with American Music* contained some especially effective passages:

The earmark of Copland's music is leanness, slenderness of sound, sharpened by the fact that it is found in connection with a strain of grandiosity. For we associate grandiosity with a Wagnerian fatness, thickness, and heaviness; and Copland's [piano] concerto, and the finale of his symphony, perhaps the two most elevated of his compositions, give us the pleasant shock of finding it both lithe and imponderous. The jarring piano and strings of the recent severe little trio [Vitebsk], sound hard, like stone or metal things. Part of this general astringency flows from Copland's preference for shrill, cock-crowing, naked effects, and part from a predilection for staccato themes, with wide intervals and defiant flourishes.[34]

Here the writing is heavily adjectival yet precise and shrewdly evaluative. At its best, Rosenfeld's criticism evoked the sense of a composer's music; at its worst it was almost inchoate. Roger Sessions once observed that Rosenfeld wrote from "feeling and intuition," not technical knowledge. For some that might have seemed a liability, but for Rosenfeld it summed up his strength as a critic. He sought to suggest and evoke, not analyze, and he tended toward visual comparisons, perhaps because his other main focus as a critic lay with painters. He also delighted in placing his favorite composers within a glimmering American mythology. With Carl Ruggles, he presented him as the ultimate Yankee:

Ruggles's harmonic schemes are of the greatest distinction. This quality, neither rich nor magnificent, and nonetheless exquisitely refined, and new to harmonic writing, ineluctably associates itself with early American furniture and [Marsden] Hartley's colour, Portsmouth doorways and Hawthorne's prose. . . . The feeling of all Ruggles's more recent, rounder compositions is intensely local. The melancholy and smothered passion of the eloquently weaving violin-music in Lilacs, middle section of Men and Mountains, is as characteristic of the New England country-side as anything by [Edwin A.] Robinson or Frost.[35]

Rosenfeld was not the only one to cultivate this extravagant style. Waldo Frank and Van Wyck Brooks, to varying degrees, each tended toward opulent language. In retrospect, their writing seems like a last gasp of Victorian excess before the crisp economies of the younger generation took over. In reviewing Henry Cowell's American Composers on American Music, Rosenfeld took issue with the style of the essays, claiming they showed "an obsession with the means of music and a neglect of its substance." For him, impressionistic writing conveyed "substance," and technical analysis missed the point.[36]

Beginning in 1927, the year he left the Dial, Rosenfeld undertook a magazine of his own, the American Caravan, which he edited at first with Van Wyck Brooks, Alfred Kreymborg, and Lewis Mumford. It published short fiction by American authors, providing an antidote to "the passive and recessive attitudes of the leading magazines." Then in 1931, the last year of the American Caravan, Rosenfeld began contributing to *Modern Music*, the "little magazine" sponsored by the League of Composers. *Modern Music*'s editor, Minna Lederman, later called Rosenfeld the "Odd Man Out" of her journal, since his roots were in "an earlier period." Those were telling words, for during the 1930s Rosenfeld increasingly became something of an anachronism. His instincts lay with the progressive ideology of early modernism, not with the social realism of this new era. In reviewing *An Hour with American Music*, Nicolas Slonimsky forecast that Rosenfeld's condescension toward Gershwin and jazz would soon make him a "lone objector." It was an ominous prediction, for Rosenfeld's deeply ingrained elitism isolated him in the years ahead.[37]

Yet the man had his season, a time when his own sensibility was perfectly attuned to developments around him. That sensibility involved the effective amalgam of being "highbrow" and daringly adventuresome. "At a moment when the American artist needed most of all, perhaps, a sense that he was at last welcome in his own country and was surrounded by those who understood him," observed Lewis Mumford not long after the critic's death in 1946. "Rosenfeld gave him precisely what he needed: appreciation, encouragement, and sometimes, in the very best sense of the word, patronage; for he brought to criticism an inexhaustible delight in art itself, art in all its manifestations, as the final wonder and justification in life."[38]

As we look over Rosenfeld's contribution, his idealism deserves recognition. At the same time, we will understand more about the progression of American art music during the entire twentieth century if we keep in mind his biases and his fixation on European models. The values he projected were inherited by subsequent generations of American composers. We continue to wrestle with them.

Widening Horizons

Modernism and the "Jazz Age"

> "Civilization's going to pieces," broke out Tom violently. . . .
> "Have you read 'The Rise of the Coloured Empires' by this
> man Goddard? . . . Well, it's a fine book and everybody
> ought to read it. The idea is if we don't look out the white
> race will be—will be utterly submerged." . . .
>
> "We've got to beat them down," whispered Daisy, . . .
>
> Tom interrupted, . . . "The idea is that we're Nordics. I
> am and you are and you are . . . and we've produced all the
> things that go to make civilization—oh, science and art and
> all that."
>
> —F. Scott Fitzgerald, *The Great Gatsby*, 1925

When Paul Rosenfeld and Carl Van Vechten ended up on either side of the high-low divide, each represented prominent factions on the American cultural landscape. Yet no matter where your eye glanced on the scene, jazz popped up. It was the single most discussed American musical genre of the 1920s, coming to represent the decade as a whole. It stood as "the symbol, or the byword, for a great many elements in the spirit of the time," declared Gilbert Seldes, a pioneering critic of American popular culture. The "Jazz Age"—as in F. Scott Fitzgerald's *Tales of the Jazz Age* from 1922—evoked rapid mechanization and the giddy good life of America's more high-rolling citizens, as much as it did a particular genre of music. At the same time jazz presented a means for expressing youthful dissatisfaction. After World War I, "conventions had tumbled," recalled the songwriter Hoagy Carmichael. "There was rebellion then, against the accepted, and the proper and the old. . . . The shooting war was over but the rebellion was just getting started. And for us jazz . . . said what we wanted to say though what that was we might not know." The bandleader Paul Whiteman also looked to jazz as "a revolt and a release" but added another dimension to its symbolism: "Through it, we get back to a simple, to a savage, if you like, joy in being alive."[1]

All these meanings and more converged in the word *jazz*, and American modernist composers faced its implications squarely. Yet an even broader issue lay behind it—that is, the rapid shift in American demographics. "America is no longer an Anglo-Saxon country," declared the composer Roger Sessions in 1927, summarily conveying the scope of the changes shaking his native land. Through the combined effects of a large influx of eastern and southern European immigrants, an internal migration of African Americans from the rural south to northern cities, and the greater accessibility through phonograph recordings and radio of music of diverse styles and peoples, the intermingling process that had been basic to the founding of America gained force during the first few decades of the 1900s, eventually becoming one of the most prominent and controversial issues of the century as a whole. As early as 1913, the American philosopher George Santayana recognized the potential impact, observing that "the civilisation characteristic of Christendom has not disappeared, yet another civilisation has begun to take its place."[2]

By the end of World War I, the outlines of a new, more pluralistic society grew ever more apparent, and in the 1920s pluralism became a defining feature of an evolving social and cultural order. Yet increased diversity brought pain alongside potential. Spurred by the anti-German sentiment of World War I, racism intensified. As Americans of northern European descent felt their dominion to be threatened, intolerance grew, finding varied means of expression. The publication of widely circulated texts such as Madison Grant's *Passing of the Great Race* of 1916 articulated intense bigotry, as did the revival of the Ku Klux Klan, which by 1923 boasted a membership between three and six million. In 1919, there were race riots in Chicago. Then, two years later, a quota system aimed at controlling ethnic balances was imposed on immigration for the first time. The new quotas permitted annual entrance of only 3 percent of the population of each nationality, as already represented in the United States; and as a way of turning back the clock, the percentages were based on the 1910 census.[3]

For American modernist composers, increased pluralism expanded the repertory of available sound sources, and their "eclectic breeding"—to call up a phrase of Virgil Thomson—inspired a challenge to long-standing European-based values, becoming a vital component in shaping modernism in the New World. Jazz was the non-European music with the greatest impact on modernist composers. It served all sorts of purposes. Besides contributing new musical materials, it provided a much-desired musical link to cultures thought to be "primitive," whether those of the African continent or the American South. It was used as a tool for articulating national identity, and it provided a means for communicating with an audience puz-

Figure 19.1. Fish, "Americans All: A Cross-Section of the Sidewalks of New York." Caricature published in *Vanity Fair* (June 1925). Reproduced by permission of Condé Nast Publications.

zled by and often hostile to the subtleties of modernism. It also appeared to be one of the most effective ways in which American composers might gain long-desired acceptance in Western Europe.[4]

The vogue for jazz among American concert composers reached its peak between 1924 and 1926, yet it had ongoing implications, profoundly affecting the musical language of Americans for decades to come. Perhaps the most significant impact of jazz on concert composers came with the challenge that it issued to well-established divisions between "highbrow" and "lowbrow" art. Looking back on the 1920s, Copland later observed, "In those days, the lines were more sharply

Figure 19.2. "Giving the Jazz Baby her Darktown Coloring." Cartoon published in *Musical America* (13 February 1926). Courtesy of Musical America Archives.

drawn between popular and classical musics." Neither seemed content to stay in its place, and it became just as radical to challenge long-cherished distinctions between them as to defy the traditional tonal language. Van Wyck Brooks devoted an entire chapter of *America's Coming-of-Age* (1915) to "'Highbrow' and 'Lowbrow,'" articulating the importance of these concepts in American culture:

> Both are used in a derogatory sense. The "Highbrow" is the superior person whose virtue is admitted but felt to be an inept unpalatable virtue; while the "Lowbrow" is a good fellow one readily takes to, but with a certain scorn for him and all his works. . . . They are equally undesirable, and they are incompatible, but they divide American life between them.

By 1924, Gilbert Seldes's *Seven Lively Arts* turned the quandary into a call for change, proposing that modes of creative expression previously considered "popular," such as movies, popular songs, and comic strips, be viewed as "art." But many in the concert world clung fast to the old categories. Even Henry Cowell, whose thinking in many respects was nothing short of revolutionary, had trouble seeing high and low art as equal: "The real division among the modern American composers now, a sharp one, is between those who regard music as something for the purpose of amusement, and those who regard it as a medium for expressing greater depths of feeling."[5]

Some American composers, such as Cowell and quite a number of his ultra-modern allies, ignored jazz altogether, preferring to launch their experiments apart from it. But just as many found themselves seduced by its sounds. The results were as varied as the composers who shaped them.

Crossing Over with George Gershwin, Paul Whiteman, and the Modernists

Actually Gershwin and I came from opposite sides of the tracks, and if we meet anywhere at all it's in my love for his music. But there it ends. Gershwin was a songwriter who grew into a serious composer. I am a serious composer trying to be a songwriter.

—Leonard Bernstein, 1959

Be proud, my Race, in mind and soul.

—Paul Laurence Dunbar, as quoted in
William Grant Still's *Afro-American Symphony*

On 12 February 1924, a "lank and dark young man" of "extraordinary talent" strode onstage at Aeolian Hall for the premiere of *Rhapsody in Blue*. With this piece, George Gershwin brought a new hybrid strain of composition directly into the spotlight. Soon a group of other composers joined him in a brief but intense movement to produce "highbrow jazz," as Virgil Thomson called it. Among the principal Americans involved were John Alden Carpenter, Aaron Copland, Louis Gruenberg, and William Grant Still; the first three made their careers in concert music, and the last straddled both the popular and concert realms. At the same time, parallel forays were being made by European modernists, ranging from Darius Milhaud and Igor Stravinsky to Ernst Krenek and Kurt Weill. Each sought a means of mediating between the rarefied aesthetic terrain of high modernism and the more accessible plains of jazz. "Jazz," in turn, was synonymous with popular music of many types. "The word has been used for so many different things," wrote Gershwin in 1926, "that it has ceased to have any definite meaning."[1]

Modernism made efforts to challenge the notion of what might be termed "acceptable" in art, whether through Dada and the machine movement or forays into popular music. At the same time, it resisted the quotidian. "Modernism constituted itself through a conscious strategy of exclusion," writes the cultural historian Andreas Huyssen, "an anxiety of contamination by its other: an increasingly consuming and engulfing mass culture." Jazz—in its broadest sense—presented native potential for new modes of expression. At the same time, its immense popularity posed a threat. The resulting "volatility" yielded a series of works that fused divergent genres. By the end of the twentieth century, with jazz ensconced at Lincoln Center and concert composers venturing into ever-wider realms of popular music, this hardly seemed so daring. But in the 1920s it meant crossing racial barriers in an era of segregation and blurring distinctions between art and entertainment.[2]

Representative American musical figures and compositions involved in transforming jazz for the concert hall are profiled on the pages that follow. Through it all, Gershwin reappears like a leitmotif. His contemporaries might not have always endorsed his work, but they could not avoid confronting it.

Rhapsody in Blue generated considerable controversy after its premiere, with strongly voiced opinions both pro and con. Carl Van Vechten hailed it as "the very finest piece of serious music that had ever come out of America," while Virgil Thomson managed both commendation and censure. On the one hand, he praised *Rhapsody in Blue* as "enormously superior to anything that the better educated musicians have done in that style." On the other, he skewered it as "some scraps of bully jazz sewed together with oratory and cadenzas out of Liszt." But Gershwin (1898–1937) may have taken his biggest artistic leap of the mid-1920s with another work: the *Concerto in F*. Commissioned by Walter Damrosch for the New York Symphony Orchestra and premiered in December of 1925, almost two years after *Rhapsody in Blue*, *Concerto in F* represented a more ambitious attempt to bridge independent musical categories. *Rhapsody in Blue* had been written for a symphonic jazz ensemble— a context somewhat familiar to its composer from his experience with theater pit orchestras. The Concerto, by contrast, placed Gershwin before a standard symphony orchestra, holding the historic weight attached to a revered musical form. Although less well known than *Rhapsody in Blue*, *Concerto in F* nonetheless gained a good deal of attention at the time, further increasing Gershwin's celebrity within the concert world. Yet its success, too, was controversial and threatening. "You must whisper softly still when you dare suggest that at last America has a music all its own," wrote Carl Engel, a composer who was also chief of the Music Division at the Library of Congress, immediately after the Concerto's premiere. This new musical realm was not rooted "at the top, in the Hermetic circles of New Music Societies, Manuscript Societies, Associations for the Promotion of Native Talent, and the like," Engel continued, "but at the bottom, in the street." Praise for Gershwin, while fulsome, was encased within a class-based frame.[3]

Concerto in F revealed both the bias that accompanied mergers of jazz with concert music and the new musical perspectives that this repertory demanded. At the Concerto's premiere, Walter Damrosch introduced Gershwin to his audience with a familiar fairy-tale image that rested upon an entrenched social code. He declared the Concerto's composer to be the first to accomplish the "miracle" of "lift[ing]" jazz to "a level that would enable her to be received as a respectable member in musical circles. . . . He is the prince who has taken Cinderella by the hand and openly proclaimed her a princess to the astonished world, no doubt to the fury of her envious sisters." Damrosch's language betrayed his highbrow bias. "Cinderella," before her magical transformation into a princess, exemplified poverty, servitude, or lowly origins. She was even dirty or—by extension—dark. At the same time, the notion of a "prince" expressed the degree to which this charismatic composer was a star—someone capable of transporting the most ordinary listener into a fantasy world of sparkling elegance. Yet Damrosch's message was clear, especially since he reiterated the core of it in other forums during the 1920s: jazz was a "very low form of art" that required a "genius" to imbue it with "real emotion."[4]

Damrosch was also demonstrating a belief that new music, even when composed by a figure as accessible as Gershwin, required mediation for audiences to accept it. Damrosch had a supportive but uneasy relationship with modernism. In January 1925, he had been adventuresome enough to present the premiere of the Symphony for Organ and Orchestra by Aaron Copland—then an unknown twenty-four-year-old. Damrosch spoke out vividly at that event as well, turning to the audience at the work's conclusion to blurt out, "Ladies and gentlemen, I am sure you will agree that if a gifted young man can write a symphony like this at twenty-three, within five years he will be ready to commit murder." And each year he conducted the New York Symphony Orchestra in a concert titled "Modern Music—Pleasant and Unpleasant." On 5 December 1926, for example, he presented the Prelude to Act II of *Phaedre* by Honegger (1926), *Fuji in Sunset Glow* by Bernard Rogers (1925), *La Bumba* by Quinto Maganini (1925), and *Music for the Theatre* by Copland. He also premiered Gershwin's *American in Paris* in 1928. Whatever the repertory being performed, Damrosch made spoken introductions his signature. The same year as *American in Paris*, he became a national celebrity when his "Music Appreciation Hour" started to be broadcast coast to coast on NBC radio. There, he framed classical chestnuts with meet-the-people explanations.[5]

With his introduction to *Concerto in F*, then, Damrosch was performing a familiar mission of helping an audience shape a perspective on the work it was about to hear. No matter how accessible this particular composition, it was still rife with unorthodox juxtapositions. The Concerto fused a standard three-movement form, used by European composers from Mozart to Rachmaninov, with African American traditions, and swathed it all in soaring strings and rippling glissandos. Expectations for a concerto were realized at the same time as gestures of American popular music were delivered in varied guises. Aspects of the blues pervaded the work's harmonic language and internal structures, figuring most prominently in the second move-

Figure 20.1. "Making Jazz Respectable." Cartoon by George Hager, published in *Musical America* (13 February 1926). Courtesy of Musical America Archives.

ment. But the concerto also had strong ties to musical theater, which the opening section for orchestra illustrates vividly. No staid exposition, it opens with the flash and flare of timpani and snare drum, conveying a sense of a curtain rising. Both timpani and snare return at the end of the same introduction to announce the appearance of the piano. This is a standard technique in the theater, whether at the start of the overture to Gershwin's *Tip-Toes*, which began with a drumroll on Broadway in December 1925, or to introduce a trapeze artist in the circus.[6]

Another theatrical device appears in the use of bustling transitions, which lace the Concerto, consistently evoking the overture to a musical comedy more than any genre from the Western European concert repertory. Like scene changes on stage, they move the action from one section to another. The first such case, heard early on in the opening orchestral segment (mm. 9–12), uses a dotted note figure to generate the second "idea" (Example 20.1). No melodically shaped theme, it has the character of a chordal vamp, with a flatted third and seventh invoking the

Example 20.1. Gershwin, *Concerto in F,* first movement, p. 1. © 1927 (Renewed) WB Music Corp. All rights for the world outside the U.S.A. owned by New World Music Company, Ltd., administered by WB Music Corp. All rights reserved. Used by permission. Warner Bros. Publications U.S. Inc., Miami, FL 33014.

Concerto in F
For Piano And Orchestra ✳

I

GEORGE GERSHWIN

blues. This same gesture occurs in different mutations throughout the orchestral introduction, growing in length and reaching upward in range until it establishes a C (m. 37) that is prolonged for fourteen bars until the piano's entrance (at m. 51). It returns after the statement of the first theme in the piano's exposition (not shown in the example here); again it serves as a transition—this time to a second theme in the piano. Another example of a "scurrying" segment in the work appears in the opening orchestral section. This is a much shorter unit—only one measure long—which spills out a stream of sixteenth notes (rehearsal 1) and functions as a link to the initial thematic area. The technique of stitching together tunes with glittering splashes of sound deserves greater recognition—even validation—in Gershwin's concert music, as it does in that of William Grant Still, who also had considerable experience in musical theater.[7]

Another key characteristic of *Concerto in F* was its construction in four-bar units, as the opening orchestral section also reveals. It unfolds in the following sequence: timpani and snare drums (mm. 1–4), first orchestral idea (mm. 5–8), second orchestral idea (mm. 9–12), scurrying violin transition (m. 13). These brief segments form the basis for the entire opening. Throughout the Concerto, Gershwin relies on this same method of construction, drawing upon a phrase structure that formed the core of American popular music, from ragtime and blues to popular song. This is the case for the initial piano theme in the first movement, which is built of two four-bar pairs (Example 20.2). There, the segments also point up the fundamental duality of the concerto's character. Like cinematic cross-cuts between one location and another, they splice aural images of the blues together with ones of the European piano-virtuoso repertory. The first half of the opening piano theme presents a parlor blues much like that at the beginning of Gershwin's Second Piano Prelude. With flatted thirds and sevenths, an undulating two-bar vamp, and persistent languorous syncopation, this segment is repeated with a migrating bass in the second four bars. Suddenly, the theme changes character, soaring in the direction of turn-of-the-century Russia, with a lyrical minor melody that floats to a high register. Yet even that section has blues-based altered chords in its accompaniment and uses a unit of construction that is two bars long. As the Concerto unfolds, this duality becomes a central characteristic, with the language of the work vacillating between the American vernacular and the bravura of European virtuosos.[8]

Both traits—use of quick transitions from musical theater and construction in four-bar units—eluded most critics of the day. There were a few strong endorsements, as in Engel's review quoted earlier. On the whole, though, critics came down much harder on *Concerto in F* than they had on *Rhapsody in Blue*. But then its pretensions—in both musical form and performance venue—raised the stakes. Lawrence Gilman wrote in the *Herald-Tribune* that *Concerto in F* was "conventional, trite, at its worst a little dull." The young composer Marc Blitzstein wrote in the *Review* that *Concerto in F* was "decidedly inferior in thematic invention and lyricism" to *Rhapsody*. "The concerto as a whole seems faintly disappointing." And

Example 20.2. Gershwin, *Concerto in F*, first movement, mm. 51–66. © 1927 (Renewed) WB Music Corp. All rights for the world outside the U.S.A. owned by New World Music Company, Ltd., administered by WB Music Corp. All rights reserved. Used by permission. Warner Bros. Publications U.S. Inc., Miami, FL 33014.

Olin Downes concurred in the *New York Times*, declaring that Gershwin had "tried" but "not succeeded." Downes then uttered a more specific complaint: "the development flags: indeed, there is not often very much of it, but rather the repetition of figures and melodies." For him and others, Gershwin's formal conception was patchwork and discontinuous, foiling traditional European expectations of unity, development, and organicism.[9]

At the same time, there was at least one critic—Abbe Niles, a leading commentator on the blues during the 1920s—who perceptively evaluated Gershwin for what he offered rather than lacked. Writing in the *New Republic* after the premiere of *Concerto in F*, Niles made comments that were revolutionary enough to pause over. He suggested that Gershwin's "episodic treatment of his material . . . may be due, less to any supposed deficiencies . . . than to the nature of the material." In other words, the same trait that had infuriated Downes struck Niles as utterly acceptable. Niles then connected Gershwin's use of form to ragtime rather than to any traditional concert-music structure: "ragtime particularly benefits by a simple, well-rounded and *brief* form—eight or sixteen bars to the strain (in the case of the blues, twelve, two or three strains), and then *finis*—or change of subject. . . . If the composer presses on into 'development,' does he not risk taking his subject out of the category of ragtime as well as robbing it of one of the very virtues which made it popular?" Niles went on to include the second movement of *Concerto in F* in *Blues: An Anthology*, which he issued together with the African American composer and publisher W. C. Handy in 1926, and he used the opening trumpet melody from that same movement as a musical example in his article about jazz for the 1929 edition of *Encyclopedia Britannica*.[10]

For Niles, "jazz," "blues," and "ragtime" were such flexible designations as to include *Concerto in F*. On the one hand, Gershwin was defying categories, while on the other he was functioning in a time and place where the dividing lines were not so firm. For many white critics and listeners in the 1920s, Gershwin did not just borrow from jazz; he embodied it.

Concerto in F did not emerge in isolation, but rather in an environment that was being intensely cultivated. One of the trendsetters in the crossover movement was the jazz-band conductor Paul Whiteman (1890–1967), who not only premiered *Rhapsody in Blue* but also aimed to establish a whole new genre of composition. One part of his multifaceted approach was to award commissions for jazz-based works, aiming to give "the unknown composer . . . his chance." Whiteman's initiative with composers has been little acknowledged, in part because history has chronicled the concert and popular realms separately. Yet for a time, he was arguably one of the most important figures in the United States in challenging the barriers between high and low art, playing a parallel role to that of Gunther Schuller or Wynton Marsalis later in the twentieth century, and his work set in place models for the populist nationalism to which so many American composers turned during the mid-1930s. Proselytizer, instigator, spokesperson, wizard of outreach, Whiteman sought to bring jazz to the broadest possible audience—not just to the connoisseurs of "race" records, as jazz and blues recordings by black musicians were labeled at the time, but to symphony subscribers. He had high artistic ambitions in mind, at the same time as he aimed for commercial success, becoming one of the best-paid popular musicians of the mid-1920s.[11]

The beginning of Whiteman's effort, with the premiere of *Rhapsody in Blue*, is the part of the saga that has become legendary. With it, he tried to establish credibility for his orchestra within the concert world. By calling the event "An Experiment in Modern Music," Whiteman noticeably avoided the problematic word *jazz* and instead sought to identify himself with vanguard movements of the day. He attracted an audience that included cabaret-goers as well as the concert-world elite—an audience presaging that for the New York premiere of Antheil's *Ballet Mécanique* three years later—and he brought instant notoriety to the issue of interpolating jazz into new compositions, turning it into one of the most fashionable topics of the moment.

After *Rhapsody in Blue* appeared, Whiteman searched for new ways to capitalize on his success. The result was a string of highly publicized "Modern Music" concerts through which Whiteman launched a campaign to commission "somebody," as the critic and composer Deems Taylor conveyed it, "to write some serious . . . music for the American jazz orchestra." He must have realized that *Rhapsody in Blue* had a better chance of flourishing among a strong group of kindred works than it did as an isolated phenomenon; he also saw a way of giving his orchestra a distinctive identity. Whiteman's initiative continued with a repeat of the "Experiment" on 21 April 1924, an event that moved even further upscale from its Aeolian Hall beginnings to Carnegie Hall, where it was staged as a benefit concert for the American Academy in Rome, and it continued until 1938, well beyond the period under discussion here.[12]

Dubbing his ensemble the "modern orchestra," Whiteman presented a series of new works over the next several years, many of which he commissioned, by Ferde Grofé, Mana-Zucca (best known as a piano virtuoso), Deems Taylor, John Alden Carpenter, Eastwood Lane, and Leo Sowerby, who was the first American composer to receive a fellowship at the American Academy in Rome (perhaps explaining Whiteman's link to that institution). Whiteman also reportedly "conferred" about commissions with others, including George Antheil, Ernest Bloch, Charles Wakefield Cadman, Leopold Godowsky, Percy Grainger, John Powell, even Igor Stravinsky. His programs carried "a general invitation" to compose special works for his orchestra, and the promotional booklet for his 1925–26 transcontinental tour included a section titled "Workshop for American Composers: Building a Repertoire for a New Medium" which expanded on this invitation, claiming that Whiteman not only had invited American composers to write for his ensemble but also had "offered to orchestrate at his own expense, rehearse as frequently as necessary for a first-class performance, and present to the public." Whiteman's concerts in the next few years continued to join new compositions with his genre of jazz, and a sense of historic opportunity infused the literature by and about his orchestra. "For the first time in musical history, I think, we have the spectacle of a performing medium outgrowing its old repertoire without developing a new one," wrote the composer-critic Deems Taylor. "The opportunity of a generation is facing modern composers, and it would be a shame and disgrace to let it go to waste."[13]

Accordingly, Whiteman featured new compositions on his concerts, and one of his competitors, the band director Vincent Lopez, got into the act as well. On 14 November 1924, Whiteman gave a concert titled "Modern American Music" in

Figure 20.2. "Paul Whiteman and Chief Arrangers in his Unique Jazz Program. Left to Right: Ferdie [*sic*] Grofe, Whiteman's Arranger; Deems Taylor, Who Wrote 'Circus Day'; Mr. Whiteman, Blossom Seeley, and George Gershwin, Composer of the Jazz Opera, '135th Street.'" Photo published in *Musical America* (9 January 1926). Courtesy of Musical America Archives.

Carnegie Hall. The program that evening included Grofé's *Broadway Night*, Mana-Zucca's *Zouave's Drill* and *Valse Brilliante*, and—once again—Gershwin's *Rhapsody in Blue*. Nine days later, Lopez and his orchestra appeared at the Metropolitan Opera House in a "Symphonic 'Jazz' Concert," performing Whithorne's "Pell Street," arranged from *New York Days and Nights*, Vladimir Heifetz's *Biblical Suite*, Fletcher Henderson's *Meanest Blues*, and *The Evolution of the Blues* by W. C. Handy and Joseph Nussbaum (the latter an arranger for Lopez). Significantly, Lopez's program featured works by whites and blacks side by side. Then on 29 December 1925, Whiteman returned with a "Second Experiment in Modern Music," featuring the opera *135th Street* (earlier titled *Blue Monday*) by Gershwin, *A Little Bit of Jazz* by Carpenter, *Mississippi* by Grofé, and *Circus Days* by Taylor. On 13 December 1928, Whiteman again presented a "Concert in Modern Music" in Carnegie Hall, which included Grofé's *Metropolis* and an arrangement of *Concerto in F* by Grofé. Many of these same compositions traveled with Whiteman and his orchestra from coast to coast.[14]

Yet in spite of Whiteman's ambitious attempt to forge a new American repertory, his initiative stalled not long after take-off. By 1926, even such vigorous supporters of symphonic jazz as H. O. Osgood and Gilbert Seldes were disheartened by the results. Osgood included an entire chapter on "The Concert Repertoire of Jazz" in his historic book, *So This Is Jazz* of 1926, concluding that "very little has happened" since the *Rhapsody in Blue.* Seldes, whose *Seven Lively Arts* of 1924 had made a powerful and pioneering argument for the acceptance of American popular culture, called *135th Street* "an extremely dreary affair." Reviews of Whiteman's concerts from the mid-1920s expressed similar criticism. Olin Downes, who had been enthusiastic after the *Rhapsody's* premiere, described himself as "disappointed . . . by the quality of the music" at a Whiteman concert in November 1924 and called Whiteman's 1928 effort "prevailingly poor and trivial." Whiteman's highly publicized recruitment campaign attracted few young composers. Those who did write for him tended to be of an older generation, with the single notable exception of Gershwin, and their music leaned in the direction of consonance and accessibility—necessary traits for Whiteman's own palate but damnable ones to composers aligning themselves with modernism.[15]

Looking back on Whiteman's work, it is striking how he aimed to legitimize jazz, doing much to shape a context in which Damrosch's "Cinderella" metaphor could seem entirely reasonable. He was a self-proclaimed "jazz missionary" who sought to give the music "a respectful hearing" in America. Whiteman's words reflected racial attitudes of the day, as well as distinctions between social classes, and they also showed the extent to which whites assumed the superiority of the European-based concert tradition. On the one hand, Whiteman took a stance shared by many Europeans then, considering jazz to be the "only *original* idea" that American musicians had produced (the emphasis is his). And he asserted these opinions with clear acknowledgment that his form of jazz stood at some distance from its African American roots. "It is a relief to be able to prove at last that I did not invent jazz," Whiteman exclaimed in *Jazz*, his book from 1926. He went on to trace its birth in New Orleans and, in the process, fused gendered images with a reference to the Ku Klux Klan. "I took it where I found it and I wish the preachers and club lady uplifters who put on sheets and pillowcases to go jazz-clanning wouldn't concentrate on me. . . . All I did was orchestrate jazz." On the other hand, Whiteman's arrangements and his whole means of packaging the music moved it away from its African American base and toward the realm of European orchestral traditions—or as a 1924–25 program book for his orchestra put it, Whiteman was involved in "subduing, without devitalizing, that wild creature known as 'Jazz.'" He was moving jazz "out of the kitchen," as Deems Taylor put it, and "upstairs into the parlor." He achieved this putative upgrading through a shrewd job of packaging, always using the adjective *symphonic* in labeling his form of jazz. He reinforced the effect by playing up his own background in classical music, especially as a violist in the Denver Symphony, and by touting the symphonic experience of many players in his band. Whiteman also boasted that his was the first jazz ensemble to play from written parts; his publicity machine went so far as to claim that he "forbade his players to depart from his script." In other words, they were not permitted to improvise.[16]

Although no huge body of compositions resulted from Whiteman's commissions, he did inspire the birth of two works that have had a wide-ranging impact. One,

Rhapsody in Blue, has been repeatedly and officially acknowledged for its historic position; the other, Ferde Grofé's *Grand Canyon Suite*, premiered by Whiteman in 1931, has not. Both have enjoyed immense popularity since, and both presaged the self-conscious nationalism embraced by American composers during the mid-1930s. *Rhapsody in Blue* may have quickly become a "shadow" hanging over American composers, making them "the hybrid child of a hybrid," as the British composer Constant Lambert once put it. Yet at least it was part of the discussion. With *Grand Canyon Suite*, despite its continuing popularity on "pops" programs, it has been largely avoided in the historical literature.[17]

As instigator of these works, Whiteman was seeking a distinctive American genre that would fuse the popular and the erudite. In one complex blend, he had the idealism to pursue an artistic vision and the practicality to court white middle-class audiences. He may not have fully succeeded, but he set important precedents for the future.

In advancing the fusion of concert music and jazz, Whiteman was joined by musicians from "the opposite side of the tracks," to return to Leonard Bernstein's image. Such illustrious virtuosi of the day as Jascha Heifetz and Fritz Kreisler joined the vogue for jazz by adding a syncopated reading of a popular tune or two to their programs. Here too there was an especially notable moment: a concert in Aeolian Hall by the soprano Eva Gauthier on 1 November 1923, three and a half months before the premiere of *Rhapsody in Blue*, that placed American popular songs alongside compositions by Arnold Schoenberg, Béla Bartók, Paul Hindemith, and Darius Milhaud. Gershwin stepped in as accompanist for the songs, which included "Alexander's Ragtime Band" by Irving Berlin, "The Siren's Song" by Jerome Kern, "Carolina in the Morning" by Walter Donaldson, and "Innocent Ingenue Baby," "I'll Build a Stairway to Paradise," and "Swanee" by Gershwin. This concert has been historicized affirmatively as a watershed in the crossover movement. But it has another side as well, raising questions of ongoing resonance about the effect of transferring performance standards from one realm of music making to another.[18]

Like Whiteman and Damrosch, Gauthier (1885–1958) talked of elevating jazz and used language similar to theirs. She too was an unabashed uplifter. A noted singer of the day, Gauthier specialized in early music, nonwestern repertories, and contemporary compositions (for example, she gave the American premiere of Stravinsky's *Three Japanese Lyrics* in 1917). For her 1923 program, she claimed to have chosen songs with "life to them, not the sentimental, saccharine, love-sick ballads we hear so much of," and she took pride in performing these tunes "with artistry." Gauthier believed that she validated popular songs by programming them, holding little respect for the performance traditions from which they came. Lamenting that such songs had "previously been relegated to the cabaret and vaudeville house, where singers with uncultivated and saw-tooth voices rasped them out," Gauthier intended to perform them "with 'tone and technic' . . . and see how the people would receive them."[19]

Gauthier was at once open-minded and unreformedly highbrow—appearing like an aesthetic precursor to Kiri Te Kanawa or Marilyn Horne, among the many divas who have continued the practice of bringing "artistry" to popular music. Critics, in turn, responded to her performance according to their own musical allegiances. "Mme. Gauthier sang these songs about as well as they can be sung, not in the vulgar and raucous manner of the coon shouter but with a certain archness, restraint and attention to detail which revealed them in the best light," reported Bernard Rogers to the concert-goers who read *Musical America*. He felt she had improved the tunes with her cultivated veneer. Henry O. Osgood, as a sympathizer for symphonic jazz, heard the concert quite differently: "She did not do well by the songs. She sang them 'straight,' just as she sang all the others of her program—and that's no way to sing jazz songs; it is like drawing a comic strip in the style of a pre-Raphaelite. The excellence of Gershwin's accompaniments only served to accentuate the insufficiency of her interpretations."[20]

These same issues surrounded Whiteman, albeit in a different configuration. As the literary critic Edmund Wilson articulated it, Whiteman had "refined and disciplined his orchestra" until it reached "a point of individuality and distinction" that suited concert-hall audiences. Yet the resulting product was "likely to embarrass dancers and diners." With these comments, Wilson joined Osgood in voicing a question at the core of the entire crossover movement: did such mainstreaming efforts leach the joy from popular idioms and compromise their integrity?[21]

These questions reverberated just as loudly in the jazz-based works by modernist composers. For a time, such music appeared in a frenzy, as in the 1925–26 concert season when at least one notable fusion event took place each month. Both the League of Composers and International Composers' Guild entered the picture, and the result was a string of new works in which presenters and performers crossed over as often as composers. It was as though the New York musical scene had been placed in a blender. Singers, dancers, and composers from the highbrow world joined with those from Broadway and Harlem. Florence Mills appeared at the International Composers' Guild, and Roger Pryor Dodge at the Metropolitan Opera. Hierarchies were being flouted, and intriguing new combinations resulted. The result was neither "pure" jazz nor "pure" modernism, but an ever-shifting middle ground in between.

Two highlights of this season were William Grant Still's *Levee Land*, presented by the International Composers' Guild on 24 January 1926, and John Alden Carpenter's *Skyscrapers* on 19 February. They were surrounded by a varied array of jazz-based compositions that included Louis Gruenberg's *Jazzberries*, which received its premiere by the League of Composers in October 1925; Aaron Copland's *Music for the Theatre*, first performed in November by the Boston Symphony Orchestra, conducted by Serge Koussevitzky; Gershwin's *Concerto in F* in early December; Whiteman's "Second Experiment in Modern Music" (including Gershwin's *135th Street*, Carpenter's *A Little Bit of Jazz*, and Deems Taylor's *Circus Days*) late that same month; and Emerson Whithorne's *Saturday's Child*, premiered by the League in March. At a time when music of any sort by an American modernist was just beginning to gain an audience in New York, these jazz-based pieces represented a significant portion of the overall total.

Among American composers experimenting with jazz, William Grant Still (1895–1978) presented a singular case. If Gershwin sat on one side of the high-low divide, with Copland and Carpenter on the other, Still covered the entire terrain. Ultimately he moved over almost completely into the world of concert music. But in the early 1920s he was doing it all—playing in the orchestra of the historic Eubie Blake and Noble Sissle musical *Shuffle Along*; working for the Pace and Handy Music Company, subsequently for the Black Swan phonograph company; producing arrangements for black revues; and beginning to compose concert music, first studying in Boston with George Wakefield Chadwick and then in

Figure 20.3. William Grant Still, press photo from late 1920s. Prints and Photographs Division, Library of Congress. All rights reserved by William Grant Still Music, Flagstaff, Arizona.

New York with Edgard Varèse. Like Gershwin and Copland, Still struggled with class-based distinctions in the musical world. But he had another major issue to confront: Still was the only African American composer among the modernists. Throughout the 1920s, he darted in and out of the modernist scene, often fully on the inside, having works performed and published by the new-music societies, but always aware of his race. Although treated well within these circles—even championed there—Still constantly faced expectations to produce work that in some way reflected his racial difference. And even though the modernists on the whole embraced him enthusiastically, he still had to function in a world where racism could be loudly articulated. One egregious example came in 1929, when a critic in the nationally disseminated magazine the *Musical Courier* congratulated the white composer John Powell—an older figure of conservative sensibility—for his *Negro Rhapsody*. According to this anonymous critic, it was "not mere 'nigger music,' but [it] is dignified, worthy music of idealistic Negro themes and rhythms." Such language, although not aimed specifically at Still, compromised the environment in which he strove to gain equal status.[22]

Still made his debut with the modernists on 8 February 1925 in a concert of the International Composers' Guild. On this program, *From the Land of Dreams* received its premiere. Composed the previous year, the piece had little to do with jazz. Still and his wife Verna Arvey later described it as an "ultramodern" work. But the composition is now lost, so descriptions are all that remain. Program notes for the concert, written by Louise Varèse, indicate that *From the Land of Dreams* was scored for a chamber ensemble of flute, oboe, clarinet, bassoon, horn, viola, cello, double bass, bells, triangle, and three sopranos "used instrumentally" and that it was about "the flimsiness of dreams." In reviews of the concert, Rosenfeld and Downes singled out Still as a figure of enormous potential, but they both also noted that his style relied heavily on that of his teacher, Edgard Varèse. Rosenfeld was especially enthusiastic, complimenting Still on his orchestration, while Downes injected an issue of ongoing concern for Still: he expected an African American composer to write music indicative of his race and musical class. Still "knows the rollicking and often original and entertaining music performed at negro revues," wrote Downes. "But Mr. Varese, Mr. Still's teacher, has driven all that out of him. Is Mr. Still unaware that the cheapest melody in the revues he has orchestrated has more originality and inspiration in it than the curious noises he has manufactured?" It was a declaration at once open-minded and deeply stereotyped, but it may have been a factor in influencing Still to turn his concert music in a new direction.[23]

With *Levee Land*, his next performance at the ICG, Still resolutely entered the realm of incorporating jazz into a concert work. He joined the movement that was gaining force among white composers, at the same time as he started to shape his own distinctive response to the ideals of the Harlem Renaissance. American modernism and the Harlem Renaissance were closely intertwined, perhaps most fundamentally in a shared sense of historic opportunity. "The most outstanding phase of the development of the Negro in the United States during the past decade has been the recent literary and artistic emergence of the individual creative artist," wrote James Weldon Johnson in 1930. "It seems rather like a sudden awakening, like an instantaneous change." Johnson was commenting on a distinct group of literary and cultural figures, at the same time as he chronicled an attitude that suffused the entire artistic scene in New York, regardless of race. Just a few years later, the white poet and literary critic Malcolm Cowley looked back on the 1920s with a parallel sense of wonder, recalling how his contemporaries then felt themselves to be "representatives of a new age" with "a sense of being somehow unique." History has tended to chronicle creative figures from this period in race-based slots. But there was growing fluidity in crossing race lines, as Still's career demonstrated.[24]

Still wrote *Levee Land* for the celebrated African American singer and actress Florence Mills, devising a sensational way of proclaiming his turn to a jazz-based style. Mills was a star of black musical theater, and she had sung in at least two shows for which Still played in the pit orchestra: *Shuffle Along* (1921) and *Dixie to Broadway* (1924). Like the premiere of *Rhapsody in Blue*, that of *Levee Land* attracted a glittering crowd, including Gershwin, Carl Van Vechten, and Arturo Toscanini.

Following the trend in black theatrical revues of the day, Still drafted a scenario for *Levee Land* made up of vignettes from southern black life. Still's text for *Levee Land* used black dialect, recalling the style of the African American poet Paul Laurence Dunbar, and its rhythms suggest the blues-inspired verse of Langston Hughes, who published *The Weary Blues* the same year. The first stanza, as printed in the Guild program, gives a sense of Still's language throughout:

Oh, baby! Baby, baby, baby.
Oh, baby! Ah feels so blue,
Sittin' on de Levee
A longin', babe, fo' you[25]

Levee Land is in four parts, "Levee Song," "Hey-Hey," "Croon," and "The Backslider." The first and fourth are texted; the second incorporates spoken, comic interjections; and the third uses a wordless vocal, much like *From the Land of Dreams* or Ellington's *Creole Love Call* recorded in 1927 by the African American singer Adelaide Hall. Throughout, Still strikes a compromise between an accessible black idiom—in this case the blues, which not only serves as a basis for some of the formal structures but permeates the harmonic language as well—and the more arcane world of modernist concert music. The scoring is very close to that of Gershwin's *Rhapsody in Blue*, with a chamber ensemble of two violins, two clarinets, bass clarinet, alto saxophone, bassoon, horn, trumpet, trombone, banjo, piano, and percussion.[26]

Yet *Levee Land* stands apart in its use of dissonance. From the outset, the piece is built on two distinct planes. On one level there is Mills's melodic line together with a core of supporting instruments that present conventional blues-derived melodies and harmonies, and on another there are chromatic third relationships that play off a trait basic to the blues but do so using modernist techniques. In the introduction, for example, the trumpet, alto saxophone, and bassoon seamlessly lead to a two-note wordless vocal (Example 20.3). But their traditional blues inflection is juxtaposed with raised thirds. The clarinets in the third measure sound D-sharp and F-sharp against D-natural in the trumpet, and the violins then pile on another layer (A-sharp and C-sharp), a third above the previous one. When the first stanza of the voice begins, a similar technique appears (Example 20.4). Mills sings a straightforward blues-derived line, well supported by a standard blues harmony and chordal vamp in the piano, violin, and bassoon. Cascading under it on another plane is a string of chromatic seconds and thirds in parallel motion.

The piece uses this same principle throughout: encircling popular African American gestures with chromaticism. By doing so, Still met both a practical necessity and an aesthetic ideal. He taught these songs to Mills orally and had the responsibility of keeping at least one layer of the ensemble within a sonic world familiar to her.[27]

Reviews of this concert focused more on the exotic presence of Florence Mills within a sanctuary of modernism than on Still's composition. Even such a buttoned-down highbrow as Rosenfeld was charmed, writing that there had "never [been] an-

Example 20.3. William Grant Still, "Levee Song" from *Levee Land*, mm. 1–14. © William Grant Still Music. All rights reserved.

other voice with the infinitely relaxed, impersonal, bird-like quality of [Mills]."
Rosenfeld, at this point, was a resolute supporter of Still.[28]

John Alden Carpenter's *Skyscrapers: A Ballet of Modern American Life* opened on
19 February 1926—one month after *Levee Land*—at the Metropolitan Opera
House and went on to a two-year run there. It too brought African American performers into the concert world, yet under radically different conditions. With *Skyscrapers*, a well-established white composer of the generation of Charles Ives and
E. B. Hill—that is, a figure older than Gershwin or Still—found an illustrious
forum for a crossover conception. He had at his disposal one of the most esteemed
performance spaces in the country, guaranteeing that this would be no "hermetic"
new-music production, to return to the image of Carl Engel. Earlier ties to jazz
on the part of both this composer and venue have already been discussed in this
chapter. Carpenter (1876–1951) had been commissioned by Whiteman the previous year, and the Metropolitan Opera House was the site two years earlier for
Vincent Lopez's concert of symphonic jazz.

Like Stravinsky's *Le Sacre du printemps* and Milhaud's *La Création du monde*, *Skyscrapers* was a ballet, in this case commissioned by Diaghilev but never performed
by him. Rather, its premiere featured the Metropolitan Opera's own corps de ballet, and it fit into a series of American dance works spanning the high-low divide,
including Carpenter's *Krazy Kat*, performed in New York in early 1922 by Adolph
Bolm with his Ballet Intime and based on the George Herriman comic strip; Cole
Porter's *Within the Quota*, produced in 1923 by the Ballet Suédois (the company
that premiered *La Création du monde* that same year); and Emerson Whithorne's
Sooner or Later, presented at the Neighborhood Playhouse in 1925 with a scenario
by Irene Lewisohn that "deal[t] fantastically with three states of existence, with
their characteristic work rhythms and entertainment—a primitive tribal life, a
mechanized city life and a resultant crystalized era," making it sound like a precursor to *Skyscrapers*.[29]

Skyscrapers had an unusual position within this cluster not only by gesturing toward popular music and dance but also by actually incorporating performers from
those worlds. In a review of *Krazy Kat*, the composer and critic Deems Taylor had
suggested that "the people who really ought to be doing ballet in this country are
the producers of reviews and musical comedies," and with *Skyscrapers*, Carpenter did
just that. The man called in to direct the Metropolitan Opera's dancers was Sammy
Lee, whose Broadway credits included *Lady Be Good!* (1924) and *Captain Jinks*
(1925). The year after *Skyscrapers*, he went on to work as choreographer for *Show Boat*,
as well as for *Yes, Yes, Yvette* (1927), both of which featured Charles Winninger. *Skyscrapers* also had a strong connection to black theater. It used a "Negro chorus, recruited from Harlem," according to a description in *Musical America*, and it included
Frank Wilson, who "organized" the chorus. An African American from the famed
Lafayette Players, Wilson also had significant experience on Broadway, appearing
with Paul Robeson in a 1924 production of Eugene O'Neill's *All God's Chillun Got*

Wings and as star of the 1927 play *Porgy*. Carpenter and his scene designer Robert Edmond Jones had strong feelings about avoiding a sense of white appropriation, as Jones expressed in an interview in *Modern Music*. "It seemed a little devious to say the least," Jones mused, "that we should take one of the Europeans who after six months spent watching Florence Mills and other cabaret stars, go home and skilfully apply the borrowed devices of our jazz."[30]

Even though Jones and Carpenter strove to give African American culture a forum and devised innovative links to Broadway, their work also clung to an old theatrical custom—using a white actor in blackface to portray the chief black character in *Skyscrapers*, a street sweeper named "White Wings" (Figure 20.4). The role was played by Roger Pryor Dodge, a popular white dancer who became a celebrated writer on jazz and dance. Blackface had been used in the premiere of Gershwin's *Blue Monday* as part of the *Scandals of 1922*, and it continued through

Figure 20.4. Performers in John Alden Carpenter's *Skyscrapers*: "Roger Dodge as 'White Wings' [a blackface character], Rita De Leporte as 'Herself' and Albert Troy as 'The Strutter.'" Published in *Musical America* (27 February 1926). Courtesy of Musical America Archives.

the American debut of Ernst Krenek's *Jonny spielt auf* in 1929 and that of Louis Gruenberg's opera *The Emperor Jones* in 1933, with Lawrence Tibbett in the title role. These last two both took place at the Metropolitan Opera House.[31]

When Carpenter and Jones concocted an elaborate scenario for *Skyscrapers*, they did so in the Diaghilev spirit of ballet-pantomime. In addition to the character of "White-Wings," there were "Herself," played by Rita De Leporte, and "The Strutter," played by Albert Troy. These character types—identified by generic labels rather than specific names—foreshadowed Marc Blitzstein's *The Cradle Will Rock* nearly a decade later. So too did the ballet's sympathetic portrayal of the dreary sameness of a worker's life. Blitzstein's characters were "Mr. and Mrs. Mister" and their children, "Sister Mister" and "Junior Mister," and the politics were didactically leftist. Carpenter, by contrast, was an odd figure to be championing the proletariat. He was of the "moneyed people," as Blitzstein characterized that class; like Ives, Carpenter was a successful businessman.

As with Carpenter's characters, his music for *Skyscrapers* also represented broadly etched parodies. Urban chaos was conveyed through Stravinskyan ostinatos; the blithe abandon of an amusement park was suggested through evocations of popular-song melodies; and the humble existence of blacks in the rural South was conjured up through elements of the blues. Like Still, he devised segregated spheres within his composition for the modernist and popular segments. For Still, those spheres were layered. With Carpenter, they appeared sequentially.

The "WORK" portion of the scenario, which opens and closes the ballet as well as recurring throughout, featured a "dreary and endless shadow-procession of the indifferent city crowd" against the backdrop of "a huge and sinister skyscraper in course of construction." Its music was built of hammered ostinatos, asymmetric rhythms, pungent chordal punctuation, and unusual instrumental ranges—all following the practice of Stravinsky, especially in *Les Noces* and *Le Sacre du printemps*. The piano has an especially prominent percussive function, with hard-hitting repetitions and erratic cross accents, while the woodwinds provide jarring punctuation (Example 20.5). As in Antheil's *Ballet Mécanique*, these emblems of primitivism came to convey the sinister assault of industrialism. They suggested an environment run amok.[32]

The scenario unfolds with "violent alternations of WORK and PLAY," and the music follows suit, interweaving ostinato-based sections with others conjuring up American popular idioms. These last occur most strikingly in Scene IV, the large centerpiece of the ballet, which depicts an "exaggeration of the Coney Island type of American amusement park." There a modernist assault gives way to a tinkling, bucolic carousel. The piano takes on a vamplike accompaniment, joined by banjo, and an alto saxophone enters, doubling with the violins to sing out a saucily syncopated melody. The overall effect is that of a pops orchestra—whether at an amusement park or skating rink.[33]

The most striking part of this portion of the work is the "Negro Scene," which opens with "the dream fantasy of the sleeping negro," acted out by the blackface

Example 20.5. John Alden Carpenter, *Skyscrapers*, p. 1. Copyright © 1926 (Renewed) by
G. Schirmer, Inc. (ASCAP). International copyright secured. All rights reserved. Reprinted by
permission.

character, White-Wings. "Through a gauze curtain just beyond him," the scenario continues, "we see gradually taking shape in the dim light a group of negroes, men and women, half-forgotten types of the poor South. We hear their actual voices, in a song, first slow and soothing, then more animated and rising at last to a fierce religious fervor." The scene ends with a dance by the chorus and White-Wings. This section is loosely built of four-bar segments, suggestive of the blues. There are also "blue" notes and call-and-response, which appear both in the division of the chorus's melody and in the orchestra's accompaniment. Again, as in the amusement-park section, the saxophone and banjo are featured (Example 20.6).

This must have been the portion of the work that inspired a front-page story in the *New York Herald-Tribune* the morning after *Skyscrapers'* premiere, where it was hailed as embodying "the spirit of jazz." In the realm of jazz, *Skyscrapers* was certainly stronger on "spirit" than substance. Its evocations of both African American idioms and popular tunes were thoroughly caricatured. This is especially so with the nonsense syllables given in Scene IV to the black chorus—"Bola, manola monabola. Fiama lo"—sketching a stereotype of an untutored, even inchoate, southern black. Like blackface, this gibberish appeared in some important works of the 1920s, reaching into the 1930s. The "Dahomey" section of *Show Boat*'s world fair scene from 1927 (the year after *Skyscrapers*) has a chorus ostensibly portraying Africans that sings "Dyunga Doe! Dyunga Doe! Dyunga Hungyung gunga Hungyung gunga go!" Another occurrence appeared in the film *Sanders of the River* from 1934, starring Paul Robeson. While including much authentic footage from Central Africa, together with indigenous music, the film also included newly composed songs with nonsensical text.[34]

And so *Skyscrapers* added up to a complex whole. By incorporating a black chorus and Broadway dancers, it not only aimed for authenticity but also showed respect for traditions beyond the Western concert hall, taking a big step past the condescending attitude toward jazz of Gauthier or Damrosch. Yet as much as *Skyscrapers* represented an earnest attempt to go beyond "apply[ing] the borrowed devices of our jazz," as Robert Edmond Jones put it, it also reflected the limits of that attitude in the mid-1920s, dishing up a hefty serving of stereotypes.

When the 1926–27 season dawned, it did not promise quite as many jazz-based compositions as the previous year. But even though the flow of such works was beginning to slow, there were some major events. Four compositions from that season bring this chapter to a close. They include Gruenberg's *The Creation: A Negro Sermon*, Still's *Darker America*, Copland's Piano Concerto, and Antheil's *Jazz Symphony*. In style, performance setting, and impact, each took the jazz movement in a different direction.

With *The Creation* and *Darker America*, the modern-music societies once again provided a forum. Both premieres took place in late November. Gruenberg's cantata, *The Creation*, was heard first, premiered by the League of Composers on 27 November 1926. Gruenberg has already been discussed as a founder of both the

American Music Guild and the League of Composers, also as the man who conducted the American premiere of *Pierrot lunaire*. During the 1920s, he produced a strong series of pieces associated with jazz, most of them premiered by the League, which peaked with his opera *Emperor Jones*, produced at the Metropolitan Opera in 1933.

If anything, *The Creation* showed how far the concept of "jazz" could be stretched. Virtually void of standard jazz emblems, whether blue notes or banjos, *The Creation* seemed to look most toward *Pierrot lunaire* as a model. Like Schoenberg's work of 1912, *The Creation* was scored "for voice and eight instruments," although Gruenberg made some different choices, especially by adding a rhythm section: flute, clarinet, bassoon, horn, viola, timpani, percussion, and piano (as compared to flute, piccolo, clarinet, bass clarinet, violin, viola, cello, and piano in *Pierrot*). Gruenberg's earlier *Daniel Jazz* used the same basic instrumentation. The instrumental part of *The Creation* was largely atonal, opening with low-lying chords rumbling from the depths of the piano to convey a sense of the chaos that preceded creation (Example 20.7).[35]

But *The Creation* had another model as well: William Grant Still's *Levee Land*. Besides being extended works for solo voice and instruments, both shared a connection in having been conceived for a singer from outside the modernist realm and in shaping the music to accommodate that performer. *The Creation* was launched by Jules (or Julius) Bledsoe, a famous African American singer and actor whose career ran parallel to that of Paul Robeson. One month before his appearance at the League of Composers, Bledsoe had starred in *Deep River*, a short-running Broadway musical, and the next year he played the role of Joe in the premiere of *Show Boat* (a role that Robeson assumed for a revival in 1932 and the film version in 1936). In 1934, Bledsoe sang the lead in a European production of Gruenberg's *Emperor Jones*.

Like *Levee Land*, although less consistently, *The Creation* had a vocal line that was largely diatonic, surrounded by a dissonant instrumental wash. Yet while Still doubled the voice with at least one instrument, Gruenberg left the singer on his own, confident of Bledsoe's training and experience. *The Creation* opens with a simple, recitative-like delivery on C, with brief forays to D and E. Its first dissonant vocal pitch enters on the word *lonely* to color the text (Example 20.7, m. 7). Soon there are far more adventuresome vocal forays; but they are contained, especially in comparison to *Pierrot*.

This work must have been considered part of the "jazz" movement both because of Bledsoe's involvement and because its text was by James Weldon Johnson. Johnson's "The Creation" was published the next year (1927) as part of *God's Trombones—Seven Negro Sermons in Verse*. In it, Johnson "took the rhetoric, idiom, and images of the Negro preacher," as one historian has characterized it. Even though the Gruenberg title came from Johnson, it also echoed one of the most famous jazz-based compositions of the 1920s—Milhaud's *La Création du monde*, which had appeared in Paris three years earlier.[36]

Example 20.7. Gruenberg, *The Creation,* pp. 1–2. © Copyright 1926. Reprinted by permission of the publisher, Gunmar Music, of Newton Centre, Massachusetts.

U. E. 8327

In an article about jazz for the *Musical Leader*, published in 1925, Gruenberg already seemed steeped in Johnson's text. "In the beginning was Rhythm," opened the article. He went on to present an evolutionary view of jazz as originating in "the beating of drums" and culminating in the United States. He wrote sympathetically of African American idioms, at the same time as he repeatedly characterized them as crude material for sophisticated transformation in the hands of composers. "When the ragtime movement started to take definite form in a unified manner such as the Cakewalk," opened one such instance, "it occurred to the white man with his superior technical knowledge to exploit this new form, and he composed music for the masses which swept our country and then Europe with its intriguing mannerisms." There lay the essence of Gruenberg's own approach. With a musical style consistently grounded more in Western Europe than in Harlem, he remained among the most highbrow of American composers experimenting with jazz.[37]

The evening after *The Creation* received its premiere, William Grant Still turned up at the ICG with a new jazz-based work. Titled *Darker America* and written for orchestra, it once again synthesized black idioms with areas of intense chromaticism, and it did so in much the same way as *Levee Land*, employing planes—or whole areas—that evoked African American traditions and juxtaposing them, either vertically or horizontally, with a dissonant fabric. Yet in overall purpose, this work moved away from sassily gesturing toward the nightclub and turned to epic racial statement, preparing the way for Still's *Afro-American Symphony* several years later. This change took Still in a completely different direction from Gruenberg and his other white colleagues. *Darker America* had a self-consciously sober ambience, conceived for a symphony orchestra that unambiguously sought to "elevate" (in Still's own term) African American idioms.[38]

Still described *Darker America* in the ICG's program as "representative of the American Negro," and he conceived a program for it that dealt with race, tracing the African American experience from a sorrowful past to a triumphant present (and future). Such litanies of progress suffused the creative arts during the Harlem Renaissance.

His ["the American Negro's"] serious side is presented and is intended to suggest the triumph of a people over their sorrows through fervent prayer. At the beginning the theme of the American Negro is announced by the strings in unison. Following a short development of this the English horn announces the sorrow theme which is followed immediately by the theme of hope, given to muted brass accompanied by strings and woodwind. The sorrow theme returns treated differently, indicative of more intense sorrow as contrasted to passive sorrow indicated at the initial appearance of the theme. Again hope appears and the people seem about to rise above their troubles. But sorrow triumphs. Then the prayer is heard (given to oboe); the prayer of numbed rather than anguished souls. Strongly contrasted moods follow, leading up to the triumph of the people near the end, at which point the three principal themes are combined.[39]

Even though the scenario of *Darker America* pointed toward the *Afro-American Symphony*, its musical style looked back to *Levee Land*. In the opening measures of *Darker America*, unison strings proclaim the mournful "American Negro" theme in G minor (Example 20.8). Immediately, as in *Levee Land*, Still injected an alien sound world but did so based on the traditional technique of call-and-response. The music for the "call" imitated black vernacular idioms of uptown New York, and that for the "response" provided a dissonant comment from downtown. Note the second beat of measure two where the horns and piano right hand enunciate G minor, and the lower strings and piano left hand interject F, C-sharp, and E. Or put another way, in the second measure the G minor of the opening melody coincides with a dissonant third (C-sharp and E). That third, in turn, has an added augmented fifth below (on F). This kind of technique—fusing together blues-derived harmonies with ones of intense chromaticism—occurs throughout the work.

Another striking aspect of *Darker America* is its form. Just as Still's program note indicates, the four musical themes appear one after another, much like characters in a pageant. Some recur, and secondary themes enter as well. There is a central development section in which the "sorrow" theme returns especially frequently, and the themes coalesce at the end to convey "the triumph of the people" that was described by Still (yet it is a quiet victory). The result is a highly sectional work, with its many parts spliced together with dramatically orchestrated transitions. Like the formal conception of *Concerto in F*, that of *Darker America* bears stronger ties to a musical comedy overture than to any European symphonic form. In a further parallel to *Concerto in F*, it was just this aspect of *Darker America* that caused Olin Downes to raise strong objections, although he admired the piece as a whole: "What is lacking [in *Darker America*] is actual development and organic growth of the ideas. This music, however, has direction and feeling in it, qualities usually lacking in contemporaneous music." Once again, it did not dawn on Downes that this kind of discontinuous formal structure might have grown out of a musical experience in another arena—in this case, Still's work as an arranger for the theater.[40]

If Gruenberg's jazz built on European models and Still's was moving toward weighty proclamations about the African American experience, Copland's Concerto for Piano and Orchestra and Antheil's *Jazz Symphony* yielded even more variations on how jazz and modernism could be mingled. Both hailed from the "art" side of the art-pop fusion, yet they did so in markedly different ways. The lineage of Copland's Concerto reached toward the *Concerto in F*, while the *Jazz Symphony* was rooted in the symphonic-jazz world of *Rhapsody in Blue*. Yet each formed a distinctive response. Both works appeared during the first half of 1927, and both brought the encounter with jazz to a culminating point. Other jazz-based compositions continued to appear after this date, but the intensity of a fad passed away.

With Copland's Concerto, jazz provided the excuse for a modernist excursion. This was gestural jazz, akin to the so-called primitivist abstractions of Pablo Picasso. With characteristic open intervals and carefully chiseled cells, Copland delivered all the expected components of jazz, from blue notes to syncopations and cross-rhythms. Yet they were persistently refracted rather than straightforwardly presented.

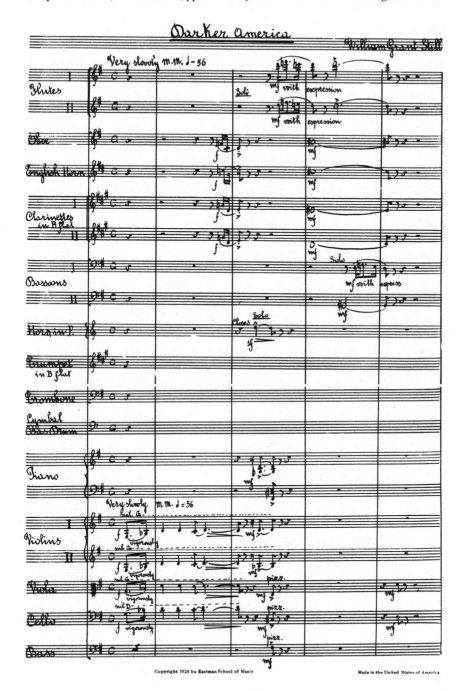

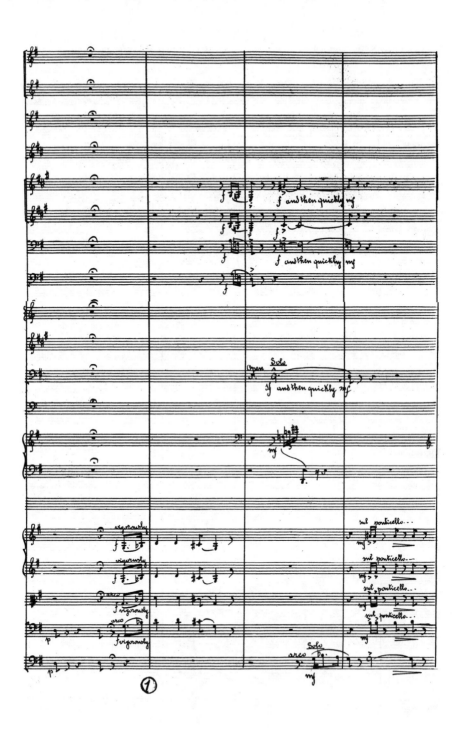

The opening presents some of the most abstracted jazz in the entire work (Example 20.9). It is built of a syncopated three-note module (introduced by trombones and trumpets), which the composer alternately stretches and compresses in both pitch and rhythm, moving it through a spectrum of timbres and ranges. This module is suggestive and pointillistic rather than toe-tapping. The second half of it plays off the major-minor third so basic to the blues, yet it does so with unorthodox contractions into major and minor seconds (note the trombone in m. 2 and m. 5). The opening piano theme then emerges from this orchestral cell. Rather than bounding off into a rollicking stint, it too focuses on essences. Soon a second theme enters—first hinted at in the woodwinds (at rehearsal 4), then forthrightly stated in the piano (immediately after rehearsal 5; Example 20.10). It resonates with the sounds of Gershwin. Its melodic shape is similar to that of Gershwin's *Piano Prelude No. 2*, and the texture in which it is delivered becomes less spiky and more linked to contemporary popular idioms (Example 20.11). In later life, Copland sought to distance his concerto from that of Gershwin. "I have no idea today whether Gershwin's *Concerto* of 1925 influenced me toward composing a piano concerto the following year," he declared in the 1980s. "I doubt it." He went on: "The melodic material of the first movement is taken from a traditional blues, one also used by Gershwin at about the same time in his *Prelude No. 2* for piano." Although the link may have been coincidental, the shape and pacing of the melodies are too close to ignore.[41]

Perhaps the most exuberantly jazz-inflected part of Copland's Concerto is the opening of the second movement (there are only two movements in the work) (Example 20.12). Copland leads directly into it from the first movement, managing yet another distinctive alignment of modernism and jazz. Void of orchestral accompaniment, this segment has the character of a cadenza, to call on the terminology of a concerto, or of a break or brief solo, in the lingo of jazz. Although precisely notated, it convincingly conveys a sense of improvised abandon, and it plays off two principal components of jazz: cross-rhythms and crushed notes. In an article by Copland about jazz, published in the January–February 1927 issue of *Modern Music*—cunningly timed to coincide with the concerto's premiere—Copland focused primarily on rhythm. He outlined various subdivisions into $3 + 3 + 2$ of the eighth notes in a measure of $\frac{4}{4}$, and he did so by calling upon examples from Gershwin's songs and the novelty piano works of Zez Confrey. He cited no music by African Americans.

The Concerto's second movement opened by subdividing the measure into two units of three (in the right hand) against three of two (in the left), both with cross-accents. The section that ensues is even more pointillistic than that of the first, with jabs of sound spiking out accents from distant registers. To enhance this effect, Copland uses crushed notes (major and minor seconds), often in a high register. Constructions of this sort, playfully presented, were common in the piano style of Zez Confrey or Gershwin.

Like *Rhapsody in Blue* and *Concerto in F*, Copland's Concerto was also arranged

Example 20.9. Copland, Concerto for Piano and Orchestra, p. 1. © Copyright 1929 by The Aaron Copland Fund for Music, Inc. Renewed. Boosey & Hawkes, Inc., sole licensee. Reprinted by permission of The Aaron Copland Fund for Music, Inc., and Boosey & Hawkes, Inc.

Example 20.10. Copland, Concerto for Piano, pp. 8–9. © Copyright 1929 by The Aaron Copland Fund for Music, Inc. Renewed. Boosey & Hawkes, Inc., sole licensee. Reprinted by permission of The Aaron Copland Fund for Music, Inc., and Boosey & Hawkes, Inc.

for two pianos, in this case by John Kirkpatrick, who later became a noted scholar and performer of the music of Charles Ives. It was published by Cos Cob Press in 1929. This arrangement gave fellow composers a chance to know the piece, just as the four-hand arrangement of *Le Sacre du printemps* had done. The work was not recorded until 1952.[42]

Copland's Concerto for Piano and Orchestra appeared slightly more than a year

after Gershwin's *Concerto in F*, and even though a cluster of composers incorporating jazz surrounded these two figures, it was Gershwin who loomed as the star of the show. The result was an undeclared contest that pitted Copland against Gershwin, in an attempt to establish Copland as America's most illustrious musical newcomer. Like a battle of the bands, so familiar in popular music, this contest had the aura of an athletic competition. It made for good sport, but in this

Example 20.12. Copland, Concerto for Piano, p. 17. © Copyright 1929 by The Aaron Copland Fund for Music, Inc. Renewed. Boosey & Hawkes, Inc., sole licensee. Reprinted by permission of The Aaron Copland Fund for Music, Inc., and Boosey & Hawkes, Inc.

case it had long-ranging ramifications. Orchestrated by the promoters of American modernism—principally Paul Rosenfeld—this contest did not seem to engage either Copland or Gershwin very much.[43]

In a review of the Copland Concerto, Rosenfeld laid out his case bluntly. Hailing the work as the first in which jazz had "borne music," which of course suggested that all previous jazz-based endeavors had yielded something less, Rosenfeld placed Copland's concerto high above what he dismissed as the "hash derivative" compositions of Gershwin. For him, only Still stood on a level with Copland. Others got into the comparative act as well. Lawrence Gilman reported in the *New York Herald-Tribune* that "unlike certain of his more naive colleagues, [Copland] does not have to seek painfully to be 'serious.'" A writer for the *Brooklyn Daily Eagle* claimed that "Mr. Copland has quite outdone Mr. Gershwin and Mr. Carpenter." Even Isaac Goldberg, who within a few years was to be Gershwin's first biographer, implied such a comparison, declaring Copland to be "the young man who seems to hold out the greatest hopes for a jazz that shall be music as well."[44]

This debate had considerable reach, undermining the validity of popular music as a form of artistic expression and setting models for a new generation of modernist rhetoric that would emerge so forcefully after World War II. One of its more intriguing offshoots involved yet another figure—Darius Milhaud—whose *La Création du monde* increasingly was held up as a precursor of Copland and the whole jazz-modernist movement. In the process, Gershwin's role, as chronicled and perceived within the concert-music world, was diminished.

Several historiographic infelicities resulted. For one thing, *La Création du monde* came to hold an exaggerated pride of chronological place over *Rhapsody in Blue*. First performed in Paris on 25 October 1923—three-and-a-half months before *Rhapsody in Blue*—*La Création du monde* has consistently been cited as appearing a year or even two years earlier. This gave it an edge. Reviews of the New York premiere of *La Création du monde*, which finally took place in December 1933, were rife with such overstatement. (As noted in Chapter 4, the work had been scheduled to be performed as part of a New York visit by the Ballet Suédois late in 1923 but was dropped from the program.) After the 1933 premiere in New York, the *New York Times* claimed that *La Création du monde* had been "written some years earlier" than *Rhapsody in Blue*. Marc Blitzstein, reporting in *Modern Music*, asserted that "this extraordinary ballet" appeared "one year before the *Rhapsody in Blue*." And Paul Rosenfeld, who included an essay about the concert in *Discoveries of a Music Critic* (1936), placed *La Création du monde* "very considerably in advance of the appearance of Gershwin's *Rhapsody in Blue*."[45]

The tendency to stretch the chronological gap between *Le Création du Monde* and *Rhapsody in Blue* has held firm over the decades, and it became one component—a crucial one—in making Milhaud a progenitor of the jazz movement in American composition and in diminishing the role of Gershwin. This helped Blitzstein and Rosenfeld validate their subject, and it was a strong tool in essays about Copland. A legitimizing ancestor, Milhaud gave Copland weight and credibility. "There are also origins in jazz which, though entirely American in their manifestations, go back, perhaps, more to Milhaud than, as is sometimes suggested, to Gershwin," wrote Arthur Berger in a historically important assessment of Copland from 1953. "It is more likely," Berger continued, "that Gershwin's motivations arose out of the same source as Copland's (namely, out of Milhaud) than that Gershwin influenced Copland."[46]

At the end of a multi-decade process, stretching from Paul Rosenfeld's reviews to Berger's biography, Copland had been historicized as an American who adopted a distinctive national idiom—jazz—but did so at the inspiration of a French highbrow contemporary rather than an American box-office star. In the process, Copland's pedigree was burnished to match the European models so revered by Rosenfeld, and Gershwin was kept in his place.

While Copland was elevated at Gershwin's expense, George Antheil was largely ignored in discussions of the jazz movement. His *Jazz Symphony* received its premiere at Antheil's Carnegie Hall extravaganza in April 1927, where it was thoroughly eclipsed by *Ballet Mécanique*. The critics were so prepared to be outraged by *Ballet Mécanique* that they simply and succinctly dismissed everything else on the program. The *Jazz Symphony* was "even staler and emptier" than the Sonata for Violin, Piano, and Drum that immediately preceded it, wrote the *Tribune* critic Lawrence Gilman. Even the sensational stroke of having the work performed by W. C. Handy's Orchestra did not seem to affect the overall impression. But the work deserves fresh consideration, as much for the nature of its borrowings as for the brand of jazz it represented.[47]

Constructed in one movement, the *Jazz Symphony* stands firmly beside *Ballet Mécanique* as a vanguard work of postmodern pastiche, and it adds on a bold layer of cross-genre sampling. Its result was as different from Copland's response to jazz as Copland's was from Gruenberg's or Still's from Carpenter's. A granddaddy to John Zorn, Antheil pushes the cinematic technique of pasting together disparate snippets even further than in *Ballet Mécanique*. The segments are shorter, the juxtapositions more outrageous. Originally intended for Paul Whiteman's orchestra but never performed by that group, the *Jazz Symphony* has an orchestration not far from that of Whiteman's band (i.e., not far from *Rhapsody*): two each of oboes and clarinets, three saxophones, three each of trumpets and trombones, one tuba, percussion, two banjos, and strings (here a full complement, not just violins, as in Whiteman's orchestra). Yet even though *Jazz Symphony* was sparked by a commission from Whiteman, Antheil tried hard to distance himself both from Whiteman's aesthetic and from connections to Gershwin. Writing to his patron Mary Louise Curtis Bok the year that he composed *Jazz Symphony*, Antheil dismissed *Rhapsody in Blue* as "a very mediocre piece," stating in a subsequent letter that his own work would "put Gershwin in the shade." He also claimed that his symphony was "a reaction towards negro jazz as away from 'sweet' jazz." Yet no matter how much

Antheil claimed to oppose "sweet" jazz, his *Jazz Symphony* begins with a sassy segment of easy-going syncopation and does so with a Latin tinge, à la Vincent Lopez (Example 20.13). After sixteen measures, the first piano abruptly enters on its own with an entirely new persona (Example 20.14). The left hand sports a chordal vamp, drawn from the opening orchestral material, while the right hand launches into a chromatic wash, saturating the spectrum with a series of migrating patterns (the first of these begins in m. 17 and the second in m. 25). Like *Ballet Mécanique*, this work draws upon the block form of Stravinsky but pushes it to extremes; it also draws upon the principle of cinematic contrast articulated by Fernand Léger.[48]

Throughout, these same sorts of juxtapositions of high and low prevail, with the pianos taking on a mechanized, cluster-banging function against changing moods in the orchestra. Large sections resemble riffs on Stravinsky, whose style is parodied just as vigorously as popular idioms of the day. Throughout much of the work it is hard to hear how it was "an expression of the American negro," as Antheil claimed. But three-quarters of the way through this suddenly changes with a snippet of wah-wah trumpet, followed by animal effects on clarinet. The clarinet phrases trace their roots to *Rhapsody in Blue* and Whiteman's orchestra, while the trumpet could have had a variety of sources, whether the recordings of the white bandleader Isham Jones or those of King Oliver, which by 1925, when Antheil composed this work, were available in the United States and abroad. Another slice of the *Rhapsody* appears near the end, when a descending clarinet glissando, passed on to alto saxophone, parodies *Rhapsody* by reversing the work's opening gesture.[49]

Following the trend set in motion by William Grant Still, Louis Gruenberg, and others, Antheil hired an African American ensemble—W. C. Handy's Orchestra—to perform his *Jazz Symphony*. Handy apparently had difficulty dealing with the score, so the African American conductor Allie Ross, who enjoyed considerable prominence as a conductor in Harlem, stepped in. Among other groups, Ross was conductor of the New Amsterdam Symphonic Orchestra, which gave concerts in Harlem during the 1920s. Still played in that orchestra for a time as well. The appearance of Handy's orchestra at Antheil's concert also should be recognized for its position in the significant history of African Americans in Carnegie Hall, beginning with a series of concerts between 1912 and 1914 by James Reese Europe and his Clef Club Orchestra. Antheil's concert may well have helped Handy in making the necessary contacts for his now-famous concert at Carnegie in 1928.[50]

All this unfolded against a scenic backdrop designed by Joseph Mullen, as discussed together with that for *Ballet Mécanique*, which featured an African American couple dancing while the man clasped the woman's buttocks. For 1927, this was all rather daring—as though Harlem had moved downtown to invade 57th Street.

Jazz and concert music have continued to intersect throughout the century. But rarely did they do so with such a sense of discovery and excitement as in these few

Example 20.13. Antheil, *Jazz Symphony*, p. 1. Copyright © 1925 (Renewed) by G. Schirmer, Inc. (ASCAP) International copyright secured. All rights reserved. Reprinted by permission.

years of the 1920s. The crossover movement then gave a jump-start to the process of racial integration on American concert stages, and it intensified the process of reaching out to the masses that is so basic to American culture.

For some of the American composers profiled here, jazz played a role in their music as the years passed. Gershwin, most notably, stuck with his jazz-based concert-music style of the 1920s right through *Cuban Overture*, *Second Rhapsody*, and *Porgy and Bess*, until his death in 1937. He remained the symbol of jazz-based composition, a figure envied and emulated, pilloried and praised. Copland did not remain as closely engaged with jazz. Some of the idiom's rhythmic and harmonic gestures settled deeply into his style; his Piano Variations, for example, while hardly a jazz-based work, has moments that subtly reveal this infusion. But in a more overt way he returned to jazz only occasionally, with his Clarinet Concerto for Benny Goodman in 1947–48 and his *Piano Blues* (including four pieces, written in 1926, 1934, 1947, and 1948). For Still, meanwhile, involvement with jazz in the 1920s spurred him on toward musical expression of his African American heritage. It also eased him into a more broadly accessible style.

The greatest legacy of all was how the minds and ears of composers in the concert world opened up to the potential for exploring popular idioms. "High" and "low" moved closer together during the 1930s and 1940s, facing a new stage of polarization when a second wave of modernism gripped American concert composers after World War II. Yet horizons had undeniably widened during the 1920s, and the sounds unleashed by these crossover composers resounded across the decades.

Epilogue

Every now and then a historical period has a glimmer to it—both for those on the scene and for those looking back. The 1920s in the United States was such a decade. Young artists and composers felt confident that they were "somehow unique" as "representatives of a new age," in the words of writer Malcolm Cowley, and enjoyed enough support from patrons and modernist activists to make their dreams come true. Far from doggedly making do, they skipped and sprinted, fueled by a sense of opportunity that few have the privilege to experience.[1]

In many ways, New York yielded a thriving marketplace for modernism during the 1920s. There, the newest music from all over the Western world was not only heard but discussed and debated, and it provided an environment for wide-ranging experimentation with new ideas. As the decade progressed, the variety of musics classified as "modernist" grew ever more varied, and by its end, a new generation of American composers and critics had come into its own. At the same time, an institutional network for new music took shape, and an aesthetic agenda was set in place that fueled American composition for the rest of the century.

Perhaps most striking of all was the way that the drive to internationalize dominated. This was not a time of cultural isolationism but rather of reaching out as boldly and ecumenically as possible. With rapid motion, the 1920s turned the Atlantic into a conduit for artistic exchange. Americans traveled abroad, Europeans visited the United States, and music by both was heard in both places. This shows up in the transnational styles that evolved during the period as much as it does in concert programs or travel itineraries. Whether Dada and its accompanying tie to machines, neoclassicism, or the pursuit of dissonance, each new artistic preoccupation of the period had practitioners on both sides of the Atlantic. New ideas migrated and mutated, assuming different forms in the hands of different personalities across the Western spectrum. The young American generation seemed especially adept at this process, whether setting out to confect new styles of their own or adapting European idioms to their personal agendas. Modernism was so deeply transnational that searching for points of origin often misses the point. The nineteenth-century image of young American students dutifully copying from European plaster casts was chucked out the window, replaced by one of them reassembling the models so thoroughly and ingeniously that the original is barely visible—but it is often there.

At the same time, though, the transatlantic playing field was by no means level. Americans may have been gaining parity with their European colleagues, but their newfound relationship to Europe remained in progress rather than being fully realized. They were increasingly gaining recognition abroad though they were not yet fully admitted into the international fraternity.

What, then, was distinctively American about the modernist movement that converged in New York? Raw ambition and a do-it-yourself work ethic stood out, whether in the founding and rapid success of composer societies or the equally quick establishment of the careers of young leaders, such as Copland and Cowell. Shrewd marketing strategies and unabashed self-promotion also thrived. Convening press conferences and interviews, as Varèse, Cowell, Antheil, and Copland all did; arranging photo opportunities for *Musical America* or *Vanity Fair*; publishing a polemic in *Modern Music*—these were tried-and-true tactics from political campaigns and business that composers adapted imaginatively. A faith in progress through community action also set Americans apart, as did a preoccupation with the perceived lack of an indigenous high-art tradition. In a climate where newness mattered above all else, this last was a real asset. While European modernists threatened to burn their museums, Americans could feel happily unencumbered.

Tension between "high" and "low" also had a special bearing on Americans. It brought potential for a national distinctiveness—as the jazz crossover compositions of Gershwin, Copland, Antheil, and others showed—at the same time as it set up a competitive field. In gaining public attention, young American composers of the 1920s not only had to grapple with their European contemporaries and with music of the European past, but they often felt themselves running behind a fast-paced industry for popular music. This was especially true within the realms of phonograph recordings and radio, where concert-music composers took awhile to gain their stride.

American's relationship to Europe also emerged as an important factor in the "high"-"low" debate—especially in the criticism of Paul Rosenfeld, which did so much to define American modernism. At the same time as American popular music—especially jazz—traveled all over the globe, becoming an emblem of American culture, Rosenfeld waged a battle against it, positioning the modernism of concert-music composers as superior. He drove a wedge between "high" and "low," earnestly hoping that native modernist expression would not be contaminated by idioms that he considered inferior. Rosenfeld posited a form of modernism circumscribed by class and gender; new music of America was to be shaped according to a set of high-art values, securely grounded in European traditions, and it was to be "virile," rising above the masterpiece mania of well-established music institutions, which he and his contemporaries persistently perceived as dominated by women. Rosenfeld's perspective not only affected how these young American composers saw themselves but it also has conditioned most writing about their music in subsequent decades. Moreover, the values he promoted remained strong in the United States, rising again with renewed force after World War II.

Which leads to another topic: the fate of the American modernist movement after the onset of the Great Depression. In some ways, it strode forward. The League of Composers continued giving concerts in New York, as did the New Music Society in California. Both organizations broadened into different media—the League through a series of radio broadcasts beginning in 1935 and New Music through the issue of recordings beginning the previous year. And musical developments of the 1920s continued to have an impact, whether in increased attention to writing for percussion ensemble—as exhibited in pieces such as Cowell's *Pulse*, Cage's *First Construction in Metal* (both 1939), and Lou Harrison's *Labyrinth* (1941)—or in ongoing fusions of jazz and concert idioms. American involvement in neoclassicism also held firm as the long lines and clean textures promoted within the aesthetic became the basis for a new, more nationalistic idiom. The musical language of Copland's *Appalachian Spring*, for example, is not so far removed from that of the *Piano Variations*. Rather the meaning and overall accessibility of the work were changed.

The single biggest difference between these two decades resulted from a radical shift in economic and political conditions. Whereas American composers during the 1920s often seemed blithely apolitical, as can happen in times of prosperity and peace, they moved out of a warp of oblivion once the Depression arrived to confront gritty questions of survival and social relevance. "It was as if we had been walking for years in a mist, on what seemed to be level ground," to call up the words of Malcolm Cowley once again, "but with nothing visible beyond a few yards, so that we became preoccupied with the design of things close at hand . . . and then as if the mist had blown away to reveal that the level ground was only a terrace, that chasms lay on all sides of us, and that beyond them were mountains rising into the golden sunlight. We could not reach the mountains alone, but perhaps we could merge ourselves in the working class and thereby help to build a bridge for ourselves and for humanity."[2]

Composers, too, joined in that quest. The Composers' Collective, which involved Copland, Cowell, Seeger, and Blitzstein, among others, convened in New York between 1932 and 1936 as an affiliate of the American Communist Party to explore various means of "merging" with "the working class." Composers initially brought their modernist products to "the people," as a slogan of the day put it. Copland, for example, performed his *Piano Variations* at the Pierre Degeyter Club in 1934. But they soon attempted to make their music relevant to a broader public, first composing "worker's songs" and later, especially after the Communist Party's Popular Front came to the fore in 1936, producing concert works steeped in the American vernacular. All this had been foreshadowed during the 1920s, whether in the social feminist mission of Claire Reis, especially in her scheme to build a new audience for modern music by attracting "the man on the street"; the musical paeans to African American history of William Grant Still; the "meet-the-people" fusions of jazz and modernism in the commissions of Paul Whiteman; or the political and spiritual vision of American dissonance of Dane Rudhyar.

As composers reached out to the masses during the 1930s, they became immersed in American culture, especially its folk traditions. But they did not lose an international gaze. The Composers' Collective, to return to that organization, included a number of visiting Europeans and immigrants among its participants—Lan Adomian, Hanns Eisler, Jacob Schaeffer—at the same time as it was an extension of similar efforts abroad. As the 1930s progressed and Nazi Germany grew ever more threatening, major European modernists—some of the same figures who had visited the United States in the 1920s—began to move to America, initiating a whole new phase in modernist transnationalism. Stravinsky, Schoenberg, Krenek, Milhaud, Hindemith, and Weill were among a major wave of composer-refugees who settled in the United States. Americans began studying composition with them, and by the end of World War II, the United States rose up as home to a new wave of modernism that was even more deeply transnational than that of the 1920s.

In the postwar period, the generation of John Cage and Milton Babbitt did not have to invent forums for their music to be heard. Composer organizations were in place, as were models for promoting and publishing new work. By bringing American modernism into the international marketplace of new music, composers of the 1920s achieved the greatest feat of all: they broke through the glass ceiling for artists from the New World, making it possible for future generations to aim ever higher.

Selected Discography

Following are selected CDs for compositions discussed in this book.

Antheil, George. *Airplane Sonata.* Marthanne Verbit, piano. Albany Records TROY 146.
———. *Ballet Mécanique* and *Jazz Symphony.* Maurice Peress, conductor. MusicMasters 67094-2.
Bauer, Marion. "Chromaticon" from *Four Piano Pieces.* Virginia Eskin, piano. Northeastern Records.
Carpenter, John Alden. *Skyscrapers.* Kenneth Klein, conductor; London Symphony Orchestra. EMI CDC-7 49263 2.
Copland, Aaron. Concerto for Piano. Garrick Ohlsson, piano; Michael Tilson Thomas, conductor; San Francisco Symphony Orchestra. RCA Red Seal 09026-68541-2.
———. *Piano Variations.* Leo Smit, piano. Sony Classical SM2K 66345.
Cowell, Henry. *The Voice of Lir* and *Dynamic Motion.* Henry Cowell, piano. Smithsonian Folkways 4081.
———. *Piece for Piano.* Robert Miller, piano. New World Records NW 80203-2.
Crawford, Ruth. Prelude No. 6. Joseph Bloch, piano. CRI 658.
———. *String Quartet 1931.* Arditti Quartet. Gramavision R2-79440. Also: Schönberg Ensemble; Oliver Knussen, conductor. Deutsche Grammophon 449 925-2.
———. Violin Sonata. Ida Kavafian, violin; Vivian Fine, piano. CRI 658.
Gershwin, George. *Concerto in F.* Phillippe Entremont, piano; Philadelphia Orchestra. Sony SBT 46338.
Gruenberg, Louis. *The Creation.* William Brown, tenor; Collage New Music Ensemble; Gunther Schuller, conductor. Gunmar GM 2015.
Harris, Roy. Piano Sonata No. 1. Richard Zimdars, piano. Albany TROY 105. Also: Johana Harris, piano. CRI 818.
Ornstein, Leo. *A la Chinoise.* Alan Feinberg, piano. Argo 436 925-2.
Piston, Walter. Three Pieces for Flute, Clarinet, and Bassoon. Members of the Boehm Quintet. Premier PRCD 1006.
Rudhyar, Dane. *Paeans* and *Granites.* William Masselos, piano. CRI 584.
Ruggles, Carl. *Angels.* Ensemble 21; Arthur Weisberg, conductor. Summit 122.
———. *Men and Mountains.* Polish National Radio Symphony Orchestra; William Strickland, conductor. CRI 715.

Seeger, Ruth Crawford. SEE Crawford, Ruth.

Sessions, Roger. Piano Sonata No. 1. Barry Salwen, piano. Koch KIC 7106.

Still, William Grant. *Darker America.* Westchester Symphony Orchestra; Siegfried Landau, conductor. Vox Box CD 5157.

Thomson, Virgil. *Susie Asado.* Nancy Armstrong, soprano; Anthony Tommasini, piano. Northeastern Records NR 250.

————. *Capital, Capitals.* Paul Kirby, Frank Kelley, Sanford Sylvan, and David Ripley, vocalists; Anthony Tommasini, piano. Northeastern Records NR 250. Also: Joseph Crawford, Clyde S. Turner, Joseph James, and William C. Smith, vocalists; Virgil Thomson, piano. Sony Classical CB 770.

Varèse, Edgard. *Hyperprism.* Orchestre National de France; Kent Nagano, conductor. Erato 4509-92137-2.

————. *Octandre.* Ensemble InterContemporain; Pierre Boulez, conductor. Sony Classical SMK 45844.

Whithorne, Emerson. "Chimes of St. Patrick's," from *New York Days and Nights.* John Kozar, piano. Preamble PRCD 1786.

Appendix

Programs of Modern-Music Societies
in New York, 1920–1931

To gain a perspective on the contemporary music heard in New York, here is a composite list of programs presented between 1920 and 1931 by the following new-music organizations:

Pro Musica Society   League of Composers
American Music Guild   Copland-Sessions Concerts
International Composers' Guild   Pan American Association

The list is arranged by composer, and, in turn, the entries under each composer's name are cited chronologically by performance date. Both European and American composers are included, as are any pre-twentieth-century works that were performed. The location of the performance appears in parentheses.

Asterisks are used to denote different types of premieres:

*   New York premiere
**   American premiere
***   World premiere

Most information about premieres comes from programs printed by the modernist organizations. I have attempted to verify it but have not been able to track down all titles. Regardless of absolute accuracy, it is intriguing to see what these organizations believed to be first performances.

The following sources—both published and unpublished—have been used in compiling this list:

"American Music Guild: Programs," uncatalogued program file at NN.
"International Composers' Guild: Programs," uncatalogued program file at NN.

"League of Composers: Programs," uncatalogued program files at NN and DLC.

The League of Composers: A Record of Performances and a Survey of General Activities from 1923 to 1935. New York: The League of Composers, [1935].

Lott, R. Allen. "New Music for New Ears': The International Composers' Guild." *Journal of the American Musicological Society* 36/2 (1983): 266–86.

Metzer, David. "The League of Composers: The Initial Years." *American Music* 15/1 (Spring 1997): 59–66.

Oja, Carol J. "The Copland-Sessions Concerts and their Reception in the Contemporary Press." *The Musical Quarterly* 65/2 (April 1979): 227–29.

"Pan American Association: Programs," DLC.

"Pro Musica: Programs," Schmitz-CtY.

Root, Deane L. "The Pan American Association of Composers (1928–1934)." *Yearbook for Inter-American Musical Research* 8 (1972): 62–66.

Wiecki, Ronald V. *A Chronicle of Pro Musica in the United States (1920–1944): With a Biographical Sketch of its Founder, E. Robert Schmitz*. Ph.D. dissertation, University of Wisconsin, 1992, 3:654–62.

ACHRON, JOSEPH
• Four Impressions for String Quartet
Russian String Quartet
League of Composers
January 12, 1930 (Art Centre)

ALFANO, FRANCO
• Two Songs from "The Gardener" of
Tagore
Lucilla de Vescovi, soprano;
LeRoy Shield, piano
League of Composers
March 23, 1924 (Klaw Theatre)

ANTHEIL, GEORGE
• Jazz Sonata (Piano Sonata No. 4)
Carol Robinson, piano
League of Composers
November 16, 1924 (Anderson
Galleries)

• String Quartet No. 2
Hans Lange String Quartet
Copland-Sessions Concerts
December 30, 1928 (The Little
Theatre)

• Airplane Sonata (Piano Sonata No. 2)
Imre Weisshaus, piano
Pan American Association of
Composers

April 21, 1930 (Carnegie Chamber
Hall)

AUBERT, LOUIS
• Brodeuses from "Crépuscules
d'automne"
Raymonde Delaunois, soprano; piano
Pro Musica
February 14, 1925 (Aeolian Hall)

BACH, JOHANN SEBASTIAN
• French Suite No. 6 in E Major,
BWV 817
Salzedo Harp Trio
Pro Musica
March 5, 1923 (Carnegie Hall)

BARLOW, SAMUEL
• Three Songs from the Chinese***
José Delaquerriere, tenor; instrumental
ensemble
International Composers' Guild
February 3, 1924 (Vanderbilt Theatre)

BARTH, HANS
• Sonata (Third Movement)
Hans Barth, piano; Sigmund Klein,
piano
Pro Musica
February 14, 1925 (Aeolian Hall)

BARTÓK, BÉLA

- String Quartet No. 2, Op. 17**
  Jacob Mestechkin, violin; Elfrida Boos,
    violin; Samuel Stillman, viola;
    Gdàl Salesski, cello
  International Composers' Guild
  March 4, 1923 (Klaw Theatre)

- Improvisations on Hungarian Peasant
    Songs**
  Claudio Arrau, piano
  International Composers' Guild
  December 2, 1923 (Vanderbilt Theatre)

- Sonata No. 2 for Violin and Piano**
  Yolanda Mero, violin; Albert Stoessel,
    piano
  League of Composers
  January 6, 1924 (Klaw Theatre)

- Sonatina for Piano
  Hyman Rovinsky, piano
  International Composers' Guild
  February 8, 1925 (Aeolian Hall)

- Improvisations Nos. 1, 3, and 5
  E. Robert Schmitz, piano
  Pro Musica
  February 14, 1925 (Aeolian Hall)

- Two Hungarian Folksongs
  Isolde Bernhart, soprano; Irene Jacobi,
    piano
  League of Composers
  October 25, 1925 (Anderson Galleries)

- String Quartet No. 1, Op. 7
  Pro Arte Quartet
  League of Composers
  October 28, 1926 (Town Hall)

- Village Scenes***
  Larry Banks, Zilla Wilson, Nancy
    Hitch, and Elinor Markey, voices;
    Brahms Quartet
  League of Composers
  Commissioned by the League
  November 27, 1926 (Town Hall)

- Sonata for Piano
  Béla Bartók, piano

Pro Musica
February 5, 1928 (Gallo Theater)

- Sonata for Violin and Piano; Seven
    Hungarian Folk Tunes (arr. Szigeti);
    Seven Peasant Dances (arr. Szekely)
  Joseph Szigeti, violin; Béla Bartók, piano
  Pro Musica
  February 5, 1928 (Gallo Theater)

BAUER, MARION

- Sonata for Violin and Piano, Op. 14
  Albert Stoessel, violin;
    Louis Gruenberg, piano
  American Music Guild
  April 29, 1922 (MacDowell Gallery)

- Star Trysts, Orientale, The Epitaph of a
    Butterfly, By the Indus
  Doria Fernanca, soprano; Imogen Peay,
    piano
  American Music Guild
  December 6, 1922 (58th Street Branch
    of the New York Public Library)

- Up the Ocklawaha
  Ruth Kemper, violin; Imogen Peay,
    piano
  American Music Guild
  December 6, 1922 (58th Street Branch
    of the New York Public Library)

- Three Preludes from Op. 15: F-Sharp
    Major*, B Minor, and D Minor*
  E. Robert Schmitz, piano
  American Music Guild
  February 7, 1923 (Town Hall)

- Sonata No. 2 for Violin and Piano***
  Mayo Wadler, violin; Arthur Loesser,
    piano
  League of Composers
  October 25, 1925 (Anderson Galleries)

- Introspection and Turbulence
  Marion Rous, piano
  League of Composers
  November 19, 1926 (Brooklyn
    Museum, in conjunction with an
    exhibition by the Société Anonyme)

BAUER (*continued*)
- String Quartet***
  Lenox Quartet
  League of Composers
  February 12, 1928 (Guild Theatre)

- Four Pieces for Piano, Op. 21
  Harrison Potter, piano
  League of Composers
  April 6, 1930 (Art Centre)

- Noël tryste, Op. 22, No. 1
  Emanu-El Choir; Lazare Saminsky,
    conductor
  League of Composers
  December 10, 1930 (Town Hall)

BAX, ARNOLD
- Piano Quartet in One Movement**
  Clarence Adler, piano; Sandor Harmati,
    violin; Nicolas Moldavan, viola;
    Emmeran Stoeber, cello
  League of Composers
  January 6, 1924 (Klaw Theatre)

- Carol for Men's Voices
  Emanu-El Choir; Lazare Saminsky,
    conductor
  League of Composers
  December 10, 1930 (Town Hall)

BEACH, JOHN
- Angelo's Letter
  Arturo de Filippi, tenor; chamber
    orchestra; Howard Hanson, conductor
  Pro Musica
  February 27, 1929 (Town Hall)

BÉCLARD d' HARCOURT,
MARGUERITE
- Four Indian Folksongs**
  Elsa Respighi, voice;
    Ottorino Respighi, piano
  International Composers' Guild
  January 24, 1926 (Aeolian Hall)

BENNETT, ROBERT RUSSELL
- Two Pieces for Flute and Piano
  Quinto Maganini, flute; Robert Russell
    Bennett, piano

Copland-Sessions Concerts
February 9, 1930 (Steinway Hall)

- Four songs from "Lyrics" by Sara
    Teasdale: The Tune, I Could Snatch
    a Day, On the South Downs,
    and An End
  Radiana Pazmor, contralto; Robert
    Russell Bennett, piano
  League of Composers
  March 1, 1931 (Art Centre)

BERCKMAN, EVELYN
- Limpidité*** and Le baptême de la
    cloche***
  Elizabeth Gutman, soprano;
    Alderson Mowbray, piano
  League of Composers
  February 13, 1927 (Anderson Galleries)

- Springtime in the Orchard
  Ethel Codd Luening, soprano;
    Russian String Quartet
  League of Composers
  January 12, 1930 (Art Centre)

BEREZOWSKY, NICOLAI
- Suite for Five Wind Instruments***
  Chamber ensemble from the New York
    Philharmonic
  League of Composers
  December 19, 1928 (Town Hall)

- Capriccio for Two Pianos***
  Paul Nordoff, piano; Edward Bredshal,
    piano
  League of Composers
  February 2, 1930 (Art Centre)

- Duo for Viola and Clarinet***
  Alexander Pripadcheff, clarinet; viola;
    Nicolai Berezowsky, piano
  League of Composers
  February 1, 1931 (Art Centre)

BERG, ALBAN
- Spring (Op. 2, No. 4)**
  Greta Torpadie, soprano; piano
  International Composers' Guild
  January 13, 1924 (Vanderbilt Theatre)

- Dem Schmertz sein recht
  Greta Torpadie, soprano;
    Rex Tillson, piano
  Pro Musica
  January 18, 1925 (Aeolian Hall)

- String Quartet, Op. 3
  Pro Arte Quartet
  League of Composers
  October 28, 1926 (Town Hall)

- Kammerkonzert**
  Oscar Ziegler, piano; chamber
    ensemble; Artur Rodzinski,
    conductor
  International Composers' Guild
  April 17, 1927 (Aeolian Hall)

BERNERS, LORD
- Lieder Album***
  Lucy Gates, voice; Rex Tillson, piano
  International Composers' Guild
  March 4, 1923 (Klaw Theatre)

- Valses bourgeoises**
  Clarence Adler, piano;
    Joseph Adler, piano
  League of Composers
  January 6, 1924 (Klaw Theatre)

BLISS, ARTHUR
- Madam Noy*
  Eva Gauthier, voice; Marie Miller,
    harp; Chamber Music Art Society
  International Composers' Guild
  March 19, 1922 (Greenwich Village
    Theatre)

- Madam Noy, The Women of Yueh***,
    and Rout
  Lillian Gustafson, voice; Lenox Quartet;
    members of the Philharmonic
    Orchestra; Arthur Bliss, conductor
  League of Composers
  November 11, 1923 (Klaw Theatre)

- Storm Music from "The Tempest"
  José Delaquerriere, tenor; Richard
    Hale, trumpet; Claudio Arrau, piano;

members of the New York
  Symphony Orchestra;
  E. Robert Schmitz, conductor
Pro Musica
February 22, 1924 (Aeolian Hall)

BLITZSTEIN, MARC
- As if a Phantom Caress'd Me***
  Elizabeth Gutman, soprano;
    Alderson Mowbray, piano
  League of Composers
  February 13, 1927 (Anderson Galleries)

- Piano Sonata***
  Marc Blitzstein, piano
  League of Composers
  February 12, 1928 (Guild Theatre)

- Four Songs for Baritone and Piano
    (Texts by Walt Whitman):
    O Hymen, O Hymenee; I am He;
    Ages and Ages; As Adam
  Benjohn Ragsdale, baritone;
    Marc Blitzstein, piano
  Copland-Sessions Concerts
  December 30, 1928 (The Little
    Theatre)

- Percussion Music for Piano
  Marc Blitzstein, piano
  League of Composers
  March 17, 1929 (Steinway Hall)

- Songs from "is 5" by e. e.
    cummings***: Mister Youse,
    You Are like the Snow,
    Jimmie's Got a Goil
  Radiana Pazmor, mezzo-soprano;
    Edwin McArthur, piano
  League of Composers
  April 6, 1930 (Art Centre)

- Surf and Seaweed (music to a film by
    Ralph Steiner)
  Ensemble from the New York
    Philharmonic; Aaron Copland,
    conductor
  Copland-Sessions Concerts
  March 15, 1931 (Broadhurst Theatre)

BLOCH, ERNEST
• Piano Quintet No. 1***
Harold Bauer, piano; Lenox Quartet
League of Composers
November 11, 1923 (Klaw Theatre)

BOWLES, PAUL
• Sonata for Oboe and Clarinet
Helen Gaskell, oboe; Alan Frank,
clarinet
Copland-Sessions Concerts
December 16, 1931 (Aeolian Hall,
London)

BRANT, HENRY
• Six Piano Pieces
Henry Brant, piano
Copland-Sessions Concerts
February 9, 1930 (Steinway Hall)

• Two Sarabandes
Imre Weisshaus, piano
Pan American Association of Composers
April 21, 1930 (Carnegie Chamber
Hall)

CAPLET, ANDRÉ
• Conte fantastique
Carlos Salzedo, harp; Letz Quartet
Pro Musica
January 18, 1925 (Aeolian Hall)

CARPENTER, JOHN ALDEN
• The Player Queen
Povla Frijsh, soprano;
Frederick Jacobi, piano
American Music Guild
April 22, 1922 (MacDowell Gallery)

CARRILLO, JULIÁN
• Sonata casi-fantasia***
Lucino Nava, French horn;
Bernard Ocko, violin; Genaro Nava,
guitarri; Lajos Shuk, cello; Emil Mix,
octavina; Margaret Kane, arpa citara;
Julián Carillo, conductor
League of Composers
March 13, 1926 (Town Hall)

CASELLA, ALFREDO
• O toi suprème
Greta Torpadie, soprano;
Carlos Salzedo, piano
International Composers' Guild
February 19, 1922 (Greenwich Village
Theatre)

• Pupazzetti and Foxtrot
Alfredo Casella, piano;
E. Robert Schmitz, piano
Pro Musica
March 5, 1923 (Carnegie Hall)

• Five Pieces for String Quartet*
French American String Quartet
International Composers' Guild
January 13, 1924 (Vanderbilt
Theatre)

• L'adieu à la vie
Raymonde Delaunois, soprano; piano
Pro Musica
February 14, 1925 (Aeolian Hall)

• Ondici pezzi infantili
Alfredo Casella, piano
Pro Musica
November 19, 1925 (Colony Club)

• Tre canzoni trecentesche and Quattro
favole romanesche di Trilussa
Judith Litante, soprano;
Alfredo Casella, piano
Pro Musica
November 19, 1925 (Colony Club)

• Pupazzetti*** (new version)
Members of the New York Symphony
Orchestra; Fritz Reiner, conductor
International Composers' Guild
December 27, 1925 (Aeolian Hall)

• Concerto for String Quartet**
Arthur Hartmann String Quartet
International Composers' Guild
February 14, 1926 (Aeolian Hall)

• L'adieu à la vie**
Greta Torpadie, soprano; chamber
ensemble; Otto Klemperer, conductor

International Composers' Guild
January 30, 1927 (Aeolian Hall)

- Serenade for Woodwind Instruments
  Chamber ensemble;
    Alexander Smallens, conductor
  League of Composers
  December 18, 1929 (Town Hall)

CASTELNUOVO-TEDESCO, MARIO
- Stelle cadenti, Op. 6, No. 2
  Marya Freund, soprano; piano
  Pro Musica
  December 14, 1923 (Aeolian Hall)

- Stelle cadenti (excerpts)
  Marya Freund, soprano;
    Carlos Salzedo, piano
  International Composers' Guild
  February 3, 1924 (Vanderbilt Theatre)

- Nocturne from "Alt Wien"
  Esther Streicher, piano
  League of Composers
  November 16, 1924 (Anderson
    Galleries)

- Three Songs from the Coplas***
  Raymonde Delaunois, soprano;
    Constance Piper, piano
  League of Composers
  November 30, 1924 (Klaw Theatre)

- Cipressi, Op. 17
  Alfredo Casella, piano
  Pro Musica
  November 19, 1925 (Colony Club)

- Under the Greenwood Tree
  Ruth Rodgers, soprano;
    Edna Smith, piano
  League of Composers
  November 19, 1926 (Brooklyn
    Museum, in conjunction with an
    exhibition by the Société Anonyme)

- Dances of King David**
  Walter Gieseking, piano
  League of Composers
  February 16, 1929 (Town Hall)

CATURLA, ALEJANDRO
- Dos danzas cubanas
  Martha Whittemore, voice;
    Crystal Waters, soprano;
    Stephanie Schehatowitsch, piano
  Pan American Association of Composers
  March 12, 1929 (Birchard Hall)

- Two Afro-Cuban Songs
  Radiana Pazmor, contralto;
    Imre Weisshaus, piano
  Pan American Association of
    Composers
  April 21, 1930 (Carnegie Chamber
    Hall)

- Bembé
  Chamber orchestra; Nicolas Slonimsky,
    conductor
  Pan American Association of
    Composers
  June 11, 1931 (Paris)

CHABRIER, EMMANUEL
- España
  Alfredo Casella, piano;
    E. Robert Schmitz, piano
  Pro Musica
  March 5, 1923 (Carnegie Hall)

CHANLER, THEODORE
- These, My Ophelia*** and Voyage in
    Provence***
  Elizabeth Gutman, soprano;
    Theodore Chanler, piano
  League of Composers
  February 13, 1927 (Anderson Galleries)

- Sonata for Violin and Piano
  Ruth Warfield, violin;
    Harry Cumpson, piano
  Copland-Sessions Concerts
  April 22, 1928 (Edyth Totten Theatre)

- Sonata for Violin and Piano
  Cyril Towbin, violin;
    Harry Cumpson, piano
  Copland-Sessions Concerts
  March 16, 1930 (Steinway Hall)

CHÁVEZ, CARLOS

- Tres exágonos***
  Colin O'More, tenor; piano
  International Composers' Guild
  February 8, 1925 (Aeolian Hall)

- Caballos de vapor (H.P.)***
  Chamber ensemble;
     Eugene Goossens, conductor
  International Composers' Guild
  November 28, 1926 (Aeolian Hall)

- Sonata for Piano
  Carlos Chávez, piano
  Copland-Sessions Concerts
  April 22, 1928 (Edyth Totten Theatre)

- Three Sonatinas: Cello and Piano,
     Piano Solo, Violin and Piano
  Hans Lange, violin; Percy Such, cello;
     Harry Cumpson, piano
  Copland-Sessions Concerts
  April 22, 1928 (Edyth Totten Theatre)

- Sonatina
  Stephanie Schehatowitsch, piano
  Pan American Association of
     Composers
  March 12, 1929 (Birchard Hall)

- Sonata for Piano
  Ilona Kabos, piano
  Copland-Sessions Concerts
  June 17, 1929 (Salle Chopin, Paris)

- Mexican Pieces***
  Paul Nordoff, piano
  League of Composers
  February 2, 1930 (Art Centre)

- Sonata for Piano
  Jesús María Sanromá, piano
  Copland-Sessions Concerts
  March 16, 1930 (Steinway Hall)

- Sonatina for Violin and Piano
  Jerome Goldstein, violin;
     Imre Weisshaus, piano
  Pan American Association of
     Composers
  April 21, 1930 (Carnegie Chamber Hall)

- Energia
  Chamber orchestra;
     Nicolas Slonimsky, conductor
  Pan American Association of Composers
  June 11, 1931 (Paris)

- Sonatina for Piano
  Aaron Copland, piano
  Copland-Sessions Concerts
  December 16, 1931 (Aeolian Hall,
     London)

CITKOWITZ, ISRAEL

- Three Songs from "Chamber Music" by
     James Joyce: Strings in the Earth and
     Air; When the Sky Star; Bid Adieu
  Marthe-Marthine, soprano; piano
  Copland-Sessions Concerts
  June 17, 1929 (Salle Chopin, Paris)

- Five Songs from "Chamber Music" by
     James Joyce: Strings in the Earth and
     Air; When the Sky Star; O It Was
     Out By Donneycarney; Bid Adieu;
     My Love Is in a Light Attire
  Ethel Codd Luening, soprano;
     Aaron Copland, piano
  Copland-Sessions Concerts
  April 13, 1930 (President Theatre)

- Sonatina for Piano
  Jacques Jolas, piano
  Copland-Sessions Concerts
  April 13, 1930 (President Theatre)

- Five Songs from "Chamber Music" by
     James Joyce
  Tatania Makushina, soprano; piano
  Copland-Sessions Concerts
  December 16, 1931 (Aeolian Hall,
     London)

CLIFTON, CHALMERS

- Interlude and Humoresque
  Gustave Langenus, clarinet;
     Chalmers Clifton, piano
  American Music Guild
  December 6, 1922 (58th Street Branch
     of the New York Public Library)

COPLAND, AARON

- Passacaglia*** and The Cat and the Mouse***
  Esther Streicher, piano
  League of Composers
  November 16, 1924 (Anderson Galleries)

- Music for the Theatre***
  Chamber orchestra from the Boston Symphony Orchestra;
  Serge Koussevitzky, conductor
  League of Composers
  Commissioned by the League
  November 28, 1925 (Town Hall)

- Two Pieces for Violin and Piano***
  Josef Stopak, violin; Aaron Copland, piano
  League of Composers
  February 13, 1927 (Anderson Galleries)

- Two Pieces for String Quartet
  Edwin Ideler, violin; Wolfe Wolfinsohn, violin; Herbert Borodkin, viola;
  Lucien Schmit, cello
  Copland-Sessions Concerts
  May 6, 1928 (Edyth Totten Theatre)

- Vitebsk***
  O. Onnou, violin; R. Maas, cello;
  Walter Gieseking, piano
  League of Composers
  February 16, 1929 (Town Hall)

- Two Pieces for String Quartet
  Le Quatuor Calvet
  Copland-Sessions Concerts
  June 17, 1929 (Salle Chopin, Paris)

- Vitebsk
  Joseph Calvet, violin; Paul Mas, viola;
  and Aaron Copland, piano
  Copland-Sessions Concerts
  June 17, 1929 (Salle Chopin, Paris)

- Vitebsk
  Ivor Karmon, violin; Evsei Beloussof, cello; Clarence Adler, piano

Copland-Sessions Concerts
March 16, 1930 (Steinway Hall)

- Piano Variations***
  Aaron Copland, piano
  League of Composers
  January 4, 1931 (Art Centre)

- Music for the Theatre
  Ensemble from the New York Philharmonic; Aaron Copland, conductor
  Copland-Sessions Concerts
  March 15, 1931 (Broadhurst Theatre)

- Piano Variations
  Aaron Copland, piano
  Copland-Sessions Concerts
  December 16, 1931 (Aeolian Hall, London)

COTAPOS, ACARIO

- Philippe l'arabe***
  Hubert Linscott, baritone; chamber ensemble
  International Composers' Guild
  April 23, 1922 (Greenwich Village Theatre)

- Three Preludes***
  Chamber ensemble; Vladimir Shavitch, conductor
  International Composers' Guild
  February 8, 1925 (Aeolian Hall)

COWELL, HENRY

- Ensemble for String Quintet with Thunder Sticks***
  Henry Cowell, thunder sticks;
  Letz Quartet
  International Composers' Guild
  February 8, 1925 (Aeolian Hall)

- Paragraphs for Two Violins and Cello
  Hans Lange, violin; Arthur Schuller, violin; Percy Such, cello
  Copland-Sessions Concerts
  December 30, 1928 (The Little Theatre)

COWELL (*continued*)

- Trio (Four Combinations for Three
    Instruments): Nos. 1, 3, and 4
    Stephanie Schehatowitsch, piano;
        Hans Lange, violin; Percy Such, cello
    League of Composers
    March 17, 1929 (Steinway Hall)

- Solo for Violin
    Jerome Goldstein, violin;
        Imre Weisshaus, piano
    Pan American Association of
        Composers
    April 21, 1930 (Carnegie Chamber
        Hall)

- Synchrony
    Orchestre Straram; Nicolas Slonimsky,
        conductor
    Pan American Association of
        Composers
    June 6, 1931 (Paris)

CRAWFORD, RUTH

- Sonata for Violin and Piano***
    Josef Stopak, violin; Irene Jacobi,
        piano
    League of Composers
    February 13, 1927 (Anderson
        Galleries)

- Two Preludes
    Richard Buhlig, piano
    Copland-Sessions Concerts
    May 6, 1928 (Edyth Totten Theatre)

- Suite No. 2 for Piano and String
        Quartet
    Colin McPhee, piano; New World
        String Quartet
    Pro Musica
    March 9, 1930 (Carnegie Chamber
        Hall)

- Home Thoughts, White Moon, Joy,
        and Sunsets
    Radiana Pazmor, mezzo-soprano;
        Ruth Crawford, piano

League of Composers
April 6, 1930 (Art Centre)

- Rat Riddles
    Radiana Pazmor, contralto;
        Imre Weisshaus, percussion;
        D. Desarno, oboe;
        Stephanie Schehatowitsch, piano
    Pan American Association of
        Composers
    April 21, 1930 (Carnegie Chamber Hall)

- Suite for Flute (Diaphonic Suite
        No. 3)***
    Frances Blaisdell, flute
    League of Composers
    March 1, 1931 (Art Centre)

DEBUSSY, CLAUDE

- Danse sacrée et danse profane
    Carlos Salzedo, harp; French American
        String Quartet; Henry Moskovitz,
        violin; Delmas-Boussagol, bass
    Pro Musica
    December 14, 1923 (Aeolian Hall)

- Trois Chansons de Charles d'Orléans:
        Dieu, qui'il la fait bon regarder! and
        Yver, vous n'estes qu'un villain
    Vocal ensemble (Clara Deeks,
        Leonore Leoni, Marguerite Price,
        Dorothy Sinott, Viola Gramm-
        Salzedo, Elias N. Caplan,
        Raymond C. Frank, Hubert Linscott,
        Raymond S. Miller)
    Pro Musica
    January 18, 1925 (Aeolian Hall)

- De fleurs from "Proses lyriques"
    Raymonde Delaunois, soprano; piano
    Pro Musica
    February 14, 1925 (Aeolian Hall)

- Danse sacrée et danse profane
    Marcel Grandjany, harp; Pro Arte
        Quartet
    Pro Musica
    December 30, 1926 (Wanamaker
        Auditorium)

- Musique pour Le roi Lear
  New York Philharmonic;
      Eugene Goossens, conductor
  Pro Musica
  January 29, 1927 (Town Hall)

DELAGE, MAURICE
- Benares: La naissance de bouddha*
  Eva Gauthier, voice; Marie Miller,
      harp; Chamber Music Art Society
  International Composers' Guild
  March 19, 1922 (Greenwich Village
      Theatre)

- Trois poèmes**
  Eva Leoni, voice; Carlos Salzedo, piano
  International Composers' Guild
  December 2, 1923 (Vanderbilt Theatre)

- Ragamalika
  Greta Torpadie, soprano; piano
  Pro Musica
  November 14, 1928 (Town Hall)

DELANEY, ROBERT
- Sonata for Violin and Piano
  Edwin Ideler, violin; Aaron Copland,
      piano
  Copland-Sessions Concerts
  May 6, 1928 (Edyth Totten Theatre)

- String Quartet No. 3
  New World String Quartet
  Copland-Sessions Concerts
  February 9, 1930 (Steinway Hall)

DINSMORE, WILLIAM
- Trio
  Wolfe Wolfinsohn, violin;
      Willem Durieux, cello;
      William Dinsmore, piano
  League of Composers
  February 1, 1931 (Art Centre)

DUKELSKY, VLADIMIR
- Le chaleur du soudan and
      Bien haute est ma fenêtre***
  Eva Gauthier, voice; LeRoy Shield, piano

International Composers' Guild
March 19, 1922 (Greenwich Village
    Theatre)

- Three Poems of Hyppolite Bogdanovitch
  Cati Andreades, soprano;
      Aaron Copland, piano
  Copland-Sessions Concerts
  February 24, 1929 (The Little Theatre)

- Sonata for Piano in E-Flat
  Nicholas Kopeikine, piano
  Copland-Sessions Concerts
  February 9, 1930 (Steinway Hall)

- Far from the City and Khodovetzki
  Lola Gorsey, soprano;
      Vladimir Dukelsky, piano
  League of Composers
  March 2, 1930 (Art Centre)

EICHHEIM, HENRY
- Malay Mosaic***
  Members of the Philadelphia Orchestra;
      Leopold Stokowski, conductor
  International Composers' Guild
  March 1, 1925 (Aeolian Hall)

- The Rivals (A Chinese Legend)
  Adolph Bolm Ballet; Ruth Page,
      dancer; Chamber orchestra from the
      Philharmonic Orchestra;
      Tullio Serafin, conductor
  League of Composers
  New York stage premiere
  March 27, 1927 (Jolson Theatre)

ENGEL, CARL
- In Twilight Garden and Marching
  Lawrence Strauss, voice; Carlos Salzedo,
      piano
  International Composers' Guild
  March 19, 1922 (Greenwich Village
      Theatre)

- Triptych for Violin and Piano*
  Albert Stoessel, violin; Edna Stoessel,
      piano
  American Music Guild
  February 7, 1923 (Town Hall)

FAIRCHILD, BLAIR
• Sonata for Violin and Piano, Op. 43
Sascha Jacobson, violin; Irene Jacobi,
piano
American Music Guild
December 6, 1922 (58th Street Branch
of the New York Public Library)

FALLA, MANUEL DE
• Four Spanish Songs
Raymonde Delaunois, soprano; piano
League of Composers
November 11, 1923 (Klaw Theatre)

• Seguidilla marciana and Jota
Raymonde Delaunois, soprano;
LeRoy Shield, piano
League of Composers
November 25, 1923 (Anderson
Galleries)

• Cinq chansons populaires
Marya Freund, soprano; piano
Pro Musica
December 14, 1923 (Aeolian Hall)

• El retablo de maese Pedro
Raymonde Delaunois, soprano;
Eva Gauthier, soprano; Rafaelo Diaz,
voice; William Simmins, voice;
Wanda Landowska, harpsichord;
Willem Mengelberg, conductor
League of Composers
New York stage premiere
December 29, 1925 (Town Hall)

• Psyché, Aria de Salud (from
Vida Breve), Nana and Polo (from
Canciones populares), and
Seguidilla marciana
Eva Gauthier, soprano; instrumental
ensemble; Willem Mengelberg,
conductor
League of Composers
December 29, 1925 (Town Hall)

• El retablo de maese Pedro
Chamber ensemble from the New York
Philharmonic; Pierre Monteux,

conductor; marionettes created and
directed by Remo Bufano
League of Composers
March 25, 1928 (Jolson Theatre)

FINE, VIVIAN
• Solo for Oboe
D. Desarno, oboe
Pan American Association of
Composers
April 21, 1930 (Carnegie Chamber
Hall)

FITELBERG, JERZY
• String Quartet No. 2
Pro Arte Quartet
League of Composers
February 2, 1930 (Art Centre)

• Piano Sonata No. 2
Jacques Jolas, piano
Copland-Sessions Concerts
April 13, 1930 (President Theatre)

FOGG, ERIC
• Two Faery Pieces: Grimm and
The Wee Folk's Market
Esther Streicher, piano
League of Composers
November 16, 1924 (Anderson
Galleries)

FOOTE, ARTHUR
• Piano Quartet in C Major, Op. 23
Albert Stoessel, violin;
Nicolas Moldavan, viola;
Emmeran Stoeber, cello;
Louis Gruenberg, piano
American Music Guild
April 11, 1923 (58th Street Branch of
the New York Public Library)

FRESCOBALDI, GIROLAMO
• Toccata cromatica per l'elevazione
Joseph Yasser, organ
League of Composers
December 30, 1927 (Town Hall)

FRY, WILLIAM

- Leonora (excerpts, arranged by
  Otto Kinkeldey)
  Vocalists; Otto Kinkeldey, piano
  Pro Musica
  February 27, 1929 (Town Hall)

GAILLARD, MARIUS-FRANÇOIS

- Un grand sommeil noir** and
  A clymène**
  Georgette Leblanc-Maeterlinck, voice;
  Marius-François Gaillard, piano
  International Composers' Guild
  December 17, 1922 (Klaw Theatre)

GARDNER, SAMUEL

- Prelude No. 3, B Minor; Slovak;
  Prelude No. 9; Prelude No. 4, C
  Major; From the Canebrake
  Samuel Gardner, violin; Stella Barnard,
  piano
  American Music Guild
  March 7, 1923 (Town Hall)

GESUALDO, CARLO

- Tu m'uccidi, oh crudele
  Choral Symphony Society (Solo Unit)
  League of Composers
  December 30, 1927 (Town Hall)

GIBBONS, ORLANDO

- Fantasia
  Russian String Quartet
  Pro Musica
  March 1, 1926 (Chickering Hall)

GNESSIN, MIKHAIL

- The Dead Princess**
  Lucilla de Vescovi, soprano;
  LeRoy Shield, piano
  League of Composers
  March 23, 1924 (Klaw Theatre)

GOOSSENS, EUGENE

- Sonata No. 1 for Violin and Piano*
  André Polah, violin; Louis Gruenberg,
  piano

International Composers' Guild
February 19, 1922 (Greenwich Village
Theatre)

- Tea-Time
  John Barclay, voice; Frederick Bristol,
  piano
  League of Composers
  November 25, 1923 (Anderson
  Galleries)

- Phantasy Quartet*
  French American String Quartet
  International Composers' Guild
  February 3, 1924 (Vanderbilt Theatre)

- Fantasy***
  Members of the State Symphony
  Orchestra; Eugene Goossens,
  conductor
  International Composers' Guild
  December 7, 1924 (Aeolian Hall)

- Pastoral and Harlequinade***
  Meredith Willson, flute; Arthur
  Foreman, oboe; Eugene Goossens,
  piano
  International Composers' Guild
  January 24, 1926 (Aeolian Hall)

- Three Pagan Hymns***
  Chamber ensemble; Eugene Goossens,
  conductor
  International Composers' Guild
  November 28, 1926 (Aeolian Hall)

- Concertino for Double String
  Orchestra**
  String orchestra; Eugene Goossens,
  conductor
  League of Composers
  December 18, 1929 (Town Hall)

GRASSE, EDWARD

- Scherzo
  Ruth Kemper, violin; Imogen Peay,
  piano
  American Music Guild
  December 6, 1922 (58th Street Branch
  of the New York Public Library)

GRIFFES, CHARLES T.
- Sonata*
  Katherine Bacon, piano
  American Music Guild
  January 3, 1923 (Town Hall)

- Songs
  Léon Rothier, tenor; LeRoy Shield,
      piano; Eva Gauthier, soprano
  Pro Musica
  March 5, 1923 (Carnegie Hall)

- Two Sketches for String Quartet Based
      on Indian Themes
  French American String Quartet
  Pro Musica
  March 5, 1923 (Carnegie Hall)

- The White Peacock
  Harold Morris, piano
  American Music Guild
  April 11, 1923 (58th Street Branch of
      the New York Public Library)

- Sonata
  Gitta Gradova, piano
  Pro Musica
  January 18, 1925 (Aeolian Hall)

- Sonata
  Jesús María Sanromá, piano
  Copland-Sessions Concerts
  March 16, 1930 (Steinway Hall)

GRUENBERG, LOUIS
- Polychromatics**
  Louis Gruenberg, piano
  International Composers' Guild
  February 19, 1922 (Greenwich Village
      Theatre)

- Concerto for Piano in One
      Movement***
  Louis Gruenberg, piano; Harold Morris,
      piano
  American Music Guild
  April 22, 1922 (MacDowell Gallery)

- Four Pieces for Violoncello***
  Lajos Shuk, cello; Louis Gruenberg,
      piano

American Music Guild
November 8, 1922 (58th Street Branch
      of the New York Public Library)

- Sonata No. 1 for Violin and Piano***
  Albert Stoessel, violin;
      Louis Gruenberg, piano
  American Music Guild
  January 3, 1923 (Town Hall)

- A Fantasy
  Lucy Gates, voice; Rex Tillson, piano
  International Composers' Guild
  March 4, 1923 (Klaw Theatre)

- Daniel Jazz***
  Colin O'More, tenor; chamber
      ensemble; Howard Barlow,
      conductor
  League of Composers
  February 22, 1925 (Times Square
      Theatre)

- Jazzberries***
  Nadia Reisenberg, piano
  League of Composers
  October 25, 1925 (Anderson
      Galleries)

- The Creation: A Negro Sermon***
  Jules Bledsoe, baritone; chamber
      ensemble from the Boston Symphony
      Orchestra
  League of Composers
  November 27, 1926 (Town Hall)

- Negro Spirituals
  George Perkins Raymond, voice; piano
  League of Composers
  November 27, 1927 (MacDowell Club)

- Four Indiscretions, Op. 20
  Pro Arte Quartet
  League of Composers
  January 12, 1928 (Town Hall)

- Daniel Jazz
  Dan Gridley, tenor; chamber ensemble;
      Louis Gruenberg, conductor
  League of Composers
  December 18, 1929 (Town Hall)

HÁBA, ALOIS

• Two Grotesque Pieces
  LeRoy Shield, piano
  League of Composers
  November 16, 1924 (Anderson
    Galleries)

HAMMOND, RICHARD

• The Vow, The Dancer, and In a Boat
    from "La flûte de jade"
  Greta Torpadie, soprano;
    Carlos Salzedo, piano
  Pro Musica
  February 22, 1924 (Aeolian Hall)

• Dans les montagnes*** and Les trois
    princesses***
  Inez Barbour, voice; piano
  League of Composers
  November 16, 1924 (Anderson
    Galleries)

• The Fiddler of Dooney
  Ruth Rodgers, soprano; Edna Smith,
    piano
  League of Composers
  November 19, 1926 (Brooklyn
    Museum, in conjunction with an
    exhibition by the Société Anonyme)

• Voyage to the East***
  Greta Torpadie, soprano; chamber
    orchestra from the Philharmonic
    Orchestra
  League of Composers
  March 27, 1927 (Jolson Theatre)

• Promenades sentimentales; Aux bois
  George Perkins Raymond, voice; piano
  League of Composers
  November 27, 1927 (MacDowell Club)

HANSON, HOWARD

• Concerto da Camera in C Minor, Op. 7
  Albert Stoessel, violin;
    Wolf Wolfinsohn, violin;
    Nicolas Moldavan, viola;
    Emmeran Stoeber, cello;
    Charles Haubiel, piano

  American Music Guild
  April 11, 1923 (58th Street Branch of
    the New York Public Library)

• Pan and the Priest
  Chamber orchestra; Howard Hanson,
    conductor
  Pro Musica
  February 27, 1929 (Town Hall)

HARMATI, SÁNDOR

• String Quartet: Adagio sostenuto and
    Scherzo
  Lenox Quartet
  American Music Guild
  April 22, 1922 (MacDowell Gallery)

• A Portrait***
  Georges Grisez, clarinet; Irene Jacobi,
    piano
  American Music Guild
  February 7, 1923 (Town Hall)

• String Quartet No. 2***
  New York String Quartet
  League of Composers
  April 12, 1931 (Art Centre)

HARRIS, ROY

• Concerto for Piano, Clarinet, and String
    Quartet***
  Lenox Quartet; Harry Cumpson, piano;
    Aaron Garodner, clarinet
  League of Composers
  February 12, 1928 (Guild Theatre)

• Sonata for Piano
  Harry Cumpson, piano
  Copland-Sessions Concerts
  February 24, 1929 (The Little Theatre)

• Concerto for Piano, Clarinet, and String
    Quartet
  Le Quatuor Calvet; Ilona Kabos, piano;
    M. Lefebvre, clarinet
  Copland-Sessions Concerts
  June 17, 1929 (Salle Chopin, Paris)

• Sonata for Piano
  Harry Cumpson, piano

HARRIS (*continued*)
League of Composers
April 6, 1930 (Art Centre)

- String Quartet
New World String Quartet
Copland-Sessions Concerts
April 13, 1930 (President Theatre)

HAUBIEL, CHARLES
- Three Part Songs for Women's Voices:
In the Forest, Requiescat, In the
Garden
Florence White, Georgia Schutt,
Katherine Metcalf, Claire Stetson of
the Parnassus Club Chorale;
Grace C. Thompson, director
American Music Guild
April 29, 1922 (MacDowell Gallery)

- Choral Variations and Fugue for Two
Pianos***
Charles Haubiel, piano;
Leopold Damrosch Mannes, piano
American Music Guild
December 6, 1922 (58th Street Branch
of the New York Public Library)

HERSCHER-CLEMENT, JEANNE
- Dans arles and Filippa, Fais,
Esclarmonde
Vocal Quartet (Grace James Robinson,
Radiana Pazmor, Raymond Frank,
Walter Leary)
Pro Musica
March 1, 1926 (Chickering Hall)

HINDEMITH, PAUL
- Suite "1922" (excerpts)**
Claudio Arrau, piano
International Composers' Guild
December 2, 1923 (Vanderbilt Theatre)

- Kleine Kammermusik, Op. 24**
Chamber orchestra; Tullio Serafin,
conductor
League of Composers
March 29, 1925 (Forty-Eighth Street
Theatre)

- Trio, Op. 34**
Gregory Besrodny, violin; Samuel
Stillman, viola; Lajos Shuk, cello
League of Composers
March 29, 1925 (Forty-Eighth Street
Theatre)

- Kammermusik No. 3**
Cornelius Van Vliet, cello; members of
the New York Symphony Orchestra;
Fritz Reiner, conductor
International Composers' Guild
December 27, 1925 (Aeolian Hall)

- Der Dämon**
Chamber ensemble; Otto Klemperer,
conductor
International Composers' Guild
January 30, 1927 (Aeolian Hall)

- Landsknechtstrinklied from "Das
Liederbuch für mehrere
Singstimmen"
Choral Symphony Society (Solo Unit)
League of Composers
December 30, 1927 (Town Hall)

- Six Songs from "Das Marienleben"
Greta Torpadie, soprano;
Aaron Copland, piano
League of Composers
December 30, 1927 (Town Hall)

- String Quartet No. 3, Op. 22
Pro Arte Quartet
League of Composers
January 12, 1928 (Town Hall)

- Die junge Magd***
Madame Cahier, contralto; chamber
orchestra from the New York
Philharmonic; Lazare Saminsky,
conductor
League of Composers
December 19, 1928 (Town Hall)

- Concerto for Organ and Chamber
Orchestra, Op. 46*
Lynwood Farnam, organist; chamber
orchestra; Alexander Smallens,
conductor

League of Composers
December 18, 1929 (Town Hall)

- Kleine Sonate
Alix Young Maruchess, viola d'amore;
Frank Bibb, piano
League of Composers
January 12, 1930 (Art Centre)

- O Herr, gib jedem seinen eignen
Tod*** and Landsknecht Trinklied
Emanu-El Choir; Lazare Saminsky,
conductor
League of Composers
December 10, 1930 (Town Hall)

- String Quartet No. 2, Op. 16
Budapest Quartet
League of Composers
January 4, 1931 (Art Centre)

HONEGGER, ARTHUR

- Three Fragments (excerpts)**
Greta Torpadie, soprano;
Bachmann String Quartet
International Composers' Guild
February 19, 1922 (Greenwich Village
Theatre)

- Sonata No. 1 for Violin and Piano**
Gustave Tinlot, violin; Carlos Salzedo,
piano
International Composers' Guild
December 17, 1922 (Klaw Theatre)

- Le chasseur perdu en forêt
John Barclay, voice; Frederick Bristol,
piano
League of Composers
November 25, 1923 (Anderson
Galleries)

- L'ombre*** and L'homme et la mer***
Chamber orchestra; Howard Barlow,
conductor
League of Composers
November 30, 1924 (Klaw Theatre)

- Concertino for Piano and Orchestra
Jésus María Sanromá, piano; chamber
orchestra from the Boston Symphony

Orchestra; Serge Koussevitzky,
conductor
League of Composers
November 28, 1925 (Town Hall)

- Three Fragments from "Pâques à New
York"
Mina Hager, mezzo-soprano; Pro Arte
Quartet
League of Composers
October 28, 1926 (Town Hall)

- Rhapsody for Two Flutes, Clarinet,
and Piano
Olga de Stroumillo, piano; musicians
from the New York Philharmonic
League of Composers
December 19, 1928 (Town Hall)

- Hommage à Ravel and Toccata for Piano
Andrée Vaurabourg Honegger, piano
Pro Musica
January 24, 1929 (Town Hall)

- Partita for Two Pianos
Arthur Honegger, piano;
Andrée Vaurabourg Honegger, piano
Pro Musica
January 24, 1929 (Town Hall)

- Poems and Song of Ronsard
Cobina Wright, soprano;
Arthur Honegger, piano
Pro Musica
January 24, 1929 (Town Hall)

- Quartet for Strings
Philharmonic String Quartet
Pro Musica
January 24, 1929 (Town Hall)

- Suite for Chamber Orchestra
Chamber orchestra
Pro Musica
January 24, 1929 (Town Hall)

- Three Fragments from "Pâques à New
York"
Cobina Wright, soprano; Philharmonic
String Quartet
Pro Musica
January 24, 1929 (Town Hall)

HORSMAN, EDWARD

• The Dream and The Shepherdess
Dicie Howell, voice; Frederick Jacobi,
  piano
American Music Guild
April 11, 1923 (58th Street Branch of
  the New York Public Library)

HOUSMAN, ROSALIE

• God's World and Tara Bindu
Dicie Howell, voice; Frederick Jacobi,
  piano
American Music Guild
April 11, 1923 (58th Street Branch of
  the New York Public Library)

IBERT, JACQUES

• Deux mouvements
Woodwind quartet
Pro Musica
February 14, 1925 (Aeolian Hall)

IL'IASHENKO, ANDREI

• Quasi Trio
Harry Cumpson, piano; Joseph Coleman,
  violin; Julian Kahn, cello
League of Composers
February 1, 1931 (Art Centre)

INCH, HERBERT

• Barcarolle
Chamber orchestra; Howard Hanson,
  conductor
Pro Musica
February 27, 1929 (Town Hall)

INFANTE, MANUEL

• Sentimento from "Dances andalouses"
Claudio Arrau, piano;
  E. Robert Schmitz, piano
Pro Musica
February 22, 1924 (Aeolian Hall)

IVES, CHARLES

• Largo and Allegro from "Three
  Quarter-Tone Pieces"
Hans Barth, piano; Sigmund Klein,
  piano

Pro Musica
February 14, 1925 (Aeolian Hall)

• Symphony No. 4 (First and Second
  Movements)
New York Philharmonic;
  Eugene Goossens, conductor
Pro Musica
January 29, 1927 (Town Hall)

• The Celestial Railroad
Anton Rovinsky, piano
Pro Musica
November 14, 1928 (Town Hall)

• The New River, The Indians, and
  Ann Street (arranged for trumpet and
  piano)
Harry Freistadt, trumpet;
  Imre Weisshaus, piano
Pan American Association of
  Composers
April 21, 1930 (Carnegie Chamber Hall)

• Three Places in New England
Orchestre Straram; Nicolas Slonimsky,
  conductor
Pan American Association of
  Composers
June 6, 1931 (Paris)

JACOBI, FREDERICK

• Love and Death; Ballad***
Povla Frijsh, soprano; Frederick Jacobi,
  piano
American Music Guild
April 22, 1922 (MacDowell Gallery)

• Circe*** and Medusa***
Nina Koshetz, soprano;
  Frederick Jacobi, piano
International Composers' Guild
April 23, 1922 (Greenwich Village
  Theatre)

• Three Preludes for Violin
Helen Teschner Tas, violin;
  Frederick Jacobi, piano
American Music Guild
November 8, 1922 (58th Street Branch
  of the New York Public Library)

- Assyrian Prayers***
  Judson House, voice; Irene Jacobi,
      piano; chamber orchestra;
      Frederick Jacobi, conductor
  League of Composers
  November 30, 1924 (Klaw Theatre)

- String Quartet on Indian Themes
  Helen Teschner Tas Quartet
  League of Composers
  November 19, 1926 (Brooklyn
      Museum, in conjunction with an
      exhibition by the Société Anonyme)

JONGEN, JOSEPH
- Quintet
  Mortimer Wilson, flute; Pro Arte
      Quartet
  Pro Musica
  December 30, 1926 (Wanamaker
      Auditorium)

KADOSA, PÁL
- Sonatina
  Imre Weisshaus, piano
  Copland-Sessions Concerts
  April 13, 1930 (President Theatre)

KAMINSKI, HEINRICH
- Magnificat
  Choral Symphony Society of New
      York; New York Philharmonic;
      Willem Mengelberg, conductor
  Pro Musica
  December 19, 1927 (Carnegie Hall)

- Prelude and Fugue**
  Paul Stassevitch, violin;
      Gottfried Federlein, organ
  League of Composers
  December 10, 1930 (Town Hall)

KLEIN, FRITZ
- Die Maschine***
  Constance Piper, piano;
      Robert O'Connor, piano; chamber
      orchestra; Howard Barlow, conductor
  League of Composers
  November 30, 1924 (Klaw Theatre)

KODÁLY, ZOLTÁN
- Pièces pour piano**
  LeRoy Shield, piano
  International Composers' Guild
  March 19, 1922 (Greenwich Village
      Theatre)

- Quartet No. 1
  French American String Quartet
  Pro Musica
  December 14, 1923 (Aeolian Hall)

- Psalmus hungaricus
  Choral Symphony Society of New
      York; New York Philharmonic;
      Willem Mengelberg, conductor
  Pro Musica
  December 19, 1927 (Carnegie Hall)

- Two Folksongs from "Székely"
  Denyse Molié, piano
  League of Composers
  March 2, 1930 (Art Centre)

- String Quartet, Op. 10
  Budapest Quartet
  League of Composers
  January 4, 1931 (Art Centre)

KOECHLIN, CHARLES
- Sonata for Two Flutes
  Sarah Possell, flute; George Possell,
      flute
  International Composers' Guild
  February 4, 1923 (Klaw Theatre)

KOSHETZ, NINA
- To the Sun
  Nina Koshetz, soprano;
      Frederick Jacobi, piano
  International Composers' Guild
  April 23, 1922 (Greenwich Village
      Theatre)

KRAMER, A. WALTER
- Interlude for a Drama
  Eva Gauthier, voice;
      A. Walter Kramer, piano;
      Chamber Music Art Society

KRAMER (*continued*)
International Composers' Guild
March 19, 1922 (Greenwich Village
Theatre)

- The Faltering Dusk, Op. 34, No. 1;
Green, Op. 39, No. 4; I Have Seen
Dawn, Op. 48, No. 1; Song Without
Words, Op. 45, No. 4
Greta Torpadie, soprano;
A. Walter Kramer, piano
American Music Guild
April 29, 1922 (MacDowell Gallery)

KRASA, HANS
- Symphony for Chamber Orchestra and
Voice
Nancy Hitch, contralto; chamber
orchestra from the Boston Symphony
Orchestra; Serge Koussevitzky,
conductor
League of Composers
November 27, 1926 (Town Hall)

KREIN, ALEXANDER
- Two Gazelles
Voice; Sarah Possell, flute;
Stephanie Schehatowitsch, piano
League of Composers
March 17, 1929 (Steinway Hall)

KRENEK, ERNST
- Dance Study
LeRoy Shield, piano
League of Composers
November 16, 1924 (Anderson
Galleries)

- Symphonische Musik**
Chamber ensemble; Otto Klemperer,
conductor
International Composers' Guild
January 30, 1927 (Aeolian Hall)

- Quartet No. 3, Op. 20
New World String Quartet
Pro Musica
November 14, 1928 (Town Hall)

LABROCA, MARIO
- Quartet for Strings
Lenox Quartet
League of Composers
October 25, 1925 (Anderson
Galleries)

- Selections from the Sinfonietta**
Chamber orchestra from the
Philharmonic Orchestra;
Tullio Serafin, conductor
League of Composers
March 27, 1927 (Jolson Theatre)

LAURENCE, FREDERICK
- Labyrinth**
Members of the State Symphony
Orchestra; Eugene Goossens,
conductor
International Composers' Guild
December 7, 1924 (Aeolian Hall)

LAZARUS, DANIEL
- Fantasy
LeRoy Shield, piano
League of Composers
November 16, 1924 (Anderson
Galleries)

LE FLEM, PAUL
- La neige and Vrai dieu, qui m'y
confortera!
Vocal ensemble (Clara Deeks,
Leonore Leoni, Marguerite Price,
Dorothy Sinott,
Viola Gramm-Salzedo,
Elias N. Caplan, Raymond C. Frank,
Hubert Linscott, Raymond S. Miller)
Pro Musica
January 18, 1925 (Aeolian Hall)

LEGINSKA, ETHEL
- Six Nursery Rhymes
Greta Torpadie, soprano;
Ethel Leginska, piano
Pro Musica
January 18, 1925 (Aeolian Hall)

LILIEN, IGNACE
• Four Beggars Songs
Marya Freund, soprano; piano
Pro Musica
March 1, 1926 (Chickering Hall)

LIPSKY, ALEXANDER
• Sonata for Violin and Piano
Ruth Breton, violin; Alexander Lipsky,
piano
Copland-Sessions Concerts
February 24, 1929 (The Little Theatre)

LOEFFLER, CHARLES MARTIN
• Bolero triste
Povla Frijsh, soprano; Frederick Jacobi,
piano
American Music Guild
April 22, 1922 (MacDowell Gallery)

• Two Rhapsodies for Oboe, Viola, and
Piano
Albert Marsh, oboe; Sandor Harmati,
viola; Harold Morris, piano
American Music Guild
January 3, 1923 (Town Hall)

• Music for Four Stringed Instruments
French American String Quartet
Pro Musica
February 22, 1924 (Aeolian Hall)

LOPATNIKOFF, NIKOLAI
• Sonatina for Piano
Colin McPhee, piano
Copland-Sessions Concerts
December 30, 1928 (The Little Theatre)

LOURIÉ, ARTHUR
• Pleurs de la Vierge Marie**
Georgette Leblanc-Maeterlinck, voice;
Gustave Tinlot, violin; Saul Sharrow,
viola; Paul Kéfer, cello
International Composers' Guild
December 17, 1922 (Klaw Theatre)

• Synthesis**
Claudio Arrau, piano

International Composers' Guild
December 2, 1923 (Vanderbilt Theatre)

• Sonata for Violin and Double Bass***
Arthur Hartmann, violin; Morris Tivin,
double bass
International Composers' Guild
December 27, 1925 (Aeolian Hall)

LUENING, OTTO
• Songs to Poems of Whitman, Blake,
and Shelley
Ethel Codd Luening, voice
Pro Musica
March 9, 1930 (Carnegie Chamber Hall)

McPHEE, COLIN
• Pastorale and Rondino***
Colin McPhee, piano
International Composers' Guild
November 28, 1926 (Aeolian Hall)

• Mechanical Principles and H_2O (scores
to films by Ralph Steiner)
Ensemble from the New York
Philharmonic; Aaron Copland,
conductor
Copland-Sessions Concerts
March 15, 1931 (Broadhurst Theatre)

MAGANINI, QUINTO
• Sonata for Flute and Piano***
Quinto Maganini, flute;
John Kirkpatrick, piano
League of Composers
February 12, 1928 (Guild Theatre)

MALIPIERO, GIAN FRANCESCO
• Ariette**
Greta Torpadie, soprano;
Carlos Salzedo, piano
International Composers' Guild
February 19, 1922 (Greenwich Village
Theatre)

• Mirinda
Raymonde Delaunois, soprano;
LeRoy Shield, piano

MALIPIERO (*continued*)
League of Composers
November 25, 1923 (Anderson
Galleries)

- String Quartet No. 2 (Stornelli e
  ballate)*
  French American String Quartet
  International Composers' Guild
  February 3, 1924 (Vanderbilt Theatre)

- Le stagione italiche (The Snow and In
  Praise of Summer)**
  Lucilla de Vescovi, soprano;
  Wilfred Pelletier, piano
  League of Composers
  March 29, 1925 (Forty-Eighth Street
  Theatre)

- Sette canzoni***
  Richard Hale, voice; Albert Rappoport,
  voice; Lucilla de Vescovi, voice;
  chamber orchestra; Tullio Serafin,
  conductor
  League of Composers
  March 29, 1925 (Forty-Eighth Street
  Theatre)

- Quattro preludi autunnali
  Alfredo Casella, piano
  Pro Musica
  November 19, 1925 (Colony Club)

- I partenti from "Poemi asolani"
  Marion Rous, piano
  League of Composers
  November 19, 1926 (Brooklyn
  Museum, in conjunction with an
  exhibition by the Société Anonyme)

- Ricercari*
  Chamber Ensemble; Otto Klemperer,
  conductor
  International Composers' Guild
  January 30, 1927 (Aeolian Hall)

MANNING, KATHLEEN LOCKHART
- Three Songs: Melancholy, Bitter Sweet,
  Magic
  Radiana Pazmor, contralto;
  Robert Russell Bennett, piano

League of Composers
March 1, 1931 (Art Centre)

MARENZIO, LUCA
- Solo e pensoso
  Choral Symphony Society (Solo Unit)
  League of Composers
  December 30, 1927 (Town Hall)

MARK, JEFFREY
- North Country Suite for Piano
  Colin McPhee, piano
  Copland-Sessions Concerts
  February 9, 1930 (Steinway Hall)

MASE, OWEN
- There Is No More to Say
  Ursula Greville, voice; Marie Miller,
  harp
  International Composers' Guild
  December 7, 1924 (Aeolian Hall)

MASON, DANIEL GREGORY
- Russians, Op. 18
  Reinald Werrenrath, baritone;
  Daniel Gregory Mason, piano
  American Music Guild
  January 3, 1923 (Town Hall)

MIASKOVSKY, NIKOLAI
- To the Unsuffering Master**
  Nina Koshetz, soprano;
  Frederick Jacobi, piano
  International Composers' Guild
  April 23, 1922 (Greenwich Village
  Theatre)

- Song of the Autumn
  Raymonde Delaunois, soprano;
  LeRoy Shield, piano
  League of Composers
  November 25, 1923 (Anderson
  Galleries)

- Sonata for Piano No. 3**
  Nadia Reisenberg, piano
  League of Composers
  March 23, 1924 (Klaw Theatre)

MIGOT, GEORGES

- Chanson and Dans le calme
  Raymonde Delaunois, soprano;
    LeRoy Shield, piano
  League of Composers
  November 25, 1923 (Anderson
    Galleries)

- Trio à la memoire de Lili Boulanger
  Elfrida Boos, violin; Jacob Mestechkin,
    cello; LeRoy Shield, piano
  League of Composers
  November 16, 1924 (Anderson
    Galleries)

- Song from "Hommage à Thibaud de
    Champagne"
  Ethel Codd Luening, soprano
  League of Composers
  January 12, 1930 (Art Centre)

MILHAUD, DARIUS

- Saudades do Brasil (excerpts)**
  E. Robert Schmitz, piano
  International Composers' Guild
  February 4, 1923 (Klaw Theatre)

- Le forgeron
  John Barclay, voice; Frederick Bristol,
    piano
  League of Composers
  November 25, 1923 (Anderson
    Galleries)

- Sonata for Flute, Oboe, Clarinet, and
    Piano**
  George Possell, flute; Auguste Duques,
    oboe?; Pierre Mathieu, clarinet?;
    Carlos Salzedo, piano
  International Composers' Guild
  February 3, 1924 (Vanderbilt Theatre)

- Catalogue de fleurs, Op. 60
  Greta Torpadie, soprano;
    E. Robert Schmitz, piano
  Pro Musica
  February 22, 1924 (Aeolian Hall)

- Chamber Symphony No. 6
  Vocal Quartet (Grace James Robinson,
    Radiana Pazmor, Raymond Frank,

Walter Leary); B. Labate, oboe;
    Vladimir Dubinsky, cello;
    E. Robert Schmitz, conductor
  Pro Musica
  March 1, 1926 (Chickering Hall)

- Two Hebrew Folk Songs, Op. 86
  Marya Freund, soprano; piano
  Pro Musica
  March 1, 1926 (Chickering Hall)

- Quartet for Strings
  Pro Arte Quartet
  Pro Musica
  December 30, 1926 (Wanamaker
    Auditorium)

- Les malheurs d'Orphée, Op. 85
  Mina Hager, Eric Morgan,
    Greta Torpadie, Rosalie Miller,
    Radiana Pazmor, John Parish,
    Irving Jackson, Dudley Marwick,
    voices; New York Philharmonic;
    Darius Milhaud, conductor
  Pro Musica
  January 29, 1927 (Town Hall)

- String Quartet No. 6
  Pro Arte Quartet
  League of Composers
  January 12, 1928 (Town Hall)

- Third Symphony
  Ruth Rodgers, soprano;
    Mildred Kreuder, contralto;
    Henry Clancy, tenor; Moses Rudinov,
    baritone; oboe; cello
  League of Composers
  December 10, 1930 (Town Hall)

- La p'tite Lilie and Actualités (music to
    films by Cavalcanti)
  Ensemble from the New York
    Philharmonic; Aaron Copland,
    conductor
  Copland-Sessions Concerts
  March 15, 1931 (Broadhurst Theatre)

MILOJEVIĆ, MILOJE

- Air Tzigane and Miryana
  Raymonde Delaunois, soprano; piano

MILOJEVIĆ (*continued*)
Pro Musica
February 14, 1925 (Aeolian Hall)

MONTEVERDI, CLAUDIO
• Ecco mormorar l'onde
Choral Symphony Society (Solo Unit)
League of Composers
December 30, 1927 (Town Hall)

• Il combattimento di Tancredi e
Clorinda**
Jeanne Palmer Soudeikine, voice;
Charles Kullman, voice; Irene Jacobi,
harpsichord
League of Composers
New York stage premiere (staged as
chamber opera)
April 25, 1929 (Metropolitan Opera
House)

MOORE, DOUGLAS
• Sonata for Violin and Piano
Hildegarde Donaldson, violin;
Douglas Moore, piano
League of Composers
March 2, 1930 (Art Centre)

MORRIS, HAROLD
• Trio in One Movement, Op. 7
Harold Morris, piano; Albert Stoessel,
violin; Lucien Schmit, cello
American Music Guild
April 29, 1922 (MacDowell Gallery)

• Love's Philosophy
Dicie Howell, voice; Frederick Jacobi,
piano
American Music Guild
April 11, 1923 (58th Street Branch of
the New York Public Library)

• Scherzo
Harold Morris, piano
American Music Guild
April 11, 1923 (58th Street Branch of
the New York Public Library)

• String Quartet
Hans Lange String Quartet

League of Composers
March 17, 1929 (Steinway Hall)

• Piano Quintet***
Harold Morris, piano; New York String
Quartet
League of Composers
April 12, 1931 (Art Centre)

NYSTRÖM, GÖSTA
• Au fond de mon coeur and Sous les
étoiles
Mildred Kreuder, contralto;
Marguerite Miller, piano
League of Composers
March 17, 1929 (Steinway Hall)

ORNSTEIN, LEO
• Nocturne (Op. 96, No. 2)*** and
Sonata No. 4***
Leo Ornstein, piano
International Composers' Guild
March 4, 1923 (Klaw Theatre)

• Sonata for Two Pianos, Op. 89
Leo Ornstein, piano; Ethel Leginska,
piano
American Music Guild
March 7, 1923 (Town Hall)

• Piano Quintet, Op. 92***
Leo Ornstein, piano; Pro Arte Quartet
League of Composers
January 12, 1928 (Town Hall)

• Six Poems, Two Dances,
and Three Moods
Leo Ornstein, piano
Copland-Sessions Concerts
March 16, 1930 (Steinway Hall)

• String Quartet, Op. 99***
Philadelphia Musical Fund String
Quartette
League of Composers
April 6, 1930 (Art Centre)

• Six Preludes for Cello and Piano***
Alexandre Barjansky, cello; Leo
Ornstein, piano

League of Composers
April 12, 1931 (Art Centre)

PANIAGUA, RAUL
- Leyenda maya
  Raul Paniagua, piano
  Pan American Association of Composers
  March 12, 1929 (Birchard Hall)

PETIT, RAYMOND
- Hymne for Voice and Flute, and
    Cantique spirituel
  Marianne de Gonitch, soprano;
    Sarah Possell, flute; Pietro Cimara,
    piano
  League of Composers
  March 17, 1929 (Steinway Hall)

PETYREK, FELIX
- Cortège nocturne
  E. Robert Schmitz, piano
  Pro Musica
  February 14, 1925 (Aeolian Hall)

- Hallelujah from "Litany"**
  Emanu-El Choir; Pan-American
    Ensemble; Lazare Saminsky, conductor
  League of Composers
  December 10, 1930 (Town Hall)

PIJPER, WILLEM
- Sonatine No. 2
  Anton Rovinsky, piano
  Pro Musica
  November 14, 1928 (Town Hall)

PISK, PAUL
- Song from "Gesänge eines fahrenden
    Spielmanns"
  Mildred Kreuder, contralto;
    Marguerite Miller, piano
  League of Composers
  March 17, 1929 (Steinway Hall)

PISTON, WALTER
- Three Pieces for Flute, Clarinet, and
    Bassoon
  Lamar Stringfield, flute; Guy D'Isere,
    clarinet; David Swaan, bassoon

Copland-Sessions Concerts
April 22, 1928 (Edyth Totten Theatre)

PIZZETTI, ILDEBRANDO
- I pastori and La madre al figlio lontano
  Greta Torpadie, soprano;
    Carlos Salzedo, piano
  International Composers' Guild
  February 19, 1922 (Greenwich Village
    Theatre)

- I pastori
  Marya Freund, soprano; piano
  Pro Musica
  December 14, 1923 (Aeolian Hall)

- Passeggiata*
  Marya Freund, soprano; Carlos Salzedo,
    piano
  International Composers' Guild
  February 3, 1924 (Vanderbilt Theatre)

- Sonata for Violin and Piano
  Arthur Hartmann, violin;
    Alfredo Casella, piano
  Pro Musica
  November 19, 1925 (Colony Club)

- Trio in A for Piano and Strings
  Chamber ensemble
  International Composers' Guild
  November 28, 1926 (Aeolian Hall)

PORTER, W. QUINCY
- Quintet for Piano and Strings
  Aaron Copland, piano; Edwin Ideler
    and Wolfe Wolfinsohn, violins;
    Herbert Borodkin, viola;
    Lucien Schmit, cello
  Copland-Sessions Concerts
  May 6, 1928 (Edyth Totten Theatre)

POULENC, FRANCIS
- Sonata for Two Clarinets**
  Georges Grisez, clarinet;
    Walter Thalin, clarinet
  International Composers' Guild
  April 23, 1922 (Greenwich Village
    Theatre)

POULENC (*continued*)

• Rhapsodie nègre*
  Boris Saslavsky, baritone;
      Lamar Stringfield, flute; Guy D'Isere,
      clarinet; Lenox Quartet
  League of Composers
  March 23, 1924 (Klaw Theatre)

POWELL, JOHN

• Sonata for Violin and Piano
  Albert Stoessel, violin; John Powell,
      piano
  American Music Guild
  March 7, 1923 (Town Hall)

• Minuetto
  Harold Morris, piano
  American Music Guild
  April 11, 1923 (58th Street Branch of
      the New York Public Library)

PROKOFIEV, SERGE

• The Sun Filled the Room***
  Nina Koshetz, soprano;
      Frederick Jacobi, piano
  International Composers' Guild
  April 23, 1922 (Greenwich Village
      Theatre)

• Two Songs Without Words
  Marya Freund, soprano
  Pro Musica
  December 14, 1923 (Aeolian Hall)

• Quintet
  Chamber ensemble from the Boston
      Symphony Orchestra
  League of Composers
  November 28, 1925 (Town Hall)

• Sarcasms, Op. 17, No. 3
  Marion Rous, piano
  League of Composers
  November 19, 1926 (Brooklyn
      Museum, in conjunction with an
      exhibition by the Société Anonyme)

• Visions fugitives, Op. 22 (March,
      Rigaudon, and Allemand) and
      The Love of Three Oranges

(Grandmother's Tale, Choses en soi;
      Two Gavottes; March)
  Serge Prokofiev, piano
  Pro Musica
  January 6, 1930 (Town Hall)

• Excerpts from The Love of Three
      Oranges and The Ugly Duckling
  Nina Koshetz, soprano;
      Serge Prokofiev, piano
  Pro Musica
  January 6, 1930 (Town Hall)

• Le pas d'acier
  Edwin Strawbridge, choreographer;
      Philadelphia Orchestra; Leopold
      Stokowski, conductor
  League of Composers
  April 10, 11, 13, 21, 22, 1931
      (Metropolitan Opera House)

PURCELL, HENRY

• The Gordian Knot Untied
  Russian String Quartet
  Pro Musica
  March 1, 1926 (Chickering Hall)

RAMEAU, JEAN-PHILIPPE

• Deuxième concert
  Carlos Salzedo, harp; Gustave Tinlot,
      violin; Paul Kéfer, cello
  Pro Musica
  February 22, 1924 (Aeolian Hall)

RATHAUS, KAROL

• Sonata No. 3***
  Walter Gieseking, piano
  League of Composers
  February 16, 1929 (Town Hall)

RAVEL, MAURICE

• Placet futile from "Trois poèmes de
      Stéphane Mallarmé"*
  Eva Gauthier, voice; Chamber Music
      Art Society
  International Composers' Guild
  March 19, 1922 (Greenwich Village
      Theatre)

- Sonata for Violin and Violoncello**
  Gustave Tinlot, violin; Paul Kéfer, cello
  International Composers' Guild
  December 17, 1922 (Klaw Theatre)

- Introduction and Allegro
  French American String Quartet; flute;
     harp; clarinet
  Pro Musica
  March 5, 1923 (Carnegie Hall)

- Les grands vents venus d'outremer
  John Barclay, voice; Frederick Bristol,
     piano
  League of Composers
  November 25, 1923 (Anderson
     Galleries)

- Trio
  E. Robert Schmitz, piano;
     Gustave Tinlot, violin;
     Paul Kéfer, cello
  Pro Musica
  December 14, 1923 (Aeolian Hall)

- Tzigane**
  Members of the State Symphony
     Orchestra; Eugene Goossens,
     conductor
  International Composers' Guild
  December 7, 1924 (Aeolian Hall)

- Trois poèmes de Stéphane Mallarmé
  Maria Dormont, voice; chamber
     orchestra of the Boston Symphony
     Orchestra; Serge Koussevitzky,
     conductor
  League of Composers
  November 28, 1925 (Town Hall)

- Chansons madécasses**
  Greta Torpadie, soprano; flute; cello;
     piano
  International Composers' Guild
  January 30, 1927 (Aeolian Hall)

- Chansons madécasses
  Greta Torpadie, soprano; Arthur Lora,
     flute; Horace Britt, cello; Maurice
     Ravel, piano

Pro Musica
January 15, 1928 (Gallo Theater)

- Histoires naturelles
  Greta Torpadie, soprano;
     Maurice Ravel, piano
  Pro Musica
  January 15, 1928 (Gallo Theater)

- Introduction and Allegro
  Carlos Salzedo, harp; Hart House
     String Quartet; Arthur Lora, flute;
     Henri Leon Leroy, clarinet
  Pro Musica
  January 15, 1928 (Gallo Theater)

- Sonata for Violin and Piano
  Joseph Szigeti, violin; Maurice Ravel,
     piano
  Pro Musica
  January 15, 1928 (Gallo Theater)

- Sonatine; Habañera from "Rhapsodie
     espagñole"; Pavane pour une infante
     défunte
  Maurice Ravel, piano
  Pro Musica
  January 15, 1928 (Gallo Theater)

RESPIGHI, OTTORINO
- Deità silvane***
  Elsa Respighi, voice; chamber
     ensemble; Ottorino Respighi, piano;
     conductor
  International Composers' Guild
  January 24, 1926 (Aeolian Hall)

RIEGGER, WALLINGFORD
- Suite for Flute Solo
  Georges Barrère, flute
  League of Composers
  February 2, 1930 (Art Centre)

- Study in Sonority
  New World String Quartet
     (plus additional violins)
  Pro Musica
  March 9, 1930 (Carnegie Chamber
     Hall)

RIEGGER (*continued*)

• Three Canons for Woodwinds
  Pan American Association Chamber
    Orchestra; Adolph Weiss, conductor
  Pan American Association of
    Composers
  March 10, 1931 (New School for Social
    Research)

• Three Canons for Woodwinds
  Chamber orchestra;
    Nicolas Slonimsky, conductor
  Pan American Association of
    Composers
  June 11, 1931 (Paris)

RIETI, VITTORIO

• Sonatina for Flute and Piano***
  George Possell, flute; Rex Tillson,
    piano
  International Composers' Guild
  January 13, 1924 (Vanderbilt Theatre)

• Sonata for Flute, Oboe, Bassoon, and
    Piano**
  Meredith Willson, flute;
    Arthur Foreman, oboe; Philip Reines,
    bassoon; Alfredo Casella, piano
  International Composers' Guild
  January 24, 1926 (Aeolian Hall)

• Quartet for Strings
  Pro Arte Quartet
  Pro Musica
  December 30, 1926 (Wanamaker
    Auditorium)

ROGERS, BERNARD

• In the Gold Room and Notturno
  Inez Barbour, voice; piano
  League of Composers
  November 16, 1924 (Anderson
    Galleries)

• Pastorale
  Chamber orchestra; Howard Hanson,
    conductor
  Pro Musica
  February 27, 1929 (Town Hall)

• String Quartet No. 2 in D Minor
  New Russian String Quartet
  League of Composers
  January 12, 1930 (Art Centre)

ROLDÁN, AMADEO

• Dos canciones populares cubanas and
    Three Songs
  Martha Whittemore, voice; or
    Crystal Waters, soprano;
    Stephanie Schehatowitsch, piano
  Pan American Association of Composers
  March 12, 1929 (Birchard Hall)

• Rítmicas (for percussion)
  Pan American Association Chamber
    Orchestra; Adolph Weiss, conductor
  Pan American Association of
    Composers
  March 10, 1931 (New School for Social
    Research)

• La rebambaramba
  Orchestre Straram; Nicolas Slonimsky,
    conductor
  Pan American Association of Composers
  June 6, 1931 (Paris)

ROTA, NINO

• Three Songs
  Dorothy Seegar, soprano
  Copland-Sessions Concerts
  February 9, 1930 (Steinway Hall)

ROUSSEL, ALBERT

• Divertissement for Piano and
    Woodwinds
  LeRoy Shield, piano; Members of the
    Philharmonic Orchestra
  League of Composers
  November 11, 1923 (Klaw Theatre)

• Serenade for Harp, String Trio, and
    Flute
  Marcel Grandjany, harp;
    Meredith Willson, flute; string trio
  Pro Musica
  March 1, 1926 (Chickering Hall)

RUDHYAR, DANE
- Luciferian Stanza*** and
  Ravissement***
  Dane Rudhyar, piano
  International Composers' Guild
  December 17, 1922 (Klaw Theatre)

- Moments*** (excerpts)
  Dane Rudhyar, piano
  International Composers' Guild
  December 27, 1925 (Aeolian Hall)

- Three Paeans
  Richard Buhlig, piano
  Copland-Sessions Concerts
  May 6, 1928 (Edyth Totten Theatre)

- Granites
  Dane Rudhyar, piano
  League of Composers
  February 2, 1930 (Art Centre)

- Sonatina
  Dane Rudhyar, piano
  Pro Musica
  March 9, 1930 (Carnegie Chamber
  Hall)

- Two "Moments"
  Imre Weisshaus, piano
  Pan American Association of
  Composers
  April 21, 1930 (Carnegie Chamber
  Hall)

- The Surge of Fire
  Pan American Association Chamber
  Orchestra; Adolph Weiss, conductor
  Pan American Association of
  Composers
  March 10, 1931 (New School for Social
  Research)

RUGGLES, CARL
- Angels***
  Capodiferro, Buono, Glicken, Ricci,
  Rubinstein, and Giannone, trumpets
  International Composers' Guild
  December 17, 1922 (Klaw Theatre)

- Toys***
  Lucy Gates, voice; Rex Tillson, piano
  International Composers' Guild
  March 4, 1923 (Klaw Theatre)

- Vox clamans in deserto***
  Greta Torpadie, soprano; chamber
  orchestra; Carlos Salzedo, conductor
  International Composers' Guild
  January 13, 1924 (Vanderbilt Theatre)

- Men and Mountains***
  Members of the State Symphony
  Orchestra; Eugene Goossens,
  conductor
  International Composers' Guild
  December 7, 1924 (Aeolian Hall)

- Portals***
  String ensemble; Eugene Goossens,
  conductor
  International Composers' Guild
  January 24, 1926 (Aeolian Hall)

- Men and Mountains
  Orchestre Straram; Nicolas Slonimsky,
  conductor
  Pan American Association of Composers
  June 6, 1931 (Paris)

SAINT-SAËNS, CAMILLE
- Septet for Two Violins, Viola, Cello,
  Bass, and Piano
  French American String Quartet; bass;
  piano
  Pro Musica
  March 5, 1923 (Carnegie Hall)

SALZEDO, CARLOS
- Four Preludes to the Afternoon of a
  Telephone***
  Marie Miller, harp; Carlos Salzedo, harp
  International Composers' Guild
  April 23, 1922 (Greenwich Village
  Theatre)

- Sonata in One Part for Harp and
  Piano***
  Marie Miller, harp; Carlos Salzedo,
  piano

SALZEDO (*continued*)
International Composers' Guild
March 4, 1923 (Klaw Theatre)

- Préambule et jeux***
Harp, flute, oboe, bassoon, French
horn, and string quintet;
Carlos Salzedo, conductor
International Composers' Guild
January 13, 1924 (Vanderbilt Theatre)

- Trois poèmes de Stéphane
Mallarmé***
Greta Torpadie, soprano;
Carlos Salzedo, piano
International Composers' Guild
February 8, 1925 (Aeolian Hall)

- Concerto for Harp and Seven Wind
Instruments***
Carlos Salzedo, harp; wind ensemble;
Artur Rodzinski, conductor
International Composers' Guild
April 17, 1927 (Aeolian Hall)

- Pentacle
Carlos Salzedo, harp; Lucille Lawrence,
harp
Pro Musica
November 14, 1928 (Town Hall)

- Concerto for Harp and Seven Wind
Instruments
Lucille Lawrence, harp; woodwind
ensemble; Carlos Salzedo, conductor
League of Composers
December 10, 1930 (Town Hall)

- Préambule et jeux
Lily Laskine, harp; chamber orchestra;
Nicolas Slonimsky, conductor
Pan American Association of Composers
June 11, 1931 (Paris)

SAMINSKY, LAZARE
- The Deceitful Day*** and
The Resurrection***
Georgette Leblanc-Maeterlinck, voice;
Lazare Saminsky, piano

International Composers' Guild
December 17, 1922 (Klaw Theatre)

- The Gagliarda of a Merry Plague***
Richard Hale, voice; Patricia
O'Connell, voice; Paul Oscard, voice;
chamber ensemble; Lazare Saminsky,
conductor
League of Composers
February 22, 1925 (Times Square
Theatre)

- Un grand sommeil noir,
Hebrew Lullaby, and Spring Garden
Ruth Rodgers, soprano; Edna Smith,
piano
League of Composers
November 19, 1926 (Brooklyn
Museum, in conjunction with an
exhibition by the Société Anonyme)

- Piano Pieces, Op. 19
Piano
League of Composers
November 27, 1927 (MacDowell Club)

- Litanies of Women**
Dorma Lee, voice; chamber orchestra
from the New York Philharmonic;
Lazare Saminsky, conductor
League of Composers
December 19, 1928 (Town Hall)

- The Daughter of Jephtha (excerpts)**
Emanu-El Choir; Ruth Rodgers,
soprano; Denyse Molié, piano;
Pan-American Ensemble;
Lazare Saminsky, conductor
League of Composers
December 10, 1930 (Town Hall)

SANJUÁN, PEDRO
- Sones de Castilla
Pan American Association Chamber
Orchestra; Adolph Weiss, conductor
Pan American Association of
Composers
March 10, 1931 (New School for Social
Research)

- Sones de Castilla
  Chamber orchestra;
    Nicolas Slonimsky, conductor
  Pan American Association of Composers
  June 11, 1931 (Paris)

SATIE, ERIK

- Choses vues à droite et à gauche**
  André Polah, violin;
    Josephine Rosensweet, piano
  International Composers' Guild
  April 23, 1922 (Greenwich Village
    Theatre)

- Sports et divertissements**
  E. Robert Schmitz, piano
  International Composers' Guild
  February 4, 1923 (Klaw Theatre)

- Le piège de Méduse (excerpts)**
  Members of the Philadelphia Orchestra;
    Leopold Stokowski, conductor
  International Composers' Guild
  March 1, 1925 (Aeolian Hall)

SCHELLING, ERNEST

- Morocco
  New York Philharmonic;
    Willem Mengelberg, conductor
  Pro Musica
  December 19, 1927 (Carnegie Hall)

SCHILLINGER, JOSEPH

- Funeral March
  Denyse Molié, piano
  League of Composers
  March 2, 1930 (Art Centre)

SCHMITT, FLORENT

- Free Sonata in Two Connected Parts**
  Gustave Tinlot, violin; LeRoy Shield,
    piano
  International Composers' Guild
  March 19, 1922 (Greenwich Village
    Theatre)

- Kerob-shal**
  Colin O'More, tenor; piccolo; flute; 2
    clarinets; piano; and string quartet

International Composers' Guild
December 27, 1925 (Aeolian Hall)

SCHOENBERG, ARNOLD

- Pierrot lunaire
  Greta Torpadie, soprano; chamber
    ensemble; Louis Gruenberg,
    conductor
  International Composers' Guild
  February 4, 1923 (Klaw Theatre)

- Herzgewächse**
  Eva Leoni, voice; harp; harmonium; and
    celesta
  International Composers' Guild
  December 2, 1923 (Vanderbilt Theatre)

- String Quartet with Voice, Op. 10**
  Ruth Rodgers, soprano; Lenox Quartet
  League of Composers
  January 6, 1924 (Klaw Theatre)

- Das Buch der hängenden Gärten
    (excerpts)
  Marya Freund, soprano; Carlos Salzedo,
    piano
  International Composers' Guild
  February 3, 1924 (Vanderbilt Theatre)

- Pierrot lunaire
  Greta Torpadie, soprano; chamber
    orchestra; Howard Barlow, conductor
  League of Composers
  February 22, 1925 (Times Square
    Theatre)

- Serenade
  Members of the Philadelphia Orchestra;
    Leopold Stokowski, conductor
  International Composers' Guild
  March 1, 1925 (Aeolian Hall)

- Quintet for Wind Instruments,
    Op. 26**
  Quinto Maganini, flute; Michel Nazzi,
    oboe; A. Williams, clarinet;
    David Swaan, bassoon; Lucino Nava,
    horn
  League of Composers
  March 13, 1926 (Town Hall)

SCHOENBERG (*continued*)

- String Quartet with Voice, Op. 10
  Ruth Rodgers, soprano; Pro Arte
    Quartet
  League of Composers
  February 16, 1929 (Town Hall)

- Die glückliche Hand
  Ivan Ivantzoff, baritone; Artist Chorus
    of the Curtis Institute; Philadelphia
    Orchestra; Leopold Stokowski,
    conductor
  League of Composers
  April 11, 12, 14, 22, 23, 1930
    (Metropolitan Opera House)

SCHUBERT, FRANZ

- Duo in A Major
  Josef Szigeti, violin; Béla Bartók, piano
  Pro Musica
  February 5, 1928 (Gallo Theater)

SCOTT, FRANCIS GEORGE

- Whistle, Whistle, Auld Wife***
  Ursula Greville, voice; Carlos Salzedo,
    piano
  International Composers' Guild
  December 7, 1924 (Aeolian Hall)

SCRIABIN, ALEXANDER

- Visual Mysticism**
  Orchestration by Forrest Lamont of
    Scriabin's Désir, Enigme, and
    Caresse dansée
  Adolph Bolm Ballet; Ruth Page,
    dancer; Chamber Orchestra from the
    Philharmonic Orchestra;
    Tullio Serafin, conductor
  League of Composers
  New York stage premiere
  March 27, 1927 (Jolson Theatre)

SERLY, TIBOR

- Sonata for Violin and Piano
  Sol Ruden, violin; William Juliber,
    piano
  League of Composers
  March 2, 1931 (Art Centre)

SESSIONS, ROGER

- Two Choral Preludes for Organ
  Joseph Yasser, organ
  League of Composers
  December 30, 1927 (Town Hall)

- Sonata for Piano (incomplete)
  John Duke, piano
  Copland-Sessions Concerts
  May 6, 1928 (Edyth Totten Theatre)

- Prelude for Organ
  Gottfried Federlein, organ
  League of Composers
  December 10, 1930 (Town Hall)

- Black Maskers
  Ensemble from the New York
    Philharmonic; Hugh Ross, conductor
  Copland-Sessions Concerts
  March 15, 1931 (Broadhurst Theatre)

- Sonata for Piano
  Irene Jacobi, piano
  Copland-Sessions Concerts
  December 16, 1931 (Aeolian Hall,
    London)

SLONIMSKY, NICOLAS

- Studies in Black and White
  Nicolas Slonimsky, piano
  League of Composers
  March 2, 1930 (Art Centre)

SMITH, DAVID STANLEY

- String Quartet in C, Op. 46
  Letz Quartet
  American Music Guild
  February 7, 1923 (Town Hall)

SNYDERMAN, TOBIE

- Sonata for Piano
  Tobie Snyderman, piano
  League of Composers
  March 1, 1931 (Art Centre)

SOWERBY, LEO

- Suite for Violin and Piano
  Sandor Harmati, violin; Harold Morris,
    piano

American Music Guild
November 8, 1922 (58th Street Branch
of the New York Public Library)

- Irish Washerwoman
Harold Morris, piano
American Music Guild
April 11, 1923 (58th Street Branch of
the New York Public Library)

STEINERT, ALEXANDER
- Lady of the Clouds***
Lucy Gates, voice; Rex Tillson, piano
International Composers' Guild
March 4, 1923 (Klaw Theatre)

- Four Lacquer Prints***
Eva Gauthier, soprano;
Frederic Persson, piano
American Music Guild
March 7, 1923 (Town Hall)

- Lady of the Clouds, Snow at
Twilight***, and Footsteps in the
Sand***
Inez Barbour, voice; piano
League of Composers
November 16, 1924 (Anderson
Galleries)

- Sonata for Violin and Piano
Barbara Lull, violin; Marian Cassell,
piano
Pro Musica
November 14, 1928 (Town Hall)

- Trio for Violin, Cello, and Piano
Paul Stassevitch, violin; Horace Britt,
cello; Alexander Steinert, piano
League of Composers
March 1, 1931 (Art Centre)

ŠTĚPÁN, VÁCLAV
- Two Czech Folksongs
Isolde Bernhart, soprano; Irene Jacobi,
piano
League of Composers
October 25, 1925
(Anderson Galleries)

STILL, WILLIAM GRANT
- From the Land of Dreams***
Chamber orchestra; Vladimir Shavitch,
conductor
International Composers' Guild
February 8, 1925 (Aeolian Hall)

- Levee Land***
Florence Mills, voice; chamber ensemble;
Eugene Goossens, conductor
International Composers' Guild
January 24, 1926 (Aeolian Hall)

- Darker America***
Chamber orchestra; Eugene Goossens,
conductor
International Composers' Guild
November 28, 1926 (Aeolian Hall)

STILLMAN, MITYA
- Sérénade for Strings
Russian Trio
League of Composers
March 2, 1930 (Art Centre)

STOESSEL, ALBERT
- Sonata in G for Violin and Piano
Albert Stoessel, violin;
Louis Gruenberg, piano
American Music Guild
April 22, 1922 (MacDowell Gallery)

- American Dance (G Minor)
Ruth Kemper, violin; Imogen Peay,
piano
American Music Guild
December 6, 1922 (58th Street Branch
of the New York Public Library)

- A Lover and His Lass
Dicie Howell, voice; Frederick Jacobi,
piano
American Music Guild
April 11, 1923 (58th Street Branch of
the New York Public Library)

- Seguedilla
Harold Morris, piano
American Music Guild
April 11, 1923 (58th Street Branch of
the New York Public Library)

STRANG, GERALD
- Two Pieces for Piano
  Imre Weisshaus, piano
  Pan American Association of Composers
  April 21, 1930 (Carnegie Chamber Hall)

STRAVINSKY, IGOR
- Two Poems of Konstantin Balmont**
  and Histoires pour enfants
  (excerpts)**
  Eva Gauthier, voice; LeRoy Shield,
  piano
  International Composers' Guild
  March 19, 1922 (Greenwich Village
  Theatre)

- Three Pieces for Clarinet
  Simeon Bellison, clarinet
  League of Composers
  November 11, 1923 (Klaw Theatre)

- Renard**
  José Delaquerriere, voice; Harold
  Hansen, voice; John Barclay, voice;
  Hubert Linscott, voice; members of
  the Philadelphia Orchestra;
  Leopold Stokowski, conductor
  International Composers' Guild
  December 2, 1923 (Vanderbilt Theatre)

- Cloches au monastère
  Marya Freund, soprano; piano
  Pro Musica
  December 14, 1923 (Aeolian Hall)

- Trois histoires pour enfantes
  Greta Torpadie, soprano;
  Carlos Salzedo, piano
  Pro Musica
  February 22, 1924 (Aeolian Hall)

- Histoire du soldat**
  Chamber ensemble; Chalmers Clifton,
  conductor
  League of Composers
  March 23, 1924 (Klaw Theatre)

- Concertino for String Quartet
  Lenox Quartet

League of Composers
November 30, 1924 (Klaw Theatre)

- Two Poems of Konstantin Balmont
  Raymonde Delaunois, soprano;
  Constance Piper, piano
  League of Composers
  November 30, 1924 (Klaw Theatre)

- Three Little Songs: La petite pie,
  Le corbeau, and Tchitcher-Iatcher
  Greta Torpadie, soprano; Rex Tillson,
  piano
  Pro Musica
  January 18, 1925 (Aeolian Hall)

- Le pigeon; Myosotis, d'amour fleurette
  Raymonde Delaunois, soprano; piano
  Pro Musica
  February 14, 1925 (Aeolian Hall)

- Sonata for Piano
  Nadia Reisenberg, piano
  League of Composers
  October 25, 1925
  (Anderson Galleries)

- Les noces**
  Madame Cahier, Marguerite Ringo,
  Richard Hale, and Colin O'More,
  voices; Alfredo Casella,
  Georges Enesco, Carlos Salzedo, and
  Germaine Tailleferre, pianos;
  Leopold Stokowski, conductor
  International Composers' Guild
  February 14, 1926 (Aeolian Hall)

- Rag-time
  Marion Rous, piano
  League of Composers
  November 19, 1926 (Brooklyn
  Museum, in conjunction
  with an exhibition by the
  Société Anonyme)

- Selections from the Suite for Chamber
  Orchestra
  Chamber orchestra from the New York
  Philharmonic; Tullio Serafin,
  conductor

League of Composers
March 27, 1927 (Jolson Theatre)

• Octet
Chamber ensemble; Artur Rodzinski,
conductor
International Composers' Guild
April 27, 1927 (Aeolian Hall)

• Histoire du soldat
Chamber ensemble from the New York
Philharmonic; Pierre Monteux,
conductor; Michio Ito, stage
direction
League of Composers
New York stage premiere
March 25, 1928 (Jolson Theatre)

• Les noces
Nina Koshetz, soprano; Gabriel
Leonoff, tenor; Sophie Braslau,
contralto; Moshe Rudinov,
contralto; Marc Blitzstein,
Aaron Copland, Louis Gruenberg,
Frederick Jacobi, pianos
League of Composers
April 25, 1929 (Metropolitan Opera
House)

• Le Sacre du printemps
Martha Graham, soloist; Philadelphia
Orchestra; Leopold Stokowski,
conductor
League of Composers
New York stage premiere
April 11, 12, 14, 22, 23, 1930
(Metropolitan Opera House)

• Oedipus rex
Opera-oratorio (staged with puppets
and chorus)
Margaret Matzenhauer, voice;
Paul Althouse, voice; Philadelphia
Orchestra; Leopold Stokowski,
conductor
League of Composers
New York stage premiere
April 10, 11, 13, 21, 22, 1931
(Metropolitan Opera House)

SWEELINCK, JAN PIETERSZOON
• Fantasia chromatica
Joseph Yasser, organ
League of Composers
December 30, 1927 (Town Hall)

• Rozette
Choral Symphony Society (Solo Unit)
League of Composers
December 30, 1927 (Town Hall)

SZELÉNYI, ISTVÁN
• Recitative
Imre Weisshaus, piano
Copland-Sessions Concerts
April 13, 1930
(President Theatre)

SZYMANOWSKI, KAROL
• Twelve Studies for Piano***
E. Robert Schmitz, piano
International Composers' Guild
January 13, 1924
(Vanderbilt Theatre)

• Songs of a Lovelorn Muzzein, Nos. 1, 2,
and 4
Greta Torpadie, soprano; Carlos Salzedo,
harp
Pro Musica
November 14, 1928 (Town Hall)

TAILLEFERRE, GERMAINE
• Sonata for Violin and Piano
Robert Imandt, violin;
Germaine Tailleferre, piano
Pro Musica
February 14, 1925 (Aeolian Hall)

TANSMAN, ALEXANDER
• String Quartet**
Lenox Quartet
League of Composers
March 23, 1924 (Klaw Theatre)

• Etude and Nocturne No. 2
E. Robert Schmitz, piano
Pro Musica
February 14, 1925 (Aeolian Hall)

TANSMAN (*continued*)

- Sinfonietta
  Chamber orchestra from the Boston
    Symphony Orchestra;
    Serge Koussevitzky, conductor
  League of Composers
  November 28, 1925 (Town Hall)

- Tragedy of the Cello**
  Adolph Bolm Ballet; chamber orchestra
    from the Philharmonic Orchestra;
    Tullio Serafin, conductor
  League of Composers
  March 27, 1927 (Jolson Theatre)

- Danse de la sorcière and Petits pièces
    polonaises
  Woodwinds of the Pan-American
    Ensemble; Alexandre Tansman,
    conductor
  Pro Musica
  December 17, 1929 (Roerich Hall)

- Dans le secret de mon Ame; Hélas;
    Sommeil; Chats de guttière; and
    Bonheur
  Cobina Wright, soprano;
    Alexandre Tansman, piano
  Pro Musica
  December 17, 1929 (Roerich Hall)

- Sonata No. 2; Two Impromptus;
    Three Mazurkas; Berceuse; and
    Burlesque
  Alexandre Tansman, piano
  Pro Musica
  December 17, 1929 (Roerich Hall)

- Suite Divertissement
  Alexandre Tansman, piano; New York
    String Quartet
  Pro Musica
  December 17, 1929 (Roerich Hall)

TAYLOR, DEEMS

- Three Songs for Soprano: The Rivals,
    A Song for Lovers, the Messenger
  Greta Torpadie, soprano;
    Frederick Jacobi, piano

American Music Guild
April 29, 1922 (MacDowell Gallery)

TCHEREPNIN, ALEXANDER

- Sonata for Violin and Piano***
  Helen Teschner Tas, violin;
    Katherine Bacon, piano
  League of Composers
  November 30, 1924 (Klaw Theatre)

- Trois bagatelles
  Denyse Molié, piano
  League of Composers
  March 2, 1930 (Art Centre)

THOMPSON, RANDALL

- The Wind in the Willows***
  Helen Teschner Tas Quartet
  League of Composers
  February 13, 1927
    (Anderson Galleries)

THOMSON, VIRGIL

- Five Phrases from the Song of Solomon
  Radiana Pazmor, mezzo-soprano;
    Aaron Copland, percussion
  Copland-Sessions Concerts
  April 22, 1928
    (Edyth Totten Theatre)

- Capital, Capitals
  Ionian Quartet (Harold Dearborn,
    tenor; Frank Hart, tenor;
    Baldwin Allan-Allen, baritone;
    Hildreth Martin, bass);
    Virgil Thomson, piano
  Copland-Sessions Concerts
  February 24, 1929
    (The Little Theatre)

- La valse grégorienne; La Seine;
    Le berceau de Gertrude Stein, ou le
    mystère de la rue de fleurus;
    Susie Asado; Preciosilla
  Marthe-Marthine, soprano;
    Virgil Thomson, piano
  Copland-Sessions Concerts
  June 17, 1929 (Salle Chopin, Paris)

- Capital, Capitals
London Singers; Virgil Thomson, piano
Copland-Sessions Concerts
December 16, 1931 (Aeolian Hall,
London)

TOCH, ERNST
- Tanz-Suite, Op. 30**
Chamber orchestra; Alexander Smallens,
conductor
League of Composers
March 13, 1926 (Town Hall)

TOMMASINI, VINCENZO
- The Veil Moves and The Absent One
Lucilla de Vescovi, soprano;
LeRoy Shield, piano
League of Composers
March 23, 1924 (Klaw Theatre)

VAN DIEREN, BERNARD
- Two Songs for Baritone and
String Quartet***
Hubert Linscott, baritone; string quartet
International Composers' Guild
April 23, 1922 (Greenwich Village
Theatre)

VARÈSE, EDGARD
- Offrandes***
Nina Koshetz, soprano; chamber
orchestra; Carlos Salzedo, conductor
International Composers' Guild
April 23, 1922 (Greenwich Village
Theatre)

- Hyperprism***
Chamber ensemble; Edgard Varèse,
conductor
International Composers' Guild
March 4, 1923 (Klaw Theatre)

- Octandre***
Chamber ensemble; E. Robert Schmitz,
conductor
International Composers' Guild
January 13, 1924 (Vanderbilt Theatre)

- Intégrales***
Members of the Philadelphia Orchestra;
Leopold Stokowski, conductor
International Composers' Guild
March 1, 1925 (Aeolian Hall)

- Intégrales
Chamber ensemble; Artur Rodzinski,
conductor
International Composers' Guild
April 17, 1927 (Aeolian Hall)

- Intégrales
Chamber orchestra; Nicolas Slonimsky,
conductor
Pan American Association of
Composers
June 11, 1931 (Paris)

VAUGHAN, CLIFFORD
- Three Songs to Poems by
Ruth Harwood***
Eva Gauthier, soprano;
Frederic Persson, piano
American Music Guild
March 7, 1923 (Town Hall)

VAUGHAN WILLIAMS, RALPH
- Bredon Hill from "On Wenlock
Edge"*
Lawrence Strauss, voice; Carlos Salzedo,
piano; Chamber Music Art Society
International Composers' Guild
March 19, 1922 (Greenwich Village
Theatre)

- Merciless Beauty
Ursula Greville, voice; members of the
State Symphony Orchestra
International Composers' Guild
December 7, 1924 (Aeolian Hall)

VERDI, GIUSEPPE
- Quartet
Pro Arte Quartet
Pro Musica
December 30, 1926 (Wanamaker
Auditorium)

VILLA-LOBOS, HEITOR

• O ginete do pierrozinho prole do bébé
  (No. 1)
  Martha Whittemore, voice; or
    Crystal Waters, soprano;
    Stephanie Schehatowitsch, piano
  Pan American Association of
    Composers
  March 12, 1929 (Birchard Hall)

VOGEL, WLADIMIR

• Etude-Toccata
  Harry Cumpson, piano
  League of Composers
  February 1, 1931 (Art Centre)

VUILLEMIN, LOUIS

• Two Dances
  Claudio Arrau, piano;
    E. Robert Schmitz, piano
  Pro Musica
  February 22, 1924 (Aeolian Hall)

WAGENAAR, BERNARD

• Sonata for Piano
  John Duke, piano
  Copland-Sessions Concerts
  December 30, 1928
    (The Little Theatre)

WATTS, WINTTER

• Like Music on the Water; Vignettes of
    Italy; The Little Shepherd's Song;
    The Nightingale and the Rose;
    The White Rose; With the Tide
  Zelina de Maclot, soprano;
    Wintter Watts, piano
  American Music Guild
  November 8, 1922 (58th Street
    Branch of the New York
    Public Library)

• Songs
  Eva Gauthier, soprano; LeRoy Shield,
    piano
  Pro Musica
  March 5, 1923 (Carnegie Hall)

WEBERN, ANTON

• Dead Flames (Op. 4, No. 5)*
  Greta Torpadie, soprano; piano
  International Composers' Guild
  January 13, 1924 (Vanderbilt Theatre)

• So ich traurig bin
  Greta Torpadie, soprano; Rex Tillson,
    piano
  Pro Musica
  January 18, 1925 (Aeolian Hall)

• Five Movements for String Quartet,
    Op. 5
  Letz Quartet
  International Composers' Guild
  February 8, 1925 (Aeolian Hall)

• Five Orchestral Pieces, Op. 10
  Chamber orchestra from the Boston
    Symphony Orchestra; Serge
    Koussevitzky, conductor
  League of Composers
  November 27, 1926 (Town Hall)

• Fünf geistliche Lieder
  Mina Hager, mezzo-soprano; chamber
    ensemble; Eugene Goossens,
    conductor
  International Composers' Guild
  November 28, 1926 (Aeolian Hall)

• Symphony for Chamber Ensemble,
    Op. 21***
  Chamber orchestra;
    Alexander Smallens, conductor
  League of Composers
  Commissioned by the League
  December 18, 1929 (Town Hall)

WEISS, ADOLPH

• Three Preludes
  Richard Buhlig, piano
  Copland-Sessions Concerts
  May 6, 1928 (Edyth Totten Theatre)

• Quartet
  New World String Quartet
  Pro Musica
  March 9, 1930 (Carnegie Chamber Hall)

- Sonata da camera for Flute and Viola***
  Samuel Levitsky, flute; Lotte Karman,
  viola
  League of Composers
  April 6, 1930 (Art Centre)

- Prelude
  Imre Weisshaus, piano
  Pan American Association of Composers
  April 21, 1930 (Carnegie Chamber Hall)

- Chamber Symphony
  Pan American Association Chamber
  Orchestra; Adolph Weiss, conductor
  Pan American Association of Composers
  March 10, 1931 (New School for Social
  Research)

- American Life
  Orchestre Straram; Nicolas Slonimsky,
  conductor
  Pan American Association of Composers
  June 6, 1931 (Paris)

WEISSHAUS, IMRE (Arma, Paul)
- Piano Study
  Imre Weisshaus, piano
  Copland-Sessions Concerts
  April 13, 1930 (President Theatre)

- Six Pieces for Solo Voice
  Radiana Pazmor, contralto;
  Imre Weisshaus, piano
  Pan American Association of Composers
  April 21, 1930 (Carnegie Chamber Hall)

- Suite for Piano
  Imre Weisshaus, piano
  Pan American Association of Composers
  April 21, 1930 (Carnegie Chamber
  Hall)

WELLESZ, EGON
- Aurora***
  Ursula Greville, voice; members of the
  State Symphony Orchestra;
  Eugene Goossens, conductor
  International Composers' Guild
  December 7, 1924 (Aeolian Hall)

- Quartet No. 4, Op. 28
  Russian String Quartet
  Pro Musica
  March 1, 1926 (Chickering Hall)

WHITE, FELIX
- I Bended Unto Me a Bough of May***
  Ursula Greville, voice; Carlos Salzedo,
  piano
  International Composers' Guild
  December 7, 1924 (Aeolian Hall)

WHITHORNE, EMERSON
- Greek Impressions (String Quartet,
  Op. 18)
  Bachmann String Quartet
  International Composers' Guild
  February 19, 1922 (Greenwich Village
  Theatre)

- New York Days and Nights (excerpts):
  On the Ferry*, A Greenwich Village
  Tragedy*, Pell Street
  E. Robert Schmitz, piano
  American Music Guild
  February 7, 1923 (Town Hall)

- Tears*** and Invocation***
  Lucy Gates, voice; Rex Tillson, piano
  International Composers' Guild
  March 4, 1923 (Klaw Theatre)

- Saturday's Child***
  Mina Hager, soprano; Colin O'More,
  tenor; chamber orchestra;
  Alexander Smallens, conductor
  League of Composers
  Commissioned by the League
  March 13, 1926 (Town Hall)

- Portrait
  Marion Rous, piano
  League of Composers
  November 19, 1926 (Brooklyn
  Museum, in conjunction with an
  exhibition by the Société Anonyme)

- New York Days and Nights
  Piano

WHITHORNE (*continued*)
League of Composers
November 27, 1927 (MacDowell Club)

- Quintet for Piano and Strings***
Harold Bauer, piano; Lenox Quartet
League of Composers
December 19, 1928 (Town Hall)

WILLIAMS, GERRARD
- Aubade
Raymonde Delaunois, soprano;
LeRoy Shield, piano
League of Composers
November 25, 1923
(Anderson Galleries)

ZANOTTI-BIANCO, MASSIMO
- Materia***
Hyman Rovinsky, piano
International Composers' Guild
February 8, 1925 (Aeolian Hall)

Notes

Following is a list of abbreviations for manuscript sources cited in the notes. For published sources, a shortform reference is used to indicate books and articles that are cited in more than one chapter. Complete information for these appear in the concluding "Bibliography."

Abbreviations for Manuscript Collections

Antheil-DLC	George Antheil Collection, Music Division, Library of Congress
Blitzstein-WHi	Marc Blitzstein Collection, Wisconsin State Historical Society, Madison
CLobS	California State University, Long Beach
Coolidge-DLC	Elizabeth Sprague Coolidge Collection, Music Division, Library of Congress
Copland-DLC	Aaron Copland Collection, Music Division, Library of Congress
DLC	Music Division, Library of Congress
Ives-CtY	Charles Ives Papers, Beinecke Library, Yale University
Modern Music-DLC	Archives of *Modern Music*, Music Division, Library of Congress
NN	New York Public Library for the Performing Arts
Oral History/American Music-CtY	Oral History/American Music Archive, Yale School of Music
Reis-NN	Claire Reis Collection (League of Composers), New York Public Library for the Performing Arts
Rudhyar-CSt	Dane Rudhyar Collection, Green Library, Stanford University
Ruggles-CtY	Carl Ruggles Collection, Beinecke Library, Yale University
Schmitz-CtY	E. Robert Schmitz and Pro Musica Collection, Yale University

Schoenberg-DLC	Arnold Schoenberg Collection, Library of Congress
Schwerké-DLC	Irving Schwerké Collection, Music Division, Library of Congress
Seeger-DCL	Seeger Collection, Library of Congress
Slonimsky-DLC	Nicolas Slonimsky Collection, Music Division, Library of Congress
Sonneck-DLC	Oscar Sonneck Collection, Music Division, Library of Congress
Thomson-CtY	Virgil Thomson Collection, Beinecke Library, Yale University
Thomson-NNC	Virgil Thomson Collection [of music criticism], Columbia University
Upton-DLC	William Treat Upton Collection, Music Division, Library of Congress
Walton-NN	Blanche Walton Collection, New York Public Library for the Performing Arts
Whiteman-MWiW	Paul Whiteman Collection, Williams College

INTRODUCTION

1. *"the capital"*: Carlos Salzedo, "Outward Shows," *Eolus* 5/2 (May 1926), 4. Salzedo was cofounder with Edgard Varèse of the International Composers' Guild. The spelling in the original text is "capitol."

2. *"grey musty presence"*: Paul Rosenfeld, "Musical Chronicle: Introit," *The Dial* 69 (November 1920), 550.

3. *Within a few weeks*: The exact dates of these performances in 1924 were as follows: *Le Sacre du printemps*, 31 January; Cowell, 4 February; *Rhapsody in Blue*, 12 February, Varèse and Ruggles, 13 January.

4. *"all its vagueness"*: David A. Hollinger, "The Knower and the Artificer," in Singal 1991, 42. Two core texts within the voluminous literature about modernism in Western culture include Berman 1994 and Everdell 1997.

5. *The city's overall cultural life*: Douglas 1995, Singal 1991, and Tashjian 1975. A number of important studies have explored various aspects of American music during this period: Mead 1981, Levy 1983, Moore 1985, Tischler 1986, Nicholls 1990, Mattis 1992, Wiecki 1992, and Metzer 1993.

6. *"the economic, spiritual"*: Blitzstein, "New Music: A Thumbnail History," typescript, 6; Blitzstein-WHi.

7. *"The air of New York"*: Edna Ferber, *A Peculiar Treasure* (New York: The Literary Guild of America, 1939), 266.

8. *"Myth and symbol"*: This is discussed by Elaine Tyler May in "'The Radical Roots of American Studies': Presidential Address to the American Studies Association, November 9, 1995," *American Quarterly* 48/2 (June 1996), 179–200.

" *'Has he talent?'* ": John Tasker Howard, *Our American Music: Three Hundred Years of It* (New York: Thomas Y. Crowell, 1930), 557.

"The Americanists": Gilbert Chase, *America's Music: From the Pilgrims to the Present*, first ed. (New York: McGraw-Hill, 1955), 488–515.

"The Pioneer and the Wilderness": Wilfrid Mellers, *Music in a New Found Land* (New York: Stonehill, 1964; rev. ed., Mellers 1987). This is the title for the first half of Mellers's book.

In literary circles: In addition to May's essay, cited above, a critique of the tendency to mythologize American culture is offered by Malcolm Bradbury, who cites Matthiesen and

Kazin as examples of it ("The Nonhomemade World: European and American Modernism," in Singal 1991, 28–41).

CHAPTER 1

1. *"Perhaps the stronger"*: Leo Ornstein, untitled and undated typescript, property of Vivian Perlis, [3].

In the middle of: Ornstein's first two recitals at the Bandbox Theatre took place on 26 January and 7 February 1915; I have not been able to pinpoint dates for the second two. The first recital was reviewed in the *New York Times* ("Mr. Ornstein's Recital," 27 January 1915); the second was announced in the *Times* on 7 February 1915 ("A Calendar of Concerts") but apparently was not reviewed.

"really startled": Carl Van Vechten, "Leo Ornstein," in Van Vechten 1916, 233.

"a breath of the intentions": "Modern Music," *291* 2 (April 1915), 1.

"the high apostle": Van Vechten 1916, 233.

2. *Born in 1893*: I am grateful to Michael Broyles for clarifying Ornstein's birthdate, which has previously been published as 1892. Broyles and Denise Von Glahn are at work on a biography of Ornstein.

3. *Tapper (1859–1915)*: A. Walter Kramer, "Bertha Fiering Tapper: Altruist [obituary]," *Musical America* 22 (25 September 1915), 9.

After the two returned: One review of Ornstein's New York debut criticized his "talent" as more apparent in "his technical proficiency than [in] any intellectual or emotional proclamation": "A Young Pianist's Debut," *New-York Tribune*, 6 March 1911 (Clippings-NN). Ornstein's story was first told in Martens 1918 (1975).

4. *In 1913 Ornstein composed*: The composition dates of *Dwarf Suite* and *Wild Men's Dance* are according to Martens 1918 (1975), 19.

"a group of Schoenberg pieces": Ibid., 24.

5. *"You see a young man"* to *"possesst by a bewildering"*: Charles L. Buchanan, "Futurist Music," *The Independent* 87 (31 July 1916), 160.

"hypnotized as a rabbit": review in *London Daily Telegraph*, as quoted in Martens 1918 (1975), 25.

Billy Sunday: Buchanan, "Ornstein and Modern Music," *Musical Quarterly* 4 (1918), 176.

6. *From 1916 through 1921*: Following is a partial list of Ornstein's concerts during the 1910s: 5 March 1911; 26 January and 7 February 1915 (Bandbox Theatre; also two other concerts in this series), 5 December 1915 (Cort Theatre), 15 January 1916 (Aeolian Hall), 25 November 1916 (Aeolian Hall), 4 March 1917 (Princess Theatre), 15 January 1918 (Aeolian Hall), 4 June 1918 (Carnegie Hall; concert on the Ampico Reproducing Piano, which was built by the American Piano Company, with the orchestra of the Metropolitan Opera House, conducted by Arthur Bodanzky), 12 November 1918 (Aeolian Hall), October 1919 (Aeolian Hall), 7 December 1919, 3 February 1920 (Carnegie Hall, a joint concert with Leopold Godowsky, Mischa Levitzki, Benno Moiseiwitsch, and Artur Rubinstein). These dates come from reviews in New York newspapers; some in Ornstein Clippings-NN.

"was no less than a graduation" to *"so enthusiastically"*: "Leo Ornstein at his Best in Last Recital," *New York Herald*, 26 November 1916 (Clippings-NN).

"intimate" to *"a modern music society"*: Paul Rosenfeld to Claire Reis, 16 August 1915, Reis-NN.

7. *"carry {his futurist style}"*: Ornstein, as quoted in liner notes for *The Music of Leo Ornstein: String Quartet No. 3*, The New Boston Quartet (Serenus 12089); the quotation is credited to "program notes written by Daniel Stepner, violinist."

"extreme nervousness": Pauline Ornstein, interview with Vivian Perlis, as summarized in Perlis 1974–75, 743.

"startled the world": Henry Cowell, "Trends in American Music," Cowell 1933, 4–5.

8. *"the irresistible urging"*: Ornstein, as reported by Buchanan, "Ornstein and Modern Music," 178.

9. *This last notion*: Much of this summary of Bergson's thought comes from two key sources: Antliff 1993 and Douglass 1986.

"process philosophy": "Henri Bergson," *The New Encyclopedia Britannica*, 15th ed., 32 vols. (Chicago: Encyclopedia Britannica, 1993), 2:129.

"always follow" to "a champion": Bergson, as quoted in Harold A. Larrabee, Introduction to Bergson 1949, viii.

10. *"creativity and intuition"*: Douglass 1986, 2.

He was also an important force: Publications of Bergson's writings in *Camera Work* are cited in Charles C. Eldredge, "Nature Symbolized: American Painting from Ryder to Hartley," in *Spiritual* 1986, 118.

"stressed the extra-intellectual": Sherrye Cohn, "Arthur Dove and Theosophy: Visions of a Transcendental Reality," *Arts Magazine* (September 1983), 86.

11. *"written at one sitting"*: Martens 1918 (1975), 41.

According to historian: Perlis 1974–75, 743.

An extreme case: Ornstein claimed to have *Three Moods* written out for a performance of the work at a League of Composers' concert (Leo Ornstein, interview with Vivian Perlis, 8 December 1972, Oral History/American Music, CtY).

"To me, you see, music": Ibid.

"The boy says": Van Vechten 1916, 239.

12. *"Spiritual energy" and "simple"*: Buchanan, "Ornstein and Modern Music," 179, 177.

"childlike": Paul Rosenfeld, "Ornstein," *New Republic* 7 (27 May 1916), 85.

"passive transmitter": Buchanan, "Futurist Music," 160.

"But it is to the very": Bergson 1911 (1944), 194–95.

"For consciousness corresponds": Ibid., 287–88.

13. *"Ornstein has often"*: Martens 1918 (1975), 47.

"When I wrote the 'Moods'": Ornstein, untitled and undated typescript, [3]. Ornstein made a similar statement in print: "You must not think that the composers who broke the limits set for music by the generation of Debussy were conscious of each other. . . . I know that I, myself, for instance, had already composed many pieces before I ever heard of Schoenberg or of Strawinsky" (Leo Ornstein, "The Trend of Ultra-Modern Composition," *Musical Observer* 21 [February 1922], 54).

14. *"I have never heard"*: Ives 1972, 27.

"there is no doubt": published in *New York Times*, 12 July 1931; as quoted in Kirkpatrick, introduction to Ives 1972, 15.

"Leo Ornstein is unquestionably": Winthrop Parkhurst, "Leo Ornstein," *The Dial* 68 (April 1920), 479–80.

15. *There is a substantial body*: Ornstein's music manuscripts are in the Yale University Libraries; his publishers are Joshua Corporation (during the 1940s) and Poon Hill Press of Woodside, California (in the 1990s). Ornstein was rediscovered by Vivian Perlis in the early 1970s, prompting some recordings of his music as well as a few publications about it, including especially: Perlis 1974–75, and a recording of Ornstein's *Three Moods* and *Quintet for Piano and Strings* by William Westney (CRI-339, recorded in 1975).

"thrilling" and "aesthetic of spontaneous": Rosenfeld 1929, 64.

16. *Of the fourteen solo*: Dates for all these Ornstein works come from Perlis, "Leo Ornstein," Hitchcock and Sadie 1986, 3:452. The only exception is *Impressions de la Tamise*, which is dated by Perlis as ca. 1920; however, it appeared on Ornstein's Paris concert in 1914.

17. *"Our personality"*: as quoted in Bergson 1949, 61–62.

18. *"diversity"*: Van Vechten 1916, 229. At his New York concert in December 1915, for example, Ornstein included "2 lovely impressionistic things by Vannin" (Ibid., 234).

19. *"a poor Russian Jew"*: Van Vechten 1916, 234.

20. *"musical anarchism" to "gives promise"*: Waldo Frank: "Leo Ornstein and the Emancipated Music," typescript, no date [1910s], and "Musical Anarchism," *The Onlooker* (1916), 18. (These are two closely related texts; thanks to Vivian Perlis for making copies available to me.) For more from Waldo Frank about Ornstein see *Memoirs of Waldo Frank*, edited by Alan Trachtenberg, introduction by Lewis Mumford (Amherst: University of Massachusetts Press, 1973), 65. In a 1923 study of Frank, Gorham Munson listed Ornstein among Frank's key friends, who also included Sherwood Anderson and Romain Rolland (Gorham Munson, *Waldo Frank: A Study* [New York: Boni & Liveright, 1923; reprint, Folcroft Library Editions, 1974], 68).

"Ornstein alone": Rosenfeld, "Ornstein," 84.

As further evidence: Leo Ornstein, "The Music of New Russia," *The Seven Arts* 1 (January 1917), 260–69.

21. *"Like a revelation"*: Emerson Whithorne, "An American Composer Bares His Futuristic Soul," *Musical America* 25/12 (20 January 1917), 13.

Claire Reis confessed: Claire Reis, interview with Vivian Perlis, 21 January 1976, Oral History/American Music-CtY.

"the first American composer": Ruggles completed this statement by complaining that Ornstein's "later things have become mushy and soft" (Ruggles, as quoted in Kirkpatrick 1968, 154).

"when modern music": Henry Cowell, Introduction to Ornstein, *The Corpse*, published in *New Music Quarterly* 1/3 (April 1928). *The Corpse* was a song from 1917 that incorporated tone clusters; Cowell chose to publish it in the third issue of *New Music*'s inaugural year.

"only two" to "intense delight": Henry Cowell, "Carl Ruggles," in Harrison 1946, 1.

"a young boy": Dane Rudhyar, interview with Vivian Perlis, 18 March 1970.

"three years ago": George Antheil, letter to Mary Louise Curtis Bok [14 January 1922], written from Philadelphia, Antheil-DLC.

CHAPTER 2

1. *"On my fifteenth birthday"*: Frank Zappa, with Peter Occhiogrosso, *The Real Frank Zappa Book* (New York: Poseidon, 1989), 33.

"new instruments" to "hypnotized": Edgard Varèse, as quoted in "Composer Varese to Give New York Abundance of Futuristic Music," *New York Review*, 11 March 1916, 3. A slightly different version of this article appeared the same month in the *New York Telegraph* and is quoted in Fernand Ouellette, *Edgard Varèse*, translated by Derek Coltman (New York: Da Capo, 1981), 46–47. Note that the spelling of Varèse's first name varies between "Edgard" and "Edgar." I consistently use the former. According to Slonimsky 1997, a final "d" was originally used, but Varèse's early publications did not include it. Around 1940 he returned to the original (p. 1431).

"new god": Paul Rosenfeld, "Musical Chronicle," *The Dial* 82 (June 1927), 539.

"hero": Olin Downes, "Music: The Philadelphia Orchestra," *New York Times*, 13 April 1927, 28.

"flatulent": Lawrence Gilman, "Stokowski Says Good By to New York Until the Autumn of 1928," *New York Herald-Tribune*, 13 April 1927.

2. *"only abuse"*: Chou Wen-Chung 1966, 163. This statement was repeated almost verbatim in an article by John D. Anderson: "Varèse and the Lyricism of the New Physics," *Musical Quarterly* 75/1 (Spring 1991), 31.

"*Few took him seriously*": Mellers 1987, 165, 168.

"*one of a now somewhat*": Elliott Carter, "On Edgard Varèse," *The New Worlds of Edgard Varèse: A Symposium*, ed. Sherman Van Solkema (I.S.A.M. Monographs, No. 11; Brooklyn, N.Y.: Institute for Studies in American Music, 1979), 1.

"*Varèse's time*": Bernard 1987, xxiv.

3. *For Carter, Milton Babbitt:* One example of this is found in an insightful lecture about Varèse given by Babbitt at the MacDowell Colony in 1965, in which Babbitt commented: "we have recognized the extent to which Varèse's music engages the same issues, represents the same kind of stage in a mainstream of musical development as that of Schoenberg, Stravinsky, Webern, and Berg, and that its eventual originality is thus most fruitfully and justly gauged in the light of its shared connections, as 'competitive' rather than as insular" (Milton Babbitt, "Edgar Varese: A Few Observations of his Music," in Boretz and Cone 1971, 41).

4. *But it is the collective:* The Varèse bibliography includes Varèse 1972; Bernard 1987; Mattis 1992.

5. "*I see only*": Edgard Varèse, letter to Madame Kauffmann, as quoted in Varèse 1972, 122.

"*the art*" and "*finished*": Marcel Duchamp, as quoted in "The Iconoclastic Opinions of M. Marcel Duchamps [*sic*] Concerning Art and America," *Current Opinion* 59/5 (November 1915), 346.

"*New York Is More Alive*" to "*Your city*": Sarah Addington, "New York Is More Alive and Stimulating than France Ever Was, Say Two French Painters," *New York Tribune*, 9 October 1915, 7.

"*all discoveries*": Varèse, as quoted in Chou Wen-Chung 1966, 153.

6. "*arranged for a tour*": "Composer Varese to Give New York Abundance of Futuristic Music."

7. "*grandiose and solemn*": Varèse 1972, 128. This event is also discussed in Mattis 1992, 114–16.

"*war concert*": "Toscanini Conducting a Recent 'War Concert' in Milan," *Vanity Fair* (January 1916), 48.

8. *He also capitalized:* "Some New Aspects of the Ballet Russe [*sic*]: Serge de Diaghileff's Dancers to Appear at the Century Theater in January," *Vanity Fair* (January 1916), 52.

9. "*seemed to possess*" to "*It has been*": as quoted in Varèse 1972, 128–30. Not all of Varèse's letters from this period have the ebullience of this report to his mother-in-law. Olivia Mattis views this Hippodrome concert quite differently, writing that "the timing of his debut could not have been worse" (p. 115). The economy was floundering then, and Varèse's spirits were evidently down. But Varèse's mixed perception of the event is a separate issue from the fact that he conceived it brilliantly and critical response was favorable.

10. *At the same time:* Barbara Tischler provides a useful tabulation by nationality of works performed by the New York Philharmonic and the Boston Symphony Orchestra during the war (Tischler 1986, 74, 85).

"*a suburb of Berlin*": Pitts Sanborn, "The War and Music in America," *Vanity Fair* 9 (January 1918), 60, 88.

11. "*brief but terrible*": Paul Rosenfeld, "The Music of Post-Straussian Germany: Impressions of Three Present-Day German Musicians Gleaned from Recent Performances of Their Work," *Vanity Fair* 19 (November 1922), 63.

"*Banishment {of German music}*": Henrietta Straus, "Music: Fair Play," *The Nation* 110 (1 May 1920), 599.

12. *Van Vechten was then:* Carl Van Vechten, "Erik Satie: Master of the Rigolo (A French Extremist in Modernist Music)," *Vanity Fair* 10 (March 1918), 57, 92.

When trouble erupted: Varèse 1972, 136–39. Alexander Scriabin faced similar censure when his companion, Tatiana Schloezer, joined him in New York in 1907. According to Nicolas Slonimsky, Scriabin was not divorced from his wife, Vera Isakovich, and he left New York to avoid "charges of moral turpitude" (Slonimsky 1992, 1672–74).

13. *"first performance":* Program, New Symphony Orchestra, 11–12 April 1919, Program Files-NN.

The remaining concerts: "The New Symphony Orchestra, Edgar Varèse Conductor, Announces Three Pairs (Six) of Concerts at Carnegie Hall," 1919, Program Files-NN.

"Edgar Varèse . . . is a Frenchman": Ibid.

14. *"cultivate the scandal"* to *"publicizing the incident":* Seigel 1995, 137.

"I should like": Edgar Varèse, "A League of Art: A Free Interchange to Make the Nations Acquainted," *New York Times,* 23 March 1919.

15. *"an informal talk"* to *"There is an urgent":* "A Talk with Mr. Varese," *New York Times,* 30 March 1919.

A similar interview: "Edgar Varese Is True Modernist," *Morning Telegraph* [New York], 20 April 1919.

16. *"scarcely a good word":* Varèse 1972, 142, 145.

"That {Varèse} has in him": Unidentified clipping, 12 April 1919, Clippings-NN.

"limped pitifully": Paul Rosenfeld, "Musical Chronicle: The New, or National Symphony Orchestra," *The Dial* 69 (December 1920), 668.

"evidently nervous" to *"Mr. Varèse is French":* James Gibbons Huneker, "Music," *New York Times,* 12 April 1919. An amusing review in *Musical Courier* described "the only familiar piece" on the program as the "Star Spangled Banner," then told of a "crass mistake during the final measures" of it, "for which the conductor must take the blame." The reviewer concluded, "Sometimes Mr. Varese had to wait for his orchestra and sometimes his orchestra . . . refused to wait for him" ("New Orchestra Heard in New York," *Musical Courier* 88/16 [17 April 1919], 17).

"patrie psychique": Van Wyck Brooks, *The Confident Years, 1885–1915,* vol. 5 of *Makers and Finders: A History of the Writer in America, 1800–1915* (New York: Dutton, 1952), 3.

17. *"New Instruments":* Winthrop P. Tryon, "New Instruments in Orchestra Are Needed, Says Mr. Varèse," *Christian Science Monitor,* 8 July 1922, 18.

18. *"We should write":* Varèse, as quoted in Ibid.

19. *"contempt":* Mueser 1975, 90.

"The name of Varèse": W. J. Henderson, "Playing of Ultra-Modern Piece Called Hyperprism Arouses Audience to Outbreak Never Before Witnessed at a Similar Entertainment," *New York Herald,* 11 March 1923 (as quoted in Klarén 1928, 12).

20. *At the opening, a trombone melody:* See Bernard 1987 (pp. 193–217) for a probing analysis of the details of *Hyperprism.*

21. *"one of the most exciting":* Ursula Greville, "An American Jaunt," *The Sackbut* 5/8 (March 1925), 230.

"lonely, incomparable" to *"We are not one":* Lawrence Gilman, "The Philadelphia Orchestra Plays Varese's 'Hyperprism' with Cheering Results," *New York Herald-Tribune,* 17 December 1924.

"I think I was present": Minna Lederman, letter to Louise Varèse, 10 March 1980, Lederman Collection, privately held.

22. *"hard of surface":* Paul Rosenfeld, "Musical Chronicle," *The Dial* 76 (March 1924), 299.

The opening oboe melody: For an analysis of the role of the initial tetrachord in *Octandre,* see Milton Babbitt, "Edgard Varese: A Few Observations of His Music," in Boretz and Cone 1971, 42–43.

23. *"Varèse has already":* Ibid., 299, 300.

24. *"Varèse stems from":* Paul Rosenfeld, "Musical Chronicle," *The Dial* 78 (May 1925), 438.

"as a small boy": Rosenfeld, "Musical Chronicle," *The Dial* 76 (March 1924), 298.

25. *"Varèse never has":* Rosenfeld, "Musical Chronicle," *The Dial* 78 (May 1925), 438.

"Intégrales is informed": Ibid., 439.

Such gendered language: Another notable use of "penetration" occurs in a historiographically significant profile of Varèse published by his student Chou Wen-Chung (1966, 161).

26. *"virtuosic genius":* Paul Rosenfeld, "Musical Chronicle," *The Dial* 80 (June 1926), 529.

27. *By the time of:* Paul Rosenfeld, "Musical Chronicle," *The Dial* 82 (June 1927), 537.

"hero": Olin Downes, "Music," *New York Times*, 13 April 1927.

"Hissing is an honor": W. J. Henderson, Review in *New York Sun* (13 April 1927), as quoted in Klarén, 1928, 22.

"The crown and sceptre": Pitts Sanborn, "A Glance Toward the Left," *Modern Music* 4/2 (January–February 1927), 25.

28. *"high priest":* Lawrence Gilman, "The Philadelphia Orchestra Plays Varese's 'Hyperprism,' with Cheering Results," *New York Herald-Tribune*, 17 December 1924.

"sense of power": Gilman, "Hisses for a Novelty at the Last Philadelphia Orchestra Concert," *New York Herald-Tribune*, 14 April 1926.

"I felt it to be": Winthrop P. Tryon, "'Amériques,' Repartitioned," *Christian Science Monitor*, 19 January 1929.

29. *"an almost hypnotic":* Platt 1985, 12.

"celebrated" to *"He was treated":* Seigel 1995, 2–3.

30. *"But the greatest":* Rosenfeld 1929, 160, 165, 167.

31. *"I am the ancestor":* Edgard Varèse, as quoted in Varèse 1972, 23.

"a virtual parricide": Larry Stempel, "Not Even Varèse Can Be an Orphan," *Musical Quarterly* 60 (1974), 46. In addition to Stempel's article probing the Varèse myth, there have followed books by Jonathan Bernard and Olivia Mattis, already cited.

32. *"unnecessary sensitiveness":* Winthrop P. Tryon, "Edgar Varèse's New Orchestra Work, 'Amériques,'" *Christian Science Monitor*, 7 July 1923.

33. *"What with the vicissitudes":* "Pan-American Concert," *New York Times*, 7 March 1933. F.D.P., "Pan-American Concert Offers Unusual Works: 41 Percussion Instruments Used in Varese Piece," *New York Herald-Tribune*, 7 March 1933.

CHAPTER 3

1. *"The influence of":* Foreword, *Exhibition of Modern Art: Arranged by a Group of European and American Artists in New York {catalogue},* Bourgeois Galleries, 3–29 April 1916, 3.

"The moment belonged": Meyer Schapiro, "Rebellion in Art," *America in Crisis*, ed. Daniel Aaron (New York: Alfred A. Knopf, 1952), 207.

2. *In 1915, the critic:* Van Vechten 1915, 36ff.

"Stravinsky is no longer": Henry Cowell, "America Takes a Front Rank in Year's Modernist Output," *Musical America* 41/23 (28 March 1925), 5.

The information about European modernism presented here is culled from clipping files at the New York Public Library (NN), scattered reminiscences (both contemporaneous and retrospective) by composers, and program notes of the 1920s. These last are a key source. It was common in the 1920s to introduce the performance of a contemporary European composition by giving its performance history in the United States.

3. *"During these formative":* Aaron Copland, "Composer from Brooklyn," in Copland 1941 (1968), 152–53.

"It was a fortunate": Ibid., 155.

4. *Thomson heard* Petrushka: Thomson wrote of Debussy and Ravel in Thomson 1966 (1977), 51. In an interview with me in New York in February 1988, he talked of hearing *Petrushka*. For more about Thomson's early exposure to European modernism see Carol J. Oja, "Virgil Thomson's Harvard Years," in Crawford, Lott, and Oja 1990, 323–45.

"consisted of one concert": Ruth Crawford, letter to Nicolas Slonimsky, 29 January 1933, Slonimsky-DLC (reprinted in Neuls-Bates 1982, 304.)

"There are few modern": George Antheil, letter to Mary Louise Curtis Bok, 14 December 1921, Antheil-DLC.

5. *But by the mid-1920s:* This account is limited to the East Coast.

6. *"There were a few":* S. Foster Damon, "Schönberg, Strindberg and Sibelius," *Harvard Musical Review* 3/6 (March 1915), 11.

"scandalized the hell": Virgil Thomson, interview with the author.

7. *"first opportunity"* to *"only a few days ago":* "Flonzaleys Play Schoenberg," *New York Post*, 27 January 1914 (Flonzaley Quartet Clippings-NN). An article in *Musical America* the following year stated: "The Flonzaleys it was who administered concertgoers of this city their first solid dose of Schönberg" (H.F.P., "Stravinsky Pieces Get First Hearing," *Musical America* [December 4, 1915], Stravinsky Clippings-NN).

8. *At the one on 28 December:* Kurt Schindler, *Arnold Schönberg's Quartet in D Minor, Op. 7* (New York: G. Schirmer, 1914).

"who, during his last trip": Ibid., 2–3.

9. *"Charles Henry Cooper":* Van Vechten 1915, 11.

10. *"The name of Igor":* "Music and Musicians," *Boston Transcript*, 1 May 1914, Schoenberg Clippings-NN.

"mounted a sophisticated": Garafola 1989, 204.

That same March: This production took place on 18–19 March 1916. Hyland was "official pianist at the Playhouse," according to Marion Bauer who recalled this event in Bauer 1943, 373.

And three years later: Schouvaloff and Borovsky 1982, 59.

These works were heard: The BSO performances are listed in Howe 1931 (1978), 223.

11. *"un-Anglo-Saxon":* Rosenfeld 1920, 97; H. F. P., "Stravinsky Pieces Get First Hearing."

In the spring of 1918: "Stravinsky by the London String Quartet," *Musical Courier* (4 April 1918), Stravinsky Clippings-NN.

And by November 1920: "Flonzaleys and Stravinsky," *New York Times*, 21 November 1920 (*New York Scrapbook*, Reel 25, NN).

12. *"The assemblage sat":* Paul Rosenfeld, "Musical Chronicle," *The Dial* 72 (January 1922), 111–13.

"Dear Friend" and *"marvellous":* Cowell, letter to Arnold Schoenberg, 22 October 1948, Schoenberg-DLC.

13. *"among the first":* Lawrence Gilman, "Bartok and His Remarkable Music," *New York Herald-Tribune*, 18 December 1927, Bartók Clippings-NN.

The Boston Symphony: The BSO performed Bartók's Dance Suite (1923) in 1926 (Howe 1931, 185).

14. *"a shy little man":* Unidentified clipping, *Radio Guide*, 5 January 1940, Scriabin Clippings-NN. Scriabin's visit was announced in "Scriabine to Play in New York Soon," *Musical America* 4 (20 October 1906), 6.

Then in 1908: Altschuler's orchestra also performed Scriabin's *Nuance for Strings* on 10 December 1918, during Prokofiev's first visit to the United States (Program, Scriabin Clippings-NN). See "Scriabin" and "Altschuler" in Slonimsky 1992, 31, 1672–74.

This was not the first: Lawrence Gilman, Program notes for the Philadelphia Orchestra, 11–12 March 1932, Scriabin Clippings-NN.

15. *"Among European modernists"*: "Alexander Scriabin, 'Prometheus: The Poem of Fire,' Op. 60," unlabeled program notes in Scriabin Clippings-NN. The quotation is identified as being from 1925.

16. *"felt certain colors"*: "'Feels Colors' as She Plays Piano: Katherine Ruth Heyman Tells of an Interesting Phase of Her Work," *Musical America* (28 August 1909), Heyman Clippings-NN. Heyman lived from 1874 to 1944.

"met Scriabin": Faubion Bowers, "Memoir with Memoirs," *Paideuma* 2/1 (Spring 1973), 61.

Heyman had earlier: "Miss Heyman's Versatility," *Musical America* (2 December 1916), Heyman Clippings-NN. Katherine Ruth Heyman, *The Relation of Ultramodern to Archaic Music* (Boston: Small, Maynard & Company, 1921).

"appreciation of Scriabin": Heyman, 136.

17. *In 1924 and 1927:* Heyman's Scriabin recitals are cited on the back of a flier for a New York recital by her on 13 April 1934, Heyman Programs-NN.

Prior to the 1927 event: Elliott C. Carter Jr. to Charles Ives, 19 February 1927, Ives-CtY.

Ives, in turn: Heyman wrote Ives on 8 June 1927, thanking him for a check: "Prometheus did certainly need a dinner!" (Ives-CtY).

"I have been puttering": Clifton Furness, letter to Ives, 24 July 1923, Ives-CtY. The Ives-Scriabin-Heyman-Furness link opens up a big topic. A letter from Furness to Ives, written on 6 April 1924, showed a continuing interest in the Russian: "I'm sending the program notes from the Boston Symphony about Scriabin['s] 'Divine Poem,' thinking you might be interested in some of the information. . . . They miss totally the point of the introduction of 'sensuousness'—the way in which Scriabin transcends this (or as you said, builds out of it) is the point and purpose of the whole work." At the end, Furness says he has complimentary tickets for Heyman's all-Scriabin recital that same month and asks Ives and his wife to join him.

18. *His* Gymnopédies: Program Notes, Boston Symphony Orchestra, Carnegie Hall, 7 and 9 March 1929, Satie Clippings-NN.

Performances of his works: Carl Van Vechten reported on the Copeland performances in: "Erik Satie: Master of the Rigolo (A French Extremist in Modernist Music)," *Vanity Fair* 10 (March 1918), 57. Eva Gauthier's recital on 12 March 1919 included some Satie songs, as mentioned in a caption for caricatures of Gauthier and Satie, published in *Musical Quarterly* 5 (1919), 468.

Of all the composers: Virgil Thomson produced *Socrate* at Harvard in 1922 after returning from his first extended stay in Paris. Oja, "Virgil Thomson's Harvard Years," in Crawford, Lott, and Oja 1990, 336–38.

"Eric {sic} Satie" to "difficult to find": "Eric [sic] Satie," *Harvard Musical Review* 2/6 (March 1914), 18–20. This article is unsigned, but Damon, who was a great devotee of Satie, was editor of the journal at the time it was published. His authorship of the article has been assumed by several writers, including Charles Norman (*The Magic-Maker: E. E. Cummings* [New York: Macmillan, 1958], 41).

19. *Where Satie gained:* The articles by Satie in *Vanity Fair* included "A Hymn in Praise of the Critics" (September 1921), 49; "A Lecture on 'The Six'" (October 1921), 61; "A Learned Lecture on Music and Animals" (May 1922), 64; "Igor Stravinsky" (February 1923), 39, 88.

Over that same span: Paul Rosenfeld, "The Musician as a Parodist of Life" (November 1921), 43, 92; "Satie and 'Socrate,'" (December 1921), 46, 100; Georges Auric, "Erik Satie and the New Spirit Possessing French Music," (July 1922), 62, 104.

20. *"sudden fame"*: Henri Prunières, "The Failure of Success" [obituary for Erik Satie], *Musical Digest* (28 July 1925), 5. A similar opinion appeared in William H. Spier, "Musical World Loses Ironic Farceur in Satie's Passing," *Musical America* (18 July 1925), 8, 10.

21. *"Up to the present"*: E. B. Hill, letter to Sonneck, 18 March 1914, Sonneck-DLC. With "Vuillermoz," Hill could have been referring to one of at least two articles by the French critic Emile Vuillermoz: "Igor Stravinsky," *La Revue Musicale* 8/5 (1912), 15–21; or "La Saison russe au Théâtre des Champs-Elysées: Le Sacre," *S.I.M. La Revue Musicale* (1913), 52–56. H.T.P. was Henry Taylor Parker, longtime Boston music critic. This Stravinsky bibliography comes from: Carroll D. Wade, "A Selected Bibliography of Igor Stravinsky," *Stravinsky: A New Appraisal of His Work*, ed. Paul Henry Lang (New York: W. W. Norton, 1963), 97–109.

22. *"I am greatly obliged"*: Hill, letter to Sonneck, 24 March 1914, Sonneck-DLC. The articles he refers to probably include: Pierre Lalo, "Remarks on the Ballet 'Le Sacre du Printemps,'" *New Music Review* 2 (1913), 440–42, and M. D. Calvocoressi, "A Russian Composer of To-day," *Musical Times* 52 (1911), 511–12. M. Montagu-Nathan published *A History of Russian Music* (London and New York, 1914). Lalo was a French music critic; Calvocoressi was a Greek music critic who settled in London; Montagu-Nathan was an English critic; and Chalmers Clifton was a student of Hill at Harvard.

23. *Instead in 1915:* E. B. Hill, "Vincent d'Indy: An Estimate," *Musical Quarterly* 1 (1915), 246–59.

"violently revolutionary" to *"It is the logical"*: Edward B. Hill, "A Note on Stravinsky," *Harvard Musical Review* 2 (April 1914), 7.

24. *The second issue of the* Musical Quarterly: All the following were published in *Musical Quarterly* 2 (1916): Egon Wellesz, "Schönberg and Beyond," 76–95; C. Stanley Wise, "Impressions of Igor Stravinsky," 249–56; and A. Eaglefield Hull, "A Survey of the Pianoforte Works of Scriabin," 601–14.

"Never before": Wellesz, 93.

CHAPTER 4

1. *"There is a growing"*: Gilbert Seldes, "Thompson's Panorama, the Woolworth Building, and Do It Now: Can a Purely American Art Be Created Out of These Elements?" *Vanity Fair* (December 1924), 39. The title for this chapter comes from: [Jane Heap], "Comments," *Little Review* (spring 1924), 57.

"startled" to *"unencumbered by"*: Edmund Wilson, "The Aesthetic Upheaval in France: The Influence of Jazz in Paris and Americanization of French Literature and Art," *Vanity Fair* 17 (February 1922), 49.

2. *The first American radio:* These statistics come from Richard Guy Wilson, "America and the Machine Age," in Richard Guy Wilson, Dianne H. Pilgrim, and Dickran Tashjian, *The Machine Age in America, 1918–1941* (Brooklyn, N.Y.: The Brooklyn Museum and Harry N. Abrams, 1986), 26.

The recording and: Gordon Mumma, "Sound Recording," in Hitchcock and Sadie 1986, 4:268.

"highbrow" and *"lowbrow"*: These terms recur throughout this book as crucial issues of the 1920s. According to Lawrence W. Levine, "highbrow" was first used in the 1880s and "lowbrow" appeared shortly after 1900 (Levine 1988, 221–22).

3. *"Composers were slow"*: Copland 1952 (1959), 113–14.

4. *"amazing results"* to *"I talk to homes"*: Walter Damrosch, "What the Radio Has Meant to Me," *Musical Leader* 52 (21 April 1927), 23.

5. *"The recording of modern"* to *"no composition of Schönberg"*: Henry Cowell, "Music of and for the Records," *Modern Music* 8/3 (March–April 1931), 32–33.

6. *"Life in ancient times"*: Luigi Russolo, "The Art of Noises: Futurist Manifesto," translated by Stephen Somervell, in Slonimsky 1994, 1019.

7. *"Aphorisms on Futurism"* to *"DIE in the Past"*: *Camera Work* 45 (January 1914), 13–15. In 1914, Edward Steichen knew enough about the futurist movement to rail against it as just another "dogma" that should be "relegated to the scrap heap—History" (Steichen, "291," *Camera Work* 47 [July 1914], 65).

"a symbol of modern": Hamilton Easter Field, "Joseph Stella," *The Arts* (October 1921), 24; as quoted in Platt 1985, 112.

"The average New Yorker": J[ane] H[eap], "Stella Exhibition," *Little Review* (Autumn 1922), 2; as quoted in Platt 1985, 113.

8. *"rhetoric of the technological"*: Marx 1964, 195.

"a special affinity": Ibid., 203.

"objects of exalted": Charles Caldwell, "Thoughts on the Moral and Other Indirect Influences of Rail-Roads," *New England Magazine* 2 (April 1832), 288–300; as quoted in Marx 1964, 195.

9. *"If America has"*: Ezra Pound, "George Antheil," *The Criterion: A Quarterly Review* 2/7 (April 1924), 323; as quoted in Whitesitt 1983, 18.

"This is by far": George Antheil, letter to Mary Louise Curtis Bok, [13 August 1925?], Antheil-DLC.

10. *"the great gallery"*: Henry Adams, *The Education of Henry Adams* (Boston: Massachusetts Historical Society, 1918; Boston: Houghton Mifflin, 1974), 380.

"lying in the Gallery": Ibid., 382.

11. *"tiny, awkward"*: Gordon 1989, 64.

"mechanical picturesque": Lambert 1936, 243.

"joyous epic": F. S. Converse, *Flivver Ten Million: A Joyous Epic* (Boston: C. C. Birchard, 1927).

"train, with its": George Gershwin, as quoted in Goldberg 1931 (1958), 139.

12. *"best known works"*: B.S., "New York Concerts, *Musical Courier* 98/5 (31 January 1929), 22.

Pacific 231 had previously: A chronicle of the performances of *Pacific 231* in Paris and the United States gives a sense of how the dissemination of modernist European works unfolded. Serge Koussevitzky conducted its premiere in Paris on 8 May 1924. That was followed by a cluster of performances in American cities: Boston on 10 October 1924, conducted by Koussevitzky; Chicago that same fall (1924) by Frederick Stock with the Chicago Symphony Orchestra; and New York with Damrosch on 31 October 1924. ["'Pacific 231' by Arthur Honegger," *Musical Leader* 48 (30 October 1924), 416; [Honegger, *Pacific 231*], *Symphony Society: Bulletin* 18 (27 October 1924), NN; "Pacific 231," [program] Philharmonic Symphony Society of New York, 19 January 1929, Programs-NN.] Toscanini's performance is reviewed in Kenneth Burke, "Musical Chronicle," *The Dial* 84 (April 1928), 356.

Damrosch broadcast: Olin Downes, "Radio and the Public Taste," *New York Times*, 20 May 1928.

"a vast complex": Henry McBride, "The Skating Rink by Fernand Léger," *New York Herald*, 18 November 1923.

Other European machine: Marion Bauer and Flora Bauer, "Music in New York," *Musical Leader* 60 (19 March 1931), 8.

13. *"Beauty is everywhere"*: Fernand Léger, "The Esthetics of the Machine," Part I, *Little Review* 9/3 (Spring 1923), 46.

14. *"ten years from now"*: "A New Substitute for Scenery and a New Kind of Concert," *Vanity Fair* (May 1925), 67.

"either moving-picture" to *"a most potent"*: Marion Bauer and Flora Bauer Bernstein, "Music in New York," *Musical Leader* 51 (12 August 1926), 5.

15. *Although his instrument:* Joseph Schillinger, "Electricity, A Musical Liberator," *Modern Music* 8/3 (March–April 1931), 29–31; William Grimes, "Leon Theremin, Musical Inventor, Is Dead at 97," *New York Times* (9 November 1993).

Theremin gave well-publicized: The program for a concert by Theremin at the Plaza Hotel on 24 January 1928 was included in a review by Marion Bauer and Flora Bauer, "Music from the Ether" [part of their column, "Music in New York"], *Musical Leader* 54 (2 February 1928), 6. A Lewisohn Stadium concert on the instrument occurred on 27 August 1928; a review of it stated that Theremin had given concerts at the Metropolitan Opera House and Carnegie Hall ("Takes Music Out of Air," *Musical Leader* 55 [30 August 1928], 7). A subsequent Carnegie Hall demonstration took place on 3 February 1929 (John Gerard, "The Thereminvox and Its Tonal Resources," *Pro Musica Quarterly* 7/3–4 [March–June 1929], 41–43).

16. *"cajoled" to "on women in investment":* E. Paige, "Princess de Broglie Makes Debut as Performer on Thereminvox," *Musical Leader* 55 (11 October 1928), 6.

Three months later: B.S., "New York Concerts," *Musical Courier* 98/5 (31 January 1929), 22.

"To give a program": Leon Theremin, as quoted in "Takes Music Out of Air."

17. *However, the instrument:* In 1971, *Rhythmicana* (or *Concerto for Rhythmicon and Orchestra*) was performed in a computer realization by Leland Smith with the Stanford Orchestra (Lichtenwanger 1986, 132–33).

18. *"a wireless instructor":* Marion Bauer and Flora Bauer, "Music in New York," *Musical Leader* 59 (25 December 1930), 8.

19. *"composer and enthusiastic proponent":* "Contributors to This Issue," *Modern Music* 6/2 (January–February 1929), [43].

"noise . . . holds": Carol Bérard, "Recorded Noises—Tomorrow's Instrumentation," *Modern Music* 6/2 (January–February 1929), 28–29.

20. *"established all the basic":* H. H. Stuckenschmidt, "Machines—A Vision of the Future," *Modern Music* 4/3 (March–April 1927), 14, 13, 9.

"The field of composition": Henry Cowell, "Music of and for the Records," 34.

CHAPTER 5

1. *"My reaction to New York":* "Antheil's 'Ballet Mécanique' Causes a Near Riot," *Musical Leader* 52 (21 April 1927), 109.

"The first few minutes" to "drowning out": Friede 1948, 60–61.

2. *"For the first time":* Antheil, letter to Bok, [?4 January 1926], written from Paris, Antheil-DLC.

"nightmare": Antheil 1945, 138.

3. *"most original":* Thomson 1966 (1977), 82.

4. *"I had been born":* Antheil 1945, 13–14.

5. *"vistas of distant":* Ibid., 14.

"a severe theoretical": Ibid., 16. Sternberg was so reactionary that he published an article titled "Against Modern'ism' [*sic*]" in *Musical Quarterly* (7/1 [January 1921], 1–7).

Yet he recognized: Whitesitt 1983, 6. Whitesitt's archival research has been invaluable in writing this chapter.

6. *"gatherings of ultras":* Antheil, letter to Stanley Hart, 9 May 1922, written from Philadelphia, Antheil-DLC.

"modern artists society": Antheil, letter to Bok, [14 December 1921], written from Philadelphia, Antheil-DLC. Antheil mentions this society in other letters as well. These plans suggest that Antheil knew Pound before reaching Europe. Pound's notorious *Antheil and the Treatise on Harmony with Supplementary Notes* (Pound 1924 [1968]) is part of Antheil's story in Europe and is discussed in Whitesitt 1983, 16–19.

7. *"I am, beyond"*: Antheil, letter to Bok, [20 December 1921], written from Philadelphia, Antheil-DLC.

Renard was published: The full score for *Histoire* was not issued until 1924. See White 1979, 239, 264, 275.

As for "Les Six": The articles from *Vanity Fair* are cited in Chapter 3, notes 18 and 19.

8. *"the new Christ"*: Harry Crosby, *Shadows of the Sun: The Diaries of Harry Crosby*, ed. Edward Germain (Santa Barbara: Black Sparrow, 1977), 146.

9. *Antheil's machine music*: See especially Whitesitt 1983, 13–14.

10. *"matrix of nonsense"*: Tashjian 1975, 14.

"yet again {with}": Rudolf E. Kuenzli, Introduction to Kuenzli 1986, 5. Another crucial source is Naumann 1996.

11. *Morton Schamberg was:* Schamberg lived from 1881 to 1918.

12. *Amid all this:* Maurice Peress first pointed out the link between Picabia's sculpture and Antheil's composition in liner notes for his 1992 recording of *Ballet Mécanique* (MusicMasters 67094-2).

The title "Ballet Mécanique": See Erica E. Hirschler, [*Ballet Méchanique*], in Susan Dodge Peters, ed., *Memorial Art Gallery: An Introduction to the Collection* (Rochester, N.Y.: Memorial Art Gallery, 1988), 212–13. Thanks to Erica Hirschler for telling me about Sheeler's drawing.

13. *Antheil connected:* George Antheil, "My Ballet Mécanique: What It Means," *Der Querschnitt* 5 (September 1925), 789–91. Also published as "My Ballet Mécanique," *De Stijl* 6/12 (1924–25), 141–44.

"My Ballet Mécanique": Ibid., 789.

"My first big work": Antheil to Stanley Hart, [9 ?March 1925], Antheil-DLC.

"We of the future": Antheil, letter to Bok, [August 1922], Antheil-DLC.

14. *All this bluster:* This manuscript is now in NN.

The revised text: The one important exception to this is the 1992 recording conducted by Maurice Peress.

15. *"the début of Dadaism"*: Tristan Tzara, "Some Memoirs of Dadaism," *Vanity Fair* (July 1922), 70.

"for decades buried": Gillmore 1988, 102.

16. *"My Ballet Mécanique"*: Antheil, "My Ballet Mécanique: What It Means," 789–90.

17. *"the best popular"*: Henderson 1983, 41. Linda Dalrymple Henderson's book provides a basis for the discussion here about the fourth dimension and art.

"New York people": Willa Cather, *The Song of the Lark*, rev. ed. (Boston: Houghton Mifflin, 1937; original publication date, 1915), 455.

18. *"The Fourth Dimension" to "the consciousness"*: Max Weber, "The Fourth Dimension from a Plastic Point of View," *Camera Work* 31 (July 1910), 25; as quoted in Henderson 1983, 168.

"harmonic use": Schamberg, statement in "Post-Impression Exhibit Awaited," *Philadelphia Inquirer*, 19 January 1913; as quoted in Henderson 1983, 173–74.

19. *"Time," wrote Antheil:* Antheil, untitled manuscript, beginning "The drawings of Miro," ca. 1927; as quoted in Whitesitt 1983, 104–5.

20. *"final ten minutes"*: Billy, "George Antheil," in "Paris Comet" [probably a column title], 10 August 1927, Antheil Clippings-NN. The comment about women is included in the original source.

21. *Whereas Satie's redundancies:* Antheil himself acknowledged a possible connection between his score and Satie's, but he did so in a typically combative way, belligerently asserting that his project was begun first (Antheil 1945, 134–35).

22. *"Everybody either thinks"*: Antheil, letter to Stanley Hart, [16 December 1921], from Philadelphia, Antheil-DLC.

23. *"attain{ed} a single":* Antheil, "My Ballet Mécanique: What It Means," 791.

"I personally consider": Antheil, letter to Nicolas Slonimsky, 21 July 1936, as quoted in Whitesitt 1983, 105.

"Now I hope to present": Antheil, "My Ballet Mécanique," 791.

"ballet obcène [sic]": Gillmore 1988, 251.

24. *"formula":* Antheil, untitled manuscript, ca. 1927; as quoted in Whitesitt 1983, 105.

25. *"had no idea":* Antheil 1945, 140.

26. *In his autobiography:* Antheil 1945, 135.

"saw and admired": Peter de Francia, *Fernand Léger* (New Haven: Yale University Press, 1983), 59. De Francia erroneously credited Virgil Thomson's autobiography as his source, so his claim raises questions.

27. *Léger also attended:* Caesar Searchinger, "The Greatest Coup of the Age," *Der Querschnitt* 4 (1924), 47–48; as quoted in Whitesitt 1983, 19.

"organization through contrast": Fernand Léger, "Notes on the Mechanical Element [1923]," as reprinted in Léger 1965, 30.

"as a method": Léger, "Notes on Contemporary Plastic Life [1923]," as reprinted in Léger 1965, 25.

28. *For the Carnegie:* The pianists are listed in the program for the concert; Eugene Goossens conducted. The additional noise-makers are cited in a front-page story about the event in the *New York Herald-Tribune* of 11 April 1927: "Boos Greet Antheil Ballet of Machines."

29. *At the core:* Stravinsky's forays into this realm included *Study for Pianola* of 1917 and a series of transcriptions for pianola of *Petrushka*, *Pulcinella*, and *Les Noces*, among other works, in the 1920s (White 1979, 619–20).

30. *"skyscraper primitive":* Gorham B. Munson, "The Skyscraper Primitives," *The Guardian* 1/5 (March 1925), 164–78. Glenn Watkins discusses this fusion meaningfully in connection with Antheil. See Watkins 1994, 329–37.

"splendid examples": Weber, "The Fourth Dimension from a Plastic Point of View," 25.

"many young artists": Guillaume Apollinaire, *Les Peintres Cubistes: Méditations esthétiques* (Paris: Eugène Figuière, 1913), 16–17; as quoted in Henderson 1983, 80.

31. *"I feel that":* Antheil, letter to Bok, [5 April 1923], written from Berlin, Antheil-DLC.

"symbolic of New York": Antheil, letter to Bok, [19 October 1925], written from Paris, Antheil-DLC.

"to express America": This quotation turned up in many publications, including "Goossens to Conduct 'Ballet Mecanique': Letter from Antheil Throws Light on Composer and His Musical Credo—How He Views Himself and Europe," *Musical Leader* 52 (24 February 1927), 5, and also program notes for the Carnegie Hall concert ("George Antheil: First American Appearance in a Concert of His Own Works," Carnegie Hall, 10 April 1927, Antheil Clippings-NN).

"first 'theme'": Antheil, "Composer's Notes on 1942–43 Re-Editing," *Ballet Mécanique* (n.p.: Templeton, 1959).

32. *"Elite subscribers":* "Antheil's 'Ballet Mecanique' Causes a Near Riot."

"All the gals": "Antheil Gives Concert of Own Music," *New York Journal*, 11 April 1927, Antheil-DLC.

"The Horse-Shoe Circle": Billy, "George Antheil," in "Paris Comet," 10 August 1927, Antheil Clippings-NN.

And a fourth: "The Riotous Return of Mr. Antheil," *Literary Digest* (30 April 1927), 26.

33. *"sensational American":* Concert flier for New York premiere, as quoted in Whitesitt 1983, 31.

"The newspapers": Lawrence Gilman, "Mr. George Antheil Presents His Compliments to New York," *New York Herald-Tribune*, 11 April 1927.

34. *The machines on stage*: Mullen's stage career was short-lived, extending from 1924 to 1931, when he began working as an interior designer (Bobbi Owen, *Scenic Design on Broadway: Designers and Their Credits, 1915–1990* [New York: Greenwood, 1991], 133).

The sets were built: "George Antheil: First American Appearance" [program].

"a gigantic Negro couple": Friede 1948, 49.

"cubistic Tin-Pan Alley": "Antheil's 'Ballet Mecanique' Causes a Near Riot."

35. *"a bitter disappointment"*: Pitts Sanborn, "G. Antheil Presents," *New York Telegram*, 11 April 1927, clipping in Antheil-DLC. Sanborn was a friend of contemporary music; he published a number of articles in *Modern Music* chronicling the performance of new works (mostly European) in New York.

"unconscionably boring": Lawrence Gilman, "Mr. George Antheil Presents His Compliments to New York." This brief excerpt barely gives a flavor of how searing the review was.

"Expected Riots": Olga Samaroff, *New York Evening Post*, 11 April 1927, clipping in Antheil-DLC.

"good vaudeville": Charles Seeger, letter to Carl Ruggles, n.d. [1927], Ruggles-CtY.

36. *"a wholly false"*: Antheil, as quoted in "Father of Mechanical Symphonics [*sic*] Dislikes Being Called Jazz Artiste," *New York Herald, Paris*, 24 October 1927; pasted into a letter from Antheil to Mrs. Bok (24 October 1927, Antheil-DLC).

"youth from the Trenton": Paul Rosenfeld, "Musical Chronicle," *The Dial* 67 (June 1922), 659.

"A great deal": Aaron Copland, "George Antheil," *League of Composers' Review* 2/1 (January 1925), 26.

"the first composer": Thomson, letter to Briggs Buchanan, as quoted in Thomson 1966, 82.

"Antheil is easily": Blitzstein 1929, 163–64.

37. *"George Antheil"*: Ned Rorem, Introduction to Pound 1924 (1968), 7.

CHAPTER 6

1. *"To us, Dane Rudhyar's"*: Paul Rosenfeld, "Musical Chronicle," *The Dial* 79 (December 1925), 528.

"a deeper, richer": Rudhyar 1923b, 13.

His perspective represented: The ultra-moderns were studied vigorously in the closing decades of the twentieth century. Two important books focusing on their compositional craft were Nicholls 1990 and Gann 1997.

2. *"metaphysically aimless" to "neo-scholasticism"*: Rudhyar 1922, 117 (Rudhyar's emphasis).

"a new mechanical world": Jane Heap, "Machine-Age Exposition," *Little Review* 11 (spring 1925), 22.

"chaotic superabundance": Ruth Crawford, letter to Nicolas Slonimsky, 29 January 1933, Slonimsky-DLC, published in Neuls-Bates 1982, 305.

3. *"dissonant counterpoint"*: Since Seeger's ideas have been explored elsewhere in considerable detail, I summarize them briefly in this chapter. For more information, see Greer 1998, Nicholls 1990, Pescatello 1992, and Seeger 1994.

Rudhyar and Seeger were: The exchange was quite angry and occurred over an article by Rudhyar about Ruggles that appeared in *Eolian Review* in 1923 (Rudhyar 1923c, followed by Seeger 1923 and Rudhyar 1924b). This is discussed in Chapter 7.

4. *In the 1970s*: Reprints of Rudhyar's articles, together with his scores, appear in the following volumes of *Soundings*: 2 (1972), 6 (1973), 7–8 (1973), and 10 (1986). Garland also wrote an obituary for Rudhyar: "Dane Rudhyar," *Soundings* 10 (1986), 4–5.

In 1987: Chase 1987, 465–67.

And four years: Tick 1991.

"to continue": Rudhyar 1982, viii. Rudhyar recounted this stage of his career in other sources, including: Rudhyar, interview with Vincent Plush, 24 November 1982, Palo Alto, California; transcript in Oral History/American Music, CtY. For a time, a newsletter devoted to Rudhyar's work, titled *To Sow*, was published in Austin, Texas. I am grateful to its editor, Patana Usuni, for his generosity in commenting on this chapter and providing information about Rudhyar.

5. *It also connected:* Shere 1972, 5, Clippings-NN.

6. *His* Claude Debussy: Rudhyar 1913.

"{Debussy's} music": Dane Rudhyar, interview with Sheila Finch Rayner, 23 May 1977, Oral History Archive, California State University, Long Beach.

But Rudhyar remained: Shere (1972) gives the dates for Rudhyar's extended trips to New York as 1922, 1925, 1926, 1928, 1929, and 1930 (p. 7). Alfred Morang, however, claimed he was there in 1923, 1925 (perhaps 1926), 1929, 1930 (Morang 1939, 21–22).

7. *All this culminated:* The information about Herz comes from Shere 1972, 4; that about La Liberté from Rudhyar, interview with Vivian Perlis, 18 March 1970, Oral History/American Music, Yale School of Music. It is also confirmed in the interview with Sheila Finch Rayner.

8. *"deeper psychic states":* Bergson, as quoted in Douglass 1986, 21.

"This music is built": Rudhyar 1923a, 46. Charles Seeger was also affected by Bergson, as Taylor Greer explores in a chapter titled "Bergson's Intuition and Seeger's Predicament" (Greer 1998).

9. *Claiming a continuity:* Basic information about theosophy is found in Sydney E. Ahlstrom, *A Religious History of the American People* (New Haven: Yale University Press, 1972), 1038–43, and Campbell 1980. See also: Peter Washington, *Madame Blavatsky's Baboon: A History of the Mystics, Mediums, and Misfits Who Brought Spiritualism to America* (New York: Schocken Books, 1993). William Quan Judge's *Ocean of Theosophy* was an important early text (New York: The Path, 1893).

10. *"universal brotherhoods":* Rudhyar 1928a, 10.

"mysterious personages": Campbell 1980, 53–54.

"the new composer": Rudhyar 1926a, 15.

11. On the Spiritual in Art: As cited in Charles C. Eldredge, "Nature Symbolized: American Painting from Ryder to Hartley," in *Spiritual* 1986, 118.

"responsibility": Wassily Kandinsky, *On the Spiritual in Art* (1912), in *Kandinsky: Complete Writings on Art*, ed. Kenneth C. Lindsay and Peter Vergo, 2 vols. (Boston: G. K. Hall, 1982), 1:213.

12. *"the one great pioneer":* Rudhyar 1926b, 899.

"The Latin reactionaries": Ibid., 900–1.

13. *"The Rise of" to "social point of view":* Rudhyar 1920, 500, 507. The Rudhyar scholar Patana Usuni has informed me that Rudhyar's name change was not legalized until 1926, when he became a citizen; hence this article was signed "Rudhyar D. Chennevière," a composite of his old and new names.

14. *With "The Relativity":* Rudhyar 1922. According to Patana Usuni, this article was written at the same time as "The Rise of the Musical Proletariat" (Rudhyar 1920); it was simply published two years later (letter to the author, 24 July 1997).

"the possibility of" to "living entit{y}": Rudhyar 1922, 108–9, 111 (Rudhyar's emphasis).

15. *"the gospel of tone":* This comes from the description for a lecture, "The Foundations of the Music to Be," that was the last of three talks by Rudhyar with the oddly antiquated title of "The New Music: Whence and Whither?" These were given in New York at the studio of Iva Krupp Bradley on three Monday evenings, March 1, 8, and 15 (probably 1926; those dates fell on Mondays in both 1920 and 1926, and the latter seems more likely), flier in Ruggles-CtY.

"deals now with": Rudhyar 1926a, 15.

"must be heard subjectively": Rudhyar 1927b, 5.

16. *"The shock of the cymbals"*: Rudhyar 1926a, 17 (Rudhyar's emphasis).

17. *"dissonant counterpoint"* to *"one of purification"*: Charles Seeger, "On Dissonant Counterpoint," *Modern Music* 7/4 (June–July 1930), 25–26.

"fusion of reason": Greer 1998, 84.

18. *"I am working now"* to *"merely another way"*: Rudhyar, letter to Ruggles, 5 March 1926, Ruggles-CtY.

"That's why I came": Rudhyar, interview with Perlis, 18 March 1970.

19. *"the common"*: Ives 1970, 35, 96.

"Notes stand as individuals": Rudhyar 1923c, 13–14.

20. *"an incantation"*: Michael Broyles, "Charles Ives and the American Democratic Tradition," *Charles Ives and His World*, ed. J. Peter Burkholder (Princeton: Princeton University Press, 1996), 125.

"That's the Negro's life": Ellington, as quoted in "Interview in Los Angeles: On *Jump for Joy*, Opera, and Dissonance as a 'Way of Life,'" reprinted in Tucker 1993, 150.

"a community of singing lines": Harrison 1946, 8.

21. Dissonant Harmony: Rudhyar 1928a. HAMSA Publications was Rudhyar's own publishing enterprise (Patana Usuni, letter to the author). The other treatise is Rudhyar 1930a.

"regeneration" to *"Dissonant music"*: Rudhyar 1928a, 10–11.

22. The New Sense of Space: Rudhyar 1930a.

"two opposite conceptions": Ibid., 4, 6.

23. *"turned back to"*: Rudhyar 1927c, 5.

"tried to start": Rudhyar, interview with Perlis.

The Rebirth of Hindu Music: Rudhyar 1928b. Rudhyar talks about the genesis of the book in his "Foreword to the Second Edition" [i.e., the reprint], also in an interview with Sheila Finch Rayner, 23 May 1975.

"never adequately": Rudhyar, "Foreword to the Second Edition," Rudhyar 1928b, vii.

24. *"be true to their souls"*: Rudhyar 1928b, 6.

25. *These are overshadowed*: *The Summons*, *The Enfoldment*, and *Release* from *Four Pentagrams* were published as *Moments* in 1930. Most of these dates come from Robert Stevenson, "Dane Rudhyar," in Hitchcock and Sadie 1986, 4: 103–4. One exception is *Paeans*, which is dated at the end of the published score: "January–March 1927, Hollywood"; Stevenson cites it as 1925. Other exceptions include dates for *Syntony No. 1*, *Four Pentagrams*, and *Syntony* (for piano); this information comes from Patana Usuni, letter to the author, 20 September 1997.

26. *"odes of joy"*: Rudhyar, "Introductory [sic]," *Three Paeans*, as published in *New Music: Quarterly of Modern Compositions* 1/2 (January 1928), [3].

27. *"tonality dies"*: Rudhyar 1927d, 5.

28. *"relentlessly harmonic"*: Straus 1995, 208.

"Rhudyar's [sic] Paeans": Elliott Carter, letter to Charles Ives, [January 1928], Ives-CtY.

"tremendously conceived": John J. Becker, review in *News-Times, South Bend* (February 1928), as quoted in *To Sow* 3/1 (Spring 1995), 26.

"powerfull [sic], intense": Chávez, letter to Rudhyar, 6[?] March 1928, Rudhyar-CSt.

"concentrated and interior": Lawrence Gilman, *New York Tribune* (28 December 1925); as quoted in *To Sow* 3/1 (1995), 26.

"power, wild joy": Rosenfeld, "Musical Chronicle," *The Dial* 79 (December 1925), 525.

CHAPTER 7

1. *"No one else speaks"*: Walton to Ruggles, 3 March 1961, Ruggles-CtY. Walton uses the spelling "exhaltation" in the original.

2. *Rudhyar published two portraits:* Rudhyar 1923c and Rudhyar 1927d.

Both of Rudhyar's articles: Seeger 1932 and Seeger, "Carl Ruggles," in Cowell 1933 (1961), 14–35. The Ruggles bibliography is by no means extensive, but Rudhyar's role in Ruggles's work has been unacknowledged within it. Jonathan D. Green states in *Carl Ruggles: A Bio-Bibliography* that Seeger's 1932 essay about Ruggles "is the first substantial article dedicated to Ruggles and his music" (Westport: Greenwood, 1995, 69). He does not even cite Rudhyar's articles. Marilyn Ziffrin briefly notes Rudhyar's article from *Eolian Review* (Ziffrin 1994, 83, 91).

"my style began": Ruggles, interview with Marilyn J. Ziffrin; cited in Ziffrin 1994, 71. Ziffrin does much to establish the importance of Seeger's relationship to Ruggles, continuing a process begun in Nicholls 1990.

3. *"The quality of sublimity":* Harrison 1946, 10.

4. *At the same time, though . . . New Masses:* Ruggles is the only composer listed on stationery for "New Masses" in 1926 (letter from the Dinner Committee of *New Masses* to Ruggles, 27 September 1926, Ruggles-CtY).

5. *"a great stimulus":* Ruggles, letter to Rudhyar, [1927], Rudhyar-CSt.

"My dear Rudhyar": Ruggles, letter to Rudhyar, 26 November [1927], Rudhyar-CSt. The program for the New Music Society concert where *Lilacs* appeared is in Mead 1981, 79.

"I think you": Rudhyar, letter to Ruggles, 26 March [1928], Ruggles-CtY.

"in which I spoke": Ruggles, letter to Rudhyar, 18 July 1928, Rudhyar-CSt.

6. *"Varèse can't pull":* Ruggles, letter to Rudhyar, 6 December 1926, Rudhyar-CSt.

7. *"Of course":* Ruggles, letter to Rudhyar, [1927].

"Ruggles is finding": Rudhyar 1927d, 3.

"neo-scholasticism" to *"{His method} produces":* Rudhyar 1927c, 5.

8. *"The finest modern":* Cowell 1925, 5.

9. *"notes stand":* Rudhyar 1923c, 13, 15.

"dissonant counterpoint": Ibid., 15.

"peculiar terminology": Seeger 1923, 16–17.

"I may have been": Rudhyar 1924b, 29.

10. *"ecstacy {sic}":* Rudhyar 1927d, 3. All the quotations in this paragraph come from the same source.

11. *"Emerson was one":* "The New Spiritual America Emerging," *Current Literature* 46 (February 1909), 180; as quoted in Linda Dalrymple Henderson, "Mysticism, Romanticism, and the Fourth Dimension," in *Spiritual* 1986, 224.

12. *"Whitmanian craze"* to *"a guide for the social":* Erkkila 1980, 176–77.

"the vital part": Pound, as quoted in ibid., 233.

13. *"an unearthly quality":* Rudhyar 1927d, 3.

"If the composer": Rudhyar, "Oriental Influence in American Music," in Cowell 1933 (1961), 185.

14. *"loveliness of the sound":* Paul Rosenfeld, "Musical Chronicle," *The Dial* 74 (February 1923), 223.

"new sense of relationship": Ruggles 1927d, 3.

15. *A three-part work:* There is a fine analysis of *Angels* in Nicholls 1990, 99.

16. *"Space is in truth":* Rudhyar 1930a, 3.

"makes a form esthetic": Ibid., 2.

"sonal energy": Ibid., 23–24.

"analytical sense" to *"a series of changing":* Ibid., 23.

"the fulness of": Ibid., 3.

17. *"apt distant glow"* and *"relative stillness":* Paul Griffiths and Marilyn J. Ziffrin, "Carl Ruggles," in Hitchcock and Sadie 1986, 4:106.

18. *Much of Ruggles's setting:* Ziffrin 1994, 86.

19. *"Ruggles very definitely":* Paul Rosenfeld, "Musical Chronicle," *The Dial* 80 (April 1926), 351.

"Jesus": Ruggles, interview with Marilyn Ziffrin, 28 January 1967, as quoted in Ziffrin 1994, 134.

20. *"majesty":* Kirkpatrick 1968, 155.

"primal simplicity": Sherrye Cohn, "Arthur Dove and Theosophy: Visions of a Transcendental Reality," *Arts Magazine* (September 1983), 86.

"monumental splendor": Kirkpatrick 1968, 157.

21. *"There are some":* Rudhyar 1920, 509.

"Dissonant music": Rudhyar 1928a, 18.

22. *"I saw Kent's exhibition":* Rudhyar, letter to Ruggles, 5 March [1926], Ruggles-CtY.

"White Thunder": Rudhyar, *White Thunder*, 1938; poem reproduced in a catalogue for The Seed Center, Palo Alto, 1974 or 1975, Rudhyar-CSt.

23. *"during our struggles":* Henrietta Straus, "Honest Antagonism," *Modern Music* 4 (January–February 1927), 8.

"ladies": Ives's embrace of a "masculine ideal" has been sympathetically analyzed by Tick 1993.

"There is a remark": Ives, letter to Jerome Goldstein, 10 October 1922, Ives-CtY.

24. *"impotent":* Edgard Varèse, lecture given at University of Southern California, Los Angeles, 1939, as quoted in Chou Wen-Chung 1966, 156.

"beautiful" to "virile-spiritual": Varèse, letter to Ruggles, [14?] November 1944, Ruggles-CtY.

25. *"curious ratio":* Seeger 1932, 589–90.

CHAPTER 8

1. *"I believe in music":* Cowell, "Credo," typescript, prepared for the program "This I Believe," 1954; Cowell-NN. I am grateful to H. Wiley Hitchcock for bringing the "Credo" to my attention; it was also quoted in Oja and Allen 1997, [2].

2. *"The Relativity":* Rudhyar 1922, 109.

"roaring pianism": Rudhyar 1926a, 16.

"new sense of tone-fulness": Rudhyar 1930a, 29.

3. *Varian introduced Cowell:* An important study of Cowell's connection to Halcyon is Johnson 1993. Halcyon's history is charted in Campbell 1980, 158–60. Its governing structure is described in Robert V. Hine, *California's Utopian Colonies* (San Marino, Calif.: The Huntington Library, 1953), 55–57.

4. *"There is a new race":* John Varian, foreword to *Tirawa* (San Diego: Troubadour, 1930); as quoted in Johnson 1993, 16.

Cowell's connection with Rudhyar: Rudhyar, interview with Clare G. Rayner, 19 May 1977, Oral History of the Arts Archive, CLobS. In an interview with Vivian Perlis, however, Rudhyar says he met Cowell in 1921 (18 March 1970, Oral History/American Music, CtY). Johnson 1993 mentions Rudhyar in passing (p. 2).

"vast beach": Rudhyar, interview with Clare G. Rayner.

"I and these people" to "Then we became": Rudhyar, interview with Vincent Plush, 24 November 1982, Oral History/American Music, CtY.

5. *"a younger man":* Rudhyar, interview with Clare G. Rayner.

6. *"quirk of history":* Mead 1981, 45–46. Program from 22 October 1925 reproduced on p. 37.

7. *"I am crazy":* Cowell, letter to Rudhyar, n.d. [ca. 1920–21], Rudhyar-CSt. These letters represent a one-sided view of Rudhyar's relationship to Cowell, since Cowell's papers, which presumably include letters from Rudhyar, are at this writing inaccessible to scholars.

"Mrs. Stevenson" was Christine: Rudhyar describes her and the Pilgrimage Play in his interview with Clare G. Rayner.

"Your most charming": Cowell, letter to Rudhyar, written from 33 Stuyvesant Street, New York City, n.d., Rudhyar-CSt.

8. *"I have just read":* Cowell, letter to Rudhyar, n.d. [1922], written from 33 Stuyvesant Street, New York, Rudhyar-CSt. Lichtenwanger dates this snippet as 1924, linking it to the wrong article by Rudhyar in the *Musical Quarterly* (Lichtenwanger 1986, 95). It should be dated 1922.

"imperilled": Rudhyar 1922, 109.

"It is the finest": Cowell, letter [1922].

9. *"The theory of Relativity":* Rudhyar 1922, 108.

"may be termed": Cowell 1930 (1996), xi.

"the possibility of": Rudhyar 1922, 108.

"A dazzling profusion": Ibid., 115–16.

"Harmonic Development": Henry Cowell and Robert L. Duffus, "Harmonic Development in Music," *The Freeman* 3/55 (30 March 1921), 63–65; 3/56 (6 April 1921), 85–87; 3/57 (13 April 1921), 111–13. Kyle Gann examines Cowell's rhythmic theories as related to over- and undertones, in: "Subversive Prophet: Henry Cowell as Theorist and Critic," in Nicholls 1997, 180–90. Undertones, of course, have no acoustical basis.

10. *"no 'true' origin":* Hicks 1993, 432.

"evidence again and again": P.G.S., "The Mystic in the Machine Age," *The Carmelite*, 21 August 1929.

11. *"programmatic mystic":* Hicks calls this same type "mystic style clusters" (Hicks 1993, 441); I am simply modifying his term to differentiate from the "abstract mystic" clusters discussed below.

"violent": Nicholls 1990, 157.

"futuristic": Hicks 1993, 441.

"the virtuoso pieces": Steven Johnson, "'Worlds of Ideas': The Music of Henry Cowell," in Nicholls 1997, 29.

12. *"separately but in a series":* Lichtenwanger describes these publications, gives a copyright date of 11 October 1922, and tells how the title must have included "Myths" for the New York concerts and then been changed to "Legends" (Lichtenwanger 1986, 90).

Included in this set: Johnson discusses *The Building of Bamba* at length (Johnson 1993, 17–19). *The Tides of Manaunaun* was performed on its own as early as 6 November 1920 in a recital at the Community House in Palo Alto (see Ray C. B. Brown, "Recital Given by California Pianist of Note," *San Francisco Chronicle*, 8 November 1920). The *Three Irish Legends* were published in *The Piano Music of Henry Cowell*, Volume 2 (New York: Associated Music Publishers, 1982). *The Tides of Manaunaun* and *The Voice of Lir* were recorded by Cowell himself for Circle records in 1952 and rereleased on Folkways in 1963; the Smithsonian reissued the disc on CD in 1993.

Cowell performed the three: There is a discrepancy in dating here, since the published score of *Voice of Lir* is dated November 1992 but Cowell performed the piece that May; perhaps the piece was in progress in May, and Cowell completed it in November.

"Mr. Cowell played": Marjory M. Fisher, "Henry Cowell Reveals Way of Playing/ Technique for Tone-Clusters and Other Innovations Demonstrated," *San Francisco News*, 30 July 1935, 15 (as quoted in Manion 1982, 215–16).

"really worth while": Redfern Mason, "Beauty Rare in Cowell's Compositions," *San Francisco Examiner,* 14 December 1922, 12 (as quoted in Manion 1982, 124–25).

"effective": "Henry Cowell," *San Francisco Examiner*, 27 April 1924, p. 12S (as quoted in Manion 1982, 148).

"Mr. Cowell is": "The Stringpiano," *Musical America* 43/15 (30 January 1926), 20.

13. *"Lir of the half tongue"*: *"The Voice of Lir*/Story according to John Varian," as published in *Piano Music of Cowell*, 2:64.

"a tone-picture": Ray C. B. Brown, "Recital Given by California Pianist of Note," *San Francisco Chronicle*, 8 November 1920, 5.

14. *"move in such fashion"*: Cowell, as quoted in Redfern Mason, "Henry Cowell Tells of Tone Clusters," *San Francisco Examiner*, 19 July 1925.

15. *"despite their exotic"*: Johnson 1993, 15.

"they seem to be": Cowell, as quoted in "World of Music," *Brooklyn Standard Union*, 24 February 1924.

16. *"Modernist music is"*: Cowell 1927, 677.

17. *"probably the most"*: "Henry Cowell/Composer-Pianist/in a Program of His Own Compositions," Palace of Fine Arts, San Francisco, 13 December [1922?], Programs-NN.

Johnson associates: Steven Johnson discusses *Dynamic Motion* at length in "'Worlds of Ideas': The Music of Henry Cowell," in Nicholls 1997, 29–32.

"table of resonance": Rudhyar 1930a, 29–30.

18. *Piece for Piano*: This work was performed by Cowell at his debut recital in London on 10 December 1923 (A. K., "Piano Played with Elbow," *London Daily News*, 11 December 1923, as cited in Manion 1982, 131).

"new lovely": Rosenfeld, Paul. "Musical Chronicle," *The Dial* 76 (April 1924), 390.

"one of his most": "Cowell Outlines Materials Used by Modernists," *Daily Palo Alto Times*, 15 May 1925, 5, as quoted in Manion 1982, 73.

19. *"Henry Cowell has invented"* to *"simple utterances"*: P.G.S., "The Mystic in the Machine Age," 3.

20. *"an impression of"*: Nicolas Slonimsky, "By Innovation Shall Hearers Recognize Him: Henry Cowell, Explorer Among Pianistic Possibilities Alights in Boston," *Boston Evening Transcript*, 9 March 1929; clipping in Slonimsky-DLC.

"His creations bring": Unnamed author and title, as quoted in Slonimsky, ibid.

21. *"ugly and meaningless"*: This is one example of the negative criticism Cowell faced (Jerome Hart, "Musical Bolshevism," *New York Times*, 30 July 1922). As discussed in Chapter 12, this is the same critic who attacked Claire Reis in response to her article: "Contemporary Music and 'the Man on the Street,'" *Eolian Review* 2/2 (March 1923).

"Certain of his works": "Henry Cowell," undated promotional brochure in which Cowell is listed as being under the "Exclusive Management of Wm. C. Gassner (The Concert Guild), Steinway Hall, New York," copy in Ives-CtY. This probably appeared around 1930 because *New Musical Resources* is advertised in it.

"imposing effect" to *"The piano seems"*: Isaac Goldberg, "Chiefly About Henry Cowell," *Disques* 2/5 (July 1931), 206–7.

22. *As for Cowell himself*: Johnson speculates about this (1993, 19–22).

23. *"forefront"*: Cowell 1927, 677.

"Dane Rudhyar . . . writes": Cowell, "Music," *The Americana Annual*, ed. A. H. McDannald (New York: Americana, 1929), 501.

24. *"For the sake"*: Cowell 1930, (1996), 138–39.

CHAPTER 9

1. *"Lightly sprinting"*: Crawford, "Lightly sprinting," untitled poem from Winter, 1928; the manuscript text was generously shared with me by Judith Tick.

"a definite": Crawford, letter to Nicolas Slonimsky, 29 January 1933, Slonimsky-DLC, as published in Neuls-Bates 1982, 304.

"worshipping": Ruth Crawford, Diary, 9 November 1928, private collection, as quoted in Tick 1991, 233–34.

"idol": Crawford to Charles Seeger, 18 January 1931, Seeger Estate, as quoted in Tick 1991, 233.

"first really": In this interview, Rudhyar went on to praise Crawford's works from the 1920s as superior to the *String Quartet* 1931, calling them less "determined" and "intentional" (as quoted in Tick 1991, 235).

2. *The event also:* Wiecki 1992, 3:748.

"vision of": Crawford, Diary, 11 November 1928, as quoted in Tick 1991, 234.

"She regarded Emerson" to *"a model for":* For more about Crawford's connection to the ideas of Whitman and the Transcendentalists see Tick 1991, 228–32. Tick's work provides the foundation on which this chapter is built.

3. *"thick resonating":* Tick 1991, 239.

4. *"hidden {spiritual} meaning":* Tick 1991, 240.

"program from" to *"distinction between":* Crawford, Diary, 29 October 1928, Seeger-DLC, as quoted in Tick 1991, 241.

5. *"To Ruth Crawford":* Charles Seeger, "Tradition and Experiment in the New Music," typescript of Version B, ca. 1930–31, Seeger-DLC. This treatise has been published in Seeger 1994.

6. *"a language of my own":* Crawford, letter to Carl Sandburg, 26 January 1931, Sandburg Collection, University of Illinois, as quoted in Tick 1991, 247.

7. *"tragic power":* Tick 1997, 215.

8. *"a kind of* Klangfarbenmelodie*":* Straus 1995, 160.

9. *"spiritual in spite":* Adolph Weiss, as quoted in Tick 1997, 222.

"evok{es} masses": Straus 1995, 159.

"heart and head": Tick 1997, 222.

"Music must flow": Crawford, letter to Vivian Fine, 1931, as quoted in ibid., 222.

"medium": Crawford, letter to Vivian Fine, 26 January 1931, personal collection of Vivian Fine, as quoted in ibid., 202.

10. "modulations of sounds": Rudhyar 1922, 112.

"continuous unfolding" to *"fluid becoming":* Rudhyar 1923a, 46.

11. *"a new type":* Rudhyar 1927d, 3.

"polyphony itself": Ibid.

"relationship between tones": Ibid.

12. *"the musical gestures":* Straus 1995, 211.

"that dissonance is": Crawford, Diary, 11 November 1928, Seeger-DLC, as quoted in Tick 1991, 234.

13. *"the concept":* Nicholls 1990, 220.

CHAPTER 10

1. *"In our humble opinion":* Marion Bauer and Flora Bauer, "Music in New York," *Musical Leader* 52 (3 February 1927), 6. This was written in response to an article by Carlos Salzedo, where he raised questions about the potential for a viable group of American composers: C. S., "Yes, We Have No—Composers!" *Eolus* 6/1 (January 1927), 26–27.

2. *"Suddenly":* D. J., "A Guild for American Composers," *Musical Digest* 2/27 (24 April 1922), 11.

"It was, indeed": Paul Rosenfeld, "Musical Chronicle," *The Dial* 67 (June 1922), 655.

In addition to: Harmati (1892–1936) emigrated to the United States in 1914 and he was among the founders of the Lenox Quartet; Haubiel (b. 1892) taught at New York University; Kramer (1890–1969) was a music critic, principally associated with *Musical America*; Morris (1890–1964) taught at Juilliard during the 1920s; Stoessel (1894–1943) helped found the music department at New York University; and Taylor (1885–1966) was a leading music critic and composer of the day.

3. *"furthering interest"*: Program, the American Music Guild, 22 and 29 April 1922, copies at DLC and NN.

4. *"I can attest"*: Bauer 1933 (1978), 285.

In fact, they: The group seems to have started out informally in the fall of 1921 and had its first publicly announced planning session in the spring of 1922 ("Music Guild Active," *Musical America* 35/2 [15 April 1922], 47).

Charles Martin Loeffler's Two Rhapsodies: These performances occurred over the entire span of concerts. For a complete listing of the American Music Guild's programs, see: McNaughton 1958, 424–28. In the appendix to the present book, music performed by the AMG is interwoven within the works performed by modern-music societies in New York during the 1920s.

5. *The AMG gave:* Information from "The American Music Guild: Announcement for the Season of 1922–1923," Programs-NN.

"bondage to Germany" to "It was the searching": Frederick Jacobi, "In Retrospect," *Modern Music* 4/2 (January–February 1927), 32–33. Other articles about Griffes included Bauer 1927, which was followed sixteen years later by Bauer 1943.

6. *"We wish to state":* "The American Music Guild: Announcement for the Season of 1922–1923," Programs-NN.

"without private patronage": D. J., "A Guild for American Composers," *Musical Digest* (24 April 1922), 11, Clippings-NN. In 1922, Jacobi tried to enlist the support of Elizabeth Sprague Coolidge for the AMG but failed. Rather than stepping in to underwrite the organization in any substantial way, she sent a check for $10 to become a "subscribing member" (Frederick Jacobi, letter to Elizabeth Sprague Coolidge, 15 October 1922; Secretary for Mrs. Coolidge, letter to Jacobi, 21 October 1922, Coolidge-DLC).

7. *"to stimulate native" to "include works":* "Compositions Published by the Composers' Music Corporation: First Annual Catalogue" (New York: Composers' Music Corporation, 1920), DLC.

The last catalog: "Complete Catalogue of Compositions" (New York: Composers' Music Corporation, 1922), DLC.

8. *"to bring forth" to "lack of confidence":* Ibid.

Whithorne served: The dates of Whithorne's tenure with the company are hard to pin down. John Tasker Howard reports that Whithorne was vice president from 1920 to 1922 (Howard 1929, 9). But Whithorne continued to use CMC stationery in 1923 (various letters from Whithorne at DLC), and in 1924 Whithorne wrote William Treat Upton about "some songs from the Composers' Music Corporation which may interest you" (letter, 26 February 1924, Upton-DLC).

9. *It was followed:* For a complete list of SPAM publications, together with a brief chronicle of its history, see Holman 1977, 50–55. Jacobi had music published by SPAM in the 1920s.

10. *"publications of leading":* Ad for the Modern Music Shop, *Little Review* 8/2 (Spring 1922), inside front cover.

11. *"one of the most":* "Jacobi's 'California' Suite Well Liked," *Musical Courier* (10 April 1919), Clippings-NN; "Contributors to this Issue [Jacobi]," *Modern Music* 5/4 (May–June 1928), [39].

"composer laureate": Henrietta Malkiel, "In the New York Manner: Emerson Whithorne, American Composer, Strives to Introduce Democracy into Music," *Musical Digest* 4/17 (14 August 1923), 15.

12. *"Les jeunes compositeurs":* Lazare Saminsky, "Les Jeunes Compositeurs Américains," *Le Monde Musical* 33/23–24 (December 1922), 428–31. Saminsky also discussed others active in the American Music Guild, including Albert Elkus, Carl Engel, Richard Hammond, A. Walter Kramer, Leo Sowerby, and Deems Taylor.

Saminsky included their music: Reviews of Saminsky's concerts: "French Critics Review American Music," *Musical Leader* 46 (4 October 1923), 322; E. F. Bauer, "Saminsky's Concert in Paris," *Musical Leader* 50 (2 July 1925), 5. Review of a concert by the Franco-American Musical Society: "American Music in Paris," *Musical Leader* 47 (8 May 1924), 435.

At the Salzburg: Emilie Frances Bauer, "New York Composers to the Fore in Europe," *Musical Leader* 45 (14 June 1923), 557.

At the festival: These ISCM performances were reported in various publications, including Alfredo Casella, "The Festival at Venice," *Modern Music* 3 (November–December 1925), 18; Louis Gruenberg, "Fourth Festival of Modern Music at Zurich," *Musical Leader* 51 (22 July 1926), 6, 18.

13. *The same was true:* Bauer's *From the New Hampshire Woods* was published in New York by G. Schirmer in 1923.

14. *Three years later:* The date of composition for *Turbulence* comes from: Marion Bauer and Flora Bauer, "Music in New York: New Quartet by Marion Bauer on Next League Program," *Musical Leader* 54 (2 February 1928), 6. See also Hisama 1996.

15. *"arbitrary":* Bauer 1933 (1978), 125.

16. *"tendencies" to "We must reflect":* Marion Bauer to Irving Schwerké, letter from Paris, 29 January 1925, Schwerké-DLC.

17. *"intensely interested":* "Frederick Jacobi," unidentified and undated program note (typescript), Clippings-NN.

"leanings toward": Bauer 1933 (1978), 174.

18. *"a series of" to "for the composer":* Frederick Jacobi, as quoted in unidentified and undated program notes for *Indian Dances* (published), Clippings-NN.

He stood close: For more information about Beach's quartet, see Block 1998, 234–42.

19. *"Those in the second":* Frederick Jacobi, [Introduction to] *String Quartet on Indian Themes* (New York: Society for the Publication of American Music and Carl Fischer, 1926).

20. *"big seller":* Emerson Whithorne, letter to William Treat Upton, 21 February 1924, Upton-DLC. After Lopez's performance of "Pell Street," Henry O. Osgood, an early American chronicler of jazz, called it the "most successful" of the composer-produced works on the program (the other two such pieces were *A Biblical Suite* by Vladimir Heifetz and *Evolution of the Blues* by W. C. Handy) (Osgood 1926, 158).

"may be mentioned": Howard 1929, 3–4.

21. *"The tumultuous chiming":* Emerson Whithorne, Epigram to "Chimes of Saint Patrick's," in *New York Days and Nights* (New York: Carl Fischer, 1922).

22. *"a block in":* Bauer 1927, 19.

23. *"The supreme function":* Louis Gruenberg, "For an American Gesture," *Modern Music* 1/2 (June 1924), 26.

24. *He studied first:* For a study of Gruenberg's life and work, see Robert Nisbett, *Louis Gruenberg: His Life and Work* (Ph.D. dissertation, Ohio State University, 1979), 12–14, 21.

Gruenberg conducted: Other Americans published by Universal during the 1920s included George Antheil, Werner Josten, Lazare Saminsky, and Alexander Steinert.

25. *"great success":* Alfredo Casella, "The Festival at Venice," *Modern Music* 3 (1925), 18.

"an early variant": Gail Levin, "'Primitivism' in American Art: Some Literary Parallels of the 1910s and 1920s," *Art Magazine* (November 1984), 102.

26. *"Emerson Whithorne was not":* Virgil Thomson, interview with the author, New York City, 29 February 1988.

CHAPTER 11

1. *"Americans of all":* Alexis de Tocqueville, *Democracy in America* (1835) (New York: Alfred A. Knopf, 1994), 2:106.

"I'm glad you made": Ruggles to Cowell, 30 July (1926), Ruggles-CtY. The emphasis here is Ruggles's.

"We are provincials": Wilson, second inaugural address, 5 March 1917; quoted in *New York Times*, 6 March 1917, 1.

2. *At first, the goal:* [E. Robert Schmitz], "Aims of Pro-Musica," *Pro-Musica Quarterly* (December 1925), 36.

"music representative": "New League to Aid Modern Composer," *Musical America* 37 (31 March 1923), 2.

"strong national bias": This comes from an important article about the League of Composers by David Metzer, in which he acknowledges the international impetus of the League's first season but sees a national emphasis as emerging soon after (Metzer 1997, 56).

3. *"There is a fundamental":* Peter Garland, "The American Experimental Tradition: A Personal Perspective," in Garland 1991, 5.

4. *"the first generation":* Straus 1995, 1.

"acceptable Europeanised": Nicholls 1990, 2.

"two rival camps": Steven E. Gilbert, "'The Ultra-Modern Idiom': A Survey of *New Music*," *Perspectives of New Music* 12/1–2 (1973–74), 284.

"While Copland": Mattis 1992, 170.

5. *"internationalization in music":* "The Franco-American Musical Society, Flyer," 1923–1924, Programs-NN. Two important accounts of the Pro Musica Society are: Perlis 1978 and Wiecki 1992. Also, Metzer 1993 provides an interesting European backdrop during the nineteenth and early twentieth centuries to these American societies (Chapter 4).

"His {Schmitz's} fight": "Virtuoso Founds American Music Library in Paris," *Chicago Tribune, Paris*, 21 December 1922 (in Pro-Musica Scrapbook, 1922–23, Schmitz-CtY).

National membership: "Membership Growth of Pro Musica," typescript itemization of membership, Schmitz-CtY.

"give equal opportunity": "The Franco-American Musical Society, Flyer," 1923–24, Programs-NN.

6. *Working toward the same goal:* "Virtuoso Founds American Music Library in Paris," *Chicago Tribune, Paris,* 21 December 1922.

7. *"Central Europe":* Schmitz to Alban Berg, no date [1925], Schmitz-CtY. Wiecki 1992 (p. 151) dates this as 13 March 1925.

8. *In 1923, the ICG:* The manifesto of the ICG is printed in Varèse 1972, 166–67. Information about international affiliates is found in Lott 1983, 269. Lott provides the first survey of the ICG's activities, which was built upon in Metzer 1993.

9. *"Since 1921":* International Composers' Guild, flyer for 1923–24 season, Ruggles-CtY.

In fact, such works: These percentages are based on the number of compositions performed, not on the total number of composers (i.e., many composers had more than one work performed and all those pieces are tallied individually). See Lott 1983, 282–86, for a complete list of ICG programs.

10. *On the whole:* These observations assume Varèse to have been the chief decision-maker for the ICG, and there is ample evidence that this was so. At various points during the ICG's existence, Varèse was accused by his contemporaries of being a "dictator"; Ruggles went so far as to condemn his "Mussolini stuff," as already recounted (Ruggles, letter to Rudhyar, 6 December 1926, Rudhyar-CSt).

11. *Antheil's* Ballet Mécanique: Antheil, letter to Stanley Hart, 1 September 1925 from Africa, Antheil-DLC.

12. *"satisfaction":* Edgard Varèse, Letter to the Editor, *Eolus* 7/1 (January 1928), 31–32; as quoted in Lott 1983, 279–80.

It was a disingenuous: Lott, interview with Louise Varèse, 6 July 1982; as cited in Lott 1983, 280.

"routine like": Varèse, letter to Ruggles, 28 March 1927, Ruggles-CtY.

13. *There were administrative:* This issue is explored more fully in Chapter 12.

"one forward-looking": Copland, "New Music in the U.S.A.," in Copland 1941 (1968), 103.

"The competition between": Copland and Perlis 1984, 117.

14. *"effect co-operation":* League of Composers, 1923–24 pamphlet, NN.

"present new and": "Brilliant Opening for League of Composers," *Musical Leader* (15 November 1923), 459.

"The League of Composers . . . had": Claire Reis, videotaped interview with Vivian Perlis, 9 July 1977, Oral History/American Music, CtY.

15. *The ICG began in:* Carlos Salzedo commented on the difference this new venue made in the size of the audience, writing in 1926 that in five years, the ICG audience had "widened from the handful that came to hear the first concerts of modern music in 1921 to the fourteen hundred who packed Aeolian Hall last February to listen to Stravinsky's *Les Noces*" ("Outward Shows," *Eolus* 5/2 [May 1926]. 5).

Those for the ICG: Carl Ruggles heard the Schoenberg *Serenade* on 1 March 1925 and wrote Henry Cowell about it afterward: "The Schönberg composition was far and away the best thing on the program. The first movement was absurdly trivial and thin, with its miserable, stinking little mandolin strumming away. Really it was pitiful. But lo! the next movement, slow and full of a melting lyricism, was beautiful. The work as a whole, however, was not the Schönberg of either the Orchestral Pieces or Pierrot" (16 March 1925, Ruggles-CtY).

16. *In 1929 it produced:* A tradition was taking shape of having composers perform this. When the ICG gave a concert presentation of the work on 14 February 1926, the pianists were Germaine Tailleferre, Alfredo Casella, Georges Enesco, and Carlos Salzedo. That June, another group of composers performed at a production of *Les Noces* in London: Georges Auric, Francis Poulenc, Vittorio Rieti, and Vladimir Dukelsky.

17. *The League's 1928:* This and the following information about Stravinsky performances come from two sources: *Stravinsky and the Dance* 1962, and Schouvaloff and Borovsky 1982.

18. *"Stravinsky, Picasso":* Lederman 1983, 9.

"the next number": "A New Publication," *Musical Courier* (14 February 1924), 38.

For various reasons, I did not focus on Minna Lederman in this book to the extent that I might have. In the years ahead, I plan to compile a volume of her unpublished writings, together with an extended biographical introduction.

19. *During its first year:* Program, League of Composers, 10 February 1924. This and all the programs listed below are in the archives of the League of Composers-NN. A listing of League programs from the 1920s appears in Metzer 1997, 59–66.

20. *According to Copland:* Copland and Perlis 1984, 101.

21. *"the Intimate study":* Announcement for the Intimate Gallery, 7 December 1925, Sheldon Cheney Papers, Archives of American Art, Washington, D.C., as quoted in Platt 1985, 15.

22. *"affiliated with":* Flyer reproduced in Mead 1981, 32. Much of the information here about the New Music enterprise is drawn from Mead's pioneering study.

"had developed theories" to "a reincarnation of": Ibid., 42.

23. *To be sure, works:* Cowell wrote Ives to ask his opinion about publishing the Schoenberg work, worrying over whether or not he should pay the fee of $100 that Schoenberg had requested: "The fee is very low, as such things go. Stravinsky would charge $5000! Still, I hate to pay for material from Europe, while I am forced to offer nothing to most of the men who write for us" (Cowell, letter to Charles Ives, 13 July 1931, Ives-CtY).

"the modern American": Mead 1981, 62.

24. *"developed indigenous"*: Henry Cowell, "Trends in American Music," in Cowell 1933 (1961), 3.

"It would be very": Henry Cowell, letter to Irving Schwerké, 7 September 1927, written from California, Schwerké-DLC.

During New Music's *first*: Rita Mead counted 600 subscribers; Cowell himself claimed it to be 700 (Mead 1981, 65–70).

25. *"exclusively {to} composers"* to *"that {its performances}"*: Manifesto, Pan American Association of Composers, February 1928, as quoted in Root 1972, 50–51. The remaining quotations from the manifesto, as given in this paragraph, come from the same source.

26. *"I regret to say"*: Cowell, letter to Ives, from Menlo Park, California, 24 November 1928, Ives-CtY.

"not take": Seeger, letter to Ruggles, 3 March, no year; Ruggles-CtY.

"a motley crew": Isaac Goldberg, "Nicolas Slonimsky and the New American Composers," *Disques* 3/5 (July 1932), 202.

27. *Beginning in 1931*: These programs are given in full in Root 1972, 62–66.

28. *"You gave me"*: Cowell, letter to Ives, from Menlo Park, California, 24 November 1928, Ives-CtY.

Ives went on: Root 1972, 55.

29. *"a usable past"*: This phrase recurred frequently in the 1920s and is first attributed to Brooks 1918, 337.

"Charles E. Ives is": Cowell, "Charles E. Ives," in Cowell 1933 (1961), 128.

30. *Long seen as*: I interpret the aesthetic orientation of the Copland-Sessions Concerts differently from when I published an article about the series some twenty years ago; there I highlighted its ties to Boulanger. See Oja 1979.

31. *In June 1927*: Henry Cowell, "How Young Hungary Expresses Individuality," *Musical America* 46/7 (4 June 1927), 11.

"a week of modern": Cowell, "Music," *The Americana Annual: An Encyclopedia of Current Events* (1928), 544.

32. *It paralleled*: The history of Cos Cob Press is discussed in Chapter 12.

33. *"combat"*: Varèse, as quoted in Michael Sperling, "Varèse and Contemporary Music," *Trend* 2/3 (May–June 1934), 126.

"We had rejected": Wallingford Riegger, "To the New Through the Old," *Magazine of Art* 32 (August 1939), 491–92; as quoted in Rossiter 1975, 218.

34. *There were isolated*: The New World String Quartet included Ivor Karmon and Raphael Galindo, violinists; Egon Kornstein, viola; Lucien Kirsch, cello.

"three talks on": Announcement card, Ruggles-CtY.

"written out carefully" to *"did not deter"*: Henry Cowell, "Carl Ruggles," in Harrison 1946, 2–3.

"Open Forum": Postcard announcing "Open Forum . . . December 14 . . . Modernism in Music . . . The Society for Ethical Culture," postmarked 1924, mailed from Cowell to Ruggles, Ruggles-CtY.

35. *"arranged"*: Programs for these concerts are in program files for the New School at NN.

36. *The New York Philharmonic*: Archives of the New York Philharmonic, [List of performances of American composers], typescript, 1993.

The role of performing: These are all cited in a list of "Various First Performances" in Daniel 1982, 1040–50.

37. *"a thoroughly co-operative"*: "American Symphonic Ensemble: A Symphony Orchestra without Conductor; announces a Series of Three Concerts" [1928–29]; flyer in Clippings-NN.

"The interpretation": "Conductorless Symphony Orchestra: Second Year/1929—Season—1930," Clippings-NN.

"radical Russia": Henry Cowell, "Conservative Music in Radical Russia," *New Republic* 59 (14 August 1929), 340.

38. *"Committee on"* to *"to play one"*: "Conductorless Symphony Orchestra: Second Year." *It managed: Portals* is listed on the 1929–30 concert flyer for the Conductorless Orchestra, and Cowell reports on his concert in a letter to Ives (15 October 1929, Ives-CtY). Specific information about the latter event is included in Lichtenwanger 1986, 118.

"Mr. Hazard very": Adolph Weiss, letter to Ruggles, 16 September 1929, Ruggles-CtY.

CHAPTER 12

1. *"It was not that"*: E. M. Forster, *A Room with a View* (1908) (New York: Alfred A. Knopf, 1923), 67.

"I do not think": Damrosch 1923, 323.

While Damrosch: An earlier version of this essay was published as Oja 1997.

2. *Minna Lederman was:* See Lederman's chronicle of *Modern Music* (Lederman 1983), and my own obituary for her, "The Mother of Them All: Remembering Minna Lederman," *Institute for Studies in American Music Newsletter* 25/2 (spring 1996), 1–2, 14.

3. *"If you want"*: George Antheil to Mary Louise Curtis Bok, 7 July 1925, written from Paris, Antheil-DLC.

4. *Women, more than men:* There were also a few male patrons supporting new music during the 1920s, most notably Ives.

In Paris, the Princesse: See Jeanice Brooks, "Nadia Boulanger and the Salon of the Princesse de Polignac," *Journal of the American Musicological Society* 46/3 (fall 1993), 415–68.

"A striking characteristic": Gilbert and Gubar 1988, 147.

"feminized": Brown 1987, 151.

"like tithing": Lederman, interview with author, 3 March 1988.

5. *In music, most:* One of the few studies of music patronage in America is unpublished: Richard Crawford, "Professions and Patronage: American Musical Economics," typescript, n.d. Material from it is incorporated in Chapter 2 of Crawford 1993.

6. *Things began changing:* See Barr 1998.

7. *"executive committee"*: Program, The New Symphony Orchestra, April 1919, Program Collection-NN. The other three women were Mrs. Newbold LeRoy Edgar, Mrs. Charles S. (Minnie) Guggenheimer, and Miss Anne Shingleur (Secretary).

"one of the principal": Varèse 1972, 154.

Whitney not only: Information about the location of the ICG's offices comes from Mattis 1992, 149.

8. *"the inchoate sense"*: Scott 1984, 127.

"Private Means": Paul Delany, "Who Paid for Modernism?" in *New Economic Criticism*, eds. Martha Woodmansee and Mark Osteen (London: Routledge, 1997), 2.

"I pity": Friedman 1978, 181.

9. *Details about Whitney's:* The most informative sources about Whitney's patronage of composers include Varèse 1972, 153–55 and 259; Friedman 1978, 387, 405; and Mattis 1992, 149–58.

"an adequate allowance" to *"by practically"*: Varèse 1972, 155, 172.

"No one will ever": Sloan, as quoted in *Juliana Force and American Art: A Memorial Exhibition, September 24–October 30, 1949* (New York: Whitney Museum of American Art, 1949), 35–36. Whitney's contribution as art patron is evaluated in Roberta K. Tarbell, "Gertrude Vanderbilt Whitney as Patron," in Patricia Hills and Roberta K. Tarbell, eds., *The Figurative Tradition and the Whitney Museum of American Art* (New York: Whitney Museum of American Art, 1980), 11–22, 171–72.

10. *She was an amateur:* "Mrs. A. M. Wertheim Architect's Bride," *New York Times,* 25 January 1934; "Mrs. Morgenthau, A Patron of Arts," *New York Times,* 26 December 1953.

11. *A child of Jewish:* Another of the Guild's patrons was Mrs. Christian Holmes, born Betti Fleischmann and heir to the yeast fortune, who came to New York from Cincinnati around 1920.

"Alma Morgenthau Wertheim was giving": Claire Reis, interview with Vivian Perlis, 29 January 1976, Oral History/American Music, CtY. All the quotations from Reis that follow come from either this interview or one on 5 February 1976.

In 1922, Wertheim: Alma Wertheim, "World-Wide Guild of Composers," *New York Times*, 26 November 1922.

12. *Wertheim also subsidized:* Minna Lederman, interview with author, 1 April 1989; Claire Reis, in an interview with Perlis, recalled the sum as $2,000/year.

13. *"a very special figure":* Lederman, letter to author, 17 July 1988.

"left the League": Ibid.

"The Alma Morgenthau chapter": Hilda Reis Bijur, interview with author, 16 November 1990.

14. *"I don't know how":* Copland and Perlis 1984, 112.

She presented Roy: Ibid., 129.

cash stipends to Israel Citkowitz: Copland wrote to Nadia Boulanger on 19 December 1927, "Mrs. Wertheim gave me $100 for Israel" (Copland-DLC).

15. *Ultimately the most:* More about Wertheim and her support of Cos Cob Press can be found in Oja 1988.

"under consideration": Olin Downes: "Old and Modern Revolutionaries," *New York Times*, 29 May 1927.

"There is a growing": "Cos Cob Press Is Launched," *Musical America* 49/7 (25 February 1929), 53.

A similar announcement: "The Cos Cob Press," *New York Times*, 17 February 1929.

16. *When Wertheim incorporated:* Herbert A. Cone, "Estate Alma Morgenthau—Cos Cob Press, Inc" [Memorandum], typescript, 28 March 1955, Copland-DLC.

For example, Nancy Cunard: For a discussion of women publishers see Shari Benstock, *Women of the Left Bank: Paris, 1900–1940* (Austin: University of Texas Press, 1986).

17. *The Morgenthau Archive:* A family history of the Morgenthaus continues a focus on males, with a brief segment about Alma. Noting that Henry Morgenthau Jr. had "real talent" as a singer, his son wrote that "a musical career was the last thing in the world [his father] had in mind for his only son. Music was all right, though, for the girls. Alma, one of my father's three sisters, trained her voice to the edge of professionalism; later she became a discriminating and demanding patron of avant garde composers like Arnold Schoenberg and Aaron Copland" (Henry Morgenthau III, *Mostly Morgenthaus: A Family History* [New York: Ticknor & Fields, 1991], 240).

Even though one: Barbara Tuchman, letter to author, 11 December 1987; Anne W. Werner, interview with author, 21 February 1988.

Most of the remaining: The papers for the League of Composers are at NN; those for Cos Cob Press are largely contained in Copland-DLC.

18. *"Keep on":* Ruggles to Walton, 7 February 1928, Walton-NN.

19. *"a pianist of professional":* Cowell, "Program Note" for a concert honoring Blanche Walton, given at the New School for Social Research, 12 April 1959; typescript copy in the collection of Mildred Baker (sister of the composer Adolph Weiss), New York City. Other basic biographical information for Walton can be found in: Richard Jackson, "Blanche Wetherill Walton," in Hitchcock and Sadie 1986, 4:474.

Instead, after losing: This and other biographical information here came from Marion Walton Putnam (Walton's daughter), interview with author, 19 April 1989, New York City.

"The one contribution": Walton, "Only a Sketch," manuscript fragment of a memoir, n.d., Walton-NN.

20. *"We appreciate so much":* Varèse, letter to Walton, 8 December 1924, Walton-NN.

"How I wish I might": Mrs. Edward MacDowell, letter to Walton, 15[?] September 1916, Walton-NN. This musicale is discussed by Judith Tick, "Ruth Crawford Seeger—A Modernist Pioneer," in Tick and Schneider 1993, xxii–xxiii.

She also hosted: "The Founding of the Society," *AMS Bulletin* 1 (1936): 1.

21. *Sometime in 1929:* Copland to Walton, "Wed," no date, Walton-NN.

This last was: Copland, party list now attached to an undated letter, "Monday," Walton-NN.

"Don't I wish": Walton, letter to Ruth Crawford, 29 December 1930, private collection.

22. *"During the crash":* Putnam, interview with author.

23. *"one of the most":* Henry Cowell, "Program Note" for a concert honoring Blanche Walton.

24. *"self-effacing":* Varèse 1972, 153.

25. *"luminous, nourishing":* Waldo Frank, letter to Claire Reis, 21 September 1956, Reis-NN.

26. *She shared progressive:* Platt discusses Katherine Dreir (1985, 8–9, 11).

27. *While Reis later claimed:* Reis discussed her potential for a concert career as part of the same series of interviews conducted by Vivian Perlis that is quoted earlier in this chapter; this one took place on 21 January 1976. Tapes and a transcript are housed in Oral History/American Music-CtY. This is an invaluable source, with the transcript running to some 300 pages.

"playing for charity": Reis, "Outline," undated typescript autobiographical statement, Reis-NN (Box 1). Reis's obituary also provides some biographical information: "Claire Raphael Reis Dies at 89; Leader in New York Cultural Life," *New York Times*, 13 April 1978.

Reis later recalled: Reis, interview with Perlis, 21 January 1976.

"The long room": Waldo Frank, *Memoirs of Waldo Frank*, edited by Alan Trachtenberg, introduction by Lewis Mumford (Amherst: University of Massachusetts Press, 1973, 65). Since Frank describes Ornstein as "just back from overseas successes," 1914 is a likely year for this event (undated by Frank); Ornstein had just returned to New York then after a highly acclaimed recital in London.

There were other connections between Frank and Reis. His first wife was Margaret Naumburg, with whom Reis started the Walden School, and Reis's husband Arthur, whom she married in 1915, was business adviser to Frank's little magazine, *The Seven Arts*, which ran from 1916 to 1917. Arthur Reis was president of Robert Reis and Company, a firm established by his father that manufactured men's underwear.

28. *"was really the beginning":* Reis, interview with Perlis, 21 January 1976.

"Four Informal Recitals": Programs for the recitals are in Reis-NN.

"giving a comprehensive" to "The point is": Paul Rosenfeld to Claire Reis, 16 August 1915, Reis-NN.

29. *In 1911, she fulfilled:* Reis, undated typescript resume; another resume, dated 6 January 1952, describes the People's Music League as founded "for the purpose of giving good music to the masses." Both in Reis-NN.

Reis's involvement: Wertheim's name turns up in "Music for the People," a pamphlet from around 1913, Reis-NN.

"first satisfying experience": Reis, "Outline," undated typescript autobiographical statement, Reis-NN.

The concerts included: Music by Buck and Cook appeared at "Special Concert under the Auspices of the Hudson Park Social Centre and the People's Music League . . . at Public School No. 95," February 17 [no year]; Gauthier and Torpadie are listed in a flyer, "Fifteen Concerts Given by the People's Music League," no date; both Reis-NN.

Bands and orchestras: Listed in a pamphlet, "Music for the People," probably published in 1913, Reis-NN.

30. *For the tenth anniversary:* Program in Reis-NN.

"My reputation": Reis, "Outline" (Reis's emphasis).

31. *Her success with:* Varèse 1972, 177.

"the folding": Ibid., 185.

32. *"took over":* Ibid., 177.

"those delicatessen parties": Edgard Varèse, as quoted in ibid., 186.

In part, he might: This has come up repeatedly, as when Olivia Mattis writes that "anti-semitism [*sic*] was . . . undoubtedly the true reason for the secession from the ICG of the Jewish composers who founded the League of Composers" (Mattis 1992, 175–76).

The bigotry of: Ruggles's biographer Marilyn Ziffrin refers generally to "Carl's anti-Semitism," suggesting that it was so well known as to require no explanation (Ziffrin 1994, 195) (Ruggles's emphasis).

"I agree with": Ruggles, letter to Cowell, 21 June 1933, Ruggles-CtY, as quoted in Mattis 1992, 176.

"How you will shine": Cowell, letter to Ruggles, 5 December 1931, Ruggles-CtY; the concert is mentioned in Copland and Perlis 1984, 190.

"League of Jewish Composers": Virgil Thomson, interview with author, 29 February 1988.

33. *"No, I definitely":* Reis, interview with Perlis, 29 January 1976.

Yet when I later: Lederman, interview with author, 21 June 1991.

34. *"great disorder":* Reis, interview with Perlis, 29 January 1976.

"People like Ruggles": Reis, "Notes Added to Music," undated typescript, Reis-NN.

"so-called musically": Reis 1923, 24, 27 (Reis's emphasis).

35. *"Of course, this":* Jerome Hart, "Modern Music: Its Appreciators and Depreciators," *The Sackbut* 4/4 (November 1923): 102. Hart was a frequent contributor to *The Freeman*, a journal for which Daniel Gregory Mason also wrote. When he earlier called Cowell's clusters "ugly and meaningless noises," Hart also dubbed the composer a "Bolshevik," suggesting that his opinions were as much anti-modernist as anti-female (Jerome Hart, "Musical Bolshevism," *New York Times*, 30 July 1922).

36. *"dictator":* Reis, interview with Vivian Perlis, 29 January 1976.

37. *"a pro":* Copland 1978, 387.

Proud to have: Hilda Reis Bijur, interview with author, 16 November 1990, New York City. It is important to note that suffragists were not necessarily feminists.

"to win the power": Brown 1987, 34.

"In those days": Reis, interview with Vivian Perlis, 21 January 1976.

38. *Also striking:* Reis discussed her connection with the Women's City Club in an interview with Perlis, 6 May 1977. The Women's City Club remained active throughout the century; through it the mission of social feminism lived on. A 1990 pamphlet described the group as "an activist organization," which focused on issues such as dropout prevention in the schools, nuclear waste disposal, family planning and abortion rights, maternal and child health issues, and "sex equity for women in all walks of life."

More immediately germane: See Shanet 1975, 207–8, 245.

"I never felt": Reis, interview with Vivian Perlis, 3 March 1976.

Each of the thirty-five: The involvement of the Countess Mercati (that is, in an earlier marriage where she was known as Mrs. Newbold Le Roy Edgar) and Mrs. Charles Guggenheimer in the ICG is cited in Varèse 1972, 140.

Mrs. Charles (Minnie) Guggenheimer: Sophie Guggenheimer Untermeyer and Alix Williamson, *Mother Is Music* (New York: Doubleday, 1960).

39. *"We were keenly":* Reis 1955 (1974), 73.

40. *"the ladies":* Lederman, interview with author, 1 April 1989.

"large Ladies' Committee": Varèse 1972, 140.

41. *Among Reis's many other achievements:* Reis 1930.

Two years later: Reis 1932.

Subsequent editions: Reis 1938 and Reis 1947.

42. *"We thought":* Lederman, stated in a private conversation with the author.

Copland and Cowell: Copland 1978 and Cowell, "Program Note," typescript version, 1959.

43. *"one of the innumerable" to "But in our civilization":* Rosenfeld, "Musical Chronicle: The New, or National, Symphony Orchestra," *The Dial* 69 (December 1920), 670.

44. *"not like":* Willa Cather, "Introduction," *My Ántonia* (Boston: Houghton Mifflin, 1918), [ii].

45. *"Women," wrote Taylor:* Deems Taylor, "Music," in Stearns 1922 (1971), 205–6.

46. *"a social function":* Paul Rosenfeld, "Thanks to the International Guild: A Musical Chronicle," in Rosenfeld 1928, 14.

"a rather good-humored": "Modern Music Guilds and Their Messages," *Christian Science Monitor* (15 May 1926), 16.

"a dues paying": Jerome Moross to Catherine Smith, 20 July 1981; quoted with the permission of Catherine Smith. Connections between misogyny and modernist music are explored in Smith 1994.

47. *"The Modern Music Jag":* W. J. Henderson, "The Modern Music Jag," *New Yorker* (21 February 1926), 21.

"Mrs. Bartow Blodgett": *Vanity Fair* 31 (February 1929), 54.

48. *"manliness complex":* Editorial, "Music and Manliness," *Musical America* (2 February 1924), 20; as cited by DuPree 1983, 311–12.

"It was true": Sherwood Anderson, *Dark Laughter* (New York: Boni and Liveright, 1925), 55.

"I know I am": Gruenberg, letter to Reis, 1 December 1951, Reis-NN. This comment was as much an outcry against McCarthyism as it was against homosexuals.

49. *"But there is":* Irving Weil, "The Wizardry of Toscanini and the Latest from America," *Musical America* (10 March 1929), 53.

"Perhaps its chief lack": Oscar Thompson, "Modern American Life Symbolized in 'Skyscrapers,'" *Musical America* 43/19 (27 February 1926), 5.

"Loeffler is": Paul Rosenfeld, "Charles Martin Loeffler," *The Dial* 68 (January 1920), 27, 32.

50. *"It is indeed striking":* Huyssen 1986, 47.

"the 'wrong'": Ibid., 53.

51. *"Yes, we want our":* Nicolas Slonimsky, "The Patient, the Doctors, the Verdicts," *Boston Globe*, undated clipping (probably January, 1929), Slonimsky-DLC. This was a review of Rosenfeld 1929.

"I pride myself": Antheil, letter to Stanley Hart, [9 March? 1925], Antheil-DLC.

52. *"To be virile":* Bok, letter to Antheil, 1 August 1930, Antheil-DLC.

53. *"silly":* Lederman, interview with author, 23 July 1987.

CHAPTER 13

1. *"Back to Principles!":* Rudhyar 1927a, 14–15.

"Labels in art": Ives 1972, 78.

2. *"International Style":* In 1931, Philip Johnson and Henry-Russell Hitchcock organized an exhibit titled "The International Style: Architecture Since 1922" at the Museum of Modern Art. In an accompanying book, the art historian Alfred H. Barr Jr.

defined "distinguishing aesthetic principles of the International Style," which bear striking parallels to those of neoclassical music: "emphasis upon volume—space enclosed by thin planes or surfaces as opposed to the suggestion of mass and solidity" and "dependence upon the intrinsic elegance of materials, technical perfection, and fine proportions, as opposed to applied ornament" (Barr, "Preface" to Henry-Russell Hitchcock and Philip Johnson, *The International Style: Architecture Since 1922* [New York: W. W. Norton, 1932; reprinted with a new foreword by Henry-Russell Hitchcock, New York: Norton, 1966], 13).

3. *"purity"*: This observation recurs throughout letters and published writings by Boulanger's pupils of the twenties. Two examples are a letter from Harris to Copland (8 December 1926, Copland-DLC) and an article about Copland by Kirkpatrick in the *Fontainebleau Alumni Bulletin* (Kirkpatrick 1928, 1).

"never singled out": Copland 1930, 1.

4. *"It is a strictly"*: Rudhyar 1927a, 12.

"curiosity": Henry Cowell, "Roy Harris, An American Composer," *The Sackbut* (April 1932), 134.

"neo-Romanticism": Charles Seeger, "Ruth Crawford," in Cowell 1933 (1961), 114.

"neo-classical ideal": Varèse, letter to José Rodriguez, written from Paris, 1 March 1933, as quoted in Mattis 1992, 174.

5. *"for every cautionary"*: Messing 1988, xiii. Much of the discussion of European neoclassicism that follows is indebted to Messing's work.

6. *According to Messing:* Boris de Schloezer, "La Musique," *La Revue contemporaine* (1 February 1923), 245–48, as translated in Messing 1988, 129–30.

"simplicity," "clarity": These terms were commonly associated with neoclassicism in literature from the 1920s (Messing 1988, xiv).

"new impersonal approach": Aaron Copland, "Stravinsky's 'Oedipus Rex,'" *New Republic* (29 February 1928), 69.

"a new classic art": Ferruccio Busoni, "Gedanken zu einer 'Neuen Klassizität,'" *Musica Viva* (October 1936), 27–28, as quoted in Messing 1988, 65–66.

"l'esprit nouveau": Guillaume Apollinaire, *Oeuvres complètes*, ed. Michel Décaudin, 4 vols. (Paris: Balland and Lecat, 1965–66), 3:900. "L'esprit nouveau et les poètes" was given as a lecture on 26 November 1917 and appeared in *Mercure de France*, December 1918 (Messing 1988, 77, 172).

"geometric principles": Gino Severini, *Du cubisme au classicisme* (Paris: Povolovsky, 1921), as paraphrased in Messing 1988, 80.

"nothing less than": Kenneth E. Silver, *Esprit de corps: The Art of the Parisian Avant-Garde and the First World War, 1914–25* (Princeton: Princeton University Press, 1989), 11.

7. *"Tendencies—?"*: Quincy Porter, letter to Irving Schwerké, 18 February [ca. 1930], from Paris, Schwerké-DLC.

"avoid neo-classicism": Roy Harris, letter to Aaron Copland, May 1928, written on stationery from Café Terminus in Paris, Copland-DLC.

"I subscribed to": Roy Harris, "Perspective at Forty," *Magazine of Art* 32/11 (November 1939), 668, as quoted in Stehman 1984, 20.

8. *"was never neat"*: Dickran Tashjian, "American Dada Against Surrealism: Matthew Josephson," in Kuenzli 1986, 48–49.

9. *"accepted an artistic"*: Copland, "The Composer in Industrial America," in Copland 1952 (1959), 109.

"We have inherited": Ibid., 101.

10. *"the younger generation"*: "The Copland-Sessions Concerts of Contemporary Music," printed in the program for the first concert, 22 April 1928, Programs-NN.

"honestly conceived": Julian Seaman, "Copland Sees Hope in Trend of Moderns," November 1929; clipping in "Modern Music Press Book," Modern Music-DLC.

CHAPTER 14

1. *"Charles can no longer"*: Margaret Drabble, *A Natural Curiosity* (New York: Viking, 1989), 176.

2. *"aggressively American"*: Gorham B. Munson, "The Skyscraper Primitives," *The Guardian* 1/5 (March 1925), 169. Coady's venture was in fact the second incarnation of a journal titled *The Soil*.

"An Internationalist is" to *"Internationalism cannot be"*: Robert Coady, from a pamphlet prepared for the American Tradition League, quoted in ibid., 174.

3. *"felt 'at home'"*: Aaron Copland, "Rubin Goldmark: A Tribute," *Juilliard Review* 3/3 (fall 1956), 15–16.

"Suppose that one": "Comment," *The Dial* 74 (March 1923), 316. Information about Copland subscribing to the *Dial* appears in Copland and Perlis 1984, 44.

4. *Rather than seeking*: Legend has it that Copland was Boulanger's first American pupil, but in fact Marion Bauer preceded him, although as a pupil of theory and counterpoint. Bauer herself credits Copland as Boulanger's "first student of composition" (Marion Bauer, "Aaron Copland: A Significant Personality in American Music," *American Music Lover* 4/12 [April 1939], 428).

"faith in the future": Copland 1930, 1. Howard Pollack discusses Boulanger's informal Wednesday-afternoon classes as an "opportunity to meet or at least observe Stravinsky, Milhaud, Poulenc, Roussel, Ravel, Villa-Lobos, and even the ancient Saint-Saëns" (Pollack 1998, 47–48).

5. *"grouped without impertinence"*: Rosenfeld 1929, 26.

"No American not yet": Paul Rosenfeld, "Musical Chronicle," *The Dial* 78 (March 1925), 258–59. Wescott was an American writer of Copland's generation, especially well known for his *Goodbye, Wisconsin* of 1928. Pollack sees Copland's relationship to Rosenfeld quite differently than I do, stating that the critic "expressed reservations about Copland's music, perhaps no more than his wont, but more than in the case of Varèse, Chávez, or Ives"; he goes on to describe how "the gulf between the two widened in the course of the 1930s" (Pollack 1998, 99).

6. *"I reported on"*: Copland and Perlis 1984, 90. Copland's longtime assistant David Walker also compiled a list, "Trips Made—Chronological Record," Copland-DLC.

He was at the Zurich: Copland 1926; Copland 1927; Copland 1931–32.

7. *"curious and unique"*: Copland, "Gabriel Fauré, A Neglected Master," *Musical Quarterly* 10/4 (October 1924), 573.

According to John: Rondino information in Kirkpatrick 1928, [2].

"quite justified": Copland, "Defends the Music of Mahler," *New York Times*, 5 April 1925.

8. *"As time goes on"* to *"musical dictation"*: Copland, "What Europe Means to the Aspiring Composer," *Musical America* 41/11 (3 January 1925), 15.

Five years later: Copland 1930, 1.

9. *"fascinating diversion"*: Copland, "America's Young Men of Promise," *Modern Music* 3/3 (March–April 1926), 13, 20.

Modeled perhaps: Malcolm Cowley, "'This Youngest Generation,'" *Literary Review of the New York Evening Post* (15 October 1921), 81–82. Copland's sequels to "America's Young Men of Promise" were: "The Composer in America, 1923–1933," *Modern Music* 10 (January– February 1933), 87–92; and "Our Younger Generation—Ten Years Later," *Modern Music* 13 (May–June 1936), 3–11.

10. *"regarded by most"*: "Contributors to this Issue," *Modern Music* 6 (January–February 1929), [43].

11. *"Aaron's view"*: Virgil Thomson, interview with the author, Chelsea Hotel, 29 February 1988.

"God bless": Harris, letter to Copland, 1928, Copland-DLC.

There were many: Oja 1988.

12. "current European fashion": Copland 1930, 1.

"All you wrote": Copland, letter to Carlos Chávez, 26 December [1931?], Copland-DLC.

13. "cultural sense": Messing 1998.

"economy of means" to "mere imitator": Berger 1934, 85.

14. "thumbnail" to "preoccupied with form": Marc Blitzstein, "New Music: A Thumbnail History," typescript, p. 5; Blitzstein-WHi.

15. "excellent specimens": Kirkpatrick 1928, 1.

"thrifty to the point": Blitzstein 1929, 165.

Other works showed: See also Pollack's discussion of Copland's Short Symphony (1931–33) as "neoclassical" (Pollack 1998, 289).

16. "But it is not": Copland 1927, 32.

"Modern music is no longer": Copland 1928, 17, 19.

17. "Self-expression": Jane Heap, "Lost: A Renaissance," Little Review 12/2 (May 1929), 6.

"The high modernists": Berman 1994, 64.

18. "I am anxious": Copland, in a small black book, written in ink in Copland's hand and stored in a folder labeled, "Diary (Poems & Philosophy) 1927–1959," p. 3, Copland-DLC.

19. "borrow from": Messing 1988, xiv.

"tons" to "began by playing": Gerald Sykes, interview with Vivian Perlis, as quoted in Copland and Perlis 1984, 173.

20. "eclecticism": Thomson 1932, 71.

"materials added": Copland 1928, 17, 19.

21. "in my own way": Copland and Perlis 1984, 182.

Copland's knowledge: Thanks to Glenn Watkins for making this point about Opus 11.

As Arthur Berger demonstrated: Berger 1953, 45–47.

"toward discipline": Blitzstein, "New Music: A Thumbnail History," p. 5.

22. "incisive rhythms": Copland 1927, 33. Berger picked up the Bartók connection, which he mentioned in passing, saying that "Copland showed himself devoted" to Bartók "in some lectures given at the New School for Social Research, during the period when the Variations were written" (Berger 1953, 43).

"a super-sensitive": Copland 1926, 29. In a letter to Israel Citkowitz, written right after the Zurich festival, Copland told him that "there was only one composition [in Zurich] that you should have heard . . . Anton Webern's Five Orchestral Pieces. The orchestral sonorities he manages to get are magical, nothing less" (Copland to Citkowitz, 12 July 1926, written from France, Copland-DLC).

23. "stem{med} directly": Blitzstein, "New Music: A Thumbnail History," 5.

"affinity": Berger 1934, 85.

Later, he zeroed: Berger 1953, 44.

24. He reviewed its Paris: Aaron Copland, "Stravinsky's 'Oedipus Rex,'" New Republic 54/691 (29 February 1928), 68–69.

"confessed a fondness": Julian Seaman, "Copland Sees Hope in Trend of Moderns," November 1929; unidentified clipping, Modern Music Press Book, Modern Music-DLC.

"[Oedipus] made a wonderful": Israel Citkowitz to Aaron Copland, 19 June 1928, [from France], Copland-DLC.

25. "It is a big work": Copland to Citkowitz, 29 May 1930, from Bedford, New York, Copland-DLC.

"To have the Variations played": Berger 1934, 86.

"a tragic peroration": "Copland," in Rosenfeld 1936, 335.

26. *"problem of rhetoric":* Thomson 1932, 71.

27. *According to sketches:* One page of sketches (with the number "5" stamped on it) gives a reduction of Copland's theme, and has "Jan 1930" written at the top in Copland's hand (Copland-DLC).

CHAPTER 15

1. *"The twenties had been":* Thomson 1966 (1977), 151.

Thomson not only studied: I explored Thomson's awakening as a modernist in "Virgil Thomson's Harvard Years," Crawford, Lott, and Oja 1990, 323–45.

"lingua franca": Thomson 1939 (1962), 92, 95.

2. *"graduation piece":* Thomson, as quoted in John Cage, "Virgil Thomson: His Music," in Hoover and Cage 1959, 134.

3. *"the greatest audacity":* Jean Cocteau, "The Public and the Artist: Reflections by a French Critic, On Music, Painting and the Creative Arts in General," *Vanity Fair* (October 1922), 61.

4. *"chose to appear":* Hoover and Cage 1959, 144.

5. *"My* Capital, Capitals": Virgil Thomson, letter to Briggs Buchanan, 17 July 1927, Thomson-CtY (reprinted in Page and Page 1988, 81–82).

6. *"a member of {Natalie}":* Thomson 1966 (1977), 95.

Around the same time: Geoffrey K. Spratt, *The Music of Arthur Honegger* (Dublin: Cork University Press, 1987), 20, 147, 527.

Gertrude Stein's "Friday": Much of this information about de Clermont-Tonnerre comes from: Natalie Clifford Barney, *Adventures of the Mind*, translated by John Spalding Gatton (New York: NYU Press, 1992), 256.

7. *"they have incense":* Thomson, letter to Alice Smith, 21 March 1918; reprinted in Page and Page 1988, 26–27.

8. *"static nature":* Hoover and Cage 1959, 145.

9. *At the same moment:* During this period, Thomson composed other pieces incorporating hymn tunes, notably *Variations on Sunday School Tunes* and *Symphony on a Hymn Tune.* The former keeps the hymns in one piece, often presenting them within bitonality, and the latter fuses recognizable snippets of hymns with arch treatment.

10. *"dissociative rhetoric":* Harold Bloom, Introduction to *Gertrude Stein: Modern Critical Views* (New York: Chelsea House, 1986), 1.

"formal word play": Lisa Ruddick, *Reading Gertrude Stein: Body, Text, Gnosis* (Ithaca: Cornell University Press, 1990), 9.

"tenderly": Thomson, *Capital, Capitals, New Music* 20/3 (April 1947).

11. *"Your investigations":* Mencken, letter to Thomson, 23 October 1924, Thomson-CtY.

12. *"86 of these hymns":* Virgil Thomson, "My Jesus I Love Thee," typescript, dated [Paris, 1925], 3, Thomson-NNC. The quotations that follow all come from this text.

13. *Unlike Benjamin Britten:* Philip Brett writes of Britten's "open secret," which "enabled him to live openly with Peter Pears" at the same time as it "gave him social and business advantages, allowing him to pursue a highly successful career as an entrepreneur, to be on warm terms with the royal family, and to collect his nation's top set of honors" (Philip Brett, "Musicality, Essentialism, and the Closet," in *Queering the Pitch: The New Gay and Lesbian Musicology*, ed. Philip Brett, Elizabeth Wood, and Gary C. Thomas [New York: Routledge, 1994], 19).

His sexuality: This is a theme that recurs throughout the book (Tommasini 1997).

14. *"two kinds":* Aaron Copland, notes in folder marked "Appreciation of Modern Music (1927)," Copland-DLC.

CHAPTER 16

1. *"What has not":* Paul Rosenfeld, "Musical Chronicle," *The Dial* 72 (June 1922), 659.

2. *"I am aware":* Roger Sessions, Notes to "Symphony No. 1," Boston Symphony Programs, 1926–27, 1874–78; as quoted in Olmstead 1985, 51.

3. *"I was struck":* Sessions to Copland, 29 April 1929, Copland-DLC.

"Sessions had always": Edward T. Cone, "In Defense of Song: The Contribution of Roger Sessions," *Critical Inquiry* 2/1 (Autumn, 1975), 97; as quoted in Olmstead 1985, 67.

4. *"Only a brief while":* Paul Rosenfeld, "Musical Chronicle," *The Dial* 75 (October 1923), 416.

"no happy hit": Ibid., 414.

5. *It then consisted:* According to Andrea Olmstead, two movements were performed at the Copland-Sessions concert (p. 55). But a review in the *Musical Leader* put it somewhat differently, reporting that "the work, played without pause, consisted of an Andante, Allegro and Andante" ("Copland-Sessions Present Interesting Program," *Musical Leader* 54 [17 May 1928], 10). The program does not give movement titles.

Sessions took two: Information about the premiere comes from Olmstead, 53. Oddly, a program from Bad Homburg, Germany, on 7 July 1931 lists Mannheimer playing the piece then at an American-music festival arranged by Irving Schwerké, music critic for the Paris edition of the *Chicago Tribune*; either Mannheimer repeated the work or the 1930 premiere date is not correct (Program booklet, "Amerikanisches Musikfest in Bad Homburg, 6 bis 8 Juli 1931, Unter dem Patronat des Amerikanischen Botschafters in Berlin," Schwerké-DLC).

"'universal' style": Copland 1931–32, 22–23.

6. *"built on the general":* Sessions, handwritten notes sent to Irving Schwerké, Schwerké-DLC.

"acquired a reputation": Cowell, "Current Chronicle: New York," *Musical Quarterly* 36 (January 1950), 95.

"Stravinsky camp": Sessions, as quoted in Olmstead 1985, 44.

7. *Meanwhile, the opening:* Olmstead connects this section to Beethoven's *Hammerklavier* Sonata, Op. 106 (Olmstead 1985, 55).

8. *"technique of irregular":* Carter 1955, 29.

9. *"a gift rich":* Blitzstein 1929, 166.

10. *"certainly Hindemith":* Peter Westergaard, "Conversation with Walter Piston," in Boretz and Cone 1971, 160, as quoted in Pollack 1981, 29.

Composers whom he also: Piston, private tape of an 80th birthday interview on WGBH, Boston, 19 January 1974, as quoted in Pollack 1981, 30.

11. *"concise pencil":* Piston, liner notes to *American Woodwind Symposium*, by the New Art Wind Quintet, Classic Editions Recordings CE 2003; as quoted in Pollack 1981, 30.

"a builder of": Nicolas Slonimsky, "Walter Piston," in Cowell 1933 (1961), 127.

12. *"confirmed" to "{Harris} lacks":* Kenneth Burke, "Musical Chronicle," *The Dial* 86 (April 1929), 357.

"a coarse work": Thomson, *Music Reviewed (1940–1954)* (New York: Vintage, 1967), 105.

"aims for continuous form": Cowell 1932, 135.

13. *"naturally conservative":* Ibid., 134.

"I am a practised {sic} listener": Goldberg 1933, 256. Harris's Concerto for Piano, Clarinet, and String Quartet was recorded by Harry Cumpson (piano), Aaron Gorodner (clarinet), and the Aeolian String Quartet (Columbia 68138–40D).

14. *He had the instincts:* Dan Stehman opens his biography of Harris by raising questions about whether or not Harris fabricated the story that he was "born in a log cabin in Lincoln County, Oklahoma, on Abraham Lincoln's birthday." Apparently Harris lost his birth certificate, and Stehman has been unable to locate a copy (Stehman 1984, 1, 249).

"*a young tonal Lochinvar*": Goldberg 1933, 253.

"*plain, driving force*": Cowell 1932, 133.

"*He . . . looked very wild*": Mary Churchill, letter to Copland, [June 1929], Copland-DLC.

15. "*chordal counterpoint*": Harris, as quoted in "Roy Harris: The Story of an Oklahoma Composer Who Was Born in a Log Cabin on Lincoln's Birthday," unpublished typescript, early 1950s, Slonimsky-DLC, 23.

16. "*autogenetic*": The sections unfold as follows: mm. 1–9, 10–17, 18–29, 30–35, 36–47. "Autogenetic" in Roy Harris, "Perspective at Forty," *Magazine of Art* 32 (November 1939), 668.

17. "*long, continuously developing*": Carter 1955, 28.

"*program*" to "*3rd rhythmic*": Roy Harris, letter to Aaron Copland, 30 January 1929, Copland-DLC.

18. "*grandly scaled 'serious'*": Stehman 1984, 219.

"*influenced by*": Cowell 1932, 135.

19. "*hollow octaves*": "The Americanism of Carlos Chavez," in Rosenfeld 1928, 278.

20. "*hermetic and inaccessible*": "Composer from Mexico: Carlos Chávez," in Copland 1941 (1968), 148. In 1929, Marc Blitzstein also wrote of Chávez as mythic modernist, calling him "completely self-taught" and claiming that his music "sounds like the music of no other composer, living or dead" (Blitzstein 1929, 168).

21. "*An original classical*": "The Americanism of Carlos Chavez," in Rosenfeld 1928, 273.

22. "*masculine*" to "*The robustness*": Paul Rosenfeld, "Carlos Chavez (American Composers. VIII)," *Modern Music* 9 (1932), 153, 158, 159.

23. "*Glad you have written*": Harris, letter to Copland, June [1926?], Copland-DLC.

24. *His music appeared*: Chávez's Sonata for Piano was performed on the following Copland-Sessions Concerts: 22 April 1928, 17 June 1929 (Paris), and 16 March 1930.

In September 1928: Barthold Fles, "Chavez Lights New Music with Old Fires," *Musical America* 48/22 (15 September 1928), 1, 21.

Cos Cob Press: *New Music* published Chávez's Sonatina for Violin and Piano in July 1928, its first year of operation; his 36 in October 1930; and his Sonata for Piano in 1933.

25. *Although in 1928*: Copland and Perlis 1984, 153–55, 170.

26. "*the presence of*": Messing 1988, xiii.

27. "*You will note*": Cowell, letter to Ruggles, 11 December 1931, Ruggles-CtY.

"*I had a very fine*": Rudhyar, interview with Vivian Perlis, 18 March 1970, Oral History/American Music, CtY.

"*What has been so heinous*": Garland 1991, 13.

28. "*All were to serve*": Thomson 1971, 51.

29. "*a university rather*": Howard Pollack has studied this lineage in Pollack 1992.

CHAPTER 17

1. "*The port of New York*": Rosenfeld 1924, 293.

"*Had I myself*": Sherwood Anderson, *A Story Teller's Story: A Critical Text*, ed. Ray Lewis White (Cleveland: The Press of Case Western Reserve University, 1968, 304; originally published in 1924).

2. "*'Le Sacre' . . . is*": Rosenfeld 1920, 201, 204.

"*In 1922 America*": Antheil 1945, 64.

3. *Yet reception*: Daniel 1982, 225.

With its first: Monteux conducted *Le Sacre du printemps* the previous week in Boston (on 25 January 1924).

"superbly": "New York Cheers Amazing Score by Igor Stravinsky," *Musical America* 39 (9 February 1924), 6. Other reviewers described the reception similarly, especially Olin Downes, "'Sacre du Printemps' Played," *New York Times*, 1 February 1924; and Lawrence Gilman, "Stravinsky's 'Sacre du Printemps' Sells Out the House at Its Repetition by the Boston Symphony," *New York Herald-Tribune*, 17 March 1924. Both the Downes and Gilman are included in Lesure 1980, 95–98.

"I want to tell": Monteux, letter to Stravinsky, 1 February 1924, written from the Biltmore in New York and published in Craft 1984, 64–65.

4. *Before Le Sacre:* "'Premières' du Sacre du Printemps," in Lesure 1980, [9].

5. *Virgil Thomson, for example:* Oja, "Virgil Thomson's Harvard Years," in Crawford, Lott, and Oja 1990, 334–35.

The critic Deems: Deems Taylor, "A Critic of Music," [review of Paul Rosenfeld's *Musical Portraits*], *The Dial* 69 (September 1920), 318.

And Carl Ruggles: Ruggles, flier for lecture, "The Whitney Studio Club announces the third of the series of talks on Modern Music by Carl Ruggles," 27 April [1922], Ruggles Collection-CtY.

6. *"The fact of prime":* Pitts Sanborn, "Honors of the Season," *League of Composers' Review* 1/2 (June 1924), 6. Sanborn contributed frequently to *Modern Music* and was a critic on the *New York Globe*.

"For there is": Virgil Thomson, "The Public and Stravinsky," typescript essay, [spring 1924], Thomson-NNC. During the 1923–24 concert season, the following major Stravinsky works were performed in New York (in addition to *Le Sacre du printemps*): *Le Chant du Rossignol* (1 November 1923, Walter Damrosch conducting the New York Symphony Orchestra); *Symphonies for Wind Instruments* (10 February 1924, Leopold Stokowski and the Philadelphia Orchestra); and *Renard* (conducted by Stokowski in the spring) (cited in W. J. Henderson, "All Things Considered," *Music Illustrated Monthly Magazine* 1 [midsummer 1924], 5.)

"Strawinsky a success": Paul Rosenfeld, "Musical Chronicle," *The Dial* 76 (February 1924), 210.

7. *"Scott met":* Edmund Wilson, *The Shores of Light: A Literary Chronicle of the 1920s and 1930s* (New York: Farrar, Straus and Young, 1952; reprint, Boston: Northeastern University Press, 1952), 377.

8. *The program opened:* Program, International Composers' Guild, 4 February 1923, Ruggles-CtY. See Metzer 1994 for a perceptive chronicle of the reception of *Pierrot lunaire* in New York.

Beginning in April: Documents chronicling these performances are included in: Bryan R. Simms, "The Society for Private Musical Performances: Resources and Documents in Schoenberg's Legacy," *Journal of the Arnold Schoenberg Institute* 3/2 (October 1979), 135–42.

Then in 1922: Willi Reich, *Schoenberg: A Critical Biography*, trans. Leo Black (London: Longman, 1971), 128. Virgil Thomson must have heard this Paris performance because on 21 April 1922 he wrote his friend Leland Poole about concerts he had attended in Paris: "[The] real musical event was *Pierrot Lunaire* of Schoenberg for semi-speaking, semi-singing voice and small orchestra. Fascinating concurrence of noises" (Thomson-CtY).

Soon after being heard: Casella described these performances in an article for *Modern Music* and stated that "little of Schoenberg's music has been heard in Italy" and that Schoenberg's art was "so alien to our temperament" that Italians faced with him a "chasm [that] can never be bridged" (Alfredo Casella, "Schoenberg in Italy," *Modern Music* 1/3 [November 1924], 7, 8).

9. *Then during a visit:* Louise Varèse states, "As Louis Gruenberg the previous autumn in Berlin had attended rehearsals and the concert conducted by Schoenberg himself and had studied the score, he was chosen to conduct the difficult work" (Varèse 1972, 186).

As with the premiere: The delay was announced in: "Schönberg's 'Pierrot Lunaire' Made Ready for First American Hearing," *Musical America* 37 (20 January 1923), 13. The article featured a photograph of Torpadie, Gruenberg, and the other musicians (Figure 17.1).

Twenty-two rehearsals: Claire Reis recalled the many rehearsals for the piece and the tortured decision to postpone the performance (Reis 1955 [1974], 11–13). The number of rehearsals for the Berlin premiere is given in Nicolas Slonimsky, "A Schoenberg Chronology," *Schoenberg*, ed. Merle Armitage (New York: G. Schirmer, 1937; reprint, Westport, Conn.: Greenwood, 1977), 226.

Reis later recalled: Claire Reis, videotaped interview with Vivian Perlis, 9 July 1977.

The audience was: The names of audience members come from Varèse 1972, 188; and Carlos Salzedo, "Music of the Young America," *Eolian Review* 2/2 (March 1923), 5. Significantly, Salzedo and Varèse only singled out European and European-American figures.

"amazed at the reception": Ibid., 5.

"the younger and youngest": Richard Aldrich, "'Pierrot Lunaire' and Others," *New York Times*, 5 February 1923.

"Perhaps you would rather": Clifton Furness, letter to Charles Ives, 22 January 1923, Ives-CtY.

"have never heard": Ives, letter to E. Robert Schmitz, 10 August 1931; published in Ives 1972, 27.

10. *The older, more conservative:* H. E. Krehbiel, "Composers' Guild Heard," *New York Tribune*, 5 February 1923; and Henry T. Finck, "Dreary Musical Tomfooleries," *New York Evening Post*, 5 February 1923. Both are cited in Lott 1983, 273.

"painstaking": Pitts Sanborn, as quoted in Varèse 1972, 187.

"A momentous event": Richard Aldrich, *New York Times*, 5 February 1923.

"When Eva Gauthier": Paul Rosenfeld, "Musical Chronicle," *The Dial* 74 (April 1923), 432.

In April 1924: "We Nominate for the Hall of Fame . . . Arnold Schönberg," *Vanity Fair* 21 (April 1924), 75.

11. *He wrote the composer:* Edgard Varèse, letter to Arnold Schoenberg, 31 August 1922, Schoenberg-DLC.

"no single German": Arnold Schoenberg, letter to Edgard Varèse, 23 October 1922 (published in *Arnold Schoenberg Letters*, ed. Erwin Stein [London: Faber & Faber, 1964], 78–79).

"we approached a number" to "Louis Grunberg {sic}": Max von Recklinghausen to Arnold Schoenberg, 19 December 1922, Schoenberg-DLC.

12. *"In fact":* Richard Hammond, "Salzburg," *Modern Music* 1/3 (November 1924), 24.

13. *"contemporary":* This and most of the other information in this paragraph comes from: P. J. Nolan, "America Shares in International Project to Form League of Music," *Musical America* 37 (20 January 1923), 1, 19.

"dissatisfaction following": Svend B. Felumb, "To Clear up the Salzburg Problem," *Modern Music* 1/1 (1924), 25–26.

14. *"The Invasion":* *Vanity Fair* 24 (March 1925), 35.

15. *Le Sacre du printemps had:* This is according to Emilie Frances Bauer, "Stravinsky Better as Composer than as Conductor," *Musical Leader* 49 (15 January 1925), 59.

"huge and lustrous": Lawrence Gilman, "Stravinsky Appears," *New York Herald-Tribune*, 9 January 1925.

"In the year 1925": Oscar Thompson, "Igor Stravinsky Makes N.Y. Debut as Conductor of the Philharmonic," *Musical America* 41 (17 January 1925), 1.

16. *"a slight, nervous":* Gilman, "Stravinsky Appears."

"there was no disposition": Thompson, "Igor Stravinsky Makes N.Y. Debut."

"It would be excessive": Gilman, "Stravinsky Appears."

17. *"in recital of his own":* [Program:] "Igor Stravinsky in Recital of His Own Compositions," 15 January 1925, Stravinsky Programs-NN. The pieces performed were all cited in French, and the titles are given here as they appeared on that program: *Prelude, Chanson du Pecheur et Air du Rossignol* (from the first act of *Le Rossignol*); *Le Printemps, La Rosée Sainte, Suite de Histoire du soldat, Berceuses du chat; Les Canards, les Cygnes, les Oies; Pastorale, Tilin bon, Faune et Bergère.*

"drew such a large": "'Sacre du printemps' Heard by 'Capacity,'" *Musical Leader* 49 (29 January 1925), 112.

Stravinsky then headed: The following sources provide information about Stravinsky's American tour: Stravinsky and Craft 1978, 252–56; Emilie Frances Bauer, "'Ultra-Modern' Concerto Disgusts New York Audience," *Musical Leader* 49 (12 February 1925), 152.

18. *"Previous visits":* Harry Cassin Becker, "Béla Bartók and His Credo," *Musical America* 47 (17 December 1927), 7. For this article, Becker traveled to Hungary to interview Bartók.

"On Our Musical": *Vanity Fair* 29 (December 1927), 86. A photo of the composer on board ship was published in *Musical America* (31 December 1927), with the caption "Bela Bartok, Hungarian Composer, upon His Arrival Here for a Concert Tour of Ten Weeks" (Figure 17.3).

19. *Immediately before:* "We Nominate for the Hall of Fame: . . . Bela Bartok," *Vanity Fair* 20 (March 1923), 71.

"stand{ing} apart": Paul Rosenfeld, "Hungary's Contribution to Ultra-Modern Music: An Introduction to the Compositions of Bela Bartok, a Magyar Composer," *Vanity Fair* 21 (August 1923), 44, 106. In a preview to Bartók's debut with the Philharmonic, Lawrence Gilman sketched the history of the performance of his music in America ("Bartok and His Remarkable Music," *New York Herald-Tribune*, 18 December 1927).

This was canceled: E. Robert Schmitz, letter to Bartók, 7 September 1924; Bartók to Schmitz, 28 October 1924; Bartók to Schmitz, 28 March 1926; all in Schmitz-CtY.

20. *"He is as great":* Henry Cowell, "Music," *The Americana Annual: An Encyclopedia of Current Events*, ed. Al H. McDannald (New York: Americana Corp., 1928), 545.

Irving Weil, writing: Irving Weil, "Bartok Bows to America in New York Hall," *Musical America* 47 (31 December 1927), 1.

"immature and rather": Olin Downes, "Music: Bela Bartok's American Debut," *New York Times*, 23 December 1927.

21. *"New loveliness":* Henry Cowell, "Music," *The Americana Annual: An Encyclopedia of Current Events*, ed. Al H. McDannald (New York: Americana Corp., 1929), 502.

His final stop: "Bartok and Szigeti Give Pro-Musica Concert," *Musical Leader* 54 (16 February 1928), 8. Bartok's itinerary is given on a typescript of Pro Musica Society events for 1928, Schmitz-CtY.

22. *"Stravinsky's 1925 American":* Stravinsky and Craft 1978, 258.

He wanted fifteen: Bartók, letter to Schmitz, 28 July 1928, written from Budapest, Schmitz-CtY.

23. *"going at evening":* "Igor Stravinsky Not a 'Modernist,'" *New York Times*, 6 January 1925.

"the latest things": Irving Weil, "Bartok Bows to America in New York Hall," 8.

"He {Bartók} finds": Marion Bauer, "Bela Bartok Talks on Modern Simplicity and Folk Music," *Musical Leader* 54 (12 January 1928), 14.

24. *"One thing I want":* As quoted in: John Alan Haughton, "Darius Milhaud: A Missionary of the 'Six,'" *Musical America* 37 (13 January 1923), 3.

25. *"But in the field":* Olin Downes, "The French Composer-Pianist and His Contacts with America—Certain Contrasts," *New York Times*, 26 February 1928.

26. *"We do not commend":* Olin Downes, "Arrival of Arthur Honegger," *New York Times*, 7 January 1929.

CHAPTER 18

1. *"When one is in Paris"*: Carl Van Vechten, "La Tigresse," *In the Garret* (New York: Knopf, 1920), 263.

"Paul Rosenfeld has heard": Roy Harris, letter to Aaron Copland, June [1926], Copland-DLC.

2. *One of the most*: For a brief chronicle of Van Vechten's work as a music critic, see Kellner 1968.

He took the lead: *Music After the Great War* was published by G. Schirmer (Van Vechten 1915); after that Alfred A. Knopf issued all of Van Vechten's books.

3. *Born in 1880*: Van Vechten served two stints as music critic with the *New York Times*, the first from 1906 to 1907 and the second from 1910 to 1913. His articles then dealt largely with music from an earlier era.

"I have determined": Carl Van Vechten, letter to Ralph Van Vechten, 7 February 1919; published in Kellner 1987, 27.

4. *"most extraordinary"*: Van Vechten, letter to Fania Marinoff, 4 June [1913], in Kellner 1987, 6.

He wrote a vivid: Van Vechten 1915, 87–88. This excerpt has been reprinted in Piero Weiss and Richard Taruskin, *Music in the Western World: A History in Documents* (New York: Schirmer Books, 1984), 441–42.

"perhaps the greatest": "Music After the Great War" in Van Vechten 1915, 23. The book by the same name also included "Igor Strawinsky: A New Composer" (dated 6 August 1915) and "The Secret of the Russian Ballet" (November, 1915), as well as the title essay of the volume that incorporated Stravinsky into a broader discussion. Van Vechten had previously submitted the first two articles to *Musical America*, only to have them rejected. The Stravinsky essays in *Music and Bad Manners* (Van Vechten 1916) were "The Bridge Burners" (dated 16 April 1916) and "A New Principle in Music" (dated 6 February 1916).

5. *"bringing some"*: "The Secret of the Russian Ballet," in Van Vechten 1915, 56.

6. *"The lack of"*: "Igor Strawinsky: A New Composer," in Van Vechten 1915, 106–8.

7. *"This young Russian"*: Ibid., 115.

8. *"new use of"*: "A New Principle in Music," in Van Vechten 1916, 217.

9. *"the dregs"*: "Waslav Nijinsky," in Van Vechten 1917, 149–50.

Only when Nijinsky: Ibid., 157ff.

10. *"It is from"*: "The Bridge Burners," in Van Vechten 1916, 169.

"seems to be conditioned": Aldrich, in the *New York Times*, 5 December 1915, as quoted in ibid., 171.

"it seems a bit": Ibid., 177.

"We may be on": Ibid., 213.

11. *"Symphony concerts"*: "Music for Museums?" in Van Vechten 1915, 38.

"cataloguers of the": Ibid., 41–42.

12. *"I shall not hesitate"*: "Music After the Great War," in Van Vechten 1915, 17–18.

13. *"When some curious"*: Carl Van Vechten, "The Great American Composer," *Vanity Fair* (April 1917), 75.

14. *Not surprisingly*: Van Vechten, 1925b.

15. *"may not be the last"*: Van Vechten 1925a, xv. The title of *Red* has nothing to do with communist ideology. As was typical of the day, "jazz" for Van Vechten included an array of popular and vernacular idioms. He was unusual, though, in recognizing African American traditions.

"the younger generation": Van Vechten 1925a, x–xi. By "young Italians" Van Vechten must have been thinking of Alfredo Casella, who toured the United States the same year *Red* was published.

"about ten years": Ibid., xii.

The same year: Many of these articles have been gathered together in Kellner 1979.

During this same: Van Vechten, *Nigger Heaven* (New York: Alfred A. Knopf, 1926).

16. *"highbrow"*: Brooks devoted one chapter of *America's Coming-of-Age* to "'Highbrow' and 'Lowbrow,'" viewing the two extremes as a source of much tension in American culture (Brooks 1915 [1990], 1–19).

17. *"Music I thought"*: Paul Rosenfeld, "Grand Transformation Scene—1907–1915," *Twice-A-Year* 5–6 (1940–41), 354. The title of this article suggests how much Rosenfeld thought his attitude about modern music had changed.

In the early 1920s: An early bibliography of Rosenfeld's writings about music, organized by periodical, is included in Mellquist and Wiese, 1948, 267–86. For a more complete listing that gives cross-references for the journal and book forms of essays, see Silet 1981.

Rosenfeld's productivity: Rosenfeld 1936. Rosenfeld died in 1946. See my bibliography for a list of books by Rosenfeld that included essays about music.

18. *Once the radical:* Rosenfeld lived exclusively off the income from an inheritance and lost some of that money in the Crash. See Mellquist, "Seraph from Mt. Morris Park," in Mellquist and Wiese 1948, xviii, xxix.

Although Rosenfeld's achievements: The first book about Rosenfeld's work was compiled not long after his death by Jerome Mellquist, a longtime friend and colleague (Mellquist and Wiese 1948). For cogent summaries of Rosenfeld's music criticism, see Potter 1980, 136–69, and Mueser 1975, 135–65.

19. *"a bonfire burning"*: Gorham Munson, *Waldo Frank: A Study* (New York: Boni and Liveright, 1923; reprint, Folcroft Library editions, 1974), 9.

"We are in": Waldo Frank and Van Wyck Brooks, quoted (in part) in Potter 1980, 1.

20. *"for the talent"*: "All-American Night," in Rosenfeld 1923, 263.

"a new spirit": Foreword, in Rosenfeld 1924, 2.

Rosenfeld saw Sessions: "Roger H. Sessions," in Ibid., 145–52.

21. *His writing appeared:* Here bibliographic citations will be given only for the anthology in which Rosenfeld's essays appeared. Citations for earlier releases, mostly in the *Dial*, can be located in Silet 1981.

This extraordinary little: The timing of Rosenfeld's departure from the *Dial* suggests that he left there so that he could write this book. When Marianne Moore wrote him in September 1927, asking if he would consider postponing his sabbatical, Rosenfeld replied that he had "a very keen feeling for doing work in the larger forms this winter" (Rosenfeld, letter to Moore, 15 September 1927, Dial/Scofield Thayer Papers, CtY).

22. *"American music is not jazz"*: Rosenfeld 1929, 11.

"Bach and Beethoven": Ibid., 17–18.

"And to-day a force": Ibid., 25–26.

"assimilation of European": Ibid., 40.

"determined musicians": Ibid., 39.

"the first American" to *"succumbed to 'nice'"*: Ibid., 40, 46. In *Musical Portraits*, Rosenfeld used similar language in an essay about Charles Martin Loeffler, saying his art was in "the dangerous vicinity of those amiable gentlemen the Chadwicks and the Converses and all the other highly respectable and sterile 'American Composers'" (Rosenfeld 1920, 266).

23. *"most advanced"*: Rosenfeld 1929, 127. Rosenfeld also included Carlos Chávez among the decade's great talents.

Henry Cowell: Ibid., 164–65.

"assuredly a gifted": Ibid., 138.

"individual": Ibid., 96.

24. *"a skyscraper"*: Ibid., 81.

"The dependence" to *"Weiss's music"*: Ibid., 92–93.

"cosmopolitan intelligence": Edmund Wilson, "Mr. Rosenfeld's Musical Chronicle," *The Freeman* 8 (27 February 1924), 595–96.

25. *Rosenfeld's view*: Brooks 1915 (1990) and Frank 1919.

"*When I began first*": Sherwood Anderson, letter to Paul Rosenfeld, "Chicago, Tuesday" [1922?], in Mellquist and Wiese 1948, 210.

"*Something, in American*": Brooks 1915 (1990), 20.

"*usable past*": Brooks 1918.

"*It is true*": Brooks 1915 (1990), 76.

26. "*the bible*": Gorham Munson, "The Fledgling Years, 1916–1924," *Sewanee Review* 40/1 (January–March 1933), 24–54.

"*a hidden treasure*": Frank 1919, 3.

"*for us of the younger*": Ibid., 8.

"*It must go down*": Ibid., 38.

"*The critics*": Ibid., 203.

27. "*charm*": Rosenfeld 1929, 28.

"*extra-American*": Ibid., 29.

"*The old-world*": Ibid., 31.

28. "*minces and simpers*": Ibid., 46.

"*pathetic {and} bosomy*": Rosenfeld, as quoted in Sherman Paul, "Paul Rosenfeld," in Rosenfeld 1924, ix.

"*Tailleferre has nothing*": Rosenfeld 1923, 151.

"*the most distinguished*": Rosenfeld 1929, 100.

29. *With yet another*: Potter writes that Rosenfeld's unpublished autobiography and his 1927 novel, *Boy in the Sun*, are dominated by an "acute sense of Jewish background" (Potter 1980, 10).

"*is the resurrection*": Rosenfeld 1920, 268.

"*that is a large*" to "*There are moments*": Ibid., 289.

30. "*But it is in the piano-music*": Rosenfeld 1920, 240–41.

"*the modern orientation*": Rosenfeld, "A View of Modern Music," *The Dial* (November 1925), 390.

31. "*a true Jew*": Frank 1919, 186.

"*New York Jew*": John Tasker Howard, as cited in Moore 1985, 71.

"*And our whole contemporary*": Daniel Gregory Mason, *Tune in America* (New York: Alfred A. Knopf, 1930), 160, as cited in Moore 1985, 145. Moore provides an important discussion of anti-Semitism among American composers and critics during this period.

32. "*the greatest fullness*": Rosenfeld 1929, 160.

33. "*Impressionistic*" *was*: This term was used in early reviews of Rosenfeld's writing, including Lewis Mumford's of *Musical Chronicle* ("Beyond Musical Criticism," *The Dial* [May 1925], 411–13). And it continues right up to the present. See Wayne Shirley, "Paul Rosenfeld," in Hitchcock and Sadie 1986, 4:94.

"*The style which*": Edmund Wilson, "Mr. Rosenfeld's Musical Chronicle," *The Freeman* (27 February 1924), 595.

"*In forests, sometimes*": Rosenfeld 1923, 285.

34. "*The earmark of*": Rosenfeld 1929, 128.

35. "*feeling and intuition*": Roger Sessions, *Reflections on Musical Life in the United States* (New York: Merlin, 1956), 132.

"*Ruggles's harmonic*": Rosenfeld 1929, 101–2.

36. *In retrospect, their writing*: An excerpt from Brooks illustrates the similarity: "America is like a vast Sargasso Sea—a prodigious welter of unconscious life, swept by ground-swells of half-conscious emotion. All manner of living things are drifting in it, phosphorescent, gayly colored, gathered into knots and clotted masses, gelatinous, unformed, flimsy, tangled,

rising and falling, floating and merging, here an immense distended belly, there a tiny rudimentary brain (the gross devouring the fine)—everywhere an unchecked, uncharted, unorganized vitality like that of the first chaos" (Brooks 1915 [1990], 78).

"*an obsession with*": Rosenfeld 1936, 280.

37. "*the passive and*": *The American Caravan: A Yearbook of American Literature*, ed. Van Wyck Brooks, Lewis Mumford, Alfred Kreymborg, and Paul Rosenfeld (New York: The Macaulay Company, 1927).

"*Odd Man Out*": Lederman 1983, 46.

"*lone objector*": Slonimsky, "The Patient, the Doctors, the Verdicts" [review of *An Hour with American Music*], *Boston Globe* (January 1929), Slonimsky-DLC.

38. "*At a moment*": Mumford, "Lyric Wisdom," in Mellquist and Wiese 1948, 48.

CHAPTER 19

1. "*Civilization's going*": F. Scott Fitzgerald, *The Great Gatsby* (1925), edited by Matthew J. Bruccoli (Cambridge: Cambridge University Press, 1991), 14.

"*the symbol*": Seldes 1924, 83.

"*conventions had tumbled*": Hoagy Carmichael, *The Stardust Road* (New York: Rinehart, 1946), as quoted in Neil Leonard, *Jazz and the White Americans: The Acceptance of a New Art Form* (Chicago: University of Chicago Press, 1962), 56.

"*a revolt and*": Whiteman and McBride 1926, 155.

2. "*America is no longer*": Roger Sessions, letter to Nicolas Slonimsky, 8 September 1927, Slonimsky-DLC.

"*the civilisation characteristic*": George Santayana, "The Intellectual Temper of the Age," in *Winds of Doctrine* (London and New York: Charles Scribner's, 1913), 1; as quoted in Henry F. May, "The Rebellion of the Intellectuals, 1912–1917," *American Quarterly* 3/2 (summer 1956), 114–26.

3. *The publication of*: For a study of American racism, see Thomas F. Gossett, *Race: The History of an Idea in America* (Dallas: Southern Methodist University Press, 1963), especially pages 339–408. *Britannica Online* states that the membership of the Ku Klux Klan peaked in the 1920s, when it "exceeded 4,000,000 nationally" ("Ku Klux Klan," *Britannica Online* [13 February 1999]).

The new quotas: The following gives an idea of how the balances had shifted in immigration patterns. During the 1850s, 36 percent of American immigrants came from Germany and 0.017 percent from Russia. By the first decade of the 1900s that had changed to 3.88 percent from Germany and 18.1 percent from Russia (see Vincent N. Parrillo, *Strangers to These Shores: Race and Ethnic Relations in the United States* [Boston: Houghton Mifflin, 1966], 469–70.)

4. "*eclectic breeding*": Thomson 1925, 118.

5. "*In those days*": Copland and Perlis 1984, 130.

"*Both are used*": Brooks 1915 (1990), 3–4.

"*The real division*": Henry Cowell, "The Development of Modern Music," *Ohio State University Bulletin* 36/3 (15 September 1931), 379.

CHAPTER 20

1. "*Actually Gershwin*": Leonard Bernstein, "Why Don't You Run Upstairs and Write a Nice Gershwin Tune?" *The Joy of Music* (New York: Simon and Schuster, 1959), 56–57.

"*Be proud, my Race*": Paul Laurence Dunbar, as quoted in William Grant Still, *Afro-American Symphony* (London: Novello, 1970).

"*lank and dark*": Olin Downes, "A Concert of Jazz," *New York Times*, 13 February 1924.

"highbrow jazz": Thomson 1925, 54.

"The word has been": Gershwin then listed examples of the range of styles subsumed under "jazz": "popular songs like 'Papa Loves Mama'; adaptations of the classics to dance rhythms; Negro spirituals; even a waltz number like Irving Berlin's 'What'll I Do'; the Rhapsody in Blue" (Gershwin, "Mr. Gershwin Replies to Mr. Kramer," *Singing* 1/10 [October 1926], 17.) In the spirit of the 1920s, I am using "jazz" and "popular music" interchangeably in this chapter.

Other terminology is problematic here. I continue to use "modernism" as broadly as I have throughout the book. During the 1920s, the term was ubiquitous, standing essentially for anything perceived as "new." In this chapter, it often becomes a synonym for "new concert music"—as opposed, that is, to jazz.

2. *"Modernism constituted"*: Huyssen 1986, vii.

3. *"the very finest piece"*: Van Vechten 1925b, 40.

"enormously superior": Thomson 1925, 54. I analyze the reception of *Rhapsody in Blue*—especially in terms of the way that it placed a wedge between Gershwin and the young American modernists—in Oja 1994. For a provocative study of *Rhapsody in Blue* as a whole, including an analysis of the music, see Schiff 1997.

"You must whisper": Carl Engel, "Views and Reviews," *Musical Quarterly* 12/2 (April 1926), 306.

4. *"miracle" of "lift{ing}"*: Quoted in Osgood 1926, 204. Similar metaphors were used repeatedly for Gershwin, as in the headline for a review of *Rhapsody in Blue* by Samuel Chotzinoff: "George Gershwin's 'Rhapsody in Blue': Thus Far the Most Successful Attempt to 'Make an Honest Woman out of Jazz,'" *Vanity Fair* (August 1924), 28.

"very low form": Damrosch 1923, 268. In 1928, Damrosch "delivered an assault on jazz . . . at the opening session of the . . . Music Supervisors' national conference" in Chicago, calling jazz "a monotony of rhythm; . . . personally, it annoys me" ("Damrosch Assails Jazz," *New York Times*, 17 April 1928). George Martin claims that Damrosch later "underwent a change," quoting him as stating in 1941 that jazz is "the only real national music our country has produced so far" (*The Damrosch Dynasty* [Boston: Houghton Mifflin, 1983], 288).

For more about the reception of jazz in the 1920s, see Ogren 1989.

5. *"Ladies and gentlemen"*: Damrosch, as quoted in Copland and Perlis 1984, 104.

6. *Aspects of the blues*: Connections between *Concerto in F* and the blues have been explored in an essay by Charles Hamm, "A Blues for the Ages," in Crawford, Lott, and Oja 1990, 346–55. For another major study of *Concerto in F*, see: Shirley 1985, 277–98.

7. *"idea"*: This term is introduced in Gilbert 1995, 91.

8. *It unfolds in*: Richard Crawford opens this avenue of discussion about Gershwin's music in "George Gershwin," in Hitchcock and Sadie 1986, 2: 203–5.

9. *"conventional, trite"*: Lawrence Gilman, "Music: Mr. George Gershwin Plays His New Jazz Concerto with Walter Damrosch," *New York Herald-Tribune*, 4 December 1925.

"decidedly inferior": Marc Blitzstein, "My Lady Jazz," *The Review* 9/6 (5 February 1926), 17.

"tried" but "not": Olin Downes, "Music: The New York Symphony," *New York Times*, 4 December 1925.

10. *"episodic treatment"* to *"ragtime particularly"*: Abbe Niles, "Lady Jazz in the Vestibule," *New Republic* 45 (23 December 1925), 138–39 (emphasis his).

Niles went on: W. C. Handy, *Blues: An Anthology*, introduction by Abbe Niles (New York: A. C. Boni, 1926). Abbe Niles, "Jazz," *Encylopedia Britannica*, 14th ed. (London: Britannica, 1929), 1982–84. Thanks to Elliot Hurwitt for providing me with this information. His essay, "Abbe Niles, Blues Advocate" is scheduled to appear in a volume edited by David Evans.

11. *"the unknown composer"*: Whiteman and McBride 1926, 287.

He had high: Whiteman's income rose steadily during the 1920s, from around $3,000 a week in 1924 (or $156,000/year) to a total of $800,000 in 1925 (evidently his highest-paying year) (DeLong 1983, 4, 84). In his own book, Whiteman dealt straightforwardly with the question of income, acknowledging that money meant a great deal to him.

12. *"somebody," as the critic:* Taylor 1924, 17.

Whiteman's initiative: "Mr. Paul Whiteman and His Orchestra," in "A Concert of American Music for the American Academy in Rome," program, Carnegie Hall, 21 April 1924, Whiteman-MWiW.

13. *"modern orchestra":* This phrase appears repeatedly throughout the literature surrounding Whiteman's orchestra, including the program note for the debut of *Rhapsody in Blue* (Gilbert Seldes and Hugh C. Ernst, "Notes" to *An Experiment in Modern Music*, Aeolian Hall, 12 February 1924, 7, Whiteman-MWiW).

Whiteman also reportedly "conferred": Cadman, Godowsky, Grainger, and Powell are cited in "Paul Whiteman: What He Has Done and Intends to Do," in "F. C. Coppicus Presents PAUL WHITEMAN and his ORCHESTRA OF TWENTY-FIVE in their first TRANSCONTINENTAL CONCERT TOUR SEASON 1924–1925," 1924, p. 5. Antheil was added to the list in the following year's edition: "Paul Whiteman: What He Has Done and Intends to Do," in "F. C. Coppicus Presents PAUL WHITEMAN and his GREATER CONCERT ORCHESTRA in their second TRANSCONTINENTAL CONCERT TOUR, SEASON 1925–1926," 1925, p. 76. Both in Whiteman-MWiW. Bloch's name was linked with Whiteman's in H. O. Osgood's review of Whiteman's February, 1924 concert: "An Experiment in Music," *Musical Courier* 88/8 (21 February 1924), 39, and the reference to the Stravinsky commission appears in DeLong 1983, 10.

"a general invitation": "Workshop for American Composers: Building a Repertoire for a New Medium," in "F. C. COPPICUS Presents PAUL WHITEMAN, SEASON 1925–1926," 1925, 15, Whiteman-MWiW.

"For the first time": Taylor 1924, 17.

14. *Nine days later:* "Symphonic 'Jazz' Concert by Vincent Lopez and His Augmented Orchestra of Forty Selected Soloists," Metropolitan Opera House, 23 November 1924, Programs-NN.

"Second Experiment": [Program], Paul Whiteman and His Greater Concert Orchestra, 29 December 1925, Programs-NN.

15. *"The Concert Repertoire":* Osgood 1926, 161.

"an extremely dreary": Gilbert Seldes, "Jazz Opera or Ballet?" *Modern Music* 3/2 (January–February 1926), 11.

"disappointed . . . by": Olin Downes, "Concerning 'Modern American Music': Recent Delusions and Experiments," *New York Times*, 23 November 1924; and Downes, "Whiteman's Jazz," *New York Times*, 8 October 1928.

16. *"jazz missionary":* Whiteman and McBride 1926, 295.

"a respectful hearing": Ibid., 11.

"only original idea": Whiteman, "The Progress of Jazz: Problems Which Confront the American Composer in His Search for a Musical Medium," *Vanity Fair* (January 1926), 52.

"It is a relief": Whiteman and McBride 1926, 20.

"subduing, without": "Paul Whiteman: What He Has Done and What He Intends to Do," in "F. C. Coppicus Presents PAUL WHITEMAN and his ORCHESTRA SEASON 1924–1925," 1924, p. 3. At least one of his 1925 programs opened with "An early discordant jazz tune," followed by "A similar tune made less blatant by modern scoring." The title was not cited ("Paul Whiteman and His Orchestra; First Time in Albany," program, 30 April 1925, Whiteman-MWiW).

"out of the kitchen": Taylor 1924, 16; these words were also cited in Whiteman's 1924–25 program booklet, p. 3.

He reinforced the effect: Whiteman and McBride 1926, 15–32; 238–41.

"forbade his players": Osgood (1926) wrote of Whiteman's claim regarding written parts (p. 106), and Whiteman's 1924–1925 (p. 3) program booklet declared improvisation as forbidden within the orchestra.

17. "shadow": Lambert 1936, 223. Lambert called *Rhapsody in Blue* a "singularly inept albeit popular piece."

18. *Gershwin stepped*: B[ernard] R[ogers], "Enter Jazz," *Musical America* 39 (10 November 1923), 9.

19. "*life to them*" to "*with 'tone and technic*'": Eva Gauthier, "Eva Gauthier Comments on Her Experiment in Jazz," *Musical Observer* 23 (July 1924), 22.

20. "*Mme. Gauthier sang*": B[ernard] R[ogers], "Enter Jazz!" 9.
"*She did not do well*": Osgood 1926, 47.

21. "*refined and disciplined*": Edmund Wilson, "The Jazz Problem," *New Republic* 45 (13 January 1926), 218.

22. *But in the early 1920s*: Still worked for the Pace and Handy publishing company as "head" of the arranging staff; when the firm dissolved in 1921 and Pace launched the Black Swan record label, Still "continued as arranger . . . and later superseded [Fletcher] Henderson as musical director" (Walter C. Allen, *Hendersonia: The Music of Fletcher Henderson and His Musicians* [Highland Park, N.J.: Walter C. Allen., 1973], 10). He also worked for Earl Carroll, Artie Shaw, Sophie Tucker, Don Vorhees, and Paul Whiteman, as well as for the CBS and Mutual networks and for Willard Robison's "Deep River Hour" on NBC (Haas 1975, 6).
Throughout the 1920s: I have written of Still's odyssey during the 1920s in Oja 1992.
"*not mere 'nigger*'": "American Orchestral Society," *Musical Courier* 98/6 (7 February 1929), 35. Although there is not space here to discuss how common the word *nigger* was in the 1920s, I offer one other illustration—a comparison of two sets of clothing in an ad for *Vogue* that was published in *Vanity Fair*. The outfit labeled "100% wrong" includes a "nigger turban," as the caption puts it ("Vogue Saves You Money," *Vanity Fair* [March 1927], 112).

23. "*ultramodern*": Arvey 1984, 67.
"*used instrumentally*": William Grant Still, as quoted in Program Notes, International Composers' Guild Concert, 8 February 1925, ICG Programs-NN.
In reviews of: Paul Rosenfeld, "Musical Chronicle," *The Dial* 68 (1925), 352; Olin Downes, "Music," *New York Times*, 9 February 1925, 15.
"*knows the rollicking*": Downes, ibid.

24. *American modernism*: Ann Douglas builds her fascinating book, *Terrible Honesty: Mongrel Manhattan in the 1920s*, around the thesis of racial intermingling during the period (Douglas 1995).
"*The most outstanding*": Johnson 1930, 260.
"*representatives of*": Cowley 1934 (1951), 8.

25. "*Oh, baby!*": Quoted in Louise Varèse, Program Notes, International Composers' Guild Concert, 24 January 1926, ICG Programs-NN. In the score available from William Grant Still Music, "Ah" is changed to "I".

26. *The scoring is very close*: The original scoring of *Rhapsody in Blue* differed slightly from that of *Levee Land* by including no bassoon and having a slightly different battery of percussion.

27. *He taught these songs*: Arvey 1984, 69.

28. "*never {been} another*": Paul Rosenfeld, "Musical Chronicle," *The Dial* 80 (1926), 352.

29. "*deal{t} fantastically*": Howard 1929, 25.

30. "*the people who really*": Deems Taylor, "America's First Dramatic Composer: John Alden Carpenter, Whose Pantomime Music May Presage an American School of Ballet," *Vanity Fair* (April 1922), 106.

The year after Skyscrapers: Bordman 1978, 403, 430.

It used a "Negro": This comes from the most vivid summary of who did what in *Skyscrapers*: Oscar Thompson, "Modern American Life Symbolized in 'Skyscrapers,'" *Musical America* 43/19 (27 February 1926), 1, 5. The program for *Skyscrapers* (copy at NN) states only that there was a "Negro Group organized by Frank Wilson."

An African American {re: Frank Wilson}: Johnson 1930, 172–73, 212.

"It seemed a little": M. L. [Minna Lederman], "Skyscrapers: An Experiment in Design: An Interview with Robert Edmond Jones," *Modern Music* 3/2 (January–February 1926), 25.

31. *Blackface had been:* For a fascinating exploration of the racial politics surrounding this work and its first production, see Metzer 1993.

32. *"dreary and endless":* These and other quotations from *Skyscrapers'* scenario are taken from the published orchestral score (New York: G. Schirmer, 1926), [pp. 1–2].

33. *The piano takes on:* For an extensive summary of music and dramatic action in *Skyscrapers*, see Pollack 1995, 224–34.

34. *"the spirit":* "'Skyscrapers' Ballet Hailed as New York's Own: Spirit of Jazz Crashes Past Portals of the Metropolitan in Premier of Phantasy by Carpenter," *New York Herald-Tribune*, 20 February 1926, 1.

35. *"for voice and eight":* Louis Gruenberg, *The Creation: A Negro Sermon* (Vienna: Universal Editions, 1926). David Baskerville has a different assessment of *The Creation*, writing that "the piece derives a kind of 'hot' flavor, not so much from the rhythm as from the elaborate clarinet part" (Baskerville 1965, 352).

36. *"took the rhetoric":* Huggins 1971, 77.

37. *"In the beginning":* Louis Gruenberg, "Jazz as a Starting Point," *Musical Leader* 49 (28 May 1925), 594.

38. *"elevate":* Still's wife, Verna Arvey, claimed that as early as 1916 Still had determined to "elevate the Blues . . . [to] a dignified position in symphonic literature" (Arvey, "Memo for Musicologists," in Haas 1975, 89–90), and Still used the term "elevate" in program notes for the *Afro-American Symphony* (Still, "Notes on: The AFRO-AMERICAN SYMPHONY," undated typescript, Collection of Judith Anne Still, Flagstaff, Arizona). According to the ICG program notes, Still scored two versions of *Darker America*, one for large orchestra (this is the published score, used in the above comparison) and another for chamber ensemble (this is the one performed by the ICG, which incorporated the same winds, no percussion, and a string quintet) (Louise Varèse, Program Notes, International Composers' Guild, 28 November 1926, ICG Programs-NN).

39. *"representative of" to "His {"the American Negro's"}":* Still, as quoted in Louise Varèse, Program Notes, ICG, 28 November 1926.

40. *"What is lacking":* Olin Downes, "Music," *New York Times*, 29 November 1926.

Once again, it did not dawn: It should be noted, though, that a few years later, Still echoed Downes's judgment of *Darker America*. Responding to a request from the critic Irving Schwerké for a copy of the score, Still wrote: "DARKER AMERICA, being an earlier work, has many faults. Lack of continuity, harmonization not altogether characteristic, insufficient development as well as other defects" (Still, letter to Irving Schwerké, 27 February 1931, Schwerké-DLC).

41. *"I have no idea":* Copland and Perlis 1984, 130–31.

42. *The work was not recorded:* This was a performance by the Rome Symphony Orchestra, conducted by Copland, with Leo Smit at the piano (Concert Hall CHF-4).

43. *Orchestrated by the promoters:* For a discussion of Copland's attitude toward Gershwin, see Oja 1994.

44. *"borne music":* Paul Rosenfeld, "Musical Chronicle," *The Dial* 82 (April 1927), 356–57.

"unlike certain": Lawrence Gilman, "A New American Concerto at the Boston Symphony Concert," *New York Herald-Tribune*, 4 February 1927.

"Mr. Copland has quite": Lawrence Cushing, [review of Copland Concerto], *Brooklyn Daily Eagle*, 6 February 1927, as quoted in Copland and Perlis 1984, 132.

"the young man": Isaac Goldberg, "Aaron Copland and His Jazz," *The American Mercury* 12 (1927), 63.

45. *"written some years":* H. H., "Orchestra Debut is Vital Concert," *New York Times*, 4 December 1933.

"this extraordinary": Marc Blitzstein, "Mid-Season in New York," *Modern Music*, 11/2 (January–February 1934), 102–3.

"very considerably": "Milhaud," in Rosenfeld 1936, 231.

46. *The tendency to stretch:* A few examples include John Tasker Howard, who placed one year between the two works (see *This Modern Music: A Guide for the Bewildered Listener* [New York: Thomas Y. Crowell, 1942], 128). In Joseph Machlis's *Introduction to Contemporary Music* (New York: W. W. Norton, 1961), a widely used music-appreciation text of its day, the span became two years (p. 222), as it is in Levy 1983, 42.

"There are also origins": Berger 1953, 48.

47. *"even staler":* Lawrence Gilman, "Music: Mr. George Antheil Presents His Compliments to New York," *New York Herald-Tribune*, 11 April 1927. The text of this review was reprinted in *Musical Leader* 52 (21 April 1927), 19, 109.

48. *Originally intended for Paul Whiteman's:* This is according to Whitesitt 1983, 31, 112.

"a very mediocre": George Antheil, letter to Bok [19 October 1925].

"put Gershwin": Antheil, letter to Bok [15 November 1925], Antheil-DLC.

"a reaction towards": Antheil, as quoted in "George Antheil: First American Appearance in a Concert of His Own Works," Carnegie Hall, 10 April 1927, Programs-NN.

49. *"an expression of":* Program Notes, "George Antheil: First American Appearance in a Concert of His Own Works."

The clarinet phrases: Thanks to Mark Tucker for helping sort out the various strains of jazz heard in this work.

50. *Among other groups:* A review in *New York Age* describes the orchestra: Lucien H. White, "Third Symphonic Concert by New Amsterdam Players" (3 December 1921).

EPILOGUE

1. *"Somehow unique":* Cowley 1934 (1951), 8.

2. *"It was as if ":* Malcolm Cowley, *The Dream of the Golden Mountains: Remembering the 1930s* (New York: Penguin Books, 1980), 117–18.

Selected Bibliography

Antheil, George. 1945. *Bad Boy of Music*. Garden City, N.Y.: Doubleday, Doran, and Company.

Antliff, Mark. 1993. *Inventing Bergson: Cultural Politics and the Parisian Avant-Garde*. Princeton: Princeton University Press.

Arvey, Verna. 1984. *In One Lifetime*. Fayetteville: University of Arkansas Press.

Barr, Cyrilla. 1998. *Elizabeth Sprague Coolidge: American Patron of Music*. New York: Schirmer Books.

Baskerville, David. 1965. *Jazz Influence on Art Music to Mid-Century*. Ph.D. dissertation, UCLA.

Bauer, Marion. 1927. "Impressionists in America." *Modern Music* 4/2 (January–February): 15–20.

———. 1933 (1978). *Twentieth Century Music*. New York: Putnam. Reprint, New York: Da Capo.

———. 1943. "Charles T. Griffes as I Remember Him." *Musical Quarterly* 29/3 (July): 355–80.

Berger, Arthur. 1934. "The Piano Variations of Aaron Copland." *Musical Mercury* 1/3 (August–September): 85–86.

———. 1953. *Aaron Copland*. New York: Oxford University Press.

Bergson, Henri. 1911 (1941). *Creative Evolution*. New York: Henry Holt. Reprint, New York: Modern Library.

———. 1949. *Selections from Bergson*. New York: Appleton-Century-Crofts.

Berman, Art. 1994. *Preface to Modernism*. Urbana: University of Illinois Press.

Bernard, Jonathan W. 1987. *The Music of Edgard Varèse*. New Haven: Yale University Press.

Blitzstein, Marc. 1929. "Four American Composers." *This Quarter* 2/1 (July–August–September): 163–68.

Block, Adrienne Fried. 1998. *Amy Beach, Passionate Victorian: The Life and Work of an American Composer*. New York: Oxford University Press.

Bordman, Gerald. 1978. *American Musical Theatre: A Chronicle*. New York: Oxford University Press.

Boretz, Benjamin, and Edward T. Cone. 1971. *Perspectives on American Composers*. New York: W.W. Norton.

Brooks, Van Wyck. 1915 (1990). *America's Coming-of-Age*. New York: B. W. Huebsch. Reprint, Mattituck, N.Y.: Amereon House.

———. 1918. "On Creating a Usable Past." *The Dial* 64 (11 April): 337–41.

Brown, Dorothy M. 1987. *Setting a Course: American Women in the 1920s*. Boston: Twayne.

Campbell, Bruce F. 1980. *Ancient Wisdom Revived: A History of the Theosophical Movement*. Berkeley: University of California Press.

Carter, Elliott. 1955. "The Rhythmic Basis of American Music." *The Score and I.M.A. Magazine* 12 (June), 27–32.

Chase, Gilbert. 1987. *America's Music: From the Pilgrims to the Present*, revised third edition. Urbana: University of Illinois Press.

Chennevière, Daniel. SEE Rudhyar, Dane.

Chou Wen-Chung. 1966. "Varèse: A Sketch of the Man and His Music." *Musical Quarterly* 52/2 (April): 151–70.

Copland, Aaron. 1926. "Playing Safe at Zurich." *Modern Music* 4 (November–December): 28–31.

———. 1927. "Baden-Baden, 1927." *Modern Music* 5 (November–December): 31–34.

———. 1928. "Music Since 1920." *Modern Music* 5 (March–April): 16–20.

———. 1930. "A Note on Nadia Boulanger." *Fontainebleau Alumni Bulletin* 5 (May): 1.

———. 1931–32. "Contemporaries at Oxford, 1931." *Modern Music* 9: 17–23.

———. 1941 (1968). *Our New Music: Leading Composers in Europe and America*. New York: Whittlesey House. Revised and enlarged as *The New Music: 1900–1960*. New York: W. W. Norton.

———. 1952 (1959). *Music and Imagination*. Cambridge: Harvard University Press.

———. 1978. "Claire Reis (1889 [*sic*]–1978)." *Musical Quarterly* 64 (July): 386–88.

———, and Vivian Perlis. 1984. *Copland: 1900 Through 1942*. New York: St. Martin's.

Corn, Wanda. 1999. *The Great American Thing: Modern Art and National Identity 1915–1935*. Berkeley: University of California Press.

Cowell, Henry. 1925. "America Takes a Front Rank in Year's Modernist Output." *Musical America* 41/23 (28 March): 5, 35.

———. 1927. "The Impasse of Modern Music: Searching for New Avenues of Beauty." *Century* 114 (October): 671–77.

———. 1930 (1996). *New Musical Resources*. New York: Alfred A. Knopf. Reprint with a new afterword by David Nicholls. Cambridge: Cambridge University Press.

———. 1932. "Roy Harris, An American Composer." *The Sackbut* 12/3 (April): 133–35.

———, ed. 1933 (1961). *American Composers on American Music: A Symposium*. Palo Alto: Stanford University Press. Reprint, New York: Frederick Ungar.

Cowley, Malcolm. 1934 (1951). *Exile's Return: A Literary Odyssey of the 1920s*. New York: Viking.

Craft, Robert, ed. 1984. *Stravinsky: Selected Correspondence*, Vol. 2. New York: Knopf.

Crawford, Richard. 1993. *The American Musical Landscape*. Berkeley: University of California Press.

Crawford, Richard, R. Allen Lott, and Carol J. Oja. 1990. *A Celebration of American Music: Words and Music in Honor of H. Wiley Hitchcock*. Ann Arbor: University of Michigan Press.

Damrosch, Walter. 1923. *My Musical Life*. New York: Charles Scribner's Sons.

Daniel, Oliver. 1982. *Stokowski: A Counterpoint of View*. New York: Dodd, Mead.

DeLong, Thomas A. 1983. *Pops: Paul Whiteman, King of Jazz*. Piscataway, N.J.: New Century.

Douglas, Ann. 1995. *Terrible Honesty: Mongrel Manhattan in the 1920s*. New York: Farrar, Straus and Giroux.

Douglass, Paul. 1986. *Bergson, Eliot, and American Literature*. Lexington: University Press of Kentucky.

DuPree, Mary Herron. 1983. "The Failure of American Music: The Critical View from the 1920s," *Journal of Musicology* 2/3 (summer): 305–14.

Elliot, Paula. 1997. *Pro-Musica: Patronage, Performance, and a Periodical. An Index to the Quarterlies*. MLA Index and Bibliography Series, No. 28. Canton, Mass.: Music Library Association.

Erkkila, Betsy. 1980. *Walt Whitman Among the French: Poet and Myth*. Princeton: Princeton University Press.

Everdell, William R. 1997. *The First Moderns: Profiles in the Origins of Twentieth-Century Thought*. Chicago: University of Chicago Press.

Frank, Waldo. 1919. *Our America*. New York: Boni and Liveright.

Friede, Donald. 1948. *The Mechanical Angel: His Adventures and Enterprises in the Glittering 1920s*. New York: Alfred A. Knopf.

Friedman, B. H., with the research collaboration of Flora Miller Irving. 1978. *Gertrude Vanderbilt Whitney*. Garden City, N.Y.: Doubleday.

Gann, Kyle. 1997. *American Music in the Twentieth Century*. New York: Schirmer Books.

Garafola, Lynn. 1989. *Diaghilev's Ballets Russes*. New York: Oxford University Press.

Garland, Peter. 1991. *In Search of Silvestre Revueltas: Essays 1978–1990*. Santa Fe: Soundings.

Gilbert, Sandra M., and Susan Gubar. 1988. *No Man's Land: The Place of the Woman Writer in the Twentieth Century, Vol. I: The War of the Words*. New Haven: Yale University Press.

Gilbert, Steven E. 1995. *The Music of Gershwin*. New Haven: Yale University Press.

Gillmore, Allan M. 1988. *Erik Satie*. Boston: Twayne.

Goldberg, Isaac. 1931 (1958). *George Gershwin: A Study in American Music*. New York: Frederick Ungar.

———. 1933. "Roy Harris," *Musical Record* 1:253–56.

Gordon, Eric A. 1989. *Mark the Music: The Life and Work of Marc Blitzstein*. New York: St. Martin's Press.

Greer, Taylor Aitken. 1998. *A Question of Balance: Charles Seeger's Philosophy of Music*. Berkeley: University of California Press.

Haas, Robert Bartlett, ed. 1975. *William Grant Still and the Fusion of Cultures in American Music*. Los Angeles: Black Sparrow.

Harrison, Lou. 1946. *About Carl Ruggles*. Yonkers, N.Y.: Oscar Baradinsky at the Alicat Bookshop.

Henderson, Linda Dalrymple. 1983. *The Fourth Dimension and Non-Euclidian Geometry in Modern Art*. Princeton: Princeton University Press.

Hicks, Michael. 1993. "Cowell's Clusters." *Musical Quarterly* 77: 428–58.

Hisama, Ellie M. 1996. *Gender, Politics, and Modernist Music: Analyses of Five Compositions by Ruth Crawford (1901–1953) and Marion Bauer (1887–1955)*. Ph.D. dissertation, City University of New York.

Hitchcock, H. Wiley, and Stanley Sadie. 1986. *The New Grove Dictionary of American Music*, 4 vols. London: Macmillan.

Holman, William Merkel. 1977. *A Comprehensive Performance Project in Clarinet Literature with a History of the Society for the Publication of American Music, 1919–1969*. D.M.A. dissertation, University of Iowa.

Hoover, Kathleen, and John Cage. 1959. *Virgil Thomson: His Life and Music*. New York: Thomas Yoseloff.

Howard, John Tasker. 1929. *Emerson Whithorne*. Studies of American Composers. New York: Carl Fischer.

Howe, M. A. DeWolfe. 1931 (1978). *The Boston Symphony Orchestra, 1881–1931*. Boston: Houghton Mifflin. Reprint, New York: Da Capo Press.

Huggins, Nathan Irvin. 1971. *Harlem Renaissance*. London: Oxford University Press.

Huyssen, Andreas. 1986. *After the Great Divide: Modernism, Mass Culture, Postmodernism.* Bloomington: Indiana University Press.

Ives, Charles E. 1970. *Essays Before a Sonata, The Majority, and Other Writings,* ed. Howard Boatwright. New York: W. W. Norton.

———. 1972. *Memos,* ed. John Kirkpatrick. New York: W. W. Norton.

Johnson, James Weldon. 1930. *Black Manhattan.* New York: Alfred A. Knopf.

Johnson, Steven. 1993. "Henry Cowell, John Varian, and Halcyon." *American Music* 11/1 (spring): 1–27.

Kellner, Bruce. 1968. *Carl Van Vechten and the Irreverent Decades.* Norman, Oklahoma: University of Oklahoma Press.

———, ed. 1979. *'Keep A-Inchin' Along': Selected Writings of Carl Van Vechten about Black Art and Letters.* Westport, Conn.: Greenwood Press.

———, ed. 1987. *Letters of Carl Van Vechten.* New Haven: Yale University Press.

Kirkpatrick, John. 1928. "On Copland's Music." *Fontainebleau Alumni Bulletin* 1 (May): [1–3, 6].

———. 1968. "The Evolution of Carl Ruggles." *Perspectives of New Music* 6/2 (1968): 146–66.

Klarén, J. H. 1928. *Edgar Varèse: Pioneer of New Music in America.* Boston: C. C. Birchard.

Kuenzli, Rudolf, ed. 1986. *New York Dada.* New York: Willis Locker and Owens.

Lambert, Constant. 1936. *Music Ho: A Study of Music in Decline,* 2d ed. New York: Charles Scribner's Sons.

Lederman, Minna. 1983. *The Life and Death of a Small Magazine ("Modern Music," 1924–1946).* I.S.A.M. Monographs, No. 18. Brooklyn: Institute for Studies in American Music.

Léger, Fernand. 1965. *Functions of Painting,* translated by Alexandra Anderson, edited by Edward F. Fry. New York: Viking.

Lesure, François, ed. 1980. *Igor Stravinsky, Le Sacre du printemps: Dossier de Presse.* Genève: Editions Minkoff.

Levine, Lawrence W. 1988. *Highbrow/Lowbrow: The Emergence of Cultural Hierarchy in America.* Cambridge: Harvard University Press.

Levy, Alan Howard. 1983. *Musical Nationalism: American Composers' Search for Identity.* Westport, Conn.: Greenwood.

Lichtenwanger, William. 1986. *The Music of Henry Cowell: A Descriptive Catalog.* I.S.A.M. Monographs, No. 23. Brooklyn: Institute for Studies in American Music.

Locke, Ralph P., and Cyrilla Barr. 1997. *Cultivating Music in America: Women Patrons and Activists Since 1860.* Berkeley: University of California Press.

Lott, R. Allen. 1983. "'New Music for New Ears': The International Composers' Guild." *Journal of the American Musicological Society* 36/2: 266–86.

Manion, Martha L. 1982. *Writings About Henry Cowell,* I.S.A.M. Monographs, No. 16. Brooklyn: Institute for Studies in American Music.

Martens, Frederick H. 1918 (1975). *Leo Ornstein: The Man—His Ideas, His Work.* New York: Breitkopf & Härtel. Reprint, New York: Arno.

Marx, Leo. 1964. *The Machine in the Garden: Technology and the Pastoral Ideal in America.* New York: Oxford University Press.

Mattis, Olivia. 1992. *Edgard Varèse and the Visual Arts.* Ph.D. dissertation, Stanford University.

McNaughton, Charles David. 1958. *Albert Stoessel, American Musician.* Ph.D. dissertation, New York University.

Mead, Rita. 1981. *Henry Cowell's New Music, 1925–1936: The Society, the Music Editions, and the Recordings.* Ann Arbor: UMI Research Press.

Mellers, Wilfrid. 1987. *Music in a New Found Land,* rev. ed. New York: Oxford.

Mellquist, Jerome, and Lucie Wiese, ed. 1948. *Paul Rosenfeld: Voyager in the Arts.* New York: Creative Age.

Messing, Scott. 1988. *Neoclassicism in Music: From the Genesis of the Concept Through the Schoenberg/Stravinsky Polemic.* Ann Arbor: UMI Research Press.

Metzer, David. 1993. *The Ascendancy of Musical Modernism in New York City, 1915–1929.* Ph.D. dissertation, Yale University.

———. 1994. "The New York Reception of *Pierrot lunaire*: The 1923 Premiere and Its Aftermath." *Musical Quarterly* 78/4 (winter): 669–99.

———. 1995. "'A Wall of Darkness Dividing the World': Blackness and Whiteness in Louis Gruenberg's *The Emperor Jones.*" *Cambridge Opera Journal* 7/1: 55–72.

———. 1997. "The League of Composers: The Initial Years." *American Music* 15/1 (spring): 45–69.

Moore, MacDonald Smith. 1985. *Yankee Blues: Musical Culture and American Identity.* Bloomington: Indiana University Press.

Morang, Alfred. 1939. *Dane Rudhyar: Pioneer in Creative Synthesis.* New York: Lucis Publishing.

Mueser, Barbara. 1975. *The Criticism of New Music in New York: 1919–1929.* Ph.D. dissertation, City University of New York.

Naumann, Francis M., with Beth Venn. 1996. *Making Mischief: Dada Invades New York.* New York: Whitney Museum of American Art.

Neuls-Bates, Carol, ed. 1982. *Women in Music: An Anthology of Source Readings from the Middle Ages to the Present.* New York: Harper & Row.

Nicholls, David. 1990. *American Experimental Music, 1890–1940.* Cambridge: Cambridge University Press.

———, ed. 1997. *The Whole World of Music: A Henry Cowell Symposium.* Amsterdam: Harwood Academic Publishers.

Ogren, Kathy J. 1989. *The Jazz Revolution: Twenties America and the Meaning of Jazz.* New York: Oxford University Press.

Oja, Carol J. 1979. "The Copland-Sessions Concerts and their Reception in the Contemporary Press." *Musical Quarterly* 65/2 (April): 212–29.

———. 1988. "Cos Cob Press and the American Composer." Music Library Association *Notes* 45 (December): 227–52.

———. 1990. *Colin McPhee: Composer in Two Worlds.* Washington, D.C.: Smithsonian Institution Press.

———. 1992. "'New Music' and the 'New Negro': The Background of William Grant Still's *Afro-American Symphony.*" *Black Music Research Journal* 12/2 (fall): 145–69.

———. 1994. "Gershwin and American Modernists of the 1920s." *Musical Quarterly* 78/4: 646–68.

———. 1997. "Women Patrons and Activists for Modernist Music: New York in the 1920s." *Modernism/Modernity* 4/1: 129–55. A slightly different version was published in Locke and Barr 1997.

———. 1999. "Dane Rudhyar's Vision of American Dissonance." *American Music* 17/2 (summer): 129–45.

———, and Ray Allen, ed. 1997. *Henry Cowell's Musical Worlds: A Program Book for the Henry Cowell Centennial.* Brooklyn: Institute for Studies in American Music.

Olmstead, Andrea. 1985. *Roger Sessions and His Music.* Ann Arbor: UMI Research Press.

———, ed. 1992. *The Correspondence of Roger Sessions.* Boston: Northeastern University Press.

Osgood, Henry O. 1926. *So This Is Jazz.* Boston: Little, Brown, and Company.

Page, Tim, and Vanessa Weeks Page, ed. 1988. *Selected Letters of Virgil Thomson.* New York: Summit Books.

Perlis, Vivian. 1974–75. "The Futurist Music of Leo Ornstein." Music Library Association *Notes* 31: 735–50.

———. 1978. *Two Men for Modern Music: E. Robert Schmitz and Herman Langinger.* I.S.A.M. Monographs, No. 9. Brooklyn: Institute for Studies in American Music.

Pescatello, Ann M. 1992. *Charles Seeger: A Life in American Music.* Pittsburgh: University of Pittsburgh Press.

Platt, Susan Noyes. 1985. *Modernism in the 1920s: Interpretations of Modern Art in New York from Expressionism to Constructivism.* Ann Arbor: UMI Research Press.

Pollack, Howard. 1981. *Walter Piston.* Ann Arbor: UMI Research Press.

———. 1992. *Harvard Composers: Walter Piston and His Students, from Elliott Carter to Frederic Rzewski.* Metuchen, N.J.: Scarecrow.

———. 1995. *Skyscraper Lullaby: The Life and Music of John Alden Carpenter.* Washington, D.C.: Smithsonian Institution Press.

———. 1998. *Aaron Copland: The Life and Work of an Uncommon Man.* New York: Henry Holt.

Potter, Hugh M. 1980. *False Dawn: Paul Rosenfeld and Art in America: 1916–1946.* Ann Arbor: Published for the University of New Hampshire by University Microfilms International.

Pound, Ezra. 1924 (1968). *Antheil and the Treatise on Harmony with Supplementary Notes.* Paris: Three Mountains. Reprint, New York: Da Capo.

Reis, Claire. 1923. "Contemporary Music and 'the Man on the Street.'" *Eolian Review* 2/2 (March): 24–27.

———. 1930. *American Composers of Today.* New York: International Society for Contemporary Music, United States Section.

———. 1932. *American Composers: A Record of Works Written Between 1912 and 1932,* 2d ed. New York: United States Section of the International Society for Contemporary Music.

———. 1938. *Composers in America: Biographical Sketches of Living Composers with a Record of Their Works, 1912–1937.* New York: Macmillan.

———. 1947. *Composers in America: Biographical Sketches of Contemporary Composers with a Record of their Works,* revised and enlarged edition. New York: Macmillan.

———. 1955 (1974). *Composers, Conductors, and Critics.* New York: Oxford University Press. Reprint, Detroit: Detroit Reprints in Music.

Root, Deane L. 1972. "The Pan American Association of Composers (1928–1934)." *Yearbook for Inter-American Musical Research* 8: 49–70.

Rosenfeld, Paul. 1920. *Musical Portraits: Interpretations of Twenty Modern Composers.* New York: Harcourt, Brace, and Howe.

———. 1923. *Musical Chronicle (1917–1923).* New York: Harcourt, Brace.

———. 1924. *Port of New York: Essays on Fourteen American Moderns.* New York: Harcourt, Brace.

———. 1925. *Men Seen.* New York: Dial.

———. 1927. *Modern Tendencies in Music.* New York: The Caxton Institute.

———. 1928. *By Way of Art.* New York: Coward-McCann.

———. 1929. *An Hour with American Music.* The One Hour Series. Philadelphia: J. B. Lippincott.

———. 1936. *Discoveries of a Music Critic.* New York: Harcourt, Brace.

Rossiter, Frank. 1975. *Charles Ives and His America.* New York: Liveright.

Rudhyar, Dane [Daniel Chennevière]. 1913. *Claude Debussy et son oeuvre.* Paris: A. Durand et fils.

——— [Rudhyar D. Chennevière]. 1919a. "The Two Trends of Modern Music in Stravinsky's Works." *Musical Quarterly* 5: 169–74.

———— [Rudhyar D. Chennevière]. 1919b. "Erik Satie and the Music of Irony." *Musical Quarterly* 5: 469–78.

———— [Rudhyar D. Chennevière]. 1920. "The Rise of the Musical Proletariat." *Musical Quarterly* 6 (October): 500–9.

————. 1922. "The Relativity of Our Musical Conceptions." *Musical Quarterly* 8 (January): 108–18. Reprinted in *Soundings* 2 (April 1972): 14–24.

————. 1923a. "The Music of Fire." *New Pearson's* (April): 45–47.

————. 1923b. "Toward a Deeper Musicality." *Eolian Review* 2/3 (June): 11–15.

————. 1923c. "Carl Ruggles and the Future of Dissonant Counterpoint." *Eolian Review* 3/1 (23 November): 13–16. Also published in *Christian Science Monitor* (23 December 1922).

————. 1924a. "Creators and Public: Their Relationship." *Musical Quarterly* 10 (January): 120–30.

————. 1924b. "A Reply to Charles L. Seeger's 'Reviewing a Review.'" *Eolian Review* 3/2 (February): 29–31.

————. 1926a. "The Birth of the XXth Century Piano: Concerning John Hays Hammond's New Device." *Eolus* 5/1 (January): 14–17.

————. 1926b. "A New Conception of Music." *Forum* (December): 892–901.

————. 1927a. "'Going Back' in Music: Where to?" *Pro Musica Quarterly* 5 (March): 10–15.

————. 1927b. "Musical Vitamines: A Modern View of Dynamism." *Musical America* 46/6 (28 May): 5, 27.

————. 1927c. "Looking Ahead into Paths Opened by the Three S's." *Musical America* 46/11 (2 July): 5, 11.

————. 1927d. "Carl Ruggles, Pioneer: As Seen by a Fellow-Modernist." *Musical America* 46/19 (27 August): 3, 20.

————. 1928a. *Dissonant Harmony: A New Principle of Musical and Social Organization*, Seed-Ideas, No. 1. Carmel, Calif.: HAMSA Publications. Republished in Rudhyar 1930b.

————. 1928b. *The Rebirth of Hindu Music.* Madras, India: Theosophical Publishing House. Reprint, New York: Samuel Weiser, 1979.

————. 1930a. *The New Sense of Space.* Seed Ideas, No. 2. Carmel, Calif.: HAMSA Publications. Published as part of 1930b.

————. 1930b. *Art as Release of Power: A Series of Seven Essays on the Philosophy of Art.* Carmel, Calif.: HAMSA Publications.

————. 1930c. "The Mystic's Living Tone." *Modern Music* 7 (April–May): 32–36.

————. 1982. *The Magic of Tone and the Art of Music.* Boulder, Colo.: Shambhala.

Schiff, David. 1997. *Gershwin: Rhapsody in Blue.* Cambridge Music Handbooks. Cambridge: Cambridge University Press.

Schneider, Wayne, ed. 1998. *The Gershwin Style: New Looks at the Music of George Gershwin.* New York: Oxford University Press.

Schouvaloff, Alexander, and Victor Borovsky. 1982. *Stravinsky on Stage.* London: Stainer & Bell.

Scott, Anne Firor. 1984. *Making the Invisible Woman Visible.* Urbana: University of Illinois Press.

Seeger, Charles. 1923. "Reviewing a Review," *Eolian Review* 3/1 (November): 16–23.

————. 1932. "Carl Ruggles." *Musical Quarterly* 18 (October): 578–92.

————. 1994. *Studies in Musicology II: 1929–1979,* ed. Ann M. Pescatello. Berkeley: University of California Press.

Seigel, Jerrold. 1995. *The Private Worlds of Marcel Duchamp: Desire, Liberation, and the Self in Modern Culture.* Berkeley: University of California Press.

Seldes, Gilbert. 1924. *The Seven Lively Arts.* New York: Harper & Brothers.

Shanet, Howard. 1975. *Philharmonic: A History of New York's Orchestra*. New York: Doubleday.

Shere, James. 1972. *Dane Rudhyar 1895–: A Brief Factual Biography with a Listing of His Works*. Berkeley: International Committee for a Humanistic Astrology.

Shirley, Wayne D. 1985. "Scoring the Concerto in F: George Gershwin's First Orchestration." *American Music* 3: 277–98.

Silet, Charles L. P. 1981. *The Writings of Paul Rosenfeld: An Annotated Bibliography*. New York: Garland Publishing.

Singal, Daniel Joseph, ed. 1991. *Modernist Culture in America*. Belmont, Calif.: Wadsworth.

Slonimsky, Nicolas. 1992. *Baker's Biographical Dictionary*, 8th ed. New York: Schirmer Books.

———, ed. 1994. *Music Since 1900*, 5th ed. New York: Charles Scribner's Sons.

———. 1997. *Baker's Biographical Dictionary of Twentieth-Century Classical Musicians*, ed. Laura Kuhn. New York: G. Schirmer.

Smith, Catherine. 1994. "'A Distinguishing Virility': Feminism and Modernism in American Art Music." In *Cecilia Reclaimed: Feminist Perspectives on Gender and Music*, ed. Susan C. Cook and Judy S. Tsou. Urbana: University of Illinois Press: 90–106.

Spiritual. 1986. *The Spiritual in Art: Abstract Painting 1890–1985*. Los Angeles County Museum of Art. New York: Abbeville.

Stearns, Harold E., ed. 1922 (1971). *Civilization in the United States: An Inquiry by Thirty Americans*. New York: Harcourt, Brace. Reprint, Westport, Conn.: Greenwood.

Stehman, Dan. 1984. *Roy Harris: An American Musical Pioneer*. Boston: Twayne.

Straus, Joseph N. 1990. *Remaking the Past: Musical Modernism and the Influence of the Tonal Tradition*. Cambridge: Harvard University Press.

———. 1995. *The Music of Ruth Crawford Seeger*. Cambridge: Cambridge University Press.

Stravinsky, Vera, and Robert Craft. 1978. *Stravinsky in Pictures and Documents*. New York: Simon and Schuster.

Stravinsky and the Dance. 1962. *Stravinsky and the Dance: A Survey of Ballet Productions, 1910–1962*. New York: The Dance Collection of the New York Public Library.

Tashjian, Dickran. 1975. *Skyscraper Primitives: Dada and the American Avant-Garde, 1910–1925*. Middletown, Conn.: Wesleyan University Press.

Taylor, Deems. 1924. "All Dressed Up and No Place to Go." *Music Illustrated Monthly Magazine* 1 (mid-summer): 15–17.

Thomson, Virgil. 1925. "The Cult of Jazz." *Vanity Fair* (June): 54, 118.

———. 1932. "American Composers. VII. Aaron Copland." *Modern Music* 9 (January): 67–73.

———. 1939 (1962). *The State of Music*. New York: William Morrow.; New York: Vintage Books.

———. 1966 (1977). *Virgil Thomson*. New York: Alfred A. Knopf. Reprint, New York: Da Capo.

———. 1971. *American Music Since 1910*. New York: Holt, Rinehart and Winston.

Tick, Judith. 1991. "Ruth Crawford's 'Spiritual Concept': The Sound-Ideals of an Early American Modernist." *Journal of the American Musicological Society* 44/2: 221–61.

———. 1993. "Charles Ives and Gender Ideology." In *Musicology and Difference: Gender and Sexuality in Music Scholarship*, ed. Ruth A. Solie. Berkeley: University of California Press: 83–106.

———. 1997. *Ruth Crawford Seeger: A Composer's Search for American Music*. New York: Oxford University Press.

———, and Wayne Schneider, ed. 1993. *Ruth Crawford: Music for Small Orchestra, Suite No. 2*. Music of the United States of America, Vol. 1. Madison: A-R Editions, published for the American Musicological Society.

Tischler, Barbara. 1986. *An American Music: The Search for an A*
New York: Oxford University Press.

Tommasini, Anthony. 1997. *Virgil Thomson: Composer on the A.*
Norton.

Tucker, Mark, ed. 1993. *The Duke Ellington Reader*. New York: C

Van Vechten, Carl. 1915. *Music After the Great War*. New York:

———. 1916. *Music and Bad Manners*. New York: Alfred A. Kn

———. 1917. *Interpreters and Interpretations*. New York: Alfred A

———. 1925a. *Red*. New York: Alfred A. Knopf.

———. 1925b. "George Gershwin: An American Composer W
Music in the Jazz Idiom." *Vanity Fair* (March): 40, 78, 84.

Varèse, Louise. 1972. *Varèse: A Looking-Glass Diary*. New York: \

Watkins, Glenn. 1988. *Soundings: Music in the Twentieth Century*
Books.

———. 1994. *Pyramids at the Louvre: Music, Culture, and Collage fr.*
modernists. Cambridge: Belknap Press of Harvard University Pr

White, Eric Walter. 1979. *Stravinsky: The Composer and His Works*
versity of California Press.

Whiteman, Paul, and Mary Margaret McBride. 1926. *Jazz*. New \

Whitesitt, Linda. 1983. *The Life and Music of George Antheil, 1900–*.
Research Press.

Wiecki, Ronald V. 1992. *A Chronicle of Pro Musica in the United State*.
Biographical Sketch of its Founder, E. Robert Schmitz. 3 parts. Ph.D.
of Wisconsin.

Ziffrin, Marilyn. 1994. *Carl Ruggles: Composer, Painter, and Storytell*
of Illinois Press.

Index

Beach, John: performance of work by, 370
Becker, John J., 110, 178, 185
    Symphonia Brevis, 192
Beckett, Samuel, 210
Beclard d'Harcourt, Marguerite, 370
Beecham, Sir Thomas, 293
Beeson, Jack, 167
Beethoven, Ludwig van, 13, 46, 81, 179, 245, 267,
    273, 304
    and neoclassicism, 234
Beethoven Association, 92
Bellison, Simeon, 293, 400
Beloussof, Evsei, 375
Benét, William Rose, 162
Bennett, Robert Russell, 264, 388
    performance of works by, 370
Bérard, Carol, 69
Berckman, Evelyn, 190
    performance of works by, 370
Berezowsky, Nicolai, 62
    performance of works by, 370
Berg, Alban, 5, 184, 192
    Dem Schmerz sein Recht, 181
    performance of works by, 370–71
    Second String Quartet, 169
Berger, Arthur, 243, 246, 248, 281, 356
Bergson, Henri, 21, 101
    Creative Evolution, 16, 17
    his influence on modernism, 16–18
    and intuition, 17–18
Berkshire Music Center, 281
Berlin, Irving, 301
    "Alexander's Ragtime Band," 329
Berlioz, Hector, 30, 133
    Requiem, 29, 93, 204
Berman, Art, 244
Bernard, Jonathan, 26
Bernays, Edward L., 48
Berners, Lord, 184
    performance of works by, 371
Bernhart, Isolde, 369, 399
Bernstein, Flora Bauer, 7, 67
    on American music, 155
Bernstein, Leonard, 28, 281, 318, 329
Besant, Annie Wood, 101, 106
    and Charles W. Leadbeater, Thought-Forms
        (Sudden Fright), 102
Besrodny, Gregory, 382
Betti, Adolfo, 48
Bibb, Frank, 383
bigotry, 125–26
Bijur, Hilda Reis, 208, 219
Biltmore Hotel, 191
Birchard Hall, 373, 374, 391, 394, 404
Bizet, Georges, 30

Black and Tan, 91–92
blackface, 337–38
Black Sun Press, 210
Black Swan (phonograph company), 331
Blaisdell, Frances, 376
Blake, Eubie: and Noble Sissle, Shuffle Along, 331,
    333
Blake, William, 124, 387
Blavatsky, Helena, 101, 102, 116
Bledsoe, Jules, 342, 380
Bliss, Arthur, 129, 180, 184
    performance of works by, 371
Blitzstein, Marc, 5, 93, 179, 188, 190, 243–44,
    246, 264, 269, 278, 323, 355, 363, 401
    on Chávez, 445n20
    The Cradle Will Rock, 223, 338
    performance of works by, 371
    Surf and Seaweed, 64–65
Bloch, Ernest, 12, 27, 47, 54, 74, 265, 286, 307,
    308, 326
    performance of work by, 372
    Piano Quintet, 189
Block, Mrs. Alexander, 286
Bloom, Harold, 257
Bodanzky, Arthur, 409n6
Bogdanovitch, Hyppolite, 377
Bok, Mary Louise Curtis, 47, 73, 74, 202, 226,
    356
Bolm, Adolph, 50, 188, 336
    See also Adolph Bolm Ballet
Bond, Carrie Jacobs, 226
Bookman, 7
Boos, Elfrida, 369, 389
Boosey and Hawkes, 210
Borodin, Alexander, 30
Borodkin, Herbert, 375, 391
Boston Symphony Orchestra, 29, 47, 48, 50, 199,
    281, 286, 293, 330, 375, 380, 383, 386,
    416n17
    chamber orchestra from, 392, 393, 402, 404
Boulanger, Lili, 389
Boulanger, Nadia, 125, 177, 179, 192, 196, 208,
    232, 234, 235, 238–39, 240, 241, 242,
    244, 252, 253, 269, 441n4
Boulez, Pierre, 28
Bourgeois, Stephan, 155, 217
Bowers, Faubion, 51
Bowles, Paul, 264, 278
    performance of work by, 372
Bradbury, Malcolm: and American culture, 408n8
Braggioti, Mario, 239
Brahms, Johannes, 33, 179, 245, 304
    Intermezzi, 162
    and neoclassicism, 234
Brahms Quartet, 369

Hammond, Richard, 159, 180, 181, 290, 430n12
   Dans les montagnes, 190
   performance of works by, 381
   Les trois princesses, 190
   Voyage to the East, 188
Handy, W. C., 356
   and Abbe Niles, *Blues: An Anthology,* 325
   Evolution of the Blues, 327, 431n20
   See also W. C. Handy's Orchestra
Hansen, Harold, 400
Hans Lange String Quartet, 368, 390
Hanson, Howard, 370, 384, 394
   Pan and the Priest, 199
   performance of works by, 381
Harlem Renaissance, 332–33, 345
Harmati, Sandor, 156, 213, 370, 387, 398, 429n2
   performance of works by, 381
Harris, Charles K., 226
Harris, Roy, 3, 125, 179, 185, 208, 210, 231, 232,
      234, 242, 264, 267, 276, 278, 280,
      281–82, 297, 305, 308
   Concerto for Piano, Clarinet, and String Quartet, 62,
      271
   his image, 272–73
   and nationalism, 6
   and neoclassicism, 271–75
   performance of works by, 381–82
   Sonata for Piano, 236, 248, 271–75
   Third Symphony, 272, 275
Harrison, Beatrice, 293
Harrison, Lou, 100, 105, 112–13, 281
   Labyrinth, 363
Hart, Frank, 402
Hart, Jerome, 218–19
   on Cowell, 438n35
Hart, Stanley, 80
Hart House String Quartet, 393
Hartley, Marsden, 45, 102, 184, 190, 309
Hartmann, Arthur, 387, 391
Harvard Musical Review, 52, 55
Harvard University, 46, 47, 51, 52, 55, 252, 253,
      281, 286
Harwood, Ruth, 403
Haubiel, Charles, 156, 159, 381, 429n2
   performance of works by, 382
Hawthorne, Nathaniel, 309
Haydn, Franz Joseph, 46, 245, 300
Hays, Sorrel Doris, 144
Hazard, Mr., 200
Heap, Jane, 63, 73, 74, 89–90, 98, 159, 244
Heifetz, Jascha, 329
Heifetz, Vladimir: *Biblical Suite,* 327, 431n20
Helen Teschner Tas Quartet, 385, 402
Hemingway, Ernest, 3
Henderson, Fletcher, 455n22
   Meanest Blues, 327

Henderson, W. J., 34, 41, 223, 227
Henry, Leigh, 213
Herriman, George, 336
Herscher-Clement, Jeanne: performance of work
   by, 382
Herz, Djane Lavoie, 47, 101, 144–48
Herz, Siegfried, 101
Herzog, George, 90
Hesselberg, Eyvind, 239
Heyman, Katherine Ruth, 51–52, 159
   and Scriabin, 51–52
Hicks, Michael, 131, 132
"highbrow" and "lowbrow," 67, 303, 315–17, 319,
   330, 362
Hill, E. B., 55, 189, 252, 286, 336
Hindemith, Paul, 47, 69, 184, 185, 187, 198,
      233, 244, 246, 269, 271, 329, 364
   Der Dämon, 172
   Das Nusch-Nuschi, 172
   performance of works by, 382–83
Hippodrome, 29
Hirsch, Louis A., 301, 302
Hitch, Nancy, 369, 386
Hitchcock, Henry-Russell, 439n2
Hofmann, Josef, 47
Holmes, Mrs. Christian, 436n11
homosexuality, 125–26, 142, 225, 253, 256,
      257–63, 278, 443n13
   and Christianity, 261–63
Honegger, Andrée Vaurabourg, 383
Honegger, Arthur, 181, 184, 187, 256, 291, 296,
      307
   Pacific 231, 65, 73, 418n12
   performance of works by, 383
   Phaedre, 320
   Skating Rink, 65
Horne, Marilyn, 330
Horowitz, Vladimir, 293
Horsman, Edward: performance of work by, 384
Hours Press, 210
House, Judson, 385
Housman, Rosalie: performance of work by, 384
Howard, John Tasker, 169, 308
   Our American Music, 6
Howe, Frederick, 217
Howell, Dicie, 384, 390, 399
Hughes, Langston, 3
   on New York City, xiii
   The Weary Blues, 333
Human, Alfred, 290
Humphrey, Doris, 188
Huneker, James Gibbons, 32, 34
Hungary: composers from, 196–97, 212–13
Hunter College Opera Workshop, 221
Hutch, Nancy, 369
Huyssen, Andreas, 225, 319

Hyland, Lilly May, 49
hymns: and Thomson, 261–63
hyperspace theory, 83–84

Ibert, Jacques: performance of work by, 384
ICG: *See* International Composers' Guild
Ideler, Edwin, 375, 377, 391
Il'iashenko, Andrei: performance of work by, 384
Imandt, Robert, 401
immigration: and composers, 12–13, 22, 27–28,
    181–83, 189, 291
  and New York's expatriate community, 28
  and quota system, 452n3
  and World War I, 12
Inch, Herbert: performance of work by, 384
Indians: *See* Native Americans
Infante, Manuel: performance of work by, 384
Institute of Musical Art, 13
  See also Juilliard School
International Composers' Guild (ICG), 23, 28, 40,
    41, 43, 74, 101, 103, 111, 113–14, 115,
    116, 119, 121, 155, 156, 157, 158, 162,
    169, 172, 178, 179, 181–88, 190, 194,
    196, 202, 212, 214, 216, 217, 218, 219,
    225, 278, 287, 289–90, 293, 330, 332,
    345, 367, 368–406 passim, 408n1,
    433n15
  conservatism within, 185
  disbanding of, 186
  and League of Composers, 222
  manifesto of, 183
  patronage of, 204–05, 206
  and Varèse's music, 32–35, 37
Internationale Komponisten-Gilde, 182
International Exhibition of Modern Art: *See*
    Armory Show
internationalism: and American modernism,
    63–69, 73, 77–80, 177–85, 187–89,
    232–35, 285–96
  and Sessions, 265–66
International Society for Contemporary Music,
    285, 290–91
  concerts of, 266, 267
  festivals of, 162, 172, 240, 246
Intimate Gallery, 190
Ionian Quartet, 402
Isakovich, Vera, 413n12
ISCM: *See* International Society for Contemporary
    Music
Ito, Michio, 188, 401
Ivantzoff, Ivan, 398
Ives, Charles, 7, 18, 26, 51, 104, 110, 152, 178,
    185, 194, 210, 225, 231, 232, 288, 298,
    301, 336, 338, 352
  The Celestial Railroad, 181
  Fourth Symphony, 129, 181, 191

  and gender, 125, 126
  General William Booth Enters Into Heaven, 172
  Majority, 105
  Memos, 288, 305
  and *New Music Quarterly,* 433n23
  as patron, 195, 435n4
  performance of works by, 384
  and Scriabin, 51–52, 416n17
  Three Places in New England, 195, 213
  Three Quarter-Tone Pieces, 181

Jackson, Irving, 389
Jacobi, Frederick, 156, 158–62, 166–68, 172, 176,
    185, 186, 188, 189, 213, 216, 217, 218,
    291, 372, 384, 387, 388, 390, 392, 399,
    401, 402
  Assyrian Prayers, 189
  Indian Dances, 167
  Jewish identity of, 166
  performance of works by, 384–85
  String Quartet on Indian Themes, 162, 167–68
  Three Preludes for Violin, 157
  Three Psalms, 167
Jacobi, Irene, 216, 369, 376, 378, 381, 385,
    389–90, 398, 399
Jacobson, Sascha, 378
Jade, Ely (pseud. of Germaine Schmitz), 202
James, Henry, 204
James, Philip, 62
Janacopoulous, Vera, 289
jazz, 301, 302
  and American modernism, 172, 313–17, 318–60
  and class, 319–20, 321, 328
  and European composers, 295–96
  impact of, 313–17
  the "legitimizing" of, 318–60
  and race, 319, 328
  and Rosenfeld, 304, 310
Jewish identity, 307–08, 451n29
  and Jacobi, 166
  and Ornstein, 22–23
  See also anti-Semitism
Johnson, James Weldon, 333
  God's Trombones—Seven Negro Sermons in Verse,
    342–44
Johnson, Philip, 439n2
Johnson, Steven, 132, 134, 137
Jolas, Jacques, 374, 378
Jolson Theatre, 377, 378, 381, 386, 398, 401, 402
Jones, Isham, 357
Jones, Robert Edmond, 188, 337–38, 340
Jongen, Joseph: performance of work by, 385
Jordan Hall (Boston), 52
journalism: and modernist music, 54–56
Joyce, James, 16, 203, 374
Judge, William Quan, 101

Marx, Leo: *The Machine in the Garden,* 63
Mas, Paul, 375
Mase, Owen: performance of work by, 388
Mason, Daniel Gregory, 219, 308, 438n35
  performance of work by, 388
Mason, Lowell, 305
mass communication: rise of, 61
Massine, Leonide, 188–89
Mathieu, Pierre, 389
Matisse, Henri, 45
Mattfeld, Julius, 183
Matthiessen, F. O.: *American Renaissance,* 6
Mattis, Olivia, 179
  on Varèse's Hippodrome concert, 412n9
Matzenhauer, Margaret, 401
Mead, Rita, 129
Mellers, Wilfrid, 26
  Music in a New-Found Land, 6
Mencken, H. L., 261
Mengelberg, Willem, 28, 187, 188, 288, 293,
  295, 378, 385, 397
Mercati, Countess, 220, 435n7
Mero, Yolanda, 369
Messing, Scott, 233, 243, 245, 279
Mestechkin, Jacob, 289, 369, 389
Metcalf, Katherine, 382
Metropolitan Museum of Art, 203, 204
Metropolitan Opera, 29, 48, 50, 172, 201, 203,
  342
Metropolitan Opera House, 68, 169, 327, 330,
  336, 338, 390, 392, 398, 401, 409n6
Miaskovsky, Nikolai, 184
  performance of works by, 388
Migot, Georges, 189
  performance of works by, 389
Milhaud, Darius, 181, 184, 187, 188, 192, 233,
  244, 287, 288, 291, 295, 302, 305, 318,
  329, 355–56, 364
  La Création du monde, 65, 66, 336, 342, 355
  performance of works by, 389
  Sonata for Two Violins and Piano, 129, 191
Miller, Marguerite, 390, 391
Miller, Marie, 371, 377, 388, 395
Miller, Raymond S., 376, 386
Miller, Rosalie, 389
Mills, Florence, 330, 333, 334–36, 337, 399
Milojeviæ, Miloje: performance of work by,
  389–90
Mix, Emil, 372
Modern Music, 4, 7, 35, 62, 69, 93, 104, 125, 157,
  160, 171, 189, 202, 203, 206, 207, 210,
  240, 241, 245, 246, 248, 276, 281, 287,
  291, 310, 337, 349, 355, 362
Modern Music Shop, 3, 156, 159–60
Moiseiwitsch, Benno, 409n6

Moldavan, Nicolas, 370, 378, 381
Molié, Denyse, 385, 396, 397, 402
Mondrian, Piet, 102
Montagu-Nathan, Montagu, 55, 417n22
Monteux, Pierre, 100, 187, 286, 378, 401
Monteverdi, Claudio: performance of works by,
  390
Moore, Douglas: performance of work by, 390
Moore, Marianne, 450n21
Morgan, Eric, 389
Morgenthau, Henry, 210
Morgenthau, Henry, Jr., 210
Morgenthau family, 436n17
Moross, Jerome, 223
Morris, Harold, 156, 380, 387, 392, 398, 399,
  429n2
  performance of works by, 390
Moskovitz, Henry, 376
Mossolov, Alexander: *Factory: Music for Machines,*
  65
Moussorgsky, Modest, 30
Mowbray, Alderson, 370, 371
Mozart, Wolfgang Amadeus, 69, 245, 300, 304
Muck, Karl, 29, 47
Muir, Lewis F., 301, 302
Mullen, Joseph, 93, 357
  stage career of, 422n34
multiculturalism, 104–05, 152
Mumford, Lewis, 309, 310
Munson, Gorham, 91, 303
Murphey, Dudley, 92
Museum of Modern Art, 89
music, modernist:
  and critics, 297–310
  as a feminized sphere, 223–27
  and gender, 213–14, 221–27
  historiography of, 178–79
  publishing of, 158–59, 191–92, 208–10
  and spirituality, 15–16, 97–152
Musical America, 7, 27, 46, 50, 52, 72, 98, 111,
  112, 114, 132, 133, 180, 197, 209, 223,
  240, 265, 289, 290, 291, 292, 293, 294,
  295, 316, 321, 327, 330, 336, 337, 362,
  429n2, 449n4
Musical Chronicle, 308
Musical Courier, 189, 290, 332
Musical Leader, 7, 67, 162, 187, 344, 444n5
Musical Mercury, 243
Musical Quarterly, 17, 49, 53, 55, 103, 130, 240
Music Appreciation Hour, 61, 320
musique concrète, 69

Nancarrow, Conlon, 70
Nason, Kathryn, 271
Nation, 30